Ethics and Politics
Cases and Comments

Fourth Edition

Edited by

Amy Gutmann

UNIVERSITY OF PENNSYLVANIA

and

Dennis Thompson

HARVARD UNIVERSITY

THOMSON

WADSWORTH

Australia • Canada • Mexico • Singapore • Spain • United Kingdom • United States

Ethics and Politics: Cases and Comments, Fourth Edition
Amy Gutmann and Dennis Thompson

Publisher: *Clark Baxter*
Executive Editor: *David Tatom*
Assistant Editor: *Anne Gittinger*
Editorial Assistant: *Cheryl Lee*
Technology Project Manager: *Michelle Vardeman*
Marketing Manager: *Janise Fry*
Marketing Assistant: *Teresa Jessen*
Advertising Project Manager: *Kelley McAllister*
Project Manager, Editorial Production: *Candace Chen*
Art Director: *Maria Epes*

Print Buyer: *Rebecca Cross*
Permissions Editor: *Chelsea Junget*
Production Service: *Linda DeMasi, Stratford Publishing, Inc.*
Copy Editor: *Leslie Connor*
Illustrator: *Stratford Publishing, Inc.*
Cover Designer: *Sue Hart*
Text & Cover Printer: *Webcom*
Compositor: *Integra Software Services, Inc.*

Printed in Canada
1 2 3 4 5 6 7 09 08 07 06 05

For more information about our products, contact us at:
Thomson Learning Academic Resource Center
1-800-423-0563

For permission to use material from this text or product, submit a request online at
http://www.thomsonrights.com.
Any additional questions about permissions can be submitted by email to
thomsonrights@thomson.com.

Thomson Higher Education
10 Davis Drive
Belmont, CA 94002-3098
USA

Asia (including India)
Thomson Learning
5 Shenton Way
#01–01 UIC Building
Singapore 068808

Australia/New Zealand
Thomson Learning Australia
102 Dodds Street
Southbank, Victoria 3006
Australia

Canada
Thomson Nelson
1120 Birchmount Road
Toronto, Ontario M1K 5G4
Canada

UK/Europe/Middle East/Africa
Thomson Learning
High Holborn House
50–51 Bedford Row
London WC1R 4LR
United Kingdom

Library of Congress Control Number: 2004116284

ISBN 0-534-62645-9

Contents

Part Two: The Ethics of Policy

Acknowledgments

This book grew out of courses we have taught at Princeton and Harvard. We are grateful to our students, who appreciated the importance of cases in understanding political ethics and who helped us choose (and in some instances write) the cases we present here. The late Donald E. Stokes, then Dean of the Woodrow Wilson School at Princeton, encouraged this project from the beginning. We are grateful to him and to the School for their early support. We also appreciate the continuing support of the University Center for Human Values at Princeton and the Edmond J. Safra Foundation Center for Ethics at Harvard.

In addition to writing several case studies, Sigal Ben-Porath, Simone Sandy, and Alex Zakaras provided excellent editorial advice for this edition. Sigal Ben-Porath and Jaime Muehl expertly managed the process of revision. We are fortunate to have enjoyed the contributions of such a proficient team.

For permission to reprint previously published work, we thank the publishers who are specifically acknowledged on the first page of the sections in which the work appears. Several individuals who kindly helped us secure permissions deserve mention: Robert Caro, Henry Finder, Elizabeth Kolbert, David Rudenstine, and Peter Zimmerman.

Introduction

Dean Acheson, secretary of state under President Truman, described the place of morality in making foreign policy in this way: "Our discussions centered on the appraisal of dangers and risks, the weighing of the need for decisive and effective action against considerations of prudence. . . . Moral talk did not bear on the issue." When one of his colleagues objected that a proposed course was morally wrong, Acheson's reply reflected the conventional wisdom of American policy makers at the time. He told his colleague that on the Day of Judgment his view might be confirmed and that he was free to go forth and preach the necessity of salvation, but that "it was not, however, a view which I would entertain as a public servant."

This view is no doubt still widely held today—though more often in private than in public. The political climate is now more favorable for ethics—or at least for talk about ethics. Corruption and misdeeds in public life have far from disappeared but public officials are less hesitant to raise ethical questions and are less reluctant to accept ethical constraints on at least some of their conduct. If they try to avoid moral questions, critics stand ready to challenge them. The controversy over the treatment of the detainees the United States had captured in Afghanistan intensified when it was disclosed in 2004 that the Justice Department had earlier concluded that torturing al Qaeda terrorists in captivity abroad "may be justified" under domestic law, and that international law may not apply to interrogations conducted as part of the U.S. war on terrorism. President George W. Bush was asked by a reporter: "When you say that you want the U.S. to adhere to international and U.S. laws, that's not very comforting. This is a *moral* question: Is torture ever justified? " At first, the president repeated the legalistic response: "The instructions went out to our people to adhere to law." But some days later, he answered in moral terms: "The values of this country are such that torture is not a part of our soul and our being."

Ethics, again expressed in terms of "values," became a salient issue early in the 2004 presidential campaign. Some of its aims are now securely institutionalized. Several presidents and executive agencies have appointed commissions, councils, and aides to advise them on ethical questions. More significantly, questions of undeniable moral content have captured a prominent place on the political agenda. Officials cannot escape talking about ethics when they address issues of military intervention, personal morality, compensation for loss of life, environmental risk, affirmative action, welfare reform, stem cell research, abortion, and even tax policy.

One reason for the growing respectability of ethics is, no doubt, that politicians have discovered that moral talk, and sometimes even moral action, help them win or stay in office. But there are also, as there have always been, good moral reasons for public officials to be guided by ethical considerations in making policy. The reasons are now even more compelling, because the scope and stakes of American politics are greater than ever.

Public officials use means—such as violence and the threat of violence—that affect the fate of all of us and future generations as well. And the goods that public institutions distribute or provide the means to obtain—such as health care and employment opportunities—are among those that people value most. Because officials and institutions act in ways that seriously affect the well-being of many other people and other societies, we should want their actions to be guided by rules that prevent them from unfairly subordinating some people's interests to those of others. Because in a democracy officials and institutions are supposed to act in our name and only on our authority, we want their actions to conform to the moral principles that we share.

Moral or ethical principles express the rights and obligations that individuals should respect when they act in ways that seriously affect the well-being of others, and the standards that collective practices and policies should satisfy when these similarly affect well-being. Ethical principles differ from the purely prudential principles common in politics. Prudence asks whether an action or policy serves the interests of particular individuals, groups, or nations. Its principles reflect and often reinforce the prevailing distributions of power in society. Ethics asks whether an action or policy could be justified to free and equal citizens who are trying to find fair terms of cooperation. Its principles evaluate and often criticize the prevailing distribution of power.

Prudence and ethics are not necessarily opposed in politics. A satisfactory political ethics must take into account the exigencies of political life, and effective political prudence recognizes the potency of moral criticism. If the conflict is between expedience and principle, few politicians would want to stand with the former. To be sure, some may argue that the free pursuit of self-interest will contribute to the public interest—at least if social and political institutions are designed correctly. But this claim does not fundamentally challenge the relevance of morality to politics. It simply proposes a supposedly more effective means of achieving moral ends in politics. If there is any dispute here, it is over the devices of moralists, not their desires.

Should we try to change the principles that motivate public officials, or should we try to restructure political institutions to elicit ethical behavior from those who are self-interested? Presumably we have to attempt both. More broadly, we may seek to change the structures of power in government and society so that citizens and officials can live together in a genuinely moral community. Whatever ways we choose to realize morality in politics, we must understand the meaning, justification, and application of moral principles and values in political life. This is the subject of political ethics.

Discussions of political ethics are not salient in the literature on U.S. politics and even in moral philosophy. Texts in U.S. government tend to concentrate on the mechanics of power, and the efficacy of policies. If they do not banish ethics from politics, they keep it safely segregated in a realm of ideals that rarely intrude into the real world of politics. The literature of moral philosophy often takes the opposite, but no less mistaken, approach. Philosophers tend to bring their principles of morality to the study of politics without change. They rarely attend to the special features of political life, the necessities of politics in general and the imperatives of democratic politics in particular. The moral values of the political process itself, so important in a democracy, usually meet with benign neglect.

Although political ethics must be consistent with a more general theory of ethics, it does not have exactly the same content as ordinary ethics because political life differs in morally significant ways from ordinary life. More than most citizens, public officials assume responsibility for protecting the rights and interests of all of us. They act in our name and on our behalf. And the environment in which they act is largely impersonal and intractable. It is often populated by powerful people and formidable institutions that are hostile to the purposes of public-spirited officials. These and other differences between public and private life do not make ethics irrelevant to politics. If anything they make it all the more important. But they do require us to take into account the special characteristics of politics as we frame our moral judgments.

We make moral judgments about two different aspects of politics, the ethics of the process and the ethics of policy. The first part of this book considers the moral problems of the methods used to achieve political goals, and the second part examines problems of the content of the goals themselves. The cases focus on problems of public policy and the officials who make it. Knowing how to think ethically about the means and ends of public policy is essential not only for officials but for all citizens who participate in the democratic process.

The moral problem of process is that politics often requires public officials to use bad means to achieve good ends—means, such as violence—that private citizens may not use except under the most extraordinary circumstances. The moral demands of ordinary politics may include the need to threaten and to use violence, the necessity to deceive and manipulate others, and the obligation to disobey orders. These otherwise immoral acts become moral, or so it is claimed, because officials are harming some people for the sake of helping more people or protecting the same people from even greater harm.

If we recognize that public officials cannot avoid using bad means to achieve good ends, we must seek moral limits on the use of these means. Machiavelli's advice to the Prince is inadequate: "He should not depart from the good if he can hold to it, but he should be ready to enter on evil if he has to." Political necessity is at best a vague and at worst a misleading standard. We want to prevent public officials not only from pursuing their self-interest with impunity but also from unfairly sacrificing the interests of some people or societies for the sake of advancing the interests of others. To admit that politicians must get their hands dirty, therefore, is not to agree with Machiavelli that "when the effect is good . . . it always justifies the action." Even utilitarians who give great weight to good consequences would not permit politicians so easily to justify using morally bad methods to achieve good ends. Utilitarians insist on a strict calculation of the costs and benefits that would rarely license the use of methods that common morality condemns. And leading critics of utilitarianism argue that some means, such as torturing innocent persons, are not justified, even when the gain in social benefits outweighs the costs.

The cases in the first four chapters of Part One invite you to examine the morally questionable means that are most commonly used in the political process: violence, deception, secrecy, violation of privacy, and manipulation. Less common but no less important is the method illustrated in Chapter 5, official disobedience, which is not necessarily a morally questionable means, but nonetheless calls upon public officials to decide whether they should blow the whistle or otherwise disobey while remaining in office rather than comply with a policy for the sake of furthering better policies in the future.

The cases in Part Two illustrate the ethical problems of determining the goals of public policy. In everyday life we must choose among the many things that we ideally would like to accomplish. But our choices generally do not raise the same difficult moral questions as in politics, because in private life we are not responsible for acting in the interests of so many other people and reconciling their conflicts over such a wide range of values. Competing preferences, scarce resources, and stakes as high as basic liberty, opportunity, and even life itself combine with the duties of office to make the choices among policy goals morally hard.

The choices confronted by public officials are typically complex and so, fittingly, are most of the cases in this book. They are full of details, ranging from scientific and legal technicalities to biographical facts about the officials who are featured. The cases are designed to represent, as far as possible, actual decisions and policies rather than hypothetical ones. One purpose of using real cases is to appreciate better the complexity that confronts the officials who make policy and the citizens who assess it. One of the most difficult but least examined steps in political ethics is to identify and frame the ethical issues themselves. Issues do not usually announce themselves as moral dilemmas; they often lie buried in a mass of facts and a welter of claims and counter-claims. Nearly all of the cases here call for some moral detective work to discover the ethical suspects among the many leads the facts may suggest.

The complexity of the cases also serves a second purpose. Moral principles in their pristine form often seem to have little critical force in politics. Either they are so general that everyone readily accepts them, or they are so extreme that almost no one takes them seriously. By trying to apply the principles to particular cases, we can begin to see exactly what difference which principles make in our political judgments. Finally, the complexity should remind us that context matters in political ethics. The cases, of course, cannot give a full account of the history of the events and institutions or the structures of social and economic power. But they should provide enough information to prompt you to ask what more must be known about the context to reach ethical conclusions. After reading each case, you should always ask what further information is necessary to arrive at an adequately informed conclusion. The information provided in the case is intended to be as much an invitation to further research as an account of the facts relevant to the case.

The subjects of some of the cases are officials at the highest levels of government making decisions of great historical significance, as in the decision to use the atomic bomb against Japan. And some are statements of policies with far-reaching implications for society now and in the future—as in the state debates over gay marriage and the national debates on abortion. We have included such cases because they raise important issues in themselves and because they illustrate principles that have wider application. But equally important are the cases that describe less famous and less momentous events in which lower level officials make decisions that directly affect relatively few people, such as the dispute about welfare reform in Wisconsin or education in Hawkins County, Tennessee. We have deliberately presented some cases that take place in cities, counties, and states. Such cases represent an important part of the moral world of politics. It is a world that both citizens and officials can more often influence because the scale of its problems is more manageable and because the patterns of its problems are more predictable. Though less dramatic than the once-in-a-lifetime dilemmas more often heard about, these decisions of normal politics cumulatively affect at least as many people.

The range of cases is intended to indicate that ethical problems may appear almost any place in political life. Ethical issues do not arrive only at great moments in history. They also dwell in the routine of everyday politics, in everything from a president's State of the Union address to congressional hearings on taxes to state deliberations about health care.

However valuable cases may be, they cannot stand alone. All of the selections in this book are meant to be read in conjunction with works in moral philosophy and political theory. Such works provide principles to help assess the cases, and the cases may sometimes suggest revisions in the principles to take account of the special features of politics. Recommended readings accompany each set of cases. The recommendations are neither exclusive nor exhaustive, and other works not mentioned may be equally appropriate. But without some substantial basis in theory, any analysis of the cases is likely to be superficial.

At the end of each set of cases are comments and questions designed to encourage discussions of the ethical issues that the cases raise. Since ethical analysis should be viewed as a process of deliberation, it is best conducted at least in part through discussion with other people. This is especially true for political ethics. In a democracy, it is only through persuading other citizens of the moral worth of our causes that we can legitimately win their support in the making of public policies.

Recommended Reading

Two good introductions to moral philosophy are Stephen Darwall, *Philosophical Ethics* (Boulder, Colo.: Westview Press, 1998); and Shelly Kagan, *Normative Ethics* (Boulder, Colo.: Westview Press, 1997). An engaging way to sample the leading contemporary approaches to ethics is Marcia Baron, Michael Slote, and Philip Petit, *Three Methods of Ethics: A Debate* (Oxford: Blackwell, 1997). Useful collections on consequentialism and nonconsequentialism are Darwall (ed.), *Consequentialism,* and Darwall (ed.), *Deontology* (both Oxford: Blackwell, 2002).

The most comprehensive guide to practical or applied ethics is the multivolume *Oxford Handbook of Practical Ethics,* edited by Hugh LaFollette (Oxford and New York: Oxford University Press, 2003). Also see Ruth F. Chadwick (ed.), *Encyclopedia of Applied Ethics* (San Diego, Calif.: Academic Press/Harcourt Brace, 1998). Useful collections sensitive to practical ethics include: Brenda Almond (ed.), *Introducing Applied Ethics* (Oxford and Cambridge, Mass.: Blackwell, 1995); Francis J. Beckwith, *Do the Right Thing: Readings in Applied Ethics and Social Philosophy,* 2nd edition (Belmont, Calif.: Wadsworth/Thomson Learning, 2002); Ruth F. Chadwick and Doris Schroeder (eds.), *Applied Ethics: Critical Concepts in Philosophy* (London and New York: Routledge, 2002); and Peter Singer (ed.), *Ethics* (New York: Oxford University Press, 1994). An antidote to the consequentialist tendency of much work in the field is David S. Oderberg, *Applied Ethics: A Non-Consequentialist Approach* (Oxford and Malden, Mass.: Blackwell, 2000).

More specifically on political ethics, see Joel Fleishman et al. (eds.), *Public Duties: The Moral Obligations of Government Officials* (Cambridge, Mass.: Harvard University Press, 1981); Andrew Sabl, *Ruling Passions: Political Offices and Democratic Ethics* (Princeton, NJ: Princeton University Press, 2002); Dennis F. Thompson, *Political Ethics and Public Office* (Cambridge, Mass.: Harvard University Press, 1987); and his *Restoring Responsibility: Ethics in Government, Business and Health Care* (Cambridge and New York: Cambridge University Press, 2004). Political ethics in the post–9/11 international context is the subject of Michael Ignatief's *The Lesser Evil: Political Ethics in an Age of Terror* (Princeton, N.J.: Princeton University Press, 2004).

For an approach to political ethics grounded in a theory of deliberative democracy, see Amy Gutmann and Dennis Thompson, *Democracy and Disagreement* (Cambridge, Mass.: Harvard University Press, 1996), which discusses most of the issues raised by the cases in this text as well as many of the cases themselves. A shorter version of the theory with some more recent examples can be found in the first chapter of *Why Deliberative Democracy?* (Princeton: Princeton University Press, 2004).

A general framework for questions about the ethics of process should be informed by the literature on the problem of dirty hands. The classic sources are Machiavelli, *The Prince* (New York: Random House, 1950); and Max Weber, "Politics as a Vocation," in H. H. Gerth and C. W. Mills (eds.), *From Max Weber* (New York: Oxford University Press, 1958). If you read only one modern work on the subject, it should be Michael Walzer, "Political Action: The Problem of Dirty Hands," *Philosophy & Public Affairs,* 1 (Winter 1972), pp. 160–80; reprinted in Marshall Cohen et al. (eds.), *War and Moral Responsibility* (Princeton, N.J.: Princeton University Press, 1974). Some other contemporary discussions are the articles by Stuart Hampshire, Bernard Williams, and Thomas Nagel in Hampshire et al. (eds.), *Public and Private Morality* (New York: Cambridge University Press, 1978), and Dennis F. Thompson, "Democratic Dirty Hands," in *Political Ethics and Public Office,* pp. 11–39.

The ethics of policy has generated a large literature in recent years, but most of the applied work is either focused on specific topics (see the Recommended Readings at the end of each chapter), or on the methods of policy analysis (see the readings at the end of Chapter 6). A selection of philosophical writing on particular policies appears in the readers compiled by the editors of *Philosophy & Public Affairs* and published by Princeton University Press. See Marshall Cohen et al. (eds.), *Equality and Preferential Treatment* (1978); *Medicine and Moral Philosophy* (1982); *Rights and Wrongs of Abortion* (1974); *War and Moral Responsibility* (1974); and Charles R. Beitz et al. (eds.), *International Ethics* (1985). On the strengths and weaknesses of utilitarianism as a method for analyzing public policy, the foundation of the dominant approach to policy analysis, see Robert Goodin, *Utilitarianism as a Public Philosophy* (New York and Cambridge: Cambridge University Press, 1995).

At the more general level, work on theories of justice by philosophers and theories of welfare and development by economists are the most relevant. The philosophical work that continues to be the most influential in the study of the ethics of policy is John Rawls, *A Theory of Justice* (Cambridge, Mass.: Harvard University Press, 1971). A shorter and more recent version of the theory, which incorporates the revisions Rawls made over the years, is Erin Kelly (ed.), *Justice as Fairness: A Restatement* (Cambridge, Mass.: Harvard University Press, 2001). For commentary and criticism on Rawls, see the *Cambridge Companion to Rawls* (New York and Cambridge: Cambridge University Press, 2002).

For two perspectives on public policy by ethically sensitive economists, see John Broome, *Ethics Out of Economics* (Cambridge and New York: Cambridge University Press, 1999); and Amartya Sen, *Development as Freedom* (New York: Doubleday, 2000).

Students can keep up with current work on political ethics and related fields by regularly reading relevant articles and reviews in *Ethics* (University of Chicago Press) and *Philosophy & Public Affairs* (Princeton University Press). Others worth consulting include the *Journal of Political Philosophy* (Blackwell), *Social Philosophy & Policy (Cambridge),* and the *Journal of Applied Philosophy* (Blackwell).

Part One

The Ethics of Process

1 Violence

Violence violates the fundamental moral prohibition against harming persons, yet governments must sometimes use violent means to defend that same fundamental principle. The most dramatic instance of the use of violence is war, and the most terrifying instruments of war are the bombs that kill civilians and destroy cities. The cases in this chapter raise questions about the morality of war—the means used to fight wars and the ends for which they are fought.

"War is cruel and you cannot refine it," General Sherman told the citizens of Atlanta who protested against the brutality of his invasion of their city during the Civil War. Many other military and political leaders as well as moral philosophers have agreed with Sherman. If your cause is just in a war, you should use any means necessary to win it. To place moral constraints on the fighting of a war, the argument goes, would simply prolong it and could increase the chances of war in the future by making war more morally respectable.

In most wars most nations nevertheless have accepted some moral constraints on their conduct (such as not torturing prisoners), and the philosophical writing on just war has long distinguished the justice of a war from the justice of the means used to fight it. The former does not necessarily determine the latter. Even in the war against Nazis, we should condemn some methods—for example, the practice of the Free French forces who enlisted Moroccan mercenaries by promising that they could, with impunity, rape Italian women. And we also distinguish moral from immoral actions of men fighting on the side of the aggressor nation: we praise General Rommel for ignoring Hitler's order to shoot all prisoners captured behind the lines.

The basic principle underlying most rules of war is that it is morally wrong to attack noncombatants. Noncombatants are defined as those who are not fighting or not supplying the means of fighting the war. Farmers and nurses are noncombatants, while munitions workers and soldiers are combatants. Different moral traditions provide different reasons for this prohibition, but all regard it as important.

At the same time, most theories of just war recognize that noncombatants will inevitably be killed in modern warfare—sometimes justifiably so. The theories then take one of two approaches: they either (1) formulate the prohibition so as to

3

justify some deaths of noncombatants or (2) specify the conditions under which the prohibition may be suspended. The most prominent example of the first alternative is the doctrine of double effect, which holds that the death of noncombatants is permissible if it is an unintended (though foreseen) side effect of a morally legitimate end. The doctrine would permit, for example, an air strike against an enemy missile site even if civilians lived nearby. The second alternative would allow civilians to be killed directly only if necessary to stop the imminent destruction of a nation. On this view, British bombing of German cities may have been justified until 1942 but not thereafter.

Some have argued that nuclear weapons make obsolete all these fine distinctions and the rules of war that depend on them. With the possible exception of tactical weapons, nuclear forces strike directly at civilian populations. The destruction of Hiroshima and Nagasaki could hardly be described as an unintended side effect. Nor was the bombing necessary to prevent the defeat of the United States. But others argue that the destructiveness of the new technology increases the need to take the old rules of war seriously.

Even some of those who favored the bombing of Hiroshima and Nagasaki recognized that it called for moral justification and believed they could provide it. Writing only a few months before President Harry S. Truman accepted his advice to use the bomb against Japan, Secretary of State Henry Stimson insisted that the "rule sparing the civilian population should be applied as far as possible to the use of any new weapon." Stimson's own defense of the use of that weapon, reprinted as the first selection in this chapter, shows how he came to terms with that moral rule. The selection that follows provides a broader account drawing on more recent historical sources of the considerations that led to the decision and its consequences.

From the beginning, there were critics of the decision. General Dwight D. Eisenhower says that he told Stimson in 1945 that he was "against it on two counts. First, the Japanese were ready to surrender and it wasn't necessary to hit them with that awful thing. Second, I hated to see our country be the first to use such a weapon." As Eisenhower's comment reveals, the controversy about the bomb usually seems at first to turn mainly on the question of military necessity (would the Japanese have surrendered soon in any case?). But that question is so contentious because it is not independent of the question of the morality of using "that awful thing."

The controversy continues to the present day, not only among academic historians but also among politicians and citizens. In 1995 the Smithsonian's National Air and Space Museum planned an exhibition featuring the *Enola Gay* (the plane from which the bomb was dropped) along with an explanatory script that raised some questions about whether the bombing was necessary. Although the rather bland script took no position on the question, the public outcry forced the curators to abandon the script and exhibit the plane alone. The controversy thus remains significant not only as a dispute about a historical event but also as a question about the moral stance that we believe our nation should take in the use of instruments of violence.

Although the United States has not used nuclear weapons again, it has sent conventional bombers on campaigns that killed civilians, often in large numbers. The most sustained and destructive missions took place during the Vietnam War. In recent years more isolated and smaller scale incidents are more typical now that the military finds itself in an era of what is called "low-intensity conflict." (The navy, more poetic in its classifications, calls it "violent peace.") "Bombing the Bunker in Baghdad" describes one such incident. During the Gulf War, the United States ordered an air strike against a command center near which civilians lived and in which, as it turned out, civilians had taken shelter. The moral question is whether the rules of war require the United States to take more care than it did to avoid civilian casualties.

When a war is clearly just, it is possible to discuss the morality of the means used without considering the ends pursued. Few people now doubt the justice of the Allies' cause in World War II, and most would accept that the U.S.-led forces in the Gulf were justified in resisting Iraq's attack against Kuwait (even if the motivation was more economic than moral). But the question of the justice of the war is itself often more difficult than these cases suggest. The decisions to intervene that U.S. officials face now are more likely to involve uncertain claims and confused boundaries than clear cases in which an aggressor nation crosses the border to impose its will on another sovereign power. And the aims of the war are not usually so simple as stopping aggression or even restoring peace. "Intervention in Somalia" provides an account of a forceful intervention that was justified on humanitarian grounds but in which the goals shifted, and the moral and logistical problems multiplied, during the intervention itself.

"Why Attack Iraq?" shows the effect of the changing circumstances on the criteria for just war. The Bush administration argued that the "new threat" of rogue nations such as Iraq and the spread of international terrorism require a revision of traditional criteria for just war. In this perilous new world the United States cannot risk waiting until a threat is "imminent and immediate" before using force. It must be prepared to strike first—to adopt what some have called a preventive strategy. (The administration and its critics sometimes used the term *preemptive,* but the definitison of that term in international law tracks more closely the traditional criteria described earlier.) Critics argue that unless one is prepared to let all nations adopt such a strategy, it is not an acceptable basis for principles of just war. They would be inclined to agree with Eisenhower, who when presented with a plan to wage preventive war to disarm Stalin's Soviet Union in 1953, said: "I don't believe there is such a thing; and, frankly, I wouldn't even listen to anyone seriously that came in and talked about such a thing."

The war against terrorism has revived the issue of the morality of torture. Because some individuals may have information that could save millions of lives, officials may be tempted to use, and perhaps may be even justified in using, techniques of interrogation that would otherwise be inhumane. "Interrogating Detainees" presents excerpts from memos and other texts that show officials trying to determine what techniques are acceptable. The assistant attorney general's memo suggests that torture may be permitted if authorized by the president in a war on terrorism. But President Bush takes an absolutist stance: "I will never order torture."

The Decision to Use the Atomic Bomb

Henry L. Stimson

In recent months there has been much comment about the decision to use atomic bombs in attacks on the Japanese cities of Hiroshima and Nagasaki. This decision was one of the gravest made by our government in recent years, and it is entirely proper that it should be widely discussed. I have therefore decided to record for all who may be interested my understanding of the events which led up to the attack on Hiroshima on August 6, 1945, on Nagasaki on August 9, and the Japanese decision to surrender on August 10. No single individual can hope to know exactly what took place in the minds of all of those who had a share in these events, but what follows is an exact description of our thoughts and actions as I find them in the records and in my clearest recollection.

It was in the fall of 1941 that the question of atomic energy was first brought directly to my attention. At that time President Roosevelt appointed a committee consisting of Vice President Wallace, General Marshall, Dr. Vannevar Bush, Dr. James B. Conant, and myself. The function of this committee was to advise the President on questions of policy relating to the study of nuclear fission which was then proceeding both in this country and in Great Britain. For nearly four years thereafter I was directly connected with all major decisions of policy on the

development and use of atomic energy, and from May 1, 1943, until my resignation as Secretary of War on September 21, 1945, I was directly responsible to the President for the administration of the entire undertaking; my chief advisers in this period were General Marshall, Dr. Bush, Dr. Conant, and Major General Leslie R. Groves, the officer in charge of the project. At the same time I was the President's adviser on the military employment of atomic energy.

The policy adopted and steadily pursued by President Roosevelt and his advisers was a simple one. It was to spare no effort in securing the earliest possible successful development of an atomic weapon. The reasons for this policy were equally simple. The original experimental achievement of atomic fission had occurred in Germany in 1938, and it was known that the Germans had continued their experiments. In 1941 and 1942 they were believed to be ahead of us, and it was vital that they should not be the first to bring atomic weapons into the field of battle. Furthermore, if we should be the first to develop the weapon, we should have a great new instrument for shortening the war and minimizing destruction. At no time from 1941 to 1945 did I ever hear it suggested by the President, or by any other responsible member of the government, that atomic energy should not be used in the war. All of us of course understood the terrible responsibility involved in our attempt to unlock the doors to such a devastating weapon; President Roosevelt particularly spoke to me many times of his own awareness of the catastrophic potentialities of our work. But we were at war, and the work must be done. I therefore emphasize that it was our common objective throughout the war to be the first to produce an atomic weapon and use it. The possible atomic weapon was considered to be a new and tremendously powerful explosive, as legitimate as any other of the deadly explosive weapons of modern war. The entire purpose was the production of a military weapon; on no other ground could the wartime expenditure of so much time and money have been justified. The exact circumstances in which that weapon might be used were unknown to any of us until the middle of 1945, and when that time came, as we shall presently see, the military use of atomic energy was connected with larger questions of national policy.

The extraordinary story of the successful development of the atomic bomb has been well told elsewhere. As time went on it became clear that the weapon would not be available in time for use in the European theater, and the war against Germany was successfully ended by the use of what are now called conventional means. But in the spring of 1945 it became evident that the climax of our prolonged atomic effort was at hand. By the nature of atomic chain reactions, it was impossible to state with certainty that we had succeeded until a bomb had actually exploded in a full-scale experiment; nevertheless it was considered exceedingly probable that we should by midsummer have successfully detonated the first atomic bomb. This was to be done at the Alamogordo Reservation in New Mexico. It was thus time for detailed consideration of our future plans. What had begun as a well-founded hope was now developing into a reality.

On March 15, 1945, I had my last talk with President Roosevelt. My diary record of this conversation gives a fairly clear picture of the state of our thinking at that time. I have removed the name of the distinguished public servant who was fearful lest the Manhattan (atomic) project be "a lemon"; it was an opinion common among those not fully informed.

"The President . . . had suggested that I come over to lunch today. . . . First I took up with him a memorandum which he sent to me from _____, who had been alarmed at the rumors of extravagance in the Manhattan project. _____ suggested that it might become disastrous and he suggested that we get a body of 'outside' scientists to pass upon the project because rumors are going around that Vannevar Bush and Jim Conant have sold the President a lemon on the subject and ought to be checked up on. It was rather a jittery and nervous memorandum and rather silly, and I was prepared for it and I gave the President a list of the scientists who were actually engaged on it to show the very high standing of them and it comprised four Nobel Prize men, and also how practically every physicist of standing was engaged with us in the project. Then I outlined to him the future of it and when it was likely to come off and told him how important it was to get ready. I went over with him the two schools of thought that exist in respect to the future control after the war of this project, in case it is successful, one of them being the secret close-in attempted control of the project by those who control it now, and the other being the international control based upon freedom both of science and of access. I told him that those things must be settled before the first projectile is used and that he must be ready with a statement to come out to the people on it just as soon as that is done. He agreed to that. . . ."

This conversation covered the three aspects of the question which were then uppermost in our minds. First, it was always necessary to suppress a lingering doubt that any such titanic undertaking could be successful. Second, we must consider the implications of success in terms of its long-range postwar effect. Third, we must face the problem that would be presented at the time of our first use of the weapon, for with that first use there must be some public statement.

I did not see Franklin Roosevelt again. The next time I went to the White House to discuss atomic energy was April 25, 1945, and I went to explain the nature of the problem to a man whose only previous knowledge of our activities was that of a Senator who had loyally accepted our assurance that the matter must be kept a secret from him. Now he was President and Commander-in-Chief, and the final responsibility in this as in so many other matters must be his. President Truman accepted this responsibility with the same fine spirit that Senator Truman had shown before in accepting our refusal to inform him.

I discussed with him the whole history of the project. We had with us General Groves, who explained in detail the progress which had been made and the probable future course of the work. I also discussed with President Truman the broader aspects of the subject, and the memorandum which I used in this discussion is again a fair sample of the state of our thinking at the time.

Memorandum discussed with President Truman April 25, 1945:

"1. Within four months we shall in all probability have completed the most terrible weapon ever known in human history, one bomb of which could destroy a whole city.

"2. Although we have shared its development with the U.K., physically the U.S. is at present in the position of controlling the resources with which to construct and use it and no other nation could reach this position for some years.

"3. Nevertheless it is practically certain that we could not remain in this position indefinitely.

"a. Various segments of its discovery and production are widely known among many scientists in many countries, although few scientists are now acquainted with the whole process which we have developed.

"b. Although its construction under present methods requires great scientific and industrial effort and raw materials, which are temporarily mainly within the possession and knowledge of U.S. and U.K., it is extremely probable that much easier and cheaper methods of production will be discovered by scientists in the future, together with the use of materials of much wider distribution. As a result, it is extremely probable that the future will make it possible for atomic bombs to be constructed by smaller nations or even groups, or at least by a larger nation in a much shorter time.

"4. As a result, it is indicated that the future may see a time when such a weapon may be constructed in secret and used suddenly and effectively with devastating power by a willful nation or group against an unsuspecting nation or group of much greater size and material power. With its aid even a very powerful unsuspecting nation might be conquered within a very few days by a very much smaller one. [A brief reference to the estimated capabilities of other nations is here omitted; it in no way affects the course of the argument.]

"5. The world in its present state of moral advancement compared with its technical development would be eventually at the mercy of such a weapon. In other words, modern civilization might be completely destroyed.

"6. To approach any world peace organization of any pattern now likely to be considered, without an appreciation by the leaders of our country of the power of this new weapon, would seem to be unrealistic. No system of control heretofore considered would be adequate to control this menace. Both inside any particular country and between the nations of the world, the control of this weapon will undoubtedly be a matter of the greatest difficulty and would involve such thorough-going rights of inspection and internal controls as we have never heretofore contemplated.

"7. Furthermore, in the light of our present position with reference to this weapon, the question of sharing it with other nations and, if so shared, upon what terms, becomes a primary question of our foreign relations. Also our leadership in the war and in the development of this weapon has placed a certain moral responsibility upon us which we cannot shirk without very serious responsibility for any disaster to civilization which it would further.

"8. On the other hand, if the problem of the proper use of this weapon can be solved, we would have the opportunity to bring the world into a pattern in which the peace of the world and our civilization can be saved.

"9. As stated in General Groves' report, steps are under way looking towards the establishment of a select committee of particular qualifications for recommending action to the executive and legislative branches of our government when secrecy is no longer in full effect. The committee would also recommend the actions to be taken by the War Department prior to that time in anticipation of the postwar problems. All recommendations would of course be first submitted to the President."

The next step in our preparations was the appointment of the committee referred to in paragraph 9 above. This committee, which was known as the Interim Committee, was charged with the function of advising the President on the various questions raised by our apparently imminent success in developing the atomic weapon. I was its chairman, but the principal labor of guiding its extended deliberations fell to George L. Harrison, who acted as chairman in my absence. It will be useful to consider the work of the committee in some detail. Its members were

the following, in addition to Mr. Harrison and myself:

James F. Byrnes (then a private citizen) as personal representative of the President.

Ralph A. Byrd, Under Secretary of the Navy.

William L. Clayton, Assistant Secretary of State.

Dr. Vannevar Bush, Director, Office of Scientific Research and Development, and president of the Carnegie Institution of Washington.

Dr. Karl Compton, Chief of the Office of Field Service in the Office of Scientific Research and Development, and president of the Massachusetts Institute of Technology.

Dr. James B. Conant, Chairman of the National Defense Research Committee, and president of Harvard University.

The discussions of the committee ranged over the whole field of atomic energy, in its political, military, and scientific aspects. That part of its work which particularly concerns us here relates to its recommendations for the use of atomic energy against Japan, but it should be borne in mind that these recommendations were not made in a vacuum. The committee's work included the drafting of the statements which were published immediately after the first bombs were dropped, the drafting of a bill for the domestic control of atomic energy, and recommendations looking toward the international control of atomic energy. The Interim Committee was assisted in its work by a Scientific Panel whose members were the following: Dr. A. H. Compton, Dr. Enrico Fermi, Dr. E. O. Lawrence, and Dr. J. R. Oppenheimer. All four were nuclear physicists of the first rank; all four had held positions of great importance in the atomic project from its inception. At a meeting with the Interim Committees and the Scientific Panel on May 31, 1945, I urged all those present to feel free to express themselves on any phase of the subject, scientific or political. Both General Marshall and I at this meeting expressed the view that atomic energy could not be considered simply in terms of military weapons but must also be considered in terms of a new relationship of man to the universe.

On June 1, after its discussions with the Scientific Panel, the Interim Committee unanimously adopted the following recommendations:

1. The bomb should be used against Japan as soon as possible.

2. It should be used on a dual target—that is, a military installation or war plant surrounded by or adjacent to houses and other buildings most susceptible to damage, and

3. It should be used without prior warning [of the nature of the weapon]. (One member of the committee, Mr. Bard, later changed his view and dissented from the third recommendation.)

In reaching these conclusions the Interim Committee carefully considered such alternatives as a detailed advance warning or a demonstration in some uninhabited area. Both of these suggestions were discarded as impractical. They were not regarded as likely to be effective in compelling a surrender of Japan and both of them involved serious risks. Even the New Mexico test would not give final proof that any given bomb was certain to explode when dropped from an airplane. Quite apart from the generally unfamiliar nature of atomic explosives, there was the whole problem of exploding a bomb at a predetermined height in the air by a complicated mechanism which could not be tested in the static test of New Mexico. Nothing would have been more damaging to our effort to obtain surrender than a warning or a demonstration followed by a dud—and this was a real possibility. Furthermore, we had no bombs to waste. It was vital that a sufficient effect be quickly obtained with the few we had.

The Interim Committee and the Scientific Panel also served as a channel through which suggestions from other scientists working on the atomic project were forwarded to me and to the President. Among the suggestions thus forwarded was one memorandum which questioned using the bomb at all against the enemy. On June 16, 1945, after consideration of that memorandum, the Scientific Panel made a report, from which I quote the following paragraphs:

"The opinions of our scientific colleagues on the initial use of these weapons are not unanimous: they range from the proposal of a purely technical demonstration to that of the military application best designed to induce surrender. Those who advocate a purely technical demonstration would wish to outlaw the use of atomic weapons, and have feared that if we use the weapons now our position in future negotiations will be prejudiced. Others emphasize the opportunity of saving American lives by immediate military use, and believe that such use will improve the international prospects, in that they are more concerned with the prevention of war than with the elimination of this special weapon. We find ourselves closer to these latter views: *we can propose no technical demonstration likely to bring an end to the war; we see no acceptable alternative to direct military use.*

"With regard to these general aspects of the use of atomic energy, it is clear that we, as scientific men, have no proprietary rights. It is true that we are among the few citizens who have had occasion to give thoughtful consideration to these problems during the past few years. We have, however, no claim to special competence in solving the political, social, and military problems which are presented by the advent of atomic power."

The foregoing discussion presents the reasoning of the Interim Committee and its advisers. I have discussed the work of these gentlemen at length in order to make it clear that we sought the best advice that we could find. The committee's function was, of course, entirely advisory. The ultimate responsibility for the recommendation to the President rested upon me, and I have no desire to veil it. The conclusions of the committees were similar to my own, although I reached mine independently.

I felt that to extract a genuine surrender from the Emperor and his military advisers, they must be administered a tremendous shock which would carry convincing proof of our power to destroy the Empire. Such an effective shock would save many times the number of lives, both American and Japanese, than it would cost.

The facts upon which my reasoning was based and steps taken to carry it out now follow.

The principal political, social, and military objective of the United States in the summer of 1945 was the prompt and complete surrender of Japan. Only the complete destruction of her military power could open the way to lasting peace.

Japan, in July 1945, had been seriously weakened by our increasingly violent attacks. It was known to us that she had gone so far as to make tentative proposals to the Soviet government, hoping to use the Russians as mediators in a negotiated peace. These vague proposals contemplated the retention by Japan of important conquered areas and were therefore not considered seriously. There was as yet no indication of any weakening in the Japanese determination to fight rather than accept unconditional surrender. If she should persist in her fight to the end, she had still a great military force.

In the middle of July 1945, the intelligence section of the War Department General Staff estimated Japanese military strength as follows: in the home islands, slightly under two million; in Korea, Manchuria, China proper, and Formosa, slightly over two million; in French Indo-China, Thailand, and Burma, over 200,000; in the East Indies area, including the Philippines, over 500,000; in the by-passed Pacific islands, over 100,000. The total strength of the Japanese Army was estimated at about five million men. These estimates later proved to be in very close agreement with official Japanese figures.

The Japanese Army was in much better condition than the Japanese Navy and Air Force. The Navy had practically ceased to exist except as a harrying force against an invasion fleet. The Air Force had been reduced mainly to reliance upon Kamikaze, or suicide, attacks. These latter, however, had already inflicted serious damage on our seagoing forces, and their possible effectiveness in a last ditch fight was a matter of real concern to our naval leaders.

As we understood it in July, there was a very strong possibility that the Japanese government might determine upon resistance to the end, in all the areas of the Far East under its control. In such an event the Allies would be faced with the enormous task of destroying an armed force of five million men and five thousand suicide aircraft, belonging to a race which had already demonstrated its ability to fight literally to the death.

The strategic plans of our armed forces for the defeat of Japan as they stood in July had been prepared without reliance upon the atomic bomb, which had not yet been tested in New Mexico. We were planning an intensified sea and air blockade and greatly intensified strategic air bombing through the summer and early fall, to be followed on November 1 by an invasion of the southern island of Kyushu. This would be followed in turn by an invasion of the main island of Honshu in the spring of 1946. The total U.S. military and naval force involved in this grand design was of the order of five million men; if all those indirectly concerned are included, it was larger still.

We estimated that if we should be forced to carry this plan to its conclusion, the major fighting force would not end until the latter part of 1946, at the earliest. I was informed that such operations might be expected to cost over a million casualties, to American forces alone. Additional large losses might be expected among our allies, and, of course, if our campaign were successful and if we could judge by previous experience, enemy casualties would be much larger than our own.

It was already clear in July that even before the invasion, we should be able to inflict enormously severe damage on the Japanese homeland by the combined application of "conventional" sea and air power. The critical question was whether this kind of action would induce surrender. It therefore became necessary to consider very carefully the probable state of mind of the enemy, and to assess with accuracy the line of conduct which might end his will to resist.

With these considerations in mind, I wrote a memorandum for the President, on July 2, which I believe fairly represents the thinking of the American government as it finally took shape in action. This memorandum was prepared after discussion and general agreement with Joseph C. Grew, Acting Secretary of State, and Secretary of the Navy Forrestal, and when I discussed it with the President, he expressed his general approval.

Memorandum for the President, July 2, 1945, on proposed program for Japan:

"1. The plans of operation up to and including the first landing have been authorized and the preparations for the operation are now actually going on. This situation was accepted by all members of your conference on Monday, June 18.

"2. There is reason to believe that the operation for occupation of Japan following the landing may be a very long, costly, and arduous struggle on our part. The terrain, much of which I have visited several times, has left the impression on my memory of being one which would be susceptible to a last ditch defense such as has been made on Iwo Jima and Okinawa and which of course is very much larger than either of those two areas. According to my recollection it will be much more unfavorable with regard to tank maneuvering than either the Philippines or Germany.

"3. If we once land on one of the main islands and begin a forceful occupation of Japan, we shall probably have cast the die of last ditch resistance. The Japanese are highly patriotic and certainly susceptible to calls for fanatical resistance to repel an invasion. Once started in actual invasion, we shall in my opinion have to go through with an even more bitter finish fight than in Germany. We shall incur the losses incident to such a war and we shall have to leave the Japanese islands even more thoroughly destroyed than was the case with Germany. This would be due both to the difference in the Japanese and German personal character and the differences in the size and character of the terrain through which the operations will take place.

"4. A question then comes: Is there any alternative to such a forceful occupation of Japan which will secure for us the equivalent of an unconditional surrender of her forces and a permanent destruction of her power again to strike an aggressive blow at the 'peace of the Pacific'? I am inclined to think that there is enough such chance to make it well worthwhile our giving them a warning of what is to come and a definite opportunity to capitulate. As above suggested, it should be tried before the actual forceful occupation of the homeland islands is begun and furthermore the warning should be given in ample time to permit a national reaction to set in.

"We have the following enormously favorable factors on our side—factors much weightier than those we had against Germany:

"Japan has no allies.

"Her navy is nearly destroyed and she is vulnerable to a surface and underwater blockade which can deprive her of sufficient food and supplies for her population.

"She is terribly vulnerable to our concentrated air attack upon her crowded cities, industrial and food resources.

"She has against her not only the Anglo-American forces but the rising forces of China and the ominous threat of Russia.

"We have inexhaustible and untouched industrial resources to bring to bear against her diminishing potential.

"We have great moral superiority through being the victim of her first sneak attack.

"The problem is to translate these advantages into prompt and economical achievement of our objectives. I believe Japan is susceptible to reason in such a crisis to a much greater extent than is indicated by our current press and other current comment. Japan is not a nation composed wholly of mad fanatics of an entirely different mentality from ours. On the contrary, she has within the past century shown herself to possess extremely intelligent people, capable in an unprecedentedly short time of adopting not only the complicated technique of Occidental civilization but to a substantial extent their culture and their political and social ideas. Her advance in all these respects during the short period of sixty or seventy years has been one of the most astounding feats of national progress in history—a leap from the isolated feudalism of centuries into the position of one of the six or seven great powers of the world. She has not only built up powerful armies and navies. She has maintained an honest and effective national finance and respected position in many of the sciences in which we pride ourselves. Prior to the forcible seizure of power over her government by the fanatical military group in 1931, she had for ten years lived a reasonably responsible and respectable international life.

"My own opinion is in her favor on the two points involved in this question:

"a. I think the Japanese nation has the mental intelligence and versatile capacity in such a crisis to recognize the folly of a fight to the finish and to accept the proffer of what will amount to an unconditional surrender; and

"b. I think she has within her population enough liberal leaders (although now submerged by the terrorists) to be depended upon for her reconstruction as a responsible member of the family of nations. I think she is better in this respect than Germany was. Her liberals yielded only at the point of the pistol and, so far as I am aware, their liberal attitude has not been personally subverted in the way which was so general in Germany.

"On the other hand, I think that the attempt to exterminate her armies and her population by gunfire or other means will tend to produce a fusion of race solidity and antipathy which has no analogy in the case of Germany. We have a national interest in creating, if possible, a condition wherein the Japanese nation may live as a peaceful and useful member of the future Pacific community.

"5. It is therefore my conclusion that a carefully timed warning be given to Japan by the chief representatives of the United States, Great Britain, China, and, if then a belligerent, Russia by calling upon Japan to surrender and permit the occupation of her country in order to insure its complete demilitarization for the sake of the future peace.

"This warning should contain the following elements:

"The varied and overwhelming character of the force we are about to bring to bear on the islands.

"The inevitability and completeness of the destruction which the full application of this force will entail.

"The determination of the Allies to destroy permanently all authority and influence of those who have deceived and misled the country into embarking on world conquest.

"The determination of the Allies to limit Japanese sovereignty to her main islands and to render them powerless to mount and support another war.

"The disavowal of any attempt to extirpate the Japanese as a race or to destroy them as a nation.

"A statement of our readiness, once her economy is purged of its militaristic influence, to permit the Japanese to maintain such industries, particularly of a light consumer character, as offer no threat of aggression against their neighbors, but which can produce a sustaining economy, and provide a reasonable standard of living. The statement should indicate our willingness, for this purpose, to give Japan trade access to external raw materials, but no longer any control over the sources of supply outside her main islands. It should also indicate our willingness, in accordance with our now established foreign policy, in due course to enter into mutually advantageous trade relations with her.

"The withdrawal from their country as soon as the above objectives of the Allies are accomplished, and as soon as there has been established a peacefully inclined government, of a character representative of the masses of the Japanese people. I personally think that if in saying this we should add that we do not exclude a constitutional monarchy under her present dynasty, it would substantially add to the chances of acceptance.

"6. Success of course will depend on the potency of the warning which we give her. She has an extremely sensitive national pride and, as we are now seeing every day, when actually locked with the enemy will fight to the very death. For that reason the warning must be tendered before the actual invasion has occurred and while the impending destruction, though clear beyond peradventure, has not yet reduced her to fanatical despair. If Russia is part of the threat, the Russian attack, if actual, must not have progressed too far. Our own bombing should be confined to military objectives as far as possible."

It is important to emphasize the double character of the suggested warning. It was designed to promise destruction if Japan resisted, and hope, if she surrendered.

It will be noted that the atomic bomb is not mentioned in this memorandum. On grounds of secrecy the bomb was never mentioned except when absolutely necessary and furthermore, it had not yet been tested. It was of course well forward in our minds as the memorandum was written and discussed that

the bomb would be the best possible sanction if our warning were rejected.

The adoption of the policy outlined in the memorandum of July 2 was a decision of high politics; once it was accepted by the President, the position of the atomic bomb in our planning became quite clear. I find that I stated in my diary, as early as June 19, that "the last chance warning . . . must be given before an actual landing of the ground forces in Japan, and fortunately the plans provide for enough time to bring in the sanctions to our warning in the shape of heavy ordinary bombing attack and an attack of S-1." S-1 was a code name for the atomic bomb.

There was much discussion in Washington about the timing of the warning to Japan. The controlling factor in the end was the date already set for the Potsdam meeting of the Big Three. It was President Truman's decision that such a warning should be solemnly issued by the U.S. and the U.K. from this meeting, with the concurrence of the head of the Chinese government, so that it would be plain that *all* of Japan's principal enemies were in entire unity. This was done in the Potsdam ultimatum of July 26, which very closely followed the above memorandum of July 2 with the exception that it made no mention of the Japanese Emperor.

On July 28 the Premier of Japan, Suzuki, rejected the Potsdam ultimatum by announcing that it was "unworthy of public notice." In the face of this rejection we could only proceed to demonstrate that the ultimatum had meant exactly what it said when it stated that if the Japanese continued the war, "the full application of our military power, backed by our resolve, will mean the inevitable and complete destruction of the Japanese armed forces and just as inevitably the utter devastation of the Japanese homeland."

For such a purpose the atomic bomb was an entirely suitable weapon. The New Mexico test occurred while we were at Potsdam, on July 16. It was immediately clear that the power of the bomb measured up to our highest estimates. We had developed a weapon of such a revolutionary character that its use against the enemy might well be expected to produce exactly the kind of shock on the Japanese ruling oligarchy which we desired, strengthening the position of those who wished peace, and weakening that of the military party.

Because of the importance of the atomic mission against Japan, the detailed plans were brought to me by the military staff for approval. With President Truman's warm support I struck off the list of suggested targets the city of Kyoto. Although it was a target of considerable military importance, it had been the ancient capital of Japan and was a shrine of Japanese art and culture. We determined that it should be spared. I approved four other targets including the cities of Hiroshima and Nagasaki.

Hiroshima was bombed on August 6, and Nagasaki on August 9. These two cities were active working parts of the Japanese war effort. One was an army center; the other was naval and industrial. Hiroshima was the headquarters of the Japanese Army defending southern Japan and was a major military storage and assembly point. Nagasaki was a major seaport and it contained several large industrial plants of great wartime importance. We believed that our attacks had struck cities which must certainly be important to the Japanese military leaders, both Army and Navy, and we waited for a result. We waited one day.

Many accounts have been written about the Japanese surrender. After a prolonged Japanese cabinet session in which the deadlock was broken by the Emperor himself, the offer to surrender was made on August 10. It was based on the Potsdam terms, with a reservation concerning the sovereignty of the Emperor. While the Allied reply made no promises other than those already given, it implicitly recognized the Emperor's position by prescribing that his power must be subject to the orders of the Allied Supreme Commander. These terms were accepted on August 14 by the Japanese, and

the instrument of surrender was formally signed on September 2, in Tokyo Bay. Our great objective was thus achieved, and all the evidence I have seen indicates that the controlling factor in the final Japanese decision to accept our terms of surrender was the atomic bomb.

The two atomic bombs which we had dropped were the only ones we had ready, and our rate of production at the time was very small. Had the war continued until the projected invasion on November 1, additional fire raids of B-29s would have been more destructive of life and property than the very limited number of atomic raids which we could have executed in the same period. But the atomic bomb was more than a weapon of terrible destruction; it was a psychological weapon. In March 1945, our Air Force had launched its first great incendiary raid on the Tokyo area. In this raid more damage was done and more casualties were inflicted than was the case at Hiroshima. Hundreds of bombers took part and hundreds of tons of incendiaries were dropped. Similar successive raids burned out a great part of the urban area of Japan, but the Japanese fought on. On August 6 one B-29 dropped a single atomic weapon on Hiroshima. Three days later a second bomb was dropped on Nagasaki and the war was over. So far as the Japanese could know, our ability to execute atomic attacks, if necessary by many planes at a time, was unlimited. As Dr. Karl Compton has said, "it was not one atomic bomb, or two, which brought surrender; it was the experience of what an atomic bomb will actually do to a community, *plus the dread of many more,* that was effective.

The bomb thus served exactly the purpose we intended. The peace part was able to take the path of surrender, and the whole weight of the Emperor's prestige was exerted in favor of peace. When the Emperor ordered surrender, and the small but dangerous group of fanatics who opposed him were brought under control, the Japanese became so subdued that the great undertaking of occupation and disarmament was completed with unprecedented ease.

In the foregoing pages I have tried to give an accurate account of my own personal observations of the circumstances which led up to the use of the atomic bomb and the reasons which underlay our use of it. To me they have always seemed compelling and clear, and I cannot see how any person vested with such responsibilities as mine could have taken any other course or given any other advice to his chiefs.

Two great nations were approaching contact in a fight to a finish which would begin on November 1, 1945. Our enemy, Japan, commanded forces of somewhat over 5 million armed men. Men of these armies had already inflicted upon us, in our breakthrough of the outer perimeter of their defenses, over 300,000 battle casualties. Enemy armies still unbeaten had the strength to cost us a million more. *As long as the Japanese government refused to surrender,* we should be forced to take and hold the ground, and smash the Japanese ground armies, by close-in fighting of the same desperate and costly kind that we had faced in the Pacific islands for nearly four years.

In the light of the formidable problem which thus confronted us, I felt that every possible step should be taken to compel a surrender of the homelands, and a withdrawal of all Japanese troops from the Asiatic mainland and from other positions, before we had commenced an invasion. We held two cards to assist us in such an effort. One was the traditional veneration in which the Japanese Emperor was held by his subjects and the power which was thus vested in him over his loyal troops. It was for this reason that I suggested in my memorandum of July 2 that his dynasty should be continued. The second card was the use of the atomic bomb in the manner best calculated to persuade that Emperor and the counselors about him to submit to our demand for what was essentially unconditional surrender, placing

his immense power over his people and his troops subject to our orders.

In order to end the war in the shortest possible time and to avoid the enormous losses of life which otherwise confronted us, I felt that we must use the Emperor as our instrument to command and compel his people to cease fighting and subject themselves to our authority through him, and that to accomplish this we must give him and his controlling advisers a compelling reason to accede to our demands. This reason furthermore must be of such a nature that his people could understand his decision. The bomb seemed to me to furnish a unique instrument for that purpose.

My chief purpose was to end the war in victory with the least possible cost in the lives of the men in the armies which I had helped to raise. In the light of the alternatives which, on a fair estimate, were open to us, I believe that no man, in our position and subject to our responsibilities, holding in his hands a weapon of such possibilities for accomplishing this purpose and saving those lives, could have failed to use it and afterwards looked his countrymen in the face.

As I read over what I have written, I am aware that much of it, in this year of peace, may have a harsh and unfeeling sound. It would perhaps be possible to say the same things and say them more gently. But I do not think it would be wise. As I look back over the five years of my service as Secretary of War, I see too many stern and heartrending decisions to be willing to pretend that war is anything else than what it is. The face of war is the face of death; death is an inevitable part of every order that a wartime leader gives. The decision to use the atomic bomb was a decision that brought death to over a hundred thousand Japanese. No explanation can change that fact, and I do not wish to gloss it over. But this deliberate, premeditated destruction was our least abhorrent choice. The destruction of Hiroshima and Nagasaki put an end to the Japanese war. It stopped the fire raids, and the strangling blockade; it ended the ghastly specter of a clash of great land armies.

In this last great action of the Second World War we were given final proof that war is death. War in the twentieth century has grown steadily more barbarous, more destructive, more debased in all its aspects.

Now, with the release of atomic energy, man's ability to destroy himself is very nearly complete. The bombs dropped on Hiroshima and Nagasaki ended a war. They also made it wholly clear that we must never have another war. This is the lesson men and leaders everywhere must learn, and I believe that when they learn it they will find a way to lasting peace. There is no other choice.

Alternatives to the Bomb
Colin Dueck

On August 6, 1945, the *Enola Gay* B-29 bomber dropped a four-ton atomic bomb—the "Fat Boy"—on the Japanese city of Hiroshima, resulting in the death of up to 130,000 people. In a public statement that same day, President Harry Truman declared that if the leaders of Japan failed to surrender unconditionally to the Allied powers, they could "expect a rain of ruin from the air, the likes of which has never been seen on earth." On August 9, a second atomic bomb was dropped on the port city of Nagasaki, and five days later, Emperor Hirohito addressed the Japanese people over the radio to tell them that their country had surrendered.

By the end of June 1945, Japan had undoubtedly lost the war. Its navy had been destroyed, its lifeline to food and raw materials was being strangled by a naval blockade, its cities were subject to a massively destructive strategic bombing campaign. The conquest of Okinawa by American forces had opened up the home islands to invasion. Aware of their declining ability to

wage war successfully, and with tentative support from Emperor Hirohito, Japanese cabinet members sent Prince Konoye on an exploratory diplomatic mission to the USSR, in the hopes of persuading Moscow to mediate a negotiated peace between Japan and the Western Allies.[1] The Japanese seemed to be showing some interest in a peace settlement, but they feared that accepting the longstanding Allied condition of "unconditional surrender" would mean the deposition of their Emperor—an unacceptable condition. American policymakers were aware of this fear; earlier success at cracking Japanese diplomatic codes allowed the United States to intercept messages from Tokyo to the Japanese embassy in Moscow. Secretary of the Navy James Forrestal noted in his diary on July 13 that Japan's foreign minister, Shigenori Togo, had instructed his ambassador in Moscow to tell the Soviets that "the unconditional surrender terms of the Allies were about the only thing in the way of [the] termination of the war and he said that if this were insisted upon, of course the Japanese would have to fight."[2] Secretary of War Henry Stimson had suggested to Truman on July 2 that Japan might very well surrender upon being offered a guarantee of the emperor's position.[3] General MacArthur had noted that a peaceful postwar transition within a defeated, occupied Japan would be impossible without the emperor's stabilizing influence. And as early as May, acting Secretary of State Joseph Grew—formerly, ambassador to Tokyo—had argued that:

> the greatest obstacle to unconditional surrender by the Japanese is their belief that this would entail the destruction or permanent removal of the Emperor and the institution of the Throne. If some indicator can now be given the Japanese that they themselves . . . will be permitted to determine their own political structure, they will be afforded a method of saving face without which surrender will be highly unlikely.[4]

The president had remarked casually to Stimson that it sounded like a good idea. American planners were inclined to agree with MacArthur that it would be best to keep the emperor, and Stimson had drafted an early version of the Potsdam declaration in which Hirohito's position was guaranteed. Yet Secretary of State James Byrnes, supported by President Truman, vetoed Stimson's draft, and the final declaration from Potsdam on July 26 gave no indication that the emperor's status was secure—this in spite of the fact that when Japan did surrender, less than three weeks later, the United States accepted the emperor's continued reign.[5] In 1948, Stimson himself admitted that on the question of guaranteeing the emperor's position, he had come to "believe that history might find that the United States, by its delay in stating its position, had prolonged the war."[6]

It is far from certain that the Japanese would have surrendered before Hiroshima if only they had been offered a guarantee of the emperor's position. It had cost American forces three months and almost 50,000 casualties to root out Japanese forces from the small island of Okinawa. The Japanese still held on to much of their conquests in China, Manchuria, and southeast Asia, and a large army—together with

a fleet of kamikaze planes—stood ready to defend the home islands from invasion.[7] Japan had lost the war, but the military situation was not so discouraging as to require virtually unconditional surrender. A negotiated peace was a possibility; the question was, On what terms? At minimum, Japan's leaders wanted to preserve not only the emperor, but the entire imperial social, economic, and political system, or *"kokutai,"* which was bound up with their own status. Before August 6, the most dovish civilian leaders in the Cabinet wanted to preserve some degree of self-rule for Japan.[8] As Foreign Minister Togo told his ambassador to Moscow on July 17, "We are not asking the Russians' mediation in anything like unconditional surrender." Such demands were incompatible with American plans for postwar occupation, disarmament, reform, and democratization of Japan, regardless of the emperor's status. More to the point, the Cabinet was divided and diplomacy incapacitated by the army's demand that Japan fight on to win a more favorable peace. Army leaders insisted upon a continuation of the Showa regime, free from American occupation; they also hoped to keep some of the territorial gains they had made through war. Indeed, army planners expected to be able to inflict such heavy losses upon American forces, in case of an invasion, that the United States would be obliged to sign a compromise peace. As General Shoichi Miyazaki put it:

> If we could defeat the enemy in Kyushu or inflict tremendous losses, forcing him to realize the strong fighting spirit of the Japanese Army and people, it would be possible, we hoped, to bring about the termination of hostilities on comparatively favorable terms.[9]

Since the army was immensely influential, with a formal veto in the Cabinet, and since civilian leaders that acted in defiance of the army risked assassination or coup d'etat, any serious efforts at peace were ruled out.[10] No diplomatic feelers were sent to the United States. Even the famous "peace mission" to Moscow in July did not have either the support of the army or formal government backing; consequently, its proposals were vague, ambiguous, and lacking in concrete specifics.[11] As the Japanese ambassador to Moscow told Togo on July 15, "Your successive telegrams have not clarified the situation. The interests of the government and the military were not clear regarding the termination of the war."[12] In any case, by this point Stalin was uninterested in mediating any peace in the Pacific, since he had more to gain by entering the war against Japan, and Prince Konoye was not allowed into Moscow.

Even *after* the bombing of Hiroshima, military leaders in the Cabinet continued to resist the prospect of American occupation, disarmament, and war crimes tribunals. They argued that Japan still had the "ability to deal a smashing blow to the enemy" and that "it would be inexcusable to surrender unconditionally." Only after a late-night Cabinet meeting on August 9 and 10, with the direct and partisan intervention of the emperor—highly unusual in itself—did they agree to surrender to the terms laid out at Potsdam, "with the understanding that the said declaration does not comprise any demand which prejudices the prerogatives of His Majesty as a Sovereign Ruler."

A July 8 report by the Anglo-American Combined Intelligence Committee to the Chiefs of Staff informed U.S. policymakers that the Japanese Army was not yet prepared to surrender. They judged that the peace feelers to the United States through Moscow were not to be taken seriously; indeed, they feared that Japan might try to make some sort of separate arrangement with the USSR. Even Joseph Grew, a champion of guaranteeing the emperor's position, believed that the July overtures were "familiar weapons of psychological warfare" designed to "divide the Allies." Truman believed there to be little reason to offer any diplomatic concessions, given the lack of any clear indication from the other side that such concessions would bring

peace. Moreover, to negotiate with Tokyo before a Soviet entry had occurred risked alienating the USSR, a powerful ally. The policy of unconditional surrender was a legacy of Franklin Roosevelt's wartime leadership, and it had strong support both in Congress and with public opinion. The memory of Pearl Harbor, and reports of war atrocities and of mistreated American prisoners of war, fed the desire for retribution.[13] Leading congressional figures were calling for Hirohito to be tried and executed as a war criminal—a view with broad public support. Consequently, even after receiving the Japanese offer of near-unconditional surrender on August 10, the American Cabinet was divided over how to respond. While Admiral Leahy advocated its acceptance, Secretary Byrnes feared "the crucifixion of the president" if Hirohito went unpunished. The reply eventually sent by the United States—and accepted by the Japanese, a few days later—was ambiguous, giving no explicit guarantee of the emperor's position; rather, it stuck to the letter of the Potsdam declaration, reiterated that the "ultimate form of government of Japan shall . . . be established by the freely expressed will of the Japanese people," and concluded that:

> from the moment of surrender the authority of the Emperor and the Japanese government to rule the state shall be subject to the Supreme Commander of the Allied Powers who will take such steps as he deems proper to effectuate the surrender terms.

State Department planners like Archibald MacLeish had said all along that the Meiji imperial system was authoritarian and feudal, a source of hypernationalism. They wanted to reform and democratize Japanese institutions under United States tutelage, and the American occupation gave them the chance to do just that. Such considerations weighed against any explicit or early guarantee of the emperor. A peace settlement based upon such a guarantee might have resulted in a less democratic postwar Japan. But had American policymakers been willing to abandon the policy of unconditional surrender in the summer of 1945—had they allowed for the continuation of both self-rule and the imperial system—there is evidence to suggest that Japan's civilian leaders might have welcomed a negotiated peace.

A second alternative to the atomic bomb, without resorting to an invasion, was to rely upon a naval blockade and conventional strategic bombing to wear down Japanese resistance—an alternative known as the "siege strategy." Up until May 1945, the United States had relied upon such a strategy. First, American submarines had destroyed Japan's merchant marine and cut off supplies of food and raw materials destined for the home islands. With most such supplies located overseas, Japan was highly vulnerable to naval interdiction; by summer, as a result, the Japanese were suffering from severe shortages of food, clothing, and raw materials vital to the war effort.[14] Second, a strategic bombing campaign was launched against Japan—beginning with precision bombing and moving to mass firebombing early in 1945. The bombing campaign was immensely destructive, resulting in hundreds of thousands of Japanese civilian casualties. In later years, a number of Truman's key advisors, including Admiral Leahy, Truman's chief of staff and head of the joint chiefs of staff, General Henry Arnold, commanding general of the Army Air Force in 1945, and Admiral King, chief of staff for the navy, estimated that this strategy of bomb-and-blockade would have forced the Japanese to surrender without the necessity of either an invasion or the atomic bomb.[15] King wrote that "had we been willing to wait, the effective naval blockade would, in the course of time, have starved the Japanese into submission."[16] And in a 1946 United States Strategic Bombing Survey, air force authorities concluded that due to the effects of conventional bombing, "certainly prior to 31 December 1945, and in all probability prior to 1 November 1945, Japan would have surrendered even if

the atomic bomb had not been dropped, and even if no invasion had been planned or contemplated."[17]

There is little or no evidence to suggest that United States military leaders made these arguments in the summer of 1945 with Truman or any other policymakers. Such postwar recollections and evaluations cannot be assumed to reflect what historical actors thought and did at the time. In looking back at the reasons for Japan's surrender, leaders from the navy emphasized the role of the blockade, just as leaders from the air force emphasized the role of strategic bombing. But the Strategic Bombing Survey of 1946 has since been shown to have doctored the evidence from interviews with Japanese authorities in favor of its conclusion.[18] King, Leahy, and Arnold may have come genuinely to believe, after the war, that neither an invasion nor the atomic bombs had been necessary. But at a critical June 18 meeting at the White House, all three of them agreed with General Marshall, chief of staff for the army, that the time had come to supplement the "siege strategy" with definite plans for an invasion.[19] Truman also agreed. The blockade had been very effective, but Japan still had food supplies to last until the end of 1945 and was capable of fighting on. The U.S. joint chiefs "doubted whether the general economic deterioration had yet reached, or would reach for some time, the point at which it would affect the ability of the nation to fight or repel an invasion." And as for the strategic bombing campaign, it appeared to have hardly influenced the morale or policy of the Japanese leadership. As Marshall put it, in reference to the March firebombing of the Japanese capital, "We had 100,000 people killed in Tokyo in one night, and it had seemingly no effect whatsoever." There was simply no guarantee that continuing the siege strategy without an invasion would bring Japan's unconditional surrender anytime soon.[20]

The third alternative strategy was to wait for the USSR to enter the war against Japan and to rely upon the Red Army to deal the final blow to Japanese forces. The Soviet declaration of war and rapid advance against the Japanese army in Manchuria was clearly critical in bringing about a Japanese surrender. For three days after Hiroshima, Japan's military leaders refused even to attend Cabinet meetings designed to discuss terms of surrender. Then, on August 8 and 9, the Soviet attack, and immediate collapse of Japanese forces in Manchuria, stunned Japan's military leaders and changed the strategic situation literally overnight. Upon learning of the defeat, Prime Minister Suzuki remarked, "Is the Kwantung [Manchurian] Army that weak? Then the game is up."[21]

American decision-makers were aware that Soviet entry might end the war without the necessity of an invasion. The Anglo-American Joint Intelligence Committee reported on April 29, 1945, that "the entry of the USSR into the war would . . . convince most Japanese at once of the inevitability of complete defeat." The same advice was offered by the committee later that summer. And on June 18, General Marshall told President Truman that "the impact of Russian entry on the already hopeless Japanese may well be the decisive action levering them into capitulation." It was for this reason that Truman went to Potsdam eager to win Stalin's promise of an early entrance into the war against Japan. As the president put it, "If the test [of the atomic bomb] should fail, then it would be even more important to us to bring about a surrender before we had to make a physical conquest of Japan."[22] Stalin's promise of entry within a month left Truman reassured. He noted in his diary for July 17 that "he'll [Stalin] be in the Jap War on August 15. Fini Japs when that comes about."[23] Truman knew that a Soviet intervention against Japan would contribute significantly to ending the war and could possibly render an invasion unnecessary. Up until July 17, he encouraged such intervention by the USSR.

On that day, however, Truman learned that the first testing of an atomic bomb had taken place in the desert of New Mexico and that it had been an astonishing success. The new weapon held out the possibility of winning the war and averting an invasion without the necessity of a Soviet intervention. Stimson wrote on July 23 that General Marshall "felt as I felt sure he would, that now with our new weapon we would not need the assistance of the Russians to conquer Japan."[24] Truman noted in his diary that the "Japs will fold before Russia comes in. I am sure they will when Manhattan [the atomic bomb] appears over their homeland."[25] Some historians now argue that Truman and his close advisor Secretary Byrnes not only viewed the use of the bomb against Japan as the quickest route to victory, but that they: (i) hoped to win the war against Japan without Soviet aid, (ii) switched to a strategy of actively *delaying* Soviet entry into the Pacific war, in order to be able to drop the bomb first, (iii) abandoned any chance of modifying the policy of unconditional surrender at Potsdam, knowing that the Japanese would refuse, for the same reason, and (iv) dropped the atomic bomb on Japan primarily for "anti-Soviet," political reasons—not only to shut the USSR out of Japan, but to impress Stalin with American power and render him more compliant on European matters.[26]

Truman excluded any guarantee of the emperor's status in the Potsdam declaration because he expected to gain nothing from such a guarantee, and in any case had no desire to make such an offer, for reasons that had nothing to do with hostility towards the USSR. But American policy towards the bomb was influenced by policy toward the USSR, and vice versa. American decision-makers had high hopes that their control over this revolutionary new weapon would, as Truman told his reparations advisor Edwin Pauley, "keep the Russians straight." Stimson did advise Truman to delay any resolution of outstanding Soviet-American disputes over Manchuria, Poland, Rumania, and Yugoslavia until the atomic bomb had been tested successfully: "it seems a terrible thing to gamble with such big stakes in diplomacy without having your master card in your hand."[27] The possession of the bomb did in fact embolden Truman to take a harder line on Eastern Europe. American decision-makers probably did, in the words of Stimson's special assistant Harvey Bundy, see "large advantage to winning the Japanese war without the aid of Russia."[28] At Potsdam, on July 23, Winston Churchill observed that "the United States do not at the present time desire Russian participation in the war against Japan." Secretary Byrnes, at the least, was anxious to end the war before Soviet forces had a chance to advance far into or past Manchuria. When asked in a 1960 interview whether there had been a special urgency to end the war out of fear of a Soviet advance, Byrnes replied:

> There certainly was on my part, and I'm sure that, whatever views President Truman may have had of it earlier in that year, that in the days immediately preceding the dropping of the bomb his views were the same as mine— we wanted to get through the Japanese phase of the war before the Russians came in.[29]

There is no direct evidence, however, to show that the United States dropped the bomb on Hiroshima in order to intimidate Moscow.[30] Although Truman and his advisors spoke of gaining diplomatic leverage with Stalin through possession of the bomb, there is no reason to believe that the primary reason for dropping the bomb on Japan was anything other than what Truman said it was—to end the war as soon as possible and save American lives. Many historians agree that concern about the Soviet Union at best "confirmed" rather than "determined" the use of the new weapon against Japan—in other words, it gave one more reason not to cancel the *Enola Gay*'s mission.[31] As with the siege strategy, U.S. decision-makers could not be *certain* that a Soviet attack would be sufficient to defeat Japan or that it would be coming anytime soon. Indeed, it was the news of the bombing of Hiroshima—and the fear of being left out

of the picture in northeast Asia—that led Stalin to move up the Soviet declaration of war from August 15 to August 8. Despite their undeniably cooling enthusiasm for such intervention by the USSR, American leaders did not actively discourage Soviet entrance into the war after mid-July.

There is evidence, however, that Truman and his advisors were eager to conclude the war against Japan as soon as possible, before any Soviet entry, most likely out of a desire both to save American lives and to prevent the USSR from gaining a foothold in Japan and its environs. The goal of keeping Soviet forces at bay seems to have provided an added reason, particularly in the case of Secretary Byrnes, to drop the atomic bomb on Japan. Stalin aimed at recovering Russia's East Asian losses from 1905, together with influence for the USSR in Manchuria, Korea, and possibly even Japan. On August 16 he asked Truman for coequal status in the occupation of Japan. Two days later Soviet troops attacked the Kurile Islands and began to move south towards Hokkaido, the northernmost of Japan's four home islands. American naval supremacy in the area probably ruled out any Soviet occupation of Japan; but the prospect of a more advanced position in the region for the USSR was of real concern to the president. The evidence suggests that had Truman and his advisors been less worried about Soviet expansion and less determined to end the war at the earliest possible moment, they might very well have been able to rely upon Moscow's declaration of war to bring about a Japanese capitulation without an invasion of the home islands and without the atomic bomb—particularly if such an approach had been supplemented by a modification in the terms of surrender.

A fourth alternative was either to stage a demonstration of the bomb for Japan in some uninhabited area or to warn Japanese leaders about the bomb beforehand in order to give them a chance to surrender. The possibility of such a warning had been raised intermittently by leading policymakers: first at the

May 31 meeting of the Interim Committee on postwar nuclear policy, attended by Stimson and Byrnes; then by Assistant Secretary of War John McCloy at the June 18 White House meeting to discuss invasion plans; and finally, by Joseph Bard, undersecretary of the navy, throughout the summer.[32] On July 25, Truman wrote in his diary that "we will issue a warning statement asking the Japs to surrender and save lives. I'm sure that they will not do that, but we will have given them the chance."[33] But despite the warning in the Potsdam proclamation of "prompt and utter destruction," no direct mention was made of the new weapon. To begin with, no one knew whether such a warning or demonstration would work. The Interim Committee concluded at its May 31 meeting that to warn the Japanese of an upcoming bombing might allow them to shoot down the bomber or move Allied POWs to the target site. A demonstration seemed equally problematic to the committee: apart from the practical difficulties of arranging such a viewing with the leaders of a wartime adversary, the United States had a limited number of atomic bombs available, and if it turned out to be a dud or failed to impress the Japanese, the demonstration would have been for nothing.[34] Robert Oppenheimer, the leading scientist on the Manhattan Project, said that he could think of no demonstration "sufficiently spectacular" to bring about a surrender.

Still, American policymakers knew that a demonstration or warning would not cost the United States very much. Some scientists who worked on the Manhattan Project have suggested that there was enough plutonium available for several bombs like the one dropped on Nagasaki ("Fat Man") and that in any case the effectiveness of the uranium bomb ("Little Boy") was already assured well before July 16. A group of such scientists based in Chicago, led by Hungarian emigré Leo Szilard, proposed warning the Japanese about the bomb, but their efforts were resisted by Byrnes and Oppenheimer, and their petition never

reached the president. American policymakers, on the whole, were simply not interested in a warning or demonstration of the bomb. They wanted not to minimize but to maximize the element of fear, shock, and surprise that would attend the first use of this terrible new weapon. Consequently, the alternative of a demonstration or warning received very little consideration. At the May 31 Interim Committee meeting, Stimson expressed the general consensus by concluding that "we could not give the Japanese any warning, that we could not concentrate on a civilian area; but that we should seek to make a profound psychological impression on as many inhabitants as possible."[35]

In the final event, even this modest admonition not to "concentrate on a civilian area" was largely ignored in the final targeting decisions. The principle of noncombatant immunity counted for little once it came into conflict with the committee's own stated and contradictory impulse to make a "profound impression" on the Japanese. The possibility of using the bomb against a strictly military target, so as to avoid civilian casualties, received scant attention. In May, General Marshall made the case for such limited use of atomic weaponry, but was quickly overruled.[36] Stimson seems to have been troubled occasionally by considerations of noncombatant immunity, and he vetoed the atomic bombing of the ancient city of Kyoto, but this seems to have been in large part out of the desire to prevent permanent Japanese hostility towards the United States, rather than by considerations of discrimination as such.[37] Mass firebombing by *conventional* weapons had already killed hundreds of thousands of civilians—in the case of the Tokyo bombing of March 9 and 10, almost 100,000 in one night—without causing any significant controversy or meeting any opposition from American policymakers. Inured to the practice of "area" bombing, Truman and his advisors did not consider using this new weapon against a strictly military target.[38]

A fifth alternative was to drop the atomic bomb on Hiroshima but to delay the bombing of Nagasaki by a few more days, in order to give the Japanese time to surrender. The bombing of Nagasaki was made virtually automatic; Carl Spaatz, commander of the Army Strategic Air Force, was directed on July 25 to drop atomic bombs on designated targets "as made ready."[39] This meant that the Japanese Cabinet had barely seventy-two hours to let the news of Hiroshima sink in before deciding on their response. According to one historian, Truman's mistake "was signing an initial order that gave release of the go-ahead of both bombs at once." Commander Spaatz recalled in later years that he had no idea why Nagasaki had been bombed. At the time, however, American policymakers feared that a single atomic bomb might not be enough to convince Japan to surrender. To demonstrate that the United States had a number of such weapons and that Hiroshima had not been a freak occurrence, Truman and his advisors were prepared to drop two or more bombs on Japan.

Japan's military leaders in fact downplayed the importance of the atomic bomb for the first three days after Hiroshima.[40] Minister of War Anawi denied that Hiroshima had been struck at all. At the critical late-night Cabinet meeting on August 9–10, army leaders continued to resist surrender until early in the morning. News of Nagasaki arrived *during* the meeting and may have been a factor in demoralizing the military and allowing the emperor to intervene in favor of surrender.[41] As Anawi put it upon hearing of Nagasaki, "the Americans appear to have a hundred atomic bombs . . . they could drop three per day. The next target might well be Tokyo." On the other hand, there is evidence to suggest that the Soviet declaration of war earlier that day had been sufficient to demoralize Japan's military leaders, in which case the bombing of Nagasaki was extraneous.[42] Since Truman received no response from Japan in the three days after Hiroshima, he saw no

reason to cancel the second bombing; but even sympathetic observers have suggested that Truman could have waited a few days longer after Hiroshima in order to give the Japanese time to respond with surrender terms.[43]

Had all five of these options failed, the sixth alternative was to go forward with the planned invasion of the Japanese home islands. Truman later claimed that an invasion would have cost anywhere from half a million to a million American lives lost, but no such estimates were made by responsible military figures at the time. The harrowing experience of exceptionally bitter fighting on Iwo Jima and Okinawa, together with being subject to kamikaze attacks, had given the Americans reason to fear heavy casualties. The planned American invasion of Japan was to have been the largest amphibious assault in military history, beginning with the November 1 landing of 767,000 soldiers and marines on the island of Kyushu (Operation Olympic) and ending with the landing of one and a half million men on the Tokyo plain some four months later (Operation Coronet). High casualties could be expected. But by the fall of 1945, the United States had clear superiority over Japan in terms of firepower, air power, and naval power. The Japanese home army, although large, was badly equipped, and production of the most basic wartime necessities had ground to a halt. Japanese capacity to resist an invasion was diminishing.[44] In a June 18 meeting with Truman at the White House, General Marshall estimated that Operation Olympic would cost the United States about 63,000 dead and wounded.[45] These numbers are roughly comparable with a June 15 report by the Joint War Plans Committee, which predicted that the entire two-stage operation would cost between 132,000 and 220,000 casualties, of which about 20 percent would have been deaths.[46] In sum, according to the best estimates of contemporary U.S. military authorities, an invasion of Japan—while costly—would not have resulted in anything like a million American lives lost.

Japan offered terms of near-unconditional surrender on August 10. Allied peace terms had not changed in the days and weeks leading up to that point. Immediately prior to the surrender, the USSR entered the Pacific war, and two atomic bombs were dropped on Japan. The role of the atomic bomb seems to have been that its sheer novelty and destructive force shocked and demoralized the Japanese Cabinet. As Kawabe Torashima, vice chief of general staff, put it, "A surprise attack with this new weapon was beyond our wildest dreams." Military leaders were given something like an honorable excuse to accept an unwelcome peace, without having to resign or attempt a coup; they could not be expected to fight against such a weapon.[47] Civilian leaders were persuaded of the necessity of surrender. And the emperor—hitherto silent in Cabinet meetings—was convinced that the time had come to make peace on Allied terms.[48] As Hirohito said to Foreign Minister Togo upon hearing of Hiroshima, "Under these circumstances, we must bow to the inevitable. No matter what happens to my safety, we must put an end to this war as speedily as possible so that this tragedy will not be repeated." The intervention of the emperor in the August 9–10 Cabinet debate allowed the civilians to win out over the more hard-line military leaders and to send near-unconditional terms of surrender to the United States. As Kido Koichi, chancellor to the emperor, said afterwards:

> The psychological moment we had long waited for had finally arrived to resolutely carry out the termination of the war. . . . There is no doubt that the military leaders were overwhelmed by the enemy's scientific prowess. We felt that if we took the occasion and utilized the psychological shock of the bomb to carry through, we might perhaps succeed in ending the war. . . . It might be said that we of the peace party were assisted by the atomic bomb in our endeavour to end the war.

As late as August 9, Cabinet officials such as Stimson and Forrestal feared that the war might drag on for weeks or even months; Japan's offer of surrender the next day came as something of a surprise.[49] It had hardly even occurred to them to abjure the use of any weapon—including the atomic bomb—that might save American lives by contributing to the war's rapid and successful conclusion. As Stimson put it, "At no time, from 1941 to 1945 did I even hear it suggested by the President, or any other responsible member of the government, that atomic energy should not be used in the war."[50] The assumption seems to have been inherited from the Roosevelt administration that the bomb would be used.[51] Certainly, the Interim Committee never really considered any other possibility. Members of the committee worked under the widely shared assumption that the bomb would help significantly in the war effort. The need for postwar cooperation with the USSR over atomic energy was in the back of their minds as they worked under intense constraints of time and information. A victorious ending to the war in the shortest possible time was of the highest priority not only to American decision-makers but also to the general public. Moreover, the Manhattan Project had been immensely expensive. As Byrnes told Leo Szilard in May of 1945, "How would you get Congress to appropriate money for atomic energy research if you did not show results for the money which has been spent already?" In such a wartime environment, neither the Interim Committee nor President Truman ever seriously considered the possibility of *not* using the bomb against Japan. Indeed, Truman appears to have believed that the "decision" to drop it was a foregone conclusion. The final order to bomb both cities actually went out on July 25 not from Truman but from General Thomas Handy, acting army chief of staff. As General Groves, the military director of the

Manhattan Project, said of the president: "As far as I was concerned, his decision was one of noninterference—basically a decision not to upset existing plans." It would have taken clear evidence of Japan's imminent defeat to convince Truman that the bombings were no longer necessary—evidence that he did not have until August 10, at which point he "interfered" to call off a third atomic bomb, adding that he "didn't like the idea of killing . . . all those kids."[52]

NOTES

1. Akira Iriye, *Power and Culture* (Cambridge, Mass.: Harvard University Press, 1981), pp. 257–60.

2. Walter Millis, *The Forrestal Diaries* (New York, Viking Press, 1951), pp. 74, 76.

3. Stimson Diary, July 2, 1945, Yale University Library, New Haven, Conn.

4. Joseph Grew, *Turbulent Era,* vol. 2 (Boston: Houghton, 1952), pp. 1446–73.

5. John Ray Skates, *The Invasion of Japan: Alternative to the Bomb* (Columbia: University of South Carolina Press, 1994), p. 249.

6. Henry Stimson and Harvey Bundy, *On Active Service* (Boston: Harper, 1948), p. 629.

7. The curators of the National Air and Space Museum, "The Crossroads: The End of World War II, the Atomic Bomb, and the Origins of the Cold War," in *Judgment at the Smithsonian* (New York: Marlowe and Co., 1995), pp. 4–5.

8. Robert Butow, *Japan's Decision to Surrender* (Stanford, Calif.: Stanford University Press, 1954), p. 161.

9. Leon Sigal, *Fighting to a Finish: The Politics of War Termination in the United States and Japan 1945* (Ithaca, N.Y.: Cornell University Press, 1988), p. 228.

10. Ibid., p. 279.

11. Barton Bernstein, "Understanding the Atomic Bomb and the Japanese Surrender: Missed Opportunities, Little-Known Near Disasters, and Modern Memory," *Diplomatic History* (Spring 1995), pp. 263–66.

12. McGeorge Bundy, *Danger and Survival* (New York: Random House, 1988), p. 87.

13. John Dower, *War Without Mercy* (New York: Pantheon Books, 1986), p. 205.

14. Robert Pape, "Why Japan Surrendered," *International Security* 18:2 (Fall 1993): 157.

15. Henry Arnold, *Global Mission* (New York: Harper, 1949), pp. 596–98; Leahy, *I Was There* (New York: Whittlerey House, 1950), p. 441.

16. Ernest J. King and Walter M. Whitehall, *Fleet Admiral King* (New York: Norton, 1952), p. 621.

17. U.S. Strategic Bombing Survey, *Japan's Struggle to End the War* (Washington, D.C.: U.S. Government Printing Office, 1946), p. 13.

18. See, for example, interrogation with Prince Konoye, November 9, 1945, Records of the U.S. Strategic Bombing Survey, RG 243, National Archives.

19. Bernstein, "Understanding the Atomic Bomb," pp. 252–55.

20. Pape, "Why Japan Surrendered," pp. 194–95.

21. Sigal, *Fighting to a Finish*, pp. 226, 237.

22. Harry Truman, *Memoirs,* vol. 1 (Garden City, N.Y.: Doubleday, 1955), p. 417.

23. Truman, "Potsdam Diary," July 17, 1945, Truman Papers.

24. Stimson Diary, July 23, 1945, Yale University Library, New Haven, Conn.

25. Truman, "Potsdam Diary," July 18, 1945, Truman Papers.

26. Gar Alperovitz, *The Decision to Use the Atomic Bomb* (New York: Knopf, 1995), pp. 312–17.

27. Stimson Diary, May 15, 1945.

28. "Notes of the Use by the United States of the Atomic Bomb," September 1946, marked as draft 3, with the initials of HHB (presumably Harvey Bundy) in the upper right, and located in Top Secret Documents of Interest to General Groves #20, MED Records.

29. Byrnes, in "Was A-Bomb a Mistake?" *US News and World Report* (August 15, 1960), pp. 65–66.

30. Alperovitz, *Decision to Use the Atomic Bomb,* p. 306.

31. Barton Bernstein, "The Struggle over History: Defining the Hiroshima Narrative," in *Judgment at the Smithsonian* (New York: Marlowe and Co., 1995), p. 193.

32. John McCloy, *The Challenge to American Foreign Policy* (Cambridge, Mass.: Harvard University Press, 1953), pp. 41–43.

33. Truman, "Potsdam Diary," July 25, 1945.

34. National Air and Space Museum, "Crossroads," p. 47.

35. Ibid., p. 43.

36. John McCloy, memorandum of meeting, May 29, 1945, Records of the Secretary of War, May 29, 1945, RG 107, National Archives.

37. National Air and Space Museum, "Crossroads," p. 42.

38. Bundy, *Danger and Survival,* p. 64.

39. General Thomas Hardy to Carl Spaatz, July 25, 1945, in Truman's *Memoirs,* vol. 1, pp. 420–21.

40. Pape, "Why Japan Surrendered," p. 191.

41. Butow, *Japan's Decision,* pp. 151–52.

42. Pape, "Why Japan Surrendered," p. 192.

43. Bundy, *Danger and Survival*, p. 97.

44. Skates, *Invasion of Japan*, p. 256.

45. Minutes of June 18, 1945, meeting, U.S. Department of State, *Foreign Relations of the United States: Conference of Berlin (Potsdam)* (Washington, D.C.: U.S. Government Printing Office, 1960), 1, pp. 907–8.

46. Joint War Plans Committee (JWPC), "Details of the Campaign against Japan," JWPC 369/1, June 15, 1945, file 384 Japan (5-3-44), Records of the Army Staff, RG 319, National Archives.

47. Herbert Bix, "Japan's Delayed Surrender: A Reinterpretation," *Diplomatic History* (Spring 1995), p. 218.

48. Hidenari Terasaki, *Showa Tenno Dokuhakuroku* (Tokyo, Bungei Shunju, 1991), p. 121.

49. Stimson Diary, August 9, 1945; Forrestal to Truman, August 8, 1945, Forrestal Diary.

50. National Air and Space Museum, "Crossroads," p. 29.

51. Bernstein, "The Struggle over History," p. 164.

52. Henry Wallace Diary, August 10, 1945, Wallace Papers, University of Iowa, Iowa City, Iowa.

Comment

The damage and loss of lives that the atomic bomb caused in Hiroshima and Nagasaki were no greater than the destruction caused by some conventional attacks such as the firebombing of Tokyo or Dresden. What (if any) features of nuclear weapons make their use more morally questionable than the use of conventional weapons?

Compare Stimson's argument for the bombing with this defense given by Truman:

> We have used [the bomb] against those who attacked us without warning at Pearl Harbor, against those who have starved and beaten and executed American prisoners of war, against those who have abandoned all pretense of obeying international laws of warfare. We have used it in order to shorten the agony of the war.

Documents now available suggest that Stimson's recollection of the estimates of probable casualties from an invasion (over a million Americans and even more Japanese) was much higher than the estimates that Truman actually received from high military officials at the time. The joint war planners of the Joint Chiefs of Staff, for example, estimated that the number of casualties from the entire two-stage invasion would range between 132,000 and 220,000 (including about 20 percent deaths). Other military officials argued that even these estimates were too high. Should these differences in estimates make any difference in our moral assessment of Truman's decision?

Evaluate the alternative courses of action that Truman considered or should have considered: (1) bombing only one city; (2) bombing an exclusively military target; (3) detonating one or two bombs over the ocean as a "demonstration"; (4) intensifying the naval and air blockade; (5) waiting until the Russians entered the war; or (6) abandoning the demand for unconditional surrender (guaranteeing the preservation of the emperor's status, the imperial system, and self-rule).

Assume that dropping the bombs actually saved more American and Allied lives than any other option open to Truman. Would that justify his decision? What if the decision reduced the total number of lives lost (including Japanese lives)?

Some historians argue that one reason Truman decided to use the bomb was to end the war quickly before Russia could enter and gain influence in the region after the war. Would this have been a morally acceptable motive?

James Conant, then president of Harvard and an influential science adviser to President Truman, argued that the bomb "must be used." It was "the only way to awaken the world to the necessity of abolishing war altogether." Given what was known at the time, how should officials have assessed the effect of the bombing on postwar efforts to prevent nuclear war? Should such effects have been a morally relevant factor in Truman's decision?

Bombing the Bunker in Baghdad

Simone Sandy

On August 2, 1990, Iraqi armed forces invaded Kuwait and subsequently occupied and annexed it. Thirty-seven nations formed an alliance to evict Iraq from Kuwait, while the United Nations responded by adopting a series of resolutions imposing sanctions.[1] Despite all diplomatic efforts and economic sanctions, Iraq refused to retreat from Kuwait. On November 29, 1990, the United Nations' Security Council resolved that if Iraq would not withdraw from Kuwait by January 15, 1991, the Member States were commissioned to use "all necessary means . . . to restore international peace and security in the area."[2] Conforming to this authorization (but not under UN command), the United States and other allied forces began air attacks on Iraq on January 17.

On Wednesday, February 13, 1991, 4:00 A.M. Iraqi time, coalition forces dropped

two 2,000-pound laser-guided bombs on a building located in Amariya, a suburb west of Baghdad. Iraqi officials reported that bodies of 197 adults and 91 children had been removed from the structure by Thursday evening. According to the Information Ministry, at least 400 people were killed and "many would never be identified, either because they were so badly mutilated or charred or because entire families had been killed."[3] Only 8 people were reported to have survived the blast.

Iraqi authorities maintained that the facility destroyed in the air raid was a civilian bomb shelter, no military personnel were inside, and allied forces had attacked it in a calculated attempt to weaken morale. American and British journalists who visited the site of the raid reported that it did appear that the structure was being used as a civilian shelter, and that they saw no evidence that it served any military function. British, Saudi, and American briefing officers, however, insisted that the building was a confirmed military site and that Iraqi officials should have realized it would be a target.

The structure was originally built as a bomb shelter in 1985, during the Iran-Iraq War. However, according to the U.S. officials, in the late 1980s the facility was "hardened to enable electronics gear to withstand the electromagnetic pulse of a nuclear blast."[4] It was also "equipped with special air filtration systems, communications gear, electronic equipment, and special wiring."[5] The facility had a steel-reinforced 10-foot-thick concrete roof, which was painted with three black circles apparently intended to resemble bomb holes.

Brigadier General Richard I. Neal (deputy chief of staff at the U.S. command in Saudi Arabia) suggested that while camouflage is typically used to hide a military post, it is unusual on a civilian air raid shelter, which, on the contrary, should have clear civil defense markings.[6] William E. Odom, a retired army general and the former head of the National Security Agency, doubted that a facility that many people might need to enter rapidly would be surrounded by chain-link and barbed-wire fencing.[7] Lieutenant General Thomas Kelly, director of operations for the Joint Chiefs of Staff, asserted the building "stopped being a bomb shelter . . . when they went back and did a whole bunch of stuff to it to turn it into a military command-and-control facility. At that point . . . it began to be a military target."[8]

Nevertheless, according to Neal and others, the building was not a high priority on the target list until approximately a week before the bombing. At that point, officials said, military trucks began to arrive at the facility with communications equipment. Then, military messages, including orders for Iraqi troops deployed inside Kuwaiti territory, were transmitted from the site. By monitoring communications to and from the site all responsible U.S. officers assured themselves the building had a military purpose. "Signal intelligence [analysis] can confirm and therefore determine the emitter location . . . so we do have all the confidence," said Saudi Colonel Ahmed Robayan.[9]

Despite the conviction of the key briefing officers, several American newspapers reported that other officials (none identified by name) and independent analysts suggested that allied forces had bombed a dual-purpose building while it was functioning in a civilian capacity. U.S. officials, it was said, should have known there were civilians in the bunker. According to *New York Times* reporter R. W. Apple, Jr., "The nagging fear, acknowledged privately by a small number of officials, was that the building served two functions and that the allies had failed to discern it. No one seemed able to give a convincing answer to one question: If photographs taken by reconnaissance planes confirmed that people in military uniforms had been in and out of the building . . . why were there no photographs showing that civilians had been in and out as well? . . . [A] senior officer said the civilians could have entered the bunker after dark . . . when the allies were not conducting reconnaissance, whereas Iraqi military people entered it in the daytime, when the reconnaissance had resumed. But that, as he conceded, raised the question of why close nighttime observation was so lacking."[10]

However, other reports suggested that the intelligence technologies used simply were not capable of adequate nighttime observation: "Intelligence officials said normal U.S. photoreconnaissance satellites are capable of observing key military targets in Iraq more than once each day, but cannot produce images of objects shrouded in darkness. Even special satellites equipped with thermal imaging sensors cannot distinguish several hundred civilians entering or leaving a building at night, they added."[11]

Target planners said that they made no particular attempt to discover any nighttime use of the Amariya building. Rather, based on monitoring its daytime activities during the weeks preceding the raid, they concluded that the site was primarily a military command post.[12] Yet, according to several senior U.S. officials, the building was first placed on the target list because "intelligence experts concluded it was a bunker designed to shelter senior Iraqi government officials from air attack."[13] Several sources (none named) said that such a bunker would be considered by U.S. military officials to be susceptible to attack.

American officials said the day after the raid that among the civilians who died may have been officials of the ruling Baath Party and their families.[14] Asked to justify continued coalition bombings in Baghdad (as opposed to raids on troops and supply lines closer to the Kuwaiti battlefield), White House Press Secretary Marlin Fitzwater said: "Their command-and-control center is there. Their military is there, just like our military is in Washington. It's as simple as that. . . . Baghdad is where this war is originated from. It's where Saddam Hussein is. It's where the military is. It's where the leadership is."[15]

Spokesmen at the White House and Pentagon maintained that there would be neither a retrospective examination of the Amariya incident specifically nor a more general inquiry into military targeting strategies.[16] Fitzwater said, "The military has looked into this. They have considered it. They discussed it publicly; announced their conclusion. We are satisfied that we've looked into it and did the right thing for the right reasons, and we will continue to attack command-and-control centers."[17]

White House and Pentagon officials also refused to disclose surveillance photos or other evidence from intelligence sources in order to prove their case to the public. "We specifically do not talk about our ability to intercept Iraqi military communications because that would then allow them to change the way they're doing it," said Lieutenant General Kelly. Still, some intelligence experts believed that Pentagon officials had taken great risk by revealing what they already had.[18]

"[T]he openness of American society, with reporters permitted and indeed expected to challenge official versions of events, puts the United States at some disadvantage in the image war with controlled societies like Iraq," Apple suggested. "The bombing represented a significant public-relations failure, augmented by the presence of Western television reporters in Baghdad who transmitted graphic pictures of survivors and mangled bodies . . . [which implied] that the United States was merciless in using force to attain its objectives."[19]

In a letter to UN Secretary General Javier Perez de Cuellar, King Hussein of Jordan urged him to send a delegation to Baghdad to guarantee that allied military operations would not violate humanitarian norms. "The bombing of the shelter is another reminder that Security Council Resolution 678, which some see as the license to launch an organized war of devastation against Iraq, is . . . devoid of legitimate basis," Hussein wrote.[20]

In contrast, Apple pointed out, "American commanders have foresworn the use of many weapons that they have readily available for their use against cities, were their aim to try to force Iraq out of the war by demoralizing the civil population. They have used no ballistic missiles, which are relatively inaccurate, nor have they used B-52s in carpet-bombing patterns."[21] Nevertheless, Lieutenant General Kelly promised that coalition forces would try harder not to harm civilians: "We'll redouble our efforts. We're looking at every resource available to us, whatever methods we can develop to minimize civilian casualties."[22]

General Schwarzkopf charged that "the very actions of the Iraqis themselves demonstrate that they know . . . we're not attacking civilian targets," mentioning that Iraq had placed military headquarters, tanks and artillery, and warplanes in schools and residential areas.[23] Some reporters and U.S. officers suggested that Iraqi authorities had strategically put civilians in the Amariya facility, believing it would draw fire, as a "macabre publicity stunt" to gain points in a propaganda war.[24]

Neal stated that the United States Central Command policy was not to go after targets such as antiaircraft weaponry and military vehicles if placed in residential areas, because commanders did not want to "bring up the civilian casualties." However, Neal said that officials may be forced to rethink this policy if the Iraqis "started putting civilians [as human shields] into

these [command and control facilities] . . .
[as a] . . . war fighting strategy."[25]

According to Kelly and Herrington, in circumstances where hundreds of civilians
might die as a result of a hit on a military target, U.S. commanders would have to decide
whether to attack on a "case by case" basis.
The United States would try to avoid civilian
casualties but at the same time had a responsibility to "successfully prosecute [the] war."[26]

NOTES

1. *The U.S. Army in Operation Desert Storm: An
   Overview* (Arlington, Va.: Association of the
   United States Army, 1991), 1.

2. *United Nations Security Council Resolutions
   Relating to the Situation Between Iraq and Kuwait*
   (U.N. Dept. of Public Information, Dec. 1991),
   Resolution 678.

3. Nora Boustany, "Iraqi Says 288 Bodies Removed
   from Bombed Structure," *Washington Post,* Feb. 15,
   1991.

4. Doyle McManus and James Gerstenzang,
   "Structure Built to Shelter Iraqi Elite, U.S.
   Says," *Los Angeles Times,* Feb. 15, 1991.

5. Ibid.

6. Interview with Lt. Col. Mike Gallagher and Brig.
   Gen. Richard Neal, Feb. 13, 1991, Dept. of
   Defense, USCENTCOM daily briefing, Riyadh,
   Saudi Arabia.

7. McManus and Gerstenzang, "Structure Built."

8. Ibid.

9. R. Jeffrey Smith, "Building Was Targeted Months
   Ago as Shelter for Leaders," *Washington Post,*
   Feb. 14, 1991.

10. "Commanders Deny Error on Target," *New York
    Times,* Feb. 14, 1991.

11. Smith, "Building Was Targeted."

12. Ibid.

13. Ibid.

14. McManus and Gerstenzang, "Structure Built."

15. Ibid.

16. Patrick E. Tyler, "U.S. Stands Firm on Bomb Attack
    and Says Investigation Is Closed," *New York Times,*
    Feb. 15, 1991.

17. McManus and Gerstenzang, "Structure Built."

18. Ibid.

19. "Commanders Deny Error."

20. Boustany, "Iraqi Says 288 Bodies Removed."

21. R. W. Apple, Jr., "Allies Study New Steps to Avoid
    Civilians in Bombing," *New York Times,* Feb. 15,
    1991.

22. Tyler, "U.S. Stands Firm."

23. Apple, "Allies Study New Steps."

24. Interview with Gallagher and Neal.

25. Ibid.

26. Interview with Lt. Gen. Thomas Kelly and Capt.
    David Herrington, Feb. 13, 1991, Defense Dept.
    regular briefing, Washington, D.C.

Comment

Did U.S. officials have sufficient evidence for believing that (1) the building they
bombed was a military target and (2) civilians were not using it as a shelter? In war,
the answers to such questions are usually uncertain, and the answers turn not only on
matters of fact but also on matters of morality. Specifically, the degree of risk that
officials should accept depends on what values are at stake. Identify the values that
you think were at stake in this decision, and try to specify what kind of uncertainty
should be tolerated in deciding to order the bombing.

U.S. Central Command policy prohibits attacks on military targets located in residential areas. This policy is stricter than the principle of double effect, which would
permit attacks on military targets even if a foreseeable (but unintended) effect is the
death of civilians. Does a nation that adopts such a policy put itself (and its soldiers) at
an unfair disadvantage in a war with an adversary who rejects the policy? General

Neal implied that the United States might abandon the policy if the Iraqis started using civilians as "shields" as part of their war fighting strategy. If the Iraqis had deliberately placed civilians in the bunker to try to protect their command center, should that have changed the moral calculus of U.S. decision makers?

Some U.S. officials believed that most of the civilians who died in the attack were officials of the ruling Baath Party. If the bunker were being used as a shelter for government officials, would the U.S. be justified in bombing it? In September 1990, before the war began, the air force chief of staff, General Michael J. Dugan, said publicly that the U.S. military has plans to "decapitate" the Iraqi leadership—by targeting President Saddam Hussein, his family, his senior commanders, his palace guard, and even his mistress. As Dugan was relieved of his command for making these comments, Secretary of Defense Richard Cheney stated, "We never discuss operational matters, such as selection of specific targets for potential air strikes. We never talk about the targeting of specific individuals who are officials in other governments." Would the United States have been morally justified in directly attacking Saddam Hussein in 1990? In 2002? Under what circumstances (if any) may a nation engage in or encourage political assassination?

Intervention in Somalia

Neal Higgins

On October 3, 1993, an American Blackhawk helicopter was shot down by small-arms fire as it attempted to withdraw from the Olympia Hotel in downtown Mogadishu, the war-ravaged capital of Somalia. Eighteen U.S. Army Rangers were killed and seventy-eight wounded in the bloody firefight that ensued, with casualties on the Somali side somewhere between five hundred and one thousand. One American was captured, and the corpse of another dragged through the streets for camera crews to broadcast to a shocked television audience. The incident quickly spelled the end of American involvement in the United Nations' attempt to bring peace and stability to the Horn of Africa.

In the wake of the tragedy, many Americans indignantly asked why Somalis

had turned so viciously on American troops who had come to Mogadishu on a mission of charity. The answer: what began as an effort to relieve human suffering and restore peace and stability had become, in the eyes of many Somalis, an effort to intervene in a civil war and impose a government upon a sovereign people. Had the UN and the United States wrongly taken sides in an internal dispute, had they overstepped their legal and moral authority, or was this a necessary albeit painful part of legitimate post–Cold War intervention in the affairs of an impoverished and increasingly unstable state?

SOMALIA'S DECLINE AND THE DECISION TO INTERVENE

Like many post–Cold War conflicts, the civil war in Somalia began with the fall of a dictator who had long profited from the superpower rivalry. General Mohammed Siad Barre had been in power since the 1969 coup which overthrew Somalia's Western-style democracy, a system plagued by the persistence of clan loyalties and tribal divisions.[1] Siad's corrupt and oppressive regime eventually spawned active, armed opposition groups—most with a strong tribal foundation—that engaged the government in a low-level civil war. The dictatorship's brutality towards those opposition groups eventually enraged both Somali clans and Siad's foreign benefactors. Chief among these was the United States, which chose to disassociate itself from Siad by eliminating funding to the Somali government. Cut adrift from American support, Siad was left unable to control the countryside or maintain basic state institutions. With the government bereft of foreign aid and internationally isolated, rebel groups from the southern and central regions of Somalia began to challenge the dictatorship for control of Mogadishu.[2]

Chief among these rebel groups was the United Somali Congress (USC), jointly led by General Mohamed Farah Aideed and Mohamed Ali Mahdi. In January 1991 the USC captured Mogadishu and ousted Siad from power. Within weeks of seizing control the group suffered an internal split, with Aideed refusing to accept Ali Mahdi as the interim president. Mogadishu soon turned into a battlefield as followers of the two rival leaders fought for control of the capital. Between November 1991 and February 1992, fighting in Mogadishu alone caused an estimated 14,000 deaths and 27,000 injuries. But the destruction wasn't limited to the capital. As Siad's forces fled Mogadishu they pursued a scorched earth policy, killing livestock, burning crops, and occasionally tangling with USC forces. With Somalia already suffering from a crippling drought, the fighting quickened the spread of famine. By mid-1992 nearly 300,000 had died and close to 700,000 more had sought refuge in Kenya and Ethiopia. Only in the northwest, where independent rebel troops had already

claimed victory over weak government forces, did stability prevail.

Although the international community had not directly responded to the turmoil in Somalia, it was well aware of the country's troubles. United Nations Security Council resolutions and international conferences had expressed concern over the situation, most nations had closed their embassies in Mogadishu, and the UN High Commissioner for Refugees, the United Nations Children's Fund, and the World Food Program had all evacuated their personnel to Kenya. Only nongovernmental organizations (NGOs) remained in Somalia, among them the International Committee of the Red Cross, Save the Children UK, and Doctors without Borders.

Despite substantial assistance from the United States and its European allies, even those NGOs still operating in Somalia experienced a range of difficulties. With gangs of armed thugs controlling both the Mogadishu ports and many of the supply routes leading to feeding centers outside the capital, looting and extortion significantly reduced the amount of food actually reaching the neediest Somalis. Furthermore, by drawing thousands of sustenance farmers who were otherwise widely dispersed into small, densely populated areas, the feeding centers often seemed to perpetuate the drought and contribute to the spread of disease. Without protection to ensure the safe delivery of food, efforts to aid the Somali people were often doing more harm than good.

Fearing an impending humanitarian disaster and succumbing to mounting public pressure, the Security Council decided to act. On January 23, 1992, in Resolution 733, the Council called on the secretary-general to send an envoy to Mogadishu, imposed an arms embargo on all of Somalia, requested the delivery of aid from member states, and established a special coordinator to oversee the delivery of humanitarian assistance. The UN quickly encountered difficulty performing all four tasks. Despite efforts to stem their flow, arms continued to seep into

Somalia from Kenya and Ethiopia, adding to the caches left from Cold War patronage. Meanwhile, officials from the Secretariat, apparently unaware of the USC's infighting, angered Aideed by initiating a dialogue with Ali Mahdi. Finally, after restoring good relations with the NGOs—many of whom felt that the UN had abandoned them when it withdrew personnel to Kenya—the new special coordinator for humanitarian assistance encountered the same difficulties that had plagued earlier attempts to deliver food and medicine.

With few of its efforts succeeding, in April the Security Council concluded that the best way to assist the Somali people would be to deploy military observers to monitor a tenuous cease-fire that had taken hold in Mogadishu and peacekeepers to guarantee the delivery of food and medicine. Cautiously leading the way was President George Bush, who authorized the use of fourteen C-130 cargo planes to airlift humanitarian supplies and transport the proposed peacekeeping force. Over the next six months the operation would successfully deliver more than 28,000 metric tons of food, but the peacekeepers—a Pakistani brigade deployed with the begrudging consent of the warring parties—did not arrive until September.[3] By that time the Security Council had already infuriated Aideed by authorizing the eventual deployment of three thousand more peacekeepers without first consulting any of the Somali factions.

Even before the UN Secretariat secured troop contributions for the expanded force, it was clear that simply sending more peace-keepers wouldn't solve the problem. The question was less how many troops the UN could muster than how well prepared those troops were for the situation on the ground. The plight of the Pakistani peacekeepers already in Mogadishu clearly illustrated the difficulties any UN force would face:

While all of the Pakistani peacekeepers had arrived by late September 1992, the force's terms of reference, based on traditional notions of what constituted peacekeeping, proved to be totally inadequate to the Somali challenge. There was no durable cease-fire to preserve and cooperation with the warring parties was either non-existent or unreliable and inconsistent. Far from fulfilling their mission to secure the airport, seaport, and lines of communication in and around Mogadishu, the lightly-armed Pakistanis struggled to protect themselves from repeated militia attacks and were pinned down in their barracks near Mogadishu airport for the first two months after arrival.[4]

With Mogadishu warehouses filling with food waiting for safe delivery and the few peacekeepers in Somalia confined to their barracks, the only solution to the mounting crisis seemed to be a more forceful approach.

AUTHORIZING UNILATERAL ACTION

With the situation in Somalia worsening by the week, Congress, the media, and the NGO community all pressured the Bush administration to take action. With looting and extortion still plaguing efforts to airlift food into Somalia, in October 1992 the White House and the Pentagon concluded that 12,000 to 15,000 troops—triple the number already authorized by the Security Council—would be needed to provide adequate protection to ensure the safe delivery of humanitarian assistance. Although those proposing such an intervention had assumed that the troops in question would be primarily Canadian or Belgian, the developing crisis soon made the deployment of American forces appear ever more likely—and ever more necessary. According to the Office of Foreign Disaster Assistance at the U.S. Agency for International Development, one-quarter of southern Somali children under the age of five had already died. The U.S. Centers for Disease Control and Prevention estimated that the southern city of Baidoa had lost 40 percent of its population and 70 percent of its children under five to hunger or disease.[5] Although some critics pointed out that death rates were beginning to decline, aid workers retorted that it was only because there were fewer people left to die. Either way, deliveries of food and medicine were still unable to safely reach those who needed them most.

Facing the possibility of even greater starvation, many in the Bush administration began to sense the need for American leadership. As U.S. special envoy to Somalia Robert B. Oakley and political adviser John L. Hirsch explain:

> Somalia had emerged as such an overwhelming humanitarian crisis that there was no longer a question of inaction. Moreover, a definable mission had emerged, one which no other nation was likely to undertake. And the goodwill to be gained for helping out in Somalia might help offset the widespread criticism that the United States was dilatory in responding to aggression in Bosnia. Such action would also help mute criticism of the United States in the Arab world for not helping their Muslim coreligionists in Bosnia.[6]

With Chairman of the Joint Chiefs of Staff General Colin Powell pushing for the strongest possible option—a multinational force with the United States at its fore—the decision went to the White House. On November 25, 1992, President George Bush decided that if the Security Council concurred and other nations volunteered assistance, the United States would lead a new operation to provide full protection for humanitarian relief operations in southern Somalia. Named the United Task Force (UNITAF), the operation would function under Chapter VII of the UN Charter, which allows member states both to act without the consent of the warring parties and, when necessary, to use force in pursuit of their objectives. Although the White House and the Pentagon viewed the threat of force as necessary to restore civil order, both hoped UNITAF would avoid hostilities. Once the operation had established a secure environment for the delivery of humanitarian assistance, UNITAF was to relinquish control to UNOSOM II, the UN's successor to its original operation.

Even with the support of the Joint Chiefs of Staff and the president's closest advisers, the decision to deploy American troops to Somalia was nevertheless controversial. Although images of starving Somali children had stirred overwhelming public support for a humanitarian intervention—producing "a moral clarity for people like few issues in recent years"—there remained troubling questions as to what role American forces should play.[7] A poll by the *New York Times* and CBS News reported that 81 percent of those surveyed believed that the United States was "doing the right thing" by sending troops to Somalia, with 70 percent agreeing that the operation was worth both the financial and political costs and the possible loss of American lives. But the poll also revealed that the public was sharply divided as to how long the United States should remain in Somalia: while 48 percent of those surveyed thought U.S. troops should stay "only as long as it takes to set up supply lines and make sure people don't starve," 44 percent said that American troops should remain "as long as it takes to make sure Somalia will remain peaceful." Whatever their thoughts on the intervention's limits or objectives, most had already concluded that American troops and leadership were required. As the *New York Times* reported on December 13:

> There are already signs the operation may become more complicated than people expect, and the moral certainty of December could easily become the political quagmire of February. But for many people Somalia has become a Christmas-season parable, making it difficult to look at the commercial iconography of plenty—golden arches, all-you-can-eat steak joints and manic Big Boys bearing overstuffed burgers—without thinking twice.[8]

Stopping only briefly to consider the implications of such an operation, most Americans had apparently decided that in cases like Somalia "action is appropriate if only because inaction is unthinkable."[9]

Much as they too may have been moved by the images of starving Somalia, critics in both Congress and the media were far slower to endorse the deployment of American troops. While some warned that the United States must "avoid getting trapped in a moral domino theory in which intervention in one place automatically seems to compel intervention in another," others called for specific details as to what American troops would be doing in Somalia and how and when they would withdraw.[10] Among the latter was Congressman David Obey, then chairman of the House Appropriations Subcommittee on Foreign Operations, who called on the Republican administration to clarify that "the primary message is not to pacify the entire country, but to secure limited territorial zones where those who seek it can receive critically needed UN assistance."[11] Fearing that the intervention could result in a political quagmire but nevertheless supportive of intervention, Obey and others wanted assurances that UNITAF would not be a repetition of America's failed efforts in Beirut and Vietnam.

Well aware of the widespread concerns about the intervention, President Bush quickly emphasized that the operation would be limited to ensuring the safe delivery of humanitarian supplies and would not be expanded to include a wider role in rebuilding the Somali state. Administration officials also reaffirmed that UNITAF's ultimate goal would be to hand control back to the UN. As one State Department official put it, the objective was "to make the UN a more credible actor," adding that the UN "wasn't a credible military actor before, now it will be. By not being a credible military actor, it wasn't a credible political actor."[12] Confirming that the Pentagon approved of the operation, Secretary of Defense Dick Cheney and General Colin Powell publicly cited four factors that had convinced them to propose and support an intervention by American troops; first, the mission was fully justifiable as an act of humanitarian intervention; second,

UNITAF was considered to be eminently "doable"; third, it was a limited operation with a set date for withdrawal; and finally, UNITAF wouldn't run the risk of an unacceptably high casualty rate.[13]

While the operation seemed to have won the support of the White House, the Pentagon, and the American public, it had yet to receive the approval of the United Nations. Although the secretary-general and his top advisors in the Department of Peacekeeping Operations welcomed the U.S. offer to lead an operation in Somalia, they expressed deep concerns about both the high degree of American involvement and the use of force. Those two aspects of the operation, they feared, could corrupt the traditional practice of peacekeeping and taint the UN's future role in the Horn of Africa. Their concerns reflected a traditional view of UN peacekeeping, one shaped by the tensions and politics of the Cold War. Developed in an era when each superpower was wary of the other's efforts to use the UN to make geostrategic gains, peacekeeping had long been bound by a certain set of rules and restrictions. To reflect the multinational nature of the United Nations—and thus ensure that the UN was enforcing the will of the international community, not that of a given superpower—peacekeeping operations had long relied on troop contributions from every corner of the globe. Even with such contributions in place, the Security Council would only deploy an operation once it was clear that the UN had won the consent of the warring parties, that the operation could remain impartial, and that peacekeepers could refrain from the use of force.

While such restrictions all helped to appease the superpowers' many concerns, they also ensured the safety of the peacekeepers themselves. As Andrei Raevsky explains:

> The consensus on "traditional" peacekeeping was that peacekeepers should not have the obligation, the soldiers or the equipment to engage violators in hostilities. International peacekeeping forces expressed and facilitated the erstwhile belligerents' will to live in

peace; they could not supervise peace in conditions of war. Turning them into a fighting force erodes international consensus on their function, encourages withdrawals by contributing contingents, converts them into a factional participant in the internal power struggle and turns them into targets of attack from rival internal factions. . . . [T]he UN tries to ensure that it is maintaining a neutral stance between the disputants, not serving the political interest of any one faction in the conflict or at the UN, and not imposing the will of a UN majority upon any party.[14]

Although the end of the Cold War had led many to speculate as to whether the UN could use force to pursue impartial humanitarian goals without first winning the consent of the warring parties, few in the Secretariat were yet willing to take that chance.

Nor were they prepared to agree that UNITAF, even as an independent American effort, should be followed by a UN peacekeeping operation. Secretary-General Boutros Boutros-Ghali even expressed doubts about UNITAF itself, arguing that the American proposal did too little to disarm the Somali warlords.[15] Although most member states of the Security Council agreed with the secretary-general, they also understood the need for immediate and effective action. On December 3, unwilling to allow the situation in Somalia to deteriorate further, the Council passed Resolution 794, granting the United States permission to lead a multinational force sanctioned by the UN but not designated as a UN peacekeeping operation. Within a week U.S. forces were ready to land in Somalia and begin Operation Restore Hope.

Armed with a peak force of 36,000 troops—27,000 of them American—and a mandate to "get the food through," UNITAF was soon active across the southern half of Somalia.[16] With the authority to use force in an impartial manner and the begrudging consent of the warring parties, the operation rapidly became "a laboratory for new theories of UN peacekeeping."[17] The U.S.-led operation represented "the first time that the

Security Council sanctioned an enforcement action under Chapter VII of the UN Charter in a theoretically sovereign state."[18] Neither the operation's size nor its historical significance was lost on the warring parties. Within a week the United States had convinced Aideed and Ali Mahdi to meet in person for the first time since the civil war began. Although the secretary-general's special representative in Somalia was present at the meeting, the number of American troops and the need for efficient American command and control had put the United States firmly in charge. By the end of the meeting the two faction leaders had agreed to both a cease-fire and a conference on national reconciliation.

Promising as the agreements seemed, both the United States and the UN realized that they meant little without monitored implementation. Hoping to avoid confrontation with UNITAF forces and curry favor with the United States, Aideed and Ali Mahdi would stop at little to appear cooperative. Well aware of the warlords' motivations, UNITAF forces nevertheless took advantage of the diplomatic opening to begin delivering humanitarian aid and developing the foundation for a lasting settlement. Although the U.S. military until then had little experience with UN operations, it was clearly capable of the type of muscular peacekeeping required to keep the food flowing into the regions under its control. By using the threat of force effectively and impartially, UNITAF accomplished a number of the objectives that had eluded the original UNOSOM effort. As former Assistant Secretary of State for African Affairs Chester Crocker surmises:

> Establishing safety for relief workers while keeping the warlords somewhat placated and off balance; maintaining and demonstrating military primacy without making a permanent adversary or national hero of any local actor; pushing the military factions toward a locally led political process while opening up that process to civilian elites and eschewing precise formulas; removing heavy weapons from areas

of conflict while fostering the restoration of police and government functions—these were undertakings of the highest order of delicacy in a militarized and fragmented society like Somalia's. UNITAF's accomplishments far exceeded the simple, publicly discussed goal of creating a "secure environment for humanitarian relief." They required strong leadership and a well-oiled quick-response military-civilian bureaucracy.[19]

UNITAF's greatest asset was the commitment of the United States and the many advantages that that commitment entailed. Unlike most ad hoc UN peacekeeping forces, UNITAF had well-established command, control, and communication structures and full access to the proper equipment, armament, and personnel. Well-equipped and well-prepared, the operation made steady progress towards its defined objectives.

But despite its many accomplishments, UNITAF unapologetically failed to address several fundamental concerns raised by the UN. First, American commanders chose not to confront the political crisis directly, instead recognizing both Aideed and Ali Mahdi as legitimate political actors—and considerably narrowing the possibility for an alternate political solution. As the *Washington Post* reported:

> U.S. military and diplomatic representatives missed no opportunity to treat Aideed and Ali Mahdi with public respect. The two warlords, whose struggle for power and extortion of relief supplies are blamed by outside observers for starving 300,000 of their countrymen to death, were cloaked by their American interlocutors in the mantle of legitimate power.[20]

Ignoring pleas from the UN Secretariat to assume control of all of Somalia, UNITAF's leadership next decided to limit the operation's efforts exclusively to the southern half of the country. Finally, and most importantly, Washington specifically refused to forcibly disarm the Somali warlords. The Pentagon suggested that disarmament would unnecessarily antagonize the warring parties and endanger the humanitarian effort, insisting

that "the creation of a benign security environment pertained only to providing security for UNITAF forces, the relief convoys and the humanitarian relief personnel." Boutros-Ghali, on the other hand, insisted "that the UNITAF mission should be much more extensive than what the United States envisioned, with an ambitious disarmament program, broader geographic extent, and longer duration."[21]

As the deadline for the withdrawal of American forces grew nearer, the disagreement over disarmament quickly evolved into a heated debate over the goals and limits of the intervention. Both the Pentagon and the newly elected Clinton administration viewed the operation's objectives as being strictly defined and clearly limited. Their goal was not to resolve the civil war, nor to end the drought, but rather to facilitate efforts to alleviate the short-term humanitarian crisis. While diplomats at the United States Liaison Office in Mogadishu were willing to encourage the emergence of grass-roots solutions to Somalia's more fundamental problems, they were not willing to plan the reconstruction of the Somali state. Although the decision to avoid more extensive engagement in Somalia may have had more to do with politics than principle, it nevertheless reflected a belief that it was neither the right nor the responsibility of the United States to take an active role in Somalia's domestic affairs beyond what was necessary to alleviate starvation and restore order. Provided with that level of assistance, the Somalis would be expected to develop their own solutions to the nation's other woes.

Faced with the imminent withdrawal of American forces, Boutros-Ghali saw the situation quite differently. While the American approach to the crisis had temporarily alleviated starvation and restored order, it had done little to provide for a lasting peace. By striving only for local disarmament and limited attempts at political reconciliation, UNITAF had succeeded in getting the food through but not in creating long-term stability. Moreover, with the warlords still armed and hungry for power, there was good reason to believe that Somali could quickly return to anarchy. As Boutros-Ghali saw it, unless the international community provided a lasting presence to cement UNITAF's gains and address Somalia's most pressing needs, the process of national reconciliation would collapse, the civil war would most likely reignite, and the drought would undoubtedly continue. Fully aware that no UN force could match the military might of the United States, the secretary-general thus insisted that the United States at least complete the demanding task of disarmament, the most important precursor to Somalia's reconstruction.

THE RETURN TO UN CONTROL

The split between the United States and the UN could not have come at a worse time. In the first three months of 1993 the warring factions were to agree to a formal cease-fire and disarmament program, then travel to the Ethiopian capital of Addis Ababa to attend conferences on both humanitarian questions and the issue of national reconciliation. Instrumental to the success of these initiatives was the continuing cooperation of the warring parties. While UNITAF had managed to maintain that cooperation through the threat of force and the promise of American assistance, the UN was to have little such luck. Problems began as early as January, when a protest coordinated by Aideed prevented the secretary-general from visiting UNOSOM staff in Mogadishu. Claiming that the UN would enslave Somalia in a trusteeship arrangement tantamount to colonization, the protesters forced Boutros-Ghali to return to the airport, cutting his visit short.[22] Although Ambassador Oakley afterwards convinced Aideed that he needed to enter into discussions with the secretary-general, the warlord's respect for the UN was doubtful at best.

Difficulties began anew at the two conferences in Addis Ababa. Although the meetings resulted in agreements on the cantonment of forces, political reconciliation, and infrastructure redevelopment, they failed to resolve the question of disarmament. Yet disarmament remained the cornerstone upon which the accords depended; if the warlords suspected that their enemies were still armed for combat, they would hardly be compelled to begin the process of national reconciliation. As Hirsch and Oakley explain:

> The most significant gap in carrying out the Addis Ababa Accords pertained to disarmament. Operation Restore Hope's strategy for maintaining a stable security environment during the transition counted heavily on effective and timely follow-up. The accords were clearly far from self-enforcing: UNITAF's mandate did not cover nationwide enforcement, the UN was unwilling and unable to accept the responsibility, and the NGOs had neither the cohesion nor the resources required to do so. The factions, each watching and waiting for the other to disarm, were either too suspicious and frightened to do so or, in some cases, had no real intention of doing so. They feared both serious attacks from their enemies and the loss of future power and position, and Aideed's SNA prepared to challenge the UN peacekeepers as soon as U.S. forces had departed.[23]

Even with Washington's refusal to pursue disarmament, a seamless transition from a strong American force to a strong UN force might have convinced Aideed to stand down. But the transition to UN control was far from seamless.

The key obstacle to a smooth transition was miscommunication between the White House and the UN Secretariat. Although the United States was actually willing to offer support for a UN disarmament program, Boutros-Ghali assumed that the Clinton administration was unprepared to assist with any disarmament whatsoever. Because he himself was unwilling to assign the task to a weaker UN force, the secretary-general insisted that disarmament must be completed before the withdrawal of American troops. To demonstrate his resolve, Boutros-Ghali refused to begin planning for the deployment of UNOSOM II until disarmament had begun. Unfazed by the secretary-general's refusal and still unwilling to disarm the warlords, the United States flatly declared that it would begin its withdrawal as planned, in January 1993.

When the time finally came for the first departure of American troops, it was clear that the UN was unprepared to assume control. Even after the Clinton administration had unequivocally stated that UNITAF would neither expand operations to the north nor pursue a comprehensive program for disarmament, the secretary-general continued to insist that both were vital to a long-term settlement. Following his advice, the Security Council assigned the duties to UNOSOM II. As a result:

> The new UNOSOM II force, which consisted of 20,000 troops and 8,000 logical support staff from thirty-three different countries, was supposed to do what UNITAF had been unable to do with 17,000 troops more: disarm the warlord militias and take charge of the remaining sixty percent of Somalia's territory.[24]

But the Security Council's vision for UNOSOM II extended far beyond nationwide disarmament. The UN operation was also ordered to undertake the most ambitious postconflict peace-building program ever attempted, one which U.S. Ambassador to the UN Madeleine Albright would dub "an unprecedented enterprise aimed at nothing less than the restoration of a country."[25]

In Resolution 794 the Security Council outlined just what that enterprise would entail. First, the secretary-general was to solicit from member states contributions "to assist in financing the rehabilitation of the political institutions and economy of Somalia."[26] Then, to begin Somalia's "rehabilitation," UNOSOM II was to assist in the repatriation of refugees and displaced persons; to help establish local, regional, and national law enforcement agencies; to begin de-mining the Somali countryside; and, finally, "to create conditions under which Somali civil society may have a role, at every level, in the process of political reconciliation and in the formulation and realization of rehabilitation and reconstruction programs."[27] Although the system of regional and national councils agreed to in the Addis Ababa Accords would remain the foundation for national reconciliation, the UN's plan to revive Somalia went far beyond anything discussed by the warlords. The Security Council had chosen to undertake the reconstruction of a failed state.

Comprehensive as the UN's vision for Somalia may have been, it was soon to encounter a host of difficulties. UNITAF had succeeded in a less challenging mission by breaking down barriers between the military, humanitarian, and political elements of its presence and maintaining the threat of force as an incentive for the Somalis to develop their own solutions. UNOSOM II, on the other hand, operated in a slow, compartmentalized, bureaucratic fashion. Hardly as strong as its American predecessors, its troops seemed ill-organized, poorly managed, and clearly unprepared for the task at hand. Between the UN's bureaucratic approach to solving Somalia's problems and the sheer inadequacy of the operation's military capabilities, a sense of insecurity began to pervade UNOSOM II. That insecurity soon distanced UN personnel in Somalia from the Somalis they were there to help. Nowhere was the growing alienation more obvious than in the UN barracks in central Mogadishu. While American troops participating in UNITAF had remained in makeshift accommodations throughout their stay in Somalia, UNOSOM II arrived with prefabricated housing and proceeded to build what eventually appeared to be a fort guarding UN personnel from the Somalis outside.[28]

Acutely aware of the UN's shortcomings, Aideed soon began to challenge UNOSOM II. By far the most powerful of the remaining warlords, Aideed knew that the UN would be loathe to confront him. On a more personal level, tensions had emerged between Aideed and the secretary-general; while Boutros-Ghali still bore a grudge from Aideed's January protest, Aideed suspected that Boutros-Ghali, as Egypt's former foreign minister, had been an ally to former Somali dictator Siad Barre. Sensing Aideed's hostility, UN officials in Mogadishu quickly concluded—as did their American counterparts—that Aideed was likely to test the new UN presence.[29] As the *New York Times* reported in November 1993, "in early summer, the Central Intelligence Agency endorsed the view, held by the United Nations and publicly supported by President Clinton at the time, that General Aideed was a disruptive force who would interfere with the rebuilding of Somalia."[30] Most analysts suspected that the warlord had little interest in sharing power and was only biding his time until the peacekeepers departed. Few, however, had any concrete suggestions as to how to handle him.

With UN officials still deciding how to deal with Aideed, relations with the warlord began to deteriorate. The tensions came to a flashpoint in mid-May, when the UN renounced an upcoming Mogadishu peace conference sponsored by Aideed as a clear ploy to seize power. As if to emphasize their point, UN officials in Somalia quickly announced that they would sponsor a competing conference, even providing free transportation to Aideed's rivals. Although SNA representatives attended the parallel peace conferences, their behavior convinced the UN that Aideed could not be included in the plans for a new nation:

> When, as a means of political pressure, some of the participants from other clans were detained by SNA militia in the Olympia Hotel, UNOSOM concluded that Aideed's ambitions could never be satisfied by genuine power-sharing and compromise. They concluded that he should be politically marginalized rather than included in continued high-level dialogue.[31]

Had UNOSOM II had the military strength of its American-led predecessor, the UN might have ultimately succeeded in marginalizing Aideed. As it was, however, the UN would succeed only in engaging him as a foe.

The End of UNOSOM II

Nowhere were the disparities between the UN peacekeepers and their American predecessors clearer than in south Mogadishu, where American marines were replaced by Pakistani peacekeepers who had different training, less firepower, and clear doubts about the level of tactical support they would receive from UNOSOM II headquarters.[32] It was here that Aideed would launch his first offensive against the UN. Realizing that his success would in part depend on the support of the city's population, the warlord first attacked UNOSOM II not on the ground but on Radio Mogadishu, at the time controlled by Aideed's Somali National Army. Decrying foreign interference in domestic problems, praising the SNA, and calling for a Somali solution to Somali problems, Aideed made it clear that he was not about to bend to UN pressure. Soon after the broadcast the SNA's heavy weaponry reappeared on the streets of south Mogadishu.

As the UN decided how to respond to this latest affront, rumors abounded that UNOSOM II intended to force Radio Mogadishu off the air.[33] On June 4, 1993, UN headquarters warned Aideed that on the following day Pakistani peacekeepers would be coming to the compound that housed the station as part of a routine weapons inspection.[34] Fearing that the UN was attempting to marginalize him, Aideed took action. On the morning of June 5, as they began patrols throughout south Mogadishu, Pakistani peacekeepers were ambushed by SNA forces hiding in crowds of women and children. Pinned down, the Pakistanis called for support from the U.S. Quick Reaction Force (QRF)—a remnant of UNITAF still under U.S. command—and

Italian armored units stationed in Mogadishu.[35] By the end of the day twenty-four Pakistanis and scores of Somalis lay dead. The Security Council quickly convened an emergency session to denounce the violence and authorize the use of "all necessary measures" leading to the detention or arrest of those responsible for the attacks. Although Aideed was not mentioned by name, he was clearly the target. By authorizing the use of force, the Security Council had thus taken its first steps towards engaging the warlord.

While many observers had long considered Aideed to be the prime obstacle to rebuilding Somalia, the decision to use force in pursuit of his arrest represented a major turning point in the intervention. Although the intention was to bring to justice those responsible for the murder of the Pakistani peacekeepers, singling out Aideed in effect meant taking sides in a civil war. Although later painted as a rash decision on the behalf of the secretary-general and his top military adviser in Somalia, at the time the change in policy had the qualified support of the United States. As the *New York Times* later reported:

> The premise of the United Nations policy—to neutralize General Aideed's power—was shared by top Administration officials throughout most of the summer, though some were uneasy that the strategy relied too heavily on military force. The United States military at first also supported the policy of confronting Aideed with force, but later came to doubt that it would be possible to capture him.[36]

Despite their reservations, administration officials publicly supported the Security Council resolution authorizing Aideed's capture. Only days after the attack on Pakistani peacekeepers, American gunships and attack helicopters pounded Aideed's headquarters in an attack broadcast across the globe. Although President Clinton lauded the strike, claiming "the military back of Aideed has been broken" and adding that "a warrant has been issued for

his arrest," it had in fact only stirred Aideed's anger.[37] With the clear impression that he was being marginalized and persecuted in a ploy orchestrated by the United States and its allies in the UN, Aideed chose retaliation over surrender. As it became clear that Aideed would refuse to yield—and would instead take every opportunity to embarrass the foreign interlocutors and disrupt the process of national reconciliation—the United States and the UN steeled their resolve and announced a manhunt for the renegade warlord.

As forces under UN and American command began the search for Aideed, the purpose of the continuing international presence in Somalia became increasingly bluffed. Rather than building the framework for a lasting settlement, UNOSOM II forces—along with the American QRF—began to focus more and more on pursuing Aideed. As they did so, engaging the SNA on a regular basis, the foreign peacekeepers began to resemble belligerents themselves. In Aideed's eyes they were certainly fair targets, even for offensive attacks. Although clearly illegal, Aideed's offensive against the peacekeepers soon began to receive greater acceptance among the Somali people. In some quarters the warlord even began to resemble a home-grown hero resisting the will of imperialist intruders.

Mobilized by the broadcasts over Radio Mogadishu, popular support for Aideed was further enhanced by the tactics used to fight the warlord. According to one force commander, when pursuing Aideed it was often "hard to avoid civilian casualties" and "very difficult to tell what the casualty numbers are on the other side."[38] The confusion over casualty figures reflected the more fundamental difficulty of defining the rules of engagement for a manhunt in the midst of a humanitarian operation. As one correspondent put it, "In the murky business of fighting war as peacekeepers, understanding the rules is half the battle."[39] Unfortunately for the peacekeepers, it was a battle they were almost destined to lose. Unlike the UN and U.S. troops, General Aideed's renegade forces were bound by no rules of engagement. Fighting an unconventional war, they often launched attacks from crowds of civilians, even using women and children as human shields. When peacekeepers accidentally killed or wounded those civilians, even in the course of defending themselves against attacks, the result was greater resentment towards the intervention. As one Somali student explained after a battle between Aideed's troops and UN peacekeepers, "If the dead men were gunmen, it is good for Somalia. But if they were not gunmen, this is an evil foreign action."[40]

Beginning in July 1993 and continuing over the next four months, the SNA and UNOSOM II forces would clash regularly, with the UN accusing the SNA of launching ambushes from crowds of women and children and the SNA retorting that the UN had fired on innocent civilians. Although UNOSOM II staged several successful raids on SNA weapons depots, the operation was ultimately unsuccessful in stopping the rebels from attacking UN personnel. Unhappy with the escalating violence and displeased with the United States' decision to have its remaining troops report to Washington rather than UN headquarters in New York, French and Italian commanders refused to use force, eventually withdrawing their units from the UN command structure.[41] Even aid agencies expressed their disenchantment over the use of force, claiming that it was making it more difficult to distribute humanitarian assistance. But the SNA continued to press UNOSOM II forces, killing four Americans with a remote controlled device that exploded under their vehicle and injuring six more with a landmine planted along a patrol route.[42] In response,

President Clinton ordered Delta Force commandos, Army Rangers, and a helicopter detachment airlifted to Mogadishu. Though acting in support of the UNOSOM II mandate, they operated under separate U.S. command. . . . Their orders were to capture Aideed and senior SNA officials whenever the opportunity arose. . . . In effect, the Rangers and Delta Force became a posse with standing authority to go after Aideed and his outlaw band.[43]

As operations became more and more focused on fighting the SNA, life in Mogadishu began to change. With the desire to capture Aideed almost an obsession, less and less attention was paid to humanitarian operations, and the situation on the streets began to deteriorate. When not on patrol, peacekeepers took shelter in the makeshift fortress in central Mogadishu. Both the media and employees of nongovernmental organizations were increasingly evacuated to Nairobi. Those who remained often had to travel with armed escorts, even on humanitarian missions.[44]

The turning point came on October 3, 1993. After a string of firefights during the first half of September had left hundreds of Somalis and dozens of Nigerian, Pakistani, and Italian peacekeepers dead or wounded, the U.S. Rangers and Delta Force commandos stepped up their raids and patrols, arresting uninvolved Somalis and even foreign relief workers as they searched—with some success—for top SNA officials.[45] Although the new Clinton administration had privately shown signs that it might seek a political solution, the events of October 3 dashed any hopes for such an outcome. Acting on reliable intelligence, U.S. Rangers descended on the Olympia Hotel in downtown Mogadishu to search for SNA officials suspected of planning attacks on UN forces. Although the Rangers successfully captured twenty-four suspects—including several of Aideed's top aides—two of their helicopters were forced down as they attempted to withdraw. The nightmarish incident that followed spelled the end of American involvement in Somalia and sent UNOSOM II on a downward spiral from which the operation would never recover. Although UNOSOM, UNITAF, and UNOSOM II had between them saved countless lives, the UN intervention in Somalia was widely deemed a failure.

Reeling from the fallout of UNOSOM II, both the United States and the United Nations would quickly denounce the premise that force could be used to pressure warring parties to consent to a foreign humanitarian presence. The Pentagon and White House came to quick agreement that U.S. forces should engage only in traditional UN operations, ones which enjoy the full consent of the warring parties. Without the assistance of American forces or forthright American leadership on the Security Council, the UN would also shy away from using force, a decision that clearly affected the troubled operation in the former Yugoslavia. The debate continues as to how the international community can and should respond to humanitarian emergencies where intervention has not won, and perhaps could never win, the consent of the internally warring parties.

NOTES

1. Robert G. Putnam, "The UN Operation in Somalia," in Ramesh Thakur and Carlyle A. Thayer, eds., *A Crisis of Expectations: UN Peacekeeping in the 1990s* (Boulder, Colo.: Westview Press, 1995), p. 86.

2. Unless otherwise noted, background information for this section is drawn from Putnam, "The UN Operation in Somalia," pp. 86–89.

3. John L. Hirsch and Robert Oakley, *Somalia and Operation Restore Hope* (Washington, D.C.: United States Institute of Peace, 1995), p. 24.

4. Ibid., p. 91.

5. Ibid., pp. 32–33.

6. Ibid., p. 42.

7. Peter Applebom, "Seared by Faces of Need, Americans Say 'How Could We Not Do This?'" *New York Times,* Dec. 13, 1992, p. A16.

8. Ibid.

9. Ibid.

10. Thomas L. Friedman, "Clinton Inherits Conflicts That Don't Follow Rules," *New York Times,* Dec. 13, 1992, p. D3.

11. "Somalia in Brief," *Atlanta Constitution,* Dec. 4, 1992, p. A13.

12. Don Oberdorfer, "Envoy to Somalia Follows Own Script," *Washington Post,* Dec. 11, 1992, p. A47.

13. Dick Cheney and Colin Powell, "U.S. Mission to Somalia Is Clear and Necessary," USIA, *East Asia/Pacific Wireless File,* Dec. 4, 1992, pp. 11–12.

14. Andrei Raevsky, "Peacekeeping Operations: Command and Control," in Ramesh Thakur and Carlyle A. Thayer, eds., *A Crisis of Expectations: UN Peacekeeping in the 1990s* (Boulder, Colo.: Westview Press, 1995), p. 12.

15. Hirsch and Oakley, *Somalia,* p. 46.

16. Ibid., p. 93.

17. Chester Crocker, "The Lessons of Somalia: Not Everything Went Wrong," *Foreign Affairs* 74, 3, (May/June 1995): 4.

18. Putnam, "UN Operation in Somalia," p. 93.

19. Crocker, "The Lessons of Somalia," p. 4.

20. William Claiborne and Barton Gellman, "Rival Warlords Sign Peace Pact in Somalia," *Washington Post,* Dec. 11, 1992, p. A1.

21. Hirsch and Oakley, *Somalia,* pp. 102–3.

22. Ibid., p. 101.

23. Ibid., p. 99.

24. Putnam, "UN Operation in Somalia," p. 96.

25. U.S.U.N. Press Release 37–(93), United States Permanent Mission to the United Nations, March 26, 1993.

26. UN Security Council Resolution 814, March 26, 1993.

27. Ibid.

28. See Michael Maren's reports from Mogadishu published in the *Village Voice* in early 1993.

29. Hirsch and Oakley, *Somalia,* p. 116.

30. Michael R. Gordon and John H. Cushman, Jr., "U.S. Supported Hunt for Aideed; Now Calls UN Policy Skewed," *New York Times,* Oct. 18, 1993, p. A8.

31. Hirsch and Oakley, *Somalia,* p. 116.

32. Ibid., p. 116.

33. Ibid., p. 117.

34. Putnam, "UN Operation in Somalia," p. 97.

35. Hirsch and Oakley, *Somalia,* p. 118.

36. Gordon and Cushman, "U.S. Supported Hunt for Aideed," p. A8.

37. Ibid., p. A8.

38. Hirsch and Oakley, *Somalia,* p. 126.

39. Bruce B. Auster, "Fighting a New Kind of War," *U.S. News and World Report,* Nov. 8, 1993, p. 60.

40. Eric Schmitt, "2 Somalis Killed in Clash," *New York Times,* Dec. 11, 1992, p. A1.
41. Putnam, "UN Operation in Somalia," p. 97.
42. Hirsch and Oakley, *Somalia,* p. 122.
43. Ibid., p. 122.
44. Ibid., p. 123.
45. Ibid., p. 125.

Comment

Evaluate the justifications for the initial intervention. Consider the reasons that officials actually gave and the reasons that they could have given. Under what circumstances and to what extent is the use of force in international politics justified for humanitarian ends?

Some critics made a point of noting that suffering and bloodshed were just as great in many other countries in the world. If so, to what extent should this fact count as a moral argument against intervention? Should our assessment of the intervention be affected if the nations that intervened were motivated by their own national interest (in addition to or instead of humanitarian concerns)?

Analyze the way the goals of the intervention changed as the mission proceeded. Should the military force have been limited to establishing security for distributing aid, or should it have provided support for nation building? Did the military adequately observe rules of engagement that would minimize the risks to civilians?

Unlike the simple cases of intervention, in which one nation responds to an attack by an aggressor, this intervention involved many nations acting collectively under the auspices of the United Nations and in a country embroiled in a civil war. To what extent do these factors—the sponsorship of the United Nations and the breakdown of civil authority—strengthen the moral case for intervention? Should officials have tried to gain the consent of leaders in Somalia (for example, by convening a peace conference)?

Why Attack Iraq?*

On March 17, 2003, U.S. President George W. Bush delivered an ultimatum to Iraqi leader Saddam Hussein: leave Iraq within forty-eight hours or face war. Two days later, American planes dropped heavy bombs on selected targets in Baghdad in the hope of killing Hussein and other top Iraqi officials. The attack marked the beginning of an invasion of Iraq—conducted mainly by U.S. and British forces—that ended on April 8 with the collapse of the government in Baghdad. Approximately 260 of the invading coalition's soldiers died during the immediate conflict, and it is estimated that some 2,300 Iraqi soldiers and more than 6,000 Iraqi civilians were killed.

The public justifications of the war given by the British and American governments focused on Iraq's alleged possession of weapons of mass destruction (WMDs) and its government's potential ties to international terrorist networks. In the months leading up to the invasion, the allied governments insisted on the full, public destruction of all Iraqi WMDs. (Some American officials, notably President Bush, also cited the need for "regime change" in Iraq.) In late March, declaring themselves dissatisfied with Iraq's lack of cooperation with weapons inspectors and convinced of Iraqi subterfuge, the allies initiated war. Iraqi officials, meanwhile, denied possession of any WMDs, denied any connection with international terrorism, and accused the allied governments of flagrant violations of international law (citing article 2, section 4, of the UN Charter, which prohibits the use of force to seize territory or overthrow the government of another state).

Saddam Hussein had governed Iraq since 1979 in a violent, repressive authoritarian style. Among his many documented atrocities was the 1988 mass slaughter of an estimated five thousands Iraqi citizens (and members of the Kurdish minority) with chemical weapons. He was nonetheless considered a U.S. ally through the end of the Cold War, and supplied with weapons and assistance during the Iran-Iraq war, which ended in 1988. His cooperative relations with the United States ended when his army instigated the Gulf War of 1991 by invading Kuwait. Only days after Kuwait's invasion, the UN Security Council, with U.S. approval, imposed strict economic sanctions on Iraq. These sanctions were kept in place until 2003, and helped perpetuate a severe economic and humanitarian crisis in Iraq throughout this period.

At the close of the Gulf War, a defeated Iraq signed a cease-fire that included, among many other provisions, plans for the

immediate destruction of all WMDs and long-range missiles, supervised by the United Nations. Over the following seven years, UN inspectors were routinely frustrated by the Iraqi government's refusal to cooperate fully with these plans. These frustrations reached a climax in December of 1998, when the inspections teams withdrew, and the British and American governments launched a four-day retaliatory bombing campaign against Iraqi weapons programs. At the time, neither the United States nor Britain took additional steps to depose Saddam Hussein or force Iraqi disarmament.

The attacks of September 11, 2001, on the World Trade Center and Pentagon evidently changed the U.S. government's attitude toward Iraq's continuing noncompliance with the 1991 disarmament provisions. Although no one then claimed that Iraq had any direct connection to the attacks, the threat of terrorism on U.S. soil strengthened the position of U.S. officials who wished to take a more aggressive approach toward Iraq. The United States and its allies became more intensely concerned with the proliferation of WMDs and their sale to terrorist networks antagonistic to the United States. George W. Bush, whose father had been president during the 1991 Gulf War, had been elected to the presidency in the previous year, and his cabinet included several of his father's former aides—notably Secretary of Defense Donald Rumsfeld, who had desired Hussein's forcible removal even at the end of the 1991 campaign. The new Bush administration began increasing diplomatic pressure on Hussein's regime.

Immediately following the 9/11 attacks, and throughout its ensuing war against terrorist groups in Afghanistan, the United States enjoyed broad support in the international community. This support began to dissolve in the fall of 2003, following Bush's threats to attack Iraq, and in light of his controversial doctrine of "preemptive" warfare. While the UN Security Council was willing to force Hussein to accept

---

*Sigal Ben-Porath and Alex Zakaras wrote the introduction and selected the excerpts presented in this section.

inspections without further restriction, several of its prominent members—France and Russia especially—were unwilling to sanction an immediate invasion of Iraq. The Bush administration's conviction that it could legitimately initiate warfare based on its anticipation of future Iraqi aggression drew intense criticism from many in the international community.

Under international pressure, Hussein declared that he would allow unrestricted inspections to resume in November of 2003. In the months that followed, inspectors made no significant progress toward discovering hidden WMDs, but continued to believe that Hussein's regime was not fully disclosing information about its weapons programs. There was also substantial disagreement in the international community about the effectiveness of inspections in the face of a corrupt, ruthless government. The public debate—both in the United States and abroad—over the looming war grew more intense during this period. It now focused not only on the WMDs, but also on the desirability of destroying a regime widely considered morally repugnant. Critics, meanwhile, emphasized the perils of American unilateralism and the dangerous precedent of a preventive war.

The swift triumph of the military operation was not matched by equal success in the rebuilding of society and government. The occupation forces were not well prepared for the chaos that followed the victory, and took longer than expected to restore order and basic services. By August of 2004, the death toll among coalition forces exceeded 1,000, and daily outbreaks of violence continued.

No significant depositories of WMDs were discovered, and their absence raised serious questions about the validity of the public justifications for war. In January of 2004, chief U.S. weapons inspector David Kay formally concluded that Iraq possessed no weapons of mass destruction. The Bush administration, however, maintained that the "jury is still out" on the question, and continued to defend the war on Iraq as a

fight against global terrorism and weapons of mass destruction. In February 2004, however, facing increasing public pressure, the president announced the launch of a formal investigation into American intelligence about Saddam Hussein's regime.

BEFORE THE WAR
JUSTIFICATIONS

The administration argued in many different forums for the war. Top administration officers including the president gave speeches at the United Nations assembly in an attempt to generate multinational support for war. The administration also worked closely with Congress to secure formal authorization for invasion, and addressed the public through a host of media venues.

EXCERPTS FROM REMARKS BY PRESIDENT BUSH

Cincinnati, Ohio
October 7, 2002

Tonight I want to take a few minutes to discuss a grave threat to peace, and America's determination to lead the world in confronting that threat.

The threat comes from Iraq. It arises directly from the Iraqi regime's own actions—its history of aggression, and its drive toward an arsenal of terror. Eleven years ago, as a condition for ending the Persian Gulf War, the Iraqi regime was required to destroy its weapons of mass destruction, to cease all development of such weapons, and to stop all support for terrorist groups. The Iraqi regime has violated all of those obligations. It possesses and produces chemical and biological weapons. It is seeking nuclear weapons. It has given shelter and support to terrorism, and practices terror against its own people. The entire world has witnessed Iraq's eleven-year history of defiance, deception and bad faith.

We also must never forget the most vivid events of recent history. On September the

11th, 2001, America felt its vulnerability— even to threats that gather on the other side of the earth. We resolved then, and we are resolved today, to confront every threat, from any source, that could bring sudden terror and suffering to America.

Members of the Congress of both political parties, and members of the United Nations Security Council, agree that Saddam Hussein is a threat to peace and must disarm. We agree that the Iraqi dictator must not be permitted to threaten America and the world with horrible poisons and diseases and gases and atomic weapons. Since we all agree on this goal, the issue is: how can we best achieve it?

Many Americans have raised legitimate questions . . .

First, some ask why Iraq is different from other countries or regimes that also have terrible weapons. While there are many dangers in the world, the threat from Iraq stands alone—because it gathers the most serious dangers of our age in one place. Iraq's weapons of mass destruction are controlled by a murderous tyrant who has already used chemical weapons to kill thousands of people. This same tyrant has tried to dominate the Middle East, has invaded and brutally occupied a small neighbor, has struck other nations without warning, and holds an unrelenting hostility toward the United States.

By its past and present actions, by its technological capabilities, by the merciless nature of its regime, Iraq is unique. As a former chief weapons inspector of the U.N. has said, "The fundamental problem with Iraq remains the nature of the regime, itself. Saddam Hussein is a homicidal dictator who is addicted to weapons of mass destruction."

Some ask how urgent this danger is to America and the world. The danger is already significant, and it only grows worse with time. If we know Saddam Hussein has dangerous weapons today—and we do—does it make any sense for the world to wait to confront him as he grows even stronger and develops even more dangerous weapons?

· · ·

We know that the regime has produced thousands of tons of chemical agents, includ-ing mustard gas, sarin nerve gas, VX nerve gas. Saddam Hussein also has experience in using chemical weapons. He has ordered chemical attacks on Iran, and on more than forty villages in his own country. These actions killed or injured at least 20,000 people, more than six times the number of people who died in the attacks of September the 11th.

And surveillance photos reveal that the regime is rebuilding facilities that it had used to produce chemical and biological weapons. Every chemical and biological weapon that Iraq has or makes is a direct violation of the truce that ended the Persian Gulf War in 1991. . . .

Iraq possesses ballistic missiles with a likely range of hundreds of miles—far enough to strike Saudi Arabia, Israel, Turkey, and other nations—in a region where more than 135,000 American civilians and service members live and work. We've also discovered through intelligence that Iraq has a growing fleet of manned and unmanned aerial vehicles that could be used to disperse chemical or biological weapons across broad areas. We're concerned that Iraq is exploring ways of using these UAVs for missions targeting the United States. And, of course, sophisticated delivery systems aren't required for a chemical or biological attack; all that might be required are a small container and one terrorist or Iraqi intelligence operative to deliver it.

And that is the source of our urgent concern about Saddam Hussein's links to international terrorist groups. Over the years, Iraq has provided safe haven to terrorists such as Abu Nidal, whose terror organization carried out more than 90 terrorist attacks in 20 countries that killed or injured nearly 900 people, including 12 Americans. . . .

We know that Iraq and the al Qaeda terrorist network share a common enemy— the United States of America. We know that Iraq and al Qaeda have had high-level contacts that go back a decade. Some al Qaeda leaders who fled Afghanistan went to Iraq. These include one very senior al Qaeda leader who received medical treatment in Baghdad this year, and who has been associated with planning for chemical and biological attacks. We've learned that Iraq has trained al Qaeda members in bomb-making and poisons and deadly gases. And we know that after September the 11th, Saddam Hussein's regime gleefully celebrated the terrorist attacks on America.

. . .

The evidence indicates that Iraq is reconstituting its nuclear weapons program. Saddam Hussein has held numerous meetings with Iraqi nuclear scientists, a group he calls his "nuclear mujahideen"—his nuclear holy warriors. Satellite photographs reveal that Iraq is rebuilding facilities at sites that have been part of its nuclear program in the past. Iraq has attempted to purchase high-strength aluminum tubes and other equipment needed for gas centrifuges, which are used to enrich uranium for nuclear weapons.

If the Iraqi regime is able to produce, buy, or steal an amount of highly enriched uranium a little larger than a single softball, it could have a nuclear weapon in less than a year. And if we allow that to happen, a terrible line would be crossed. Saddam Hussein would be in a position to blackmail anyone who opposes his aggression. He would be in a position to dominate the Middle East. He would be in a position to threaten America. And Saddam Hussein would be in a position to pass nuclear technology to terrorists.

Some citizens wonder, after 11 years of living with this problem, why do we need to confront it now? And there's a reason. We've experienced the horror of September the 11th. We have seen that those who hate America are willing to crash airplanes into buildings full of innocent people. Our enemies would be no less willing, in fact, they would be eager, to use biological or chemical, or a nuclear weapon.

Knowing these realities, America must not ignore the threat gathering against us. Facing clear evidence of peril, we cannot wait for the final proof—the smoking gun—that could come in the form of a mushroom cloud. As President Kennedy said in October of 1962, "Neither the United States of America, nor the world community of nations can tolerate deliberate deception and offensive threats on the part of any nation, large or small. We no longer live in a world," he said, "where only the actual firing of weapons represents a sufficient challenge to a nation's security to constitute maximum peril."

Understanding the threats of our time, knowing the designs and deceptions of the Iraqi regime, we have every reason to assume the worst, and we have an urgent duty to prevent the worst from occurring. . . .

. . .

There is no easy or risk-free course of action. Some have argued we should wait—and that's an option. In my view, it's the riskiest of all options, because the longer we wait, the stronger and bolder Saddam Hussein will become. We could wait and hope that Saddam does not give weapons to terrorists, or develop a nuclear weapon to blackmail the world. But I'm convinced that is a hope against all evidence. As Americans, we want peace—we work and sacrifice for peace. But there can be no peace if our security depends on the will and whims of a ruthless and aggressive dictator. I'm not willing to stake one American life on trusting Saddam Hussein. . . .

Some worry that a change of leadership in Iraq could create instability and make the situation worse. The situation could hardly get worse, for world security and for the people of Iraq. The lives of Iraqi citizens would improve dramatically if Saddam Hussein were no longer in power, just as the lives of Afghanistan's citizens improved after the Taliban. The dictator of Iraq is a student of Stalin, using murder as a tool of terror and control, within his own cabinet, within his own army, and even within his own family.

On Saddam Hussein's orders, opponents have been decapitated, wives and mothers of political opponents have been systematically raped as a method of intimidation, and political prisoners have been forced to watch their own children being tortured.

America believes that all people are entitled to hope and human rights, to the non-negotiable demands of human dignity. People everywhere prefer freedom to slavery; prosperity to squalor; self-government to the rule of terror and torture. America is a friend to the people of Iraq. Our demands are directed only at the regime that enslaves them and threatens us. When these demands are met, the first and greatest benefit will come to Iraqi men, women and children. The oppression of Kurds, Assyrians, Turkomans, Shi'a, Sunnis and others will be lifted. The long captivity of Iraq will end, and an era of new hope will begin. . . .

EXCERPTS FROM PRESIDENT BUSH'S
STATE OF THE UNION ADDRESS

January 28, 2003

Almost three months ago, the United Nations Security Council gave Saddam Hussein his final chance to disarm. He has shown instead utter contempt for the United Nations, and for the opinion of the world. The 108 U.N. inspectors were sent to conduct—were not sent to conduct a scavenger hunt for hidden materials across a country the size of California. The job of the inspectors is to verify that Iraq's regime is disarming. It is up to Iraq to show exactly where it is hiding its banned weapons, lay those weapons out for the world to see, and destroy them as directed. Nothing like this has happened. . . .

The dictator of Iraq is not disarming. To the contrary; he is deceiving. From intelligence sources we know, for instance, that thousands of Iraqi security personnel are at work hiding documents and materials from the U.N. inspectors, sanitizing inspection sites and monitoring the inspectors themselves. Iraqi officials accompany the inspectors in order to intimidate witnesses.

Iraq is blocking U-2 surveillance flights requested by the United Nations. Iraqi intelligence officers are posing as the scientists inspectors are supposed to interview. Real scientists have been coached by Iraqi officials on what to say. Intelligence sources indicate that Saddam Hussein has ordered that scientists who cooperate with U.N. inspectors in disarming Iraq will be killed, along with their families. . . .

EXCERPTS FROM COLIN POWELL'S
APPEARANCE BEFORE THE UNITED
NATIONS SECURITY COUNCIL

February 5, 2003

Let me set the stage with three key points that all of us need to keep in mind: First, Saddam Hussein has used these horrific weapons on another country and on his own people. In fact, in the history of chemical warfare, no country has had more battlefield experience with chemical weapons since World War I than Saddam Hussein's Iraq.

Second, as with biological weapons, Saddam Hussein has never accounted for vast amounts of chemical weaponry. . . .

We believe Saddam Hussein knows what he did with it, and he has not come clean with the international community. We have evidence these weapons existed. What we don't have is evidence from Iraq that they have been destroyed or where they are. That is what we are still waiting for.

Third point, Iraq's record on chemical weapons is replete with lies. It took years for Iraq to finally admit that it had produced four tons of the deadly nerve agent, VX. A single drop of VX on the skin will kill in minutes. Four tons. The admission only came out after inspectors collected documentation as a result of the defection of Hussein Kamal, Saddam Hussein's late son-in-law. UNSCOM also gained forensic evidence that Iraq had produced VX and put it into weapons for delivery. Yet, to this day, Iraq denies it had ever weaponized VX . . .

. . . [W]e have more than a decade of proof that he remains determined to acquire nuclear weapons. . . . People will continue to debate this issue, but there is no doubt in my mind, these elicit procurement efforts show that Saddam Hussein is very much focused on putting in place the key missing piece from his nuclear weapons program, the ability to produce fissile material. He also has been busy trying to maintain the other key parts of his nuclear program, particularly his cadre of key nuclear scientists.

. . . Our concern is not just about these elicit weapons. It's the way that these elicit weapons can be connected to terrorists and terrorist organizations that have no compunction about using such devices against innocent people around the world.

. . . [W]hat I want to bring to your attention today is the potentially much more sinister nexus between Iraq and the Al Qaeda terrorist network, a nexus that combines classic terrorist organizations and modern methods of murder. Iraq today harbors a deadly terrorist network headed by Abu Musab Al-Zarqawi, an associate and collaborator of Osama bin Laden and his Al Qaeda lieutenants. . . .

Iraqi officials deny accusations of ties with Al Qaeda. These denials are simply not credible. Last year an Al Qaeda associate bragged that the situation in Iraq was "good," that Baghdad could be transited quickly. . . .

. . . Some claim these contacts do not amount to much. They say Saddam Hussein's secular tyranny and Al Qaeda's religious tyranny do not mix. I am not comforted by this thought. Ambition and hatred are enough to bring Iraq and Al Qaeda together, enough so Al Qaeda could learn how to build more sophisticated bombs and learn how to forge documents, and enough so that Al Qaeda could turn to Iraq for help in acquiring expertise on weapons of mass destruction.

· · ·

With this track record, Iraqi denials of supporting terrorism take the place alongside the other Iraqi denials of weapons of mass destruction. It is all a web of lies. . . .

There is one more subject that I would like to touch on briefly. And it should be a subject of deep and continuing concern to this council, Saddam Hussein's violations of human rights.

Underlying all that I have said, underlying all the facts and the patterns of behavior

that I have identified [are] Saddam Hussein's contempt for the will of this council, his contempt for the truth and most damning of all, his utter contempt for human life. . . .

BEFORE THE WAR
CRITICISMS

EXCERPTS FROM SENATOR BYRD'S CRITICISM

October 3, 2002

Senator Byrd (D-W.Va.) delivered the following remarks as the Senate opened debate on Senate Joint Resolution 46, a resolution authorizing the president to use whatever force he deems necessary in Iraq or elsewhere.

The newly bellicose mood that permeates this White House is unfortunate, all the more so because it is clearly motivated by campaign politics. Republicans are already running attack ads against Democrats on Iraq. Democrats favor fast approval of a resolution so they can change the subject to domestic economic problems.

Before risking the lives of American troops, all members of Congress—Democrats and Republicans alike—must overcome the siren song of political polls and focus strictly on the merits, not the politics, of this most serious issue.

The resolution before us today is not only a product of haste; it is also a product of presidential hubris. This resolution is breathtaking in its scope. It redefines the nature of defense, and reinterprets the Constitution to suit the will of the Executive Branch. It would give the President blanket authority to launch a unilateral preemptive attack on a sovereign nation that is *perceived* to be a threat to the United States. This is an unprecedented and unfounded interpretation of the President's authority under the Constitution, not to mention the fact that it stands the charter of the United Nations on its head.

Representative Abraham Lincoln, in a letter to William H. Herndon, stated: "Allow the President to invade a neighboring nation whenever he shall deem it necessary to repel an invasion, and you allow him to do so whenever he may choose to say he deems it necessary for such purpose—and you allow him to make war at pleasure. Study to see if you can fix any limit to his power in this respect, after you have given him so much as you propose." . . .

If he could speak to us today, what would Lincoln say of the Bush doctrine concerning preemptive strikes?

In a September 18 report, the Congressional Research Service had this to say about the preemptive use of military force:

The historical record indicates that the United States has never, to date, engaged in a "preemptive" military attack against another nation. Nor has the United States ever attacked another nation militarily *prior* to its first having been attacked or *prior* to U.S. citizens or interests first having been attacked, with the singular exception of the Spanish-American War. The Spanish-American War is unique in that the principal goal of United States military action was to compel Spain to grant Cuba its political independence.

The Congressional Research Service also noted that the Cuban Missile Crisis of 1962 "represents a threat situation which some may argue had elements more parallel to those presented by Iraq today—but it was resolved without a "preemptive" military attack by the United States."

· · ·

Think for a moment of the precedent that this resolution will set, not just for this President but for future Presidents. From this day forward, American Presidents will be able to invoke Senate Joint Resolution 46 as justification for launching preemptive military strikes against any sovereign nations that they perceive to be a threat. Other nations will be able to hold up the United States as the model to justify their military adventures. Do you not think that

India and Pakistan, China and Taiwan, Russia and Georgia are closely watching the outcome of this debate? Do you not think that future adversaries will look to this moment to rationalize the use of military force to achieve who knows what ends? . . .

Congress has a responsibility to exercise with extreme care the power to declare war. There is no weightier matter to be considered. A war against Iraq will affect thousands if not tens of thousands of lives, and perhaps alter the course of history. It will surely affect the balance of power in the Middle East. It is not a decision to be taken in haste, under the glare of election year politics and the pressure of artificial deadlines. And yet any observer can see that that is exactly what the Senate is proposing to do.

· · ·

The last UN weapons inspectors left Iraq in October of 1998. We are confident that Saddam Hussein retained some stockpiles of chemical and biological weapons, and that he has since embarked on a crash course to build up his chemical and biological warfare capability. Intelligence reports also indicate that he is seeking nuclear weapons, but has not yet achieved nuclear capability. It is now October of 2002. Four years have gone by in which neither this administration nor the previous one felt compelled to invade Iraq to protect against the imminent threat of weapons of mass destruction. Until today. Until 33 days until election day. Now we are being told that we must act immediately, before adjournment and before the elections. Why the rush?

Yes, we had September 11. But we must not make the mistake of looking at the resolution before us as just another offshoot of the war on terror. We know who was behind the September 11 attacks on the United States. We know it was Osama bin Laden and his al Qaeda terrorist network. We have dealt with al Qaeda and with the Taliban government that sheltered it—we have routed them from Afghanistan and we are continuing to pursue them in hiding.

So where does Iraq enter the equation? No one in the Administration has been able to produce any solid evidence linking Iraq to the September 11 attack. Iraq had biological and chemical weapons long before September 11. We knew it then, and we know it now. Iraq has been an enemy of the United States for more than a decade. . . .

No one supports Saddam Hussein. If he were to disappear tomorrow, no one would shed a tear around the world. . . . But the principle of one government deciding to eliminate another government, using force to do so, and taking that action in spite of world disapproval, is a very disquieting thing. I am concerned that it has the effect of destabilizing the world community of nations. I am concerned that it fosters a climate of suspicion and mistrust in U.S. relations with other nations. The United States is not a rogue nation, given to unilateral action in the face of worldwide opprobrium.

·   ·   ·

A U.S. invasion of Iraq that proved successful and which resulted in the overthrow of the government would not be a simple effort. The aftermath of that effort would require a long-term occupation. The President has said that he would overthrow Saddam Hussein and establish a new government that would recognize all interest groups in Iraq. This would presumably include the Kurds to the north and the Shiite Muslims to the south. Because the entire military and security apparatus of Iraq would have to be replaced, the U.S. would have to provide interim security throughout the countryside. This kind of nation-building cannot be accomplished with the wave of a wand by some fairy godmother, even one with the full might and power of the world's last remaining superpower behind her.

To follow through on the proposal outlined by the President would require the commitment of a large number of U.S. forces—forces that cannot be used for other missions, such as homeland defense—for an extended period of time. . . .

There are many formulas to calculate cost in the form of dollars, but it is much more difficult to calculate cost in the form of deaths. Iraq may be a weaker nation militarily than it was during the Persian Gulf war, but its leader is no less determined and his weapons are no less lethal. During the Persian Gulf War, the United States was able to convince Saddam Hussein that the use of weapons of mass destruction would result in his being toppled from power. This time around, the object of an invasion of Iraq is to topple Saddam Hussein, so he has no reason to exercise restraint.

·   ·   ·

Before we rush into war, we should focus on those things that pose the most direct threat to us—those facilities and weapons that form the body of Iraq's weapons of mass destruction program. The United Nations is the proper forum to deal with the inspection of these facilities, and the destruction of any weapons discovered. If United Nations inspectors can enter the country, inspect those facilities and mark for destruction the ones that truly belong to a weapons program, then Iraq can be de-clawed without unnecessary risk or loss of life. That would be the best answer for Iraq, for the United States, and for the world. But if Iraq again chooses to interfere with such an ongoing and admittedly intrusive inspection regime, then and only then should the United States, with the support of the world, take stronger measures.

·   ·   ·

Everyone wants to protect our nation and our people. To do that in the most effective way possible, we should avail ourselves of every opportunity to minimize the number of troops we put at risk. Seeking once again to allow the United Nations inspection regime to peacefully seek and destroy the facilities and equipment employed in the Iraqi weapons of mass destruction program would be the least costly and most effective way of reducing the risk to our nation, provided that it is backed up by a credible threat of force if Iraq once again attempts to thwart the inspections. We can take a measured, stepped approach that would still leave open the possibility of a ground invasion if that should become necessary, but there is no need to take that step now.

I urge restraint. President Bush gave the United Nations the opening to deal effectively with the threat posed by Iraq. The UN embraced his exhortation and is working to develop a new, tougher inspection regime with firm deadlines and swift and sure accountability. Let us be convinced that a reinvigorated inspection regime cannot work before we move to any next step, and let us if we must employ force, employ the most precise and limited use of force necessary to get the job done. . . .

EXCERPTS FROM REMARKS BY REPRESENTATIVE DENNIS KUCINICH (D-OHIO)

October 3, 2002

The resolution which this Congress is facing says: "Whereas in 1990 in response to Iraq's war of aggression against an illegal occupation of Kuwait, the United States forged a coalition of nations to liberate Kuwait and its people in order to defend the national security of the United States and enforce United Nations Security Council resolutions relating to Iraq."

. . . [I]n the Persian Gulf War there was an international coalition. World support was for protecting Kuwait. There is no world support for invading Iraq.

The resolution goes on to say: "Whereas after the liberation of Kuwait in 1991, Iraq entered into a United Nations sponsored cease-fire agreement pursuant to which Iraq unequivocally agreed, among other things, to eliminate its nuclear, biological, and chemical weapons programs and the means to deliver and develop them, and to end its support for international terrorism;

"Whereas the efforts of international weapons inspectors, United States intelligence agencies, and Iraqi defectors led to the discovery that Iraq had large stockpiles of chemical weapons and a large scale biological weapons program, and that Iraq had an advanced nuclear weapons program that was much closer to producing a nuclear weapon than intelligence reporting had previously indicated."

But the key issue here . . . is that U.N. inspection teams identified and destroyed nearly all such weapons. A lead inspector, Scott Ritter, said that he believes that nearly all other weapons not found were destroyed in the Gulf War. Furthermore . . . the Central Intelligence Agency . . . has no up-to-date accurate report on Iraq's capabilities of weapons of mass destruction.

The resolution . . . says: "Whereas Iraq, in direct and flagrant violation of the cease-fire, attempted to thwart the efforts of weapons inspectors to identify and destroy Iraq's weapons of mass destruction stockpiles and development capabilities, which finally resulted in the withdrawal of inspectors from Iraq on October 31, 1998."

. . . [T]he Iraqi deceptions always failed. The inspectors always figured out what Iraq was doing. It was the United States that withdrew from the inspections in 1998, and the United States then launched a cruise missile attack against Iraq 48 hours after the inspectors left. And it is the United States, in advance of a military strike, the U.S. continues to thwart, and this is the administration's word, weapons inspections . . .

The resolution says: "Whereas Iraq both possesses a continuing threat to the national security of the United States and international peace and security in the Persian Gulf region and remains in material and unacceptable breach of its international obligations by, among other things, continuing to possess and develop a significant chemical and biological weapons capability, actively seeking a nuclear weapons capability, and supporting and harboring terrorist organizations."

. . . [T]here is no proof that Iraq represents an imminent or immediate threat to the United States of America. . . . A continuing threat does not constitute a sufficient cause for war. The administration has refused to provide the Congress with credible evidence that proves that Iraq is a serious threat to the United States and that it is continuing to possess and develop chemical and biological and nuclear weapons.

Furthermore, there is no credible evidence connecting Iraq to al Qaeda and 9-11, and yet there are people who want to bomb Iraq in reprisal for 9-11. Imagine . . . if after this country was attacked by Japan at Pearl Harbor in 1941, if instead of retaliating by bombing Japan, we would have retaliated by bombing Peru. Iraq is not connected by any credible evidence to 9-11, nor is it connected by any credible evidence to the activities of al Qaeda on 9-11. . . .

[The resolution says:] "Whereas the current Iraqi regime has demonstrated its capability and willingness to use weapons of mass destruction against any other nations and its own people; Whereas the current Iraqi regime has demonstrated its continuing hostility toward, and willingness to attack, the United States, including by attempting in 1993 to assassinate former President Bush and by firing on many thousands of occasions on United States and Coalition Armed Forces engaged in enforcing the resolutions of the United Nations Security Council."

The counterpoint of this . . . is that the Iraqi regime has never attacked, nor does it have the capability to attack, the United States. . . .

The resolution states: "Whereas Iraq continues to aid and harbor other international terrorist organizations, including organizations that threaten the lives and safety of American citizens."

The key issue here . . . is that any connection between Iraq's support of terrorist groups in the Middle East . . . is an argument for focusing great resources on resolving the conflict between Israel and the Palestinians. It is not a sufficient cause for the United States to launch a unilateral preemptive strike against Iraq. Indeed, an argument could be made that such an attack would exacerbate the condition in the Middle East and destabilize the region.

The resolution states: "Whereas the attacks on the United States of America of September 11, 2001 underscored the gravity of the threat posed by the acquisition of weapons of mass destruction by international terrorist organizations."

. . . [T]here is no connection between Iraq and the events of 9–11. However, this resolution attempts to make the connection over and over and over. . . .

The resolution goes on to say, "Whereas Iraq's demonstrated capability and willingness to use weapons of mass destruction, the risk that the current Iraqi regime will either employ those weapons to launch a surprise attack against the United States or its Armed Forces or provide them to international terrorists who would do so, and the extreme magnitude of harm that would result to the United States and its citizens from such an attack, combine to justify action by the United States to defend itself." . . .

The key issue here is that there is no credible evidence that Iraq possesses weapons of mass destruction . . . there is no credible evidence that Iraq has the capability to reach the United States with such weapons, if they have them, and many of us believe no evidence has been presented that they do.

. . .

The resolution says, "Whereas United Nations Security Council Resolution 678 authorizes the use of all necessary means to enforce United Nations Security Council Resolution 660 and subsequent relevant resolutions and to compel Iraq to cease certain activities that threaten international peace and security, including the development of weapons of mass destruction and refusal or obstruction of United Nations weapons inspections. . . ."

. . . [T]he U.N. Charter, and we participate in the United Nations, we helped form the United Nations, we helped set up this international framework of law that is represented by the United Nations, that the United Nations Charter forbids all Member nations, including the United States, from unilaterally enforcing U.N. resolutions.

We cannot do this on our own. We cannot decide that some nation is in violation of U.N. resolutions and we take it upon ourselves to render justice. . . .

If we believe in international law, then we ought to look to what this country did in 1991 when it joined the United Nations' effort on this matter on global security and not go it alone, not initiate a unilateral action or attack or preemptive strike.

The resolution here says, "Whereas the Iraq Liberation Act (Public Law 105-338) expressed the sense of Congress that it should be the policy of the United States to support efforts to remove from power the current Iraqi regime and promote the emergence of a democratic government to replace that regime."

. . . [T]his sense of Congress's resolution which is referred to in that paragraph was not binding. Furthermore, while Congress supported democratic means of removing Saddam Hussein, and I voted for that, we clearly did not endorse the use of force contemplated in this resolution.

AFTER THE WAR
JUSTIFICATIONS

EXCERPTS FROM REMARKS BY PRESIDENT BUSH FROM THE *USS ABRAHAM LINCOLN*

May 1, 2003

In this battle, we have fought for the cause of liberty, and for the peace of the world. . . . When Iraqi civilians looked into the faces of our servicemen and women, they saw strength and kindness and goodwill . . . In the images of falling statues, we have witnessed the arrival of a new era. . . .

In the images of celebrating Iraqis, we have also seen the ageless appeal of human freedom. Decades of lies and intimidation could not make the Iraqi people love their oppressors or desire their own enslavement. Men and women in every culture need liberty like they need food and water and air.

Everywhere that freedom arrives, humanity rejoices; and everywhere that freedom stirs, let tyrants fear. . . .

We have difficult work to do in Iraq. We're bringing order to parts of that country that remain dangerous. We're pursuing and finding leaders of the old regime, who will be held to account for their crimes. . . . We're helping to rebuild Iraq, where the dictator built palaces for himself, instead of hospitals and schools. And we will stand with the new leaders of Iraq as they establish a government of, by, and for the Iraqi people. The transition from dictatorship to democracy will take time, but it is worth every effort. Our coalition will stay until our work is done. Then we will leave, and we will leave behind a free Iraq. . . . [A]nyone in the world, including the Arab world, who works and sacrifices for freedom has a loyal friend in the United States of America. . . .

Our commitment to liberty is America's tradition—declared at our founding. . . . The advance of freedom is the surest strategy to undermine the appeal of terror in the world. Where freedom takes hold, hatred gives way to hope. When freedom takes hold, men and women turn to the peaceful pursuit of a better life. American values and American interests lead in the same direction: We stand for human liberty.

EXCERPTS FROM REMARKS BY PRESIDENT BUSH ON WEAPONS OF MASS DESTRUCTION

February 11, 2004

On September the 11th, 2001, America and the world witnessed a new kind of war. We saw the great harm that a stateless network could inflict upon our country, killers armed with box cutters, mace, and 19 airline tickets. Those attacks also raised the prospect of even worse dangers—of other weapons in the hands of other men. The greatest threat before humanity today is the possibility of secret and sudden attack with chemical or biological or radiological or nuclear weapons.

In the past, enemies of America required massed armies, and great navies, powerful air forces to put our nation, our people, our friends and allies at risk. In the Cold War, Americans lived under the threat of weapons of mass destruction, but believed that deterrents made those weapons a last resort. What has changed in the 21st century is that, in the hands of terrorists, weapons of mass destruction would be a first resort—the preferred means to further their ideology of suicide and random murder. These terrible weapons are becoming easier to acquire, build, hide, and transport. Armed with a single vial of a biological agent or a single nuclear weapon, small groups of fanatics, or failing states, could gain the power to threaten great nations, threaten the world peace.

America, and the entire civilized world, will face this threat for decades to come. We must confront the danger with open eyes, and unbending purpose. I have made clear to all the policy of this nation: America will not permit terrorists and dangerous regimes to threaten us with the world's most deadly weapons.

Meeting this duty has required changes in thinking and strategy. Doctrines designed to contain empires, deter aggressive states, and defeat massed armies cannot fully protect us from this new threat. America faces the possibility of catastrophic attack from ballistic missiles armed with weapons of mass destruction. So that is why we are developing and deploying missile defenses to guard our people. The best intelligence is necessary to win the war on terror and to stop proliferation. So that is why I have established a commission that will examine our intelligence capabilities and recommend ways to improve and adapt them to detect new and emerging threats.

We're determined to confront those threats at the source. We will stop these weapons from being acquired or built. We'll block them from being transferred.

We'll prevent them from ever being used. One source of these weapons is dangerous and secretive regimes that build weapons of mass destruction to intimidate their neighbors and force their influence upon the world. These nations pose different challenges; they require different strategies.

The former dictator of Iraq possessed and used weapons of mass destruction against his own people. For 12 years, he defied the will of the international community. He refused to disarm or account for his illegal weapons and programs. He doubted our resolve to enforce our word—and now he sits in a prison cell, while his country moves toward a democratic future. . . .

Over the last two years, a great coalition has come together to defeat terrorism and to oppose the spread of weapons of mass destruction—the inseparable commitments of the war on terror. We've shown that proliferators can be discovered and can be stopped. We've shown that for regimes that choose defiance, there are serious consequences. The way ahead is not easy, but it is clear. We will proceed as if the lives of our citizens depend on our vigilance, because they do. Terrorists and terror states are in a race for weapons of mass murder, a race they must lose. Terrorists are resourceful; we're more resourceful. They're determined; we must be more determined. We will never lose focus or resolve. We'll be unrelenting in the defense of free nations, and rise to the hard demands of dangerous times.

AFTER THE WAR
OPPOSITION

EXCERPTS FROM REMARKS BY SENATOR ROBERT C. BYRD

October 17, 2003

This speech was delivered in response to the bill, sponsored by the Bush administration, asking for an additional $87 billion to fund the continuing war in Iraq.

This entire adventure in Iraq has been based on propaganda and manipulation. Eighty-seven billion dollars is too much to pay for the continuation of a war based on falsehoods.

... We were told that we were threatened by weapons of mass destruction in Iraq, but they have not been seen. We were told that the throngs of Iraqi's would welcome our troops with flowers, but no throngs or flowers appeared. We were led to believe that Saddam Hussein was connected to the attack on the Twin Towers and the Pentagon, but no evidence has ever been produced. We were told in 16 words that Saddam Hussein tried to buy "yellow cake" from Africa for production of nuclear weapons, but the story has turned into empty air. We were frightened with visions of mushroom clouds, but they turned out to be only vapors of the mind. We were told that major combat was over but 101 [as of October 17] Americans have died in combat since that proclamation from the deck of an aircraft carrier by our very own Emperor in his new clothes. Our emperor says that we are not occupiers, yet we show no inclination to relinquish the country of Iraq to its people.

Those who have dared to expose the nakedness of the Administration's policies in Iraq have been subjected to scorn. Those who have noticed the elephant in the room—that is, the fact that this war was based on falsehoods—have had our patriotism questioned. Those who have spoken aloud the thought shared by hundreds of thousands of military families across this country, that our troops should return quickly and safely from the dangers half a world away, have been accused of cowardice.

. . .

The right to ask questions, debate, and dissent is under attack. The drums of war are beaten ever louder in an attempt to drown out those who speak of our predicament in stark terms. Even in the Senate, our history and tradition of being the world's greatest deliberative body is being snubbed. This huge spending bill has been rushed through this chamber in just one month. There were just three open hearings by the Senate Appropriations Committee on $87 billion, without a single outside witness called to challenge the Administration's line.

Ambassador Bremer went so far as to refuse to return to the Appropriations Committee to answer additional questions because "I don't have time. I'm completely booked, and I have to get back to Baghdad to my duties." Despite this callous stiff-arm of the Senate and its duties to ask questions in order to represent the American people, few dared to voice their opposition to rushing this bill through these halls of Congress. Perhaps they were intimidated by the false claims that our troops are in immediate need of more funds.

. . .

Mr. President, taking the nation to war based on misleading rhetoric and hyped intelligence is a travesty and a tragedy. It is the most cynical of all cynical acts. It is dangerous to manipulate the truth. It is dangerous because once having lied, it is difficult to ever be believed again. Having misled the American people and stampeded them to war, this Administration must now attempt to sustain a policy predicated on falsehoods. The President asks for billions from those same citizens who know that they were misled about the need to go to war. We misinformed and insulted our friends and allies and now this Administration is having more than a little trouble getting help from the international community. It is perilous to mislead. . . .

I cannot support the politics of zeal and "might makes right" that created the new American arrogance and unilateralism which passes for foreign policy in this Administration. I cannot support this foolish manifestation of the dangerous and destabilizing doctrine of preemption that changes the image of America into that of a reckless bully. . . .

Comment

No war has attracted a greater variety of justifications than the U.S. invasion of Iraq in 2002. The United States was justified in going to war because Iraq (1) violated UN resolutions; (2) failed to cooperate with the inspectors; (3) posed a security threat to its neighbors; (4) supported or harbored terrorists; (5) possessed weapons of mass destruction; (6) posed a security threat to the U.S.; (7) would benefit from being liberated from the rule of a vicious dictator; (8) would benefit from becoming a democracy; and (9) could, with a new regime, lead other Arab nations to bring about a stable peace in the Middle East. Which (if any) of these are consistent with the principles of just war? To what extent are the corresponding criticisms (such as those made by Senators Byrd and Kucinich) based on ethical (as distinct from prudential and constitutional) considerations?

The most distinctive justification, as interpreted by the administration, was the sixth. But Iraq did not pose an "imminent and immediate" threat, the traditional test for a preemptive war. As explicated by Michael Walzer, the traditional criteria for justifying a first strike are: "a manifest intent to injure, a degree of active preparation that makes that intent a positive danger, and a general situation in which waiting, or doing anything other than fighting, greatly magnifies the risk." The potential injury must be grave—the loss of territorial integrity or political independence. In contrast, the Bush doctrine, suggested in the excerpts in this section and elaborated in the statement of the National Security Strategy (released in September 2002), denies that the traditional test is sufficient to deal with the "new threat" that has emerged in the world of "terrorists and rogue states" with weapons of mass destruction. U.S. security strategy should shift toward "first strikes" (or what some called "preventive war"). To what extent do these new threats require a revision of the criteria for just war?

The justifications given before and after the war differ in some respects (as do the criticisms). It is worth asking why, and whether the shift should affect our assessment of the justifications (and criticisms). When no weapons of mass destruction were discovered, defenders of the war tended to emphasize other justifications (Iraq and the world are better off without Saddam Hussein in power). We should not immediately conclude, as some critics have done, that this shift shows that the original justifications were mere rationalizations. A justification for a decision should be assessed from the perspective of what was known, or could have been known, at the time the decision was made. Other critics dismiss all of the justifications listed above; they believe that the real reason was for the administration and its corporate friends to gain greater influence over the production of Iraqi oil. But in assessing whether the war was just, we should not focus primarily on the motivations of the decision makers, but on the best justifications that they gave or could have given. The motivations may be significant for judging their character (and deciding whether to support them in the future), but actual motives bear only indirectly on the justice of the war itself.

If you conclude that the war was not justified, what is the least drastic change in the circumstances in Iraq that in your view would justify an invasion? If you conclude that the war was justified, what is the least drastic change that would reverse your conclusion?

Interrogating Detainees

In response to a White House request, the Justice Department in August 2002 wrote a memorandum on the "standards of conduct for the interrogation" of detainees captured in Afghanistan, including members of al Qaeda, who were being held by the CIA. The memo concluded that torturing al Qaeda terrorists in captivity abroad "may be justified," and that international laws against torture may not apply to interrogations conducted in the U.S. war on terrorism. Later, Defense Department lawyers used the same reasoning to assess rules governing interrogation of al Qaeda detainees at the Department's center at Guantanamo Bay, Cuba. In December 2002, Secretary of Defense Rumsfeld approved a list of specific techniques that could be used to interrogate the Guantanamo detainees. When the memos and other related documents were disclosed in June 2004, administration officials stated unequivocally that the government had strictly observed the international conventions barring torture, and that all detainees had been treated humanely (except in the case of the abuse at Abu Ghraib prison in Iraq, which was not authorized). In a press conference in early June, President Bush was asked a "moral question": "Is torture ever justified?" His response emphasized that his administration obeys the law: "The instructions went out to our people to adhere to law." Later in the month, he responded more directly to the moral question: "The values of this country are such that torture is not a part of our soul and our being."

EXCERPTS FROM A JUSTICE DEPARTMENT MEMORANDUM ON STANDARDS FOR INTERROGATION

ADDRESSED TO COUNSEL TO THE PRESIDENT, WHITE HOUSE

August 1, 2002
Jay S. Bybee, Assistant Attorney General

U.S. Department of Justice
Office of Legal Counsel
Office of Assistant Attorney General
[Jay S. Bybee]
Washington, D.C. 20530
August 1, 2002

Memorandum for Alberto R. Gonzales
Counsel to the President
Re: Standards of Conduct for Interrogation
under 18 U.S.C. §§ 2340-2340A

Section 2340A makes it a criminal offense for any person "outside the United States [to] commit[] or attempt[] to commit torture." Section 2340 defines the act of torture as an: act committed by a person acting under the color of law specifically intended to inflict severe physical or mental pain or suffering (other than pain or suffering incidental to lawful sanctions) upon another person within his custody or physical control.

. . . We conclude that for an act to constitute torture as defined in Section 2340, it must inflict pain that is difficult to endure. Physical pain amounting to torture must be equivalent in intensity to the pain accompanying serious physical injury, such as organ failure, impairment of bodily function, or even death. For purely mental pain or suffering to amount to torture under Section 2340, it must result in significant psychological harm of significant duration, e.g. lasting for months or even years. We conclude that the mental harm also must result from one of the predicate acts listed in the statute, namely: threats of imminent death; threats of infliction of the kind of pain that would amount to physical torture; infliction of such physical pain as a means of psychological torture; use of drugs or other procedures designed to deeply disrupt the senses, or fundamentally alter an individual's personality; or threatening to do any of these things to a third party. . . . The legislative history simply reveals that Congress intended for the statute's definition to track the Convention's definition of torture and the reservations, understandings, and declarations that the United States submitted with its ratification. We conclude that the statute, taken as a whole, makes plain that it prohibits only extreme acts.

Section 2340's definition of torture must be read as a sum of these component parts. . . . Each component of the definition emphasizes that torture is not the mere infliction of pain and suffering on another, but it is instead a step well removed. The victim must experience intense pain or suffering of the kind that is equivalent to the pain that would be associated with serious physical injury so severe that death, organ failure, or permanent damage resulting in a loss of significant body function will likely result. If that pain or suffering is psychological, that suffering must result from one of the acts set forth in the statute. In addition, these acts must cause long-term mental harm. Indeed, this view of the criminal act of torture is consistent with the term's common meaning. Torture is generally understood to involve "intense pain" or "excruciating pain," or put another way, "extreme anguish of body or mind." . . . In short, reading the definition of torture as a whole, it is plain that the term encompasses only extreme acts.

. . .

Under the current circumstances, we believe that a defendant accused of violating Section 2340A could have, in certain circumstances, grounds to properly claim the defense of another. The threat of an impending terrorist attack threatens the lives of hundreds if not thousands of citizens. Whether such a defense will be upheld depends on the specific context within which the interrogation decision is made. If an attack appears increasingly likely, but our intelligence services and armed forces cannot prevent it without the information from the interrogation of a specific individual, then the more likely it will appear that the conduct in question will be seen as necessary. If intelligence and other information support the conclusion that an attack is increasingly certain, then the necessity for the interrogation will be reasonable. The increasing certainty of an attack will also satisfy the imminence requirement. Finally, the fact that previous al Qaeda attacks have had as their aim the deaths of American citizens, and that evidence of other plots have had a similar goal in mind, would justify proportionality of interrogation methods designed to elicit information to prevent such deaths.

To be sure, this situation is different from the usual self-defense justification, and, indeed, it overlaps with elements of the necessity defense. Self-defense as usually discussed involves using force against an individual who is about to conduct the attack. In the current circumstances, however, an enemy combatant in detention does not himself present a threat of harm. He is not actually carrying out the attack; rather, he has participated in the planning and preparation for the attack, or merely has knowledge of the attack through his membership in the terrorist organization. Nonetheless, leading scholarly commentators believe that interrogation of such individuals using methods that might violate Section 2340A would be justified under the doctrine of self-defense, because the combatant by aiding and promoting the terrorist plot "has culpably caused the situation where someone might get hurt. If hurting him is the only means to prevent the death or injury of others put at risk by his actions, such torture should be permissible, and on the same basis that self-defense is permissible." . . . Thus, some commentators believe that by helping to create the threat of loss of life, terrorists become culpable for the threat even though they do not actually carry out the attack itself. They may be hurt in an interrogation because they are part of the mechanism that has set the attack in motion, . . . just as is someone who feeds ammunition or targeting information to an attacker. Under the present circumstances, therefore, even though a detained enemy combatant may not be the exact attacker— he is not planting the bomb, or piloting a hijacked plane to kill civilians—he still may be harmed in self-defense if he has knowledge of future attacks because he has assisted in their planning and execution.

Further, we believe that a claim by an individual of the defense of another would be further supported by the fact that, in this case, the nation itself is under attack and has the right to self-defense. This fact can bolster and support an individual claim of self-defense in a prosecution, according to the teaching of the Supreme Court in In re Neagle, 135 U.S. 1 (1890). In that case, the State of California arrested and held deputy U.S. Marshal Neagle for shooting and killing the assailant of Supreme Court Justice Field. In granting the writ of habeas corpus for Neagle's release, the Supreme Court did not rely alone upon the marshal's right to defend another or his right to self-defense,. Rather, the Court found that Neagle, as an agent of the United States and of the executive branch, was justified in the killing because, in protecting Justice Field, he was acting pursuant to the executive branch's inherent constitutional authority to protect the United States government. That authority derives, according to the Court, from the President's power under Article II to take care that the laws are faithfully executed. In other words, Neagle as a federal officer not only could raise self-defense or defense of another, but also could defend his actions on the ground that he was implementing the Executive Branch's authority to protect the United States government.

If the right to defend the national government can be raised as a defense in an individual prosecution, as Neagle suggests, then a government defendant, acting in his official capacity, should be able to argue that any conduct that arguably violated Section 2340A was undertaken pursuant to more than just individual self-defense or defense of another. In addition, the defendant could claim that he was fulfilling the Executive Branch's authority to protect the federal government, and the nation, from attack. The September 11 attacks have already triggered that authority, as recognized both under domestic and international law. Following the example of In re Neagle, we conclude that a government defendant may also argue that his conduct of an interrogation, if properly authorized, is justified on the basis of protecting the nation from attack.

　　　・　・　・

As we have made clear in other opinions involving the war against al Qaeda, the nation's right to self-defense has been triggered by the events of September 11. If a government defendant were to harm an enemy combatant during an interrogation in a manner that might arguably violate Section 2340A, he would be doing so in order to prevent further attacks on the United States by the al Qaeda terrorist network. In that case, we believe that he could argue that his actions were justified by the executive branch's constitutional authority to protect the nation from attack. This national and international version of the right to self-defense could supplement and bolster the government defendant's individual right.

. . . [W]e conclude that torture as defined in and proscribed by Sections 2340-2340A, covers only extreme acts.

Severe pain is generally of the kind difficult for the victim to endure. Where the pain is physical, it must be of an intensity akin to that which accompanies serious physical injury such as death or organ failure. Severe mental pain requires suffering not just at the moment of infliction but it also requires lasting psychological harm, such as seen in mental disorders like posttraumatic stress disorder. Additionally, such severe mental pain can arise only from the predicate acts listed in Section 2340. Because the acts inflicting torture are extreme, there is significant range of acts that though they might constitute cruel, inhuman, or degrading treatment or punishment fail to rise to the level of torture.

Further, we conclude that under the circumstances of the current war against al Qaeda and its allies, application of Section 2340A to interrogations undertaken pursuant to the President's Commander-in-Chief powers may be unconstitutional. Finally, even if an interrogation method might violate Section 2340A, necessity or self-defense could provide justifications that would eliminate any criminal liability.

EXCERPTS FROM THE DEFENSE DEPARTMENT'S APPROVAL OF TECHNIQUES OF INTERROGATION

PROPOSED COUNTER-RESISTANCE STRATEGIES AND REQUEST FOR APPROVAL

Memo for Commander, Joint Task Force, Department of Defense

DEPARTMENT OF DEFENSE
JOINT TASK FORCE 170
GUANTANAMO BAY, CUBA
APO AE 09860

11 October 2002

MEMORANDUM FOR Commander, Joint Task Force 170

SUBJECT: Legal Brief on Proposed Counter-Resistance Strategies

. . .

(b) (U) Torture is defined as "an act committed by a person acting under color of law *specifically intended* (emphasis added) to inflict severe physical or mental pain or suffering (other than pain or suffering incident to lawful sanctions) upon another person within his custody or physical control." The statute defines "severe mental pain or suffering" as "the *prolonged mental harm caused by or resulting* (emphasis added) from the intentional infliction or threatened infliction of severe physical pain or suffering; or the administration or application, or threatened administration or application, of mind altering substances or other procedures calculated to disrupt profoundly the senses of the personality; or the threat of imminent death; or the threat that another person will imminently be subjected to death, severe physical pain or suffering, or the administration or application of mind-altering substances or other procedures calculated to disrupt profoundly the senses or personality.

. . .

4. ANALYSIS: The counter-resistance techniques proposed in the JTF-170-J2 memorandum are lawful because they do not violate the Eighth Amendment to the United States Constitution or the federal torture statute as explained below. An international law analysis is not required for the current proposal because the Geneva Conventions do not apply to these detainees since they are not HPWs.

(a) Based on the Supreme Court framework utilized to assess whether a public official has violated the Eighth Amendment, so long as the force used could plausibly have been thought necessary in a particular situation to achieve a legitimate governmental objective, and it was applied in good faith effort and not maliciously or sadistically for the very purpose of causing harm, the proposed techniques are likely to pass constitutional [muster]. The federal torture statute will not be violated so long as any of the proposed strategies are not specifically intended to cause severe physical pain or suffering or prolonged mental harm. Assuming that severe physical pain is not inflicted, absent any evidence that any of those strategies will in fact cause prolonged and long lasting mental harm the proposed methods will not violate the statute.

(b) Regarding the Uniform Code of Military Justice, the proposal to grab, poke in the chest, push lightly, and place a wet towel or hood over the detainee's head would constitute a per se violation of Article 128 (Assault). Threatening a detainee with death may also constitute a violation of Article 128, or also Article 134 (communication of a threat). It would be advisable to have permission or immunity in advance from the convening authority, for military members utilizing these methods.

(c) Specifically, with regard to Category I techniques, the use of mild and fear related approaches such as yelling at the detainee is not illegal because in order to communicate a threat, there must also exist an intent to injure. Yelling at the detainee is legal so long as the yelling is not done with the intent to cause severe physical damage or prolonged mental harm. Techniques of deception such as multiple interrogator techniques, and deception regarding interrogator identity are all permissible methods of interrogation, since there is no legal requirement to be truthful while conducting an interrogation.

(d) With regard to Category II methods, the use of stress positions such as the proposed standing for four hours, the use of isolation for up to thirty days, and interrogating the detainee in an environment other than the standard interrogation booth are all legally permissible so long as no severe physical pain is inflicted and prolonged mental harm intended, and because there is a legitimate governmental objective in obtaining the information necessary that the high value detainee on which these methods would be utilized possesses, for the protection of the national security of the United States, its citizens, and allies. Furthermore, these methods would not be utilized for the "very malicious and sadistic purpose of causing harm," and absent medical evidence to the contrary, there is no evidence that prolonged mental harm would result from the use of these strategies. The use of falsified documents is legally permissible because interrogators may use deception to achieve their purpose.

(e) The deprivation of light and auditory stimuli, the placement of a hood over the detainee's head during transportation and questioning, and the use of 20 hour interrogations are all legally permissible so long as there is an important governmental objective, and it is not done for the purpose of causing harm or with the intent to cause prolonged mental suffering. There is no legal requirement that detainees must receive four hours of sleep per night, but if a U.S. Court ever had to rule on this procedure, in order to pass Eighth Amendment scrutiny, and as a cautionary measure, they should receive some amount of sleep so that no severe physical or mental harm will result. Removal of comfort items is permissible because there is no legal requirement to provide comfort items. The requirement is to provide adequate food, water, shelter, and medical care. The issue of removing published religious items or materials would be relevant if these were United States citizens with a First Amendment right. Such is not the case with the detainees. Forced grooming and removal of clothing are not illegal, so long as it is not done to punish or cause harm, as there is a legitimate governmental objective to obtain information, maintain health standards in the camp and protect both the detainees and the guards. There is no illegality in removing hot meals because there is no specific requirement to provide hot meals, only adequate food. The use of the detainee's phobias is equally permissible.

(f) With respect to the Category III advanced counter-resistance strategies, the use of scenarios designed to convince the detainee that death or severely painful consequences are imminent is not illegal for the same aforementioned reasons that there is a compelling governmental interest and it is not done intentionally to cause prolonged harm. However, caution should be utilized with this technique because the torture statute specifically mentions making death threats as an example of inflicting mental pain and suffering. Exposure to cold weather or water is permissible with the appropriate medical monitoring. The use of a wet towel to induce the misperception of suffocation would also be permissible if not done with the specific intent to cause prolonged mental harm, and absent medical evidence that it would. Caution should be exercised with this method, as foreign courts have already advised about the potential mental harm that this method may cause. The use of physical contact with the detainee, such as pushing and poking, will technically constitute an assault under Article 128, UCMJ.

5. RECOMMENDATION: I recommend that the proposed methods of interrogation be approved, and that the interrogators be properly trained in the use of the approved methods of interrogation. Since the law requires examination of all facts under a totality of circumstances test, I further recommend that all proposed interrogations involving category II and III methods must undergo a legal, medical, behavioral science, and intelligence review prior to their commencement.

DEPARTMENT OF DEFENSE
JOINT TASK FORCE 170
GUANTANAMO BAY, CUBA
APO AE 09960

JTF-J2

11 October 2002

MEMORANDUM FOR Commander, Joint Task Force 170

SUBJECT: Request for Approval of Counter-Resistance Strategies

1. PROBLEM: The current guidelines for interrogation procedures at GTMO limit the ability of interrogators to counter advanced resistance.

2. Request approval for use of the following interrogation plan.

a. Category I techniques. During the initial category of interrogation the detainee should be provided a chair and the environment should be generally comfortable. The format of the interrogation is the direct approach. The use of rewards like cookies or cigarettes may be helpful. If the detainee is determined by the interrogator to be uncooperative, the interrogator may use the following techniques.

(1) Yelling at the detainee (not directly in his ear or to the level that it would cause physical pain or hearing problems)

(2) Techniques of deception:

(a) Multiple interrogator techniques.

(b) Interrogator identity. The interviewer may identify himself as a citizen of a foreign nation or as an interrogator from a country with a reputation for harsh treatment of detainees.

b. Category II techniques. With the permission of the OIC, Interrogation Section, the interrogator may use the following techniques.

(1) The use of stress positions (like standing), for a maximum of four hours.

(2) The use of falsified documents or reports.

(3) Use of the isolation facilities for up to 30 days. Request must be made through the OIC, Interrogation Section, to the Director, Joint Interrogation Group (JIG). Extensions beyond the initial 30 days must be approved by the Commanding General. For selected detainees, the OIC, Interrogations Section, will approve all contacts with the detainee, to include medical visits of a non-emergent nature.

(4) Interrogating the detainee in an environment other than the standard interrogation booth.

(5) Deprivation of light and auditory stimuli.

(6) The detainee may also have a hood placed over his head during transportation and questioning. The hood should not restrict breathing in any way and the detainee should be under direct observation when hooded.

(7) The use of 28-hour interrogations.

(8) Removal of all comfort items (including religious items).

(9) Switching the detainee from hot rations to MREs.

(10) Removal of clothing.

(11) Forced grooming (shaving off facial hair, etc.)

(12) Using detainees' individual phobias (such as fear of dogs) to induce stress.

c. Category III techniques. Techniques in this category may be used only by submitting a request through the Director, JIG, for approval by the Commanding General with appropriate legal review and information to Commander, USSOUTHCOM. These techniques are required for a very small percentage of the most uncooperative detainees (less than 3%). The following techniques and other aversive techniques, such as those used in U.S. military interrogation resistance training or by other U.S. government agencies, may be utilized in a carefully coordinated manner to help interrogate exceptionally resistant detainees. Any of these techniques that require more than light grabbing, poking, or pushing, will be administered only by individuals specifically trained in their safe application.

(1) The use of scenarios designed to convince the detainee that death or severely painful consequences are imminent for him and/or his family.

(2) Exposure to cold weather or water (with appropriate medical monitoring).

(3) Use of a wet towel and dripping water to induce the misperception of suffocation.

(4) Use of mild, non-injurious physical contact such as grabbing, poking in the chest with the finger, and light pushing.

Excerpts from the General Counsel Recommendation and Secretary of Defense Approval

November 27, 2002/December 2, 2002 (See document on page 67.)

President Bush's Comments on Torture

Press Conference, Thursday, June 10, 2004

QUESTION: Mr. President, the Justice Department issued an advisory opinion last year declaring that, as commander in chief, you have the authority to order any kind of interrogation techniques that are necessary to pursue the war on terror. Were you aware of this advisory opinion? Do you agree with it? And did you issue any such authorization at any time?

BUSH: The authorization I issued was that anything we did would conform to U.S. law and would be consistent with international treaty obligations. That's the message I gave our people.

QUESTION: Have you seen the memos?

BUSH: I can't remember if I've seen the memo or not, but I gave those instructions.

. . .

QUESTION: Mr. President, I wanted to return to the question of torture. What we've learned from these memos this week is that the Department of Justice lawyers and the Pentagon lawyers have essentially worked out a way that U.S. officials can torture detainees without running afoul of the law. So when you say that you want the U.S. to adhere to international and U.S. laws, that's not very comforting. This is a moral question: Is torture ever justified?

BUSH: Look, I'm going to say it one more time. Maybe I can be more clear. The instructions went out to our people to adhere to law. That ought to comfort you. We're a nation of law. We adhere to laws. We have laws on the books. You might look at these laws. And that might provide comfort for you. And those were the instructions from me to the government.

GENERAL COUNSEL OF THE DEPARTMENT OF DEFENSE
1600 DEFENSE PENTAGON
WASHINGTON, D. C. 20301-1600

GENERAL COUNSEL

2002 DEC -2 AM 11: 03

OFFICE OF THE
SECRETARY OF DEFENSE

ACTION MEMO

November 27, 2002 (1:00 PM)

DEPSEC _____

FOR: SECRETARY OF DEFENSE

FROM: William J. Haynes II, General Counsel [signature]

SUBJECT: Counter-Resistance Techniques

- The Commander of USSOUTHCOM has forwarded a request by the Commander of Joint Task Force 170 (now JTF GTMO) for approval of counter-resistance techniques to aid in the interrogation of detainees at Guantanamo Bay (Tab A).

- The request contains three categories of counter-resistance techniques, with the first category the least aggressive and the third category the most aggressive (Tab B).

- I have discussed this with the Deputy, Doug Feith and General Myers. I believe that all join in my recommendation that, as a matter of policy, you authorize the Commander of USSOUTHCOM to employ, in his discretion, only Categories I and II and the fourth technique listed in Category III ("Use of mild, non-injurious physical contact such as grabbing, poking in the chest with the finger, and light pushing").

- While all Category III techniques may be legally available, we believe that, as a matter of policy, a blanket approval of Category III techniques is not warranted at this time. Our Armed Forces are trained to a standard of interrogation that reflects a tradition of restraint.

RECOMMENDATION: That SECDEF approve the USSOUTHCOM Commander's use of those counter-resistance techniques listed in Categories I and II and the fourth technique listed in Category III during the interrogation of detainees at Guantanamo Bay.

SECDEF DECISION

Approved [signature] _____ Disapproved _____ Other _____

Attachments
As stated

cc: CJCS, USD(P)

However, I stand for 8-10 hours a day. Why is standing limited to 4 hours?

D.R. DEC 0 2 2002

PRESIDENT BUSH'S STATEMENT TO REPORTERS

June 22, 2004

Look, let me make very clear the position of my government and our country. We do not condone torture. I have never ordered torture. I will never order torture. The values of this country are such that torture is not a part of our soul and our being.

EXCERPTS FROM SENATOR PATRICK LEAHY'S REACTION

Statement on the floor of the Senate, June 23, 2004

[I]n August 2002 the Justice Department advised the White House that torturing al Qaeda terrorists in captivity abroad "may be justified." The memo argued that the President has absolute authority in the "war against terrorism" and that international treaties against torture, which the United States ratified, "may be unconstitutional." And, this report continued, Congress is completely powerless when the President acts as Commander in Chief.

· · ·

[W]e now know that the White House and the Pentagon were actively working to circumvent the law. Guidelines for interrogating prisoners were applied routinely in multiple locations in ways that were illegal. It is also clear that U.S. officials knew the law was being violated and for months, possibly years, did virtually nothing about it. Instead, they detailed their lawyers to find legal loopholes and interpretations that would redefine torture and devise innocuous sounding labels for their interrogation techniques, such as "sensory deprivation" or "stress and duress."

· · ·

The individuals who committed those acts are being punished, as they must be. But what of those who gave the orders or set the tone or looked the other way? What of the White House and Pentagon lawyers who tried to justify the use of torture in their legal arguments? These lawyers have twisted the law, advising the President that for an abuse to rise to the level of torture it must go on for months or even years, and be so severe as to generate the type of pain that would result from organ failure or even death.

· · ·

And what of the President? Last March, referring to the capture of U.S. soldiers by Iraqi forces, President Bush said, "We expect them to be treated humanely, just like we'll treat any prisoner of theirs that we capture humanely. If not, the people who mistreat the prisoners will be treated as war criminals."

At the same time, the President's own lawyer, ignoring the Torture Convention altogether, called the Geneva Conventions "quaint" and "obsolete." Today, soldiers who have spoken out about the crimes they witnessed and the involvement of their superiors have been threatened and punished by the Defense Department they have honorably served.

. . . [O]ne need only review history to understand why the law makes no exception for torture. The torture of criminal suspects flagrantly violates the presumption of innocence on which our criminal jurisprudence is based, and confessions extracted through torture are notoriously unreliable.

Once exceptions are made for torture it is impossible to draw the line, and more troubling is who would be in charge of drawing it. If torture is justified in Afghanistan, why is it not justified in China, or Syria, or Argentina, or Miami?

If torture is justified to obtain information from a suspected terrorist, why not from his wife or children, or from his friends or acquaintances who might know of his activities or his whereabouts? This has happened in many countries, and decades later those societies are still trying to recover.

The United States cannot become the model of justice our forefathers envisioned if we continue to tolerate the twisted logic that has been given currency with increasing regularity in U.S. military prisons and in the White House since 9/11. Some argue it is a new world since those terrible attacks on our country three years ago. And to some degree, they are right, which is why we have reacted with tougher laws and better tools to fight this war. But do we really want to usher in a new world that justifies inhumane, immoral and cruel treatment as any means to an end?

As a nation of laws, and as the world's oldest democracy and champion of human rights, we must categorically reject the dangerous notion that is now in our midst—seeking our assent, or our silence—that torture can be legally justified and normalized.

JEREMY BENTHAM ON TORTURE*

Suppose an occasion [were] to arise, in which a suspicion is entertained, as strong as that which would be received as a sufficient ground for arrest and commitment as for [a] felony—a suspicion that at . . . this very time [a] considerable number of individuals are actually . . . suffering, by illegal violence[,]

inflictions equal in . . . intensity to those which if inflicted by the hand of justice, would universally be spoken of under the name of torture. For the purpose of rescuing from torture these hundred innocents, should any scruple be made of applying equal or superior torture, to extract the requisite information from the mouth of one criminal, who having it in his power to make known the place where at . . . this time the enormity was practicing or about to be practiced, should refuse to do so? . . . [C]ould any pretence be made . . . by the man who to save one criminal, should determine to abandon a hundred innocent persons to the same fate?

---

*From the *Bentham Papers,* unpublished manuscript, Box 074-429, 27 May 1804, "Evidence, Forthcomingness, Ch. Extraction, §.6. Extraordinary." University College London, Bentham Project see UC lxxiv. 429. We are indebted to Irena Nicholl for providing the text for this quotation.

Comment

Much of the dispute about interrogation techniques proposed and used in Afghanistan and Guantanamo was couched in legal terms—how the laws and treaties on torture and inhumane treatment should be interpreted and where and to whom they applied. But political ethics asks more fundamental questions about the morality of the techniques. We can begin by asking what the reporter who questioned President Bush called the "moral question": Is torture ever justified? Analyze Bentham's hypothetical, modifying it to cover various other circumstances and to specify conditions (if any) that would justify using torture. Some people, and not only those who reject Bentham's utilitarianism, take an absolutist stance: Torture is never justified. Examining the reasons for this position should help clarify what is wrong with torture. Some people think it is worse to torture than deliberately to kill a person. What reasons can be given for holding this view?

In analyzing these and similar cases, proceed in two steps: (1) Determine if the action in question should count as torture and (2) decide if the action, whether or not it is torture, should be permitted. This approach avoids the common definitional tactic, in which the hard question of whether painful and coercive treatment of a detainee is evaded by defining torture very narrowly to include only "extreme acts" that are most obviously unjustified. The first step of determining whether an action should count as torture does not involve merely a legal or linguistic issue: it requires a moral judgment, which should be informed by identifying the features of the act of torture that are questionable on their face, even if not yet subject to an all-things-considered analysis. The second step invites you to engage in such an analysis and ask not only when torture might or might not be justified, but also when other inhumane or degrading acts serving similar purposes might or might not be permitted.

To what extent should "mental pain and suffering" count as torture? Because such suffering is often subjective and people vary so much in their psychological responses, a rule that prohibited such suffering, some argue, would be too broad and would limit the government's ability to conduct effective interrogation. Others argue that some forms of psychological pressure affect everyone in especially painful ways—for example, "the use of scenarios designed to convince the detainee that death or severely painful consequences are imminent for him and/or his family."

The Defense Department guidelines limit the technique of subjecting detainees to "stress positions . . . (e.g., standing)" to "a maximum of four hours." This prompted Rumsfeld to remark: "I stand for 8–10 hours a day. Why is standing limited to 4 hours?" The question is not as facetious as it might seem: In providing an adequate answer, we can see more clearly that part of what makes torture and similar acts wrong is the context in which they occur. (The question also alerts us to the difficulty of drawing absolutely clear lines between what is torture and what is not torture.)

The moral debate about torture should not be sidestepped by assuming that the techniques are usually not productive. Although "confessions extracted through torture are notoriously unreliable," they may also yield small pieces of accurate information, which when combined with the results of many other interrogations, can provide important leads in terrorist investigations. Even when torture and similar techniques generally do not produce reliable information, they may have other useful effects in a war against terrorism. We need to ask whether they should be permitted even when they are useful.

Recommended Reading

The best contemporary discussion of the morality of war is still Michael Walzer, *Just and Unjust Wars* (New York: Basic Books, 1977). A valuable recent analysis, which discusses Walzer's view and the Iraq war, is David Luban, "Preventive War," *Philosophy & Public Affairs,* 32 (Summer 2004), pp. 207–48. Other general discussions worth consulting are Douglas Lackey, *The Ethics of War and Peace* (Englewood Cliffs, N.J.: Prentice-Hall, 1989); Richard Norman, *Ethics, Killing and War* (New York: Cambridge University Press, 1995); James Turner Johnson, *Morality and Contemporary Warfare* (New Haven, Conn.: Yale University Press, 1999); and Simon Chesterman, *Just War or Just Peace? Humanitarian Intervention and International Law* (Oxford, England: Oxford University Press, 2002). A variety of views on this topic may be found in these collections: Charles Beitz et al. (eds.), *International Ethics* (Princeton, N.J.: Princeton University Press, 1985), especially parts 2 and 3; Jean Bethke Elshtain (ed.), *Just War Theory* (Oxford: Blackwell, 1992); Terry Nardin (ed.), *The Ethics of War and Peace* (Princeton, N.J.: Princeton University Press, 1996); Terry Nardin and David R. Mapel, *Traditions of International Ethics* (New York: Cambridge University Press, 1992); and Deen K. Chatterjee and Don E. Scheid (eds.), *Ethics and Foreign Intervention* (Cambridge: Cambridge University Press, 2003). On the morality of violence in general, see Vittorio Bufacchi, "Why Is Violence Bad?" *American Philosophical Quarterly,* 41 (April, 2004), pp. 169–81.

For historical background and the continuing controversy over the decision to drop the atomic bomb, see Philip Nobile (ed.), *Judgment at the Smithsonian. The Uncensored Script of the Smithsonian's 50th Anniversary Exhibit of the Enola Gay* (New York: Marlowe, 1995). A "revisionist" interpretation can be found in Gar Alperovitz, *The Decision to Use the Atomic Bomb and the Architecture of an American Myth* (New York: Knopf, 1995). An account sympathetic to the decision makers is McGeorge Bundy, *Danger and Survival: Choices about the Bomb in the First Fifty Years* (New York: Random House, 1988), ch. 2. A philosopher's criticism of Truman is Elisabeth Anscombe, "Mr. Truman's Degree," in Anscombe, *Ethics, Religion and Politics* (Minneapolis: University of Minnesota Press, 1981), pp. 62–71. On the ethics of the first Gulf War, see Jean Bethke Elshtain et al., *But Was It Just? Reflections on the Morality of the Persian Gulf War* (New York: Doubleday, 1992).

On torture, see the seminal philosophical analysis by Henry Shue, "Torture," *Philosophy & Public Affairs,* 7 (Winter 1978), pp. 124–43. More recent discussions include: David Sussman, "What's Wrong With Torture?" *Philosophy & Public Affairs,* 33:1, (Winter 2005); Michael Ignatieff, *The Lesser Evil: Political Ethics in an Age of Terror* (Princeton, N.J.: Princeton University Press, 2004); Fritz Allhoff, "Terrorism & Torture," *International Journal of Applied Philosophy,* 17 (Fall, 2003), pp. 105–18.

2 Deception and Secrecy

The successful ruler, Machiavelli teaches, must be "a great liar and hypocrite." Politicians must appear to be moral even though they are not, because politics requires methods that citizens would find morally objectionable if they knew about them. We do not know how many politicians follow Machiavelli's advice today (those who do so most successfully may seem to be the least Machiavellian). We do know that many public officials have tried to justify deception, and so have some political commentators and political theorists.

Deception involves intentionally or negligently causing someone to believe something that the deceiver knows or should know to be false. Political deception is not always easy to recognize, because it seldom comes in the form of an outright lie. More often, officials give us half-truths, which they hope we will not see are half-lies. Or they offer us silence, which they hope will cause us to ignore inconvenient truths. Sometimes officials provide so much information that the truth is deliberately obscured, lost in a plethora of facts and figures. Thus the first task in analyzing a case of alleged deception is to decide whether deception actually occurred and precisely in what ways.

Those who want to justify political deception usually grant what ordinary morality maintains—that lying is generally wrong. But they go on to argue that no one (except perhaps Kant) believes that deception is always wrong. The general presumption against it can therefore be rebutted in certain circumstances, such as those that politicians often confront. Politics is supposed to make deception more often justifiable for several reasons: (1) political issues are complex and difficult to understand, especially when they must be presented in the mass media or in a short time; (2) the harmful effects of some political truths can be severe and irreversible; (3) the political effects result as much from what people believe as from what is actually true; and (4) organizing coalitions and other kinds of political action requires leaders to emphasize one part of the truth to some people and another part to others (telling the whole truth and nothing but the truth could make compromise impossible).

But, at least in a democracy, these reasons cannot give political leaders a general license to deceive whenever and wherever they think it necessary. Unless we can find out what officials have actually done—not just what they appear to have done—we cannot hold them accountable. At most, the special features of politics may justify exceptions to the general presumption against deception that should hold in a democracy.

If we conclude that deception may sometimes be necessary, our task should be to define carefully the conditions under which citizens should permit public officials to engage in deception. The main factors we should consider are: (1) the importance of the goal of the deception; (2) the availability of alternative means for achieving the goal; (3) the identity of the victims of the deception (other officials, other governments, all citizens); (4) the accountability of the deceivers (the possibility of approving the deception in advance or discovering it later); and (5) the containment of the deception (its effects on other actions by officials).

"Disinformation for Qaddafi" and "The Iran-Contra Affair" describe two foreign policy ventures in which deception was a key element; the first was formally approved by the president and key officials within the administration. The two episodes also differ with respect to their goals, the victims of the deception, the possibilities of holding the deceivers accountable, and chances of containing the deception. Instead of examples of blatant and acknowledged political lies (such as Clinton's denial of an affair), we have selected cases in the gray area of deception.

The debate about the 2003 war in Iraq offers a rich array of accusations of deception. The case presented here concentrates on only one instance: President Bush's statement in his 2003 State of the Union address that Iraq attempted to acquire nuclear materials from an African nation. Unlike other statements justifying the war mentioned in the previous chapter (such as the allegations of the close connections between Iraq and al Qaeda), there is less dispute about the facts to which this statement refers. At the time, most intelligence analysts and some senior officials (though probably not Bush himself) believed that the statement was misleading, if not completely false. The Bush administration plays a role in the other recent case—"Standard of Candor"—but here the charge of deception is directed against a critic of the administration, Richard Clarke, who defended the policy when he worked for Bush but published a critique of it after he resigned.

The problem of deception is closely related to some forms of nondisclosure, notably secrecy. Secrecy is often the means that politicians use to deceive citizens and each other. It can also itself constitute deception—for example, when the president's national security adviser failed to tell Congress and even some of his colleagues about some critical facts that would have shown a connection between the U.S. support of the Contras and the arms for hostages negotiations with Iran.

There is an important moral difference between deception and secrecy. No presumption against secrecy exists in private life as it does against deception: keeping confidences and respecting privacy in private life are more often virtues than vices. Even in public life, where there is a presumption against secrecy, secrecy still has some positive value. The need for confidentiality sometimes provides strong reasons to keep secrets. The presumption against secrecy therefore is more easily rebutted than the presumption against deception. As a consequence, our moral analysis may have to be more complex in the case of secrecy.

Those who justified the secrecy of the task force appointed by Hillary Clinton and those who defended the quite different one established later by Dick Cheney used similar arguments. Their critics (some of whom switched sides) also raised similar objections. Paired, the cases invite the comparative question: if you criticize (or defend) the secrecy of one, must you criticize (or defend) the secrecy of the other?

Disinformation for Qaddafi

Christine Huang

By spring of 1986, the Reagan administration had evidence that Libya's leader Colonel Muammar el-Qaddafi had supported and encouraged terrorist acts against U.S. citizens and U.S. installations abroad. Fearing a resurgence of terrorist activity and wishing to capitalize on the deterrent value of the April 14 U.S. air raid on Libya, the administration seized on the opportunity provided by a new intelligence report in July questioning Qaddafi's mental stability. The report triggered an inter-agency review of U.S.-Libyan policy. The State and Defense Departments, the Central Intelligence Agency, and the White House began to consider what steps might be taken to maintain the National Security Council, launching a new phase of the administration policy, first adopted in 1985, to undermine the Qaddafi regime.

On August 6, the State Department's Office of Intelligence and Research distributed a seven-page memorandum to senior midlevel officials in advance of an upcoming interagency meeting. The memo called for a "disinformation" and

"deception" campaign to bring attention to Qaddafi's continuing terrorist activities, to exaggerate his vulnerability to internal opposition, and to play up the possibility of new American military action against him. Under the heading of Qaddafi's vulnerability to internal opposition, the State Department memorandum explicitly stated as its goal: "to continue Qaddafi's paranoia so that he remains preoccupied, off balance." If, according to the memo, Qaddafi believed that the army and other elements in Libya may be plotting against him, he might increase the pressure on the Libyan army thus prompting a "coup or assassination attempt."

The Crisis Pre-Planning Group (CPPG) of senior representatives from the State and Defense Departments, the CIA, and the White House met on August 7 at 4:30 in the White House situation room and endorsed the overall plan outlined in the State Department memo. A meeting of the National Security Planning Group (NSPG) was scheduled for August 14 to consider the next steps the administration would take against Qaddafi. (The NSPG is the key cabinet-level forum in which the president and his top aides discuss and make decisions on the most sensitive policy matters.)

On August 12, President Reagan received a memorandum from his national security affairs advisor, Admiral John Poindexter, summarizing a proposed program of disinformation against Libya. "One of the key elements" of the new strategy, the Poindexter memo said, "is that it combines real and imaginary events through a disinformation program—with the basic goal of making Qaddafi think that there is a high degree of internal opposition to him within Libya, that his long trusted aides are disloyal, that the U.S. is about to move against him militarily." The purpose of taking additional steps against Libya, according to the memo, was to deter terrorism, moderate Libyan policies, and "bring about a change of leadership in Libya."

The president, Poindexter, and nine other key officials met at the White House on August 14 at 11 A.M. The overall plan as outlined by Poindexter was approved by Reagan and codified in general terms in a formal National Security Decision Directive signed by the president. Details of the plan were left to Poindexter, the State Department, and the CIA. The Reagan directive ordered covert, diplomatic, and economic steps designed to deter Libyan sponsored terrorism and to bring about a change of leadership. The principal means outlined in the directive was a campaign of disinformation. Neither the memoranda themselves nor the meetings held to discuss them addressed the details of any strategy on the dissemination of false stories to reporters.

Although Poindexter's memo said that "the current intelligence community assessment is that Qaddafi is temporarily quiescent in his support of terrorism," soon after the meeting, one or two members of the NSC staff told reporters that the United States had new intelligence indicating that Qaddafi was stepping up his terrorist plans.

On August 25, the *Wall Street Journal* on page one reported that "the U.S. and Libya are on a collision course again" and added that "the Reagan administration is preparing to teach the mercurial Libyan leader another lesson. Right now, the Pentagon is completing plans for a new and larger bombing of Libya in case the President orders it."

The report quoted a senior U.S. official as saying of Qaddafi, "There are increasing signs that he's renewed planning and preparations for terrorist acts." The article went on to describe the administration's new "three-pronged program of military, covert, and economic actions" intended "to preempt more Libyan-sponsored terrorism, exacerbate growing political and economic tensions in Libya, and remind Col. Qaddafi and his inner circle that promoting terrorism may be hazardous to their health." The program included joint exercises with Egypt in the Mediterranean, possible joint action with France to drive Libyan troops out of Chad, increased support for dissident military officers, businessmen, and technocrats inside Libya and for Libyan exiles who wanted "to oust Col. Qaddafi," and with European cooperation, tightening the economic and political sanctions adopted in the spring of 1985 by the Common Market and by the Tokyo economic summit.

All three network television evening news programs repeated the substance of the *Journal*'s report that night, citing unidentified administration officials. The August 26 issues of many major newspapers quoted unidentified and identified officials who seemed to confirm the *Journal*'s article, though there was no explicit official confirmation.

On August 25, in Santa Barbara near the ranch where President Reagan was on a three-week vacation, White House spokesman Larry Speakes said, "Our policy toward Libyan-backed terrorism is unequivocal and unchanged. We will employ all appropriate measures to cause Libya to cease its terrorist policies. We certainly have reason to believe that the Libyan state, headed by Col. Qaddafi, has not forsaken its desire to cause—to create—terrorist activities worldwide, and the capability is still there to do so." In an off-the-record statement at a news conference the next day, Speakes described the *Journal*'s article as being "highly authoritative but not authorized."

Fearing that reports of impending American military action against Libya might produce more concern in Europe than in Libya, administration officials in Washington sought to soften the public line on August 27. White House, State Department, and Pentagon officials said they had indications of planned new Libyan terrorist activities aimed at Americans. They stressed, however, that they had nothing approximating a "smoking gun" to justify sending American bombers once again to strike Libya. The officials described new American diplomatic efforts to toughen economic and political sanctions against Libya as the main thrust of administration policy. Vernon A. Walters, the U.S. delegate to the United Nations, was expected to travel to Europe the following week to explore widening these sanctions. One key official expressed the fear that "these panic stories will undercut the Walters mission. The Europeans will ask us for the hard evidence, and we won't have any. It will look like we are crying wolf once again."

Bob Woodward in the *Washington Post* on October 2 disclosed the details of the administration's "secret and unusual plan of deception." The *Post* account said that beginning with the *Journal's* August 25 report, the American news media reported as fact much of the false information generated by the deception plan described in the August memos.

The White House denied that the administration had planted false reports with news organizations in the United States as a means of bringing pressure on Qaddafi. Mr. Speakes said that the information provided to the *Wall Street Journal* "was not a part of any plan or memo drafted by Poindexter and approved by the President and the U.S. Government." Defending the statements he made in August, the White House spokesman reiterated that "the information contained in the *Wall Street Journal* in these various intelligence reports was information from intelligence sources. That was hard, that was firm."

Responding to the *Post's* article in an interview on October 2 at the White House with select news columnists and broadcast commentators, President Reagan at first said, "I challenge the veracity of that entire story," but acknowledged that "there are memos back and forth. I can't deny that here and there they're going to have something to hang it on."

Secretary of State George Shultz told reporters on the same day in New York that he knew of "no decision to have people go out and tell lies to the media" but that "if there are ways in which we can make Qaddafi nervous, why shouldn't we?" He noted Winston Churchill's statement in World War II that "in time of war the truth is so precious it must be attended by a bodyguard of lies," adding that "insofar as Qaddafi is concerned we don't have a declaration of war but we have something darn close to it."

In a statement issued on October 2 in reference to the August 25 report, *Wall Street Journal* managing editor Norman Pearlstine said, "We remain convinced, as reported in the *Journal,* that the U.S. government in late summer believed Libya had resumed its active support for terrorism and that the U.S. was considering a range of options aimed at deterring such Libyan actions. We reported this based on not one source, but on information provided by a number of sources here and abroad." Pearlstine concluded by saying, "If, indeed, our government conducted such a domestic disinformation campaign, we were among its many victims." Leaving for a weekend retreat at Camp David, Maryland, on October 3, the president insisted for the second consecutive day that the administration had been trying merely to deceive Qaddafi rather than to mislead the press into printing inaccurate reports. "We are not telling lies or doing any of these disinformation things that we are cited with doing."

The Justice Department asked the Federal Bureau of Investigation to conduct an inquiry into the *Post's* October 2 report and the *Journal's* August 25 article. The probe was referred to a new unit in the FBI's Washington field office that was set up under a reorganization in the spring of 1985 to assign veteran agents to pursue leaks of classified information.

The Senate Select Committee on Intelligence initiated an inquiry. Bernie McMahon, the committee staff director, told the Associated Press on October 3 that the staff had concluded that the administration had not deliberately attempted to plant false stories in the U.S. news media. In an interview on the same day, the chairman of the Senate Intelligence Committee, Dave Durenberger, said that individual White House aides may have provided false information without the approval of their superiors, leading to inaccurate stories about Libya by major news organizations, but added that it would take "a quantum leap" to assume that the actions of a few White House officials constituted a formal administration policy of lying to American reporters.

Comment

Although Colonel Muammar el-Qaddafi was the intended victim of the deception—described in the 1986 directive signed by President Reagan—journalists and the public were also deceived by the campaign of disinformation that ensued. Was the deception of the press and the public necessary to carry out the directive? If so, was the deception justified? More generally, are public officials justified in trying to "manage the news" to the extent necessary to achieve an important, widely shared foreign policy objective? Evaluate the defense of deception that is implicit in Secretary of State Shultz's response to reporters. The Senate Select Committee concluded that the administration did not have a formal policy of lying to American reporters. If we accept this conclusion, could we still hold the administration morally responsible for deceiving the press and the public?

The Iran-Contra Affair
David Nacht

The Iran-Contra Affair was a set of American foreign policy initiatives conducted in secret by a small number of executive branch officials, mainly members of the National Security Council Staff, during the Reagan administration between 1984 and 1986. The affair involved two principal parts: (1) the secret sale of arms to Iran in order to gain the release of American hostages held by Iranian allies in Lebanon and (2) the establishment of a covert mechanism to fund and arm the Nicaraguan insurgency, known as the Contras, at a time when the Congress had cut off funds to the Contras.

This case highlights the actions of two main officials in the affair, Admiral John Poindexter, the national security advisor to the president of the United States, and his aide, Lieutenant Colonel Oliver North. After the affair became public knowledge, two committees of Congress held joint hearings for eight months, at which the "star" witnesses were Adm. Poindexter and Lt. Col. North. Testifying under oath, they were granted immunity for their statements under the terms of the Fifth Amendment preventing self-incrimination.[1] North was fired from his post on the NSC staff, and Poindexter was forced to resign.

In order to preserve the secrecy of the Iran and Nicaragua activities, Adm. Poindexter made sure that few individuals knew about them. The secretary of state, for instance, apparently lacked detailed knowledge of almost all of the activities; the same was true for the chairman of the Joint Chiefs and the secretary of defense. In his relentless effort at compartmentalization, Admiral Poindexter even appears to have excluded the president from knowledge of major aspects of the affair. The director of the Central Intelligence Agency, William Casey, knew about—and in fact may have planned—many of the activities, although this may not have been in accord with Poindexter's wishes, but rather because of Casey's special friendship with Lt. Col. North. Selected members of the CIA, Defense Department, and State Department, private individuals, and members of certain foreign governments, all of whose participation was deemed by Poindexter and North to be necessary for the success of the mission, were also made aware of the initiatives. However, Congress was not told, even though there are legally required procedures for informing congressional leaders of highly secretive covert operations. Moreover, after an investigation began, Casey, North, and Poindexter fabricated cover stories, and the latter two destroyed documents in an effort to deceive the investigators.

THE SETTING

Public disclosure of both the Iran and the Nicaraguan initiatives was bound to cause controversy. The United States and Iran had been on uncomfortable terms since the seizure of the American diplomats in Tehran in 1979 by the Iranian Revolutionary Guards. Moreover, the Reagan administration had been pursuing a vocal antiterrorism campaign waged largely against Iran and Libya. President Reagan had officially designated Iran as a terrorist nation, forbidding it, under the terms of the amended Arms Export Control Act, to receive arms from the United States. Moreover, the president had personally asked the West European allies not to sell arms to Iran.

The diversion of funds to the Contras, although closer in spirit to stated American foreign policy, concerned many because it flouted a congressional ban on such assistance, and Reagan administration officials had falsely testified that the administration was not arming the Contras. The administration had actively opposed the ruling Sandinista regime in Nicaragua by successively condemning the regime, boycotting Nicaraguan goods in the United States, mining Nicaraguan harbors, and organizing and funding the Contras. The administration's efforts to obtain material support for the rebel force had been hampered by congressional resistance. Congress voted down a number of administration requests to arm the Contras. In December 1981, President Reagan authorized a National Intelligence Finding establishing U.S. support for the Contras. A year later on December 21, 1982, Congress passed the first of five Boland Amendments, named after the congressman who wrote the legislation, barring the CIA or the Department of Defense from spending money directed "toward overthrowing the government of Nicaragua or provoking a military exchange between Nicaragua and Honduras." In September 1983, President Reagan signed another finding authorizing "the provision of material support and guidance to the Nicaraguan resistance groups."

On December 8, 1983, Congress responded by placing a $24 million cap on funds to be used for supporting the Contras directly or indirectly by "DOD or CIA or any other agency involved in intelligence activities." In October 1984, Congress stopped all funding for the Contras "by any agency involved in intelligence activities."[2] It was at this point that Lt. Col. North essentially took over the role which the CIA had been performing as the logistics coordinator for the Contras.

AIDING THE CONTRAS

Lt. Col. North was a marine who had been "detailed" to the NSC staff. His boss, Robert "Bud" McFarlane, the national security advisor, was another marine colonel. North served on a committee on the NSC staff charged with combating terrorism abroad. Although his position was not very senior, North was self-confident and eager to take the initiative in carrying out policies. He formed friendships with McFarlane, with McFarlane's successor, Adm. Poindexter, and with the director of the CIA, William Casey. North used his personal relationships to learn the priorities of the senior policymakers and to build their trust in him. He appears to have had at least tacit approval for most or all of his activities from the successive national security advisors.

North became the NSC liaison to the Contras. He was charged with "keeping them alive, body and soul" in spite of the cutoff in congressional funding. He interpreted the legal limitation as a prohibition on funding the Contras with money appropriated by Congress. Therefore, his strategy was to get money from other sources—foreign governments and private citizens: "I made every effort, counsel, to avoid the use of appropriated funds. And, as I said, that was why the decision was made in 1984, before this proscription ever became law, to set up outside entities, and to raise non-U.S. government monies by which the Nicaraguan freedom fighters could be supported."[3]

In December 1984, he initiated the effort to raise foreign funds by asking Secretary Shultz to solicit funds from the sultan of Brunei for Contra use. (Shultz's meeting the sultan and the payment that followed actually did not occur until June 1986.) North, State Department officials, and private citizens solicited a total of $34 million for the Contras from foreign sources between June 1984 and the beginning of 1986. An additional $2.7 million was raised from private contributors.[4]

President Reagan authorized the policy to raise funds from foreign sources and private contributors for the Contras; however, he may not have had the legal authority to conduct these activities. (No Court ruling has yet been issued). President Reagan himself took part briefly in the fundraising, meeting with large donors of both the foreign and private domestic variety, and Adm. Poindexter has testified that "I am confident that he [the president] was aware that these people were making contributions to support the Contras."[5] However, this activity was kept from the Congress. Elliot Abrams, the assistant secretary of state, actively misled a congressional committee about administration fundraising efforts. He later acknowledged his distortions, stating that unless members of Congress asked "exactly the right question, using exactly the right words, they weren't going to get the right answers."[6]

Rumors of NSC staff support for the Contras reached Congress and the press by June 1985. In August 1985, representatives Michael Barnes and Lee Hamilton wrote separate letters to National Security Advisor McFarlane asking for information about these rumors. In October, McFarlane received three additional requests. McFarlane responded to these requests with statements that Col. North later described as "false, erroneous, misleading, evasive, and wrong."[7] Col. North maintains that Col. McFarlane authorized him to submit misleading documents to Congressman Barnes. Col. McFarlane has testified in response that he was unaware of the full extent of the activities of Col. North. Col. McFarlane has admitted, however, that he lied in his letter of response to Congressman Hamilton of October 7, denying NSC participation in third-country fundraising for the Contras. There is also convincing evidence that he lied regarding his knowledge of Col. North's activities in coordinating logistics for the Contras.[8]

Col. McFarlane repeated these false denials in meetings with senators Leahy and Durenberger on September 5, 1985, and with members of the House Intelligence Committee on September 10. He also gave false testimony after he resigned to the Senate Select Committee on Intelligence in December 1986 concerning his knowledge of NSC staff activities. Although he claimed that he relied on press accounts for his information, McFarlane actually received memos from Col. North via computer notes, which turned up after McFarlane testified. McFarlane worked closely with North and Poindexter to cover up the NSC role in the arms sale.[9]

From July 1985 until the operation was discovered in November 1986, North, with the clear approval of Adm. Poindexter, Robert McFarlane's successor as national security advisor, employed a network of private firms, CIA agents, CIA proprietary firms, nonprofit anticommunist organizations, some State Department officials—notably Assistant Secretary of State Elliot Abrams and the U.S. ambassador to Costa Rica, Lewis Tambs—and a few private individuals to aid the Nicaraguan rebels with logistics and fundraising efforts. The bulk of the money was handled by two individuals who controlled a network of firms, known to the congressional committees investigating the Iran-Contra Affair as "The Enterprise." The Enterprise was a partnership between Albert Hakim, an Iranian-born businessman, and ex-U.S. General Richard Secord, in close coordination with Lt. Col. North. The Enterprise served in a covert capacity as an informal contractor to the U.S. government and to the Contras.

The president was not told about The Enterprise because, according to Adm. Poindexter, it was an "unnecessary detail." William Casey was informed, although Poindexter instructed North not to tell Casey because as director of the CIA, he could be called on to testify before Congress. Poindexter also hid the operation from Donald Regan, the president's chief of staff, because "he talked to the press too much. I was afraid he'd make a slip."[10] The Congress and public were not informed of The Enterprise until the Iran-Contra investigation.

At an undetermined point in 1985, Col. North decided, with the approval of Adm. Poindexter, that the residual profits from the Iran arms sale ought to go toward assisting the Contras. Only a small fraction of the total Iran arms profits actually reached the Contras. According to the congressional committees' investigation, about $3.8 million out of the $16.1 million profit from the Iran arms sales went to support the Contras.[11]

Adm. Poindexter has testified that he did not distinguish among funds coming from private donations, the Iranian arms sales, or foreign sources in terms of their ownership. He argues that he had the authority to let Col. North and The Enterprise use the funds as they saw fit. The funds were used to cover expenses for the many operations, for buying arms for the Contras, for public relations in the United States on behalf of the Contras, and as a source of profits for Secord and Hakim. Some were also spent on a security system for the home of Col. North.[12]

Secord and Hakim controlled most of the money raised for the Contras. At one time when North visited Contra forces and wrote that "the picture is, in short, very dismal, unless a source of bridge funding can be found," there were over $4.8 million in funds in accounts controlled by Secord and Hakim of which North did not know.[13] The Enterprise took in total revenues of $4 million from the arms sales to Iran and the Contras, and private donations from people who thought they were contributing to the Contras.[14]

All of these operations were kept secret from the Congress. Except for some of the fundraising from foreign sources, and the domestic public relations effort, the State Department was also not informed. The president was not told at this time about the diversion of funds from the Iran arms sale to the Contras.

Based on further press accounts, a new congressional inquiry was launched in June 1986. In the House Intelligence Committee's "Resolution of Inquiry," dated July 1, the president was directed to provide the House of Representatives with information and documents on: contacts between NSC staff and private individuals or foreign governments about Contra provisions; the extent to which NSC staff provided military advice to the Contras; and contacts between NSC staff and certain private individuals who were known consultants to the Contras.

Adm. Poindexter replied to the request by referring to McFarlane's response from the previous year and not mentioning any details. Since Poindexter knew that McFarlane's letter had not been accurate, he continued the deception that his predecessor had begun. The House Intelligence Committee also interviewed Col. North as part of their inquiry. Months later, in his testimony to the Iran-Contra committees, North admitted to lying in that interview.[15]

Both Col. North and Adm. Poindexter acknowledge that they misled Congress and both defend their actions. In his testimony North defended the right of the executive to resist informing the Congress about sensitive matters: "[I sent] . . . answers . . . to the Congress that were clearly misleading. . . . I believed then, and I believe now that the executive was fully legitimate in giving no answer to those queries."[16] When Mr. Nields, the House chief counsel, asked Col. North how he could reconcile lying to Congress with a belief in democratic principles, North responded:

> . . . I did it because we have had incredible leaks, from discussions with closed committees of the Congress. I . . . was a part of, some

people know, the coordination for the mining of the harbors in Nicaragua. When that one leaked, there were American lives at stake, and it leaked from a member of one of the committees, who eventually admitted it. When there was a leak on the sensitive intelligence methods that we used to help capture the Achille Lauro terrorists, it almost wiped out that whole channel of communications. I mean, those kinds of things are devastating. They are devastating to the national security of the United States, and I desperately hope that one of the things that can derive from all of this ordeal is that we can find a better way by which we can communicate those things properly with the Congress.[17]

In a celebrated statement, Col. North concluded that "I think we had to weigh in the balance the difference between lies and lives."[18]

Critics, including the Senate counsel, Arthur Liman, have argued that Col. North could have revealed to Congress the general policy of aiding the Contras without revealing specific information that would have threatened lives. North maintains that a flaw in the oversight mechanism of Congress prevents the executive from feeling confident that Congress can maintain the confidentiality of sensitive matters. Moreover, he argued that a national debate on the subject would inevitably have led to the leaking of sensitive material.

Adm. Poindexter also admits to deceiving Congress, and he expected Col. North to do the same: "I did think he would withhold information and be evasive, frankly, in answering questions. My objective all along was to withhold from the Congress exactly what the NSC staff was doing in carrying out the president's policy."[19] Poindexter justifies this deception on the grounds that had Congress known the truth, it would have acted to stop the NSC activities. Since those activities did not, in his view, violate the law, they could be conducted in secret:

> that what Colonel North was doing in terms of supporting the democratic resistance was within the letter of the law at the time, although obviously very sensitive, very controversial.

We wanted to avoid more restrictive legislation, and so any activity that he would have been involved with on Central America we wanted to keep highly compartmented.[20]

THE IRAN INITIATIVE[21]

In spite of strident rhetoric on the part of both countries, Iran and the United States each had interests in reestablishing ties with one another. Iran wanted weapons and diplomatic support in its war against Iraq, and the United States wanted to diminish the likelihood that Iran would turn pro-Soviet. There were discussions underway between Israeli and American officials concerning the possibility of U.S. sale of arms to Iran in 1984 and 1985. The Israelis maintained a secret communications channel with senior Iranian officials, about which the senior officials of the NSC gradually became aware. Throughout 1985, the number of American hostages taken increased dramatically, placing great pressure on the Reagan administration to do something to bring them home, in spite of public commitments not to give in to terrorist demands. The change in attitude within the administration was expressed in the context of broader U.S.-Iranian relations in a memo to McFarlane by two NSC staffers, Howard Teicher and Donald Fortier, dated June 11, 1985. They called for a radical shift in U.S. policy toward Iran in order to advance American and limit Soviet influence in Iran. One of the steps they recommended was the occasional shipment of arms to Iran. In June, the Iranians transmitted their desire to obtain U.S.-made weapons such as the TOW and HAWK missiles. A number of private businessmen including an Israeli, an Iranian, and a Saudi exerted their influence on NSC officials in an effort to broker a deal. National Security Advisor McFarlane circulated a draft memo on June 17 to Secretaries Shultz (State) and Weinberger (Defense) and the director of central intelligence, Mr. Casey, suggesting that the United States could sell arms via the Israelis to Iran as part of a broader strategy for improving U.S.-Iranian relations and to help bring the hostages home. Both Shultz and Weinberger replied in memos that they opposed the arms sales.

After a briefing by McFarlane, President Reagan approved, on a still undetermined date in August, the shipment of U.S.-manufactured arms by Israel to Iran. On August 30, 1985, the Israelis shipped 100 TOW missiles to Iran. They sent an additional 408 TOWs on September 14. On September 15, a U.S. hostage, the Reverend Benjamin Weir, was released. In November, there was another arms sale. It remains unclear whether the president was informed of this sale; he does not remember. North, McFarlane, and Poindexter were all directly involved in the sale, and Shultz was briefed. Eighteen HAWK missiles were transferred to Iran, but they did not meet Iranian specifications, and the Iranians returned all but one of them to the Israelis. After this sale, a covert action finding was prepared by the CIA for the president to sign, approving the arms sales.

On December 7, the president met with senior officials, including McFarlane, who had just resigned as national security advisor, and Poindexter, concerning arms sales to Iran. As a result of the meeting, McFarlane, now a private citizen acting as an agent of the U.S. government, was sent to London to negotiate with a Mr. Ghorbanifar, an Iranian middleman who had brokered the previous sales.

According to his own accounts, the president was interested in proceeding with the Iran arms sales if the hostages could be freed. He signed another finding on January 17, 1986, authorizing the direct sale of American arms via the CIA to the Iranians. This decision marked a change from the previous policy of agreeing to resupply Israel with arms that they sold to Iran. Neither Secretary Shultz nor Secretary Weinberger was informed of this shift in policy, which was developed by the president and Adm. Poindexter. At this point the arms sales became coordinated within the NSC staff, as part of a broader policy aimed at the release of the hostages entitled Operation Recovery. Col. North assumed direct control over the operation under the authority of Adm. Poindexter. North brought in The Enterprise to help with the shipments.

Negotiations with the Iranians had been strained since the unsuccessful shipment of the HAWKS in November. North and McFarlane arranged a meeting with the Iranians to attempt to improve relations. Adm. Poindexter briefed the president in May 1986 in the two weeks preceding the trip, but he did not inform Shultz or Weinberger, and neither did the president. Although no U.S. hostages had been taken during the summer, three more were taken in September and October.

The taking of these hostages led North, McFarlane, and Poindexter, and probably Casey, to mistrust Ghorbanifar. Col. North sought to establish a "second channel" to Iran to replace Ghorbanifar. Acting under presidential authorization, North, along with a CIA agent and Secord, met with the second channel, an individual whose identity has not been revealed, in Frankfurt on October 5–7, 1986. They set up a second meeting in Frankfurt, at which, without presidential authorization, but possibly with Adm. Poindexter's approval, Col. North agreed that the United States would ship more TOWs and HAWKS, supply military intelligence, and pressure the Kuwaiti government to release some terrorist prisoners in exchange for the release of one or two American hostages. U.S. officials continued to negotiate with the Iranian officials through December 1986, after the affair had been made public. The talks broke down, however, and U.S. policy turned actively anti-Iran in the summer of 1987.

On November 3, 1986, the Lebanese paper Al-Shiraa disclosed that the United States had been selling arms to Iran in exchange for the release of hostages held in Lebanon. The White House issued a series of statements the following week denying the reports; the statements had been prepared in large measure by Poindexter.[22] On November 12 and 13 the cover-up continued, as Poindexter spread inaccurate accounts of the affair to the cabinet, members of Congress, and the press. He did not mention the Nicaragua connection, and he did not refer to two of the three findings signed by the president. He also omitted most of the arms shipments to Iran. On November 18, Poindexter withheld information from State Department counsel, Abraham Sofaer. That same day, Poindexter spoke with Casey about preparing false testimony for a congressional appearance.[23]

On November 19, the president held a news conference reiterating the false claims he had made during his televised address.[24] Secretary Shultz confronted the president about his factual errors on the following day. Meanwhile, McFarlane, Poindexter, and North were constructing inaccurate chronologies of the affair. Because they communicated with each other via computer messages which the congressional committees later retrieved, we have a record of their attempt. The record strongly suggests that their intention was to cover up what they could. For example, in some of their accounts, they claimed the HAWK shipments were really oil equipment, when they had been the officials who had devised the oil equipment deception to preserve secrecy in the first place.[25] On November 21, Director Casey made the same false claim in his testimony to the Intelligence Committee.

Under considerable public pressure, the attorney general, Edwin Meese, decided to launch an investigation into the affair because of conflicting stories about what had actually taken place. When he informed Poindexter of this, Poindexter and North began a massive effort to destroy the evidence of their actions. They both shredded documents; North also altered the documents, deleting references to the NSC staff's ties to the Contras.[26]

When testifying, North admitted that he shredded documents for reasons other than to preserve national security:

LIMAN: Do you deny, Colonel, that one of the reasons that you were shredding documents that Saturday, was to avoid the political embarrassment of having those documents be seen by the attorney general's staff?
NORTH: I do not deny that.[27]

Moreover, North lied to Meese during his interview with the attorney general. Meese confronted North with a document, which Bradford Reynolds, the assistant attorney general, had uncovered, mentioning the diversion of funds from Iran to Nicaragua. North claimed that "no one at CIA knew about it," when Casey, in fact, had known. North also lied about the nature of the Contra supply operations.[28]

BUREAUCRATIC IRREGULARITIES

In the Iran-Contra Affair, many normal bureaucratic procedures were ignored in an effort to maintain secrecy. Both initiatives, which could be considered to be major acts of foreign policy, were handled as covert operations and kept secret from as many senior officials in the government as possible. For instance, U.S. officials negotiated with high-level Israeli and Iranian politicians without the knowledge of the secretary of state. To maintain this secrecy, Adm. Poindexter and Director Casey evidently believed that they had to deceive Secretary Shultz, with whom they dealt on a regular basis, about the activities of Lt. Col. North.

The National Security Council staff was not formed with the purpose of undertaking covert operations or foreign policy initiatives, but for easing the presidential decision-making process, yet the NSC staff took over the job of resupplying the Contras when the CIA was expressly barred from doing so by Congress. The answer to the legal question of whether the NSC staff was included in the cut-off remains uncertain: the Boland Amendment cut-off included "DOD, CIA and other agencies engaged in intelligence activities." In general, the NSC is not considered an intelligence agency, but Executive Order 12333 stated that the NSC was "the highest Executive Branch entity that provides review of, guidance for, and direction to the conduct of all national foreign intelligence, counter-intelligence, and special activities, and attendant policies and programs."[29] Moreover, the covert operations conducted by Col. North included CIA and ex-CIA personnel and were of the type which might normally be conducted by the CIA. Poindexter and North, however, received legal advice from the president's Foreign Intelligence Advisory Board to the effect that the NSC was not covered by the Boland Amendment.

JUSTIFIABLE DECEPTION?

In the congressional hearings, Adm. Poindexter and Lt. Col. North acknowledged their attempts to deceive executive branch officials, the Congress, and the public, but they maintained that their acts of deception were justifiable. The House counsel, John Nields, asked Col. North about the covert operations:

MR. NIELDS: And these operations—they were covert operations?
LT. COL. NORTH: Yes they were.
NIELDS: And covert operations are designed to be secret from our enemies?
NORTH: That is correct.
NIELDS: But these operations were designed to be secrets from the American people?
NORTH: Mr. Nields, I'm at a loss as to how we could announce it to the American people and not have the Soviets know about it . . .
NIELDS: Well, in fact, Col. North, you believed that the Soviets were aware of our sale of arms to Iran, weren't you?
NORTH: We came to a point in time when we were concerned about that.

A few minutes later, Col. North elaborated on his statement:

LT. COL. NORTH: I think it is very important for the American people to understand that this is a dangerous world; that we live at risk and that this nation is at risk in a dangerous world. And that they ought not to be led to believe, as a consequence of these hearings, that this nation cannot or should not conduct covert operations. By their very nature, covert operations or special activities are a lie. There is great deceit, deception practiced in the conduct of covert operation[s]. They are at essence a lie. We make every effort to deceive the enemy as to our intent, our conduct and to deny the association of the United States with those activities. The intelligence committees hold hearings on all kinds of activities conducted by our intelligence service. The American people ought not to believe by the way you're asking that question that we intentionally deceived the American people, or had that intent to begin with. The effort to conduct these covert operations was made in such a way that our adversaries would not have knowledge of them or that we could deny American association with it, or the association of this government with those activities. And that is not wrong.[30]

Col. North claimed that he had been granted authority for all of his deceptions: "I sought approval for every one of my actions and it is well documented. I assumed when I had approval to proceed from . . . Bud McFarlane or Adm. Poindexter, that they had indeed solicited and obtained the approval of the President."[31] Colonel North was supported by Poindexter who testified, "I didn't tell Col. North that I was not going to tell the president."[32] North admitted, however, that following orders is insufficient grounds for breaking the law. Both he and Adm. Poindexter have argued, however, that their activities did not break the law because they did not use money appropriated by the Congress.[33]

Adm. Poindexter's deception was, in many respects, similar to that of Col. North. However, North did not withhold information from his immediate superiors. Adm. Poindexter claims that he deliberately, intentionally failed to inform President Reagan of the diversion of funds to the Contras in an effort to protect the president from responsibility for a politically controversial act. Poindexter argued in his testimony that he was justified in not telling the president for three reasons: the diversion of funds from Iran to the Contras was legal; the diversion was essentially a "detail" of the larger policy of aiding the Contras; and the president would have supported the policy had he known about it:

My impression was that it was clear to me that these were third country or private-party funds that would result from the arms sale to the Iranians. . . . I felt that it was in terms of supporting and implementing the president's policy, that it was entirely consistent. The president never really changed his policy with regard to supporting the Contras since the early decision back in 1981. It seemed that his method of financing was completely consistent with what we had been doing in terms of private parties and third countries. I knew that it would be a controversial issue. I had at that point worked with the president for three of those five-and-a-half years, very directly, meeting with him many times a day, often spending hours every day with him. So I not only clearly understood his policy, but I thought I understood the way he thought about issues. I felt that I had the authority to approve Col. North's request. I also felt that it was, as I said, consistent with the president's policy, and that if I asked him, I felt confident that he would approve it. But because it was controversial, and I obviously knew it would cause a ruckus if it were exposed, I decided to insulate the president from the decision and give him some deniability; and so I decided . . . at that point not to tell the president.[34]

As of May 1988, no court has ruled on the legality of either the arms sale or the diversion of funds. However, a grand jury returned a conspiracy indictment against Adm. Poindexter, Col. North, Richard Secord, and Albert Hakim. Also, Col. McFarlane pleaded guilty to four misdemeanor counts.

Col. McFarlane struck a deal with the independent counsel, Lawrence Walsh, in which McFarlane agreed to testify as a witness for the prosecution against Adm. Poindexter and Col. North and to plead guilty to the misdemeanors in exchange for his freedom from felony indictments. After his court appearance, McFarlane told reporters, "I did indeed withhold information from Congress."[35]

The indictment against Poindexter and North included their cover-up attempt as illegal activity:

> From August 1985 through November 1986, in order to conceal and cover up their illegal activities and to perpetrate the scheme, the conspirators, including the defendants JOHN M. POINDEXTER and OLIVER L. NORTH, deceived Congress and committees of Congress by making false, fictitious, fraudulent and misleading statements and representations, concerning, among other things, the involvement of officials of the United States, including members of the NSC staff, in support of the military and paramilitary operations in Nicaragua by the Contras at a time when the Boland Amendment I was in effect. . . .[36]

Following his indictment, Lt. Col. North resigned from the Marine Corps in order to be in a position to subpoena "testimony and records from the highest-ranking officials of our government" during his trial.[37] This action furthered speculation that President Reagan would pardon North, and possibly Poindexter as well, on the grounds that they had only been following his orders. The *Wall Street Journal* editorial board previously argued in favor of pardons for North and Poindexter for precisely these reasons on November 30, 1987.[38] As of May 1988, President Reagan has neither pardoned nor ruled out the possibility that he would pardon Poindexter and North, who have both pleaded not guilty, but whose trials have not yet begun.

The majority and minority reports of the congressional committees differ in their judgments of the affair and its participants. Almost no aspect of the affair—legal, policy, or moral—commands complete acceptance by the members of Congress or others who have studied the issue. The public also holds varying and changing views. In August, at the height of the hearings, more than half of the American public thought President Reagan had lied and was continuing to lie about the affair. They did not like the way he had handled Iranian policy. The president's job approval rating was in the forty percent range, down from his usual mid-sixties. Nevertheless, as a result of other factors, his personal popularity had returned to high levels by December.

The public did not like Adm. Poindexter, but many praised Col. North, who was as passionate and inspiring on the witness stand as Poindexter was detached and pedantic. Nevertheless, a month after North's testimony was over, a number of polls indicated that most people did not believe North had been justified in deceiving the Congress. Additionally, while public support for aiding the Contras rose dramatically during North's testimony, it dropped equally dramatically in the next two months.[39]

NOTES

1. In the House of Representatives, the Select Committee to Investigate Covert Arms Transactions with Iran was chaired by Representative Lee Hamilton. In the Senate, the Select Committee on Secret Military Assistance to Iran and the Nicaraguan Opposition was chaired by Senator Daniel Inouye. The transcript of the public sessions of Col. North was sold under the title, *Taking the Stand* (New York: Pocket Books). The president appointed a panel to review the affair, known as the Tower Commission, which released a report. Much of the closed testimony by Adm. Poindexter was released in a sanitized version by the Senate committee. The committees released a final report in November 1987 with two titles, S. Rept. No. 100-216 and H. Rept. No. 100-413. This case is based substantially on these sources.

2. John Tower, Edmund Muskie, and Brent Scowcroft, *The Tower Commission Report* (New York: Bantam Books and Times Books, 1987), pp. 55–59, 450–452.

3. *Taking the Stand,* p. 243.

4. *Report of the Congressional Committees Investigating the Iran-Contra Affair,* p. 4.

5. *Poindexter Closed Testimony to the Committees,* May 1987, p. 203. Also see p. 53.

6. *Report of the Congressional Committees*, p. 20.
7. Cited in ibid., p. 123.
8. Ibid., p. 127.
9. *Tower Report*, pp. 527, 536.
10. Cited in *Report of the Congressional Committees*, p. 139.
11. Ibid., p. 331.
12. Ibid., p. 341.
13. *Taking the Stand*, p. 552.
14. *Report of the Congressional Committees*, p. 11.
15. Ibid., p. 141.
16. *Taking the Stand*, p. 245.
17. Ibid., p. 253.
18. Ibid., p. 256.
19. Cited in *Report of the Congressional Committees*, p. 142.
20. *Poindexter Closed Testimony to the Committees*, May 1987, p. 47.
21. This section is based substantially on the *Tower Report*.
22. *Report of the Congressional Committees*, p. 294.
23. Ibid., p. 301.
24. Ibid., p. 298.
25. Ibid., p. 298–300.
26. Ibid., p. 306–7.

27. *Taking the Stand*, p. 362.
28. *Report of the Congressional Committees*, p. 312.
29. *The Chronology* (Warner, 1987), p. 67, compiled by the National Security Archive.
30. *Taking the Stand*, pp. 9, 12.
31. Ibid., p. 13.
32. *Poindexter Closed Testimony to the Committees*, May 1987, p. 70.
33. *Taking the Stand*, p. 487.
34. *Poindexter Closed Testimony to the Committees*, May 1987, pp. 70–71.
35. *New York Times*, March 12, 1988, p. 1.
36. As reproduced in the *New York Times*, March 17, 1988, p. D26.
37. *New York Times*, March 19, 1988, p. 1.
38. *Wall Street Journal*, Nov. 30, 1987, p. 20.
39. For opinion poll data, I have relied upon an extensive collection of *New York Times*/CBS, Roper, *LA Times, Newsweek, Time* and other polls collected by the Congressional Research Service of the Library of Congress. This data is computerized at the Library of Congress in the "CRS Survey Poll File" under the title "Iran-Contra Affair Polls, October 1986 to Present."

Comment

Unlike most public officials who engage in deception, Admiral John Poindexter and Colonel Oliver North did not deny that they did so. They justified their deception on grounds that their secret actions (1) were necessary to national security; (2) did not violate the letter of the law; and (3) would have been undermined, through leaks and hostile legislation, had they (or anyone else) informed Congress. Consider to what extent their various deceptive statements and actions satisfy their own criteria of justification. What relevant moral considerations are overlooked by their criteria? Does North, in his response to the House chief counsel, succeed in reconciling his approval of lying to Congress with a belief in democratic principles? Are there any conditions under which lying to Congress can be reconciled with democratic principles?

Unlike North, Poindexter deliberately withheld information not only from Congress but also from his immediate superiors, thereby doubly avoiding accountability. Assess Poindexter's justification for concealing information about "The Enterprise" from the president's chief of staff, Donald Regan. Did Poindexter's deliberate failure to inform the president about the diversion of funds to the Contras constitute deception? If so, of whom? Assume that Poindexter was correct in believing that the president would not want to know about the diversion of funds: is Poindexter then justified in not informing the president (or, as some have suggested, perhaps even obligated not to inform him)?

One of the most striking features of the deception chronicled in this case is its pervasiveness. The targets of deception included not only journalists and the American public but also many high-level executive branch officials and congressmen who would normally have been informed about foreign policies of this importance. North and Poindexter seem to have been guided by presumptions favoring deception rather than veracity, and secrecy rather than openness in government. Their testimony provides few if any principled reasons to limit deception and secrecy when public officials act in a cause they believe to be just. What principles could establish a strong presumption in favor of veracity and openness? What political institutions or procedures could guard against unjustified deception by public officials who are motivated either by self- interest or by a passionate dedication to the public interest?

The case and comment are based primarily on information revealed during the congressional hearings. Does information disclosed since then or do any subsequent events change your moral assessment of the actions of either North or Poindexter?

George W. Bush on Iraq's Nuclear Weapons*

In his 2003 State of the Union address, President George W. Bush made a forceful case for war against Iraq. Among the many facts he offered in support of this case were two pieces of evidence concerning Saddam Hussein's nuclear ambitions. Bush alleged that Hussein had recently attempted to buy both enriched uranium and high-strength aluminum tubes from an African nation in order to build nuclear weapons. The President had used these allegations several times in the months leading up to war—the specter of a nuclear Iraq loomed large in the administration's pro-war rhetoric. Vice President Cheney, in an August 2002 speech, had warned that a "nuclear" Saddam "could . . . be expected to seek domination of the entire Middle East, take control of a great portion of the world's energy supplies, directly threaten

America's friends throughout the region, and subject the United States or any other nation to nuclear blackmail."

In February 2002, the CIA had commissioned Joseph Wilson, former U.S. Ambassador to Gabon, to investigate an intelligence report that Iraq had purchased uranium ore from Niger in the late 1990s. Wilson found that there was no evidence to support this claim, and reported this finding to the CIA. Wilson was therefore surprised to find that the administration continued to rely on this allegation, and came forward after the State of the Union address to argue that "some of the intelligence related to Iraq's nuclear weapons program was twisted to exaggerate the Iraqi threat." ("What I Didn't Find in Africa," The New York Times, July 6, 2003). Subsequently, in July 2004, a report by the British Commission and the Senate Intelligence Committee concluded that Iraq may have made an attempt to procure uranium from Niger, but neither found evidence that Iraq had actually purchased any uranium from Niger.

*Alex Zakaras wrote the introduction and selected the excerpts presented in this section.

Other analysts also began to raise questions about the accuracy of the administration's evidence. The allegation concerning aluminum tubing, among others, came under attack. Analysts at the International Atomic Energy Agency argued that no evidence could be found to support this claim, and that Iraq posed no imminent nuclear threat. Administration officials have since admitted that both of these statements (concerning the uranium and the aluminum tubing) should have been removed from the president's address, though they still denied that the statements were false.

EXCERPTS FROM PRESIDENT BUSH'S STATE OF THE UNION ADDRESS, JANUARY 28, 2003

The United Nations concluded in 1999 that Saddam Hussein had biological weapons materials sufficient to produce over 25,000 liters of anthrax; enough doses to kill several million people. He hasn't accounted for that material. He has given no evidence that he has destroyed it.

The United Nations concluded that Saddam Hussein had materials sufficient to produce more than 38,000 liters of botulinum toxin; enough to subject millions of people to death by respiratory failure. He hasn't accounted for that material. He's given no evidence that he has destroyed it.

Our intelligence officials estimate that Saddam Hussein had the materials to produce as much as 500 tons of sarin, mustard and VX nerve agent. In such quantities, these chemical agents could also kill untold thousands. He's not accounted for these materials. He has given no evidence that he has destroyed them.

U.S. intelligence indicates that Saddam Hussein had upwards of 30,000 munitions capable of delivering chemical agents. Inspectors recently turned up 16 of them, despite Iraq's recent declaration denying their existence. Saddam Hussein has not accounted for the remaining 29,984 of these

prohibited munitions. He has given no evidence that he has destroyed them.

From three Iraqi defectors we know that Iraq, in the late 1990s, had several mobile biological weapons labs. These are designed to produce germ warfare agents and can be moved from place to a place to evade inspectors. Saddam Hussein has not disclosed these facilities. He has given no evidence that he has destroyed them.

The International Atomic Energy Agency confirmed in the 1990s that Saddam Hussein had an advanced nuclear weapons development program, had a design for a nuclear weapon and was working on five different methods of enriching uranium for a bomb.

The British government has learned that Saddam Hussein recently sought significant quantities of uranium from Africa.

Our intelligence sources tell us that he has attempted to purchase high-strength aluminum tubes suitable for nuclear weapons production.

Saddam Hussein has not credibly explained these activities. He clearly has much to hide.

The dictator of Iraq is not disarming. To the contrary, he is deceiving. . . .

EXCERPTS FROM THE STATEMENT OF DIRECTOR-GENERAL OF THE INTERNATIONAL ATOMIC ENERGY AGENCY, U.N. SECURITY COUNCIL MARCH 7, 2003

Mohamed ElBaradei: Mr. President, my report to the council today is an update on the status of the International Atomic Energy Agency's (IAEA) nuclear verification activities in Iraq pursuant to Security Council Resolution 1441 and other relevant resolutions.

When I reported last to the council on February 14, I explained that the agency's inspection activities have moved well beyond the reconnaissance phase—that is, re-establishing our knowledge base regarding Iraq nuclear capabilities—into the investigative phase, which focuses on the central question before the IAEA relevant to disarmament—whether Iraq has revived or attempted to revive its defunct nuclear weapons program over the last four years. . . .

Mr. President, in the last few weeks, Iraq has provided a considerable volume of documentation relevant to the issues I reported earlier as being of particular concern, including Iraq's efforts to procure aluminum tubes . . . and its reported attempt to import uranium.

I will touch briefly on the progress made on each of these issues.

Since my last update to the council, the primary technical focus of IAEA field activities in Iraq has been on resolving several outstanding issues related to the possible resumption of efforts by Iraq to enrich uranium through the use of centrifuge. For that purpose, the IAEA assembled a specially qualified team of international centrifuge manufacturing experts.

With regard to the aluminum tubes, the IAEA has conducted a thorough investigation of Iraq's attempt to purchase large quantities of high-strength aluminum tubes. As previously reported, Iraq has maintained that these aluminum tubes were sold for rocket production.

Extensive field investigation and document analysis have failed to uncover any evidence that Iraq intended to use these 81-millimeter tubes for any project other than the reverse engineering of rockets.

The Iraqi decision-making process with regard to the design of these rockets was well-documented. Iraq has provided copies of design documents, procurement records, minutes of committee meetings and supporting data and samples.

A thorough analysis of this information, together with information gathered from interviews with Iraqi personnel, has allowed the IAEA to develop a coherent picture of the attempted purchase and intended usage of the 81-millimeter aluminum tubes as well as the rationale behind the changes in the tolerance.

Drawing on this information, the IAEA has learned that the original tolerance for the 81-millimeter tubes were set prior to 1987 and were based on physical measurements taken from a small number of imported rockets in Iraq's possession.

Initial attempts to reverse-engineer the rockets met with little success. Tolerance was adjusted during the following years as part of ongoing efforts to revitalize a project and improve operational efficiency. The project language for a long period during this time became the subject of several committees, which resulted in the specification and tolerance changes on each occasion.

Based on available evidence, the IAEA team has concluded that Iraqi efforts to import these aluminum tubes were not likely to have been related to the manufacture of centrifuge, and moreover that it was highly unlikely that Iraq could have achieved the considerable redesign needed to use them in a revived centrifuge program.

However, this issue will continue to be scrutinized and investigated. . . .

With regard to uranium acquisition, the IAEA has made progress in its investigation into reports that Iraq sought to buy uranium from Niger in recent years. The investigation was centered on documents provided by a number of states that pointed to an agreement between Niger and Iraq for the sale of uranium between 1999 and 2001.

The IAEA has discussed these reports with the governments of Iraq and Israel, both of which have denied that any such activity took place.

For its part, Iraq has provided the IAEA with a comprehensive explanation of its relations with Niger and has described a visit by an Iraqi official to a number of African countries, including Niger in February 1999, which Iraq thought might have given rise to the reports.

The IAEA was able to review correspondence coming from various bodies of the government of Niger and to compare the form, format, contents and signature of that correspondence with those of the alleged procurement-related documentation.

Based on thorough analysis, the IAEA has concluded with the concurrence of outside experts that these documents which formed the basis for the report of recent uranium transaction between Iraq and Niger are in fact not authentic. We have therefore concluded that these specific allegations are unfounded. However, we will continue to follow up any additional evidence if it emerges relevant to efforts by Iraq to illicitly import nuclear materials. . . .

At this stage, the following can be stated:

One, there is no indication of resumed nuclear activities in those buildings that were identified through the use of satellite imagery as being reconstructed or newly erected since 1998, nor any indication of nuclear-related prohibited activities at any inspected sites.

Two, there is no indication that Iraq has attempted to import uranium since 1990.

Three, there is no indication that Iraq has attempted to import aluminum tubes for use in centrifuge enrichment. Moreover, even had Iraq pursued such a plan, it would have encountered practical difficulties in manufacturing centrifuge out of the aluminum tubes in question. . . .

STATEMENT BY GEORGE J. TENET, DIRECTOR OF CENTRAL INTELLIGENCE JULY 11, 2003

Legitimate questions have arisen about how remarks on alleged Iraqi attempts to obtain uranium in Africa made it into the President's State of the Union speech. Let me be clear about several things right up front. First, CIA approved the President's State of the Union address before it was delivered. Second, I am responsible for the approval process in my Agency. And third, the President had every reason to believe that the text presented to him was sound. These 16 words should never have been included in the text written for the President.

For perspective, a little history is in order. There was fragmentary intelligence gathered in late 2001 and early 2002 on the allegations of Saddam's efforts to obtain additional raw uranium from Africa, beyond the 550 metric tons already in Iraq. In an effort to inquire about certain reports involving Niger, CIA's counter-proliferation experts, on their own initiative, asked an individual with ties to the region to make a visit to see what he could learn. He reported back to us that one of the former Nigerian [*sic*] officials he met stated that he was unaware of any contract being signed between Niger and rogue states for the sale of uranium during his tenure in office. The same former official also said that in June 1999 a businessman approached him and insisted that the former official meet with an Iraqi delegation to discuss "expanding commercial relations" between Iraq and Niger. The former official interpreted the overture as an attempt to discuss uranium sales. The former officials also offered details regarding Niger's processes for monitoring and transporting uranium that suggested it would be very unlikely that material could be illicitly diverted. There was no mention in the report of forged documents—or any suggestion of the existence of documents at all.

Because this report, in our view, did not resolve whether Iraq was or was not seeking uranium from abroad, it was given a normal and wide distribution, but we did not brief it to the President, Vice-President or other senior Administration officials. We also had to consider that the former Nigerian officials knew that what they were saying would reach the U.S. government and that this might have influenced what they said.

In the fall of 2002, my Deputy and I briefed hundreds of members of Congress on Iraq. We did not brief the uranium acquisition story.

Also in the fall of 2002, our British colleagues told us they were planning to publish an unclassified dossier that mentioned reports of Iraqi attempts to obtain uranium in Africa. Because we viewed the reporting on such acquisition attempts to be inconclusive, we expressed reservations about its inclusion but our colleagues said they were confident in their reports and left it in their document.

In September and October 2002 before Senate Committees, senior intelligence officials in response to questions told members of Congress that we differed with the British dossier on the reliability of the uranium reporting.

In October, the Intelligence Community (IC) produced a classified, 90-page National Intelligence Estimate (NIE) on Iraq's WMD programs. There is a lengthy section in which most agencies of the Intelligence Community judged that Iraq was reconstituting its nuclear weapons program. Let me emphasize, the NIE's Key Judgments cited six reasons for this assessment; the African uranium issue was not one of them.

But in the interest of completeness, the report contained three paragraphs that discuss Iraq's significant 550-metric ton uranium stockpile and how it could be diverted while under IAEA safeguard. These paragraphs also cited reports that Iraq began "vigorously trying to procure" more uranium from Niger and two other African countries, which would shorten the time Baghdad needed to produce nuclear weapons. The NIE states: "A foreign government service reported that as of early 2001, Niger planned to send several tons of pure 'uranium' (probably yellowcake) to Iraq. As of early 2001, Niger and Iraq reportedly were still working out the arrangements for this deal, which could be for up to 500 tons of yellowcake." The Estimate also states: "We do not know the status of this arrangement." With regard to reports that Iraq had sought uranium from two other countries, the Estimate says: "We cannot confirm whether Iraq succeeded in acquiring uranium ore and/or yellowcake from these sources." Much later in the NIE text, in presenting an alternate view on another matter, the State Department's Bureau of Intelligence and Research included a sentence that states: "Finally, the claims of Iraqi pursuit of natural uranium in Africa are, in INR's assessment, highly dubious."

An unclassified CIA White Paper in October made no mention of the issue, again because it was not fundamental to the judgment that Iraq was reconstituting its nuclear weapons program, and because we had questions about some of the reporting. For the same reasons, the subject was not included in many public speeches, Congressional testimony and the Secretary of State's United Nations presentation in early 2003.

The background above makes it even more troubling that the 16 words eventually made it into the State of the Union speech. This was a mistake.

Portions of the State of the Union speech draft came to the CIA for comment shortly before the speech was given. Various parts were shared with cognizant elements of the Agency for review. Although the documents related to the alleged Niger-Iraqi uranium deal had not yet been determined to be forgeries, officials who were reviewing the draft remarks on uranium raised several concerns about the fragmentary nature of the intelligence with National Security Council colleagues. Some of the language was changed. From what we know now, Agency officials in the end concurred that the text in the speech was factually correct—i.e., that the British government report said that Iraq sought uranium from Africa. This should not have been the test for clearing a Presidential address. This did not rise to the level of certainty which should be required for Presidential speeches, and CIA should have ensured that it was removed.

EXCERPTS FROM VICE PRESIDENT CHENEY'S APPEARANCE ON MEET THE PRESS SEPTEMBER 14, 2003

MR. RUSSERT: Let me turn to weapons of mass destruction. I asked you back in March what you thought was the most important rationale for going to war with Iraq. There's the question, and here is your answer: "... the combination of [Saddam's] development and use of chemical weapons, his development of biological weapons, his pursuit of nuclear weapons. . . ." I want to talk about something very specific. And that was the president's State of the Union message when he said that the British had learned that Saddam was acquiring uranium from Africa. That was in January. In March the head of the International Atomic [Energy] Agency, ElBaradei, issued this statement: "A key piece of evidence linking Iraq to a nuclear weapons program appears to have been fabricated, the United Nations' chief nuclear inspector said in a report. . . . Documents that purportedly showed Iraqi officials shopping for uranium in Africa two years ago were deemed 'not authentic' after careful scrutiny by U.N. and independent experts, Mohamed ElBaradei, director general of the International Atomic Energy Agency, told the U.N. Security Council. Also, ElBaradei reported finding no evidence of banned weapons or nuclear material in an extensive sweep of Iraq using advanced radiation detectors. 'There is no indication of resumed nuclear activities,' ElBaradei said."

Eight days after that, you were on MEET THE PRESS, and we . . . talked about that specifically. Let's watch:
(Videotape, March 16, 2003):
MR. RUSSERT: And even though the International Atomic Energy Agency said he does not have a nuclear program, we disagree.
VICE PRES. CHENEY: I disagree, yes. And you'll find the CIA, for example, and other key parts of our intelligence community, disagree. And we believe he has, in fact, reconstituted nuclear weapons. I think Mr. ElBaradei, frankly, is wrong. And I think if you look at the track record of the International Atomic Energy Agency and this kind of issue, especially where Iraq is concerned, they have consistently underestimated or missed what it was Saddam Hussein was doing. I don't have any reason to believe they're any more valid this time than they've been in the past.
(End videotape)

MR. RUSSERT: Reconstituted nuclear weapons. You misspoke.
VICE PRES. CHENEY: Yeah. I did misspeak. I said repeatedly during the show weapons capability. We never had any evidence that he had acquired a nuclear weapon.
MR. RUSSERT: Now, Ambassador Joe Wilson, a year before that, was sent over by the CIA because you raised the question about uranium from Africa. He says he came back from Niger and said that, in fact, he could not find any documentation that, in fact, Niger had sent uranium to Iraq or engaged in that activity and reported it back to the proper channels. Were you briefed on his findings in February, March of 2002?
VICE PRES. CHENEY: No. I don't know Joe Wilson. I've never met Joe Wilson. A question had arisen. I'd heard a report that the Iraqis had been trying to acquire uranium in Africa, Niger in particular. I get a daily brief on my own each day before I meet with the president to go through the intel. And I ask lots of questions. One of the questions I asked at that particular time about this, I said, "What do we know about this?" They take the question. He came back within a day or two and said, "This is all we know. There's a lot we don't know," end of statement. And Joe Wilson—I don't know who sent Joe Wilson. He never submitted a report that I ever saw when he came back.

I guess the intriguing thing, Tim, on the whole thing, this question of whether or not the Iraqis were trying to acquire uranium in Africa. In the British report, this week, the Committee of the British Parliament, which just spent 90 days investigating all of this, revalidated their British claim that Saddam was, in fact, trying to acquire uranium in Africa. What was in the State of the Union speech and what was in the original British White papers. So there may be difference of opinion there. I don't know what the truth is on the ground with respect to that, but I guess—like I say, I don't know Mr. Wilson. I probably shouldn't judge him. I have no idea who hired him and it never came . . .
MR. RUSSERT: The CIA did.
VICE PRES. CHENEY: Who in the CIA, I don't know.
MR. RUSSERT: This is what concerns people, that the administration hyped the intelligence, misled the American people. This article from **the** *Washington Post* about pressuring from Cheney visits: "Vice President Cheney and his most senior aide made multiple trips to the CIA over the past year to question analysts studying Iraq's weapons programs and alleged links to al Qaeda, creating an environment in which some analysts felt they were being pressured to make their assessments fit with the Bush administration's policy objectives, according to senior intelligence officials. With Cheney taking the

lead in the administration last August in advocating military action against Iraq by claiming it had weapons of mass destruction, the visits by the vice president and his chief of staff 'sent signals, intended or otherwise, that a certain output was desired from here,' one senior agency official said."

VICE PRES. CHENEY: In terms of asking questions, I plead guilty. I ask a hell of a lot of questions. That's my job. I've had an interest in the intelligence area since I worked for Gerry Ford 30 years ago, served on the Intel Committee in the House for years in the '80s, ran a big part of the intelligence community when I was Secretary of Defense in the early '90s. This is a very important area. It's one the president's asked me to work on, and I ask questions all the time. I think if

you're going to provide the intelligence and advice to the president of the United States to make life and death decisions, you need to be able to defend your conclusions, go into an arena where you can make the arguments about why you believe what you do based on the intelligence we've got.

MR. RUSSERT: No pressure?

VICE PRES. CHENEY: Shouldn't be any pressure. I can't think of a single instance. Maybe somebody can produce one. I'm unaware of any where the community changed a judgment that they made because I asked questions.

MR. RUSSERT: If they were wrong, Mr. Vice President, shouldn't we have a wholesale investigation into the intelligence failure that they predicted? . . .

Comment

We now know that the evidence relied on by the Bush administration to conclude that Iraq had weapons of mass destruction was faulty and some even fabricated. But the question of deception arises only if the administration knew or should have known that the claims they were making on the basis of such evidence were false. At the time they made most of these claims, Bush and his colleagues probably sincerely believed that Saddam Hussein had a substantial number of weapons of mass destruction. Whether they exaggerated the quality of the evidence or pressured intelligence officials to slant it remains controversial. But in at least one instance—the claim, highlighted in this case, that Iraq sought nuclear material from Niger—there is no doubt that the statement was believed to be misleading by many officials at the time it was made. This claim potentially counts as what might be called negligent deception—an all too common phenomenon in government, in which officials, acting without full information, make a false statement that they do not know to be false but is known by other officials to be false, and is intended by those other officials to mislead the public.

The questions we should ask in such cases are: should the official who made the statement have taken steps to verify it? Did the official create conditions that discouraged other officials from challenging the statement (or perhaps that even encouraged other officials to put forward the statement in the first place)? Did the officials who knew the statement to be false intend to mislead anyone? And did the official who made the statement, once he learned that it was false, correct the record, and take action to avoid similar deceptions in the future? In this case, if Bush could not be expected to have known, who should have known and told him? His National Security adviser and her deputy? His vice president? The director of the CIA? After the statement was challenged, Cheney continued to defend it. Is he justified in saying that the dispute is merely a "difference of opinion" and "I don't know what the truth is"?

Some might defend the statement by pointing out that it is literally true: Bush said only that the "British government had learned that . . ." and "Our intelligence sources tell us that . . ." Others argue that, though the statement may be false or misleading, it is not significant. As Tenet stated: the claim about the pursuit of uranium in Africa was "not fundamental to the judgment that Iraq was reconstituting its nuclear weapons program." To what extent do either of these arguments defend against the charge of deception?

The twist the story took in July 2004—when a Senate committee and a British commission suggested that the original statement might be true after all—prompted some defenders of the administration to call for an apology from critics who had doubted it earlier. Admittedly, anyone who at the time believed that the statement was false, and presented it as true is guilty of deception. But the president and at least some of his senior advisers believed at the time that it was true. What should matter is what the truth is, and if the president's statement is true now, it was true when it was made. Yet we may be uneasy about completely excusing officials who reach, on the basis of inadequate evidence, conclusions that happen to be true, or (as in this case) reach a conclusion that on the best available evidence at the time was regarded as probably false. Consider what if any political vices other than deception may have shown themselves in this case.

Most of the controversy about this statement and other alleged deceptions in the debate leading up to the war turned on whether the administration was misleading the public. Both sides evidently assumed that the deception would not be justified; they were arguing only about what counts as deception. But in wars in the past, presidents and other officials have believed, sometimes for good reason, that they had to make misleading or false statements (for example, to preserve the element of surprise in an attack or to protect the troops). In the case of the Iraq war, what if any circumstances would justify what kinds of deception by officials?

A Standard of Candor

THE COUNTERTERRORISM
COORDINATOR DEFENDS
AND CRITICIZES
THE BUSH ADMINISTRATION'S
ACTIONS BEFORE 9/11

More than a year after 9/11—the day in 2001 that terrorists flew planes into the World Trade Center and the Pentagon—President George W. Bush created a bipartisan commission to provide a "full and complete accounting" of the government's response to the attacks, and how to prevent such attacks in the future. The commission began its work in December 2002, and for the most part conducted its business relatively quietly until March 2004. By that time, new revelations about the failures of the government to respond to the terrorist threat and the continuing terrorist activity abroad had given the commission's task more urgency, and its proceedings more publicity. But the most important cause of the greater public attention was the publication of a new book, *Against All Enemies,* and the subsequent testimony of its author, Richard Clarke.

As the chief counterterrorism official in the White House under four presidents, Clarke was well informed and widely respected. His book was sharply critical of the Bush administration's efforts to deal with terrorism during its first eight months in office. In his book, Clarke charges that the administration failed to take al Qaeda seriously before the attacks despite "repeated warnings," and afterward tolerated a lackluster, bureaucratic response to the attacks. He wrote that Condoleezza Rice, the national security adviser, downgraded the counterterrorism office when she arrived in the White House; she even gave "the impression she had never heard the term" *al Qaeda.* As counterterrorism chief, Clarke never had the "chance to talk with [Bush] about terrorism" until after the attacks, though he had regularly briefed President Clinton on this subject. He accuses Bush and others, especially Vice President Richard Cheney and Deputy Secretary of Defense Paul Wolfowitz, of "belittling" the danger of al Qaeda and insisting that Iraq must be responsible for the attacks. Although others had made many of the same criticisms (and Bush himself had acknowledged that he did not "feel that sense of urgency" before 9/11), Clarke's account attracted greater attention because of his unique position, the forcefulness of his criticism, and the vigorous response of the White House.

When Clarke testified before the commission on March 24, 2004, several members sharply challenged his account of the Bush administration's efforts to deal with terrorist threats. Commission member James R. Thompson, former governor of Illinois, probed what he regarded as inconsistencies between Clarke's book and his testimony to the commission (which were both very critical of the Bush administration), and his earlier statements in a press briefing in October 2002 and other settings (which were more positive). Clarke denied that there were inconsistencies, but acknowledged that while he was still working for the administration, he believed that he had an obligation "to put the best face" on the facts that he could for the administration. "I was asked to highlight the positive . . . and to minimize the negative. . . ." To Thompson, that suggested that "there is one standard of candor and morality for White House special assistants and another . . . for the rest of America."

CLARKE'S TESTIMONY

The following is an excerpt from the transcript of hearings by the National Commission on Terrorist Attacks Upon the United States: March 24, 2004

JAMES R. THOMPSON, Commission member [former Gov. of Illinois]

RICHARD CLARKE, former National Coordinator for Counterterrorism for National Security Council

THOMPSON: Mr. Clarke, as we sit here this afternoon, we have your book and we have your press briefing of August 2002. Which is true?

CLARKE: Well, I think the question is a little misleading.

The press briefing you're referring to comes in the following context: *Time* magazine had published a cover story article highlighting what your staff briefing talks about. They had learned that, as your staff briefing notes, that there was a strategy or a plan and a series of additional options that were presented to the national security adviser and the new Bush team when they came into office.

Time magazine ran a somewhat sensational story that implied that the Bush administration hadn't worked on that plan. And this, of course, coming after 9/11 caused the Bush White House a great deal of concern.

So I was asked by several people in senior levels of the Bush White House to do a press backgrounder to try to explain that set of facts in a way that minimized criticism of the administration. And so I did.

Now, we can get into semantic games of whether it was a strategy, or whether it was a plan, or whether it was a series of options to be decided upon. I think the facts are as they were outlined in your staff briefing.

THOMPSON: Well, let's take a look, then, at your press briefing, because I don't want to engage in semantic games. You said, the Bush administration decided, then, you know, mid-January—that's mid-January, 2001—to do 2 things: one, vigorously pursue the existing the policy—that would be the Clinton policy—including all of the lethal covert action findings which we've now made public to some extent. Is that so? Did they decide in January of 2001 to vigorously pursue the existing Clinton policy?

CLARKE: They decided that the existing covert action findings would remain in effect.

THOMPSON: OK. The second thing the administration decided to do is to initiate a process to look at those issues which had been on the table for a couple of years and get them decided. Now, that seems to indicate to me that proposals had been sitting on the table in the Clinton administration for a couple of years, but that the Bush administration was going to get them done. Is that a correct assumption?

CLARKE: Well, that was my hope at the time. It turned out not to be the case.

THOMPSON: Well, then why in August of 2002, over a year later, did you say that it was the case?

CLARKE: I was asked to make that case to the press. I was a special assistant to the president, and I made the case I was asked to make.

THOMPSON: Are you saying you were asked to make an untrue case to the press and the public, and that you went ahead and did it?

CLARKE: No, sir. Not untrue. Not an untrue case. I was asked to highlight the positive aspects of what the administration had done and to minimize the negative aspects of what the administration had done. And as a special assistant to the president, one is frequently asked to do that kind of thing. I've done it for several presidents.

. . .

THOMPSON: So you believed that your conference with the press in August of 2002 is consistent with what you've said in your book and what you've said in press interviews the last five days about your book?

CLARKE: I do. I think the thing that's obviously bothering you is the tenor and the tone. And I've tried to explain to you, sir, that when you're on the staff of the president of the United States, you try to make his policies look as good as possible.

THOMPSON: Well, with all respect, Mr. Clarke, I think a lot of things beyond the tenor and the tone bother me about this.

. . .

THOMPSON: Mr. Clarke, in this background briefing, as Senator Kerry has now described it, for the press in August of 2002, you intended to mislead the press, did you not?

CLARKE: No. I think there is a very fine line that anyone who's been in the White House, in any administration, can tell you about. And that is when you are special assistant to the president and you're asked to explain something that is potentially embarrassing to the administration, because the administration didn't do enough or didn't do it in a timely manner and is taking political heat for it, as was the case there, you have a choice. Actually, I think you have three choices. You can resign rather than do it. I chose not to do that. Second choice is . . .

THOMPSON: Why was that, Mr. Clarke? You finally resigned because you were frustrated.

CLARKE: I was, at that time, at the request of the president, preparing a national strategy to defend America's cyberspace, something which I thought then and think now is vitally important. I thought that completing that strategy was a lot more important than whether or not I had to provide emphasis in one place or other while discussing the facts on this particular news story.

The second choice one has, Governor, is whether or not to say things that are untruthful. And no one in the Bush White House asked me to say things that were untruthful, and I would not have said them.

In any event, the third choice that one has is to put the best face you can for the administration on the facts as they were, and that is what I did.

I think that is what most people in the White House in any administration do when they're asked to explain something that is embarrassing to the administration.

THOMPSON: But you will admit that what you said in August of 2002 is inconsistent with what you say in your book?

CLARKE: No, I don't think it's inconsistent at all. I think, as I said in your last round of questioning, Governor, that it's really a matter here of emphasis and tone. I mean, what you're suggesting, perhaps, is that as special assistant to the president of the United States when asked to give a press backgrounder I should spend my time in that press backgrounder criticizing him. I think that's somewhat of an unrealistic thing to expect.

THOMPSON: Well, what it suggests to me is that there is one standard of candor and morality for White House special assistants and another standard of candor and morality for the rest of America.

CLARKE: I don't get that.

CLARKE: I don't think it's a question of morality at all. I think it's a question of politics.

THOMPSON: Well, I . . .

(APPLAUSE)

THOMPSON: I'm not a Washington insider. I've never been a special assistant in the White House. I'm from the Midwest. So I think I'll leave it there.

CLARKE'S BOOK

The following are quotations from Richard Clarke's Against All Enemies *(New York: Simon and Schuster, 2004):*

George W. Bush . . . failed to act prior to September 11 on the threat from al Qaeda despite repeated warnings and then harvested a political windfall for taking obvious yet insufficient steps after the attacks, and who launched an unnecessary and costly war in Iraq that strengthen the fundamentalist, radical Islamic terrorist movement worldwide (p. x).

Clinton left office with bin Laden alive, but having authorized actions to eliminate him and to step up the attacks on al Qaeda. . . . He had seen earlier than anyone that terrorism would be the major new threat facing America, and therefore had greatly increased funding for counterterrorism and initiated homeland protection programs. . . . [H]e put in place the plans and programs that allowed America to respond to the big attacks when

they did come, sweeping away the political barriers to action.

When Clinton left office many people, including the incoming Bush administration leadership, thought that he and his administration were overly obsessed with al Qaeda. After all, al Qaeda had killed only a few Americans. . . . In January 2001, the new administration really thought Clinton's recommendation that eliminating al Qaeda be one of their highest priorities, well, rather odd, like so many of the Clinton administration's actions, from their perspective (pp. 225–26).

CLARKE'S PRESS BRIEFING

The following are excerpts from a transcript of a background briefing that Richard Clarke gave to a small group of reporters with the approval of the White House in early August 2002. At the time Clarke was still working for the administration, but he had resigned as counterterrorism chief, and had been serving as special adviser to the president for cyberspace security since October 2001. He resigned from that post in January 2003.

CLARKE: Actually, I've got about seven points, let me just go through them quickly. Um, the first point, I think the overall point is, there was no plan on Al Qaeda that was passed from the Clinton administration to the Bush administration.

Second point is that the Clinton administration had a strategy in place, effectively dating from 1998. And there were a number of issues on the table since 1998. And they remained on the table when that administration went out of office—issues like aiding the Northern Alliance in Afghanistan, changing our Pakistan policy—uh, changing our policy toward Uzbekistan. And in January 2001, the incoming Bush administration was briefed on the existing strategy. They were also briefed on these series of issues that had not been decided on in a couple of years.

And the third point is the Bush administration decided then, you know, in late January, to do two things. One, vigorously pursue the existing policy, including all of the lethal covert action findings, which we've now made public to some extent.

And the point is, while this big review was going on, there were still in effect, the lethal findings were still in effect. The second thing the administration decided to do is to initiate a process to look at those issues which had been on the table for a couple of years and get them decided.

So, point five, that process which was initiated in the first week in February, uh, decided in principle, uh, in the spring to add to the existing Clinton strategy and to increase CIA resources, for example, for covert action, five-fold, to go after Al Qaeda.

The sixth point, the newly-appointed deputies—and you had to remember, the deputies didn't get into office until late March, early April. The deputies then tasked the development of the implementation details, uh, of these new decisions that they were endorsing, and sending out to the principals.

Over the course of the summer—last point—they developed implementation details, the principals met at the end of the summer, approved them in their first meeting, changed the strategy by authorizing the increase in funding five-fold, changing the policy on Pakistan, changing the policy on Uzbekistan, changing the policy on the Northern Alliance assistance.

And then changed the strategy from one of rollback with Al Qaeda over the course of five years, which it had been, to a new strategy that called for the rapid elimination of Al Qaeda. That is in fact the timeline.

QUESTION: When was that presented to the president?

CLARKE: Well, the president was briefed throughout this process.

QUESTION: But when was the final September 4 document? (interrupted) Was that presented to the president?

CLARKE: The document went to the president on September 10, I think.

QUESTION: What is your response to the suggestion in the [Aug. 12, 2002] *Time* [magazine] article that the Bush administration was unwilling to take on board the suggestions made in the Clinton administration because of animus against the—general animus against the foreign policy?

CLARKE: I think if there was a general animus that clouded their vision, they might not have kept the same guy dealing with terrorism issue. This is the one issue where the National Security Council leadership decided continuity was important and kept the same guy around, the same team in place. That doesn't sound like animus against uh the previous team to me.

QUESTION: You're saying that the Bush administration did not stop anything that the Clinton administration was doing while it was making these decisions, and by the end of the summer had increased money for covert action five-fold. Is that correct?

. . .

CLARKE: All of that's correct.

QUESTION: So, just to finish up if we could then, so what you're saying is that there was no—one, there was no plan; two, there was no delay; and that actually the first changes since October of '98 were made in the spring months just after the administration came into office?

CLARKE: You got it. That's right.

QUESTION: It was not put into an action plan until September 4, signed off by the principals?

CLARKE: That's right.

Comment

Clarke was widely regarded in government as someone who would "tell it like it is," without regard to what his superiors or anyone else might think. Thompson's suggestion that in either the book or his earlier press conference Clarke had not been truthful was therefore especially striking. And so was Clarke's acknowledgement that he had "highlight[ed] the positive . . . and minimize[ed] the negative aspects of what the administration had done." Even the most honorable officials sometimes bend the truth, for good and bad reasons. And even accusations brought for the most political motives may be valid. The question is whether Clarke engaged in deception, and if so was it excusable or justifiable?

The first task in analyzing a case of this kind is to try to determine whether the statements Clarke made in the press briefing and those he made in the book are inconsistent, as Thompson maintained. (We include only excerpts from the book, but they should be sufficient to indicate the general view expressed there.) Do not let the dispute about terminology—was it a "plan" or only a "strategy"?—distract you from the main issue: was Clarke's view about the Bush administration's effort so much more positive in the press briefing than in the book as to count as deceptive? It was evidently more positive in the press briefing, but was it so much more so that it was deceptive? Politicians and other officials often try to "put the best face" they can "on the facts as they are." That is not only unavoidable in politics but also to some degree desirable. We have to ask how much spin (and for what reasons and under what conditions) is morally acceptable (or excusable).

If Clarke did not present the whole truth in the press briefing, is he right that his role as special assistant justified his actions? It is certainly "unrealistic" to expect a special assistant to the President "to spend . . . time in [a] press backgrounder criticizing him." But consider whether that (or resignation) was Clarke's only alternative.

Thompson evidently believes that Clarke's justification implies that White House special assistants (and presumably others in similar roles) are held to lower standards of "candor and morality" than "the rest of America." Is that a necessary implication of Clarke's justification? Officials have some obligations that private citizens do not have, but former officials also may have distinctive obligations, including a duty to contribute to public debate on issues about which they have special knowledge.

Why does it matter whether Clarke's earlier and later views are inconsistent? The inconsistency (to the extent that it exists) may reflect on his character, but it does not necessarily discredit his claim that the Bush administration did not devote enough attention to counterterrorism. The moral focus shifts when we judge his contribution to the public debate on the administration's policy on terrorism rather than his character. Some might argue that Thompson's line of questioning (perhaps deliberately) distracted the hearing from this substantive issue. In reply, Thompson might well contend that because Clarke's testimony was so important to reaching a judgment about that issue, his credibility was not only a legitimate but an essential subject for the hearings.

A Tale of Two Task Forces*

HILLARY CLINTON'S TASK FORCE

President Bill Clinton created the now notorious task force on National Health Care Reform on January 25, 1993. He appointed his wife, Hillary Clinton, chair of the task force, which consisted of top cabinet members and White House advisors. He directed the task force to "listen to all parties" and then "prepare health care reform legislation to be submitted to Congress within 100 days of our taking office."

On the same day, the president also formed an interdepartmental working group, which was to be responsible for gathering information and researching health care policy alternatives. The working group consisted of (1) several hundred permanent federal employees, (2) about forty "special government employees" hired by federal agencies and the Executive Office for a limited time, and (3) an indefinite number of consultants who were to attend the working group sessions intermittently. Ira Magaziner, the senior advisor to the president for policy development, headed the working group. He was the only member of the task force who attended the working group meetings. The president himself had no direct contact with the working group.

With the exception of a single meeting—held on March 29, 1993, at which interested parties were invited to contribute recommendations—all of the task force's meetings were closed to the public. The working group meetings were also held behind closed doors. The task force dissolved on May 30th after presenting its recommendations to the president.

While the task force was still active, several groups—including the Association of American Physicians and Surgeons (AAPS), which represents physicians, and the American Council for Health Care Reform, which represents health care consumers—tried to gain access to its meetings. They cited the Federal Advisory Committee Act of 1972 (FACA), which stipulated that advisory committees must remain open to public scrutiny. Congress passed FACA in 1972 to control the growth and operation of the "numerous committees, boards, commissions, councils, and similar groups which have been established to advise

officers and agencies in the executive branch of the Federal Government." FACA allowed an exemption for "any committee which is composed wholly of full-time officers or employees of the Federal Government." Citing this exemption, the Clinton administration denied the AAPS and allied groups access to the meetings, and these groups then filed a suit against the task force in district court.

The AAPS argued that the task force should not be exempt from FACA because Hillary Clinton herself was not a federal employee. It also claimed that the working groups should also be open to the public because they had hired private consultants. Behind these technical claims lay the broader assertion that information gathering and policy formulation should remain accessible to citizens. Public scrutiny would, among other things, ensure that the advisory committees consulted a broad range of expert opinions. It would help keep the government accountable to the public interest.

The president's lawyers defended the secrecy of the Task Force and the working groups using several separate lines of argument. First, they argued that public scrutiny of the president's interactions with his close advisors (the task force) was unconstitutional and would interfere with the president's ability to receive confidential advice vital to carrying out his executive responsibilities. Second, they maintained that the working groups only served to gather information and were therefore not real advisory committees (and not subject to FACA).

While waiting for the case to come to trial, the plaintiffs sought a temporary injunction allowing them access to the task force meetings. The district court issued an equivocal response, ruling that the task force itself was subject to the FACA, but only when it was not directly advising the president. It also ruled that the working groups, because they were fact-gathering organs and not advisory committees, could remain closed to the public. When the case came to trial in the circuit court, the verdict

---

*Alex Zakaras wrote the introductions and selected the excerpts presented in this section.

(issued in June of 1993) was more favorable to the Clinton administration: it established that the task force was in fact protected from public scrutiny because of its close proximity to the president.

AMICI CURIAE BRIEF BY THE REPORTERS COMMITTEE FOR FREEDOM OF THE PRESS, RADIO-TELEVISION NEWS DIRECTORS ASSOCIATION, NEWSLETTER PUBLISHERS ASSOCIATION, INC., AMERICAN SOCIETY OF NEWSPAPER EDITORS, SOCIETY OF PROFESSIONAL JOURNALISTS AND THE ASSOCIATED PRESS (APRIL 5, 1993)

In order to insure meaningful public access to the President's Task Force on National Health Care Reform, the Federal Advisory Committee Act (FACA) must apply to the Task Force interdepartmental working group.

Application of the FACA to the Task Force's interdepartmental working groups ("working groups") is essential to achieving the openness and accountability of the Task Force mandated by the FACA. The court below correctly recognized the FACA's goal of openness, stating that it was intended "to increase the accountability of advisory committees by opening their meetings to the general public and forcing disclosure of their purpose, membership, costs, and activities." This openness is vital to the role of the news media in informing and educating the public about issues of national concern. . . .

Issues of national health care reform are of vital importance to the American people. Their participation in the formulation of a national health care plan is essential to the democratic process. News media access is particularly important because many persons rely on press reports, television and radio broadcasts and trade journals for information concerning advisory committee actions. The news media have a "statutory right under the (FACA) as well as a First Amendment privilege to report on the manner in which Government affairs are conducted."

Appellants . . . make many references in their brief to the high priority given to their mission. This view of the critical nature of our nation's health care is shared by the American public. The President himself recognizes Americans' overwhelming concerns about the cost and availability of health care in the United States. (Remarks on Health Care Reform and an Exchange with Reporters, January 25, 1993, 29 weekly Compilation of Presidential Documents 96, February 1, 1993.) The extensive news coverage of the creation of the Task Force and of its . . . work is a result of the public's desire to be informed about the Task Force's progress.

Without reporting by the nation's news media, Americans would have little means of learning about the Task Force's work. Indeed, were this holding applied to media access to other advisory committees, the public would be cut off from an enormous part of the governmental process. The number of advisory committees created each year bears witness to the importance of these committees to the formulation of national policies. During fiscal year 1992, for example, 64 federal departments and agencies sponsored 1,230 advisory committees, which were composed of a total of 29,020 individuals, held 4,645 meetings and issued 1,241 reports. Issues of national importance addressed by advisory committees include AIDS, homelessness, drug abuse and environmental contamination. . . . News media access to the Health Care Task Force and advisory committees in general is essential to an informed public.

The court below, however, thwarted the goals of the FACA in this case. After deciding that the FACA applied to the Task Force, the court decided that the working groups were not subject to the FACA because they were not created by the President and were only fact-gathering groups. This holding denies the public access to the testimony of private citizens before the Task Force's working groups on issues which affect their health and economic well-being. The news media, likewise, are denied the ability to report these events to the public. . . .

The working groups, composed of government employees and outside consultants, play an essential role in the Task Force's duties. The President's spokesman, in his press briefing after the district court's decision, said that the working groups do all the "nuts and bolts" work of the Task Force—"that is always how it was contemplated."

By the administration's own admission, the working groups are the heart of the Task Force; to exclude them from public scrutiny is to severely limit the public's view. . . . The Health Care Task Force's working groups, which were created by the president for the purpose of gathering information into reports for his review and for review by the Task Force, perform the type of functions that by law must be open to public view. To hold otherwise is to render meaningless the intent of the FACA. . . .

The lower court's analysis is flawed because it fails to distinguish the uncontested ability of the President to consult with his advisors at will from the legally mandated requirement that formal committee meetings be held in public view. The FACA does not in any way limit the President's right to confer with advisors behind closed doors; rather, it simply mandates that should the President create a formal committee structure to approach an issue of national concern, the work and process of the committee and its subgroups should not be shrouded in secrecy away from public view. Limiting the public's access to only those meetings where facts are gathered bars the public from the policy making process that results from the evaluation of those facts. This violates the spirit and the intent of the FACA. Because separation of powers is not violated in providing the openness Congress intended, the FACA is not unconstitutional as applied in this case, and should be applied to the Task Force without limitation.

EXCERPTS FROM JUDGE LAURENCE SILBERMAN'S OPINION

AAPS et al. v. Hillary Rodham Clinton, D.C. Circuit Court, Decided June 22, 1993

Applying FACA to the Task Force does not raise constitutional problems simply because the Task Force is involved in proposing legislation. Instead, difficulties arise because of the Task Force's operational proximity to the President himself—that is, because the Task Force provides advice and recommendations directly to the President. The Supreme Court has recognized that a President has a great need to receive advice confidentially:

> [There is a] valid need for protection of communications between high Government officials and those who advise and assist them in the performance of their manifold duties; the importance of this confidentiality is too plain to require further discussion. Human experience teaches that those who expect public dissemination of their remarks may well temper candor with a concern for appearances and for their own interests to the detriment of the decision-making process. Whatever the nature of the privilege of confidentiality of Presidential communications in the exercise of Article II powers, the privilege can be said to derive from the supremacy of each branch within its own assigned area of constitutional duties. [*United States v. Nixon,* 418 U. S. 683, 70506 (1974)]

Article II not only gives the President the ability to consult with his advisers confidentially, but also, as a corollary, it gives him the flexibility to organize his advisers and seek advice from them as he wishes. . . . In this regard, FACA's requirement that an advisory committee must be "fairly balanced in terms of the view represented" would—if enforceable and applied to groups of presidential advisers—restrict the President's ability to seek advice from whom and in the fashion he chooses. The ability to discuss matters confidentially is surely an important condition to the exercise of executive power. Without it, the President's performance of any of his duties—textually explicit or implicit in Article II's grant of executive power—would be made more difficult. In designing the Constitution, the Framers vested the executive power in one man for the very reason that he might maintain secrecy in executive operations. As Alexander Hamilton wrote in the Federalist Papers:

> Decision, activity, secrecy, and dispatch will generally characterize [*sic*] the proceedings of one man, in a much more eminent degree, than the proceedings of any greater number; and in proportion as the number is increased, these qualities will be diminished. THE FEDERALIST No. 70, at 472 (J. Cooke, ed.,1961)

The Framers thus understood that secrecy was related to the executive's ability to decide and to act quickly—a quality lacking in the government established by the Articles of Confederation. If a President cannot deliberate in confidence, it is hard to imagine how he can decide and act quickly.

This Article II right to confidential communications attaches not only to direct communications with the President, but also to discussions between his senior advisers. Certainly Department Secretaries and White House aides must be able to hold confidential meetings to discuss advice they secretly will render to the President. . . . A statute interfering with a President's ability to seek advice directly from private citizens as a group, intermixed, or not, with government officials, therefore raises Article II concerns. This is all the more so when the sole ground for asserting that the statute applies is that the President's own spouse, a member of the Task Force, is not a government official. For if the President seeks advice from those closest to him, whether in or out of government, the President's spouse, typically, would be regarded as among those closest advisers. . . .

We believe it is the Task Force's operational proximity to the President, and not its exact function at any given moment, that implicates executive powers. . . . The President's confidentiality interest is strong regardless of the particular role the Task Force is playing on any given day. Indeed, the two functions naturally interrelate and can only be divided artificially. If public disclosure of the real information-gathering process is required, the confidentiality of the advice-giving function inevitably would be compromised.

DICK CHENEY'S TASK FORCE

Shortly after taking office in 2001, President George W. Bush created the National Energy Policy Development Group (NEPDG), a council of advisors who would make recommendations to him in the area of energy policy. Bush appointed Vice President Dick Cheney to chair the group, which was to consist of top administration officials, including the secretaries of the Interior, of Energy, of Commerce, and others. In May of 2001, the Bush administration submitted its completed National Energy Policy to Congress. Though the policy was never fully enacted into law, Democrats in Congress began to raise questions about the policy's origins and development.

Representatives John D. Dingell and Henry A. Waxman raised concerns that the NEPDG's meetings "had included exclusive groups of non-governmental participants— including political contributors—to discuss specific policies, rules, regulations, and legislation." Prominent Democrats and environmental groups throughout the country also challenged the policy on these grounds, complaining that the composition of the group showed bias in favor of the interests of the energy industry (and against environmental concerns). The *San Francisco Chronicle* later reported that executives of the Enron energy corporation—a major contributor to Bush's political campaigns and a company destroyed by corporate fraud—had exerted direct influence on the content of the energy policy.

Dingell and Waxman argued that the public had a right to know how the administration had gone about formulating its policy recommendations. Democracy, in their view, required that the process of policy making—not only its results—remain open to public scrutiny. They therefore asked the

General Accounting Office (GAO) to undertake an investigation of the NEPDG. They asked the administration to reveal the identities of its members, the attendees at its meetings, the dates and locations of these meetings, and the criteria by which "nonfederal entities" had been selected for participation. The GAO began an investigation in May 2001. (The GAO is an instrument of the Legislative Branch, established in 1921 to review the management of public funds and conduct investigations of public expenditures for Congress' benefit.)

Cheney argued that the GAO's inquiry was unconstitutional and potentially damaging to the presidency. He argued that it threatened the president's ability to solicit confidential information from top advisors and violated the principle of separation of powers. If each of its interactions with advisors and experts were subject to intense public scrutiny, the executive would find itself unduly constrained—there would be a "chilling effect," on the president's interaction with his advisors. At issue here were the crucial issues of publicity and confidentiality: how much protection from public scrutiny should the president, his cabinet, and his advisors, enjoy while they were gathering information and preparing drafts of legislation? Unable to persuade Cheney to release the documents, the GAO, in February 2002, took the unprecedented step of filing a lawsuit against the administration. The lawsuit was decided in favor of the administration by U.S. District Court Judge John Bates. Bates ruled that the courts should refrain from intervening in such delicate constitutional matters involving the separation and balance of power, especially considering that the plaintiff has suffered no direct injury. The comptroller general of the GAO, David Walker, decided not to appeal the decision (citing lack of support among Republican congressional leaders), though he felt that the court's ruling would undermine Congress' investigative power and encourage executive secrecy. A separate lawsuit, filed jointly by Judicial Watch

and the Sierra Club with the aim of forcing the administration to disclose these identities, was taken up by the Supreme Court in 2004 and sent back to the district court for further review.

The arguments offered on both sides of this case are similar to those given in 1993 about President Clinton's Task Force on National Health Care Reform. The extent of secrecy, however, differs. The Clinton administration complied with a separate GAO investigation of its Task Force and published the names of the nongovernmental consultants hired by the working group. Cheney has not revealed the names of the NEPDG's nongovernmental consultants, and has maintained that these should remain secret.

VICE PRESIDENT CHENEY'S BRIEF (U.S. DISTRICT COURT, MAY 21, 2002)

Comptroller general David M. Walker seeks to place this Court in the middle of an asserted inter-branch dispute over access to executive branch documents. Specifically, he sought (and continues to seek), based on a request from two individual legislators, documents from the Vice President regarding the process by which the Vice President and top presidential advisers assisted the President in the development of the President's National Energy Policy. In response, the Vice President explained that the Comptroller General's request exceeded his statutory authority and sought unconstitutionally to interfere with the functioning of the presidency. . . .

The Vice President's Message to the House and Senate stated clearly why the Comptroller General's suit cannot stand as a matter of Constitutional Law:

> If the Comptroller General's misconstruction of the statutes . . . were to prevail, his conduct would unconstitutionally interfere with the functioning of the Executive Branch. For example, due regard for the constitutional separation of powers requires respecting the independence of the President, the Vice President and the President's other senior advisers as they execute the function of developing

recommendations for policy and legislation—a core constitutional function of the Executive Branch. Also, preservation of the ability of the Executive Branch to function effectively requires respecting the confidentiality of communications among a President, a Vice President, the President's other senior advisers and others. A President and his senior advisers must be able to work in an atmosphere that respects confidentiality of communications if the President is to get good, candid advice and other information upon which wise decision-making depends. . . .

The Comptroller General alleges a right to documents concerning the discharge of the President's constitutional functions in the possession of the President's closest advisers, and indeed the President himself. That alleged right is completely inconsistent with the constitutional system of separation of powers. . . .

There can be no question that the virtually unlimited right of access that the Comptroller General asserts would significantly interfere with the process by which the Executive Branch obtains information and exercises its constitutional functions. As the D. C. Circuit has explained, the "mere presence" of legislative agents, even if they "remain completely silent," has significant "potential to influence" the decision-making process that they are observing. The chilling effect recognized by the D. C. Circuit will be no different if the stages of the decision-making process are reviewed after the fact than if the observations occur while the decision-making process is still ongoing.

Indeed, plaintiff's own arguments contemplate the aggressive regulation of the President's information-gathering and policy-developing powers. He contends that Congress needs to know about the behind-the-scenes operation of the NEPDG to evaluate "the desirability of additional appropriations restrictions to control the use of public money for energy policy development in the future." Furthermore, he assumes that Congress could impose such

restrictions on the Executive to prevent "establishment[s] within the White House" from being "responsib[le] for energy policy development." . . .

Even if this Court balances the intrusion on executive power with the legislative interest at stake, . . . the Comptroller General's asserted authority would be just as unconstitutional. The threat to the President posed by this case is great because the intrusion is so extensive. On the other hand, the Legislature has no legitimate interest in the information the Comptroller General seeks, and has other means to pursue it in any event. . . .

The Comptroller General's asserted authority to intrude into the President's methods of informing himself for the purpose of proposing policy initiatives "'impermissibly undermine[s]' the powers of the Executive Branch, . . . or 'disrupts the proper balance between the coordinate branches.'" It is hard to imagine a more direct assault on the President's core executive powers than the asserted authority of a congressional agent to superintend the deliberative process by which the Vice President and others formulated policy recommendations for and on behalf of the President. The information that the Comptroller General seeks would expose information-gathering and policy-making activities (including deliberations) at the heart of the Executive Branch. Despite his protestations of restraint, the broad categories of information plaintiff requests in this lawsuit speak for themselves. He asks this Court to require disclosure of everyone that the Vice President met with while he was serving as a close presidential adviser discharging express constitutional functions at the request of the President, the "purpose" and "agenda" of each of those meetings, and even what decision-making process the Vice President and his staff followed in "determin[ing] who would be invited to the meetings." . . .

The Comptroller General's asserted authority strikes at the heart of the Executive's constitutional functions. At a minimum, it would intrude upon powers that are textually committed to the Executive—a result that, even taken alone, must weigh heavily in the balance (if it does not dispose of the need for the balancing). Moreover, . . . plaintiff's action "implicates executive powers" because it would interfere with a group that has "operational proximity to the President." In addition, plaintiff's claim would compromise executive branch deliberations by undercutting the President's well-recognized need for confidentiality. (See, e. g., *United States v. Nixon*, 418 U. S. 683, 708 (1974): "A President and those who assist him must be free to explore alternatives in the process of shaping policies and making decisions and to do so in a way many would be unwilling to express except privately.") [In a 1997 case, a district judge commented:] "[T] he critical role that confidentiality plays in ensuring an adequate exploration of alternatives cannot be gainsaid. If presidential advisers must assume they will be held to account publicly for all approaches that were advanced, considered but ultimately rejected, they will almost inevitably be inclined to avoid serious consideration of novel or controversial approaches to presidential problems." As the court in AAPS explained, "[A] group directly reporting [to] and advising the President must have confidentiality in each stage in the formulation of advice to him." But requiring "disclosure of the real information-gathering process" would "inevitably . . . compromise" the "confidentiality of the advice-giving function." The Comptroller General's claim in this case would compromise the confidentiality of advice within the Executive Branch because he asserts, after all, the authority to investigate not only the "results" of the NEPDG's deliberations, but also the deliberative "process" itself.

Against those great intrusions, plaintiff can offer no bona fide congressional interests. As an initial matter, Congress's legitimate interests are non-existent when it comes to investigating the discharge of functions within the exclusive province of another branch. Congress's non-textual investigative authority is derivative of its legislative authority and Congress could not validly regulate the process by which the Vice President and President formulate presidential recommendations. Notwithstanding that limitation, plaintiff has suggested several hypothetical reasons why Congress might be interested in the process by which the NEPDG developed its policy recommendations. By and large, those conjectural interests rely on untenable assumptions about Congress's powers—for example, that Congress needs to know whether the NEPDG consulted with a sufficient number of people so that it can determine whether it should exercise its purported power to "attach riders to appropriations laws that prohibit the executive branch from developing comprehensive energy policies through private task force meetings with only selected members of the public." . . .

Even if plaintiff could identify some legitimate legislative interest in the information, that peripheral interest would clearly be insufficiently weighty to justify intrusion upon the President's exercise of his constitutional powers and his interest in confidential information-gathering and deliberations. . . .

Congress has already received the most important information it needs to accomplish its legislative functions: the President's actual policy proposals and initiatives, along with his judgment that those measures are necessary and expedient. Congress may use that information to reach its own independent conclusions about the recommendations. It can also obtain information to assist that process from its own sources, and does not need to know what sources were used in the development of the NEPDG's recommendations. Even so, if Congress truly is interested in further details about the President's proposals and initiatives, it may attempt to employ its own information-gathering powers. . . .

REPRESENTATIVE HENRY
A. WAXMAN'S REMARKS TO CONGRESS
(FEBRUARY 12, 2003)*

Last Friday, February 7, the General Accounting Office abandoned its efforts to obtain basic records about the operations of the White House task force on energy policy. This action received only limited attention, and few people fully understand its profound consequences.

When we have divided government, the public can expect Congress to conduct needed oversight over the Executive Branch. But today we are living in an era of one-party control. This means the House and the Senate aren't going to conduct meaningful oversight of the Bush Administration.

When there is one-party control of both the White House and Congress, there is only one entity that can hold the Administration accountable . . . and that is the independent General Accounting Office.

But now GAO has been forced to surrender this fundamental independence.

When GAO decided not to appeal the district court decision in *Walker v. Cheney,* it crossed a divide. In the Comptroller General's words, GAO will now require "an affirmative statement of support from at least one full committee with jurisdiction over any records access matter prior to any future court action by GAO." Translated, what this means is that GAO will bring future actions to enforce its rights to documents only with the blessing of the majority party in Congress. This is a fundamental shift in our systems of checks and balances. For all practical purposes, the Bush Administration is now immune from effective oversight by any body in Congress.

Some people say GAO should never have brought legal action to obtain information about the energy task force headed by Vice President Cheney. But in reality, GAO had no choice. The Bush Administration's penchant for secrecy has been demonstrated time and again. The Department of Justice has issued a directive curtailing public access to information under the Freedom of

---

*Available at www.fas.org/sgp/congress/2003/h0212 03.html.

Information Act. The White House has restricted access to presidential records. The Administration has refused to provide information about the identity of over 1,000 individuals detained in the name of homeland security. The White House deliberately picked this fight with GAO because it wants to run the government in secret.

GAO's efforts to obtain information about the Cheney task force began with a routine request. The task force was formed in January 2001 to make recommendations about the nation's energy future. During the course of the task force's deliberations, the press reported that major campaign contributors had special access to the task force while environmental organizations, consumer groups, and the public were shut out. Rep. Dingell, the ranking member of the Energy and Commerce Committee, and I felt that Congress and the public had the right to know whether and to what extent the task force's energy recommendations may have been influenced by well-connected outside parties. Accordingly, we asked GAO to obtain some basic information on the energy task force's operations, such as who was present at each meeting of the task force, who were the professional staff, who did the Vice President and task force staff meet with, and what costs were incurred as part of the process. We did not request, and GAO did not seek, information on internal communications.

From the start, the White House assumed a hostile and uncompromising position, arguing that GAO's investigation "would unconstitutionally interfere with the functioning of the Executive Branch." Stand-offs between Congress and the White House are not new, of course. Typically, they are resolved through hard bargaining and compromise. But the White House made clear that it wasn't willing to bargain or to compromise. Even when GAO voluntarily scaled back its request—dropping its request for minutes and notes—the Vice President's office was intransigent.

The White House's contempt for legitimate congressional requests for information was apparent even in the one area in which it conceded GAO's authority. The Vice President acknowledged that GAO was entitled to review the costs associated with the task force. However, the only information he provided to GAO about costs were 77 pages of random documents. Some of the pages consisted of simply numbers or dollar amounts without an explanation of what the money was for; other pages consisted only of a drawing of cellular or desk phones. Without an explanation—which the Administration refused to provide, of course—the information was utterly useless.

The statutes governing GAO's authority spell out an elaborate process which the agency must follow before initiating any litigation against the Executive Branch. The statute even gives the White House authority to block litigation by certifying that disclosure "reasonably could be expected to impair substantially the operations of the Government."

In this case, GAO followed the letter and the spirit of that statute, even giving the White House an opportunity to file a certification. But the White House position was that GAO had no right even to ask for documents. Faced with an Administration that had no interest in reaching an accommodation, GAO was left with a stark choice: GAO could drop the matter, effectively conceding the White House's position that it was immune from oversight, or it could invoke its statutory authority to sue the Executive Branch. Reluctantly, on February 22, 2002, GAO filed its first-ever suit against the Executive Branch to obtain access to information.

It's not hard to figure out why the White House was so eager to pick a fight with GAO. After all, GAO provides the muscle for Congress' oversight function. Over the past century, Congress has increasingly turned to GAO to monitor and oversee an Executive Branch that has ballooned in size and strength. Moreover, because it has earned a reputation for fairness and independence, GAO is particularly threatening to an Administration that doesn't want to be challenged on any front.

GAO's effort failed at the trial level. In December, the district court in the case issued a sweeping decision in favor of the Bush Administration, ruling that GAO has no standing to sue the Executive Branch. The judge who wrote the decision was a recent Bush appointee who served as a deputy to Ken Starr during the independent counsel investigation of the Clinton Administration. The judge's reasoning contorted the law, and it ignored both Supreme Court and appellate court precedent recognizing GAO's right to use the courts to enforce its statutory rights to information.

This brings us to last week. Before deciding whether to pursue an appeal, the Comptroller General consulted with congressional leaders. He found no support among Republican leaders for an appeal. And he decided not to appeal.

The judge's ruling raised major institutional issues about Congress' power to investigate the Executive Branch. But Republican leaders put party ahead of the institution and partisanship ahead of principle.

The hypocrisy about this issue on the Republican side is simply breathtaking. During the 1990s, it was Republicans in Congress who embarked on a concerted effort to undermine the authority of the President. Congressional committees spent over $15 million investigating the White House. They demanded—and received— information on the innermost workings of the White House. They subpoenaed top White House officials to testify about the advice they gave the President. They forced the White House to disclose internal White House documents—memos, e-mails, phone records, even lists of guests at White House movie showings. And they launched countless GAO investigations into everything from President Clinton's Health Care

Task Force to his working group on China Permanent Normal Trade Relations.

And if the White House resisted, these same leaders insisted that Congress and the public's right to know was paramount. Defending his numerous demands for White House records, for example, Rep. Dan Burton insisted on the House floor that "public disclosure of the facts is the essence and in large part the purpose of congressional oversight. The American people have a right to know the facts." And other Republican leaders reiterated this message over and over again on countless television talk shows.

But now that President Bush and Vice President Cheney are in office, suddenly these priorities have changed. Oversight is no longer a priority. In fact, it's something to be avoided at all costs, including sacrificing the independence of GAO. Even when GAO asks for the most basic information—what private interests met with a White House task force—the answer is that GAO is not entitled to ask these questions.

By pressuring GAO to accept a badly flawed court decision, Republican leaders placed expediency over principle. In the short term, they will get what they want—a Bush White House that is accountable to no one. In the long term, however, they have done lasting damage to the balance of powers between Congress and the White House. Consider this irony: In their eagerness to undermine the Clinton White House, Republicans in Congress tried to tear down the presidency. Now, in their eagerness to protect the Bush White House, they are willing to tear down Congress.

The implications of GAO's decision not to appeal are enormous. Without a realistic threat of legal action, GAO loses most of its leverage. In effect, the agency's ability to conduct effective independent investigations is emasculated. And in the process, core American values of open government and accountable leaders have been sacrificed.

The Comptroller General has stated that his decision not to appeal will have little impact on the day-to-day operations of GAO. There is some truth to this. Much of what GAO does every day are routine audits of government programs that virtually everyone supports. GAO will be able to continue this routine work. And if a Republican-controlled committee ever urges GAO to pursue a controversial investigation of the Bush Administration, GAO may be able to do this. But don't hold your breath.

What has been lost, however, is something very precious: it is GAO's ability to be more than an auditor of government books. To truly serve Congress and the American people, GAO needs the ability to take on important assignments even if they are not supported by the majority party, and it needs the authority to carry them out effectively even if they are controversial. This essential independence is now gone.

For the first time in its history, GAO's shield of nonpartisanship has been pierced. In this new world, partisan considerations matter. Congressional Republicans can dictate GAO action; congressional Democrats can't. That is a sea change in GAO's mission.

In the last eight years, some of our most important congressional powers have been misused for partisan purposes. We've seen the power to subpoena documents or individuals abused and twisted beyond recognition. The power to immunize witnesses was trivialized. The power to hold officials in contempt became a cheap political tool. And the power to impeach a President was reduced to a campaign strategy.

Now the General Accounting Office, with its well-deserved reputation for superb work, becomes the latest casualty of partisanship. We are losing something very special here, and it is slipping away almost without notice.

Comment

Both task forces sought to function in secrecy, and both were suspected of trying to conceal conduct that critics considered improper. Some critics charged that the secrecy was in the service of deception. The task forces claimed to be considering the public interest, but (these critics suggested) were actually carrying out the agenda of particular groups (advocates of managed care and a single-payer health system in the case of the Clinton task force, and representatives of the energy industry in the case of the Cheney task force). Secrecy may enable executives "to decide and act quickly," but it also permits them to act deceptively. What practices or procedures might better facilitate decisive action while reducing the risk of deceitful action?

Regardless of whether there was any deception, critics complained that the secrecy undermined accountability. This complaint appeals to an important value in democratic politics, which can generally be overridden only by compelling considerations. In these cases, the primary consideration favoring secrecy also expressed an important democratic value: citizens want their leaders to make decisions on the basis of the best advice they can secure, and without confidentiality such advice is less likely to be forthcoming. (Although the separation of powers argument may have some independent constitutional force, its ethical significance rests mainly on this same value of the importance of confidential advice.) How should we assess this claim in these cases? Is it consistent to appeal, as the defenders of the Clinton groups did, to the importance of "advice giving" while insisting that the function of the groups is only "information gathering"?

We should try to be more specific about what citizens need to know for the purposes of accountability. Which aspects of the process should be known—how the members were chosen, who they were, when they met, what their agenda was, who said what at the meetings, what their recommendations were? It seems more acceptable to preserve confidentiality while the deliberations are in progress, but Cheney's supporters maintained that publicity "after the fact" would also have a "chilling effect" on the deliberations. The claims of the two task forces differed in how much they sought to keep secret and for how long: do those differences have any ethical significance (or should both task forces be regarded as essentially right or wrong in their claim)?

We should also ask, more fundamentally, why citizens need to know anything about the process itself. Why not judge the outcome only on its merits? The recommendations and ultimately the policy that the president proposes should arguably be their chief concern.

If you object to the secrecy of the Cheney task force, must you also object to that of the Clinton task force? Waxman's charge of "hypocrisy" against the Republicans who criticized the Clinton's task force but defended Cheney's should prompt you to examine more closely the similarities and differences between the two, and the justifications that were given or could be given for each.

Recommended Reading

The most comprehensive treatment of the problem of deception is Sissela Bok, *Lying: Moral Choice in Public and Private Life* (New York: Random House, 1979), especially ch. 1, 2, 3, 6 to 8, and 12. The appendix provides substantial excerpts from works by Augustine, Aquinas, Bacon, Grotius, Kant, Sidgwick, Harrod, Bonhoeffer, and Warnock. See also Hannah Arendt, "Truth and Politics," in P. Laslett and W. G. Runciman (eds.), *Philosophy, Politics and Society,* third series (Oxford: Blackwell, 1967), pp. 104–33; Christine M. Korsgaard, "The Right to Lie: Kant on Dealing with Evil," *Philosophy & Public Affairs,* 15 (Fall 1986), pp. 325–49; and Bernard Williams, *Truth and Truthfulness* (Princeton: Princeton University Press, 2002).

On secrecy, Bok again provides a valuable overview in *Secrets: On the Ethics of Concealment and Revelation* (New York: Pantheon, 1982), especially chs. 8, 12, 14, 17, and 18. On political secrecy, see Dennis F. Thompson, *Restoring Responsibility* (Cambridge, England: Cambridge University Press, 2004), ch. 6. The classic contrast between utilitarian and deontological views of publicity can be brought out by comparing Immanuel Kant, "On the Disagreement Between Politics and Morality," *Perpetual Peace,* Appendix II, in *Political Writings,* pp. 125–30: and Jeremy Bentham, "Of Publicity," in *Essay on Political Tactics, Works,* vol. 2, pp. 310–17.

For a discussion of the principle of publicity in political ethics, see Amy Gutmann and Dennis Thompson, *Democracy and Disagreement* (Cambridge, Mass.: Harvard University Press, 1996), ch. 3. The most influential contemporary philosophical discussion of the principle is John Rawls, *A Theory of Justice* (Cambridge, Mass.: Harvard University Press, 1970), pp. 130–36, 177–82; and *Political Liberalism* (New York: Columbia University Press, 1993), lecture 6.

3 Privacy of Officials

The difference between the ethical demands of private and public life has never been more plainly put than by an anonymous supporter of Grover Cleveland in the presidential campaign of 1884. Cleveland's opponent, James G. Blaine, had corruptly profited from public office but lived an impeccable private life. Cleveland had a reputation for public integrity, but had been forced to acknowledge fathering an illegitimate child. Cleveland's supporter declared:

> I gather that Mr. Cleveland has shown high character and great capacity in public office, but that in private life his conduct has been open to question, while, on the other hand, Mr. Blaine, in public life has been weak and dishonest, while he seems to have been an admirable husband and father. The conclusion that I draw from these facts is that we should elect Mr. Cleveland to the public office which he is so admirably qualified to fill and remand Mr. Blaine to the private life which he is so eminently fitted to adorn.

Yet the separation between private and public life is not so sharp as Cleveland's supporter implies. Some kinds of otherwise private immoralities affect public responsibilities and raise challenging questions about the privacy of public officials.

To what extent should the private lives of public officials be publicized? The question has become more pressing as the media have become more probing. The answer is usually not simple. It depends on a comparison of competing values. On the one hand, citizens have a right to know. In order to hold officials accountable, citizens may need to know quite a bit about their private life. Their private conduct may be highly relevant to judging their fitness for office, and their performance in office. On the other hand, officials do not completely give up their right to privacy when they enter public office. Privacy is important not only for preserving a sense of personal dignity, but also for protecting the quality of public discourse. Stories about private life have the tendency to dominate other forms of information, and to lower the overall quality of political discussion. Even during the first six months of its public life, the Clinton-Lewinsky affair dominated media discussion of not only new policy proposals on Social Security, health insurance, and campaign finance reform, but also attempts to explain the U.S. position on Iraq in preparation for military action.

The most general answer to the question of what privacy officials can legitimately claim is the familiar "relevance" standard: private conduct should be publicized to the extent that it is relevant to the performance in public office. Private conduct can be relevant in several different ways, each of which requires making some ethical as well as empirical assessments.

First, some conduct loses the protection of privacy if it contravenes the law. Sexual conduct that would otherwise be private becomes a legitimate subject for the press when it violates the law (assuming that the law itself is morally justified). Sexual harassment is not a private matter. Even some conduct that does not violate the law may still be relevant if it reveals a pattern of unwanted sexual advances to persons in subordinate positions. The press therefore could not be faulted for publicizing Senator Bob Packwood's sexual encounters, which the Senate Ethics Committee in 1995 found constituted a "pattern of abuse of his position of power and authority."

Second, private conduct may tell us something about an official's competence to do the job even if evidence about previous performance in similar jobs is available and more reliable and relevant than information about private life. Someone who cannot manage his own personal finances may not be the best choice for a position in the Treasury Department. Private conduct may also be relevant to assessing the competence of the people he appoints. Although citizens may not care if the chair of the House Administration Committee has an affair, they may legitimately object if he gives his mistress a job on the Committee staff, especially if she proclaims: "I can't type. I can't file. I can't even answer the phone."

Third, private conduct may reveal aspects of personal character that affect an official's public integrity. People who do not keep promises in their private dealings may not be trustworthy in their public dealings. If the character trait is specifically related to the job, the case for its relevance is stronger, even if the connection is only symbolic. William Bennett had to give up smoking when he was head of the Drug Enforcement Agency. But private and public character are not identical. Perhaps even more than other people, politicians are quite capable of compartmentalizing their lives. Nor is private virtue a sign of public virtue. Most of the leading conspirators in the Watergate scandal led impeccable private lives.

Fourth, private conduct may affect job performance as a result of public reaction. In the early days of the Clinton-Lewinsky scandal, many people said that while they themselves did not think the conduct was relevant to Clinton's job performance, the expectation that other people, including foreign leaders, would have less confidence in him made it relevant. When an official's private life becomes so scandalous that it casts doubt on his judgment, it tends to undermine his effectiveness on the job. Perhaps the chair of the Ways and Means Committee should be able to date an Argentine striptease dancer, but when he appears on a Boston burlesque stage to praise her performance, citizens take notice. We should be careful about appealing to these kinds of reactive effects. The anticipated reaction of other people should rarely if ever count as a sufficient reason to publicize further what would otherwise be private. The missing step in any such argument is the assumption that the private conduct itself is morally wrong, and that therefore the anticipated reactions of other people are morally justified.

Even if the private conduct is relevant, unlimited publicity is not necessarily justified. Just as relevance is a matter of degree, so is publicity. The fact that a story about a private scandal is likely to be published elsewhere ("If we don't run it, somebody else will") is not itself sufficient. It makes a difference where the story is published—a difference that is becoming more important in the era of cyberpublicity. Publication in the *New York Times* or the *Wall Street Journal* gives a story more credibility, and has a greater effect on political discourse, than does publication in the tabloids or on the Internet. Nor do journalists or citizens escape responsibility for publicizing private conduct by repeating the reports of others. This tactic, which may be called *meta-reporting,* is increasingly common. The more respectable press writes about the fact that the less respectable press is writing about a private scandal. The *New York Times* published a story about the unsubstantiated rumors that the *Daily News* published about President Clinton and Monica Lewinksy—complete with miniature reproductions of the front pages of the *News.*

The cases in this chapter describe the two most prominent controversies about private conduct of public officials in recent U.S. history: the dispute about the nomination of Clarence Thomas to the Supreme Court, and the scandal that led to the impeachment of Bill Clinton. In both cases, the privacy question is doubly complex: First, there is the difficulty of determining what is legitimately considered private conduct and then the problem of deciding how to balance the values of privacy and publicity. Also in both cases, the privacy question is mixed with other ethical issues. "The Confirmation of Justice Thomas" brings out some of these complexities by presenting a conflict between the claims of privacy of Justice Thomas and his accuser, Anita Hill, and the demands of publicity in the democratic process. This case also raises issues of sexual harassment and racial discrimination that are relevant to the problem of equal opportunity presented in Chapter 8. "The Investigation and Impeachment of President Clinton" provides material for judging not only Clinton's conduct, but also that of other officials who carried out the investigation and impeachment. His conduct may not have been private in any significant sense, but it also may not have been relevant to his public role to the degree that his accusers believed. The issues in the case go beyond privacy, and involve questions about the meaning of sexual harassment, the legitimacy of deception, the scope of publicity, and the grounds for impeachment.

The Confirmation of Justice Thomas*

Jillian P. Dickert

Only days after it was announced, President George Bush's July 1991 nomination of federal appeals court Judge Clarence Thomas to sit on the Supreme Court grew intensely politicized. The stakes were high: if confirmed, Thomas would gain a seat on the nation's highest court at the young age of forty-three, making it possible for him to decide cases through the 2030s. Opponents feared the impact that the lifetime appointment of the conservative black jurist would have on a court poised to review so many high-profile, consequential cases in the coming years. In the 1991–92 term alone, the Supreme Court was preparing to decide such politically sensitive issues as the rights of antiabortion protesters, school prayer, "hate speech," and school desegregation, and many believed that the Court would soon rule on whether to overturn the 1973 *Roe v. Wade* decision that legalized abortion nationwide.

In late September—as the fourteen members of the Senate Judiciary Committee prepared for their vote on the nomination— a *confidential* statement from Anita Hill, Thomas's former subordinate at the Equal Employment Opportunity Commission (EEOC) and the U.S. Department of Education, described in graphic language how Thomas had sexually harassed her over a three-year period in the early 1980s. Hill had made it clear that she wanted her charges heard by the Senate Judiciary Committee, but not made public. The Judiciary Committee and its staff would have to decide how to handle a private charge and also deal with their public responsibilities.

A BOOTSTRAPS SUCCESS STORY

On July 2, 1991, President Bush announced the nomination of Clarence Thomas to fill Justice Thurgood Marshall's seat on the Supreme Court. Standing before the president's oceanfront home in Kennebunkport, Maine, Thomas addressed the nation, his voice choked with emotion. "As a child, I could not dare to dream that I would ever see the Supreme Court, not to mention be nominated to it," said Thomas, who rose to

*Funding was supplied by the Program in Ethics and the Professions at Harvard University. Copyright © 2000 by the President and Fellows of Harvard College and by Princeton University.

his current status from an impoverished early childhood in racially segregated rural Georgia. "Only in America could this have been possible." The appointment would elevate Thomas from his seat on the U.S. Court of Appeals for the District of Columbia, for which the Senate Judiciary Committee had approved Thomas only fifteen months earlier by a vote of 13–1.[1]

Believing that no government program could replace the kind of self-discipline that was instilled in him by the grandfather who raised him and reinforced by the Catholic nuns who schooled him, Thomas was opposed to various forms of preferential treatment for minorities. In 1983, Thomas said that only "God . . . school, discipline, hard work, and 'right from wrong' " saved him from a life like that of his sister, who was raised by other relatives and later supported four children on welfare.[2] Thomas was expressing these views at the same time Republican party activists were hoping to nurture and promote a black elite that could directly challenge the traditional—and predominantly Democratic—civil rights leadership.[3]

After graduating from Yale Law School, Thomas rose quickly through the ranks of the Reagan and Bush administrations. In 1981, President Reagan appointed him assistant secretary for civil rights in the Department of Education, and just one year later, Thomas was made chairman of the EEOC. In his eight-year tenure at the EEOC, Thomas redefined how the federal government handled job discrimination complaints. By the time he left the agency in 1990, Thomas had: (1) changed EEOC policy to emphasize individual redress rather than the use of class action lawsuits that relied on statistical evidence to prove widespread job discrimination at large corporations; (2) largely abandoned the use of minority hiring goals and timetables by employers to correct racial and ethnic disparities; and (3) yielded the agency's once dominant role on civil rights issues to the Justice Department.[4]

Thomas's record at the EEOC drew fire from many liberal groups, who charged that Thomas "dismally" failed to enforce anti-discrimination laws. They pointed to thousands of age discrimination complaints that had lapsed for lack of action during his tenure.[5] Some critics claimed his conservative views were a betrayal for a man who in law school was himself a beneficiary of affirmative action. (Yale Law School actively recruited minority students in the early 1970s.)[6] Thomas responded to this criticism: "I have been extremely fortunate. I have benefited greatly from the civil rights movement, from the justice whom I am nominated to succeed."[7]

President Bush insisted race played no part in his selection of Thomas to replace Justice Marshall, the Supreme Court's first and only black justice. "Judge Thomas's life is a model for all Americans, and he's earned the right to sit on this nation's highest court," Bush said. "The fact that he is black and a minority has nothing to do with this sense that he is the best qualified at this time."[8]

THE POLITICS OF SUPREME COURT NOMINATIONS

In Article II, Section 2, the U.S. Constitution states that the president "shall nominate, and by and with the Advice and Consent of the Senate, shall appoint . . . Judges of the Supreme Court." As an important check on presidential power, the Senate's power to consent also involves the power to reject: of the 144 Supreme Court nominees prior to Thomas, 27 (nearly one out of five) were rejected, withdrawn, or not acted on by the Senate. The Senate's power to consent often has meant the exercise of a clearly political judgment. When the president and Senate majority have been of the same party, consent has been given to more than 90 percent of the nominations. When they have been of different parties, more than half of the nominees have not been confirmed.[9]

President Reagan's 1987 nomination of federal appeals court Judge Robert Bork led to a confirmation battle described as bitterly partisan. Bork's opponents used his extensive "paper trail" of articles, books, and judicial opinions to convince senators that his theory of "original intent" was sharply at odds with much of recent U.S. constitutional law. Bork, the first Supreme Court nominee since 1970 to be rejected by the Senate, predicted after his defeat: "A president who wants to avoid a battle like mine . . . is likely to nominate men and women who have not written much, and certainly nothing that could be regarded as controversial by left-leaning senators and groups."[10] In fact, neither of the two subsequent nominees, Anthony Kennedy and David Souter, were outspoken conservatives, and neither was subjected to broad opposition.

After ten consecutive Republican apointments over twenty-two years, the Democrat-controlled Senate in 1991 began expressing frustration with so-called "stealth" nominees who, during their confirmation hearings, endorsed conventional wisdom and claimed to have "no agenda" for the Court, only to emerge as staunch conservatives once on the bench. Critics pointed to Justice Souter. During his confirmation hearings, Souter refused to discuss his views on abortion. Later, in his first term on the Court, Souter joined with four other justices to uphold a ban on abortion counseling at federally funded clinics.

Judge Thomas's written opinions—which, during his fifteen months on the bench, dealt largely with criminal law and regulatory issues—were not considered revealing of his overall constitutional philosophy. With the retirement of Justice Marshall, the Court's last consistently liberal justice, Senate Democrats seemed to gain greater resolve to exercise their power to reject.

THE CAMPAIGN BEGINS

On July 11, members of the Congressional Black Caucus voted overwhelmingly to oppose Thomas,[11] promising to organize a national campaign by black leaders to fight the selection.

In August, the National Association for the Advancement of Colored People (NAACP) and the AFL-CIO announced their opposition in a dual press conference. The Leadership Conference on Civil Rights, a coalition of 185 organizations claiming that Thomas "demonstrated a consistent hostility to many of the Supreme Court's most fundamental civil rights decisions" followed suit soon after.[12]

Several other liberal-leaning organizations and women's groups joined in the campaign to defeat Thomas. Abortion rights activists feared that Thomas's expressed views on natural law (a philosophy typically identified with the premise that there are laws given by a higher authority than government that override any governmental authority) could signal his opposition to legalized abortion. Thomas had never decided an abortion case or commented directly on the correctness of *Roe v. Wade,* but in a 1987 speech for the conservative Heritage Foundation, he praised an antiabortion article by conservative Lewis E. Lehrman as a "splendid example of applying natural law."[13]

To counter this opposition, Thomas's backers quickly painted him as a by-the-bootstraps success story with few strongly held views on specific legal issues. Senator John Danforth (R-Mo.), Thomas's most outspoken defender in the Senate, described him as a "compassionate kind of conservative, not rigid or ideological in his views. His very motive is that he empathizes with ordinary people, he's one of them."[14] Senate Minority Leader Bob Dole (R-Kans.) praised Thomas as a "man whose very life exemplifies the American dream."[15] "Does he understand [that] all men, all women are not always treated equally?" asked U.S. Department of Labor Secretary Lynn Martin, who led the newly formed group Women for Judge Thomas. "Clarence Thomas understands. He knows the inequities, the indignities, the insensitivity."[16]

Thomas's personal story of success in overcoming obstacles appeared to impress his opponents as well as his supporters. The high-profile groups joining in the fight against Thomas had difficulty generating a groundswell of opposition across the country, which frustrated anti-Thomas lobbying efforts on Capitol Hill. "The basic feeling is that Republicans have the Democrats over a barrel on this one," said Senator Charles Grassley (R-Iowa), one of six Republicans on the fourteen-member Senate Judiciary Committee, which would be holding hearings that September on whether to recommend that Thomas be confirmed by the full Senate. A few Senate Democrats even predicted Thomas's confirmation weeks before the Judiciary Committee's September hearings. In early August, Senator Paul Simon (D-Ill.) told the *Washington Post,* "I think the situation is that he is probably going to be approved." Thomas, Simon noted, "is a likable person" and "in some ways the personality things are the toughest things that we deal with here. It's easier to say no on an issue than to say no on a person."[17]

THE COMMITTEE HEARINGS

By the time the Senate Judiciary Committee hearings opened on September 10, many expected Thomas to be approved by the panel of eight Democrats and six Republicans. Thomas needed eight of the fourteen votes to be favorably recommended to the full Senate, which traditionally follows the lead of the Judiciary Committee. In his opening statement, Biden made it clear that the "single most important task for the committee" was to ascertain how Thomas would apply to the Constitution his philosophy of natural law. By conceding that Bush had "the right to appoint a conservative" and that any Bush appointee would inevitably move the Court to the right, Biden seemed to conclude that only if Thomas espoused an "extreme, activist" agenda, would he be deemed unfit for the high court.

During his hearings, Thomas described his interest in natural law not as a constitutional philosophy but as an off-hours interest in political theory. He distanced himself from his earlier hard-line conservatism, mainly recapping the status of current court decisions and offering little about his own views. Thomas referred frequently to his impoverished youth in Pin Point, Georgia and his compelling descriptions of racism and poverty seemed to deter members of the all-white, all-male committee from asking questions about affirmative action—a politically sensitive topic on which Thomas had been outspoken throughout his career.

Democrats were persistent in their efforts to determine Thomas's position on abortion, however, barraging him with more than thirty questions on the issue. In each instance, Thomas said he could not answer without compromising his impartiality. Finally, Thomas told Senator Patrick Leahy (D-Vt.) that he had no "personal opinion" on the *Roe v. Wade* decision,[18] and in fact, could not "recollect commenting one way or another" on it, not even in a private setting, in the eighteen years since the ruling. Thomas said that his only experience discussing the case was "in the most general sense that other individuals express concerns one way or the other and you listen and you try to be thoughtful. If you are asking me whether or not I have ever debated the contents of it, the answer is no, senator."

Leahy was incredulous. "With all due respect, judge, I have some difficulty with your answer," he retorted, pointing out that Thomas had been immersed in a wide variety of conservative policy debates over the past eighteen years and had cited *Roe v. Wade* in a footnote to a law review article, mentioned the abortion issue in a reference to an article about natural law and fetal right to life, and discussed black voters' views on abortion in a newspaper article. "I cannot believe all of this was done in a vacuum, absent some very clear considerations of *Roe v. Wade*," said Leahy.

Unable effectively to make issue of Thomas's views, committee Democrats expressed concern that the nominee was being purposely vague and backtracking from or contradicting earlier statements in

order to win confirmation. Biden accused the nominee of engaging in "sophistry" after trying to draw him out on natural law. Senator Howard Metzenbaum (D-Ohio) was just as blunt. "It's difficult to accept the notion that the moment you put on that judge's robe, all the positions and views you held prior to going on the bench just magically disappear."

Backed by committee Republicans, Thomas sought to allay the Democrats' concerns. He argued that he had been "consistent on this issue of natural law" and pointed repeatedly to his previous Senate hearings (for the federal appeals court), where he suggested that he would follow a more traditional approach to constitutional interpretation. Thomas claimed to have "no agenda" for the Court, elaborating that "a judge must not bring to his job, to the court, the baggage of preconceived notions, of ideology, and certainly not an agenda. . . ."

For the most part, the Republicans' strategy for the hearings seemed obvious: steer questioning away from specific substantive issues and focus on Thomas's personal background and character. Only Senator Arlen Specter (R-Pa.) appeared to have prepared probing questions for Thomas; in Specter's view, Thomas had "shifted" positions several times during his career on the legality of minority preference programs and set-asides.

After five full days of testimony from Thomas,[19] Democrats complained that they knew little more about Clarence Thomas than at the start of the hearings. The disappointment of Senator Herb Kohl (D-Wis.) was plain. "I think Judge Thomas has demonstrated that he can go through an entire hearing process and confront some very difficult questions by not answering them. Who is the real Clarence Thomas?" Kohl asked. "We really don't know." Other Democrats seemed at least as unhappy with the nomination process as they were with the nominee. "It seems that somehow it has emerged that if you are evasive, you have a better chance of being confirmed, and that seems to me to be a clearly flawed kind of situation," said Simon.[20]

Committee Republicans defended Thomas's candor and willingness to answer many questions, and argued that any short-comings in the process should be blamed on the Democrats. "Clarence Thomas gave a lot of answers. He just didn't give answers to everything they wanted, so they're griping and complaining," charged Senator Orrin Hatch (R-Utah).

With few clues to Thomas's constitutional philosophy, most senators were left without any firm reason to oppose his appointment and many recognized that his personal story of success over obstacles had struck a chord with Americans. When the hearings ended on Friday, September 20, several senators stated that—although the vote might be close—it was almost certain that the committee would approve Thomas.

THE SEXUAL HARASSMENT ALLEGATIONS

Meanwhile, behind the scene of the hearings, a time bomb was ticking on the nomination, threatening to shatter the public image of Thomas's character. As Thomas was testifying before the Judiciary Committee on national television, Anita Hill, a black, tenured law professor at the University of Oklahoma, was privately telling committee staffers that Thomas had sexually harassed her while they worked together at the Department of Education and the EEOC from 1981–1983. Hill charged that, during this period, Thomas frequently asked her out despite her refusals to date him and spoke to her about sexual topics in vivid detail. After a brief discussion of work, Thomas would typically "turn the conversation to discussion about his sexual interests," often describing films he had seen depicting group sex and women having sex with animals, Hill said. Although Thomas had not explicitly threatened her job if she would not date him, Hill said she feared retaliation.

Hill said Thomas's misconduct began when she worked as his attorney-advisor at the Education Department in 1981, stopped for a while when he started dating someone else, then resumed when she began working as his special assistant at the EEOC. According to Hill, when she resigned from her post at the EEOC to accept a teaching job at Oral Roberts Law School, Thomas warned that she could ruin his career if she revealed his behavior. Hill never filed a formal complaint against Thomas—as chairman of the EEOC, the agency charged with handling sexual harassment claims, Thomas was, in effect, the nation's chief enforcement officer on the subject.[21]

The behavior Hill described would have constituted sexual harassment under the guidelines set forth by the EEOC in 1980, which expanded the definition of sexual harassment and declared it illegal sex discrimination under the federal job discrimination law administered by the EEOC. The EEOC's 1980 definition of sexual harassment—issued before Thomas was chairman of the agency—included, for the first time, unwelcome sexual advances resulting in a hostile working environment. "Verbal sexual abuse" was not legally recognized as a form of sexual harassment in a federal court until mid-1983, and the EEOC's guidelines were not confirmed by the Supreme Court until 1986.[22] Nevertheless, in 1980, unwelcome sexual advances of any kind were generally considered unacceptable in the American workplace.

HOW THE CHARGES WERE HANDLED

Thomas was not the first nominee before the Judiciary Committee who had faced a sexual harassment charge. According to Senate Judiciary Committee Chief Counsel Ron Klain, "the Judiciary Committee deals with this stuff all the time"—although mainly with district court nominees. Typically such charges emerge as committee staffers conduct their routine investigations before a nominee's hearings begin. If a charge is determined to have merit, Klain said, "that person is confidentially approached, and [usually] that person just withdraws and the public never knows about it—there's no big deal." Klain added that the "quiet, outside-the-media-spotlight ways" used to deal with such charges are "not available in the context of the Supreme Court nomination due to its highly public nature."

The sexual harassment allegations against Thomas were first uncovered during the summer of 1991 by the Alliance for Justice, a public interest group opposed to Thomas. The Alliance received the tip at a dinner party from a lawyer who attended Yale Law School with Hill.[23] In July and August, the Alliance passed on the information—along with other allegations of Thomas's personal misconduct—to several members of Senator Metzenbaum's staff.

News of the allegations spread amongst several staffers for Metzenbaum and Senator Edward Kennedy (D-Mass.) as they investigated and coordinated a response. During the first nine days of September, at least two staff members contacted Hill. When Hill was first contacted, she did not volunteer anything but suggested that the sexual harassment charge be investigated further. In a later conversation, Hill said she was willing to talk about the issue but wasn't sure how far she wanted it to go. It was suggested that Hill might be more comfortable discussing the matter with James Brudney, a chief Metzenbaum lawyer with whom she had attended Yale Law School.

On Tuesday, September 10—the first day of the committee's hearings on Thomas—Hill detailed her allegations in a telephone conversation with Brudney. Hill told Brudney she did not wish to testify publicly and expressed reservations about making allegations if no other woman made similar charges. Brudney discussed with Hill the law on sexual harassment, some alternative methods of informing the committee of her charges, and how the committee might proceed once informed. Some possible outcomes were also discussed, including the possibility that the nominee might withdraw.[24] When the call ended, Brudney understood that Hill was undecided about whether she wished to report her allegations to the committee.

Brudney immediately advised Metzenbaum and the senator's senior staff about Hill's charges. Metzenbaum responded that the charges were too serious for a single member or staff to deal with and should be referred to Senator Biden as chairman of the Judiciary Committee. Brudney explained this to Hill, who replied that she felt a responsibility to go forward and was willing to proceed with Biden's staff. On the following day, September 11, Brudney relayed Hill's allegations to Harriet Grant, chief counsel for the Judiciary Committee's nominations unit. Grant took charge of handling all subsequent conversations with Hill for Senator Biden and the full committee staff.

During a September 12 conversation with Grant, Hill described Thomas's alleged misconduct in detail. Hill repeated her concern that a single complainant would not be believed and again expressed her desire for confidentiality—according to Grant, Hill did not want the nominee to know her name or that she had stated her concerns to the committee. Grant assured Hill that her charges would be kept confidential, but "little could he done" unless Thomas was informed and given the opportunity to respond. Grant did not push Hill to go further.[25] As the conversation ended, Hill mentioned an unnamed friend who could corroborate her charges but was also uncomfortable about coming forward. Grant told Hill that "the next logical step in the process would be to have Hill's friend contact the committee if she so chose." (Grant says that, in dealing with Hill, she followed a "rape crisis center counseling mode," such that "you give the victim every opportunity to come forward, but you don't pressure them, and it ultimately has to be within that person's control and that person's decision" to come forward.) Susan Hoerchner, a California workers' compensation judge who was a Yale classmate of Hill's, telephoned Grant on September 17. Hoerchner told Grant that Hill had complained to her about Thomas's behavior in the spring of 1981 and said that it caused

Hill to doubt her own professional abilities. Like Hill, Hoerchner expressed a strong desire for confidentiality.

The full committee staff under Biden had no other contact with Hill between Thursday, September 12 and Thursday, September 19—a full week. Senator Biden was briefed during this time and all agreed that nothing further could be done to investigate Hill's allegations unless Hill agreed Thomas could be told of the charges.[26] No committee staffer was sent to Oklahoma to question Hill more thoroughly, and Biden decided at this time not to tell other committee members of her allegations. Biden, according to his staff, felt strongly that he was not going to circulate "some anonymous charge."[27] At this point, Biden, Kennedy, and Metzenbaum were the only senators on the Judiciary Committee who knew of Hill's charges.

In the meantime, Brudney, having heard nothing from Grant, called Hill on September 13 and 15. (Brudney later said he "felt responsible for Hill because he had placed her in a difficult situation" and did not want Hill to feel that he or his colleagues "had deserted her."[28]) Through his conversations with Hill and another Metzenbaum staffer who had spoken with Grant, Brudney gained the impression that Grant had misunderstood the scope of Hill's request for confidentiality and that Hill was upset with the committee's response.[29]

In response to Brudney's concerns about a possible misunderstanding, Kennedy's staff contacted two of Leahy's chief staffers, Ellen Lovell and Ann Harkins, who suggested that Grant place another call to Hill to determine whether she in fact meant to "cut off all committee activity through her request for total anonymity." Harkins calculated that at least ten people already knew of Hill's allegations and warned that their "disclosure could embarrass the committee if nothing more was done." However, Ted Kaufman, Biden's chief of staff, was "adamant" in his belief that it would be wrong to push Hill in any way, given her request for confidentiality. Later

that evening, Senator Leahy briefly discussed with Biden the possibility of additional investigative efforts. Biden, too, "believed nothing more should be done."[30]

Hill called Grant on Thursday, September 19; Thomas had finished testifying three days before and other witnesses were before the committee. Hill told Grant she was afraid that Grant had misunderstood her concerns; Hill, in fact, had wanted all members of the committee to know about her complaint and was willing to use her name if necessary. Grant says she "repeated: 'before committee members could be apprised of [her] concerns, the nominee must be afforded an opportunity to respond; that is both committee policy and practice.'" According to Grant's notes of the conversation, Hill said she needed to know her options, wanted to make choices, and did not want to abandon the matter. At this point, Grant felt that clear instructions from her superiors were in order and deferred any further response.[31]

On Friday morning, September 20—the final day of Thomas's hearing—Grant called Hill back and explained that, in order to proceed, Hill's allegations would need to be given to the Federal Bureau of Investigation, and the bureau would interview Hill, Thomas, and anyone else with relevant information. (Judiciary staffers agreed that the committee's limited investigative capacity required the use of the FBI to conduct the field interviews.) Hill responded that she was unsure of the "utility" of an FBI investigation and wanted to discuss the idea with someone she had been using for advice. Hill then spoke with Brudney and Georgetown University law professor Susan Ross (whom Brudney had proposed as a possible advisor familiar with the law on sex discrimination) about her concern that FBI interviewers would distort her charges against Thomas. It was suggested that Hill prepare a written statement in her own words.[32]

On Saturday, September 21, Grant called Hill for a response to the FBI question. According to Grant, Hill told her that "she did not want to go through with the FBI investigation, because she was not convinced that the information would be communicated to the committee members in a way with which she was comfortable." Hill said she did not know if the FBI was experienced in handling matters of this sort, and told Grant she would call back with another option. Early Monday morning, September 23, Hill called Grant and said that she had prepared a statement outlining her allegations against Thomas and wanted it to be made available to the members of the Judiciary Committee. Then, Hill told Grant, she would submit to an interview with the FBI "if necessary."[33] Hill's written statement reaffirmed her desire for confidentiality: "I make this statement for the benefit of the Committee only," Hill wrote.

At Grant's request, Hill faxed her personal statement to Grant that afternoon. A copy of the four-page statement was then delivered to the office of Ranking Minority Member Strom Thurmond (R-S.C.), and an FBI investigation was initiated immediately. That evening, the FBI interviewed Hill in Oklahoma and informed the White House of her charges.[34] Thomas was interviewed by the FBI two days later on Wednesday, September 25; he denied Hill's allegations.[35] On the afternoon of the 25th, the FBI completed its report and immediately delivered copies to the Senate and the White House. The FBI report contained background information from interviews and record checks, a synopsis of the investigation, and a supplemental report on sexual harassment allegations.[36] Those who saw the report said "it read like a bad wire [service] story, a collection of he-said, she-said quotes that reached no conclusion."[37]

In a conversation with Grant on September 25, Hill asked Grant for an explicit assurance that her statement would be circulated to all members of the Judiciary Committee, as she had previously requested. Grant—unsure about how Biden planned to proceed—assured Hill that the information would be made available to all members, but said she could not guarantee that hard copies of the statement itself would be physically distributed. Hill was upset.[38]

That same day, Chairman Biden—under White House pressure to confirm Thomas before the Supreme Court started its term on October 7—proceeded to schedule the committee vote on the nomination for Friday, September 27 (two days later), even though he knew his colleagues would not be briefed on Hill's charges until just before the vote. Klain later said Biden acted out of "the desire to protect Hill's confidentiality"; the press had begun to get suspicious. Committee rules dictate that nominees be voted on seven days after their hearings end, and ten days had already passed while the investigation was under way. Klain explained that "even with that [three-day] delay, I was getting press calls every day, asking: 'Why are you putting this thing off? What's going on?'"

Immediately after receiving the completed FBI report on September 25, Biden began notifying all Democratic members of the Senate Judiciary Committee on Hill's allegations and Thomas's denial. He also briefed Senate Majority Leader George Mitchell (D-Maine) and Minority Leader Bob Dole (R-Kans.), but the allegations were not shared with the full Senate. A committee aide later told the *New York Times* that "some committee members were briefed [orally] on Wednesday evening and the rest on Thursday [the 26th]," one day before the scheduled committee vote. The aide said that "at these briefings by Biden's staff, the senators were told they could see Ms. Hill's affidavit and the FBI report if they chose, and some took advantage. And some did not."[39] In fact, only senators Simon, DeConcini (D-Ariz.), and Specter asked for and reviewed the FBI report prior to Friday's scheduled vote.[40]

Biden left it up to the committee's ranking minority member, as was customary, to advise all Republican committee members about the sexual harassment allegations and the FBI report. Senator Thurmond did not do so.[41] Most Republican senators learned of Hill's allegations from other colleagues, but some complained they did not know about the FBI report before the vote.[42]

Meanwhile, Hill contacted several of her friends for help in getting her statement to the committee. One of Hill's friends, Kim Taylor, contacted Professor Charles Ogletree at Harvard Law School and informed him in very general terms of the sexual harassment allegations, repeating Hill's concern that her statement had not been circulated within the committee. (Hill's name was not mentioned.) Ogletree, in turn, called his Harvard colleague, Professor Laurence Tribe, and passed on the information. Tribe was able to reach Klain—a former student of Tribe's—at the Judiciary Committee on September 27, the morning of the vote. Tribe told Klain that "a group of women professors on the West Coast" were concerned that an unidentified woman's allegation of sexual harassment had not been circulated to the committee. Klain, who declined to discuss the subject with Tribe, assured him that any allegations had been thoroughly investigated.[43]

Klain immediately reported Tribe's call to Biden early that morning and recommended distribution of Hill's statement to all Democratic members of the Judiciary Committee. Less than an hour before the scheduled 10:00 A.M. vote, Judiciary staff delivered the document to each Democratic senator on the committee in individual envelopes marked "Personal and Confidential, For Senator's Eyes Only." All Democratic members read the statement. The committee hearing concluded at 12:46 P.M., and by 3:15 P.M. every copy of the statement was retrieved in its original envelope by Senator Biden's office and destroyed. It was not clear why Hill's statement had not been distributed to the committee's Republican members as well.

DEADLOCK

On September 27, the Senate Judiciary Committee failed, by a vote of 7–7, to recommend Thomas's nomination to the full Senate. The vote fell along party lines, except for DeConcini, who voted with Republicans for Thomas, referring to the nominee's "remarkable life story" in his speech and stating that he believed Thomas was capable of growing into a fine jurist. In announcing their votes for Thomas, committee Republicans also highlighted his struggle and his career. All seven Democrats voting against Thomas cited reasons unrelated to the harassment charges for their "no" votes—primarily his reluctance to give direct answers to questions. No member pushed for postponement of the Committee vote in order to hold a closed-door session with Hill.

In opposing Thomas, Biden cast the last vote needed for the Committee to deadlock but said he did so "with a truly heavy heart." "This is about what [Thomas] believes, not about who he is. . . . For this senator, there is no question with respect to the nominee's character, competence, credentials or credibility," Biden said. Perhaps recognizing that the committee deadlock might encourage Thomas's opponents to publicize Hill's charges, Biden then gave what appeared to be a warning to his colleagues: he urged "everyone else to refrain from personalizing this battle, to the extent that it is one, on the floor of the Senate . . . I don't expect it to happen off the floor, but I hope it won't happen on the floor in the Senate." Biden apparently considered the matter of the sexual harassment charges closed.

After the deadlock, the panel voted 13–1 to send Thomas's name to the full Senate without recommendation. The lone dissenter was Simon, who said the committee should not send nominations to the Senate without guidance; the panel had never before done so.[44] The 7–7 vote against Thomas was far more negative than had been anticipated at the start of the hearings. Senators were moved by the committee deadlock. "Certainly, if it was much closer to unanimous, with more of the moderate liberals voting with him then [it] would feel much easier to say 'OK, I'll support him,' " said James Jeffords (R-Vt.).[45]

Meanwhile, knowledge of Hill's "confidential" allegations was beginning to spread among the interested Washington community. The sexual harassment allegations were mentioned during at least two dinner parties on Saturday evening, September 28, and made their way back to Judiciary staffers.[46] In addition, two news reporters, Timothy Phelps of *Newsday* and Nina Totenberg of National Public Radio, were going after the story. Phelps had picked up on Senator Biden's speech warning Thomas's opponents to "stay away from personal attacks," and in an article published on September 28, Phelps described Biden's admonition as "an apparent reference [to what] sources said was a reopening of the FBI background investigation on Thomas to check opponents' allegations of personal misconduct."[47]

According to Klain, it was difficult for the Judiciary Committee to gauge how many people actually knew about Hill's charges. "Because it was confidential," Klain explained, "no one was discussing how unconfidential it might have become."

FULL SENATE DEBATE AND LAST MINUTE STRATEGIES

On October 3—with Hill's charges still considered confidential by the Judiciary Committee—the debate on Thomas's confirmation moved to the Senate floor. The first two days of full Senate debate revealed that while Democrats were deeply divided over the nomination, they were united in attacking President Bush for pursuing what they described as a racial, political, and ideological agenda for the Supreme Court. The harshest criticism came from Senator Bill Bradley (D-N.J.), who called the nomination "a stunning example of political opportunism." Bradley contended that Thomas's nomination conveyed "many subtle and not so subtle messages," including the suggestion that blacks do not need government intervention, that "white America has no responsibility for the failure of blacks," that "tokenism is the only acceptable form of affirmative action" and that "an administration [which] nominates a black for the U.S. Supreme Court has answered the critics of its racial policies."

The full Senate vote on Thomas's confirmation was scheduled for Tuesday, October 8. Thomas's confirmation hinged on fifty-one votes—a bare majority of the one hundred senators. By Friday, October 4, thirteen of the fifty-seven Democrats in the Senate had announced their support for Thomas, and none of the forty-three Republicans had yet voiced opposition; according to Danforth, forty-one Republicans were committed to his confirmation. But the vote was likely to be a close one: Thomas's opponents claimed they could muster more than forty votes against him. If so, Thomas would take his seat on the court with the largest number of negative votes ever recorded.[48]

As the Senate prepared for a weekend recess on Friday, October 4, Thomas's opponents had only four more days to change the minds of at least six senators. One possible avenue of attack was a filibuster, which could have delayed the nomination until sixty senators voted to shut it down.[49] While Republicans said they feared such a maneuver, Democrats seemed loath to start one.[50] Even Leahy—one of Thomas's strongest critics—declared himself "totally opposed to a filibuster," and Simon stated, "I don't exclude that possibility, but I don't have any such plans."[51] Hatch pointed out that a filibuster had often been used in the past by those opposed to civil rights, and to start one on Thomas would be "just the greatest irony of all. . . . Can you imagine liberals using a filibuster on the second black nominated to the Supreme Court?"[52]

Those who knew about Anita Hill had another option: publicize her sexual harassment charges. Whether the allegations could be proved or not, Thomas's confirmation was likely to be put in grave jeopardy. Charges of sexual harassment involve a violation of the law, and under Thomas's own guidelines for evaluating sexual harassment charges filed at the EEOC, it was plausible to believe that the benefit of the doubt would have been given to Hill.

However, a public disclosure of Hill's charges or her personal statement would have breached her stated desire for confidentiality. It would have violated Senate rules as well: a senator or staff member found to have disclosed such confidential information was subject to expulsion or dismissal.[53] What is more, disclosure of a confidential FBI report would have constituted a federal crime. Yet Senate leak probes rarely led to conclusive outcomes, and for the most part, anonymous leakers escaped detection: only two senators had ever been disciplined by the Senate for breaking secrecy rules, and both cases were a century old.[54] Those who contemplated whether or not to publicize Hill's allegations had little more than a weekend left to decide what to do.

THE LEAK

Sometime between October 1 and 5, just days before the scheduled Senate vote on the nomination of Clarence Thomas to the Supreme Court, the contents of Anita Hill's confidential statement to the Senate Judiciary Committee were leaked to two reporters: Timothy Phelps of *Newsday* and Nina Totenberg of National Public Radio.[55] Hill's sexual harassment allegations were then reported in *Newsday* on the evening of October 5 and broadcast on NPR the following morning. The story instantly became the lead item on most network news programs. By Monday, it made front-page headlines of newspapers across the country. Virtually overnight, the Senate Judiciary Committee found itself at the core of a nasty and embarrassing controversy that riveted the nation.

Hill confirmed reports that she told the FBI that Thomas had sexually harassed her in the early 1980s, but declined to discuss the details with Phelps on Saturday since he seemed not to have hard copy of her statement to the committee. However, when Totenberg began reading verbatim from the statement, Hill granted the reporter an interview. (Hill said she wanted to be able to respond to the information before it was made public.) As she detailed her allegations for Totenberg, Hill explained that, initially,

she had decided against telling her story, but when Senate staffers approached her in early September, she felt an obligation to provide information about the nominee. "Here is a person who is in charge of protecting rights of women and other groups in the workplace and he is using his position of power for personal gain for one thing," Hill said of Thomas, "and he did it in a very ugly and intimidating way."

As word of the allegations spread over the weekend, the White House and Thomas's supporters mounted a swift counterattack. White House Deputy Press Secretary Judy Smith immediately responded that a "full, thorough and expeditious" FBI investigation of Hill's charge had been ordered on September 25, and after reviewing the FBI's report, the White House had "determined that the allegation was unfounded." President Bush stressed that he did not believe Hill's charge, while White House spokesman Marlin Fitzwater called her accusation "absolutely" untrue, a "smear."

Meanwhile, Simon called Saturday for the postponement of the full Senate vote scheduled for Tuesday, October 8. "I think it is a serious enough charge that the committee ought to look at it and if necessary the vote ought to be postponed," Simon told reporters. On Sunday, Metzenbaum said the allegations were "very disturbing" and suggested the full Senate review them before voting. Leahy agreed: "I can't imagine a senator feeling that he or she can vote on this without reading the [FBI] report."[56]

In a statement released Monday, October 7, Biden rejected the idea that the full Senate vote should now be delayed. "The Senate and [Judiciary] committee leadership and all Democratic members of the committee were briefed regarding Professor Hill's allegations several days before the Senate set a vote on the Thomas nomination. They all had the right to object to a [full Senate] vote on Tuesday at 6 P.M., and none did. At the same time, none believed that the information which we then possessed necessitated a delay in voting. I see no reason why the addition of public disclosure of the allegations—but no new information about the charges themselves—should change the decision." Senate Majority Leader George Mitchell concurred: the members who demanded a delay "knew what was in the FBI report before they scheduled the [full Senate] vote and they went ahead. So why change now? It would be pure politics."

HILL'S PRESS CONFERENCE

Hill introduced herself to the public on Monday, October 7, in a nationally televised news conference from Oklahoma. Assailing the Judiciary Committee for seeming to ignore her repeated allegations against the nominee, Hill described how she struggled for nearly two weeks in September to put before the committee a confidential account of her harassment: "The control of the timing and release of this information has never been with me," said Hill. "It was not until the 20th of September that an FBI investigation was suggested to me. It was at that time I was told that this is the way to get the information before the committee . . . so to say that I perhaps delayed it is not true." Hill said she "was very surprised" that the committee had not called her to testify: "I felt that they had an obligation to hear what I was saying once I had come forward."

Hill denied that she was a "political opportunist," as the White House and some committee members sought to portray her.[57] Hill asked that others "look at the fact that this has taken a great toll on me personally and professionally. . . . There is no way that I would do something like this for political purposes." Finally, Hill demanded an "official resolution" of the situation:

> My integrity has been called into question by people who have never spoken to me, [who] have not considered the facts carefully as far as I know, and I want an official resolution of this because at this point the issue is being deflected. People are talking about this as a political ploy. And all that is, is an attempt not to deal with the issue itself.

It is an unpleasant issue. It's an ugly issue, and people don't want to deal with it generally, and in particular in this case. . . . If the members of the Senate carefully consider this and investigate it and make a determination, then I have done what I'm obligated to do. . . . But until that happens, I think that none of us [has] done our jobs.

At the end of her one-hour press conference, Hill expressed her willingness to talk with senators and cooperate with any further investigation.

COMMITTEE ON THE DEFENSIVE

"The Judiciary Committee didn't screw up on anything," Biden snapped at reporters questioning the handling of Hill's charges.[58] Shortly after Hill's press conference, Biden released a chronology of his full committee staff's contacts with Hill in September. His statement emphasized two points. First, the Judiciary Committee's "handling of the investigation was guided by Hill's repeated requests for confidentiality," which "initially precluded the committee from conducting a complete investigation until she chose to have her name released to the FBI for further and full investigation, which (as is customary) includes the nominee's response." Second, "Hill's wishes with respect to the disposition of this matter were honored. The Republican leadership and all Democratic members of the committee were fully briefed of her allegations and all were shown a copy of her statement prior to the committee's vote on the Thomas nomination."[59]

Meanwhile, other members of the Judiciary panel fiercely defended Thomas—and their own actions. For instance, before Hill finished her statement to the press, DeConcini called his own news conference to declare that he believed the nominee's denials. Hatch took the Senate floor that night to say that, impressive as she may have been, "the facts do not line up on Ms. Hill's side." And Specter—who had questioned Thomas about Hill's charges before the committee vote—told reporters that, given "the lateness of the allegation, the absence of any touching or intimidation, and the fact that she moved with him from one agency to another, . . . I felt I had done my duty and was satisfied with [Thomas's] responses." (When asked later about his comment, Specter, a former prosecutor, said he did not understand that touching was not required in a sexual harassment suit; that verbal harassment was also against the law.[60])

"THEY JUST DON'T GET IT"

"What disturbs me as much as the allegations themselves is that the United States Senate appears not to take the charge of sexual harassment seriously," declared Senator Barbara Mikulski, a Democrat from Maryland and one of two women in the Senate. Many people were critical that Biden did not fully discuss Hill's charges with all panel members. They were angry that the committee neither questioned Thomas personally nor brought Hill to Washington to hear her side of the story, yet some Judiciary Committee members seemed automatically to believe Thomas over Hill. Many felt the public reaction of some committee members revealed not only that they did not give the matter much weight but also that they did not understand the law on sexual harassment. Critics pointed out that with just two women members—one from each party—and no minority members, the Senate operated like an exclusive club for white men only.[61] Over and over, the question was repeated: were the fourteen members of the Judiciary Committee, all white men over fifty, capable of sensitively evaluating sexual harassment allegations?

Thousands of phone calls from constituents demanding that senators get to the bottom of Hill's charges, intense lobbying by women's groups, and exhaustive newspaper and television coverage underscored the extent of many women's anger. "They just don't get it" became the phrase of the week. "They are men," said Representative Nancy Pelosi, a California Democrat.

"They can't possibly know what it's like to receive verbal harassment, harassment that is fleeting to the man, and lasting and demeaning to the woman."

Many Republican women joined female Democrats in lashing out at the Judiciary Committee's handling of the issue. "It's an outrage that people's character has been sullied because the Senate did not deal properly with the information," declared Representative Nancy Johnson (R-Conn.). Johnson was joined by Senator Nancy Kassebaum (R-Kans.). "I think it was most unfortunate that the Judiciary Committee didn't assume greater responsibility when they had seen [Hill's] affidavit in the FBI report" and "more thoroughly [examine] these charges," Kassebaum said.

THE SENATE DEBATE CONTINUES

On the Senate floor, some erosion of Thomas's support set in almost immediately, and by early morning Tuesday, the pressure to delay the vote was intense. Many Democrats called for a postponement of the Senate vote. One by one, senators took to the floor, agreeing that the matter had "touched a nerve" with women on Capitol Hill, and any "rush to judgment," as several senators put it, would surely be taken by many to mean that the Senate considered Hill's charges trivial. Simon hammered the message home: "I think there is, in a body that is ninety-eight males to two women, a lack of sensitivity toward women's concerns and black and Hispanic concerns. . . . If there were twenty women who were members of the Senate we could delay the vote right now." Other senators complained that the Judiciary Committee had let them down by not informing them of allegations in the first place.

Meanwhile, Republicans focused on the fact that a breach of Senate rules had occurred. In his floor speech, Senate Minority Leader Bob Dole demanded an inquiry into the disclosure of Hill's confidential allegations. "I think many of us felt when the vote was postponed until Tuesday there would be a weekend revelation. We're not totally naive in this body," said Dole, a Thomas supporter. "Somebody on the [Judiciary] committee has been driving this to this result." In declaring his opposition to a delayed vote, Danforth contended that Hill's charges had come to light in the Senate through an infraction of the rules and therefore were not valid. "Think about voting down the nomination of Clarence Thomas solely on the basis of a violation of Senate rules. Talk about scandal," declared Danforth. "I guess if we want to defeat somebody, we destroy them—no holds barred. What are the rules of the Senate? Rules are made to be broken."

Kennedy tried to deflect all the talk about rules, remarking that "it is not a question of having the Senate train run on time, but whether we can stop the Senate train from running off the track." Kennedy also asked for a delayed vote, suggesting that Hill's claims "call into question Judge Thomas's views on women and sex discrimination in the workplace." Specter surprised many Republicans when he joined in the push for a postponement, saying "the Senate is on trial at this point." In the end, even Biden said he favored a delay "in light of the fact that Ms. Hill has lifted all conditions of anonymity."

THE TURNING POINT

Less than two hours before the floor vote, Danforth took the floor to request a forty-eight-hour delay of the vote. Danforth reported that Thomas was requesting time to "clear his name." Danforth quoted Thomas—who had been publicly silent up to this point—as saying: "They have taken from me what I have worked forty-three years to build: my reputation." Danforth then distributed the following statement signed by Thomas:

1. As I told the Federal Bureau of Investigation on September 28, 1991, I totally and unequivocally deny Anita Hill's allegations of misconduct of any kind toward her, sexual or otherwise.[62] These allegations are untrue.

2. At all times during the period she worked with me, our relationship was strictly professional. During that time and subsequently, the relationship has been wholly cordial.

3. I am terribly saddened and deeply offended by these allegations.

Danforth later told reporters, "If he is telling the truth and he loses the nomination because of this, that to me is an earth-shaking development—to have the nomination of Clarence Thomas for associate justice of the United States Supreme Court lost because of the illegal distribution or leaking of the content of an FBI report. . . ."[63]

Although Danforth portrayed Thomas as seeking the delay, most agreed that the postponement was forced on Republicans and the White House; according to Dole, the tide seemed to be running so strongly against Thomas that night that the nominee might have been rejected altogether.[64] "There are some who would have rolled the dice at 6 P.M.," said Dole. "It seemed to me a gamble that shouldn't be taken. . . . I couldn't put together fifty votes at 6 o'clock."[65]

At 8:11 P.M. on Tuesday, October 8, the Senate agreed by unanimous consent to put off the vote on Thomas's nomination for one week. "The delay approved," Mitchell said, "is important to the integrity of the Senate, the integrity of the confirmation process, the integrity of the Supreme Court, and the integrity of the individuals involved."

NEGOTIATING THE GROUND RULES

With the vote now delayed until Tuesday, October 15, senators began negotiating the ground rules for a new set of Senate Judiciary Committee hearings on the Thomas nomination. The hearing process, Chairman Biden cautioned, "is incredibly difficult in cases where women have been victimized. We must be careful that the victim not be victimized by the system." However, Biden said, the hearings would be public: "We are going to ventilate this subject to give Professor Hill the opportunity to make her case in full and we are going to give the nominee the opportunity to make his defense in full."

After heated debate, the Judiciary Committee ultimately agreed that, out of courtesy for the nominee, Thomas would be given the opportunity to testify first if he wanted and again at the hearings' conclusion in order to rebut any charges made against him. At a caucus of the committee, Biden also made a controversial ruling that there would be no questioning about the personal lives of either Thomas or Hill during the hearings, including questions relating to whether Thomas had viewed pornography at home[66] and questions about Hill's sex life.

Biden announced that the Judiciary Committee would subpoena witnesses if necessary but that the scope of the inquiry would be limited to allegations of sexual harassment, either by Hill or any others who might step forward. Danforth wanted the hearings limited to Hill's accusation, but Biden insisted that if any other credible allegations of sexual harassment appeared, they should be covered; but "anyone who wants to make charges against Thomas would have to be willing to testify in public session." Both parties agreed that there would be no surprise witnesses, but Biden later admitted he "wouldn't be very surprised if someone doesn't come out of the blue and say something."

MORE CHARGES ARISE

In fact, just two days later, the Senate Judiciary Committee disclosed the name of another woman accusing Thomas of improper sexual advances at the EEOC. Angela Wright—assistant metropolitan editor for the *Charlotte Observer* newspaper in North Carolina—was subpoenaed to testify at the new round of public hearings. Wright told the committee that Thomas had persistently tried to date her, commented on the size of her breasts, and once showed up unannounced at her apartment while she worked as chief spokeswoman for the EEOC from 1984–85. The committee also subpoenaed

Rose Jourdain, a former speech writer for Thomas at the EEOC, who said Wright confided in her at the time that Thomas's remarks about "her figure, her body, her breasts" had bothered her. Wright insisted she was not "stating a claim of sexual harassment" against Thomas, and that she found his conduct "at the most annoying and obnoxious." "My desire is not to keep Clarence Thomas off the Supreme Court," stated Wright, a registered Republican. However, Wright said, "I know enough about the man to know he's quite capable of doing what she [Hill] said he did. . . . We are talking about a general mode of operating." Wright had never met Hill.

Soon after Wright's name was disclosed, White House officials questioned her honesty. They described her as "the classic disgruntled employee" and promised to produce a witness to refute her charges. On October 10, the White House also issued a statement criticizing the Judiciary Committee for neglecting what it called the "normal practice" of first seeking an FBI investigation.

The committee also received a sworn affidavit from Sukari Hardnett, a special assistant to Thomas at the EEOC from 1985–86. In her affidavit, Hardnett testified that Thomas's treatment of women at work was more than that of "a mentor to protégés." "If you were young, black, female, reasonably attractive and worked directly for Clarence Thomas," Hardnett wrote, "you knew full well you were being inspected and auditioned as a female. . . . And you knew when you had ceased to be an object of sexual interest because you were barred from entering his office and treated as an outcast, or worse, a leper." Although Hardnett also said she was not charging Thomas with sexual harassment, she stated that she "found his attention unpleasant, [and] sought a transfer. . . ."

THE THOMAS-HILL HEARINGS

The Senate Judiciary Committee hearings reconvened on Friday, October 11, continuing over the long Columbus Day weekend.

The first two days of proceedings were carried live on ABC, NBC, and CBS; on public television; and on CNN and other cable networks. (On Sunday, only public television stations ran the hearings.) Friday morning, Thomas testified first, followed by seven hours of afternoon testimony from Hill. After Hill was finished, Thomas again testified before the committee during "prime time" that evening and all day Saturday. On Sunday, witnesses appearing on behalf of Hill and Thomas began their testimony at noon and continued through the wee hours of the morning. Neither Thomas nor Hill appeared before the committee on Monday. The full Senate vote was scheduled for Tuesday, October 15, at 6:00 P.M.

In his opening statement, Biden explained the ground rules of the hearings. The primary responsibility of the committee was, in Biden's view, fairness. "That means making sure we do not victimize any witness who appears here and that we treat every witness with respect. . . . Fairness means understanding what a victim of sexual harassment goes through, why victims often do not report such crimes, why they often believe that they should not or cannot leave their jobs. . . . Fairness also means that Judge Thomas must be given a full and fair opportunity to confront these charges against him, to respond fully, to tell us his side of the story, and to be given the benefit of the doubt." Biden then informed all witnesses that "they have the right under Senate Rule 26.5 to ask that the committee go into closed sessions if a question requires an answer that is quote 'a clear invasion of their right to privacy,' end quote."

The Judiciary Committee decided that Biden, Leahy, and Heflin would conduct almost all the questioning for the Democrats. For the Republicans, Hatch would question Thomas and any witness called to support him, while Specter would interrogate Hill and her supporters. A senator from each party would ask questions for thirty minutes, then give way to a senator

from the other party. Biden reminded his colleagues that he, as chairman, had "the power to rule out of order questions . . . not relevant to [the] proceedings, namely private conduct; out-of-the-workplace relationships; and intimate lives and practices of Judge Thomas, Professor Hill, and any other witness that comes before us." Biden emphasized that "this is not a hearing about the extent and nature of sexual harassment in America," and decided not to allow testimony from sexual harassment experts who might explain Hill's behavior. In addition, Biden ruled out the use of polygraph tests to resolve contradictions between Hill and Thomas, stating that polygraph tests were "not the appropriate way to get the truth," and it would be a "sad day for the civil liberties in this country" if they became the basis for important decisions.[67]

CONFLICTING TESTIMONY

In his three appearances before the committee, Thomas categorically denied all of Hill's charges.[68] Appearing to be near tears at times and almost shaking with rage at others, Thomas claimed that he was a victim of historical racial stereotypes about the alleged sexual prowess of black men. He assailed the Senate Confirmation process as "a circus" and a "national disgrace"—from his standpoint as a black American, it was "a high-tech lynching for uppity blacks who deign to think for themselves." According to Thomas, interest groups opposed to his confirmation "concocted" Hill's story in collusion with liberal Senate staffers. Thomas charged that "unless you kowtow to an old order, this is what will happen to you. You will be lynched, destroyed, caricatured by a committee of the U.S. Senate rather than hung from a tree." Thomas refused to discuss his private life with the committee. "I will not provide the rope for my own lynching," Thomas said, and declared: "I would have preferred an assassin's bullet to this kind of living hell that they have put me and my family through."

Thomas added that he would "rather die than withdraw" his nomination.

In her testimony, Hill directly contradicted her former boss with graphic detail. For seven hours on Friday, Hill recounted her story of how Thomas had humiliated her with his constant talk of women's breasts, the size of his penis, and accounts of movies of group sex and bestiality. She denied that liberal groups and others opposed to Thomas had prompted her appearance and expressed personal anguish in discussing the alleged sexual harassment on national television. "It is only after a great deal of agonizing consideration that I am able to talk of these unpleasant matters to anyone except my closest friends," Hill said. "Telling the world is the most difficult experience of my life."

Sunday afternoon, a panel of four witnesses appeared to corroborate Hill's story. All four witnesses—who had never met each other before the hearings—described Hill as an honest, reserved woman who confided in them about her situation in the early 1980s, at the time of the alleged harassment.[69] After Hill's four corroborating witnesses finished, sixteen character witnesses were presented on Thomas's behalf,[70] many of them women who had worked with Thomas at the EEOC or the Department of Education. Each described Thomas's character as impeccable and swore they could not imagine Thomas ever doing what Hill described.

PARTISAN STRATEGIES

The hearings were rife with partisan bickering and personal attacks. Committee Republicans initially blamed Democrats for publicizing Hill's charge, demanded an FBI investigation into the leak, and tried to turn the debate to whether Thomas was victimized by the Senate confirmation process. Republicans then launched what many reporters called a "scorched-earth" strategy to discredit Hill, suggesting that she was mentally unstable and merely fantasizing about the sexual

harassment as part of a conspiracy to defeat Thomas. Senator Alan Simpson (R-Wyo.) claimed that letters, faxes, and statements were pouring into his office "over the transom," warning that he "watch out for this woman."[71] Specter and Hatch repeatedly questioned why, if Thomas had harassed her as she claimed, Hill did not file complaints about the alleged incidents. Why, they asked, had Hill followed Thomas from one agency to another, and then kept in contact with him over the years? (Republicans submitted into the record telephone logs kept at the EEOC showing that Hill had telephoned Thomas ten or eleven times in the eight years since her departure from the agency.)[72]

Democrats on the committee did not move forcefully to rebut the Republican's attack on Hill's character, and for the most part, Hill stood alone against the senators. Hill told the committee she moved with Thomas to the EEOC because, if she quit, she would have been jobless—there was a hiring freeze in the federal government at the time, and she wanted to stay in civil rights. Hill said she did not file a complaint against Thomas for fear of retaliation, and later kept cordial, but distant contact with him for professional reasons. Regarding the telephone logs, Hill claimed that, in most cases, she was simply returning Thomas's calls, while some of the other reported phone calls had never been made.

When asked why the Democrats were not more aggressive vis-à-vis the Republicans, Leahy replied, "I will not smear and lie just because they do." Biden agreed. "I think the Republicans were more partisan in their objective" while "we were trying to find out the truth. We could have gone in there and said we aren't going to listen to what he says, and everything she says will be put in a positive light. I didn't think that was the way to conduct his hearing."

Committee Democrats generally appeared stunned by Thomas's angry charges of racism, and seemed almost apologetic in having to ask Thomas about the issue of sexual harassment. All respected Thomas's refusals to discuss his personal life. Not a single committee member asked Thomas about a statement made by a friend and former Yale Law School classmate of his, Lovida Coleman Jr. Coleman said that Thomas "at least once humorously described an X-rated film to [her] and other colleagues," and acknowledged that this had occurred more than once.[73] The subject was not mentioned at all until very late Sunday night, when Leahy asked a witness testifying for Thomas if he was aware of Coleman's statement. The witness—a former dean at Oral Roberts University—said he could not imagine Thomas ever watching a pornographic film.

Biden later conceded that he "could have brought in the pornography stuff." "I could have decimated him at that," said Biden, "but it would make a lie of everything I fought for."[74] Simon later said he agreed with Biden's decision: "I am not sure there is a direct link between watching pornographic films and sexual harassment," adding that he too "felt uneasy getting into that field."[75]

ANGELA WRIGHT

Before Thomas left the stand on Saturday, Biden reassured him: "The presumption [of innocence] is with you, judge." According to Biden, sexual harassment "doesn't happen in isolated instances— it's a pattern. If there's not a pattern," he told Thomas, "to me, that's probative," or legally meaningful. Late Sunday night, however, Biden announced that Angela Wright and Rose Jourdain—whom Hill's supporters believed might have helped establish Biden's required "pattern"— would not testify publicly as originally planned, despite the fact that Thomas had been given the opportunity on Friday to try to discredit Wright. (Thomas testified that he "aggressively and summarily" fired Wright because of reports that she "referred to another male member of [his] staff as a faggot.")[76] On Sunday night,

Biden stated that he would have preferred to have the two women testify in person, but because of the late hour, agreed to enter the unsworn, seventy-page transcript of their telephone interviews with Judiciary staff into the record of the hearings.[77]

Cynthia Hogan, a Judiciary Committee lawyer who led the committee's questioning of Wright, explained that although she "thought Angela Wright was a very credible witness" and "conveyed that to Senator Biden who accepted that," Biden soon learned that he was the only committee member who wanted Wright to appear. According to Hogan:

> Anita Hill's lawyers had lobbied the other Democratic members of the committee to say they don't want Angela Wright called. I think they bought into some of the stuff the Republicans were saying, and they thought that her reputation wasn't maybe as great or she would somehow taint Anita Hill. I think this was terrible advice. . . . At the same time, I was dealing with Angela Wright's lawyers who watched what happened to Anita Hill and said to me, "she doesn't want to testify, but she doesn't want to publicly say [that]."[78] . . . We did not want to put her on without a corroborating witness, and her corroborating witness [Jourdain] was in the hospital until late in the afternoon on Sunday. We had arranged to have an ambulance pick her up and bring her [to the hearings]. . . . Then out of the blue, the Republicans—who were clearly terrified of Angela Wright—said: "We don't want her to testify and we will accept the transcript of her deposition *unrebutted*." . . . Which to a lawyer means they're accepting it as basically true, so we thought this was a tremendous victory.

Hogan said she was "horrified" when no major news outlet treated the deposition as significant the following day and concedes that the committee "misjudged the way it would be perceived by the press and other senators."

Later that night, Biden announced that both Hill and Thomas would pass up the chance to address the senators again on

Monday. Just after 2:00 A.M., with many questions left unanswered, Biden gaveled the hearings to a close.

THE BENEFIT OF THE DOUBT

On Tuesday, October 15, the Senate confirmed Thomas for the Supreme Court by a vote of 52–48. It was the closest confirmation vote in the twentieth century and a much slimmer victory than had been predicted before the uproar. Voting in favor of Thomas were eleven Democrats and forty-one Republicans; forty-six Democrats and two Republicans voted against Thomas.[79] Both sides estimated that Thomas lost about ten votes that he might have had before the sexual harassment allegations emerged.[80]

The two women in the Senate ultimately voted in line with their respective parties. Kassebaum continued to support Thomas while Mikulski's vote was an outraged "no." In Mikulski's view, committee members "approached this not as a hearing, but as an inquisition. . . . The message for women is: your courage in coming forward will be met with suspicion and scorn . . . [and] unproven, unsupported charges of being mentally unbalanced, fantasizers, jealous, or opportunists." In voting for Thomas, Kassebaum said "it would be manifestly unfair for the Senate to destroy a Supreme Court nominee on the basis of evidence that finally boils down to the testimony of one person, however credible, against his flat, unequivocal, and equally credible denial."

While no Judiciary Committee members changed their votes after the second round of hearings, members intensely debated whether or not Thomas should have been given the benefit of the doubt. DeConcini said he sympathized with Thomas in his ordeal, saying Thomas "does not deserve to be punished for something that is inconclusive." Hatch insisted that "if you believe both of them, anybody who believes in the system of jurisprudence and our system of fairness will give Clarence Thomas the

benefit of the doubt." Kennedy argued the opposite. "There is a very strong likelihood that Professor Hill is telling the truth," Kennedy asserted. "In a case of this vast magnitude, where so much is riding on our decision, the Senate should give the benefit of the doubt to the Supreme Court and to the American people, not to Judge Clarence Thomas." Senator Robert Byrd (D-W.Va.) agreed. "This is not a court case; this is a confirmation hearing. . . . A credible charge of the type that has been leveled at Judge Thomas is enough, in my view, to mandate that we ought to look for a more exemplary nominee."

In a statement issued after the roll call was completed, President Bush said, "Judge Thomas has demonstrated to the Congress and to the nation that he is a man of honesty, dedication, and commitment to the Constitution and the rule of law. The nation and the Court benefit from having a man of principle who is sensitive to the problems and opportunities facing all Americans."

REFORMING THE PROCESS

The day after the confirmation vote, the Senate began a grim reappraisal of the entire process surrounding Supreme Court nominations. While some senators argued that the public hearings exemplified democracy in action, others contended that they illuminated the politicization that has characterized Senate confirmation hearings since the 1987 defeat of Bork's nomination. Sam Nunn (D-Ga.) and others proposed that the Senate refrain in the future from public hearings on confidential allegations, even if they have been leaked to the news media. "Now we have seen the consequences of fulfilling the momentary desire to accommodate the public's 'right to know' and providing for resolution of allegations in a trial-type public hearing," Nunn said. "The appetites we have struggled to control in the past were not suppressed, and the Senate now faces public revulsion, rather than accolades, for our indulgence."

President Bush agreed that the Judiciary Committee should have met privately to examine sexual harassment accusations against Thomas rather than broadcast the "graphic detail" of the charges around the country. "I was thinking of my little grandchildren hearing some of the graphic sex allegations," Bush complained. Joseph Lieberman (D-CT) was skeptical, however. He argued that serious charges could not be kept secret by a committee from the full Senate and questioned whether they could be kept confidential after being disseminated to one hundred people. In this case, Americans would have suspected a "cover-up" if public hearings were not held, Lieberman argued.

For his part, Biden said he regarded the events surrounding the Thomas nomination as a "terribly ugly chapter on Capitol Hill,"[81] but continued to believe the committee's handling of Hill's charges, prior to their public disclosure, was proper. Still, Biden told the *Washington Post* "there was no question that this would have to come out" once the allegations were made to Senate staff and that "the best thing would have been for [Hill's] allegation to have been made public from the outset." Aware that his critics believed that a committee investigator should have gone to Oklahoma in September to interview Hill and try to convince her to come forward, Biden defended his actions: "It would have been immoral for me to have done that," he said. "Going out and pushing her and cajoling her . . . would be thrusting an incredible burden on someone who is going to go through a difficult decision that is going to have a dramatic impact on her life." "I know others think differently," Biden acknowledged.

Epilogue

More people watched the Thomas confirmation hearings than any act of American governance ever before in history.[82] According to Gallup polls completed the week of the Senate vote, Americans generally approved of the way Biden ran the hearings but were dismayed by the overall confirmation process and the behavior of the Senate. Biden received a favorable response from 63 percent of those polled—the highest rating for a member of the Judiciary Committee.[83] However, 66 percent of those responding to an ABC News poll the same week said they disapproved of the Senate's handling of the confirmation process, and Gallup researchers found that 48 percent of respondents had less confidence in Congress as a result of the hearings, compared with 21 percent who had more.[84] A *New York Times*/CBS News poll taken on October 13 revealed that 58 percent of those polled believed the hearings would result in "nothing good," while 36 percent believed "something good" was accomplished by the hearings. In the same poll, 59 percent believed the committee's questions and testimony went too far for what should be allowed in a public hearing, while 33 percent believed the questions and testimony were appropriate.

In a survey of one hundred state and federal judges conducted by the *National Law Journal* after the hearings, one out of three believed the process had damaged the credibility of the Supreme Court, while many more believed that Bush and Congress had been harmed. Eighty-five judges rated the Senate Judiciary Committee's skill in examining the witnesses as "fair" or "poor." Fewer than half the judges surveyed said that they would want to be nominated to the nation's highest court.[85]

Notes

1. Senator Metzenbaum dissented.

2. *Washington Post,* July 2, 1991, p. Al.

3. Ibid., p. A7.

4. Ibid., Sept. 10, 1991, p. Al.

5. During his 1990 judicial confirmation hearings, Thomas admitted this was "the worst event during [his] tenure." Thomas blamed the growing backlog of unaddressed cases on a lack of funds. (*Washington Post,* Sept. 10, 1991, p. Al).

6. *Washington Post National Weekly Edition,* Sept.16–22, 1991, p. 9.

7. *Congressional Quarterly Weekly Report,* July 13, 1991, p. 1902.

8. *Washington Post,* July 2, 1991. p. Al.

9. Stanley Feingold, "Sure It's Politics; When Wasn't It? The Senate's Role in Supreme Court Nominations," *National Law Journal,* Sept. 2, 1991, p. 18.

10. Ibid., p. 18.

11. The group's lone Republican, freshman Gary Franks of Connecticut, was the only dissenting voice.

12. Not all civil rights groups opposed Thomas. The National Urban League voted to take no position on Thomas. "I think it is important that we have a racially diverse Supreme Court, even if he is not my candidate," said John Jacob, the league's president at that time. (*Washington Post,* Aug. 1, 1991, p. Al).

13. Lehrman's article described *Roe* as a "coup against the Constitution" leading to a "holocaust" for fetuses (*Congressional Quarterly Weekly Report,* Aug. 3, 1991, p. 2364).

14. *Washington Post,* July 2, 1991, p. Al.

15. Ibid.

16. *Congressional Quarterly Weekly Report,* Aug. 5, 1991, p. 2170.

17. *Washington Post,* Aug. 3, 1991. p. Al.

18. Like Souter, Thomas did say he believes the right to privacy—the legal underpinning for the Court's recognition of a constitutional guarantee to abortion—is a fundamental constitutional right for married couples. But he declined to say whether or not he believes that right extends beyond the marital setting.

19. Thomas completed his testimony on September 16. During the remainder of the week, through September 20, other witnesses testified before the committee on behalf of or against the nominee. These included special interest groups, legal scholars, and individuals who knew or had worked with Thomas.

20. *Washington Post,* Sept. 21, 1991, p. A7.

21. Between 1980 and 1991, fifteen harassment complaints had been filed against EEOC employees. Of those, several were rejected by the agency as unjustifiable, one was settled "with corrective action" and the fate of the others was either pending or unknown (*Boston Globe,* Oct. 10, 1991, p. 31).

22. The EEOC's new guidelines were severely critiqued in a 1980 Reagan transition team report coauthored by Thomas. Complaining that the guidelines would lead "to a barrage of trivial complaints against employers around the nation," and that "the elimination of personal slights and sexual advances which contribute to an 'intimidating, hostile or offensive working environment' is a goal impossible to reach," the report advised that "expenditure of the EEOC's limited resources in pursuit of this goal is unwise" (Timothy M. Phelps and Helen Winternitz, *Capitol Games: Clarence Thomas, Anita Hill, and the Story of a Supreme Court Nomination* [New York: Hyperion, 1992], p. 382).

23. It was later reported that this "tip" might have originated from a conversation held between Hill and her Yale law school friend, Gary Phillips, within days of Bush's nomination of Thomas. When Phillips asked Hill what she thought about the nomination of her former boss, Hill apparently replied: "I never told you this before, but I was sexually harassed by Clarence Thomas." Over the next few weeks, Phillips reportedly told friends he knew a woman who had been harassed by Thomas, and the story quickly "made the rounds" (*U.S. News & World Report,* Oct. 12, 1992). Phillips said that, at the time, Hill was "struggling personally with whether to say anything," and "wasn't planning to because she thought people wouldn't believe her," among other reasons (*Washington Post,* Oct. 9, 1991, p. A9).

24. This represents Hill's account of her conversations with Brudney, as stated before the Senate Judiciary Committee on Oct. 11, 1991.

25. Peter Fleming, Jr., *Report of Temporary Special Independent Counsel Pursuant to Senate Resolution 202,* May 4, 1992, p. 32.

26. Ibid., p. 33.

27. Phelps and Winternitz, *Capitol Games,* p. 213.

28. Fleming, *Report,* p. 33. According to Fleming's report, Brudney says that during these conversations, he did not encourage Hill to press her charges. Hill, however, recalls Brudney's stance as more persistent, and says she told Brudney on several occasions that it was her decision to make. "From Hill's perspective, the difference in approach was her own experience that allegations of sexual harassment are often disbelieved, whereas Brudney was confident that Hill's statements, with evidence of a contemporaneous complaint to a friend in 1981, would be credited," the report says.

29. Ibid., pp. 33–34.

30. Ibid., p. 35.

31. Ibid., p. 36.

32. Ibid., pp. 36–38.

33. Ibid., pp. 38–39 and p. 88.

34. The FBI regards the White House as its "client agency" in its background investigations of nominees. For that reason, any investigative assignments requested by the Senate must pass through the White House (Ibid., p. 40).

35. Both the *New York Times* and the *Washington Post* later reported, apparently inaccurately, that Thomas told the FBI he had asked Hill out a few times, but eventually dropped all advances after she declined.

36. *Washington Post,* Oct. 8, 1991, p. A7.

37. *Newsweek*, Oct. 21, 1991, p. 28. According to the FBI's Civil Rights and Special Inquiries section head, the bureau serves only as an information-gatherer, and avoids offering conclusions about the validity of allegations as a general rule (*Washington Post*, Oct. 8, 1991).

38. Fleming, *Report*, pp. 41–42.

39. *New York Times*, Oct. 8, 1991, p. A22. To ensure Hill's confidentiality, committee members were required to scan the FBI report in the presence of a committee staffer and then return it when finished.

40. Fleming, *Report*, pp. 42–43.

41. Ibid., p. 43.

42. *U.S. News and World Report*, Oct. 21, 1991, p. 36.

43. Fleming, *Report*, pp. 45–46.

44. *Washington Post*, Sept. 28, 1991, p. Al.

45. *New York Times*, Sept. 29, 1991, Section 1, p. 24.

46. Fleming, *Report*, p. 50.

47. *Newsday*, Sept. 28, 1991. At this point, Phelps had learned from others that the FBI was investigating Hill's charges of sexual harassment. However, he did not know what the specific allegations were and did not have enough information for a full story. (See Phelps and Winternitz, *Capitol Games*, p. 228).

48. The record was held by Chief Justice William Rehnquist, who drew 33 votes against when he was elevated to associate justice in the 1980s (*Washington Post*).

49. A motion to postpone the Senate vote would have required the unanimous consent of the Senate.

50. *Congressional Quarterly Weekly Report*, Sept. 28, 1991, p. 2786.

51. *Washington Post*, Sept 28, 1991, p. Al.

52. Hatch spoke as he was seated next to Thurmond, who held the personal record of 24 hours and 19 minutes for a filibuster against a civil rights bill in 1957 (*Washington Post*, Sept. 28, 1991, p. Al).

53. Rule 29.5, the general Senate rule against disclosure of confidential information, provides: "Any senator who shall disclose the secret or confidential business or proceedings of the Senate shall be liable, if a Senator, to suffer expulsion from the body; and if an officer, to dismissal from the service of the Senate, and to punishment for contempt." (Rule 29.5, Standing Rules of the Senate, reprinted in S. Doc. No. 101-1, at 62).

54. *Congressional Quarterly Weekly Report*, Oct. 12, 1991, p. 2956.

55. Contrary to the impression created by early press reports, the contents of the FBI report had not been disseminated outside the Senate in whole or in part (Fleming, *Report*, p. 5).

56. *Washington Post*, Oct. 6, 1991, p. Al.

57. Hill described herself as both a conservative and a Democrat (CBS, *Sixty Minutes*, Feb. 2, 1992).

58. *New York Times*, Oct. 9, 1991, p. A18.

59. Not all Republican members of the Senate Judiciary Committee were fully informed of Hill's charges before the September 27 committee vote.

60. *New York Times*, Oct. 8, 1991, p. A21.

61. Congress exempts itself from most federal labor laws, including those governing sexual harassment.

62. Thomas was formally interviewed by the FBI on September 25. It is unclear why his statement said September 28.

63. No portion of the FBI report was leaked.

64. *New York Times*, Oct. 9, 1991. p Al.

65. Ibid., pp. Al, Al8.

66. Two owners of video stores in Washington had indicated to journalists that they had rented pornographic movies to Thomas in recent years (Phelps and Winternitz, *Capitol Games*, p. 393).

67. On Sunday, Hill's lawyers released the results of a polygraph test conducted by Paul K. Minor, former chief polygraph examiner for the FBI. According to Minor, it indicated "no deception" in Hill's answers to questions about her charges. Thomas did not take a polygraph test. (Polygraph tests were generally not admissible in court, and there was no scientific consensus about their reliability. However, Presidents Reagan and Bush vastly expanded the use of polygraphs in the 1980s, routinely administering them in the course of "leak" and national security investigations, while liberal Democrats were traditionally critical of their use).

68. On Saturday, Thomas said that the FBI agent who interviewed him on September 25 later told him the bureau had incorrectly reported that Thomas admitted to asking Hill out on a few dates.

69. One witness (Joel Paul, a law professor at American University) said that during Hill's 1987 interview for a teaching position at American University, Hill told him that she had left her job at the EEOC because she had been sexually harassed by her supervisor.

70. According to *Newsweek*, Biden initially tried to shorten the list of witnesses supporting Thomas, but backed down after the Bush administration threatened to hold a press conference to denounce the committee for being unfair (Oct. 21, 1991, p. 26).

71. Simpson did not elaborate on the sources of content of the statements, but after critics demanded he do so, Simpson eventually put some of the material in the *Congressional Record*.

72. It is standard procedure in many federal offices to maintain daily records of office telephone calls for several years. The EEOC phone logs did not indicate whether Hill had initiated the calls or returned previous calls from Thomas.

73. Coleman, a Washington lawyer, also said that neither she nor other students "were offended by his amusing accounts. Indeed, we would have been

hypocrites to have been offended since very few of us failed to attend one or more similar films that were shown on the Yale University campus while we were in school." Coleman also described Thomas as "particularly sensitive and caring regarding the professional and personal concerns of the women he knows and with whom he has worked," and said she seriously doubted that he had sexually harassed Hill (*New York Times,* Oct.10, 1991, p. B14).

74. *Washington Post,* June 19, 1992.

75. Senator Paul Simon, *Advice & Consent: Clarence Thomas, Robert Bork and the Intriguing History of the Supreme Court's Nomination Battles* (Washington, D.C.: National Press Books, 1992), pp. 120–121.

76. The *Charlotte Observer* stated that when they called Thomas for a reference in 1990, Thomas described Wright as "an excellent employee" and told them Wright had resigned her post at the EEOC.

77. Biden later admitted that the committee might have halted the hearings to investigate whether there was a "pattern of behavior" on Thomas's part. However, Biden said, "had we announced we were holding up this hearing . . . he [Thomas] would have been cannibalized" (*Washington Post,* June 19, 1992).

78. Wright later told *U.S. News & World Report* that Biden's staff "is lying"—that Hogan "pressured" her attorney to withdraw his client as a live witness and instead submit her statement for the record. Wright said she finally succumbed when "it became apparent that hardly anyone would be around" to hear her story late that night (*U.S. News & World Report,* Oct. 12, 1992).

79. Jeffords (Vt.) and Bob Packwood (Ore.) were the only Republican senators to oppose Thomas.

80. *Congressional Quarterly Weekly Report,* Oct.19, 1991, p. 3030.

81. *Wall Street Journal,* Oct. 11, 1991, p. A10.

82. Senator Joseph R. Biden, Jr., "Reforming the Confirmation Process: A New Era Must Dawn," June 25, 1992, p. 23. (139 Cong. Rec. S8771-01)

83. *Boston Globe,* Oct. 16, 1991, p. 6.

84. Ibid.

85. Of the one hundred judges surveyed, seventy-five were state judges while twenty-five were federal judges. Ninety-four judges were male, with forty-five Democrats and thirty-six Republicans (*National Law Journal,* Oct. 28, 1991, pp. 1, 22).

Comment

Was the Senate Judiciary Committee justified in making Hill's charges public? Anita Hill initially had made her statements on the condition that they be treated as confidential. Confidentiality is not the same as privacy with respect to personal matters, but it implicates some of the same values. Hill said she had come forward only reluctantly, out of a sense of duty, to provide the information and let the Committee investigate. If the chief counsel of the Judiciary Committee reasonably understood Hill to be insisting on a degree of confidentiality that included not telling the nominee about her identity, then the Judiciary Committee had a strong reason to keep her allegations secret. Respecting her request confronted the committee with a moral dilemma. The committee could ignore the charges, in which case they would fail in their constitutional duty to examine Thomas's qualifications thoroughly. Or they could consider the charges without telling Thomas, in which case they would violate Thomas's right to confront his accusers. (The question that faced some members and staff—whether to leak information about Hill's charges—should be considered in the context of the issue of official disobedience, raised in Chapter 5.)

Clarence Thomas also had a claim to privacy. He believed that a public hearing on the allegations would be a degrading intrusion into his private life even if he could prove the allegations were false. But the allegations were also relevant to one of the most important questions that Congress decides: who is qualified to sit on the

Supreme Court. Thomas did not have a right to this job, and the hearings were not a criminal trial, contrary to what the chairman of the committee implied. The committee believed that Thomas's rights could be adequately protected if he were given a fair chance to defend himself in a proper forum.

Some argue that public hearings in a case like this tend to reinforce racist and sexist attitudes in this country. Staging a dramatic confrontation between two black citizens in the atmosphere of a "high-tech lynching" was unlikely to reduce racial prejudice. And the spectacle of the all-male, all-white committee sitting in judgment of Hill and Thomas was not a positive lesson in equal justice. Others argue that public hearings were desirable precisely to expose these attitudes and inequalities. Furthermore, if we do not publicly confront and collectively discuss issues such as sexual harassment, gay and lesbian rights, or racial justice, we may never learn how to do so responsibly.

Even if we decide that the value of publicity outweighs the claims of privacy in this case, we might not conclude that full public hearings were required. An executive session of the committee, closed to the press and the public, might have been acceptable to Hill, fairer to Thomas, and still consistent with the committee's constitutional responsibilities. In principle, the hearings could have been kept confidential, with full records to be released at a specified future date. In practice, in this instance, by the time the committee had to decide about the hearings, too many people already knew too much about the case, and too many stood to lose or gain too much by its outcome.

A decision to hold open hearings need not remove all ethical limits on publicity. The committee refused to pursue some lines of investigation that risked even greater exposure of the personal lives of the witnesses. For example, they did not permit Thomas's supporters to introduce testimony about Hill's past relationships with men, and they did not seek records of videos that Thomas rented for his personal use, even though some of this information would have been relevant to the committee's deliberations, at least to assessing the credibility of witnesses. Were they justified in setting these limits on publicity? Should they have set more limits? Had the committee held closed hearings it might have been less justified in limiting the inquiry in these ways. Making the hearings public let citizens judge for themselves whether the inquiry into the allegations had been extensive enough.

The Investigation and Impeachment of President Clinton*

Jillian Dickert

In 1994, Independent Counsel Kenneth Starr began investigating President and Mrs. Clinton's dealings, while Clinton was governor of Arkansas, with the Whitewater land development company and with Madison Guaranty, a failed savings and loan. Though his "Whitewater" probe had resulted in several indictments, guilty pleas, and convictions of Arkansas business and political figures, none of Starr's investigative threads had led directly to the president until the matter of Clinton's sexual contact with Monica Lewinsky, a young, former White House employee, came under his purview.

A former federal appeals judge and solicitor general, Starr had been a top aide in the Reagan Justice Department and Bush's top advocate before the Supreme Court. However, Starr had never before prosecuted a case and his appointment by the judicial panel overseeing independent counsels raised criticism. Before his appointment was announced, Starr had spoken out publicly in favor of Paula Corbin Jones's sexual harassment lawsuit. Jones, a clerk at the Arkansas Industrial Development Commission, claimed that Clinton kissed her, put his hands under her clothing and requested oral sex in a hotel room in 1991, while he was governor of Arkansas. Starr had disputed Clinton's assertion that a president should be immune from civil lawsuits while in office, and had volunteered to file a friend-of-the-court brief to support the contention that Jones's case should go forward.

On May 8, 1994, Jones went to court seeking $700,000 in damages from Clinton for "willful, outrageous and malicious conduct" and emotional distress. A series of legal appeals brought the Jones case all the way to the Supreme Court. Repeated attempts to settle the lawsuit failed. Then, in May 1997, the Court rejected Clinton's presidential immunity arguments, unconvinced that the Jones suit was a burden on the Office. Arkansas Judge Susan Webber Wright scheduled Jones' trial court date for May 1998.

*Research assistance was provided by Jennifer Sekelsky. Funding was supplied by the Program in Ethics and the Professions at Harvard University and the Center for Human Values at Princeton University. Copyright © 2000 by the President and Fellows of Harvard College and by Princeton University.

Meanwhile, in April 1997, former Clinton White House secretary Linda Tripp contacted *Newsweek* reporter Michael Isikoff about President Clinton's relationship with Monica Lewinsky, a 23-year-old, former White House intern and employee. Tripp claimed that the president was having sex in the Oval Office and "phone sex" with Lewinsky. Tripp had been a public affairs assistant at the Pentagon since 1996, the same year Lewinsky had also been transferred there unwillingly. Isikoff did nothing with Tripp's information at that time.

In September 1997, Tripp consulted with New York literary agent Lucianne Goldberg about a half-million dollar deal on an insider-tell-all book Tripp could write about the Clinton White House. At Goldberg's suggestion, Tripp began to record her telephone conversations with Lewinsky as "evidence" for convincing Isikoff to write a *Newsweek* piece that could serve as a "teaser" for Tripp's book. Tripp began taping Lewinsky that fall; altogether she recorded about 20 hours of their conversations on 17 cassettes.

Most of the taped conversations centered on Lewinsky's career woes; Lewinsky had long been upset about her transfer out of the White House. Together Tripp and Lewinsky came up with the idea of recruiting the assistance of Clinton's good friend Vernon Jordan, a well-connected lawyer and Washington power broker, to help with Lewinsky's job search. In December, Jordan telephoned several senior corporate executives in New York to help Lewinsky land job interviews, including one at Revlon, which offered Lewinsky a public relations job on January 9. Jordan was under Starr's scrutiny because of a consulting contract he helped arrange for a key Whitewater figure, so Lewinsky's contacts with Jordan proved crucial for justifying the eventual involvement of Office of the Independent Counsel (OIC) in the Lewinsky matter.

Tripp, meanwhile, tipped off Paula Jones's lawyers about Lewinsky. Thinking that Lewinsky might corroborate Clinton's alleged pattern of sexual misconduct, they subsequently amended Jones's lawsuit to present

Clinton as a sexual "predator" who deprived Jones of career advancements for having rebuffed him sexually, but ensured that those providing him with "sexual favors" received jobs or other workplace benefits. This new strategy would open consensual affairs—not just unwanted advances—to investigation if there was evidence that government benefits were offered. Jones's lawyers thus subpoenaed Lewinsky for the trial. But Lewinsky signed a sworn affidavit stating, "I have never had a sexual relationship with the President."

Tripp continued to record her conversations with Lewinsky through December 1997. Goldberg told lawyers working for Jones that Tripp's December 22 tape of Lewinsky proved that "Vernon Jordan told her to lie." These lawyers quietly informed a key figure in Starr's office about Tripp's taping. Intrigued, Starr agreed to work with Tripp. Her tapes and a "sting" operation (where Tripp wore a body wire in Lewinsky's presence) provided the OIC with the evidence to convince the Justice Department that Starr should expand his investigation of Clinton in January 1998. Tripp also provided the Jones legal team with an hour-long description of Lewinsky's relationship with Clinton to enable them to question the president about it during his January 17 Jones deposition. After defining "sexual relations" as "when [a] person knowingly engages in or causes contact with the genitalia, anus, groin, breast, inner thigh, or buttocks of any person with an intent to arouse or gratify the sexual desire of any person," Jones's lawyer asked Clinton about his relationship with Lewinsky. Clinton's response was: "I have never had sexual relations with Monica Lewinsky. I've never had an affair with her."

The night before Clinton's deposition, Tripp's lawyer gave *Newsweek* reporter Isikoff a copy of the December 22 tape. *Newsweek* also learned that the Justice Department had authorized Starr's investigation of the Lewinsky matter and possible obstruction of justice. But after a heated internal debate, the magazine decided to hold the story. Isikoff explained this to Goldberg, who in turn leaked the story to Internet gossip columnist Matt Drudge. The Drudge Report set off a media feeding frenzy that included over 4,000 Clinton-Lewinsky stories during the week of January 21. The *Washington Post* headline read: "Clinton Accused of Urging Aide to Lie; Starr Probes Whether President Told Woman to Deny Alleged Affair to Jones Lawyers." Not to be outdone, *Newsweek* posted an Internet version of the story the magazine held over the weekend, which made public for the first time vast amounts of new information, including an extensive account of the December 22 tape, with direct quotes and details of Starr's "sting" operation.

On January 26, 1998, President Clinton denied any wrongdoing before a prime-time television audience: "I did not have sexual relations with that woman, Ms. Lewinsky. I never told anybody to lie, . . . " Starr's investigation of the Lewinsky matter continued for nine months as details and rumors leaked out and were spread by the media. The White House settled into a brazen-it-out, scandal-response counteroffensive—Starr called it "stonewalling"—to slow down the march of events and attack Starr's investigation as a part of a "vast right-wing conspiracy" against Clinton. Executive privilege claims bought the president months of legal wrangling. Meanwhile, on April 1, Judge Wright dismissed the Jones lawsuit entirely—a dramatic move that led to Starr being bombarded with questions about his continuing investigation, which had cost the public over $40 million from the beginning of his Whitewater probe. Starr also came under heavy fire for allegedly leaking confidential information. On June 19, the judge overseeing Starr's grand jury, Norma Holloway Johnson, issued a secret ruling sanctioning Starr for "serious and repetitive . . . prima facie violations" of Rule 6(e), which requires that testimony and other evidence given to a grand jury be kept secret.

In August 1998, Lewinsky turned over a semen-stained dress to the OIC as part of an agreement granting her immunity from prosecution. President Clinton submitted a blood sample that, it was later determined, matched the DNA on the dress. Then, on August 17, the president testified before Starr's grand jury in a videotaped but "secret" five-hour session. Afterwards, Clinton addressed the nation in a speech in which he finally acknowledged having had sexual contact with Lewinsky. Public opinion polls continued to show—as they did throughout 1998—that while many Americans disapproved of Clinton's behavior, a large majority approved of his public performance as president and wanted Starr's investigation to end immediately without impeachment. But many commentators said that Clinton's speech was not contrite enough. On September 3, Connecticut Democrat Joseph Lieberman, Clinton's friend since 1970, gave an anguished speech on the Senate floor saying Clinton's "disgraceful" behavior—"extramarital sexual relations with an employee half his age . . . in the workplace, in the vicinity of the Oval Office" and "willfully deceiving the nation about his conduct"—was "not just inappropriate [but] immoral."

During his August 17 grand jury appearance, it was later revealed, Clinton did not specifically acknowledge touching Lewinsky in any sexual way, and otherwise refused to provide intimate details. Starr therefore brought Lewinsky back in late August for additional testimony about their sexual encounters. A good deal of information from this final interrogation would go into Starr's final report, in order to counter Clinton's assertion that he did not technically have "sexual relations" with Lewinsky under the definition provided by Jones's lawyers.

THE CONGRESS

On the afternoon of September 9, 1998, two black Dodge vans loaded with boxes of secret investigative materials about the president of the United States pulled up to the Capitol steps. Independent Counsel Kenneth Starr's long-awaited report had finally arrived—much to the surprise of the House of Representatives, just back from summer recess. It was a full nine months since the story of President Clinton's sexual contacts with a young, former White House employee, Monica Lewinsky, exploded onto the Washington political scene, dominating news headlines with a continuous drumbeat of misconduct allegations. Now, with a 445-page referral and 18 boxes of supplementary materials, Starr was serving Congress with what he described as "substantial and credible information" of impeachable offenses by the president. Never before in the 20-year history of the independent counsel statute had an impeachment report been sent to Congress, and only one president, Andrew Johnson, had ever been impeached—over a century before.

The delivery of the Starr report threw Washington into a state of agitation. Although in August, the president had finally admitted to a relationship with Lewinsky that was "not appropriate" and "wrong," and many details about that relationship had been leaked to the media in bits and pieces since January, Starr was now supplying two vans full of non-public information—including raw grand jury testimony. The impeachment referral came with a warning that the boxes contained "confidential" information of a "personal nature," which the House was urged to "treat as confidential." Under pressure to hold the president accountable for his actions, yet facing an outcry over a long-running and controversial investigation, the House of Representatives would ultimately need to decide how to handle Starr's materials while fulfilling its constitutional duty to assess whether further inquiry was warranted.

THE DECISION

"We are in a new era of openness in this Congress, as demanded by the American people," declared House Rules Committee chair Gerald Solomon [R-N.Y.], commencing the committee's September 10 deliberations over how to handle the confidential impeachment materials delivered one day earlier by the Office of the Independent Counsel (OIC). Solomon's resolution called for the immediate release of Starr's 445-page report, sight unseen, and the rest of the 18 boxes of materials by September 28, after some redaction by the House Judiciary Committee in executive session. The report itself contained a 25-page introduction, a 280-page narrative of events, and a 140-page section laying out possible grounds for impeachment. Included with the report were six binders of 2,000 pages of additional materials. The other 17 boxes contained raw transcripts of the testimony of over 75 witnesses as well as video and audio tapes, including the president's testimony and the Tripp tapes. Solomon said his resolution "attempts to strike an appropriate balance between House members' and the public's interest in reviewing this material, and the need to protect innocent persons." The resolution would also empower the Judiciary Committee to assess whether any potential "high crimes and misdemeanors" in Starr's report justified the initiation of impeachment proceedings against President Clinton.

Leaders of the U.S. House of Representatives had just begun to consider how to handle an impeachment referral when the OIC materials arrived at the Capitol. The House had no standing rules for impeachment, and Democrats had been complaining that they were being kept in the dark about Republican plans. House Minority Leader Dick Gephardt [D-Mo.] urged his colleagues to proceed with caution: "Next to declaring war, this may be the most important thing we do, so we have to do it right. We have to do it objectively, fairly and in a nonpartisan way."

On the morning of September 9, before Starr's report was delivered, leaders of both parties met on their first day back from summer recess and made a commitment to work together in a bipartisan manner. As ranking Judiciary Committee Democrat

John Conyers [Mich.] described it, "We're taking every human effort to control what is the most prevalent disease inside the beltway: . . . the leaks. We think that a lot of people might be unnecessarily hurt by material or information that could be . . . somewhere in some part of the reports [or] . . . the supplemental materials. And so we're torn between keeping this thing under lock and key, or making it available to our colleagues."

At the meeting, Conyers and Judiciary chair Henry Hyde [R-Ill.] proposed that they, as committee leaders, go through all of the OIC boxes jointly before deciding what should be made public—a proposal backed by Gephardt, also in attendance. House Speaker Newt Gingrich [R-Ga.] wanted at least the 445-page Starr report released immediately, but did eventually agree with the bipartisan plan to screen it and the rest of the material first to remove salacious or irrelevant information. However, Gingrich—who later said he viewed the Judiciary Committee as "the most anti-openness group in the House"—gave the power to draft the procedural resolution concerning Starr's referral to Solomon, the Rules chair, rather than Hyde.[1] Solomon then decided to ignore the agreement made earlier by House leaders when, he later told the *Washington Post,* he overheard Judiciary Democrat Barney Frank [Mass.] criticizing Hyde's proposal—which included giving the chair an unprecedented power to charge reluctant witnesses with contempt, without a full House vote—to reporters. "We weren't about to be subjected to that," Solomon said. "If they were going to be that way, let it all come out."[2]

Clearly angry that the deal had been broken, Conyers thundered at the Rules hearings: "The House of Representative is not the U.S. Postal Service . . . [or] a delivery system for Kenneth W. Starr. We cannot, we ought not, we should not release anything to anybody unless we know what it is we are releasing." Reminding the committee that Starr's letter stipulated that some materials contained confidential personal information,

Conyers asked, "Can somebody explain to me what danger will befall a member of Congress if we adhere to what the independent counsel himself told us to do?" Abbe Lowell, the Judiciary's chief Democratic investigator, pleaded for patience: "People's lives are at stake. . . . It ought to be that the House could take a moment to reflect."

House Democrats also complained that the resolution did not provide the president with an opportunity to review and respond to the material before making it public. They pointed out that House ethics rules required that the subject of any investigation be given at least a week before a scheduled vote to review alleged violations, and that Speaker Gingrich was allotted that much time to respond to House Ethics Committee charges made against him in 1997. Others pointed to the 1974 Watergate proceedings in opposing the Starr report's release. None of the materials then sent to Congress by special prosecutor Leon Jaworski were made public until after seven weeks of evidentiary hearings, and a great deal of Jaworski's referral—especially the secret grand jury materials—were still under seal at the National Archives in 1998. Jaworski's referral contained only one briefcase full of raw evidence and a 60-page report that he called a "road map" to it, with no analysis or argument—and only a few senior committee members and lawyers were permitted to see it. In addition, the House Judiciary Committee heard all testimony in private sessions, and President Nixon's counsel was allowed to be present at every stage of the proceedings and to cross-examine witnesses. From the perspective of Sheila Jackson-Lee [D-Tex.], "that was not secrecy to destroy the process, but secrecy to protect freedom and the process."

But as Solomon pointed out, Democrats were divided over whether or not to make Starr's report public. Some, most prominently John Dingell [D-Mich.], wanted it released quickly—especially given the approaching November elections. In a

New York Times editorial appearing on September 10, Dingell wrote: "Let's face it: the damaging details are already out . . . [and] the selective or staged release of the report would only further contribute to public cynicism and distrust of government. Taxpayers spent $40 million on this document. They have a right to know what's in it." Charles Rangel [D-N.Y.] agreed: "There is no question that the substance of the accusations have to be made public because it's going to be leaked anyway, and everyone between now and the election will be putting their spin on it." Both however agreed that sensitive grand jury testimony and names should be omitted, and that the president should be allowed to see the report at least 48 hours before its release. Yet another Democrat, Peter Deutsch [Fla.], argued that if the Starr report was released immediately, then the supporting materials should also be released in their entirety "so people can look at those source documents and very well might come up with totally different conclusions than Mr. Starr came up with."

Most Republicans, in control of the House, supported releasing the Starr referral and opposed giving the president an advance copy because, as Hyde told the White House, "we are unwilling to give you a public relations advantage any greater than the one you have had for the past eight months." Speaker Gingrich added that House "members would never tolerate the President and his counsel getting a document they had never seen." Asked about his certainty that Starr's report did not contain material harmful to innocent people, House Majority Leader Dick Armey replied that "there is general agreement, a sense of comfort about what you're going to run into there." Armey said that the Judiciary Committee had received OIC assurances that the 445 pages could be made public without harm.[3]

On September 10, after three hours of debate, the committee voted along party lines against giving Clinton 48 hours to see the charges Starr had made against him. By voice vote the resolution to release the Starr report was adopted and sent to the full House for a vote on the following day.

On the morning of September 11, two days after delivering its referral, the OIC realized that Congress was about to put the full text of the Starr report on the Internet. Alarmed, Brett Kavanaugh—part of the OIC legal team who wrote the report—quickly drafted a letter to Gingrich warning him that it included "highly explicit" material that was "almost certainly inappropriate for wide public dissemination." But Starr decided against sending the letter, concluding that it was not the OIC's place to interfere with the House impeachment process.[4]

House members were thus in the extraordinary position of being asked to vote to publish confidential documents about the president of the United States that none of them had ever seen. By noon, after only two hours of debate, the House voted overwhelmingly, 363 to 63—with all Republicans, 138 Democrats, and one independent voting for the resolution—to release the Starr report immediately to the general public.

That afternoon, the 112,000-word report from Independent Counsel Starr was posted on the Internet, and heavy traffic quickly overwhelmed government and news servers—with House sites alone facing 3 million hits per hour, up from an average of 66,000.[5] Several major newspapers also reprinted the full Starr text and the 23,000-word preemptive rebuttal issued concurrently by President Clinton's lawyers, along with an enormous number of related stories (20 in the *New York Times* and 12 in the *Washington Post*)—easily eclipsing all other national and world events. Newspaper editors issued warning notices, such as "may be offensive to some readers," to accompany the Starr report, due to its many references to various types of sex acts.

The report charged President Clinton with 11 counts of wrongdoing: five counts of lying under oath (in *Jones v. Clinton* and before Starr's grand jury); four counts of obstruction of justice (working with Monica Lewinsky to conceal their relationship); one count of witness tampering (attempting to influence his secretary Betty Currie's grand jury testimony); and one count of abuse of constitutional authority (for the White House executive privilege claims). The narrative recounted several new details of 10 White House sexual encounters between Clinton and Lewinsky, including liaisons that occurred while the president was talking on the telephone to House members. It also reported the results of a DNA test of Lewinsky's semen-stained dress, in which the FBI concluded that the odds of the stain coming from someone other than Clinton were one in nearly eight trillion.

In its introduction, the Starr report stated: "All Americans, including the president, are entitled to enjoy a private life, free from public or governmental scrutiny. But the private concerns raised in this case are subject to limits." First, the report stated: "Congress and the Supreme Court have concluded that embarrassment-related concerns must give way to the greater interest in allowing aggrieved parties to pursue their claims. . . . To excuse a party who lied or concealed evidence on the ground that the evidence covered only 'personal' or 'private' behavior would frustrate the goals that Congress and the courts have sought to achieve in enacting and interpreting the nation's sexual harassment laws. That is particularly true when the conduct that is being concealed—sexual relations in the workplace between a high official and a young subordinate employee—itself conflicts with those goals." Second, Starr's report pointed out, "Judge Wright required disclosure of the precise information that is in part the subject of this referral, . . . [and] the President was duty-bound to testify truthfully and fully" in the Jones case. Third, given the nature of his office, "the President has a manifest duty to ensure that his conduct at all times complies with the law of the land," the report stated.

Regarding the amount of personal information, Starr stated in his report that the length and detail of the narrative portion was "crucial to an informed evaluation of the testimony, the credibility of witnesses, and the reliability of other evidence." "The President's testimony unfortunately has rendered the details essential," the report explained. "The President's defense to many of the allegations is based on a close parsing of the definitions that were used to describe his conduct. We have, after careful review, identified no manner of providing the information that reveals the falsity of the President's statements other than to describe his conduct with precision."

Attorney David Kendall presented the rebuttal to Starr for President Clinton. "The amount of lurid, graphic detail here far exceeds any legal justification" and is "intended to humiliate the President and force him from office," he argued. "This is personal and not impeachable." Kendall pointed out that "the issue of sex is mentioned more than 500 times, in the most graphic, salacious and gratuitous manner" in the Starr report—versus only two brief mentions of the Whitewater matter, regarding which Starr leveled no charges. Contrasting the aggressive legal advocacy in the report with Jaworski's "roadmap" approach during Watergate, Kendall called Starr's referral "a portrait of biased recounting, skewed analysis and unconscionable overreaching" that failed to acknowledge exculpatory evidence. "Spectacularly absent," Kendall noted, was Lewinsky's statement that "no one ever asked me to lie and I was never promised a job for my silence." Kendall also argued that Currie was never on any witness list for the Jones case, and the executive privilege claims that Starr called abuse of power were "nothing more than an assertion of constitutionally protected rights."

House members from both sides of the aisle were shocked by the explicit sexual details contained in the Starr report, and in light of the public outcry, several began to second-guess their decision. "I've probably never read anything that graphic before," said Mark Edward Souder [R-Fla.], a conservative

who had demanded Clinton's resignation. "I don't think anyone in this country is comfortable with such detailed probing of someone's sex life." On the Democratic side, John Murtha [Pa.] said: "I'm not sure I would have voted to release the report if I had known the vulgarity."

House Democrats began to defend Clinton. Judiciary member Zoe Lofgren [D-Calif.] was one of them: "The standard for impeachment is a destruction of the constitutional form of government, and all we've got is the President had a girlfriend and lied about it. . . . I'm trying to find the place where he [Starr] makes the case that a sex scandal threatens the Constitution." Nancy Pelosi [D-Calif.] went further: "Four years of investigation have vindicated the President for his public conduct, since all we're left with is his private life." Albert Wynn [D-Md.] added, "If you open up anyone's private life to public inspection it would look pretty lurid."

CHARGES OF HYPOCRISY

Surrounding the release of Starr's report, rumors about whose sexual indiscretions might next be publicized swirled about the Capitol. On September 5, impending local newspaper reports forced Representative Dan Burton [R-Ind.] to confess an extramarital affair he had 15 years ago while in the state legislature. Editor Vic Caleca of the *Indianapolis Star and News* told PBS's *NewsHour* that he ran the story because he saw "a disconnect between what he [Burton] stands for"—"bedrock, conservative values"—and "the fact that a child resulted from the affair." Representative Helen Chenoweth [R-Idaho]—who had a long-term affair with a married man in the 1980s—was next on September 10, right after she began airing commercials urging Clinton to resign over the Lewinsky matter. Editor Karen Baker explained the *Idaho Statesman*'s perspective: "We've heard reports about this for several years and we had decided it was not a story . . . until she made it an issue with her TV commercials. That makes it newsworthy in my mind."[6]

Then, on September 16, *Salon* Internet magazine headlined a story, "This Hypocrite Broke Up My Family" about a previously undisclosed extramarital affair that 74-year-old Judiciary chair Henry Hyde had in his 40s. "Aren't we fighting fire with fire, descending to the gutter tactics of those we deplore?" *Salon* asked. "Frankly, yes. But ugly times call for ugly tactics. . . . In the brave new world that has been created by the Clinton-Lewinsky scandal, the private lives of public figures are no longer off-limits."

In an election year, the ongoing impeachment drama heightened the lust some held for further revelations of public officials' past affairs. Pornography publisher Larry Flynt—who had written Starr a letter stating that his report had "broken historic ground in disseminating pornographic materials to a broader and more diverse community of Americans"—assumed center stage in fulfilling that desire. In October, Flynt took out a full-page ad in the *Washington Post* offering up to one million dollars to anyone who could "provide documentary evidence of illicit sexual relations with a congressman, senator or member of the executive or judiciary branches." Meanwhile, Senate Majority leader Trent Lott [R-Mich.] suggested that politicians who had broken their marriage vows consider another line of work.

VIDEOTAPE MADE PUBLIC

Coming just as the House Judiciary Committee began debating which portions of Starr's supplementary materials should be kept secret, the "outing" of Chairman Hyde added rancor to the closed-door deliberations. The 37-member Judiciary committee was considered to be one of the most politically polarized panels in Congress, noted for its nearly complete lack of moderate members—a stark contrast with the committee in place during the Watergate

hearings, which included 10 conservative southern Democrats and moderate Republicans. In 1997, all GOP Judiciary members voted with the party at least 85 percent of the time.[7] In addition, the Republican side consisted of 20 white Christian males plus the newly elected Mary Bono, while the 16 representatives on the Democratic side included five African Americans, one openly gay man, six Jews, and three women.

During the week-long Judiciary debate, Hyde said, "there was a general view among Democrats not to reveal anything, and a general view among Republicans to reveal as much as possible." Most of it focused on whether to release Starr's videotape of President Clinton's grand jury testimony. "The president's videotaped testimony is no longer grand jury material," argued Christopher Cox [R-Calif.], adding that releasing it "in total, in context . . . gives the president the best opportunity to have his case appreciated on its merits, and likewise for the independent counsel to have his allegations understood in their context."

After a series of party-line votes, the Judiciary Committee released the president's videotape, subject to 120 cuts, along with 2,800 pages of supplementary evidence from Starr on September 21. On October 2, the committee published an additional 5,000 pages of material, including edited transcripts of Linda Tripp's tapes as well as her grand jury testimony and that of Betty Currie, Vernon Jordan and White House counsel Bruce Lindsey.

Ranking Democrat Conyers, the only Judiciary member to have served on the Watergate inquiry, was clearly dismayed at the outcome. "This time we've dumped process and fairness on its head and, instead, we've released material without hardly having an opportunity to take out the offensive parts, the parts that would injure people, the parts that are unfair." Barney Frank [D-Mass.] was equally miffed: "We have given the prosecutor total dominance on the grounds that it wasn't going to be made public. And so now we have apparently set the precedent that everybody can expect that there will be a total destruction of grand jury secrecy. . . . Ambitious prosecutors will now be timing juicy prosecutions for 'sweeps week' " on TV. Characterizing GOP strategy, Frank added: "The public is not sufficiently anti-Clinton now. This is designed to build up support for impeachment."

A *New York Times* editorial, however, endorsed the committee's decision to release the videotape of the president's grand jury testimony: "Full disclosure and the free flow of information are the oxygen of democracy. . . . Only rare exceptions may be justified to protect the privacy of individuals peripheral to the case." On the morning of September 21, the video was carried live and unedited by all the major TV and cable networks, generating high ratings as it preempted regularly scheduled children's programming. CBS anchor Dan Rather gave the following warning before airing it: "If you are usually watching Tele-Tubbies at this hour, you probably shouldn't be watching this. Now ask your mother's permission, you go ask her right now." NBC was the only network to stop the tape when the OIC prosecutors' questions turned sexually explicit.

During his testimony about Monica Lewinsky, the president refused to answer questions about specific sexual acts, saying, "This is an indirect way to get me to testify on matters that have no direct bearing on whether I committed perjury. . . . I'm not trying to be evasive here. I'm trying to protect my privacy, my family's privacy, and I'm trying to stick to what the [Jones] deposition was about." Regarding the definition of "sexual relations" Jones's lawyers used, Clinton explained that he had interpreted the word "cause" to imply force, since her complaint was about sexual misconduct. Clinton described the Jones lawsuit as "bogus" and told prosecutors: "They thought they could just take a wrecking ball to me. . . . [I]n the face of their repeated, illegal leaking, it was not my responsibility

to volunteer a lot of information. I was determined to walk through the minefield of this deposition without violating the law, and I believe I did."

After the videotape ran on national TV, White House press secretary Mike McCurry called it "arguably an unnecessary day in the life of our country, an awful day." But despite predications of a presidential disaster, the public reaction was positive. A CNN-USA Today poll showed that the president's job approval rating jumped from 60 to 66 percent after the airing. The Starr report had not described Clinton's explanations in detail, and many Americans sympathized with the president. Judiciary Republican Lindsay Graham [S.C.] noted that people "put themselves in his position, and they didn't like it."

President Clinton did, however, receive criticism for some of his responses—such as "it depends how you define alone" and "it depends on what the meaning of 'is' is"—which some, like *Time* magazine, described as "chronic weaseling." Senate Minority Leader Tom Daschle [D-S.D.] agreed publicly "with those who have grown impatient with hairsplitting over legal technicalities." But any admission of perjury would leave Clinton open to criminal indictment by Starr, not to mention providing ammunition to a resurrected Jones case.

With that no doubt in mind, Clinton's lawyers settled the Jones case on November 13 for $850,000. The settlement did not require Clinton to apologize to Jones.

ELECTIONS

By late September, Democrats' complaints about Clinton were outweighed by their anger over the way Republicans were running the impeachment process. Judiciary Republicans were pushing for an open-ended impeachment inquiry that could include matters unrelated to the Lewinsky affair. Bob Barr [R-Ga.] declared: "We are witnessing nothing less than the symptoms of a cancer on the American presidency. If we fail to remove it, it will expand to destroy the principles that matter most to all of us." Democrats offered instead a resolution to censure Clinton for "reprehensible conduct with a subordinate."

Although Republicans dismissed the Democrats' proposals, Chairman Hyde promised to "use all [his] strength to ensure that this inquiry does not become a fishing expedition," and argued that the Judiciary Committee could rely on grand jury testimony collected by Starr rather than call witnesses and lengthen the inquiry. Less than a month before the November 3 elections, the Republican resolution to open a formal inquiry into whether Clinton should be impeached passed the committee 21–16, a straight party-line vote. The impeachment resolution was then sent to the House floor for an October 8 decision. No Republicans spoke against it; most stated that they were seeking "the truth," and that "no man is above the law." On the Democratic side, the refrain was that Republicans were out for a "partisan witch hunt" and "the American people are being railroaded." The full House vote was 258–176 in favor of an open-ended inquiry. Thirty Democrats voted for it—fewer than expected—some of whom said they just wanted to get the issue "off the table" while campaigning for re-election.

The House then adjourned on October 21 and turned its attention to the November elections, now just 13 days away. In every midterm election since 1938, the party of the president has lost an average of 32 House seats.[8] But Republicans faced a growing "impeach the impeachers" movement. Rather than the big gains expected, the GOP lost a stunning five seats. The elections cut the Republican majority in the House to 223–210 and left the 55–45 GOP majority in the Senate unchanged. Gephardt chalked it up to public distaste for impeachment: "It's almost as if they're saying collectively: 'Enough already! Enough! Bring it to an end.'"

"My leadership totally overplayed the problems of the President," conceded Representative Chris Shays [R-Conn.], as House Republicans maneuvered to oust Speaker Gingrich from his post. At first Gingrich blamed the media for the Lewinsky scandal drumbeat, but three days after the elections—and after his longtime friend, Bob Livingston [R-La.] announced his candidacy for Speaker—Gingrich stepped down, and later announced that in January, he would resign from Congress altogether.

THE IMPEACHMENT INQUIRY

In November, Chairman Hyde announced that the House Judiciary Committee impeachment inquiry would focus on a list of 81 written questions for President Clinton and one witness: Independent Counsel Kenneth Starr. But first, the House Judiciary Committee heard testimony from 19 scholars on the history of impeachment, the Constitution, and what constitutes an impeachable offense. On that topic, Arthur Schlesinger, former aide to President Kennedy, stated that "lying about one's sex life, I'm sure, is the last thing the Framers had in mind." Other scholarly witnesses said that a censure resolution might be unconstitutional. Then, on November 17, the Judiciary Committee released the Tripp tapes. They were aired on national TV and marked the first time most people heard Lewinsky's voice.

Starr testified two days later for 12 hours, and emphasized as a "critical turning point" the December 17, 1997 conversation during which Clinton told Lewinsky she was on the Jones witness list. "At that point, the president's intimate relationship with a subordinate employee was transformed into an unlawful effort to thwart the judicial process," Starr stated. "The evidence suggests that the president chose to engage in a criminal act: to reach an understanding with Ms. Lewinsky that they would both make false statements under oath." Aiding Republican efforts to classify Clinton's alleged misconduct as an "act of bribery" that clearly constituted an impeachable offense, Starr said he believed "that perjury does take the same dimension in our law as bribery because it is a corruption of the court system."

Democrats made much of Starr's acknowledgment that he had concluded "some months ago" that there was no presidential wrongdoing in matters pertaining to either the Whitewater, FBI files, or travel office investigations—asking why Starr had not informed Congress of that sooner, before the elections. Others asked whether Starr would be willing to release the media from its confidentiality pledges to him so that the alleged OIC leaks could be investigated. Starr dodged both of these questions.

"Let's presume . . . that Linda Tripp is a really nasty person," said Bob Barr [R-Ga.], taking Democrats' and other's criticisms to task as he questioned Starr about his report. "Let's presume further . . . that Lucianne Goldberg is a crafty manipulator . . . that Monica Lewinsky is an over-sexed blabbermouth . . . that there really is a vast right-wing conspiracy out there somewhere, maybe at work here today. Let's presume Paula Jones was interested in just the money . . . that the independent counsel [law] is not a perfect statute and . . . that, horror of horrors, you use tobacco products. Would any of that, in your professional judgment, change the conclusions contained in your referral?" Starr's answer was no, it would not: "The facts have a real power to them. And it was Justice Brandeis who said, 'Facts, facts, facts; give me facts.' And that's what we've sought to do . . . in this referral."

When Starr finished his testimony, Republicans gave him a standing ovation; Democrats sat in silence. The next day Starr's ethics advisor, Sam Dash, resigned in protest of Starr's testimony before the Judiciary Committee. Dash wrote to Starr, "Against my strong advice, you decided to . . . serve as an aggressive advocate for the proposition that . . . the President committed impeachable offenses." In his opinion, Starr had "no right or authority under the law . . . to advocate for a particular

position," and thus had "unlawfully intruded" into the impeachment proceedings.

The Judiciary Committee called no factual witnesses. Democrats complained that Republicans were simply accepting Starr's version of the events. Hyde countered that "We haven't called a lot of witnesses because you've pled 'nolo contendere.' " Hyde, however, did threaten to subpoena the president if he did not immediately answer the committee's 81 questions. Clinton finally responded in late November, reiterating his previous denials of any legal wrongdoing. The Republican position supporting impeachment seemed to harden in light of Clinton's continued "legalistic" responses, which some viewed as arrogant.

Final arguments by majority and minority counsel were made on December 10. For the Democrats, Abbe Lowell underscored the case against impeachment by quoting Chairman Hyde's own words in 1987 during the Iran-Contra affair that: " 'It seems too simplistic to condemn all lying. In the murkier grayness of the real world, choices often have to be made. All of us at some time confront conflicts between rights and duties, between choices that are evil and less evil, and one hardly exhausts moral imagination by labeling every untruth and every deception an outrage.' " For the Republicans, David Schippers reminded the committee: "Lies are lies are lies." "This is not about sex or private conduct," Schippers said. The president "employed the power and prestige of his office and of his cabinet members to mislead and to lie to the American people," he argued, adding: "It almost worked."

On December 11, less than 10 minutes after President Clinton again expressed "profound remorse"—this time from the Rose Garden—for his behavior in the Lewinsky matter, the House Judiciary Committee began its vote on four articles of impeachment that grouped together all the charges against Clinton in Starr's report. All four passed easily, once again along party lines—except for Republican

Lindsay Graham's vote against Article II, which charged Clinton with perjury in *Jones*. Despite the historical significance of the votes and the extent of the scandal coverage in 1998, the Judiciary hearings received scant coverage on network TV.

CASUALTIES OF WAR

Although censure was strongly favored by Democrats as the impeachment articles moved to the House floor, Speaker-designate Livingston vowed to fight a censure alternative. "Censure of the President would violate the careful balance of separation of powers and the scheme laid out by the Framers to address the issue of executive misconduct," Livingston said, announcing his intention to vote for impeachment. Greg Ganske [R-Iowa] reflected the opinion of many Republicans: "The idea that Congress should simply apply a 'wrist-slap' censure is another effort to put the president above the law." Anyone still on the impeachment fence was urged privately—and then publicly by Steve Buyer [R-Ind.] on December 16—to review the still-secret reports about "Jane Doe Number Five," a woman whom Jones's lawyers claimed Clinton had "forcibly raped and sexually assaulted . . . and then bribed and/or intimidated . . . into remaining silent. . . ." ("Jane Doe Number Five" denied any misconduct by Clinton.); 45 Republicans took that advice.[9]

But the censure deadlock was quickly overshadowed by dramatic new developments. On December 17, just as the House readied for its final vote on impeachment, President Clinton ordered a surprise round of military air strikes on Iraq—a show of force designed to respond to President Saddam Hussein's repeated refusals to allow United Nations weapons inspections. Livingston put off the impeachment vote by one day, despite charges by Senate Majority Leader Trent Lott and others that the bombing was an effort to thwart the impeachment process. When Livingston resumed the proceedings the next day while American

fighter pilots were still in the air, Democrats were outraged. "This is wrong! This is wrong! This is wrong!" Gephardt thundered. Impeachment opponents called it a "coup d'état."

Before the day was over, Livingston dropped a bombshell of his own on the floor of the House, announcing that he too had "on occasion strayed" from his marriage. Livingston's stunning admission came in light of impending media stories owing to the efforts of Larry Flynt. Although the affairs were kept secret when he ran for Speaker, Livingston had told CNN in November: "I'm not running for saint. I'm not looking to be canonized. I'm just a regular person." Flynt said his goal with the Livingston revelation was "to expose hypocrisy"—"if these guys are going after the president, they shouldn't have any skeletons in their closet"—and warned other Congress members: "This is only the beginning."[10] Shortly afterward, Livingston said he would end his political career altogether.

Congress members responded with a standing ovation as Livingston left the House floor. On the Democratic side, David Obey [Wis.] fought back tears as he cried out: "How many more good people are going to be destroyed next?" On the Republican side, Richard Baker [La.] asked: "Where in God's name does the line of the public right to know end, and the individual right of personal liberty begin?" But most Republicans saw a clear distinction between Livingston's admission and the president's statements. Robert Ney [R-Ohio] said Livingston was "telling the truth and the other end of Pennsylvania Avenue couldn't tell the truth if he had a gun to his head."

Amidst the tumult, the Republican-dominated House forged ahead on impeachment, calling it a "vote of conscience." After three hours of debate on December 19, a vote on a censure motion supported by Democrats and some moderate Republicans was ruled irrelevant to the debate. Democrats staged a walkout. But minutes later they returned, and the House narrowly approved two of the four articles of impeachment: a vote of 228–206 for perjury before the grand jury and 221–212 for obstruction of justice in the Jones lawsuit.[11] With these near party-line votes, Clinton was impeached, the first president to wear that badge of dishonor in over 100 years, and only the second in all of U.S. history.

The vast majority of Americans were not pleased with the impeachment of President Clinton. Immediately after the vote, Clinton's approval ratings jumped from 63 to 73 percent, while the Republican Party's dropped from 43 to 31 percent.[12] Several polls showed over 60 percent of the American public did not want a full Senate trial and over 50 percent wanted no trial at all.[13] Then, four moderate Republicans who voted for at least one article of impeachment announced before Christmas that they favored censure in the Senate.

"THE SERGEANT-AT-ARMS WILL PLEASE CLOSE THE DOORS"

"Hear ye, hear ye, hear ye," boomed the sergeant-at-arms at the January 7 opening of the Senate trial, commanding senators "to keep silent on pain of imprisonment." Chief Supreme Court Justice William Rehnquist presided over the deliberations, all of which were to be held behind closed doors, due to nineteenth-century Senate secrecy rules that required a two-thirds majority to change. At the outset, two Democratic senators, Tom Harkin [Iowa] and Paul Wellstone [Minn.], announced that they would try to adjust the rules to open the debate to the public, since in modern times, closed Senate sessions were usually held only when classified information was under discussion. "A secret debate is wrong," Harkin said. "It's danger-ous, and it's not representative of the open traditions of American democracy." Well-stone added that the American people would be "much more likely to believe in the process if it's open to them." They faced significant Senate opposition. As Mitch McConnell [R-Ky.] argued: "We are much better able to relate to each other and reach compromises when we are not under the glare of cameras, which I must confess leads some to the temptation to grandstand and be partisan." Other senators saw themselves as impeachment "jurors," which implied delib-erating in secret. But Harkin noted that nowhere in the Constitution were they referred to as jurors, and Justice Rehnquist agreed, ruling that, "the Senate is not simply a jury, it is a court."

Senate leaders of both parties seemed determined from the start to avoid the pub-lic's wrath and work together in a dignified, bipartisan fashion. As Senator Edward Kennedy [D-Mass.] said later, "Everyone had a sense that . . . the Senate was on trial. It wasn't just the President." As the trial got underway, the key point of contention between the parties concerned whether to call witnesses—essentially a proxy for the debate over the trial's length. While Republi-cans appeared somewhat torn on the issue, Democratic opposition to calling witnesses seemed firm. Nonetheless, senators managed in their closed-door caucus to vote 100–0 for a bipartisan compromise on some initial trial ground rules. After hearing opening argu-ments from the House managers and the president's lawyers—to which senators could submit written questions—the Senate would then decide on the most controversial matter: whether to call witnesses or end the trial.

Over three days beginning January 14, the House prosecutors made the case for impeachment. James Sensenbrenner [R-Wis.] gave the case overview, saying that Clinton had made "perjurious, false and misleading statements under oath" and encouraged Lewinsky and others to do so. "Some have said that the false testimony given by the President relating to sex should be excused," he continued, "since, as the argument goes, everyone lies about sex. I would ask the Senate to stop and think about the consequences of adopting that attitude. Our sexual harassment laws would become unenforceable, since every sexual harassment suit is about sex, and much of the domestic violence litigation in our country is at least partly about sex." In closing, Hyde told senators, "The matter before you is a question of the willful, premeditated, deliberate corruption of the nation's system of justice through perjury and obstruction of justice. These are public acts."

Next came three days of defense from the president's lawyers, who disputed the prosecutors' interpretations of both the events and the Constitution—now with more emphasis on "the facts." Attorney Charles Ruff called the two impeachment articles "empty vessels" in which the House had stirred up a "witches' brew" of theories "constructed out of sealing wax and string and spider's webs . . . that would lend to a series of otherwise innocuous and indeed exculpatory events a dark and sinister cast." Deputy White House Counsel Cheryl Mills took issue with the argument that sexual harassment laws would be damaged unless Clinton was convicted. "I'm not worried about civil rights," Mills declared, "because this president's record on civil rights, on women's rights, on all of our rights is unimpeachable."

Meanwhile, president Clinton delivered his second State of the Union address during the Lewinsky scandal, again impressing many with a strong performance under pressure, and bumping his approval ratings up to a lofty 76 percent.

THE TRIAL

Once the arguments for and against impeachment ended, the debate over witnesses was revived. In a December 30 letter to Majority Leader Lott, Hyde had written: "[T]he constitutional duty of the House of Representatives as the accusatory body differs greatly from the Senate's constitutional duty as an adjudicatory body. As the entity granted the sole power to try an impeachment—i.e., to determine the guilt or innocence of President Clinton—the Senate should hear from live witnesses." The House prosecutors had a list of at least 15

they wanted to call—especially Monica Lewinsky, since their impeachment case depended in large part on discrepancies between how Lewinsky and Clinton had described their physical encounters to Starr as they pertained to the Jones lawyers' definition of "sexual relations."

But senators from both parties demanded that the witness list be cut way back. "I don't want to create a spectacle. And I'm not by myself," Richard Shelby [R-Ala.], a conservative and no Clinton apologist, told MSNBC. John Warner [R-Va.] was also concerned about a lengthy trial: "If you decide to grant witnesses, it's questionable whether you could ever cap the number the President's lawyers could call, because it would seem to raise the issue of denying the President his right to defend himself." Democrats were particularly opposed to calling Lewinsky—worried, like Christopher Dodd [D-Conn.] that "the Senate is going to become a sort of burlesque stage." Joseph Biden [D-Del.] told PBS *NewsHour:* "She's in a position where . . . if she changes her position on the Senate floor, she loses her immunity [from prosecution]. What makes anybody possibly think that anything Monica Lewinsky could say on the floor would be different than the 20 times she's testified under oath already?" Biden added that senators "should make independent judgments about whether we think we need witnesses and not being so deferential to the House. They made their case. Who the heck are they?"

The proceedings were thrown into turmoil on the afternoon of January 22 with Byrd's surprise announcement that he would motion to dismiss the charges against Clinton as "the best way to promptly end this sad and sorry time for our country." Byrd explained in a statement: "I am convinced that the necessary two-thirds for conviction are not there and . . . are not likely to develop. . . . [L]engthening this trial will only prolong and deepen the divisive, bitter, and polarizing effect that this sorry affair has visited upon our nation."

Several Democrats endorsed Byrd's plan, and Senate Judiciary Chair Orrin Hatch [R-Utah] agreed, as long as the "adjournment motion" acknowledged that the House vote on impeachment was "the highest form of censure possible under our system." But Hyde and the House prosecutors rejected it as "sending a terrible message . . . [that] obstruction is OK even though it is an effort to deny a citizen her right to a fair trial," and argued, "history and justice demand a full record of the truth." Several Republican senators including Phil Gramm [R-Tex.] concurred: "It seems to me we have a constitutional duty to see this through." Sam Brownback [R-Kans.] added later on PBS *NewsHour,* "We've had 15 impeachment trials in the history of the republic. Not a single one was dismissed."

During January 25th summations, Clinton lawyer Nicole Seligman argued that the impeachment process "seems long ago to have lost all sense of proportionality," and because it involved overturning an election, convicting a president required the highest standards. "Charges arising out of the President's efforts to keep an admittedly wrongful relationship secret are, by no means, by no analysis, of that caliber," Seligman argued. House manager Charles Canady [R-Fla.] countered that the Senate had nearly dismissed an elected senator, Bob Packwood [R-Ore.], who resigned in 1995 after being accused of sexual harassment and attempting to cover it up. To draw a parallel with the charges against Clinton, Canady described Packwood's alleged offenses as "a violation of his policy of trust to the Senate and an abuse of his position as a United States Senator."

On January 26, the Senate rejected the Harkin-Wellstone proposal to open to the public its debate over the witness issue and Byrd's motion to dismiss. It was a largely party-line vote, 43–57—a full 24 votes short of the two-thirds majority needed to change Senate rules—with a majority of Democrats voting for open debates and a majority of Republicans preferring secrecy.

In practice, however, the secrecy rule did not keep senators from appearing on TV after deliberations ended each day. Several remarked about the closed-door effects, but even those assessments tended to differ by party. In the opinion of Chuck Hagel [R-Neb.], the Senate "stripped away the theater;" while the closed hearings led Robert Torricelli [D-N.J.] to conclude: "Senators are theatrical even in the privacy of their home showers."

The next day the Senate voted 56–44 against the motion to dismiss the trial and for a resolution to call three witnesses selected by the House managers. Wisconsin's Russell Finegold was the only Democrat to vote with Republicans to continue the trial; the party unity meant that the Senate was 10 votes short of that required to convict the president. Nevertheless, the Senate issued subpoenas ordering Lewinsky, Vernon Jordan, and White House communications advisor Sidney Blumenthal—whom House prosecutors wanted to question about his alleged "whisper campaign" to label Lewinsky a "stalker"—to submit to private interviews. A further vote was still needed regarding whether to question them live, and the White House threatened to drag out the proceedings if that occurred. But the resolution gave Minority Leader Daschle a veto over calling more witnesses or expanding the trial, foreclosing any chance for House prosecutors to call other "Jane Does" who had testified in the Jones trial.

From the perspective of most senators, the three witness depositions essentially reaffirmed previous testimony and failed to produce a smoking gun. By February 4, House managers had limited their request for live witnesses to one: Lewinsky. However, more than two-thirds of the Senate, including 25 Republicans, voted against the idea of having her appear live. That vote was 70–30, but the Senate approved a motion by 62–38—nine Democrats voting in favor—to allow videotaped depositions to be shown during floor arguments. Selective portions of Lewinsky on videotape were aired by both sides on February 6, including her statement that: "For me, the best way to explain how I feel what happened was . . . no one asked or encouraged me to lie, but no one discouraged me, either." Both sides continued to find different meanings in her words.

As the vote on whether to remove the president from office approached, Kay Bailey Hutchinson [R-Tex.] joined Harkin in filing a motion to make the final Senate deliberations public, while CNN distributed a brief making the case for openness to all 100 senators. "I just can't imagine something of this magnitude not being debated in public," said Kent Conrad [D-N.D.]. "We are public servants; we don't belong to some private organization, and we have to be held accountable," declared Harkin. But Lott continued his opposition because, his spokesman said: "The Senate is now approaching a mode where it's most like a jury, and at no time in the history of trial-by-jury have those deliberations been public." Other Republicans said they did not want to allow Democrats to vocally condemn Clinton's behavior or the House prosecutors while they voted for acquittal. On February 9, a bipartisan majority of senators—including 14 Republicans—did vote to open the final proceedings, but the 59–41 vote was eight votes short of the supermajority needed to suspend the rules. The Senate did, however, agree to allow members to have their statements published afterwards.

On February 12, 1999, after five weeks of testimony and debate, the Senate acquitted President Clinton of both articles of impeachment—no surprise, since most senators had already announced how they intended to vote. But neither article commanded even a simple majority, as an unexpected number of Republicans joined all 45 Democrats in voting not guilty. Ten Republicans joined the Democrats in voting down Article I charging perjury before a federal grand jury, and five joined them in voting down Article II, which alleged presidential obstruction of justice. Afterwards, Senator John Chafee [R-R.I.] told

PBS *NewsHour:* "I think that the Senate really acquitted itself in excellent fashion."

Consideration of a bipartisan censure resolution sponsored by Dianne Feinstein [D-Calif.] and Robert Bennett [R-Utah] was blocked by Texas Republican Phil Gramm's procedural move requiring 67 votes to take up the censure motion. But many senators delivered sharp rebukes of the president in public speeches. Olympia Snowe [R-Maine], who voted to acquit, castigated Clinton after the vote: "As a woman who has fought long and hard for sexual harassment laws, I resent that the President has undermined our progress. . . . No matter how consensual this relationship was, it involved a man with tremendous power, with authority over a 21-year-old subordinate, in the workplace—and not just any workplace." Robert Bennett [R-Utah] who voted to convict, was even harsher: "Bill Clinton will go down in history as the most accomplished, polished liar we have ever had serving in the White House."

Speaking briefly about the vote in the Rose Garden that day, President Clinton again expressed "how profoundly sorry I am for what I said and did to trigger these events and the great burden they have imposed on the Congress and on the American people." Now, Clinton continued, "This can be and this must be a time of reconciliation and renewal for America."

NOTES

1. Jeffrey L. Katz, "Gingrich's Role is Scrutinized in Impeachment Drama," *CQ Weekly*, Sept. 26, 1998.
2. *Washington Post*, Feb. 14, 1999.
3. Jeffrey L. Katz, "Promises of Bipartisanship Will Be Put to an Early Test," *CQ Weekly*, Sept. 12, 1998.
4. Michael Isikoff, *Uncovering Clinton: A Reporter's Story* (New York: Crown Publishers, 1999), p. 353.
5. *Washington Post*, Sept. 12, 1998.
6. Quoted in the *Washington Post*, Sept. 11, 1998, p. D01.
7. Cited in Dan Carney, "Along Clinton's Political Gantlet: A Panel Noted for Both Partisanship, Civility," *CQ Weekly*, Sept. 5, 1998.

8. Marc Birtel, "House: The Scandal Recedes," *CQ Weekly*, Oct. 24, 1998.

9. Jeffrey Toobin, *A Vast Conspiracy* (New York: Random House, 2000), p. 363. All of these Republicans eventually voted to impeach Clinton.

10. Flynt told the *Los Angeles Times* (Dec. 27, 1998) that he was not surprised that Livingston resigned, because "he [Livingston] put out a statement that none of the women worked for him, that he wasn't involved with any of them in a professional capacity," but Flynt's investigation suggested otherwise.

11. Article II (perjury in the Jones case) failed by a vote of 205–229 and Article IV (abuse of power) failed 148–285.

12. The poll was conducted by CNN/Gallup/*USA Today*.

13. From CNN-Gallup and CBS News polls.

Comment

The Starr report declared: "All Americans, including the president, are entitled to enjoy a private life, free from public or governmental scrutiny. But the private concerns raised in this case are subject to limits." The grounds for limiting privacy in this case include the need to investigate allegations of sexual harassment and perjury. A claim of privacy should not protect anyone from punishment for offenses of this kind, but allegations should not be enough to override privacy. The question is how much evidence and of what kind is sufficient to justify what degree of interference with privacy. Public officials have less claim to privacy, but democratic citizens may wish to grant them more privacy in some cases in order to protect the democratic process from being degraded. Through a political version of the Gresham's law, information about private life tends to drive out other forms of information and to lower the overall quality of public discourse and democratic accountability.

We should also ask, what other reasons, in addition to the limits that Starr cites, would justify disclosing what would otherwise be private conduct of a public official. The motives of neither the accusers nor the defenders were as high minded as their rhetoric implied, but the positions of both rest on important values, and should be considered on their merits.

"This is not about sex or private conduct," Representative Schippers insisted. Clinton's accusers generally maintained that their objection was not to the sexual misconduct but to the abuse of power, including lying to the courts and the public. No one is above the law. But his defenders argued that without the prurient appeal of the accounts of sex, the accusations would not have had much effect. They believed that the conduct, even if not completely private, had relatively little relevance to the public office, and that any subsequent deception, even if not justified, was a response to the overzealous prosecution of Starr and the hostility of his political opponents in Congress. Even if his relationship with Lewinsky showed a disrespect for women in private, his "record on women's rights" in public was "unimpeachable."

Some critics see the sexual misconduct itself as relevant, quite apart from the alleged harassment or deception. They believe that it manifests a general lack of self-discipline, and exposes a general character flaw that reflects poorly on any political leader. They deny any sharp distinction between private and public character. Others, including some friends of Clinton, consider the misconduct relevant because it shows poor judgment. Clinton must have known that if his relationship with Lewinsky were exposed, the ensuing reaction would weaken his presidency. The risk he took (not only with his own future but also with that of his colleagues, his policies, and the office) was irresponsible. That other people might react negatively is not in general a sufficient justification for publicizing conduct or even for condemning an official who engages in it. Exposing a gay legislator whose constituents are homophobic would not be justified. Consider whether the Clinton case is different in this respect.

Evaluate the specific decisions that Starr and his staff took in this case: pressuring Lewinsky to cooperate, leaking grand jury testimony, releasing the videotape of Clinton's testimony, including detailed sexual descriptions in the report, and advocating impeachment (prompting Dash's resignation). Also consider the actions of Lucianne Goldberg, Linda Tripp, Matt Drudge, and the *Newsweek* editors and reporters, who were instrumental in bringing the scandal to light.

Both the House Judiciary Committee and the Senate confronted the question of what to make public. The reasons against publicity were based on the president's privacy only in an indirect way. Some members of the Judiciary Committee were concerned that some of the material might harm other people and that the president should, as a matter of fairness, have a chance to object or at least respond to the accusations in the report before it was released. The "vulgarity" of the report (as Representative Murtha suggested) would reflect badly on the Congress and degrade the public forum. In the Senate, some of the same concerns about discussing prurient matters in public led some members to favor closing the trial. McConnell argued for keeping the proceedings secret to avoid the "temptation to grandstand and be partisan." Others considered the Senate deliberations to be analogous to those of a jury. The challenge is to find the right balance between publicity and privacy in deliberations in which the public takes a legitimate interest.

The exposure of Clinton's escapades evidently provoked a retaliation and seemed to license the exposure of the sexual improprieties (mostly adultery) of several other prominent officials. Consider the similarities and differences between Clinton's case and those of each of the others: Dan Burton, Newt Gingrich, Henry Hyde, Helen Chenoweth, and Bob Livingston. It is hard to regard these disclosures as justified retribution, but perhaps some may be considered warranted exposures of hypocrisy. Still, as the exposure wars continued, many were inclined to agree with the sentiment expressed by Representative Obey: "How many more good people are going to be destroyed next?"

Recommended Reading

For a sample of the various approaches to the value of privacy, see Ferdinand Schoeman (ed.), *Philosophical Dimensions of Privacy* (Cambridge, England: Cambridge University Press, 1984); and Judith Wagner Decew, *In Pursuit of Privacy* (Ithaca, N.Y.: Cornell University Press, 1997). A philosophical analysis with reference to the Clinton-Lewinsky scandal can be found in the first part of Thomas Nagel's *Concealment and Exposure* (New York and Oxford: Oxford University Press, 2002). For different views on the relevance of private lives of public officials, compare Frederick Schauer, "Can Public Figures Have Private Lives?" *Social Philosophy and Policy,* 17 (2000), pp. 299–306; and Dennis F. Thompson, "Private Life and Public Office," *Restoring Responsibility* (Cambridge, England: Cambridge University Press, 2004). For an earlier but more comprehensive treatment of the subject, see Dennis F. Thompson, *Political Ethics and Public Office* (Cambridge, Mass.: Harvard University Press, 1987), pp. 123–47.

There are now dozens of books on each of the episodes featured in this chapter, though almost none of the books deals systematically with ethical issues. Students would be better advised to examine the primary sources. Thomas's confirmation hearings are available in Nina Totenberg and Anita Millca (eds.), *Complete Transcripts of the Clarence Thomas-Anita Hill Hearings* (Chicago: Academy Chicago, 1994). The transcript of the impeachment proceedings, the Starr Report, and other documents related to the Clinton-Lewinsky scandal are conveniently collected by the *Washington Post* at http://www.washingtonpost.com/wp-srv/politics/special/clinton/itranscripts.htm. Although polemical in some respects, Richard Posner's *An Affair of State* (Cambridge, Mass.: Harvard University Press, 1999) is the most suggestive for discussions about the theoretical implications of the scandal and subsequent proceedings.

The privacy claims of public officials raise issues that are distinct from those raised by the forms of nondisclosure considered in Chapter 2, which involve concealing official rather than personal activities, sometimes in order to deceive the public. But some of the recommended readings at the end of that chapter are relevant to the questions considered in this chapter. See especially the readings on secrecy and on the concept of publicity.

4 Manipulation

In an editorial entitled "The Reform Movement Is Failing to Manipulate Voters" issued during the primary season in 2000, a progressive political organization by the name of Transparency Now criticized John McCain, Ralph Nader, and Bill Bradley, among others, for refusing to "lower" themselves into the real world of politics. "Great—and good—political leaders have always recognized that if you want to lead large groups of people, you have to inspire them and appeal to their emotions, not just win them over with the better argument. That means you have to manipulate them . . . that includes [being willing] to run negatively-toned advertisements. . . ."

The manipulative politician may be a figure of disrepute, but the politician who completely shuns manipulative politics is not likely to succeed. He is likely to be criticized even by supporters for putting his own sense of "misplaced honor" ahead of the goals of a movement, party, or institution. Politics, a conventional view suggests, is essentially a strategic process in which the agents seek to gain advantage by using any legal means they can, including manipulation. Anyone who wants to participate in politics in a serious way therefore must be prepared to manipulate and be manipulated.

Yet the suspicion of the manipulative politician persists, and for good reason. Manipulation is the attempt to "influence, manage, use, or control persons or procedures to one's advantage by artful or indirect means." We speak of manipulating not only people but also the system (though with the ultimate aim of manipulating people in the system). The artful and indirect strategies characteristic of a manipulative politics, carried too far or practiced too often, can undermine the transparent and trustful relationships necessary for a healthy democracy. We should respect this suspicion by granting a presumption against manipulation, and treat it like other necessary vices in politics. Its use calls for justification. The central question, then, should be: Under what conditions is which kind of manipulation justified in politics?

Manipulation has two features that should give the ethical politician pause. It involves attempts to influence other people's actions (1) toward your ends without regard to theirs; and (2) with means that disregard or circumvent their rational faculties. When your ends are the same as theirs, the manipulation is benevolent. But this kind of manipulation is presumably more common among friends than among politicians. When the nonrational means produce what their reason in a more deliberative mood would recommend, the manipulation may be warranted, even desirable. But in politics the attempt to bypass reason is usually a sign that, if reason were more in control, it would not approve the action in question.

Manipulation is closely related to deception. One of the most common ways to manipulate people is to deceive them about your true purposes. But not all manipulation is deceptive. A politician can manipulate potential supporters by openly exploiting their weaknesses (offering membership in an exclusive club, or the chance to win a lottery prize). A politician can also indirectly manipulate opponents by directly manipulating the procedures in an electoral or legislative process. The opponents may be well aware of what is going on, but unable to do anything about it. Even when manipulation is deceptive, its use adds a further problematic element. As an attempt to induce people actively to serve your own purposes, it involves using another person directly as a means. Deception is typically a defensive, protective strategy: it is intended to deflect others from interfering with your plans. Manipulation is more aggressive: it is intended to induce others to do your bidding. With deception, one acquires the kind of power that Hobbes's sovereign pursued: the liberty to go one's own way unimpeded. With manipulation, one secures the kind of power that Machiavelli's prince sought: the ability to make others go your way unapprised.

The examples presented in the first section of this chapter illustrate manipulation in three different settings: campaigns, legislatures, and electoral adjudication. The most familiar objects of manipulation are potential voters. In campaigns, we have seen the manipulated and they are us. Campaign managers use the tools of advertising and public relations to sell us on the virtues of their candidates, and increasingly to persuade us of the vices of their opponents. No doubt some of this communication is informative and fulfills important purposes of the democratic process. But some serves the ends of candidates more than those of voters, and uses the means of demagogues more than those of deliberators. Attack ads are a case in point. The small collection of negative ads exhibited in the section that follows, most of which do not make substantially false claims, raise the question of how far an ethical candidate may go in attacking his opponent. Another way that candidates manipulate voters is through the ballot itself. Proponents of term limits in several states managed to enact a requirement that, next to each name on the ballot, a notation must appear indicating the candidate's position on this question. The proponents knew that most voters favored term limits, and believed that such a notation would cause many voters to ignore other issues they might have considered and to vote against candidates who opposed term limits. In other cases, candidates have even gone so far as to change their names in an effort to cause voters to think better of them.

One of the most potent tools of manipulation in campaigns is money. The most pervasive problem of money's use is the corruption that results from the favors that contributors expect and often receive from politicians. What may candidates offer voters, and how may they offer it? As an essential part of a campaign, candidates promise benefits to voters, but they may not promise direct payments in return for a vote because that would be bribery, which is both morally corrupt and illegal. But may candidates offer money for simply voting—or even for *not* voting? A proposal to hold a lottery for which all voters are eligible and the payment to community leaders to stay at home on election day should provoke questions about using money as a means to influence voters.

Politicians themselves are also vulnerable to manipulation, as the account of Lyndon Johnson's machinations in the Senate shows. Taking advantage of his role as Democratic majority leader, Johnson artfully controlled the agenda, deciding who would speak, to whom speakers would yield, and at what time a vote would take place. In this episode, he used whatever rhetorical means he thought would work to stage a "drama" that was intended to persuade senators who would normally oppose an amendment to a civil rights act. With a mixture of disingenuousness and wile, he outmaneuvered the Republican minority leader and the liberal wing of his own party. They did not know they had been manipulated until it was too late.

In the second case of legislative manipulation, the Texas redistricting caper, the scheming was obvious to all and engaged in by both parties. Both manipulated the procedures in order to manipulate each another. The Republicans redrew the districts to bring more Republicans into the legislature. They took advantage of the absence of any law prohibiting redistricting between censuses, even though customarily redistricting had only taken place once after each census every ten years. The Democrats took advantage of a rule that required a quorum for any vote in the legislature. They not only refused to show up for the vote but temporarily left the state to avoid being arrested and forced to vote.

The controversy over counting the votes in Florida after the presidential election in 2000 provided a fertile occasion for partisan wrangling, legal maneuvering, and political scheming. Both sides sought to manipulate the procedures to their advantage, but most observers thought that George Bush's teams were more aggressive than Al Gore's in pressing their case. Gore was criticized by some of his own supporters for being too reluctant to use means that might have been considered manipulative.

Crafty Communications*

NEGATIVE ADS

JOHNSON VERSUS GOLDWATER

Images reprinted with permission from the American Museum of the Moving Image.

During the 1964 campaign, President Lyndon Johnson portrayed his Republican opponent Barry Goldwater as a dangerous extremist, who might start a nuclear war. In one of Johnson's ads, a young girl licks an ice cream cone while the voice of a female announcer warns that Barry Goldwater supports nuclear testing. In another ad, a young girl counts daisy petals in a field while a voice counts down to a nuclear explosion.

HELMS VERSUS HUNT

In the 1984 North Carolina Senate race, Jesse Helms launched an 18-month

negative campaign centered around the theme, "Where do you stand, Jim?" directed against his opponent, Jim Hunt, who was serving as Democratic governor. One ad, published in 150 small daily and weekly newspapers outside urban areas, featured a photograph of Reverend Jesse Jackson visiting Governor Hunt with a comment by Jackson saying that he hoped to register 200,000 black voters in North Carolina. Below was the caption: "Ask yourself: Is this the proper use of taxpayer funds?"

BUSH VERSUS DUKAKIS

Images reprinted with permission from the American Museum of the Moving Image.

As governor of Massachusetts, Michael Dukakis had supported prison reform, including a weekend release program that was widely thought to be successful. However, one of the convicts who received a weekend pass, Willy Horton, committed rape while he was out of the prison.

---

*Jaime Muehl assisted with the selection of the ads and the descriptions of the ads and ballot notations.

A conservative political action committee highlighted this incident in a dramatic ad that linked Dukakis to Horton and implied that Dukakis was soft on crime.

BUSH VERSUS KERRY

Bush Ad (March 2004)

BUSH: I'm George W. Bush and I approve this message.
ANNOUNCER: A President sets his agenda for America in the first 100 days. John Kerry's plan: To pay for new government spending, raise taxes by at least $900 billion. On the War on Terror: Weaken the Patriot Act used to arrest terrorists and protect America. And he wanted to delay defending America until the United Nations approved. John Kerry: Wrong on taxes. Wrong on defense.

FactCheck.org comments:

In its first attack ad to hit the airwaves, the Bush campaign accuses Kerry of proposing to raise taxes by $900 billion. Kerry denies that. And Bush's ad fails to mention that Kerry's "new government spending" would benefit millions of Americans who lack health insurance. According to a study by Emory University professor Kenneth Thorpe, which the Bush campaign's own background material cites as a credible authority, Kerry's plan would provide coverage for 26.7 million who currently have no coverage.

But Kerry's ambitious health-care plan would indeed cost an estimated $895 billion over 10 years. And Kerry has also promised to cut the current $500-billion federal deficit in half. Can he pay for all that while raising taxes only for the wealthy? Those numbers don't quite add. [http://www.factcheck.org, 11 March 2004]

Kerry Ad (April 2004)

ANNOUNCER: While jobs are leaving our country in record numbers, George Bush says sending jobs overseas "makes sense" for America. His top economic advisors say "moving American jobs to low cost countries" is a plus for the U.S. John Kerry's proposed a different economic plan that encourages companies to keep jobs here. It's part of a "detailed economic agenda" to create 10 million jobs. John Kerry. A new direction for America.
KERRY: I'm John Kerry and I approved this message.

FactCheck.org comments:

A Kerry ad has Bush saying that sending jobs overseas "makes sense." But Bush didn't say that. The quote is actually from Bush's Council of Economic Advisers. The Kerry campaign claims Bush signed the report containing those words, but that's wrong, too. Some Bush administration officials do indeed defend the practice of contracting for white-collar services overseas as one aspect of free trade, which they say creates jobs in the U.S. Textbook economics supports that notion. But the Kerry ad goes too far when it makes the President seem to be rooting for the loss of U.S. jobs using words he never used. [http://www.factcheck.org, 3 April 2004]

SHAM ISSUE ADS

Campaign finance law strictly regulates what candidates and some organizations, notably corporations and unions, can spend on political ads to support the election of candidates. But it does not regulate ads that only take positions on issues. Those are protected by the First Amendment. The distinction between express advocacy (for the election of a candidate) and issue advocacy, was first enunciated in *Buckley v. Valeo* (424 U.S. 1 at 44). In accord with that opinion, the criterion for express advocacy was whether a communication used what became known as the magic words: "vote for," "elect," "support," "cast your ballot for," "Smith for Congress," "vote against," "defeat," and similar terms. Subsequent court decisions broadened the test somewhat to include statements such as those that "provide in effect an explicit directive" to vote for named candidates. The distinction was anything but clear in practice, and candidates and their managers soon found ways to write ads that would stay within the letter of the law but in effect serve their campaign strategy. By 1996, these "sham issue" ads had proliferated, and were used by candidates of both parties throughout the country. One of the most cited examples:

> Who is Bill Yellowtail? He preaches family values, but he took a swing at his wife. Yellowtail's explanation? He "only slapped her," but her nose was broken. He talks law and order, but is himself a convicted criminal. And though he talks about protecting children, Yellowtail failed to make his own child support payments, then voted against child support enforcement. Call Bill Yellowtail and tell him we don't approve of his wrongful behavior. Call 406 443 3620. (Richard Briffault, "Issue Advocacy: Redrawing the Elections/Politics Line." *Texas Law Review* 77 [June 1999]: 1764–66.)

The campaign reform act signed into law in March 2002 seeks to deal with these sham issue ads by adopting a broader concept than express advocacy. It defines an "electioneering communication" (which is subject to regulation) as a broadcast ad that clearly identifies a federal candidate within 30 days of a primary or 60 days of a general election and is targeted to his or her constituency.

Informative Ballots?

BALLOT NOTATIONS

In a statewide initiative in 1996, the voters of Missouri overwhelmingly passed a requirement that any nonincumbent congressional candidate who refused to take a term limit pledge be branded with this notation on the ballot: "declined to pledge to support term limits." Any incumbent candidate who did not take legislative action in support of the term limit amendment had the notation "disregarded voters' instruction on term limits" printed beside his or her name on the ballot. Missouri voters adopted this term limit requirement

after an Arkansas law that prohibited congressional candidates from serving more than two Senate terms or three House terms had been declared unconstitutional.

Along with other critics, Donald J. Gralike and Mike Harmon, candidates for Congress, objected to the ballot notation as a form of coercion. It forces candidates either to abandon their principled opposition to term limits or to reduce significantly their chances of election. The notations, the critics charged, used pejorative language which is inappropriate on a public document. Furthermore, notations are unfair because they are read in the voting booth, where there is no opportunity for the candidate to respond. They give proponents the last word at the most critical moment in an election—just before the vote is cast.

Proponents of the notation device argued that the law was an exercise of the people's right to instruct their representatives. They maintained that ballot notations do not prevent candidates from opposing term limits. Although they may put a certain amount of pressure on candidates to support term limits, that kind of influence is a perfectly legitimate part of normal democratic politics. It was the voters who adopted ballot notations in the first place, and the issue was debated fully in the public forum prior to the election. The state was not coercing or "punishing" candidates for their choices, and any perceived consequence of a candidate's stance on term limits (i.e., a loss of votes) was meted out by the voters themselves. Finally, the rights of voters, not the rights of candidates, should be the main concern.

The Supreme Court eventually struck down the Missouri law [*Cook v. Gralike* (531 U.S. 510)]—but without deciding the merits of ballot notations themselves. Although the court's opinion and one of the three concurring opinions expressed disapproval of ballot notations, the grounds on which the justices agreed chiefly concerned only the authority of states to regulate congressional elections. Under the elections clause of the

Constitution, states may regulate only the "time, place and manner" of elections; that authority, the Court held, does not include the right to require ballot notations, which do not merely inform voters but disadvantage candidates.

By Any Other Name

THE ANTI-ESTABLISHMENT CANDIDATE

Luther Devine "L. D." Knox wanted to be governor of Louisiana, but thought correctly that as someone who was not a party regular, he did not have much of a chance. Then it occurred to him that he might capitalize on exactly his outsider status. Before the campaign began, he went to court and officially changed his name to "None of the Above." He submitted his application to be put on the ballot under his new name. The attorney general refused his request. He said that "None of the Above" was misleading and deceptive. "None of the Above" argued that his new name made an important point: it accurately conveyed a message (his outsider status) that was the main point of his campaign. The courts were not impressed, and L. D. Knox, aka "None of the Above," did not win the governorship.

HONORING A ROLE MODEL

Carol Moseley Braun, the first African American woman to be elected to the Senate, was a highly popular figure in Chicago politics especially among black voters in the 1990s. When 21-year-old Lauryn Kaye Valentine decided to run for a seat on city council, she said she was inspired by Senator Moseley Braun. She admired the senator so much that she legally changed her name to "Carol Moseley Braun." The other Carol Moseley Braun accused Valentine of "name trickery" and identity theft. The Chicago Board of Elections refused to allow Valentine to appear on the ballot under her new name, declaring it "false and misleading."

FOR LOWER TAXES

Byron Anthony Looper, property assessor in Putnam County, Tennessee, was the only opponent to state Senator Tommy Burks in the 1998 election. Looper was believed not to have much chance to defeat the incumbent, but he hoped that by emphasizing his opposition to taxes, he could make a respectable showing. He changed his middle name from Anthony to "Low Tax." Unfortunately, he did not stop with that tactic. A few weeks before the election, Tommy Burks's body was found dead in his pickup truck. "Low Tax" Looper was arrested and indicted for the murder.

Pecuniary Persuasion

LOTTERIES

WIN $2,000 CASH

Congratulations, I have checked the voter list at the courthouse and found that you are a registered voter.

Would you like to be 1 of 10 voters who will win $100.00 cash on election day? Would you like to be THE voter who will win $1,000.00 cash on election day? If so, bring this card with you to the Expo building on election day, September 18, 1984. After you vote, drop this card in the "Concerned Voter Box".

. . . This is a voter turnout drive sponsored by ELLIS L. PRESTAGE, candidate for Supervisor, District 4. You do not have to vote for Ellis L. Prestage to be eligible to win. Ellis L. Prestage encourages you to vote for the candidate of your choice.

Ellis L. Prestage distributed 4,000 of the postcards with this message to registered voters in east Cleveland prior to a Special Democratic primary election for district supervisor in 1984. He defeated his opponent

Tommy E. Naron by a narrow margin (995 to 985). The County Democratic Executive Committee certified the results of the election, declaring Prestage the Party's nominee for Supervisor. Naron filed a protest, objecting to the postcards among other tactics. The Executive Committee dismissed the protest, and a special judicial tribunal upheld the election results.

When the state supreme court decided the case, it criticized Prestage's postcard tactic: "such a scheme encourages the electorate, whose motivation to vote should be a sense of civic duty, to go to the polls out of an ignoble desire for short-term financial enrichment." *Naron v. Prestage,* 469 So. 2d 83, 86 (Miss. 1985). The court also commented that the lotteries are "clearly undesirable" because, if they become common in campaigns, they will further disadvantage candidates of "modest means." Nevertheless, the court permitted the lottery in this case mainly because the candidate "expressly disclaimed any attempt to influence the direction of that vote." Also, if Prestage's offer were treated as a gift under the statute, which prohibits candidates from offering anything of value to voters, candidates could no longer sponsor many of the other events that they commonly sponsor such as fish fries, barbeques, and musical shows. Nor was Prestage's offer technically a bribe—which is something of value given to a public official with the intent to influence an official act. The scheme was not even a lottery under the law: the participants did not have to give the organizers anything in order to win. They did not even have to vote for Prestage.

More recently, some reformers have proposed a regular national lottery to increase turnout in elections:

> . . . In each state or territory during a presidential election, the federal government would contribute 25 cents per voter into a state voter lottery. A single voter in each state would win the lottery, notwithstanding who they voted for, so long as they voted during the month-long period that the polls

would remain open. A lottery of this sort would get almost everyone eligible to the voting booth for the chance of realizing two American dreams—the chance of becoming instantly wealthy and the opportunity to exercise a meaningful vote. (Bowie, Nolan A., "Voting, Campaigns, and Elections in the Future: Looking Back from 2008" in Henry Jenkins and David Thorburn, Eds., *Democracy and New Media* [MIT Press, 2003] p. 161.)

WALKING-AROUND MONEY

Ed Rollins, campaign manager for Christie Todd Whitman's victory over incumbent Jim Florio in the 1993 New Jersey gubernatorial contest, boasted afterward that their success was partly the result of his efforts to discourage black voters from turning out. He said he had given some $500,000 worth of contributions to black churches in order to persuade black ministers to refrain from endorsing Florio in the pulpit the Sunday before the election. He also suggested that some key election workers—mainly those in Democratic neighborhoods who were supposed to help get party loyalists to the polls—were paid to stay at home on Election Day.

Democratic party officials had initially attributed the low voter turnout in black neighborhoods to Florio's lackluster campaigning, but after hearing Rollins' claims, they went to court seeking to have Whitman's narrow victory overturned. The Justice Department and the state attorney general launched an investigation into the charges. Whitman denied Rollins' account, and said she would step down if any illegal campaign tactics were discovered.

Rollins' comments provoked angry responses from many in the black community. "To suggest that the black vote or the black church is up for sale is a racist lie," Reverend Edward Verner, head of Newark's black ministers' organization, told *Time.* But some black party activists acknowledged that it is a common practice in the state to use campaign money to secure endorsements.

One asserted: "You can buy black preachers by the dozen very cheaply."

The use of "walking-around money"—small sums given to community leaders to encourage turnout of voters likely to favor your candidates—has been a common practice in many states, and is legal in most, including New Jersey. Some critics, however, argued that trying to suppress the vote is quite different from this practice of encouraging the vote. Others saw no difference: both are efforts to help your own candidate in a competitive contest, in which both sides can use either of the tactics. Other observers thought that the critical distinction is between suppressing black votes and suppressing white votes.

In face of the growing controversy, Rollins began to recant. He now claimed he had fabricated this story as a "head game," an attempt to demoralize a rival political strategist, James Carville. Under questioning during the Democratic party lawsuit, he revised his story again, saying that he had merely advised a campaign official, Lonna Hooks, to "tell wavering black leaders [that] whatever their favorite charity may be, there are other ways of helping them besides state funding Florio has." He said he never authorized her to "commit resources." But Hooks denied that any such a conversation ever took place. In the end, the federal investigation found no evidence of illegal activity.

Comment

Many critics condemn negative ads, and many voters say they disapprove of them. But negative ads often have more effect than positive ads, and sometimes convey at least as much useful and relevant information. Their vice is not only that they tend to exaggerate their claims but also that they often seek to manipulate their audiences. In 1964, Goldwater's positions did seem more bellicose, more likely to risk nuclear war, than Johnson's. In this respect the daisy petal ad correctly captured a difference between the candidates at the time (although Johnson would later escalate the war in Vietnam and may even have known that he would do so). But the powerful emotional appeal of the ad was designed to play on visceral fears of viewers and to evoke a response that went beyond any criticism of Goldwater that could be rationally justified. The manipulative technique used in a Republican ad in 2000 attacking Al Gore's prescription drug plan by warning against letting "bureaucrats decide" and trying to stimulate a subliminal response by repeatedly flashing "RATS" on the screen for a 30th of a second—was as inappropriate as it was ineffective. Yet it seems unrealistic to insist that ads should never use emotional appeals that make claims that cooler heads would reject.

The notorious Willy Horton ad is harder to justify. It not only exaggerates the risks of the weekend release program, but it is also designed to exploit racial prejudices. But assuming that the risks of the program were not negligible, would it have been acceptable to run an ad that portrayed a white felon who had committed a crime while on release? To answer this and similar questions, we would need to formulate criteria to distinguish emotional appeals that should be acceptable from those that should be condemned, and apply them to the examples cited here, and others from more recent campaigns.

The intention of the political organizers who wanted the term limit notation on the ballots was not primarily or simply to inform voters. It was to encourage the defeat of candidates who did not support term limits. But the notation did give voters a true and relevant piece of information. It simply stated a fact, without any emotional overlay. Nor does the objection of the two Missouri congressional candidates who challenged the law seem compelling: "the ballot label can cost votes, and thus will have a coercive effect on candidates and their campaigns." Admittedly, the notations put pressure on candidates to support term limits, but so does any kind of effective political communication. The effect on the voters, however, is more problematic. By focusing attention on a single issue at the critical moment of decision in the voting booth, the notation is likely to cause some voters to ignore other issues they would regard as relevant if they were not being intentionally distracted by the notation. Arguably this is a form of manipulation. But what if one believes that term limits *are* the single most important issue? After all, an overwhelming majority of the voters of Missouri thought it was important enough to pass the initiative that put the notations on ballots. We might still be wary of permitting any single message to have such a prominent place on the ballot, and to have such potential power to distract voters from other issues they themselves would in more reflective moments consider more important.

"None of the Above" may have wanted only to convey his disdain for other politicians, "Low Tax" Looper his commitment to fiscal responsibility, and the newly christened "Carol Moseley Braun," her admiration for the original Carol Moseley Braun. But these candidates must have also foreseen that their new names would achieve a positive effect on voters only by conveying messages that were both misleading and not likely to be subjected to rational reflection. The name-changing tactic is not likely to become a serious threat to the democratic process; the point of considering these examples is to clarify what aspects of a political communication should raise ethical questions. Is the problem that these candidates deliberately took an action in order to manipulate voters? Or is it the effect on voters that should be of concern? If so, then should we object to candidates by the real name of Kennedy (even one named John F. Kennedy) whose electoral successes in Massachusetts exceed those of comparable candidates less fortunately named? No doubt the fact that the message is misleading is part of what is objectionable in these and other problematic communications, but the way the message is presented, and the way it works its effects on the minds of voters, should also be of concern.

If the money candidates spend is such a great advantage and such a potent influence in political campaigns, why should we object to giving some of it directly to voters? To be sure, we might prefer that the "motivation to vote should be a sense of civic duty" rather than a "desire for short-term financial enrichment." But why should the short-term (and relatively modest) enrichment from direct payments, as in a lottery, be considered worse than the long-term (relatively hefty) benefits that contributors expect in return for their campaign pledges? In both cases, the persuasion is pecuniary, and in neither case entirely so. We are rightly suspicious of the influence of money in politics: It reflects and reinforces the broader inequalities in society, and it persuades by means that are often unrelated to the merits of the view at issue.

When money is used as that kind of means, it constitutes a form of manipulation. But money is not the only political influence that seeks to persuade by means other than reason. Moreover, money's influence can be enlisted to support what most people would regard as desirable ends, such as increasing voter turnout. Even walking around money is sometimes defended as a contribution to civic vitality. Even if the defense is disingenuous, it points to serious questions. Should our objection be to the use of money as such, or to its use for partisan ends? Would we object if both parties were limited to spending the same amount of walking-around money and only on low-income voters? Some critics of Rollins suggested that they would not have complained if he had used the money to encourage his supporters to go to the polls. Does the distinction that their criticism assumes between discouraging and encouraging turnout have ethical significance?

Lyndon Johnson, Master Manipulator*

In the late afternoon of July 31, 1957, Senate majority leader Lyndon Baines Johnson (D-Tex.) slumped in his chair in his office in the U.S. Capitol building in Washington, D.C. He had worked tirelessly for the past seven months trying to win passage of a (potentially) historic civil rights bill. But his efforts to gain support for the bill had stalled over a single amendment. The amendment, which would extend the right to a jury trial in certain types of civil rights cases, threatened to put an end to the civil rights bill. Some senators were vowing to filibuster any bill that omitted the amendment. Other senators were vowing to reject any bill that included it.

In many respects, the country was due for some new civil rights legislation. No new federal civil rights legislation had been passed in the twentieth century. The most recent federal civil rights legislation was enacted in 1871 (an 1875 law was overturned eight years later by the Supreme Court). Civil rights bills in 1950, 1948, 1946, 1938, and 1936 had all been defeated before they could be brought to the Senate floor for a vote. The country remained a deeply segregated union: schools, housing, public transportation, movie theaters, and restaurants were divided along racial lines.

In the South, horrific violence against black Americans, even against uniformed soldiers just returned from the war, went unpunished. It was commonplace for black voters to be harassed or prevented from voting. And these were the black voters who had registered to vote (only 20 percent of all eligible blacks were registered to vote). In the North, race riots were ravaging Chicago and Detroit. And televisions were delivering vivid images of these and other civil rights abuses into living rooms across the nation. Many were hoping that the Johnson-led civil rights bill would diminish, if not eliminate, some of the more egregious injustices suffered by African Americans.

The current bill, however, was lowering expectations almost on a weekly basis. Senate debate had already removed a wide range of civil rights issues from the four-part bill. Johnson had successfully negotiated agreements on the first two parts, which established a Civil Rights Division within the

*Introduction by David Kiron.

Department of Justice and a bipartisan congressional Commission on Civil Rights. The third part would have allowed the U.S. attorney general to seek court orders against violators of many types of civil rights. But it was defeated. This defeat was a significant blow to many civil rights supporters, who believed that any civil rights legislation that omitted the protections set forth in the third part of the bill might undermine the civil rights movement.

The fourth part focused on granting the attorney general the authority to sue on behalf of black Americans in connection with violations of the Fifteenth Amendment, which protected the right to vote. This part of the bill empowered the attorney general to initiate lawsuits against any individual who violated another individual's voting rights in the name of the United States. Under federal law, individuals who were held in criminal contempt of such lawsuits (that is, lawsuits brought in the name of the United States) did not have the right to a jury trial.

And so, the Johnson-led civil rights bill had come to focus on voting rights. However, even this narrow focus was a source of controversy. Southern and western senators were insisting on an amendment that would extend the right to a jury trial to individuals cited by federal judges in lawsuits involving voting rights violations. These senators wanted language that would protect their constituents from the political whim of federal judges, who in the past had demonstrated a willingness to use judicial power for political ends. More specifically, they wanted the bill to incorporate the following language:

Any person who, in the Attorney General's opinion, shall intimidate, threaten or coerce . . . any other person for the purpose of interfering with his right to vote, and against whom the Attorney General moved in either a criminal or a civil injunction proceeding, should be entitled to a trial by a jury of his peers.

Many civil rights proponents, e.g., liberal Democrats, opposed this amendment on the grounds that it would perpetuate unjust jury verdicts in southern states. Just two months before, an all-white jury had acquitted two white men who had confessed to bombing Negro churches and ministers' homes in Montgomery, Alabama. "It is this kind of justice, dispensed by these kinds of juries, that the opponents of the civil rights bills in Congress are trying to tack onto this bill. How could anyone who cared about civil rights vote for this amendment?" asked Charles Potter [D-Mich.]. Republicans also objected to the amendment, contending that jury trials would promote anarchy by interfering with the enforcement of court orders.

Although both proponents and opponents of the amendment appeared to support the right to vote, neither side could agree on the appropriate role of jury trials in civil rights cases involving violations of the right to vote. Yet, without agreement on the appropriate role of jury trials in such cases, there could be no new civil rights legislation to advance voting rights. The amendment seemed to create an unbridgeable chasm between the two sides. Noted journalist James Reston described the situation in these terms:

Every so often the play of history turns up an issue so full of personal and regional conflict, so grounded in moral philosophy, and so subject to the clash of ancient but contending principles, that it stands apart from all the normal preoccupations of political life. Such an issue is now before the Senate.

The decade that followed the end of World War II was ripe for new civil rights legislation. African Americans were uniting around a young spiritual leader, Martin Luther King, Jr. Calls for federal action, for new laws to abolish the poll tax and end lynchings, were increasing. And Democrats, who held a majority in the Senate, but had not had a successful presidential candidate in two terms, were increasing their focus on black Americans as a source of electoral support.

Major Players

Thirteen months shy of his 50th birthday, Johnson had become the youngest Senate majority leader in American history just a few years before. His rapid ascent to the most powerful position in the Senate reflected his abilities as a power broker and negotiator, his extraordinary attention to detail, and his political aspirations, which were well known to include the presidency. "Power just emanated from him," said one journalist. Another reporter observed, "He had the bearing of a man in command." Johnson's crusade to win passage of the civil rights bill, however, risked not only his reputation as a leader, but also his future as a viable presidential candidate. For Johnson, any civil rights bill, however watered down, would be better than no bill at all. If he could not establish a common ground among senators on the amendment, the bill would fail, and the racial imbroglio that haunted the country would worsen.

Seventy-two-year-old Joseph O'Mahoney (D-Wyo.) sponsored the jury trial amendment, out of concern that the civil rights bill, as then framed, violated the constitution's guarantee of a right to a trial by jury. O'Mahoney had long stood against the unwarranted expansion of executive authority. Twenty years before, O'Mahoney had undermined Roosevelt's effort to expand the Supreme Court and nominate additional justices more inclined to favor his political agenda. When the court-packing bill appeared to be doomed and Roosevelt wanted it removed from the Senate docket, O'Mahoney forced the "undemocratic [and] obnoxious bill" to the Senate floor, where he renounced it as "a measure which should be so emphatically rejected that its parallel will never again be presented to the representatives of the free people of America."

The first senator to cosponsor O'Mahoney's amendment was the 33-year-old junior senator from Idaho, Frank Church (D-Idaho). Sometimes mistaken for a page boy, Church was often referred to as Senator Sunday School for his youthful idealism. At the time, Church had fallen into disfavor with Johnson after voting against some Johnson-supported legislation. Church not only cosponsored the O'Mahoney amendment, but also suggested that the amendment offer African Americans a new civil right, the right to sit on juries. This right had been restricted to registered voters. Church's addition to O'Mahoney's amendment would give any competent citizen at least 21 years of age the right to sit on a jury. This would appeal to liberal opponents who were most concerned with the unjust consequences of all-white juries. Although Church's addendum to the amendment was largely symbolic, i.e., southern juries would still carry whites and a single white juror could prevent a conviction, Johnson held out the hope that Church's addendum might secure some common ground among rival senators. Johnson wanted to present Church's addendum the following day.

Senate minority whip William Knowland, a long-time civil rights supporter, was the Eisenhower administration's point person on blocking the amendment. The 49-year-old Knowland (R-Calif.) was a twelve-year Senate veteran, known as a tenacious and stubborn legislative negotiator. Like Johnson, he hoped to one day run for the presidency. Unlike Johnson, his commitment to civil rights for African Americans had never been in doubt. Knowland believed that he had the votes to block the amendment. And he began increasing the pressure on Johnson to bring the amendment to the Senate floor for debate and a vote.

Moving toward a Vote

Johnson knew that Church's addendum would garner a few additional votes. But he was not sure that it would be enough. Like Knowland, Vice President Richard Nixon wanted to enact enforceable civil rights legislation, and had become personally involved in the fight. Nixon was often seen in Senate offices cultivating and securing votes against the amendment. On Sunday television talk shows, liberal and Republican opponents of the amendment began gloating that Johnson did not have the votes to pass the amendment.

In fact, Johnson's own preliminary vote count showed that he had come up short. He could rely on at most forty-five senators, yet he needed support from at least three more senators to pass the amendment. The final outcome would be determined on the floor of the Senate the next day. Johnson still had a trick or two up his sleeve, but even he was not sure it would be enough.

FROM MASTER OF THE SENATE: THE YEARS OF LYNDON JOHNSON*

ROBERT A. CARO

It was almost time for the curtain to rise—for the drama that Lyndon Johnson was staging for the Church Addendum to begin—and Johnson had it all arranged. He had assembled an all-star cast of orators—fiery old O'Mahoney, fiery young Church, fiery little Pastore—and even the minor roles had been filled with care: a slow-talking, fast-thinking southerner with great presence, Herman Talmadge, was playing "the presiding officer." Johnson had given all of them their cues, and Church could hardly wait for his moment, but it was dinnertime, and many senators had left the floor to eat. Johnson told him to wait a little longer. He wanted a full house, and at about eight o'clock, when most senators had finished dinner, he asked for a quorum call. And when the floor was again full of senators—almost every desk occupied—the curtain went up.

O'Mahoney had the opening lines—two or three eloquent minutes: "Mr. President, it is my purpose tonight . . . to explain to the Senate, and to those who may be listening in the galleries, the reasons why I believe, from

_____

*New York: Alfred A. Knopf, 2002, reprinted with special permission from the author and publisher.

the depth of my soul, that the trial-by-jury amendment" should pass. Defeating it won't help Negroes to vote, O'Mahoney said. "Denial of trial by jury will not hasten a wise and permanent solution of the grave social problem of racial discrimination that is before us. . . . It will only make matters worse than they are, for trial by jury for criminal offenses is itself a civil right guaranteed to every citizen." And then, recalls Bethine Church, who was seated in the gallery, "Frank looked up at me, and I knew it was going to come."

Standing up at his desk in the back row, Church shouted, "Mr. President, will the Senator yield?" and O'Mahoney acted surprised at the interruption, and pretended reluctance. "I yield only with the understanding that I shall not lose the right to the floor," he said. Johnson, playing himself as Majority Leader, delivered his line in the charade. "Mr. President," he said, "I ask unanimous consent that the Senator from Wyoming may yield for not to exceed two minutes, with the understanding that he shall not lose the floor." Presiding Officer Talmadge intoned, "Without objection, so ordered," and Church introduced his amendment, saying it "is designed to eliminate whatever basis there may be for the charge that the efficacy of trial by jury in the Federal courts is weakened by the fact that, in some areas, colored citizens, because of the operation of State laws, are prevented from serving as jurors." Standing tall and straight among the freshmen in the back row, he said, "We believe the amendment constitutes a great step forward in the field of civil rights. We believe also that it can contribute significantly in forwarding the cause to which most of us are dedicated—the cause of enacting a civil rights bill in this session of the Congress." Then, as if he was unsure of the answer, he asked if O'Mahoney "would be agreeable to modifying [his] amendment to include the addendum I have before me." It turned out that O'Mahoney was indeed agreeable. "It was perfectly appropriate for the Senator from Idaho to offer this amendment, which I [am] so happy to accept," O'Mahoney assured him with a straight face.

Ardent Johnson supporter that he was, Richard Neuberger could barely contain himself. In a reference to a hokey stage melodrama of the nineteenth century, he muttered: "What's next week? *East Lynne*?"

Stilted though it may have been, the opening scene captured the critics. Daughter of a governor, niece of a senator, born to politics, Bethine Clark Church glanced automatically over at the Press Gallery when O'Mahoney agreed to accept the amendment, and what she saw was rows of reporters jumping up "like a wave" and running up the stairs to the telephones in the Press Room.

Then the rest of Johnson's scenario unfolded. The Rhode Island bantam with the nimble mind asked for recognition from the chair. No one—not even Johnson's staff—knew "what John Pastore was going to do," says Solis Horwitz, who had been invited to sit, on a folding chair, next to Johnson to watch the show. "[Lyndon] did, because he said, 'Now you just watch the little Italian dancing master and see what happens here.'"

Johnson had cast Pastore in a demanding role: that of a skeptic and doubter who, by giving voice to his doubts, convinces himself that they are groundless and is converted into a true believer. The subject of his doubts, of course, was the jury trial amendment; Johnson had arranged with Pastore to, in Mann's words, "feign skepticism" of the amendment, to raise the questions about it that many senators were asking, and then to think through the answers to the questions out loud—and finally, seeing the validity of the answers, to be convinced by them, to "almost imperceptibly dissolve his skepticism into outright support" for the amendment. The Rhode Islander began to ask questions of O'Mahoney—the questions that many senators, uncertain about the amendment, were asking themselves: Would the amendment, for example, permit a southern registrar who had been jailed by a judge for civil contempt and then freed when he promised to register Negroes then be able to violate his promise and be in effect immune from punishment because that violation would be criminal con-

tempt, and he would therefore be eligible for trial before a sympathetic jury that would not convict him? When O'Mahoney replied that there was no danger of this, because the judge would have ordered the registrar to register Negroes, and any violation of this order would still be civil, not criminal, contempt, Pastore said, "I think the Senator from Wyoming is moving a little too quickly. I think I know what he means, but I do not believe the *Record* is abundantly clear"—and led O'Mahoney through the reasoning again step by step until the densest senator could grasp it. And with each question that he asked, Pastore reiterated that he was asking it only to try to resolve his own doubts, that he still had "an open mind. . . . I have not as yet definitely resolved the matter in my own mind." As he assured himself on point after point—after saying, on point after point, "I have not been able to make up my mind"—his "misgivings" about the amendment faded, to be replaced by support.

"All of this had been preplanned," Horwitz was to realize, "and [Pastore] did one of the most effective jobs that was ever done." His colloquy with O'Mahoney riveted the attention of both sides of the aisle. There were senators—Republican conservatives from the Midwest, most of them—who still had sincere questions about the amendment. From far across the floor, Thye of Minnesota, hater of Democrats, interrupted to ask a question of a Democrat. "The Senator from Rhode Island was making a very impressive statement," Thye said. "He asked a question. I am as vitally concerned with the answer to that question as [he] is. . . . If he [O'Mahoney] has the answer, I hope he will give it." And while O'Mahoney was giving it—during the entire long colloquy, in fact—the Chamber was so still that although the two Democrats desks, both in the third row, were somewhat far to the side of the Chamber, and only three desks apart, no one in the Chamber had any difficulty hearing them. By the time Pastore finished "resolving" his doubts—in favor of the jury trial amendment—and said earnestly, "I cannot subscribe to the argument" that the amendment "would be emasculating the bill. . . . I cannot go along with that argument," he had convinced others. The show Johnson had staged produced the result he wanted. "The impact of Pastore's performance was profound," Mann writes. "He played the role of an earnest, undecided senator. But he had actually led his colleagues through a crafty, subtle argument for the amendment." All through Senate history, there had been speeches that made senators rethink their views. This was one of them. It "actually changed some votes," George Reedy says. And the next morning—Thursday, August 1—brought to Lyndon Johnson's office the telegram he had been waiting for: a statement signed by the presidents of the twelve railroad brotherhoods. It was much shorter than John L. Lewis' and quite straightforward: "WE FAVOR THE ENACTMENT OF AN AMENDMENT TO THE CIVIL-RIGHTS BILL THAT WOULD PRESERVE OR EXTEND THE RIGHT TO TRIAL BY JURY." Now Johnson had all the ammunition he needed. That morning, Welly Hopkins telephoned him to ask how things were going. They were going just fine, Johnson said. Hopkins recalls that Johnson mentioned "certain senators. . . . He said, 'I've got them. I'm just going to pick my time to call them. That's when I'm going to put it to a vote.'" And that day, August 1, Lyndon Johnson sprang his trap.

William Knowland walked straight into it—blind till the last. That very Thursday morning, at about the same time that Johnson was telling Hopkins that everything was going fine, Knowland was telling reporters—and the White House and Vice President Nixon—that everything was going fine, and reiterating his confidence that "at least thirty-nine or forty" Republican senators would join at least a dozen Democratic liberals in voting against the jury trial amendment. Asked by a reporter whether Church's addendum would strip away any of the Republican votes, the Republican Leader said he thought not. That morning, copies of the brotherhoods' telegram were delivered to the offices of

individual senators, to be followed by visits from Cy Anderson and other union lobbyists. Pastore's logic had had time to sink in. And that morning, Lyndon Johnson made his calls—and after several of them, erased the number that he had placed next to senators' names in one column on his tally sheet and wrote a number in the other column. Richard Russell was also keeping his own very careful tally sheet, and early that afternoon he told Johnson, "I'm ready to vote. I've got fifty votes."

Knowland, however, still believed his own vote count. At any time he might realize the truth, and if he did, he would naturally change tactics: stop pressing for an early vote, and instead try to delay one. Votes had been changing back and forth for days and White House pressure might well change some back again; a delay would afford time for that pressure to do its work. So Johnson made it very difficult for Knowland to change tactics. In a private talk now, he said he assumed that Knowland still wanted to vote as soon as possible. Knowland said he did, and Johnson quickly made those feelings public, interrupting an exchange about the bill, he said, "I have conferred with the Minority Leader. I know how anxious he is for an early vote. I . . . am equally anxious to vote [and] I express the hope that we may be able to call the roll before the evening is over." Turning to Knowland, who was standing next to him, he said, "I would assume that meets with the pleasure of my friend from California." His friend from California said, "Yes . . . I wish to say that I am encouraged by the remarks of my good friend, the Senator from Texas, that he feels we may be approaching a time when we can get a vote."

Later that afternoon, the GOP had yet another encounter with reality. While Knowland couldn't count, Nixon could, and coming to the Capitol, he did so—and promptly launched a frantic Republican lobbying campaign. One after another, GOP senators were summoned to the Vice President's Room, "for," in Douglas Cater's words, "the kind of subtle persuasion an administration in office can exert." General Persons hurried over from the White House, and so did Postmaster General Arthur B. Summerfield, who, as Cater puts it, "suddenly found it a matter of convenience to discuss postmaster appointments. Deputy Attorney General William P. Rogers arrived to answer senators' technical questions. But at 5:40 P.M., Lyndon Johnson asked for recognition from the chair to propose a unanimous consent agreement to set a time for the vote on the jury trial amendment. And the Majority Leader didn't propose his own agreement, but rather the very same agreement that had been proposed on Wednesday—had been proposed three times on Wednesday—by the Minority Leader. "Mr. President," Lyndon Johnson said, "yesterday the distinguished Minority Leader offered a unanimous consent agreement. I wish to offer the same agreement today with two modifications." The modifications would bring on the vote even faster than the distinguished Minority Leader had wanted; Knowland had, for example, allowed six hours for debate on the amendment. "In view of the fact that we have spent a good deal of time today on the bill, I am reducing the . . . hours from six to four," Johnson said. Knowland, aware now that the vote would be, at the least, very close, said he still preferred six, and Johnson suavely said that that was fine with him. Knowland could offer no other objection—he could hardly object to an agreement he himself had proposed over and over, telling the Senate each time how vital its passage was. As they realized the significance of Johnson's proposal, and the reason why he had made it, liberal senators from both sides of the aisle gathered in little groups on the floor, trying to think what they could do about it. But they could do no more than Knowland had. If Knowland had proposed the agreement yesterday, they had supported it, with equal vehemence; they were hardly in a position to object to it now. Spessard Holland, in the chair, asked, "Is there objection to the unanimous consent request?" There was only silence. "The Chair hears none, and it is so ordered," Holland said.

Johnson then addressed the chair again. The vote on the jury trial amendment would probably take place that very evening, he said. "It is the intention of the leadership to remain here until a vote is had."

Irving Ives asked: "When does the debate start? Does it start right now?"

"Right now," Lyndon Johnson said. Checkmate.

The rest was anticlimax. Offstage, off the floor, the Republican efforts intensified now that the Vice President was directing them in person. Aware now that every vote was needed, the GOP managed to contact Maine's Senator Frederick G. Payne, who had been recuperating from a heart attack and was at his fishing camp in the Maine woods, and persuaded him to fly to Washington for the vote.

Other attempts were less successful, however. Schoeppel and Butler had been two votes of which Knowland had been confident, but now it was suddenly realized that that confidence had not been justified. General Persons telephoned the White House to have Eisenhower speak to the two senators in person. Ann Whitman had to tell the General that the President was out on the golf course, at Burning Tree. Whitman managed to get in touch with him there, and he agreed to see Schoeppel, but when Persons attempted to contact the Senator to arrange a time for the appointment, it proved so difficult that it became obvious that Schoeppel was "avoiding" Persons. "Senator Butler also would not come to see the President," Whitman wrote in her diary.

That evening, Joe Rauh and Paul Sifton, chief lobbyist for Reuther's UAW, bumped into Nixon and Rogers right outside the Chamber. "They stopped us and we compared notes on how the votes were going to go, and it was clear it was going to go very badly," Rauh was to recall. "It was clear that Johnson had the votes." Nixon could barely contain his anger. Encountering Johnson in the Senate Reception Room, he said, smiling tightly, "You've really got your bullwhip on your boys tonight, Lyndon." As he started to walk by, Johnson replied angrily, "Yes, Dick, and from the way you've been trying to drive your fellows, you must have a thirty-thirty strapped to your hip, but it's not doing you any good." "Just wait," Nixon said grimly (and incorrectly). "You'll find out."

POSTSCRIPT

On August 1, 1957, the Senate approved O'Mahoney's amendment by a margin of 51 to 42. Eisenhower and Nixon were publicly furious at the outcome. Knowland reportedly cried. A few weeks later the House passed the bill after key members received pressure from Johnson. President Eisenhower signed the new civil rights legislation into law on September 9, 1957.

Comment

This account not only shows a master of manipulation in action, but exposes the complexities that are likely to arise in many actual uses of manipulative techniques. It should give pause to anyone who would try to reach simple conclusions about the legitimacy of such techniques. Many of the familiar markers of right and wrong are absent or mixed. The manipulation in this case apparently did not preclude rational persuasion: O'Mahoney's performance may have been one of those speeches in Senate history that "made senators rethink their views." The victims of manipulation—the minority leader, the vice president and the Senate liberals—were not weak or vulnerable. Arguably, they should have seen sooner what was going on. More than voters, legislators should be expected to be able to protect themselves against manipulation. But the agents of manipulation—Johnson and his cast of speakers—cannot be easily defended by appealing to the justice of their cause. Johnson may have believed that the bill was a necessary step in making progress toward civil rights for blacks, and that it would not pass without this amendment. But the most stalwart champions of civil rights and even moderate supporters of the cause in the Republican party were opposing him; they saw the amendment as a step backward. That Johnson later became a champion of civil rights is not obviously relevant to a judgment about his actions in this episode. Neither concern for the immediate victims of manipulation nor an appeal to the justice of the cause of the manipulators therefore seems decisive. To assess the actions in this case, we need to look more closely at the specific techniques.

Consider whether each of the following actions should be regarded as manipulative, and if so to what extent it is justified (taking care not to confuse the question of whether an action is manipulative with whether it is justified): (1) selecting speakers in advance and giving them instructions about what they should say; (2) arranging for a liberal Senator (Church) to present a reassuring amendment to the amendment; (3) ensuring in advance that O'Mahoney would accept the Church amendment but not too eagerly; (4) Pastore's appearing to have an "open mind," raising skeptical questions, and then announcing support for the amendment; (5) letting Knowland continue to believe he had the votes; (6) taking advantage of Knowland's prior agreement to set the early time for the final vote; (7) scheduling the vote and the debate to maximize the amendment's chances of passage; and

(8) on the other side, the Republicans' "frantic" lobbying campaign against the amendment. Should your conclusions change if you were confident that the amendment would advance (or retard) the cause of civil rights?

Even if you do not find any single action objectionable, you might still find the set of actions taken together questionable. They turned what could have been an occasion for legislative deliberation into a preplanned performance that left little room for real exchange of views or even any genuine political negotiation and compromise. Some would say that we should not expect more from legislatures. Many legislative debates are stage-managed, and benign manipulation of this kind is necessary to get legislation passed. In this drama, there was certainly plenty of politicking, but what happened offstage was more important than what the audience saw. The audience, we should keep in mind, is the democratic public, to whom the legislators should be accountable. In any assessment of this episode and similar cases of manipulation, we need to consider the individual actions and their cumulative impact, including the effects not only on the agents directly involved but on the democratic process more broadly considered.

The Texas Redistricting Caper
David Kiron

Late Sunday night, May 11, 2003, 47 Texas House Democrats climbed aboard two charter buses for a 300-mile trip from Austin, Texas to a Holiday Inn in Ardmore, Oklahoma. By the end of the following day, four more House Democrats had joined them at the hotel. Back at the state house in Austin, an angry House speaker, Tom Craddick (R), enlisted the aid of Texas Rangers, state troopers, and the Homeland Security department to help find the missing House Democrats. Craddick even issued civil warrants for their arrest.

Eventually, more than 300 police from the state Department of Public Safety were deployed. Police were pulled off criminal and narcotics probes to participate in the search. Some lawmakers' homes were placed under surveillance. Police searched (unsuccessfully) for one lawmaker at a hospital where his newborn twins were being treated.

The House Democrats took the extraordinary step of leaving the state, and risking arrest, to prevent a vote on a congressional redistricting bill that was expected to produce up to seven new Republican members in the 2004 Texas delegation to the U.S. House of Representatives. Under Texas House rules, the legislative body could not consider new legislation without the presence of a quorum, that is, at least two-thirds of the 150 House Representatives, which consisted of 62 Democrats and 88 Republicans. The absent 51 Democrats were just enough to prevent a quorum.

The Democrats and Republicans blamed one another for the stand-off, in effect destroying the spirit of bipartisanship the two groups had achieved in recent years. In a written statement, the missing Democrats singled out one Republican in particular, "We did not choose our path, Tom DeLay did. This misbegotten plan is a monument to Tom DeLay's ego, appetite for power, and disregard for our constitutional rights."[1] Texas Governor Rick Perry (R) called the Democrats' behavior "analogous to the pouting child who doesn't like the way the game is going and stomps off the field."[2] House speaker Craddick criticized them for neglecting their legislative duties and preventing consideration of other important legislation.

Public reaction was polarized. Sympathizers called them "heroes," and the press nicknamed them "Killer D's," after a group of Texas Democrats, who 24 years earlier disappeared from the state house, in a successful effort to prevent a vote on a controversial bill to move the date of the state's Republican presidential primary.[3]

Conservative talk shows mocked them, calling the group "Sons of Bees." Craddick called them "cowards" and "Chicken D's." Some House Republicans passed around playing cards with their pictures, similar to the cards of most-wanted Iraqi leaders. After the Democrats were discovered in Oklahoma, protestors surrounded the Ardmore Holiday Inn, waving posters that read, "Osama bin Laden. Saddam Hussein. Texas Democrats."

The next few days were filled with anticipation, as the media and Craddick waited to see if all 51 Democrats would remain in Oklahoma through Thursday, May 15, the deadline for House representatives to give preliminary approval to new bills in the legislative term ending June 2. On Friday, May 16, the representatives returned to the Austin-based state house. They were greeted by a cheering crowd. A sign read, "Welcome Home, Texas heroes." When they entered the chambers, the gallery erupted in applause, as their Republican colleagues sat quietly at their desks.

The Republicans vowed to continue their efforts to pass the redistricting bill. Governor Perry announced that he would call a special session to consider the bill (among others). The high level of acrimony between the two parties reflected the significance of the map to both state and nation. At stake were "not only the careers of a half-dozen senior Democratic lawmakers and the Republicans lined up to replace them, but also control of Congress itself. In a very real sense, the fight in Austin will affect the wallets, rights and security of millions of Americans, and the nation's direction on health care, Social Security, taxes, civil liberties and foreign policy for years to come," one observer noted.[4]

THE STAKES

In Texas, the bill threatened to eradicate the last remnant of Democratic advantage in state government. Republicans held all 29 statewide elected offices, and controlled both the state senate, 19 (R) to 12 (D) and the state house, 88 (R) to 62 (D). After several decades controlling the Texas legislature, the Democrats' advantage had been reduced to a 17 to 15 majority in Texas' congressional delegation. If successful, the redistricting bill would create a Republican majority in and remove senior Democrat incumbents from the congressional delegation.

From the Republican standpoint, redistricting would accurately reflect the fact that the GOP had won 57 percent of total votes cast for congressional candidates in all Texas counties. "The majority of the voters here in the state of Texas support President Bush and his policies. The majority of the congressional delegation does not. That's not fair," said Texas Lieutenant Governor David Dewhurst.[5] Republicans were also anxious to use this opportunity to correct what they believed to be gerrymandering by previous Democrat-led legislatures. Finally, Republicans were concerned that if they gave in to the Democrats this time, the Democrats would leave the state whenever things did not go their way.

At the national level, the redistricting plan was expected to strengthen, in the 2004 election, the Republican majority in the 435-member U.S. House of Representatives. The Republicans already held a 229–205 advantage over Democrats (one member was an independent). A stronger majority in the House meant that passage of controversial legislative bills, such as the 2002 Republican-sponsored Medicare bill, which passed by a single vote in the House, would require fewer compromises with opponents. Given the opportunity to further the Republicans' legislative agenda, the bill's success was a high priority for Majority Leader DeLay (R-Texas) and President Bush's chief political strategist, Karl Rove. For the same reasons, the bill's defeat was a priority for many Democrats.

THE REDISTRICTING PROCESS

The Constitution requires states to conduct a census every 10 years, in part, to reapportion the 435 seats to the U.S. House of Representatives. Depending on demographic trends, a state may lose or gain seats, each of which represents a congressional district.[6] It is up to the states to determine how to draw the lines that define a congressional district. In creating congressional districts, states must abide by federal and state laws. States must observe the 1965 Voting Rights Act, which protects minority voting interests, and the Supreme Court requirement that congressional districts have the same population. Specific state requirements differ. Texas is one of 16 states that is required by the Voting Rights Act to obtain federal approval for its congressional redistricting plans.

Politicizing the redistricting process is a venerable tradition in American history. One of the original signatories to the Declaration of Independence, Massachusetts governor Elbridge Gerry (D), used redistricting to fight off his Federalist adversaries by creating a congressional district that resembled a salamander. Thus was born the term, *gerrymander,* which today refers to the politically biased creation of odd-shaped congressional districts.

There are several ways to adjust congressional districts to obtain political advantage. One is to redraw district lines so that two

incumbents of the same political party are pitted against each other in a single, new district. Another approach is to concentrate your party's strength in one area to reduce competition in several other adjoining districts. Another approach is to distribute your opponent's strength among several adjacent districts. The latter strategy is particularly effective against long-tenured incumbents.

Redistricting does not always accomplish its intended effects. In 1991, Georgia Democrats tried to use redistricting to eliminate the lone Republican in its 10-member House delegation, Newt Gingrich.[7] The Democratic plan backfired when Gingrich moved to a Republican dominated district. And, when the state legislature complied with a federal mandate to increase black-majority seats by concentrating Democrat-leaning minorities in a few districts, other districts were left with fewer minorities. In effect, the redistricting created several new Republican dominated districts. In the next election, Gingrich and fellow Republicans won 8 of Georgia's 11 U.S. House seats, an unlikely achievement if not for the Democrats' tactics.

Over the years, partisan redistricting plans had left few U.S. House seats open to competition. In the 2000 election, 397 members won by at least 10 percentage points.

In Texas, the 2003 Republican effort to redraw congressional districts was, in part, a response to the Democratic inspired congressional map drawn in 1991. At that time, the 1990 Census had apportioned to Texas an additional three congressional seats. Democrats controlled the Texas House and Senate, and a Democrat was governor. The Democrats legislated a redistricting map that was, by many accounts, torturous and convoluted. House Rep. Martin Frost (D) led the successful charge, which at the time appeared to create new House districts for blacks and Hispanics without undermining the political base of Democratic incumbents, who relied on votes from blacks and Hispanics. One observer called it, "the shrewdest gerrymander of the 1990s."[8]

Republicans believed that the map did not fairly represent their gains among Texas voters. Republicans filed several lawsuits: one alleged that the new maps were designed to protect Democratic incumbents; another alleged that the Democratic plan did not do enough for minorities under the Voting Rights Act. In 1994, the courts embraced the Democrats' plan. Many credited the map's chief cartographer, Rep. Martin Frost (D-Texas), with its final approval.

The map, however, did little to prevent Republican gains in Texas government in elections during the rest of the decade. After the 2000 election and the 2000 census, Democratic infighting and disputes with Republicans prevented the Texas state legislature from agreeing on a new redistricting map. In 2001, the state asked a 3-judge panel to arbitrate the dispute. The panel then drew a map that was similar to, and based on, the 1991 map.[9]

In the 2002 election, Republicans were elected to every statewide office. For the first time in 130 years, a Republican majority ruled both the Texas House and Senate, and a Republican governor occupied the governor's mansion. On the heels of this victory, House Majority Leader DeLay, urged the state legislature to revise the 2001 congressional districting map on the grounds that the state of Texas, rather than a panel of judges, should be the entity that maps the state's congressional districts. Democrats were concerned that this mid-census initiative, which had never been attempted in modern history, would be replicated in Republican dominated states. Republicans in Colorado were also trying to redraw the state's most recently approved redistricting map.

In June 2003, Governor Perry ordered the Texas legislature to reconvene for a 30-day special session to consider the redistricting legislation.

SPECIAL SESSIONS

The prospect of getting 51 representatives, who varied in age, health, and family situation, to agree to stay away for 30 days stopped the House Democrats from leaving a second time. All members of the Texas legislature worked part-time as legislators. For some House members, a month-long furlough would have created onerous financial and family burdens. "Thirty days is a long time to be away from your family," observed Sen. Todd Staples (R). On Saturday, July 6, the House Redistricting Committee convened and, with almost no discussion, approved a map, called Plan 01268C, that set new boundaries for Texas' congressional districts. On the following Monday, July 8, a full House considered the bill for 10 hours. Republicans made little effort to counter Democratic objections. At the end of the day, by a vote of 83–62, the House officially approved Plan 01268C. The bill then moved to the state Senate for approval.

Some Republicans in the state senate objected to the plan. Sen. Kip Averitt (R-Waco) said, "It's a silly map. I can't support that. I can't support splitting my county."[10] Another Republican senator, Bill Ratliff (R-Mount Pleasant) said, "I cannot vote for the House map, because it obliterates Northeast Texas, the part of the state I represent." After partisan and further intra-party wrangling among Republicans, the Democratic Senators used their one-third minority to block discussion of the bill on Monday, July 28. Then, in a surprise move, Lt. Gov. Dewhurst ended the first special legislative session a day early.

Governor Perry immediately called a second 30-day legislative session.[11] However, by the time Dewhurst convened the second session later in the afternoon, 11 Democratic senators had fled to New Mexico on private charter jets (donated by supporters). They believed that Dewhurst was going to suspend the quorum rule that required a two-thirds vote to debate any piece of legislation. If the rule had been suspended, the senators could have been forced to vote on the redistricting bill. The senators were also concerned that Dewhurst, even if he did not suspend the rule, might lock the Senate chambers until the

Democratic senators agreed to vote on the redistricting measure, which if the vote followed strictly party lines, would favor the Republican plan. Sen. John Whitmire (D-Houston) explained their position, "They [Republicans] forced us to use this option. We were not going to be locked up and forced to do something we knew was wrong."[12]

ANOTHER WAITING GAME

New Mexico's governor, Bill Richardson, greeted the senators as they disembarked from their planes in Albuquerque. Richardson stationed New Mexico state troopers at the Democrats' hotel to protect the senators from bounty hunters or others who might seek their return to Texas. The Texas senators planned on staying until, at least, the end of the 30-day session.

In early August, each side tried to pressure the other to end the stalemate. Senate Democrats filed a suit in U.S. district court alleging that the governor did not have the authority to call two special sessions on redistricting on the grounds that special sessions are limited to emergencies. Republican state senators, in turn, voted to fine the absent senators $1,000 for each day of absence from the second special session.

On August 26, the second special session ended without a vote on the map. Polls were showing that the public was split in its support for the two embattled parties. A week later, the Democrats suffered a defection. On September 2, Sen. Whitmire returned to Texas, saying that it was time to fight the issue on the Senate floor. With Whitmire, the Republicans had a quorum. The Democrats were forced to return home, or face a vote on the bill while in abstentia.

In the month that followed, Majority Leader DeLay traveled to Austin and played a critical role in placating recalcitrant Senate Republicans. He acted as a shuttle diplomat, transporting map drafts from Senate office to Senate office. Finally, on October 10, the Texas legislature passed a congressional redistricting bill.

JUDICIAL CHALLENGE

In December 2003, the Justice Department announced that the Texas redistricting plan did not violate the Voting Rights Act. Texas Democrats were, predictably, bitter about the decision. Rep. Frost said in a statement that the plan was "the single greatest setback for minority voting rights in the 38-year history of the Voting Rights Act. It would have been laughed out of any other Justice Department—Republican or Democrat." Rep. Thomas M. Reynolds (R-N.Y.) chairman of the National Republican Committee, said the Justice Department's approval "shows that the map is legal and fair, and will be upheld. We look forward to contesting next year's elections under the new map."[13]

In April 2004, the redistricting plan passed its final hurdle, when the U.S. Supreme Court declined to consider the Democrats' federal case, and its central issue: whether congressional redistricting legislation between censuses was unconstitutional.[14]

NOTES

1. R. Jeffrey Smith, "In Texas Feud, a Plane Tale of Intrigue," *Washington Post,* June 7, 2003.

2. Jay Root and Karen Brooks, "Redistricting Fight Closes Texas Legislature," *Oakland Tribune* (or *Fort Worth Star-Telegram*), May 13, 2003.

3. The bill would have allowed Democrats to change their party affiliation, vote for a Republican candidate, John Connally, and then change their party affiliation again, in time to vote in the Democratic presidential primary.

4. Todd J. Gillman, "Texas Congressional Redistricting Fight Will Have National Repercussions," *Dallas Morning News,* July 6, 2003.

5. S. G. Ratcliffe, "New Map, Same Pain for Dems," *Houston Chronicle,* July 18, 2003.

6. Each congressional district had a population of roughly 650,000 people.

7. Richard E. Cohen, "The House on the Line," *National Journal,* April 8, 2000.

8. *Almanac of American Politics* cited in Jay Root, "Battle over Texas Redistricting May Get Ugly, Expensive," *Fort-Worth Star,* June 29, 2003.

9. The new map incorporated three new districts to represent the three new seats the census allotted the state.

10. R. G. Ratcliffe, "Senators Rebuke House on Remap, Eye Own Plan." *Houston Chronicle,* July 9, 2003.

11. Clay Robison and Janet Elliott, "Texas Democrats on the Run Again," *Houston Chronicle,* July 29, 2003.

12. Ibid.

13. Edward Walsh, "Justice Dept. Clears Texas Redistricting; Democrats' Lawsuit Is Still Pending," *Washington Post,* Dec. 20, 2003.

14. There are no federal laws that explicitly prohibit mid-census redistricting. However, some state constitutions do prevent mid-census redistricting. In fact, a Republican effort to conduct a mid-census redistricting in Colorado was thwarted when the courts noted that mid-census redistricting in the state violates specific language in Colorado's constitution. Unlike Colorado's constitution, Texas' state constitution does not explicitly prohibit redistricting between censuses.

Comment

Both parties tried to manipulate the system, and thereby manipulate each other. Deception was not a central element in the strategy of either side: Their intentions and actions were transparent, even if some of the tactics were surreptitious. But manipulation was key: attempts to use procedures for partisan advantage by artful or indirect means were prominent at every stage. In assessing its use, we should distinguish two kinds of judgments—those that take current norms and laws as given and those that challenge them.

Given the system, it would be hard to fault any party that uses its majority status to redistrict for partisan advantage. Partisan gerrymandering is not only constitutional but also traditional, an accepted and even celebrated part of American democracy. In this case, the Republicans could also claim that they deserved to have more seats. So the objection to their decision to redistrict must focus on the timing. Is the absence of any explicit rule stipulating that redistricting should occur *only* after the decennial census sufficient to justify their departing from the traditional schedule? Even if the Republicans were wrong to undertake redistricting under these circumstances, their action does not necessarily justify the Democrats' efforts to prevent a vote. And even if the Democrats were acting in technical violation of the law, their actions do not automatically warrant House speaker Craddick's decision to enlist the aid of Texas Rangers, state troopers, and the Department of Homeland Security to search for the missing Democrats. Nor does the Senate Democrats' behavior necessarily justify suspending the two-thirds rule or locking members in the chamber, as Lieutenant Governor Dewhurst allegedly intended to do. Each of these actions requires a specific judgment, which though it may take into account the improper actions of other agents should consider the particular wrong and its consequences for the democratic process.

Two supporting players in this drama deserve some attention as well. What should we think of Republicans such as Kip Averitt or Democrats such as John Whitmire, who deserted their respective parties? That Averitt wanted to protect his seat is neither surprising nor sinful in politics, and that he objected to splitting the county made a point that has merit. Whitmire was not wrong to acknowledge that the manipulative tactics were failing, and that the battle should now be concluded on the floor of the Senate. But actions of both these renegades cost their parties dearly, at least in the short run. Another influential actor in this drama—Tom DeLay—was not in Texas at all, but according to some accounts was managing much of the manipulation himself from Washington. Apart from the tactics he used, was DeLay justified in intervening at all? The answer depends in part on the extent to which the national party and members of Congress have a legitimate interest in the way that Texas chooses representatives to send to Congress. But if they do have such an interest, perhaps all members of Congress, or even all voters, should have a say about the procedures that shape the representational system in the states.

Taking this possibility seriously entails exercising the kind of judgment that challenges current norms and laws. This case provides an opportunity to question whether partisan gerrymandering is desirable and even if it is, whether the politicians should have control over the redistricting process. They are managing a process, cleverly and sometimes deviously, that influences and often determines whether they and their partisan colleagues will win future elections. The process may not always disadvantage one party over the other: bipartisan gerrymandering is common enough. But it can disadvantage voters who wish to see more turnover in government and more competition in the electoral process. Whatever may be wrong about manipulation is compounded when the manipulators have such a flagrant conflict of interest. Many observers therefore have proposed that redistricting be conducted by an independent commission. However, others point out that there are no objective or neutral standards for redistricting, that drawing district lines is an unavoidably political process, and that members of any commission, though they would perhaps be less partisan would also be less publicly known and less democratically accountable. Defenders of the current practice argue that there is nothing unethical about trying to gain advantage for one's party, if everyone knows that this is the way the game is played and each party, as has usually been the case over time in the country as a whole, has the opportunity to decide how to draw the districts. Is taking turns at manipulation fair play?

Statesman or Sap? Al Gore in Florida in the 2000 Election

David Kiron

Three television networks, ABC, CBS and NBC, declared Texas governor George W. Bush winner of the U.S. presidential election in the early morning hours on the day after the 2000 election.[1] From a hotel room in cold and drizzly Nashville, Tennessee, Vice President Al Gore called Bush to congratulate him on his victory. An hour later, Gore called back. He had heard that the vote count in Florida, the decisive swing state, favored Bush by only 1,784 votes; the smallest margin in the history of the Electoral College. "Circumstances have changed dramatically since I first called you," Gore said. "The state of Florida is too close to call." "Are you saying what I think you're saying? You're calling back to retract your concession?" Bush said. "You don't have to be snippy about it," replied Gore. "You do what you have to do," Bush responded.

Because the margin of victory was less than half of one percent of the state's popular vote, Florida law required an automatic recount. By Thursday, the recount was finished, and Bush's unofficial lead had dwindled to 327 votes.[2] The Bush campaign promptly used this automatic recount to affirm its victory. In the days that followed, former Secretary of State James Baker, Bush's post-election campaign manager, would proclaim over and over, "The vote in Florida was counted . . . the vote in Florida has been recounted. . . ." The Bush campaign acted vigorously to protect and build upon its slim lead.

The Gore campaign did not predict the outcome in Florida, nor did it claim victory. Instead, it focused on the message "Count all the votes." Gore believed that counting all the votes would be fair to both candidates (and the nation's voters) and reveal the truth about who won the election. His message quickly garnered broad public support.

Under Florida law, Gore had the right to call for manual recounts in each of the state's 67 counties. But to expedite a resolution to the election process and protect the country from a protracted battle over the presidency, Gore asked for recounts in four mostly Democratic counties—Broward, Miami-Dade, Palm Beach, and Volusia. The Gore campaign expected Bush's team to respond by asking for recounts in several Republican counties. Baker, however, surprised Gore's team by filing a lawsuit in federal court. The lawsuit argued that Gore's pursuit of selective recounts was unconstitutional.

Again and again, in circumstances repeated throughout the 36-day post-election process, Gore's efforts to preserve the integrity of the post-election process appeared to jeopardize his chance to win the presidency. So much so, that some observers wondered whether Gore was "a statesman or a sap?"[276]

BACKGROUND

In a presidential election, the winner of a given state's popular vote wins all of the state's votes in the Electoral College (except in Maine and Nebraska). The presidential candidate with the most votes in the Electoral College wins the presidential election. Each state is apportioned a certain number of votes in the Electoral College based on population, or more specifically, the number of senators and congressmen the state sends to Congress. As of Sunday, November 13, Gore had 255 electoral votes to Bush's 246 votes. Electoral votes from Florida (25), New Mexico (5) and Oregon (7) remained undecided. The candidate who won Florida's popular vote would also win the presidency.

In Florida, the Bush campaign had a home field advantage of sorts. Florida's governor was Bush's brother Jeb. Many of the best law firms in the state worked in some capacity for Jeb Bush. Since Gore would be seeking Florida lawyers to help him use the Byzantine laws that covered Florida's elections, conflicts of interest would prevent some of the best lawyers from working for Gore. Florida's secretary of state, Katherine Harris (R), a strong Bush supporter, would be coordinating the recount. Bush also had a large group of loyal supporters, including former Secretary of State James Baker, a long-time aid to the Bush family, who became Bush's post-election campaign manager.

The two campaigns had different attitudes toward the post-election period. The Bush campaign viewed the post-election activities as an extension of the pre-election political campaign. It was a political fight that they intended to win. The Bush team sent political operatives into the streets to stir public support. The Gore campaign made a considered decision to avoid street fighting. Against the advice of President Clinton, Gore rejected street protests "as incompatible with the solemnity of the recount process."[82] Jesse Jackson, who had come to carry the fight for votes into

Florida's streets, was asked to desist. Gore's attitude toward political protest did, however, align with the attitude of the person Gore chose to represent him in the post-election period, former Secretary of State Warren Christopher, who was well known for his integrity and professionalism. For Gore, it was important that the public see his victory, if it came to that, as legitimate.

And legitimacy was something lacking so far in the Florida election. Because of a confusing ballot hundreds if not thousands of Jewish residents in Palm Beach County believed that they had mistakenly voted for Pat Buchanan, someone they believed to be an anti-Semite. Reports were proliferating (later debunked) that African Americans had been blocked from voting in certain counties and that some ballots cast by African Americans had been lost. With thousands of ballots in other counties, it was nearly impossible to detect voter intent from ballots that had passed through defective voting machines. Some ballots had semi-perforations, with little pieces of paper, called chads, hanging semi-attached. Some ballots had multiple perforations, some had no perforations at all. There was no standard in the state for determining voter intent from such a variety of ballots, even if Gore's requests for manual recount were allowed.

COUNT ALL THE VOTES

On Saturday, November 11, Gore's senior team met in Washington to take stock of its position and plan strategy. After reviewing his legal options, his closest advisors were pessimistic about reversing the vote totals. William M. Daley, Gore's campaign chairman said, "Look, you got screwed. But people get screwed every day. They don't have a remedy. Black people get screwed all the time. They don't have a remedy. But sometimes there's no remedy. There's nothing you can do about it." Christopher added, "You can run again . . . you don't want to be known as a sore loser. You don't want to

fight for too long. You've got to have your eye on history and the future."[56]

Gore was reluctant to concede. He had responsibilities to a wide range of constituents, including his running mate, Senator Joseph Lieberman (D-CT), their closest supporters, then Democrats generally, and finally the country as a whole. Gore reportedly said that "an immediate surrender would be a violation of his obligations to the people who had supported him, all the people in all the circles."[56]

MANUAL RECOUNTS

Gore's decision to pursue recounts in only four counties was directly opposed to the advice of his recount expert, Jack Young, who had co-authored a book on the subject. Young wanted Gore to protest the counts in all counties. Young's idea, carefully detailed and argued in his book, was to pursue a recount that was, in effect, "an audit of the election."[28] Young said, "If you're ahead, you want the rules of the recount to be as narrow as possible. . . . But, if you're behind you want the scope of the recount to be as broad as possible. You want the recount to monitor the election for fairness."[28] Gore however was reluctant to file 67 different lawsuits and appear litigious.

The Bush campaign had less concern with appearing litigious. Gore's selective protests violated the equal protection section of the Fourteenth Amendment, argued the Bush team in federal court. By favoring some votes over others, selecting some votes to recount and not others, Gore was violating the one person, one vote rule of law. As a matter of law, the criticism was weak. The Florida law that allowed protests from candidates in Gore's position was similar to laws in other states. Eventually, the U.S. Supreme Court disregarded this criticism. However, by emphasizing Gore's selectivity among counties, Baker undermined public support for the view that Gore truly wanted to count every vote. Christopher and Daley, who thought they were doing the state and country a service by not demanding manual recounts in all of the counties, were "flabbergasted" by Baker's accusations.

ABSENTEE BALLOTS

SEMINOLE AND MARTIN COUNTIES

In a national effort to expand the use of absentee ballots, ostensibly to reduce the need for wealthy voters to make the trek to the polling booths, the Republican Party hired contractors to distribute preprinted absentee-ballot applications to party members. In Florida's Republican dominated Seminole and Martin counties, the contractors sent out forms that omitted a place for voter-identification numbers. Without these numbers, the forms could not be legally processed. Thousands of Republican absentee votes were returned without these important numbers. Local Republicans' resolution of these problems was controversial.

In Seminole County, the Republican supervisor of elections allowed local party members to use her office space to add voter-identification numbers to thousands of applications. In Martin County, Republican officials returned the applications to Republican Party members, who added the identification numbers and then returned the corrected forms. In these two counties, Bush gained more than 7,500 votes from absentee ballots. According to Toobin, "The privileged treatment for the Republican voters may well have violated state election law."[198]

When Democratic officials discovered what had happened, they wanted to throw out all of the absentee ballots in the two counties. Gore, however, was reluctant to back the local officials, or file a protest himself. Gore could have asked for a limited revote in both counties that involved all of those people who had originally requested an absentee ballot. Or, he could have adopted the suggestion of his

renowned lead attorney David Boies, who won a landmark government anti-trust suit against Microsoft. Boies said:

> In Miami and Palm Beach, the Republicans are saying you have to observe the letter of the law. They say if the ballots don't comply with every technical requirement, then they should be thrown out. But in Seminole and Martin, they say they want to respect the intent of the voter, even if they break some rules along the way. But they can't have it both ways. If we include Seminole and Martin, we flush them out. And if we get a consistent opinion from the judge, we win either way. A hard line gets rid of all the absentee ballots in Seminole and Martin. And a soft intent-of-the-voter standard gets us our votes in Miami and Palm Beach.[200]

Success with any of these tactics might have been enough to decide the election in Gore's favor. But, against the recommendation of Ronald Klain, his chief strategist in Florida, Gore rejected Boies's plan, which seemed to be the most promising approach. Gore was concerned that Boies's plan would be seen as, again, not wanting to count all of the votes. He proposed that a group of Democrats file separate lawsuits challenging the Seminole and Martin votes. Gore would officially stay neutral.

OVERSEAS MILITARY BALLOTS

Absentee ballots from overseas provided Gore with another opportunity to challenge the vote count process. Florida was one of the few states that accepted overseas ballots after the election. It allowed a 10-day grace period for late arriving ballots. Between November 7 and November 17, more than 2,500 ballots arrived from overseas.

All overseas ballots had to bear clear evidence that they were cast on or before election day and mailed from outside the United States. Florida state law required all overseas ballots to have foreign postmarks. However, Florida officials were receiving overseas ballots without postmarks, witnesses, or even signatures. More than 300 had domestic postmarks from towns with large military presences, such as Norfolk and San Diego.

The Bush campaign expected to increase its lead with military absentee votes, but many of these ballots were arriving with flaws, and might not pass the state's legal standards. They were also concerned that civilian absentee votes from Israel would produce a windfall of votes for Gore. In several counties, Republican lawyers assured the canvassing boards, erroneously, that mail from overseas military members was routinely postmarked when it arrived in this country. Military mail was, in fact, postmarked at the point of origin, a ship at sea or an overseas base. Lawyers representing Bush argued for a lax standard in Republican counties that were expected to net Bush additional votes.

In Democratic counties expected to net Gore additional votes, the Bush team argued for a stricter standard. The Bush team produced a 52-page document that listed how to challenge defective civilian ballots, and how to defend equally flawed military ballots before canvassing boards. It included two forms: one to challenge defective civilian ballots and another to protest equally defective military ballots. The Bush team's document did not become public until years after the election. Gore's legal team circulated a memo that contained a single all-purpose protest form. It did not distinguish between military and civilian ballots. This memo was leaked.

The political outcry over the leaked memo was rapid and devastating. "It is a very sad day in our country when the men and women [who] are serving abroad and facing danger . . . are denied the right to vote [because] of some technicality out of their control," said war hero General Norman Schwarzkopf.[130] Karen Hughes, communications director for the Bush campaign added, "No one who aspires to be commander in chief should seek to unfairly deny the votes of the men and women he would seek to lead."

When the counting of absentee ballots finished on Saturday, November 18, Bush had gained 1,380 votes to Gore's 750; a net gain of 630 votes. The absentee ballots from Israel never materialized. The next day, Senator Lieberman appeared on *Meet the Press* and tried, unsuccessfully, to limit the damage from the leaked memo. "The vice president and I would never authorize, and would not tolerate, a campaign that was aimed specifically at invalidating absentee ballots from members of our armed services. . . . I would give the benefit of the doubt to ballots coming in from military personnel." [131]

Bush's team used Lieberman's comments to protest the exclusion of absentee ballots that had already been rejected. Over the Thanksgiving week, counties reconsidered hundreds of absentee ballots, eventually allowing 288 additional ballots. This so-called Thanksgiving Stuffing gave Bush a net gain of 109 votes. In all, the overseas absentee ballots expanded Bush's unofficial lead from 300 to over a thousand votes.

Gore's team was well aware of the tactics being employed by Baker and his team of lawyers, but even so, Gore chose to ignore advice from several quarters to challenge overseas military ballots on grounds that Bush had benefited from unequal treatment of absentee ballots. Furthermore, under Florida law, if the number of improper absentee ballots arriving after the election exceeded the margin of victory—as it appeared to be in this case—a judge could, under some circumstances, disqualify all absentee ballots arriving after the election and base the results on only those ballots cast and received by election day.[3] Gore however did not pursue this option.

Gore explained his reasons for not protesting the military ballots to Joe Sandler, Democratic National Committee general counsel, "If I won this thing by a handful of military ballots, I would be hounded by Republicans and the press every day of my presidency and it wouldn't be worth having."[4]

Months after Bush became president, news organizations performed their own recounts and their results supported Gore's original message to count all the votes:

> According to a comprehensive analysis by a consortium of news organizations, Gore would have won if there had been a statewide recount of all disputed ballots, but not if the recount had taken place in only the four counties that Gore's request targeted.[5]

The official "certified total" in Florida:
BUSH: 2,912,790
GORE: 2,912,253
Leader and margin (pct. of all votes): Bush by 537 (0.009%)

NOTES

1. This case draws heavily from Jeffrey Toobin's *Too Close to Call*, Random House, 2001. All quotes are from Toobin unless otherwise noted.
2. The public announcement that the automatic recount was finished was premature: 18 of Florida's 67 counties did not even start the automatic recount.
3. David Barstow and Don van Natta Jr., "Examining the Vote; How Bush Took Florida: Mining the Overseas Absentee Vote," *New York Times,* July 15, 2001.
4. Ibid.
5. Ford Fessenden and John M. Broder, "Study of Disputed Florida Ballots Finds Justices Did Not Cast the Deciding Vote," *New York Times,* Nov. 12, 2001, sec. A, p. 1.)

Comment

To be or not to be a sap? To be or not to be a statesman? Those are not the questions. Gore did not face such a stark choice. Like the choices that politicians typically confront in competitive situations, the decisions that Gore and his advisers made were based on a mixture of strategic and ethical considerations. His team appealed to principle to defend the decision to call for a recount in only the four counties that appeared to have the most egregious violations: candidates should not prolong elections by excessive litigation. They also thought it was to their advantage to limit the recount. But requesting a recount in all the counties would have respected another principle, that all votes be treated equally. A statewide recount would also have better served Gore's electoral interest, though no one knew at the time that he would have won the broader recount. Because his decisions were legitimately a mix of prudence and principle, some that seem to reflect an exaggerated ethical sensitivity actually may have been only strategic miscalculations.

If it is too simple to say that Gore lost because he was too ethical, it is probably correct to assume that his team took a more moralistic view of the postelection process than did the Bush team. Because Bush and his advisers saw the process as a continuation of the campaign by other means, they were inclined to use techniques fit for a competitive struggle. They were willing to play hardball and within the bounds of the law to manipulate the system if necessary. Because Gore's team saw the process as an adjudicative procedure, they were more reluctant to exploit the rules or their opponents' weaknesses. (They probably also believed that most of the public shared this view of the process and that taking a more high-minded approach would ultimately better serve their political interests.)

When the results of an election remain in dispute, we should not expect politicians to cease being politicians just because the ballots have been cast. But neither should we favor a postelection process that essentially reruns the campaign.

We should seek some balance between competitive and adjudicative views (which in their pure form were held by neither team). To see what such a balance might mean in specific contexts, consider first whether Gore's team was justified in taking these key actions, which reflected their less manipulative approach: (1) refusing to allow supporters to organize street protests; (2) requesting recounts in only four counties instead of the entire state; (3) declining to bring suit to require consistent standards in counting absentee ballots; and (4) accepting that technically invalid overseas military ballots should be counted. Although Gore has been criticized more often for failure to press his case aggressively enough, at least one criticism has been directed against his decision on November 11 to reject the advice of his senior advisers to quit: "You don't want to be known as a sore loser. You don't want to fight for too long." Would quitting at that point have been the right thing to do?

The Bush team's decisions invite a different question—not whether the team failed to manipulate enough but whether they manipulated too much. Consider these actions: (1) taking the dispute to court (while complaining that Gore was refusing to accept the results of the election); (2) objecting to selective recounts while rejecting a statewide recount; (3) defending the practice of adding the missing voter identification numbers on absentee ballots; (4) favoring different standards for counting absentee ballots than for overseas military ballots; and (5) enlisting General Schwarzkopf to attack Gore for trying to deny the right to vote to "the men and women [who] are serving abroad and facing danger."

Here, as in many other cases, manipulation was accompanied by other (potential) political vices. Some of the statements that both teams made were deceptive and some hypocritical. Some of the actions could be considered unfair (if not quite cheating, then violating the spirit of fair competition). Some might be seen as moral self-indulgence—caring too much about personal integrity at the expense of political commitment—and perhaps even as kind of betrayal—letting down one's supporters by not fighting hard enough for the cause. It is worth trying to distinguish these various elements in the decisions and actions, but it is equally important to consider them in the context of the general strategy that each team adopted. Each combined the elements in different ways to carry out a distinctive strategy of manipulation.

Recommended Reading

The great theorist of manipulation is Niccolò Machiavelli [see his *The Prince* (New York: Random House, 1950)]. He is less Machiavellian than is generally assumed, and dispenses his hardnosed counsel with the hope, not as explicit as moralists might wish, that the ruthless means he recommends will be used for good ends. The general question of justifying the use of dubious means (such as manipulation) to pursue desirable ends falls within the purview of the problem of dirty hands. See the references to articles by Walzer and Thompson in the recommended reading in the Introduction.

A philosophical analysis of manipulation is found in Patricia Greenspan, "The Problem with Manipulation" *American Philosophical Quarterly,* 40 (April 2003), pp. 155–65. Among the few contemporary works that systematically discuss the concept of political manipulation: one by a political theorist Robert E. Goodin, and another by a political scientist William H. Riker, are the most instructive; see respectively, *Manipulatory Politics* (New Haven: Yale University Press, 1980); and *The Art of Political Manipulation* (New Haven: Yale University Press, 1986). Alan Wertheimer's analysis of exploitation and related concepts is relevant to understanding the nuances of manipulation, *Exploitation* (Princeton: Princeton University Press, 1996).

For a sample of the extensive literature on the effects of campaign communication, see Stephen Ansolabehere and Shanto Iyengar, *Going Negative: How Political Advertisements Shrink and Polarize the Electorate* (New York: Free Press, 1997); and Samuel L. Popkin, *The Reasoning Voter: Communication and Persuasion in Presidential Campaigns* (Chicago: University of Chicago Press, 1994).

Ballot notations and redistricting practices are criticized in Dennis F. Thompson, *Just Elections: Creating a Fair Electoral Process in the United States* (Chicago: University of Chicago Press, 2002), pp. 40–42, 92–98, 173–79; "Election Time: Normative Implications of Temporal Properties of the Electoral Process in the United States," *American Political Science Review,* 98 (February 2004), and the references there. Charles R. Beitz examines competing principles of fairness in the electoral process in his *Political Equality: An Essay in Democratic Theory* (Princeton: Princeton University Press, 1989).

An absorbing account of the postelection struggle in 2000 is Jeffrey Toobin, *Too Close To Call* (New York: Random House, 2001). For contrasting assessments of the political ethics of the various actors and actions in that drama, see Ronald Dworkin (ed.), *A Badly Flawed Election: Debating Bush v. Gore, the Supreme Court, and American Democracy,* (2002); Jack Rakove (ed.), *The Unfinished Election of 2000* (New York: Basic Books, 2001); and Cass R. Sunstein and Richard A. Epstein (eds.), *The Vote* (Chicago: University of Chicago Press, 2001).

5 Official Disobedience

What should public officials do when they disagree with a policy or decision of their government? For officials who have not been elected, this question poses a particularly difficult dilemma. They are bound to carry out the orders of others; yet they should not act contrary to their own moral convictions. Their duty to carry out policy rests in part on the requirements of the democratic process. We do not want officials whom we cannot hold accountable to impose their own views on us, overriding the policies determined by the democratic process. We also usually assume that officials consent to the terms of office. They know in advance what is expected of them, and they should not hold office if they cannot accept a policy once it is formulated. On this view, the moral responsibilities of the nonelected public official are completely captured by the imperative "obey or resign."

Critics of this view argue, first, that it underestimates the discretion that administrators exercise in modern government. Neither the law nor their superiors can determine all decisions that administrators make, and they must use their own judgment on many occasions. Second, if all public officials followed this imperative, public offices would soon be populated only by people who never had any inclination to disagree with anything the government decided to do. Men and women of strong moral conviction would always resign. Third, officials have broader obligations to the public—not merely obligations to their own consciences or to their superiors. "Obey or resign" presents too limited a menu of moral options. Depending on how serious the moral violation is and the good that officials can do by opposing it, officials may be warranted in staying in office and expressing their opposition in other ways. They may, for example, organize internal opposition, issue public protests, refuse to carry out the policy personally, support outside opponents of the policy, or directly obstruct the implementation of a policy.

The methods of disobedience that seem the most difficult to accept are those that are illegal or violate governmental procedures and lawful orders of superiors. The justification for such tactics resembles in part the rationale for civil disobedience by citizens. A democratic society benefits from permitting moral dissent. Extreme measures are sometimes necessary to force democratic majorities and governments to recognize that they have made a serious mistake, and sometimes officials are the only people in a position to bring such a mistake to public attention. But since it is an extreme measure, civil disobedience is generally thought to be justified only under certain conditions. Those who disobey must: (1) act publicly; (2) act nonviolently; (3) appeal to principles shared by other citizens; (4) direct their challenge against a substantial injustice; and (5) exhaust all normal channels of protest.

The cases in this chapter—three instances of disobedience, a successful threat to resign, a quiet but unsuccessful dissent, a strong dissent stopping short of disobedience, and two failures to violate standard procedures that stood in the way of the right action—can help clarify whether official disobedience is justified, if so under what conditions, and whether the alternatives are better.

The first pair of cases in this chapter invite a comparison of two instances of unauthorized disclosure (otherwise known as *leaks*). Otto Otepka, a State Department official, passed classified information to a congressional staff member in an effort to undermine the department's policy on security clearance, which he believed endangered national security. Daniel Ellsberg gave the classified *Pentagon Papers* to the *New York Times* to encourage opposition to the Vietnam War. The challenge to readers who wish to defend one and criticize the other is to find a principled basis for making the distinction. But justifying a principle that would defend both or a principle that would condemn both is not as simple as it might seem at first.

George Shultz did students of political ethics a great service when he made quite different decisions about whether to dissent on two issues he faced at the same time while serving as secretary of state. When the White House issued a directive that required polygraph testing of all federal officials with access to sensitive information, Shultz publicly threatened to resign, and the president rescinded the directive. But when Shultz discovered the scheme to trade arms for hostages in the Iran-Contra affair, he objected privately but made little effort to resist it, and it continued because the same official at about the same time took quite different approaches to two difficult moral issues. The cases considered together offer a rare opportunity for comparative ethical analysis.

FBI Agent Rowley faulted her organization, especially the officials in the Washington headquarters, for failing to "connect the dots" in the evidence showing a potential terrorist threat to the United States. She did not blow the whistle until she concluded that the new director was ignoring her dissent and resisting proposals to undertake the major reforms that she believed were needed in the bureau. She went outside of channels—disobeying or at least disregarding standard procedures—to bring public attention to the continuing structural problems in the organization.

In the case of the space shuttle *Challenger,* nobody involved in the decision-making process that culminated in its disastrous launching threatened to resign or publicly protested. Yet two senior engineers protested as strongly as they believed possible, short of disobeying or threatening to resign. Evaluating their actions can help clarify both the moral advantages and limitations of lawful dissent in organizations with close connections to government, as well as in government itself. History did not exactly repeat itself in the *Columbia* disaster some 17 years later. Some of the same problems remained but most of the dissent was even more muted. Dissent—and disobedience even more—seemed to be in disrepute when it was needed most.

The Odd Couple

Taylor Branch

The public reaction to two whistle-blowers, Otto F. Otepka and Daniel Ellsberg, clearly illustrates the disorienting spells cast upon fervent observers by the spectacle and drama of disclosures that involve national security. Otepka violated our national security by slipping classified documents to veteran Red-hunter Julien G. Sourwine, counsel to the Senate Internal Security Subcommittee. He was fired for his transgressions in 1963, lost his position as chief of the State Department's security-evaluation division, became a martyr of the right wing, and is considered by some to be the first whistle-blower in the modern period. Ellsberg violated our national security by slipping classified documents, later to be called the Pentagon Papers, to numerous senators and newspapers. He was indicted for his transgressions in 1971, lost his security clearance at the RAND Corporation, became a martyr of the left wing, and is often considered the capstone whistle-blower of recent years.

While these two men are ideological opposites, there are unmistakable similarities between their respective exploits, viewed on a suitably high plane of reflection after all the human juices and interesting particulars have been drained away to leave the arid generalities in which lawyers earn their keep. Like colliding planets, Ellsberg and Otepka still operate by the same laws of motion in some ways, following their higher instincts regarding the public interest as they see it, exposing treachery in places of power regarding questions of life and death. These similarities suggest that anyone who wants to

fight institutional rigor mortis by encouraging people to speak out from within the government is obliged by honesty and consistency to take his Otepkas with his Ellsbergs, and vice versa—to take a man like Otepka, who thought his bosses were ruining the country by being too sweet to communists everywhere, with one like Ellsberg, who thought his former colleagues were ruining the country by killing numerous people and lying about the whole affair. Regardless of who is right on the lofty worldview questions, the comments on the two men by prestigious newspapers and politicians suggest a strange kinship that bears some examination.

Otepka had been in the government for twenty-seven years and in the Office of Security for ten years when he was fired on November 5, 1963, on charges of "conduct unbecoming an officer of the Department of State." President Kennedy, setting a precedent for dealing with criticism from the right, assuaged a Calley-like tide by announcing that "I will examine the matter myself when it comes time," but he was killed before the review process got underway. It seems that, Otepka, described by *Reader's Digest* as a "tall, quiet, darkly handsome man," by *Newsweek* as "a sad-eyed, introverted man," and by the *New York Times* only as "stocky," (descriptions indicative of the impact of political position on the eye), had been running afoul of important people in the Kennedy Administration for some time.

In 1955, for example, he had refused to dispense with the formalities of the security clearance procedure for Walt W. Rostow, when Secretary of State Dulles wanted Rostow on the State's Committee on Operations. Subjecting Rostow to a full-dress examination of his character was considered an affront to his dignity. When President

Kennedy wanted Rostow on the team in 1961, Otepka again refused to waive security proceedings, which, some say, is why Rostow ended up in the White House while Otepka was at State, rather than going through the State security mill. (Apparently Otepka was a bit troubled by the internationalist leanings of Rostow's writings on economic development, hesitant to be taken in by possible ruses like Rostow's "non-Communist Manifesto," *The Stages of Economic Growth.* Also, as a professor, Rostow's commitment against communism was suspect a priori. Although subsequent events and the Pentagon Papers were to show that Otepka was dead wrong in his doubts about Rostow, some beneficiaries of hindsight have wished that he had possessed more clout in his efforts to keep Rostow out of the government.)

In addition to the Rostow rebuke, Otepka had nettled the new administration by locating and firing the State Department employee who had leaked a secret survey of U.S. prestige abroad to the Kennedy campaign forces in 1960. The survey, showing a dip in America's international esteem, was used with telling effect by John Kennedy in the campaign to show that the Republicans were blowing things in foreign policy, partly by following what seemed to be a deliberate path toward national weakness. Otepka had also been critical of the lax security procedures for the Cuba desk officers at the State Department, one of whom, William Wieland, was considered by the Republican Party almost single-handedly responsible for delivering Cuba into the enemy camp. Otepka testified before a Senate committee that he had dissented from the decision to clear Wieland without further study of his inner proclivities, and so much stir was created over Wieland that President Kennedy was forced to defend him publicly in a press conference.

Finally, Otepka had refused to waive security investigations for six men of decorum whom Secretary Rusk wanted in 1962 for the Advisory Committee on Management Improvement to the Assistant Secretary of State for International Organization Affairs. The six, which included Harding Bancroft, Sol Linowitz, and Andrew Cordier, were chosen to that august and rather useless body to study whether or not American employees of international organizations should be required to pass U.S. Security investigations. The issue itself was one of some controversy, spurred on by a letter to the *New York Times* on July 30, 1962, that attacked the security regulations as a dangerous legacy of the McCarthy era. The letter came from Leonard Boudin, who is now the chief attorney for Daniel Ellsberg. In any case Otepka refused to waive security clearances for men who were going to study the need for security clearances, and that kind of zeal to check out the private leanings of prestigious people had long since aggrieved the Kennedy Administration.

John F. Reilly, Assistant Secretary of State for Security. was so intent upon getting rid of his anachronistic subordinate, the John Wayne rough rider on the New Frontier, that he bugged Otepka's telephone and set up an elaborate system of surveillance to catch him in an act of shame that would stand up as evidence for doing him in. Reilly's sleuths scoured Otepka's "burn bag," a receptacle used to mark for instant destruction items like doodle pads and carbon paper and other parts of the afterbirth of state secrets that might leave telltale signs, and finally scored one day when they found classification stamps which Otepka had clipped from classified documents. Thus declassified informally, the documents were being sent by Otto over to old J. G. Sourwine at the Senate Internal Security Subcommittee, where they were used to help surprise and embarrass Otto's bosses regarding how lightly they took the red menace right here at home. The burn bag also contained a used typewriter ribbon, an instant replay of which revealed that Otepka had worked up a primer of questions for Sourwine that he could use to catch State Department officials in factual errors regarding the communist question.

OTTO'S HIGHEST LOYALTY

When the State Department used the burn bag evidence to fire Otepka, the fireworks and orations began. The *Chicago Tribune* skipped over the classified document problem to define the issue as a test of the principle of patriotism: "There can be no doubt that this case reflects an intention by the Kennedy Administration to conduct a purge of patriots." The Charleston, South Carolina, *News & Courier* agreed: "To reprimand a U.S. citizen for doing his duty would be a shame and an outrage." *Reader's Digest* later published an article called "The Ordeal of Otto Otepka," subtitled, "Why have State Department employees been using tactics of a police state to oust a dedicated security officer whose only sin seems to be loyalty to his country?" which pretty well summed up the conservative presentation of the problem. The police state argument reflects the tactical guideline that it is easier to attack the process by which the opponent operates than the substance of what he says. However, it also bore some risk of the "corner problem," by which people paint themselves into a corner through the hasty use of principles whose future application might haunt them. In this case, the *Digest*'s forthright position against a police state was quite risky. It not only made it tougher to argue in subsequent tirades that the State Department was undisciplined and namby-pamby, but it also would require a redefinition of the issues when the wiretapping and surveillance of J. Edgar Hoover came to the fore. Most conservative journals ignored the classification question and the he-broke-the-rule point of view, except perhaps to note in passing that classification was nonsense in general and that Otepka's leakage of secret material did not hurt the national interest anyway, but rather struck another blow against the pinkos in the State Department.

Meanwhile, in the Senate, members surveyed the Otepka affair and concluded that the main issue at stake was, as is so often the case, the dignity of the U.S. Senate.

Conservative Senator Williams of Delaware remarked that, "In this instance, all that Mr. Otepka was guilty of was cooperating with a congressional committee." Senator Dominick of Colorado thanked Senator Dodd for having "pointed out the very difficult position Senate committees would find themselves in if it continued to be held that the executive branch could prevent any of its employees from coming before Senate committees, either by threatening them with dismissal or by verbally preventing them from testifying under that threat." Dodd, a foreign policy buff, defined the question in terms of national survival: "If those forces bent on destroying Otepka and the no-nonsense security approach he represents are successful, who knows how many more Chinas or Cubas we may lose?" But Dodd, too, was anxious about the powers of himself and his colleagues, and he entered a long discourse with Senators Strom Thurmond and Frank Lausche on November 5, the day Otepka's dismissal was consummated, which Thurmond climaxed by declaring that the Kennedy Administration's action would "nullify our system of government by tending to destroy the constitutional system of checks and balances." There was no commander-in-chief talk on that day, no talk about how the President's powers were essential to survive in a hostile international environment. The conservatives were safe from the corner problem, however, because the war in Vietnam had not yet begun. The doves in the Senate would not really discover the checks and balances principle until about 1968, leaving the conservatives ample time to switch over to the commander-in-chief line without undue embarrassment.

"ORDERLY PROCEDURES ARE ESSENTIAL"

The liberals in the Senate were exceedingly mousy about Otepka as the supporters of the Kennedy Administration sought to ride out the storm in public silence. This does not necessarily mean that they were apathetic, for some Otepka supporters claim that there was great pressure to let the Otepka fervor die out like the groundswell for General MacArthur. Clark Mollenhoff, a straightforward, very conservative reporter for the *Des Moines Register,* made a speech about the obstacles to coverage of the case:

> I realize the broad range of direct and indirect pressures brought to discourage a defense of Otepka, for I met most of them at some stage from my friends in the Kennedy Administration. One put it crudely: "What are you lining up with Otepka and all those far-right nuts for? Do you want to destroy yourself?"
>
> There were also hints that I could be cut off from the White House contacts and other high Administration contacts if I continued to push for the facts in the Otepka case.

Liberal newspapers made slightly more noise in the dispute than their compatriot senators, and their editorial writers swept aside all the chaff about higher loyalty and patriotism and the dignity of Congress to focus on the principles at stake, with a fixity that is born of discipline. The *Washington Post,* for example, zeroed in on the law and order question, following the rule that it is always best to attack on matters of procedure: "For all of Senator Dodd's sputtering, he must know that what Otto Otepka did was not only unlawful but unconscionable as well. Mr. Otepka certainly knew this himself—which is no doubt why he did it covertly instead of candidly. He gave classified information to someone not authorized to receive it." The *New York Times* took a similar line, with slightly greater emphasis on propriety: "The disturbing aspect of this case is that both Mr. Otepka and members of the Senate subcommittee have defended their actions on ground of 'higher loyalty.' . . . Orderly procedures are essential if the vital division of powers between the legislative and executive branches is not to be undermined. The use of 'underground' methods to obtain classified documents from lower level officials is a dangerous departure from such orderly procedures."

The liberal press also used words like "controversial," "McCarthyism," "tattle," and "infidelity" as often as possible in connection with Otepka's name. This strategy, following from the rule that it is often useful to adopt your opponent's principles and turn them back on him in verbal counter-insurgency, amounted to McCarthyism turned on its head, as Marx did to Hegel, or guilt by association with McCarthy. Thus, when Otepka defended himself by citing the government employees' Code of Ethics (which charges employees to place loyalty to conscience, country, and the "highest moral principles" above "loyalty to persons, party, or government department"), the *Washington Post* news story stated that "the last time that issue was raised with public prominence, it was raised by Senator McCarthy in sweeping form. . . ." A *New York Times* story by Neil Sheehan in 1969 continued this theme of the beat-them-at-their-own-game campaign: "The enthusiastic pursuit of 'subversive elements' in the government loosed by the late Senator Joseph McCarthy slowed to a desultory walk in later years, but Mr. Otepka . . . did not change."

"HIS TRAINED JACKAL, JACK ANDERSON"

Otepka returned to the public light in 1969, when President Nixon made good on his campaign promise to review the case "with a view to seeing that justice is accorded this man who served his country so long and well." The Subversive Activities Control Board seemed like an appropriate resting spot for a seasoned personnel sniffer, who could spend the rest of his days perusing political groups for loyalty blemishes. Actually, the SACB was a secondary choice for Otepka, who really wanted to go back to the State Department but was frustrated in his desire by Secretary of State Rogers, who did not want him. Senator Dirksen, claiming Otepka as a constituent and an ideological brother, suggested the SACB spot and went to work with the other conservative senators to give the board and its $36,000-a-year members something to do. They knew that Otepka would be an additional burden in the annual battle with the liberals over the fact that the SACB members are so inert that they appear strikingly like welfare recipients, at ten times the poverty standard.

The task of selling Otepka himself was undertaken with the old principles of patriotism and higher loyalty. In the Senate, the four hoariest members of the Judiciary Committee—Eastland, McClellan, Dirksen, and Hruska—assembled for a confirmation hearing to pay homage to the SACB nominee. "You have been punished because you attempted to protect your country," said Chairman Eastland to Otto, and the four senators respectfully declined to ask the witness anything other than his name.

And Senator Dodd, now deceased, led the fight on the floor of the Senate and helped organize Otepka Day, on which patriots around the nation celebrated his resurrection. Every time Senator Dodd took the floor to wax eloquent about Otepka's higher mission against international communism, he represented the largest collection of loyalty contradictions ever assembled in one place—a veritable one-man intersection of passions on the morality of exposure. For since Dodd had first praised Otepka for exposing the State Department with pilfered documents and denounced the State Department for firing the higher patriotism of Otepka, Dodd himself had been exposed for pocketing campaign contributions and other financial misdealings. While Dodd praised the patriot who exposed corruption in the State Department, he fired the infidel who exposed corruption in himself—his administrative assistant of twelve years, James Boyd. Boyd's medium of exposure, the Drew Pearson/Jack Anderson column, decided to switch in the Otepka affair—exposing the exposer, Otepka, because of his leanings to the right. In this vortex of half-hero, it was not surprising that Dodd would resort to arguments tinged with the ad hominem, "The press campaign against

Otto Otepka has been spearheaded by Drew Pearson, the lying character assassin and his trained jackal, Jack Anderson."

In the end, however, Dodd regained the lofty, joined by the honey tongue of Senator Dirksen—who read to the Senate a moving letter from Mrs. Otepka, describing the hardships the family had faced since Otto had been demoted in 1967, while his dismissal was still being appealed, to a $15,000-a-year job that was so "demeaning" that Otto protested by taking a leave without pay and forced her to go to work to support him. What is $36,000 for a patriot, asked Dirksen and Dodd of their fellow senators, and the two crusaders went to their graves knowing that the world would be better with Otepka on the SACB. Otepka, for his part, called the Senate confirmation "my vindication," and a well-deserved one to boot, because as he later wrote, "I have disagreed only with those who quarrel with the truth. I shall continue to disagree."

NAILING DOWN THE CASE

The vindication did not come easily, for during the period when Senate confirmation was pending, the *New York Times* practiced an enthusiastic brand of beat-them-at-their-own-gamism. Reporter Neil Sheehan was dispatched to check up on Otepka's acquaintances, and began his April 4, 1969, story as follows: "A fund with John Birch Society ties has paid about 80 percent of the $26,500 in legal costs incurred by Otto F. Otepka in his four-year fight to win reinstatement as the State Department's chief security evaluator." The story went on to pin down Otepka's "ties" to the Birchers by declaring that "last summer he attended the four-day annual God, Family, and Country rally in Boston, organized by Birch Society leaders." Sheehan also tracked down James M. Stewart, chief fund-raiser of the American Defense Fund, which channeled money to Otepka's lawyers. Stewart looked and acted like a Bircher, although Sheehan wrote triumphantly that he "would neither affirm nor deny whether he was a member of the Birch Society," saying, like Pete Seeger, "I am not answering that question because it is irrelevant." Beyond such waffling on the affiliation question, Stewart further hanged himself with his reading material, because Sheehan found out, after a hard-nosed inquiry, that "he does subscribe to a number of Birch Society publications."

Having established that Otepka's legal defense was being solicited by a man who might as well have been a Bircher, if he were not in fact a bona fide one, and that Otepka himself was hanging around in right-wing crowds, the editorial board of the *New York Times* concluded that Otto was ineligible for membership on the SACB. According to the April 8, 1969, editorial, "The disclosure that Otto Otepka received $22,000 from a fund with extreme right-wing associations should be enough to kill his nomination to the Subversive Activities Control Board. After this, senators of conscience cannot vote to confirm Mr. Otepka in a $36,000-a-year job, where his work, if any, will be to judge the loyalty of American citizens and organizations."

Rather than taking the political view that the whole SACB concept is unconstitutional and therefore should not be supported—or the resigned view that the SACB is a useless bit of welfare, doing nothing, but that it was a shame for the President to use his discretion to appoint, in the *Times'* view, a schmuck like Otto—the editorial rested its case on the assertion that Otto was too tainted to do the job right as a subversive-hunter, and that a neutral mainstreamer would be more efficient. The *Times* thus ventured onto the turf of subversive-hunting and declared Otepka ineligible by the very standards the SACB uses to ferret out dangerous organizations.

An average newspaper might have rested its case there, but fortunately the *Times* is not an average newspaper and therefore was possessed of a "wait a minute" person on the board—the long view of responsibility. Apparently, such a person noticed that the Otepka editorial might look like McCarthyism to some readers, and told his colleagues that such an impression, left uncorrected, would be detrimental to the *Times'* historical commitment against Joe McCarthy's methods. So the argument was sealed with the addition of the following mop-up paragraph:

> The far right doubtless will cry "guilt by association," the charge made long ago by civil libertarians against the likes of Mr. Otepka, but there is a crucial difference here. Mr. Otepka's link to Birchites is no youthful indiscretion of many years ago but an activity carried on as recently as last summer.

Thus, the editorial board took the precautionary measure of protecting its flank against charges of McCarthyism by recalling the best case against old Senator Joe— the telling point about the unfairness of using "youthful indiscretions" that the *Times* itself had once made—and beating it down. This done, the *Times* had at least as strong an indictment against Otepka as McCarthy would have had against his victims if he had not ruined it all by rummaging through their old college notebooks.

The fact that Otto's sins did not fall in the "youthful indiscretion" category probably did carry some weight with a liberal readership—with people who remembered going to the verbal barricades for Alger Hiss and others like him over whether their doings on the left were permanent blemishes of character or merely the wanderings of callow youth. Those people who (perhaps for tactical reasons) had said that what was really wrong with Joe McCarthy was his reliance on outdated evidence, his once-a-subversive-always-a-subversive line, would be relieved to learn that Otepka, unlike Hiss, was still at it. "As recently as last summer," concluded the *Times,* in an apparent reference to the God, Family, and Country rally that Sheehan had uncovered. (Some sources suggest that the freshness of Otto's blight could have been established also by the subscription dates on James Stewart's magazines.) Anyone who bought all of McCarthyism except for the Senator's attacks on people for what they did in the past would be sympathetic to disqualifying Otto from the SACB for associations that persisted well into his maturity.

"HIS PECULIAR INFIDELITY"

After Sheehan wrote another story for the Sunday *Times* on April 20, emphasizing Otepka's right-wing associations and his likeness to a bureaucratic version of Joe McCarthy, Senator Strom Thurmond strode to Otto's battlements by declaring on the Senate floor that the *Times* had deliberately smeared Otepka. He charged that *Times* executive editor Harding Bancroft had commissioned the Sheehan investigation in order to get even with Otto for vexation caused back in 1962, when Bancroft was examined for loyalty before going on the Advisory Committee on Management Improvement to the Assistant Secretary of State for International Organization Affairs, or ACMIASSIOA. The *Times* had no comment on this counter-smear, holding to its position that its interest in Otepka sprang from the logical force of the youthful indiscretion editorial.

Whatever the motivation behind the Sheehan articles, their spirit caught on in the Senate, culminating in Senator Stephen Young's speech against the Otepka nomination on June 24, minutes before the vote. Senator Young avowed that James Stewart, who raised money to give to Otepka's lawyer to use in Otepka's defense, had, on June 16, 1969 "attended a fund-raising party at the home of Julius W. Butler . . . an admitted fund-raiser for the John Birch Society and active in several John Birch front organizations. . . . The guests at Mr. Butler's home last week included Robert Welch, founder and head of the John Birch Society, who spoke at length spewing forth the usual John Birch lunatic obsessions. Mr. and Mrs. James Stewart, I am told, were in charge of the refreshments that were served at the meeting and were introduced to the crowd and received with applause."

All this failed, and the Senate confirmed Otepka by a vote of 61 to 28. The *Washington Post* emphasized the fidelity question in its editorial lament: "Otto Otepka's long and unfaithful service to the State Department certainly entitled him to some reward from those on Capitol Hill who were the beneficiaries of his peculiar form of infidelity." The *New York Times,* as is its custom, focused on the who-are-you question to bewail Otto as a "living symbol of some of the worst days of the McCarthy-McCarran era."

THE ELLSBERG REVERSE

Two years after his investigation of Otepka, Neil Sheehan was ensconced in a New York hideaway as head of a *New York Times* writing team that prepared stories based on the top-secret Pentagon Papers—slipped to the *Times,* the *Washington Post,* and other parties by Daniel Ellsberg. Rather than investigating the left-wing associations of Ellsberg (such demented pariahs as Noam Chomsky, SDS leaders, the staff of the *Harvard Crimson,* and the editors of the *Washington Monthly*), or noting the glazed-eyed, Martin Lutherish manner in which Ellsberg had been starting speeches by confessing himself as a war criminal, Sheehan stuck to the material at hand and exposed the deceptions perpetrated by Ellsberg's former bosses. It is possible that Sheehan's views on classified material had changed over the two years since 1969, as had his views on the war in Vietnam. As late as 1967 Sheehan had described himself as only half way along the path from war support to war opposition in a *Times* magazine article entitled "No Longer a Hawk, But Not Yet a Dove." By 1971, he had progressed far enough to write a piece in the *Times* speculating on the possible criminality of people behind him on the path, and this progress helped both Sheehan and Ellsberg decide that the classified document issue paled in significance compared with the overriding injustice of the war.

Of course, the decisions regarding publication of the Pentagon Papers were not made by

Sheehan, but by the management of the *Times* and the other papers involved. By 1971, the editors of the *Times* had decided that the real issue involved in the exposure of classified documents was not orderly procedures, but the people's right to know as embodied in the freedom of the press. A June 15 editorial in the *Times* stated that the paper felt it had an obligation to publish the Pentagon Papers "once these materials fell into our hands." The *Times,* almost as disposed to see conflicts in light of its own powers as the Senate is likely to see them turning on Senate dignity, defined its position so narrowly that it left Dan Ellsberg out in the cold. Rather than presenting the Pentagon Papers as a joint venture between Ellsberg and the newspaper, the *Times* argued that retribution for "declassifying" the Pentagon Papers was a matter between Ellsberg and the government. The *Times* took responsibility for the papers only when they fell on its doorstep out of nowhere, after which their news value required publication. (There is considerable circumstantial evidence that the *Times* was not as passive in the matters as it implies.)

The *Times'* forthright exposition of press duties in matters hot enough to be classified must have convinced Otto Otepka that *he* could in the future slip classified documents to the *New York Times* and expect to see them published. He must have been heartened by the *Times'* objectivity—by the fact that the editors took no overt political or moral positions regarding why the war papers should be read in spite of their classifications, and that there was no editorial at all on the war series until the government stupidly tried to suppress it and introduced the freedom of the press question. The editors then said that the people should have a chance to read the papers, that neither the government nor the press should stand in the way of such fireside enlightenment, and that no one but the people can really tell what they mean. Otto must have reasoned that the people could also decide what his documents meant—that they could supply the political judgment if the press would only give them the chance, as the *Times* said it should.

Of course, Otto is no fool at $36,000-a-year, and he might have concluded that the *Times'* opinion on the war really did have something to do with its willingness to publish the Pentagon Papers, despite appearances and circumstantial evidence to the contrary. He might have guessed that the *Times* would not have published material like the Pentagon Papers in 1961, 1968, or even in 1969 when he joined the SACB. Even so, the newspaper's changing views on the war would also help get Otto exposure. His previous efforts to sully the reputations and political judgment of war criminals like Walt Rostow and McGeorge Bundy had not been appreciated at all, but the *Times* seemed to have come around enough on the war that it would go for a batch of documents on such men now. Both the *Times'* increasing readiness to examine the doings of war criminals and its agnosticism about the actual meaning of the Pentagon Papers should logically work in Otto's favor—and get his documents at least in the back pages. Nevertheless Otepka must fear lest the strictures about orderly procedures reappear, rising ever above the freedom of the press to leave him out in the cold again.

Despite apparent abandonment by the *New York Times,* the need for orderly procedures was identified as the central issue in the Pentagon Papers controversy by such newspapers as the Richmond *Times-Dispatch.* This journal, which had been all courage and patriotism and Paul Revere when Otto was riding, might well have dipped into the *Washington Post*'s clipping file on Otepka for its editorial on Ellsberg: "If each clerk, administrative assistant, or under secretary could ignore departmental policy and decide for himself how information should be classified, nothing would be safe." Senator Gordon Allot, a supporter of Otto, chimed in with his attention similarly focused on the rules, as he felt they should apply to the *New York Times.* "The point is that the *Times* has neither the right nor the duty to decide which classified documents should be classified in which way."

The State Department has been one of the few bastions of consistency in the Otepka and Ellsberg matters, opposing both men on the procedural grounds of loyalty and classification rules. But while the State Department has seen both the Ellsberg and Otepka cases through a monocle, most of the rest of us have been so wall-eyed on the matter that we have seen no parallel between them at all. When columnist Carl Rowan suggested that Otepka was "a sort of Daniel Ellsberg in reverse," most of his readers were shocked at the connection proposed, even a reverse one. One reader, Otto Otepka, scoffed at such a kinship in an interview with UPI reporter Marguerite Davis, who wrote that "Otepka said he gave no classified documents to newspapers but merely provided senators, at their request, with information to support his own sworn testimony." Thus, even Otto—convicted by the *New York Times* on a technicality—distinguishes himself from Dan Ellsberg on a technicality, and a misleading one at that since part of the "information" he gave the senators was a batch of classified documents.

FIDDLING OVER RULES

It is highly ironic that the cases of these two men, whose purposes are so far apart ideologically that it is dangerous to suggest a similarity at any level, have been argued on virtually interchangeable principles. None of them—the Senate's right to know, the people's right to know, freedom of the press, orderly procedures, or national security—went to the heart of the matter. Both men made an essentially moral choice, much like the civil rights sit-ins, to take a specifically illegal step in order to dramatize an injustice that they felt transcended the classification system. Otepka thought the classification system was important, but that the Administration's spinelessness in the Cold War was more important. Ellsberg thought the classification system was important (which is why his decision produced such personal anguish), but that the history of the Vietnam war was more important in its lessons about the past and the nature of the war. Both men made their decisions in the midst of ethical conflict, and any evaluation of them demands that you take a position on why that stand is or is not worthy of support. In other words, given that it is possible for something to be important enough to transcend the classification regulations, you have to make a political judgment about the purposes of Otepka and Ellsberg.

It is well for those of us who support what Ellsberg did—because the Pentagon Papers changed some minds on the war—to keep the Otepka episode in mind. Thinking of his arguments and the furor around him should keep people from being opportunists in debate—from latching on to the arbitrary rules that pop up here and there, like prairie dogs, around any such controversy. These rules, and the sonorous platitudes that editorial writers and politicians trumpet in their names, provide ludicrously poor guidance in evaluating as serious and complex a matter as the Pentagon Papers. By themselves, the rules make an ungrounded compass, each one pointing east for Ellsberg and west for Otepka, in a spectacle that is nearly comic in the conviction people work up over principles like orderly procedures.

Arguing in support of Dan Ellsberg on the basis of the obvious weaknesses in the classification system is shaky because it runs headlong into opposite impulses regarding Otepka. But more importantly, such an argument misses the point. It is like speaking out for a sit-in because of improprieties in the disturbing-the-peace laws, when the real issue is race. Whatever positive force there is in what Ellsberg did comes from the nature of the war and what the Pentagon Papers say about the war—from political and moral issues that have no simple ground rules. When the debate strays from that central question, it loses both its passion and its logic, leaving a dusty bag of rules that Otto Otepka can use just as well. When the discussion centers on personalities and sideline skirmishes, it makes fewer converts for the antiwar message of the Pentagon Papers and Ellsberg, and thus detracts from what he is trying to accomplish.

Daniel Ellsberg and the Pentagon Papers
David Rudenstine

Daniel Ellsberg was born in 1931 in Chicago. His parents were middle-class Jews who converted to Christian Science and eventually moved to Detroit, where Ellsberg grew up. In 1948 Ellsberg entered Harvard on a scholarship, studied economics, became president of the Advocate, an undergraduate literary magazine, and was elected to the editorial board of the *Crimson,* the college daily newspaper. By his junior year he was married to Carol Cummings, a Radcliffe sophomore and the daughter of a Marine colonel.

He graduated summa cum laude and third in his class in 1952. After another year of study as a Woodrow Wilson Fellow at King's College, Cambridge University, Ellsberg entered the Marines in 1954, where he excelled and obtained the distinction of Marksman. He served as a rifle platoon leader, rifle company commander, and operations officer. Whereas other lieutenants usually had to surrender their command within a few weeks to captains, Lieutenant Ellsberg was not replaced because his company "won more awards than any other in the battalion and was foremost in inspections and on maneuvers." After Egyptian leader Gamal Abdel Nasser seized the Suez Canal in 1956 Ellsberg extended his enlistment for eight months, so that he could accompany his battalion to the Sixth Fleet in the Mediterranean.

In 1957 Ellsberg returned to Harvard as a junior member of its Society of Fellows, "the most illustrious assemblage of young scholars in American academia," to work on his doctorate, which he earned in 1962. In March 1959 Ellsberg delivered the Lowell Institute Lectures at the Boston Public Library on "The Art of Coercion: A Study of Threats in Economic Conflicts and War," an outgrowth of his academic interest in the theory of bargaining, a popular interest among academics during the 1950s. About the same time Henry Kissinger, a Harvard professor, invited Ellsberg to give two lectures at his seminar on "the conscious political use of irrational military threats." . . . Following his honorable discharge from the Marines, Ellsberg worked as a strategic analyst in the Santa Monica office of the RAND Corporation, a civilian research institute as well as "the brain trust" of the Air Force. He helped to perfect plans for nuclear war against the Soviet Union, China, and other communist states. While there he was given clearances beyond top secret—clearances designated by codes so secret that even members of Congress were unaware of them. Ellsberg then gained potential access to the nation's most highly classified secrets. . . .

Ellsberg left RAND in August 1964, immediately after the United States retaliated for alleged North Vietnamese attacks on U.S. vessels in the Gulf of Tonkin. He joined the Defense Department at the highest possible civil service level, the "super-grade" rank of GS-18. He became an assistant to John T. McNaughton, McNamara's assistant secretary of defense for international security affairs, whom Ellsberg had known for a couple years. McNaughton headed the Pentagon's foreign-policy office and played a key role within the Pentagon on Vietnam issues. McNaughton told Ellsberg that he was spending 70 percent of his time on Vietnam and that he wanted Ellsberg to spend 100 percent of his time on it. Ellsberg knew little

From *The Day the Presses Stopped: a History of the Pentagon Papers Case,* by David Rudenstine (Berkeley: University of California Press, 1996). Copyright © 1996 by David Rudenstine. Reprinted by permission of University of California Press.

about Vietnam, but he was eager to learn and anxious to observe the government's decision-making process from the inside. During the spring of 1965 he helped plan for the dispatch in June of U.S. ground troops to Vietnam. He also defended Rolling Thunder, the code name for U.S. air attacks against North Vietnam, to members of Congress and to audiences on college campuses.

The following year Ellsberg's personal life disintegrated when his wife insisted on a divorce. Ellsberg had two children and became despondent. That, combined with a sense of romanticism, a need to prove himself, and a sense of duty that he should be with the soldiers in Vietnam since he helped develop the plans that put them there, led Ellsberg to want to return to Vietnam. McNaughton had become "skittish" about Ellsberg because he boasted about what he knew—a characteristic that became heightened by his divorce. As a result McNaughton let Ellsberg leave the Pentagon without a struggle. Ellsberg volunteered to fight in Vietnam as a Marine company commander but was informed that he ranked too high in the civilian bureaucracy for such "mundane" military duty. He then managed to find another way to return to Vietnam—by becoming a special liaison officer under retired Major General Edward G. Lansdale, "a free-wheeling expert on counterinsurgency." Lansdale was returning to South Vietnam as a member of the State Department, attached to the U.S. embassy in Saigon. Officially, Lansdale and his team were assigned to act as a liaison between the embassy and Saigon's Rural Reconstruction Council, a group that theoretically coordinated the government's pacification programs. In fact Lansdale's operation was trying to reform the Saigon regime and develop an effective pacification program.

During his Vietnam tour as a civilian, Ellsberg studied the pacification program and went out on patrol with Marine units in central Vietnam and accompanied Army units in the Mekong Delta. During these military operations he carried a carbine, was repeatedly caught in combat, and risked his life on several occasions. Years later, Ellsberg vividly recalled these patrols: "a couple of times when I was with the lead squad going through a paddy, Vietcong rose from the paddy we had just walked through and fired at the people behind us." . . .

Ellsberg's Vietnam experiences profoundly affected him. When he arrived in Vietnam in 1965, Ellsberg thought "the war's tactics morally justified on the assumption that the war itself was necessary." A few years later he himself summed up his views to a *Look* reporter: "I had accepted the official answer, . . . namely that there was a civil war going on, that we had a right to intervene and pick one side or the other if our interests were involved, and our interests were involved. That if the wrong side should win this war, it would be worse for the Vietnamese people, worse for the United States and for world peace. It would mean victory for the people who wished us ill and who would behave more aggressively in other parts of the world, which we would also have to counter." However, by the spring of 1967, when a severe case of hepatitis caused Ellsberg to return to the United States, he had become discouraged by the continuing violence of the war and by the unwillingness of the United States to change its approach. Overwhelmed by the war's futility, he felt a growing sense that "the programs we were pursuing had no chance of succeeding." He was convinced that the programs in Vietnam "were not in any way proceeding as people thought they were back in Washington," and he had essentially concluded that the United States "should get out of the war."

. . .

This was Ellsberg's frame of mind when, in the late summer of 1967, Halperin and Gelb asked him to join the staff of the Pentagon Papers project. Ellsberg has stated that Halperin and Gelb "were very anxious to get" him to become one of the so-called Pentagon historians and that he was one of the first people they approached. From a personal point of view Ellsberg thought it was "crucial" for him to become part of the staff, since he viewed the study as a way of rethinking U.S. policy and discussing what had gone wrong. Ellsberg has said that he insisted as "the price . . . [of] participating as a researcher" that he be permitted to read "the whole study," but neither Halperin nor Gelb recall such an understanding.

Ellsberg chose the Kennedy administration's 1961 policy in Vietnam for his assignment, largely because he felt more familiar with this period. He spent roughly four months locating documents and assembling research material. Then, in December 1967, he wrote approximately 350 pages of a draft report. He wanted to return to the West Coast to finish the draft, but Gelb objected because he worried that Ellsberg would not complete the work if he left Washington. Ellsberg left anyway and has claimed that his essay remained largely intact when the full study was eventually concluded. Leslie Gelb has stated, however, that "very few of Ellsberg's words finally appeared."

Ellsberg's attitudes, perspective, and values continued to shift during 1968. In early April he attended a conference on "America in a Revolutionary World" at Princeton University. For the first time in his life he met "activists" from the antinuclear movement of the 1950s and the civil rights and antiwar movements of the 1960s. At his luncheon table he sat across from a young woman from India who was dressed in a sari and who had a dot of red dust on her forehead. Her name was Janaki. At one point during the conversation Janaki said: "I come from a culture in which there is no concept of 'enemy.'" Ellsberg was confused by the statement and captivated by the woman. He felt that he came from a culture "in which the concept of 'enemy' was central, seemingly indispensable: the culture of RAND, the Marines, the Defense and State Departments, international and domestic politics, game theory and bargaining theory."

Identifying and understanding the enemy had been part of Ellsberg's "daily bread and butter, part of the air I breathed." Now he was "intrigued" by this Indian woman and what he considered her "Gandhian algebra." He talked with her throughout the day and into the evening. He learned about her life and her commitment to nonviolence. He asked what books she thought he should read if he wanted to learn more about Gandhi and his way of thinking. At the end of the day they learned that Martin Luther King had just been killed and that "Washington was burning."

Clearly, Ellsberg was deeply disoriented and in the process of major shifts in thought and belief. Indeed, his deepening rejection of his prior support of the war; his sudden fascination with nonviolence; his apparent willingness to accept that there are cultures with no concept of enemy; and his later recollection that this was the day "when my life started to change": all of these, as well as other factors, suggest a set of beliefs and attitudes that were in the midst of intense and radical change.

Tumultuous public events of the late winter and spring of 1968 fueled Ellsberg's evolution. The Tet offensive, which had occurred shortly before Ellsberg met Janaki, seemed to intensify his conviction that the violence in Vietnam was senseless and immoral. The assassination of Senator Robert F. Kennedy—only a couple months after King's—caused Ellsberg to lose confidence in the efficacy of traditional political processes. After the Democratic party rejected a peace plan at its Chicago national convention Ellsberg felt even less confidence in the political system. Increasingly unanchored and without a political compass, Ellsberg got little work done, dated many women, and began psychoanalysis with Doctor Lewis Fielding in Beverly Hills.

. . .

Soon after his election in 1968, Nixon appointed Henry Kissinger as his national security adviser. One of Kissinger's first moves was to telephone Henry Rowen, president of RAND and a former Pentagon official, to ask him to prepare a paper that listed the administration's possible options for the Vietnam War. Rowen asked Ellsberg to take on the assignment and he accepted. On Christmas Day Rowen, Ellsberg, and another RAND official flew to New York and met with Kissinger at Nixon's transition headquarters in the Pierre Hotel. Ellsberg's paper did not include a "win" or a "threat" option, but it did list an option of unilateral withdrawal by the United States. Thomas C. Schelling, a Kissinger colleague from Harvard, commented on the absence of the "win" and "threat" alternatives. Ellsberg told the group that he did not think "there is a win option in Vietnam" but that he would include a "threat" option even though he did not understand "how threatening bombing is going to influence the enemy because they have experienced four years of bombing." Before the paper was completed Kissinger arranged for the elimination of the "withdrawal" alternative. Shortly thereafter, Kissinger asked Ellsberg to prepare an exhaustive list of questions about Vietnam that could be presented to various parts of the government, including the Defense and State Departments, the CIA, and the American Embassy in Saigon. In February 1969 Kissinger again asked Ellsberg to return to Washington, this time to summarize the answers to the questionnaire. Ellsberg worked on the project through most of March.

It was around this time (and for reasons that are not clear) that Ellsberg decided he wanted to read the entire Pentagon Papers. He was working on a Defense Department project at the RAND Corporation, but he did not need access to the classified study to complete his research. Nor did he seem to have any larger political purpose for reading the report. What seems likely is that, given his own deep involvement with Vietnam and his complete change of viewpoint, he was beginning his own search into the historical records to understand what had happened in Vietnam; to trace his own relation to the war as it had evolved; and perhaps to find a far greater clarification or revelation of the

entire experience than had so far been fully grasped by anyone.

Ellsberg asked Henry Rowen to help him gain access to the top secret Pentagon study. Since Morton Halperin and Paul Warnke had stored a copy of the report at RAND, Rowen contacted Halperin, who telephoned Gelb. But Gelb did not trust Ellsberg to protect the confidentiality of the study and would not consent to the request. Shortly afterward, Halperin contacted Gelb again, this time pressing harder, arguing that Ellsberg had worked on the project, that he was doing an assignment for the Pentagon, that access to the classified report would be useful, and that Ellsberg had all the requisite security clearances. He added he did not believe they had any reasonable basis for turning Ellsberg down. All these reasons made it awkward for Gelb to continue his objections. Halperin passed the word along to Rowen, so Ellsberg gained access to the secret history.

Ellsberg's six-month study of the Pentagon history greatly affected his thinking. It was not any one document or any one incident or series of incidents that had such an impact on him. What was most striking was the fact that American policy in 1969 appeared to be a direct descendant of the policy pursued by the Truman administration immediately following World War II. As Ellsberg explained to a reporter in 1971: "The startling thing that came out of them was how the same sets of alternatives began to appear to each President, and ultimately the choice was neither to go for broke and adopt military recommendations, nor negotiate a settlement to get out. The decisions year after year were to continue the war, although all predictions pointed to a continued stalemate with this kind of approach and thus to prolong the war indefinitely." As a consequence of his analysis, Ellsberg came to see the war not as "Kennedy's war or Johnson's War" but as the result of a "pattern of behavior that went far beyond any one" president. "It was a war," Ellsberg concluded, "no American President had . . . the courage to turn down or to stay out of." When Ellsberg

applied these insights to the Nixon administration, he concluded that "Nixon was the
fifth President in succession to be subjected
to the same pressures that had led four other
Presidents to maintain involvement; that his
assurances that he had no intention of staying
in Indochina were no more to be believed
than other Presidents' assurances . . . that
whatever his feelings were as of '69, the
more he got involved, the more sure it was
that he would stay involved."

Even before he studied the Pentagon
Papers, Ellsberg had already begun to
change his view of what Nixon was prepared
to do in Vietnam. He wanted to believe
Kissinger's representations that the Nixon
administration intended to extricate the
United States from the war, and he had initially hoped that the conflict would soon
begin to wind down. By September 1969,
however, Ellsberg had concluded that Nixon
and Kissinger intended to escalate hostilities
in hopes of coercing North Vietnam to accept
a political settlement acceptable to the
United States. Specifically, Ellsberg thought
Nixon would not go into the 1972 elections
without having mined Haiphong harbor.
Ellsberg believed this because of information that Halperin, who had by now resigned
from the national security staff, had passed
on to him.

About the same time Ellsberg attended
a conference at Haverford College organized by the War Resisters International.
Ellsberg did not think of himself as a pacifist, and indeed he mentioned once that he
particularly admired the character played
by John Wayne in the *The Sands of Iwo
Jima*. Now, however, he noticed that those
whom he admired were often women and
nonwhite, and he now "wanted to meet
people who did see themselves" as pacifist.

Ellsberg was impressed by the draft
resisters he met at Haverford. He found
them "conscientious, reasonable, and not
fanatics. . . . They just seemed to feel that
they could not collaborate in the war and
were prepared to go to jail." But it was a
young man named Randy Kehler who most

affected Ellsberg. Kehler had been impressive earlier at the conference. He was one of
the organizers of the entire session, and
Ellsberg noted that Kehler "listened carefully, responded thoughtfully and with good
sense. Of the many younger American
activists I had met at the conference, he was
the one I most wanted to see more of."
Kehler struck Ellsberg as having a "simple
and direct manner," as well as "warmth and
humor." When Kehler finally spoke on a
panel on the last day of the conference,
Ellsberg was "surprised" to learn that, like
himself, Kehler spoke of friends who had
recently gone to prison and of his own
impending imprisonment because of draft
resistance. He spoke with fervor. Some in the
audience stood silently; others applauded.

While listening to Kehler, Ellsberg began
to cry. His friend Janaki was to speak next,
but he was too upset to stay. He left the
amphitheater and made his way down the
back corridor to a men's room. Once inside
he began "to sob convulsively, uncontrollably." He remained there alone, for over an
hour, without getting up, his head sometimes tilted back against the wall, sometimes
in his hands.

It was at this moment that Ellsberg began
to consider seriously what he might do to
change American war policy in Vietnam.
He also felt that, if he were going to
take a major risk, he wanted to be certain
he could have a major impact. Because
Ellsberg had been close to power and to
people in power, it is most unlikely that he
could imagine being an unsung imprisoned
war resister or another anonymous body in
a protest crowd. What is more likely is that
Ellsberg imagined he would be in the center
of events, with a central role in whatever
drama was to be enacted.

Before long Ellsberg found himself
thinking of the 7,000-page top secret report
that was in the RAND safe. Reading the
report had convinced him that U.S. efforts
to maintain or to escalate the war would fail
to bring North Vietnam to the bargaining
table, and he began to believe that others

might be similarly affected if they could see the documents. He also thought he might be able to change the political calculus, so that Nixon would begin to be more fearful of political attacks from the antiwar constituency than from those who would attack him if North Vietnam were to win the war—or at least to hold its own indefinitely. Ellsberg brooded over whether he could actually leak the classified study. He had been a RAND employee, a Pentagon employee, a White House consultant, and a confidant of high-ranking Pentagon and State Department officials. Could he actually betray his friends, his colleagues, and the trust that had been placed in him by making the top secret report public?

Ellsberg's indecision ended on September 29, when he learned that Secretary of the Army Stanley R. Resor had decided not to file charges against six Special Forces men accused of assassinating an alleged South Vietnamese double agent. Ellsberg thought that in its most immediate sense the army's decision to drop charges meant that military officials could not be trusted to hold soldiers responsible for their conduct. But, more generally, what was left of Ellsberg's faith in the military's willingness to enforce its own rules was undermined by Resor's announcement.

Ellsberg telephoned Anthony Russo, his friend from Vietnam and RAND who was also strongly opposed to the war. Ellsberg asked Russo if he knew of a photocopy machine that could be used to duplicate the Pentagon Papers. Lynda Sinay, Russo's girlfriend, ran her own advertising agency, and she agreed to let the two men use the agency's machine. Ellsberg had no trouble bringing the top secret documents out of RAND or returning them. He would fill his briefcase with parts of the study about 11:30 P.M., carry the briefcase past the security guard, who did not examine his bags; presumably because he knew Ellsberg. Ellsberg would photocopy the documents for several hours, have breakfast at a local restaurant, and return the documents to his RAND safe early in the morning. He followed this pattern for several weeks, sometimes making as many as forty or fifty copies of a particular document. On occasion Russo would help Ellsberg, and at least once Ellsberg's two children helped out.

. . .

Ellsberg consulted a few lawyers, whom he has refused to identify, about whether his disclosure of the report would subject him to any criminal liability. Ellsberg's memory of what he was advised is vague and incomplete. But it seems likely, given that Ellsberg came to believe that he ran the risk of long-term imprisonment if he made the Pentagon Papers public, that the lawyers told him he would be liable under existing espionage laws if he gave the documents to anyone not authorized to receive them. Consequently, the best way for Ellsberg to avoid criminal liability was to give the papers to someone who had the proper security clearance. One option that Ellsberg aggressively pursued, for example, was to give the documents to a member of Congress who had the requisite clearances and would be willing to make the papers public in Congress or at a congressional committee hearing so they might be published in the *Congressional Record*. Members of Congress are protected from criminal prosecution by the Constitution in accordance with the speech and debate clause for actions they undertake consistent with official duties and responsibilities. Ellsberg did remember that the lawyers advised him that "the surest way to get myself in prison for a long time" was to give the Pentagon Papers to the press.

In early October Ellsberg met with Senator J. William Fulbright, chairman of the Foreign Relations Committee and the Senate's leading dove; he also had the necessary security clearances. Ellsberg told him about the Pentagon Papers, gave him some documents from the study, plus a summary of the entire study and what he thought it revealed. Fulbright had previously scheduled public hearings before the Foreign Relations Committee on Vietnam, with the aim of considering legislation to stop funding for the war. Fulbright invited Ellsberg to be a witness and to make public whatever he wanted. But shortly thereafter, Fulbright backed away from his intention to hold public hearings. He told Ellsberg he had changed his mind, because "I believe the President's own statement that he is trying to wind down the war in Vietnam." Ellsberg tried to persuade Fulbright to change his mind by convincing him that Johnson had deceived him over the Tonkin Gulf Resolution. But Ellsberg could not budge Fulbright, and eventually Fulbright informed Ellsberg that there was no support in his committee for testimony critical of the war. Fulbright, however, did tell Ellsberg that he would write Secretary of Defense Melvin Laird and request that the classified history be declassified and released to his committee. . . .

Ellsberg eventually concluded that Fulbright was not going to make the documents public. He was frustrated and unsure of what to do next. He spoke with more lawyers about the possibility of a war crimes investigation in which he might appear as a witness and disclose the documents. In this way, particularly if the documents were subpoenaed, he hoped that his criminal liability would be minimized. But the lawyers apparently did not think the proposal was practical and did not follow up his suggestion.

At this point Ellsberg began to explore several alternatives. He became a consultant to Senator Charles Goodell and helped to prepare testimony the senator gave before the Senate Foreign Relations Committee in February 1970. Goodell was testifying in support of a bill that would require the withdrawal of U.S. troops from Vietnam. In the process Ellsberg gave Fulbright more pages from the classified history, including the Joint Chiefs of Staff study of the Tonkin Gulf incident, hoping the senator would make the documents public. He also gave a substantial portion of the study to Marcus G. Raskin and Richard J. Barnet, who were based at the Institute for Policy Studies and were writing a book on the Vietnam War. But as active as Ellsberg was in trying to

find an outlet for the Pentagon Papers, he was still unable to do so. . . .

In January 1971 Ellsberg turned to Senator George McGovern for possible help. McGovern was a sponsor of a major end-the-war amendment and the first announced candidate for the 1972 Democratic party presidential nomination. Ellsberg told McGovern that he was in possession of classified documents that would expose the misguided nature of U.S. policy in Vietnam and, if revealed, could hasten the end of the war. McGovern was initially interested in discussing the study with Ellsberg but then abruptly decided against any involvement in an effort to place classified documents in the public domain. He terminated further conversations with Ellsberg, stating he did not trust him. McGovern counseled Ellsberg to turn the papers over to the *Times* or the *Post*. But that makes little sense if McGovern was convinced the documents were authentic, and he seems to have accepted their authenticity. Distrust may well have played some role in McGovern's decision. But McGovern also must have realized that disclosure of the top secret history might strike a large portion of the public as irresponsible and thus undermine his effort to convince the public that he had the stature to be president.

By late January 1971 Ellsberg was so frustrated that he took a step that essentially ended his relationship with Kissinger. At a conference sponsored by MIT Ellsberg took advantage of the question period to ask Kissinger, who had made a presentation, about the administration's estimate of the Asian casualties that would result from Vietnamization. Kissinger hesitated and then characterized Ellsberg's question as "cleverly worded" and stated that "I answer even if I don't answer." Kissinger then tried to avoid the question, but Ellsberg interrupted, repeated the question, and stated: "can't you just give us an answer or tell us that you don't have such estimates?" Kissinger did not answer the question, and the student moderator, sensing the sudden tension in the room, abruptly ended the panel discussion.

· · ·

In February Ellsberg began to give more serious consideration to the advice that several political leaders, including McGovern, had given him: to give the classified study to the *New York Times*. Ellsberg had been reluctant to do this, because he feared the possibility of criminal prosecution. But he no longer had any other apparent option. He had asked many prominent members of Congress, including Senator Fulbright, Senator McGovern, Senator Charles Mathias, and Representative Paul N. (Pete) McCloskey, to release the documents, but all had refused. His efforts with Kissinger had also come to naught. The issue Ellsberg had to decide now was which reporter to contact. His most likely prospect was Neil Sheehan of the *New York Times*. . . .

Ellsberg and Sheehan had met in Vietnam and again in Washington. Ellsberg has claimed that he even leaked information to Sheehan during the late 1960s and that he was favorably impressed with how Sheehan had dealt with the information and had protected him. In December 1970 Ellsberg became convinced that Sheehan might be the right reporter to get the Pentagon Papers to the public when he read Sheehan's highly critical book review of Mark Lane's *Conversations with Americans* in the *Times*. In the course of the review Sheehan called for an inquiry into "war crimes and atrocities" committed by the U.S. military in Vietnam, an idea Ellsberg supported. Sheehan wrote that the "country desperately needs a sane and honest inquiry into the question of war crimes and atrocities in Vietnam by a body of knowledgeable and responsible men not beholden to the current military establishment." Sheehan thought the "men who now run the military establishment cannot conduct a credible investigation." Sheehan claimed that the "need" for such an inquiry was "self-evident," since "too large a segment of the citizenry" believed such acts had occurred.

Nevertheless, Ellsberg did not contact Sheehan until mid-February. When they met, Sheehan showed Ellsberg a draft of a long essay, eventually published in the *New York Times* book review section, reviewing thirty-three antiwar books and addressing the question of whether the United States had committed war crimes in Vietnam. Ellsberg was impressed, but he did not give Sheehan the Pentagon Papers. Ellsberg returned to Washington during the last weekend in February. He was scheduled to participate in a panel discussion at the National War College on Vietnam on Monday. He met with Raskin and discussed his frustration with making the Pentagon Papers public. Raskin urged Ellsberg to discuss with Sheehan the possibility of having the *Times* publish the papers. Ellsberg was persuaded. He telephoned Sheehan on the last Sunday in February. They met at Sheehan's Washington home and spent the night discussing the war.

Ellsberg told Sheehan of the study and what it contained. Sheehan already knew of the study; he had probably even discussed it with Raskin, Barnet, and Ralph Stavins, all of the Institute for Policy Studies, when they contacted him after Sheehan's December book review was published. Ellsberg asked Sheehan's advice on what he should do with the history. From the start Sheehan took the position that he could not help Ellsberg unless he read the study. He also told Ellsberg that he could not make any commitments on behalf of the *Times* and that the *Times* would not make any commitments until its editors had read the study.

Ellsberg told Sheehan that he had two conditions that had to be met before he could give the study to the *Times*. One, he wanted the *Times* to devote substantial space so that a great portion of the 7,000 pages were published. Two, he wanted the newspaper to print documents. It would not be enough to print a report based on the documents. Ellsberg wanted readers to read the documents themselves. Sheehan made it clear to Ellsberg that he and the *Times* editors had to see the documents first. The meeting ended without either man making a commitment of any kind. . . .

After several discussions Ellsberg agreed to make the papers available to Sheehan. On Friday, March 19, Sheehan and his wife, Susan, a writer, traveled to Cambridge, Massachusetts, and checked into the Treadway Motor Inn as Mr. and Mrs. Thompson. As previously arranged, Sheehan met with Ellsberg, who took him to an apartment in Cambridge. Ellsberg allowed Sheehan to read the Pentagon Papers, the Joint Chiefs of Staff report on the Tonkin Gulf incident, and early drafts of some historical studies that ultimately became part of the Pentagon Papers. He withheld from Sheehan the four volumes that traced the diplomatic history of the war from 1964 to 1968, so as to minimize any criticism that he had jeopardized peace discussions, and the footnotes, out of fear they might compromise U.S. intelligence interests.

The understanding between Ellsberg and Sheehan remains unclear to this day. What seems likely is that Ellsberg gave Sheehan permission to read the classified material and to make notes on what he read. He did not give Sheehan permission to copy or to duplicate the documents in any way. Sheehan accepted these terms, and Ellsberg gave Sheehan a key to the apartment so he could come and go as he pleased over the weekend.

Ellsberg must have realized he was taking a risk by leaving Sheehan unmonitored with thousands of pages of newsworthy, top secret documents. Sheehan was an able news reporter who had already publicly called for a war crimes investigation. Sheehan might well look upon the secret history not only as evidence of war crimes but as the spark that might prompt an official war crimes inquiry. Indeed, the whole situation suggested that Ellsberg wanted and expected Sheehan to do precisely what he told him not to do: photocopy the documents.

Ellsberg wanted the documents out and the *Times* was the best option he had for making them public. But Ellsberg did not want to give Sheehan the documents, because lawyers had told him he ran the risk of going to prison if he gave the documents to the press. Thus, Ellsberg may have decided that the best way

to reduce his risk of criminal prosecution was not to give Sheehan the documents but to place him in a situation in which he could do precisely what Ellsberg told him not to do.

Once alone with the documents, Sheehan apparently swiftly proceeded to photocopy the documents. From a pay phone Sheehan called William Kovach, the *Times*'s Boston correspondent. Sheehan told Kovach he wanted to copy some important documents he had obtained from MIT and that he had to return them by Monday morning. He also told Kovach he needed money to pay for the photocopying. Kovach called the owner of a photocopy shop in Bedford who agreed to hire additional help for the weekend so the job could be completed by Monday morning. Sheehan and his wife loaded the documents into several shopping bags and took a taxi to Bedford. Kovach telephoned the *Times*'s New York office and asked that $1,500 be wired to him, which it was. Although the photocopying machines in Bedford broke before the job was completed, a second shop was located, and the job was completed by the end of the weekend. It is not known if Sheehan or Ellsberg saw or spoke to each other at the conclusion of the weekend.

Although Sheehan has not offered a public explanation for his actions, he was likely motivated by several considerations. As did Ellsberg, Sheehan believed that the disclosure of the secret Pentagon history might well shorten the war and force a war crimes investigation. Sheehan was unsatisfied with his reporting assignment, and his prospects at the *Times* seemed limited. Getting his hands on McNamara's secret Vietnam history may have been a way of resuscitating his reporting career and his chances of becoming a *Times* editor. It would also give him a crack at winning a Pulitzer Prize.

Sheehan and Ellsberg stayed in touch with each other during the next several weeks. Apparently Sheehan never told Ellsberg he had photocopied the documents, and Ellsberg never told Sheehan—at least in so many words—that he could do so. What they said to each other is not known, but the conversations served to keep each somewhat informed of the other's actions. Ellsberg, who was still hoping to orchestrate the disclosure of the Pentagon Papers, wanted to stay abreast of Sheehan's activities. Sheehan, worried that Ellsberg might give the papers to another reporter, wanted to stay informed of Ellsberg's movements.

Comment

Do you agree that "anyone who wishes to justify civil disobedience by officials must take his Otepkas with his Ellsbergs"? Both Otepka and Ellsberg broke the law and acted alone in secret and in the service of what they believed to be an important public interest. It is tempting to try to distinguish the two acts of disobedience by saying that one sought the right end and the other did not. But this evades the problem of what means are justifiable when society disagrees about the ends. Consider whether these differences in the means make any moral difference: (1) releasing information to the press or to a congressional staffer; (2) extensive or negligible efforts to appeal to other officials; (3) some or no likelihood that release of information could endanger national security; and (4) status as a private citizen or as a public official at the time of the act.

The State Department's view about such disobedience would treat Otepka and Ellsberg alike; both were wrong. Evaluate the best argument you can construct for this view. An alternative position that also treats Otepka and Ellsberg alike would conclude that both were justified. One difficulty with this conclusion is that neither acted publicly, as the traditional theory of civil disobedience requires. Should official disobedience always have to be public to be legitimate? Does the comparison of Ellsberg and Otepka suggest any revisions in the traditional criteria of civil disobedience when they are applied to public officials?

George Shultz and the Polygraph Test
Don Lippincott

On December 19, 1985, Secretary of State George Shultz, widely considered to be a politically discreet team player (unlike his

Reprinted by permission of the Case Program, Kennedy School of Government, Harvard University. Copyright 1986 by the President and Fellows of Harvard College.

predecessor, Alexander Haig), stung the administration when he publicly threatened to resign. This action was not based on a substantive disagreement over foreign policy. Rather, Shultz was demonstrating—in no uncertain terms—his strong opposition to an administration plan to require polygraph (lie detector) tests for all government officials with access to "highly classified information." Roughly 182,000 government employees—including some agency heads like Shultz—were to be affected by this plan, including about 4,500 members of the State Department. In remarks to reporters in the department, Shultz proclaimed that his first lie detector test would be his last, adding, "The minute in this government that I am told that I'm not trusted is the day I leave."[1]

BACKGROUND: THE REAGAN ADMINISTRATION AND THE POLYGRAPH

From the outset, the Reagan Administration has been strongly interested in crushing espionage activities within the U.S. government. While the problem has plagued governments since time immemorial, a rash of recent revelations about spying in the United States has alarmed many Reagan officials as well as much of the public. Among the recent examples of espionage within the government was the late 1983 arrest of a California engineer accused of selling secret defense papers to the Poles. (The engineer's wife, who worked for a California company doing military research, had security clearance.) At the end of 1984, an ex-CIA employee was arrested on the charge of spying for Czechoslovakia. Then, in what the *Washington Post* termed "the year of the spy," 1985 witnessed an unprecedented wave of spying accusations within the U.S. government. In June, the FBI nabbed three members of the Arthur Walker family, who had apparently been passing important naval intelligence information to the Soviets for years. According to one administration official, these arrests were only "the tip of the iceberg."[2] This claim was substantiated in late November when arrests of four alleged spies in five days grabbed the nation's attention.

Former Ambassador to the United Nations Jeane Kirkpatrick offered her views of the problem of espionage in an editorial in the *Washington Post:*

> Whether the spy works for money (as the Walker ring apparently did) or for love of another country or ideology (as the Rosenbergs did), spying can seriously damage national security. The Walkers, for example, have apparently compromised our communication system and endangered aspects of our defenses.
>
> That the Soviet Union encourages such betrayals of national security is beyond reasonable doubt. They also rely on spying to promote development. Documents captured when the French government broke a major spy ring two years ago (and expelled 47 Soviet officials) confirmed that the Soviets rely heavily on planned theft and stolen technology and field large networks of spies to steal the desired technology.
>
> Spying is big, serious, dirty business and does us real harm. Recent disclosures suggest, moreover, that it may be increasing.[3]

Whether spying has been increasing or whether there is simply better counterespionage today is a debatable issue. What's clear is that the wave of spying revelations has whetted the appetite of certain administration officials—such as CIA Director William Casey—for tighter security controls. The polygraph has been one of his favorite tools. The CIA and National Security Agency use the device to screen the backgrounds of all prospective employees, with random examinations given subsequently. The State Department does neither.

On another front, the administration has proposed on more than one occasion that polygraphs be used to help prevent leaks from government employees to the press. Ex-Ambassador Kirkpatrick offers her views of how leaks have affected the Reagan Administration:

> For five years leaks—of information and disinformation—have plagued the Reagan Administration, embarrassing the government, complicating policy-making and creating international problems. Leaks have been used at high, high levels of government to undermine

policy rivals and advance personnel ambitions. They have caused real damage to policies and policymakers. They have undermined our government's dignity. They have called into question the president's competence.[4]

Throughout the Reagan years, Congress has been decidedly more hesitant about supporting government use of polygraphs (although it did authorize a pilot Defense Department polygraph clearance program—for 3,500 employees and contractors in 1986 and twice that number in 1987—in the summer of 1985). For instance, when President Reagan sought approval of an order to require government employees to submit to the polygraph during investigations of leaks to the media, Congress blocked the move. Moreover, during the 99th Congress, Congress was also "seriously considering a [bill] to ban the use of polygraphs in the private sector."[5]

While admitting the seriousness of the threat to national security posed by espionage, polygraph opponents argue that the tests are an invasion of privacy as well as a form of harassment. Opponents also contend that the polygraph is hardly an infallible instrument. They have argued that not only do polygraphs often "miss" known spies—such as Larry Wu-Tai Chin, an ex-CIA employee who spied for China for more than thirty years—but they also intimidate and run the risk of jeopardizing the careers of innocent people, who are not trained to react with the icy calm (or feigned emotion) that CIA and KGB "spooks" utilize to beat the system. They also point out that the results of polygraphs "are not used as evidence in Federal court . . . because of the[ir] notorious unreliability."[6] An article in the *National Journal* entitled "To Tell the Truth," discussed some competing views concerning the reliability of polygraph tests for preemployment screening:

Use of the test for [employment] screenings raises the loudest objections from civil libertarians. One objection is that "there is little research or scientific evidence to establish polygraph test validity in screening situations," as the congressional Office of Technology Assessment (OTA) concluded in 1983. The CIA and NSA, though, say that despite its limitations in actually finding liars, the test often compels confessions.[7]

DEJA VU

The Reagan administration had discussed instituting more widespread use of polygraphs, prior to issuing its new directive in late 1985. On at least one occasion, news leaks had been the major impetus for the discussion. The *Washington Post* sketched an interesting vignette of the earlier episode:

Shortly before noon on Sept. 14, 1983, [White House aide Michael] Deaver entered the Oval Office to find Edwin Meese III (then White House counselor) and William P. Clark (then national security affairs adviser) in an intense and apparently confidential conversation with Reagan about a paper they wanted him to sign. The paper, Deaver discovered, would have authorized the FBI to use polygraphs to investigate top officials who were privy to highly classified decision-making about Lebanon.

Two days earlier, NBC News had reported that Reagan was secretly considering air strikes against Syrian positions in Lebanon where Marines were being shelled heavily. Meese and Clark were furious at the leak and determined to identify the culprit.

Deaver described the Oval Office scene he had encountered to James A. Baker III (then White House chief of staff) while the two were driving to lunch. According to a later account, Baker was so alarmed that he ordered the car back to the White House, where Baker and Deaver barged into a luncheon meeting of Reagan with Shultz and Vice President Bush.

Shultz and Bush were startled to learn of the plan and like Deaver and Baker, they criticized any requirement that top officials submit to polygraphs. If asked to prove his veracity with a polygraph, Shultz declared, "Here's a secretary of state who isn't going to stay."[8]

The Meese-Clark paper ultimately went unsigned by the president.

AUGUST 1985: DIRECTIVE 196

The most recent directive emerged from the administration's National Security Planning Group (NSPG), a small National Security Council (NSC) committee chaired by National Security Adviser Robert McFarlane and including Schultz, CIA Director William Casey and Defense Secretary Caspar Weinberger. In an August committee meeting about possible countermeasures of spying, Casey had been the chief advocate of employing the polygraph tests, which were already in wide use at the CIA and National Security Agency. Casey apparently claimed that it was vital for national security to monitor all agency personnel handling highly classified information. According to the *Washington Post,* at this meeting:

> Shultz reportedly expressed his deeply felt view that what he termed "so-called lie detector tests" are misleading and ineffective, and that their imposition on public servants in non-secret jobs carries the message that their loyalty and character is in question.[9]

The meeting apparently produced no decision on the Casey recommendation. A subsequent article reported that the defense secretary had experienced a change of heart after learning of Shultz's position:

> Weinberger was "no big fan" of lie detectors, but when he discovered Shultz's opposition, the defense secretary "fell in love with polygraphs," one involved official sa[id].[10]

THE PRESIDENT SIGNS

On November 1, President Reagan signed National Security Decision Directive 196, affirming the NSC committee recommendation that:

> The U.S. government adopt, in principle, the use of aperiodic non-lifestyle, CI (counterintelligence)-type polygraph examinations for all individuals with access to U.S. government sensitive compartmented information

(SCI), communications security information (COMSEC) and other special access program classified information.

Though a member of the committee, Shultz only learned of the decision when the White House mailed him a copy of the five-page directive shortly after it was signed. He was not pleased. According to one aide, who informed the secretary that certain State Department officials would threaten to resign if they were forced to submit to the polygraph, Shultz tersely replied, "And I'm one of them."[11]

GEORGE SHULTZ

An economist by trade, the sixty-five-year-old Shultz left the deanship of the University of Chicago's School of Business to join the ranks of government service as Nixon's secretary of labor in 1969. Subsequently, Shultz served as the budget director (1970–72)* and secretary of the treasury (1972–74). When Shultz returned to government in 1982 to replace the resigning secretary of state, Alexander Haig, he was president of Bechtel, Inc., a San Francisco–based engineering firm. He was also teaching part-time at Stanford University.

In addition to having a reputation as a consummate team player, George Shultz is widely regarded as a man of high integrity with a "deep sense of personal rectitude."[12] A significant portion of this assessment is based on Treasury Secretary Shultz's much-publicized refusal to provide President Nixon with information on the tax returns of certain individuals on Nixon's enemies' list.

As far as President Reagan was concerned, the generally even-tempered Shultz was a welcome relief from the combative, ambitious Alexander Haig. Ex-White House aide Michael Deaver described the

---

*Shultz's deputy at the budget bureau was Caspar Weinberger, a long-time competitor if not adversary.

president's behavior during an Oval Office meeting with Shultz several months before he joined the Reagan team:

> As I watched, the president just visibly relaxed with Shultz. He has a marvelous staff style that appeals to Reagan, and he is a tough guy, a good interlocutor and a consummate government official. It was clear the president was very comfortable with Shultz.[13]

On substantive matters, Shultz's record as Reagan's secretary of state had been relatively smooth up to the end of 1985—the only major foreign policy failure being Lebanon and especially the terrorist killing of 245 U.S. marines there in 1983. At the same time, critics claimed that his tenure had no major foreign policy successes— e.g., no breakthroughs in the Middle East or Latin America or with the Soviet Union. Former Undersecretary for Political Affairs Lawrence Eagleburger compared him to some highly respected predecessors: "There is a bit of the moralism of [John Foster] Dulles in Shultz. And he is solid and steady with a style reminiscent in some ways of [Dean] Rusk. . . . It's possible to say someone was a good secretary of state because he took events and prevented them from making things worse." Another government official added: "Shultz is very self-possessed. He likes power, he likes to run things and he likes to have his own way."[14]

REAGAN PLAN REVEALED

Information about the new polygraph requirement was shielded from the public until the *Los Angeles Times* broke the story about the directive on December 11, a week before Shultz's outburst. The *Times* revealed that the president's directive would require thousands of federal employees and contractor personnel with access to highly classified information to submit to lie detector tests on an irregular and random basis. The White House responded to the story the next day through press spokesman Larry Speakes, who announced that the

president was attempting to address espionage and unauthorized information disclosures (leaks). While the directive was designed to target "a selective number of individuals who have highest levels of access" to secret information, according to Speakes, he denied that the action was related to recent and highly publicized revelations about spy activity within the U.S. government. Speakes also emphasized that "the new directive would be used mainly for counterespionage rather than for trying to identify officials who help journalists."[15] When asked by reporters for copies of the directive, Speakes claimed he could not provide it because the directive was itself a classified document. As the *New York Times* reported, "[T]his produced a round of laughter, . . . since news of the directive had already appeared in the *Los Angeles Times*."[16]

While these revelations were coming out in the national press, George Shultz was in Europe visiting several heads of state and foreign ministers. When reporters there questioned him about his opinion on the White House directive, Shultz refused to discuss the matter on the grounds that it was a domestic policy issue and should be discussed when he returned to the United States.

SHULTZ RETURNS

Only hours after his return to Washington from Europe on December 18, Shultz requested—and got—a private meeting with President Reagan. Apparently this meeting neither changed the nature of the directive nor mollified Shultz. The next day Shultz went public with what amounted to his ultimatum. After the secretary made clear his "grave reservations," one senior White House official told the *New York Times* that it was nonetheless unlikely that Shultz would resign, adding, however, that, "This is one thing that sends him through the roof. It touches a nerve."[17]

Reacting only hours after Shultz's strong criticism of the polygraph, the CIA issued a statement claiming that "selective, careful use" of polygraph tests was

EXHIBIT 1. SECRETARY OF STATE GEORGE SHULTZ'S REMARKS TO THE PRESS
(DECEMBER 19) CONCERNING HIS VIEWS ON POLYGRAPH TESTING

Personally, I have grave reservations about so-called lie detector tests because the experience with them that I have read about—I don't claim to be an expert—it's hardly a scientific instrument.

It tends to identify quite a few people who are innocent as guilty, and it misses at least some fraction of people who are guilty of lying, and it is, I think, pretty well demonstrated that a professional, let us say, a professional spy or a professional leaker, can probably train himself or herself not to be caught by the test.

So the use of it as a broad-gauged condition of employment, you might say, seems to me to be questionable. That's my viewpoint. . . . The minute in this government that I am told that I'm not trusted is the day that I leave.

EXHIBIT 2. CIA WRITTEN STATEMENT (ISSUED DECEMBER 19)

Thousands of people in the intelligence community submit to polygraph examinations in recognition of the need to protect the nation's secrets and because of the proved usefulness of the polygraph as an investigative tool.

They understand that the government, in granting access to the nation's secrets, also bestows a special trust as well as a shared responsibility for protecting those secrets. The number of leaks of sensitive, classified information in recent years makes clear that a growing number of those given special trust have not lived up to their obligations. The reality is that the loss of classified information is severely damaging our foreign policy and our intelligence capabilities.

The use of polygraphing in the intelligence community has proven to be the best deterrent to the misuse of sensitive information. There is an acute need to extend its selective, careful use to branches of government that receive that information.

The director of Central Intelligence and his predecessors voluntarily have been polygraphed, believing in the importance of setting an example in that all those with access must do what they can to protect our secrets and to cooperate in identifying those who do not.

essential for those "branches of government" (i.e., the State Department) that received classified information. (See Exhibit 2.) The CIA spokesman also pointed out that CIA Director "Casey and all his predecessors had voluntarily taken polygraph tests" to set an example for their employees. In an interview on television, Caspar Weinberger said that taking the test "wouldn't bother me a bit."[18]

THE WHITE HOUSE RETREATS

The following afternoon, after another meeting between the secretary and President Reagan, the White House issued a statement which said that the president believed polygraph tests to be "a limited, though sometimes useful tool when used in conjunction with other investigative and security procedures in espionage cases." The statement added that the secretary "fully shares the president's view of the seriousness of espionage cases and agrees with the need to use all legal means in the investigation of such cases."[19] In effect, the White House was backing down from its earlier position, expressed in NSDD 196, that increased and widespread use of polygraphs was necessary and should be implemented. Nonetheless, CIA Director Casey and other secret agency heads could still use the tests as a screening test for employment.

After his meeting with Shultz, the president, when asked if the secretary would have to take a lie detector test, responded, "Neither one of us are going to," adding, "I just explained to him that what he read in the press in Europe was not true."[20] A State Department official told the *New York Times* that the White House statement indicated that the president and Shultz agreed that such "tests should be limited to cases of suspected espionage," adding that the secretary "believed his public comments had helped modify the president's position."[21]

POSTSCRIPT

Three days later, the Christmas Eve edition of the *Washington Post* ran a front-page article under the headline, "President Said to Be Unaware of Sweep of Polygraph Order." In this article, "administration sources" claimed that the president "was not fully aware of the sweeping nature" of the directive in question, nor were several other key administration figures, including Chief White House Counsel Fred Fielding and Treasury Secretary (and ex-Chief of Staff) James Baker.[22] The Christmas edition of the *Post* contained an article in which Larry

Speakes denied the claim about Reagan, asserting that the president had been "fully aware of the scope" of the directive.[23]

NOTES

1. *New York Times*, Dec. 20, 1985, p. 30.
2. Ibid., June 7, 1985, p. 1.
3. *Washington Post*, Dec. 29, 1985, p. 29.
4. Ibid.
5. *National Journal*, Jan. 18, 1986, p. 184.
6. *New York Times*, Dec 20, 1985, p. 30.
7. *National Journal*, Jan. 18, 1986, p. 184.
8. *Washington Post National Weekly Edition*, Feb. 17, 1986, p. 8.
9. *Washington Post*, Dec. 21, 1985, p. A8.
10. *Washington Post National Weekly Edition*, Feb. 17, 1986, pp. 6–8.
11. Ibid.
12. Ibid.
13. Ibid.
14. *National Journal*, Feb. 15, 1986, p. 377.
15. *New York Times*, Dec. 12, 1985, p. A19.
16. Ibid.
17. *New York Times*, Dec. 20, 1985, p. 1.
18. Ibid.
19. Ibid, Dec. 21, 1985.
20. Ibid.
21. Ibid.
22. *Washington Post*, Dec. 24, 1985, p. 1.
23. Ibid, Dec. 25, p. A16.

George Shultz and the Iran-Contra Affair

Taeku Lee

ARMS FOR HOSTAGES

On June 17, 1985, Robert McFarlane, President Reagan's national security advisor, circulated a draft document (NSDD: National Security Decision Document) to Secretary of State Shultz, Secretary of Defense Weinberger, and Director of Central Intelligence

Casey, which set out immediate and long-term objectives for U.S. relations with Iran. This NSDD draft included the recommendations to: "Encourage Western allies and friends to help Iran meet its import requirements so as to reduce the attractiveness of Soviet assistance and trade offers, while demonstrating the value of correct relations with the West. This includes a provision of selected military equipment as determined on a case-by-case basis."[1]

On June 29, 1985, Secretary Shultz responded in writing to the NSDD draft, arguing that the proposed policy was "perverse" and that to "permit or encourage a flow of Western arms into Iran is contrary to our interest both in containing Khomeinism and in ending the excess of this regime. We should not alter this aspect of our policy when groups with ties to Iran are holding U.S. hostages in Lebanon." Weinberger's initial response to the draft was simply to write "almost too absurd to comment on" in the margin.[2]

On August 6 and 8, 1985, Shultz and other National Security Council (NSC) principals met with the president to discuss David Kimche's proposal to ship U.S.-made arms via Israel to Iran, with the understanding that four hostages would be released. McFarlane testified that Casey, White House Chief of Staff Regan, and Vice President Bush had been in favor of the transfer of arms and Shultz and Weinberger had been opposed to it. McFarlane's testimony also indicated President Reagan's approval of the arms transfers on the condition that they should not contribute to further terrorism or alter the balance of the Iran-Iraq War.[3]

On November 18, 1985, McFarlane updated Shultz on the details of the arms transfer, which was scheduled to occur on November 21. Shultz testified, "I complained to Mr. McFarlane that I had been informed so late that it was impossible to stop this

This revised and expanded version of a case originally prepared by Taeku Lee was edited by Simone Sandy, copyright © 1996 by the President and Fellows of Harvard College. Reprinted with permission of the Program in Ethics and the Professionals. Except where otherwise indicated in the endnotes, the section "Arms for Hostages" is a compilation based on *The Chronology: The Day by Day Account of the Secret Military Assistance to Iran and the Contras,* copyright © 1987. Text has been modified and is reprinted with the permission of the National Security Archive.

operation. I nonetheless expressed my hope that the hostages would in fact be released."[4]

The November 1985 arrangement ultimately collapsed. On November 30, McFarlane resigned as national security advisor; Vice Admiral John Poindexter replaced McFarlane on December 4. The same day, Lieutenant Colonel Oliver North brought a new arms-for-hostages deal to Poindexter.[5]

On December 6, 1985, a full-scale White House meeting on the Iran initiative was called at Shultz's insistence. Thus far, only one hostage had been released after three arms shipments to Iran. State Department officials considered this meeting an opportunity for Shultz to protest continuation of the program.[6]

On December 7, 1985, NSC principals met at the White House. Both Shultz and Weinberger left this meeting with the impression that the arms component of negotiations with Iran was finished. Shultz returned to the State Department with news that Weinberger and Regan also strongly opposed further arms initiatives with Iran. After this meeting, Secretary Weinberger believed that he and Shultz had persuaded the president "that it might be a good thing to achieve these objectives, but it wouldn't work, and that this was not a good way to do it."[7]

According to the Tower Commission report, "the initiative seemed to be dying" until January 2, 1986, when Amiram Nir brought a proposal to Poindexter to exchange 3,000 (U.S. made) Israeli TOW missiles and twenty Hizballah prisoners held by Israeli-supported Lebanese Christian forces for the release of five U.S. hostages in Beirut. The president signed a draft Covert Action Finding approving this plan. (This draft may have been signed by mistake, however, President Reagan did not recall signing this draft.)[8]

On January 7, 1986, President Reagan met with Bush, Shultz, Weinberger, Attorney General Meese, Casey, Regan, Poindexter, and McFarlane. Although the president made no decisions at this meeting, several participants recalled leaving the meeting persuaded that he supported the Nir proposal. During the days following this meeting, Poindexter, Regan, Casey, and North reportedly considered ways to bypass Shultz and Weinberger in pursuit of this effort.[9]

Secretary Shultz on the January 7 meeting:

I recall no specific decision being made in my presence, though I was well aware of the president's preferred course and his strong desire to establish better relations with Iran and to save the hostages. . . . I stated all of the reasons why I felt it was a bad idea, and nobody in retrospect has thought of a reason that I didn't think of. I mean, I think this is all very predictable, including the argument against those who said, well, this is going to be a secret or it is all going to be deniable; that is nonsense. So, all of that was said.

And in that January 7 meeting, I know that I not only stated these things, but I was very concerned about it, and I expressed myself as forcefully as I could. That is, I didn't just sort of rattle these arguments off. I was intense. The president knew that. The president was well aware of my views. I think everybody was well aware of my views. It wasn't just saying oh, Mr. President, this is terrible, don't do it. There were reasons given that were spelled out and which are reasons that you would expect. . . . I took the initiative as the person in the room who was opposed to what was being proposed. I cannot give you a full accounting, but it was clear to me by the time we went out that the President, the Vice President, the Director of Central Intelligence, the Attorney General, the Chief of Staff, the National Security Advisor all had one opinion and I had a different one and Cap [Weinberger] shared it. . . .[10]

Don Regan on the January 7 meeting:

The president was told, but by no means was it really teed up for him of what the downside risk would be here as far as American public opinion was concerned. There was no sampling. No one attempted to do this. The NSC certainly didn't in any paper or any discussion say that. I don't believe the State Department in its presentation arguing against this really brought out the sensitivity of this. None of us was aware of that, I regret to say.[11]

Secretary Weinberger on the January 7 meeting:

The only time that I got the impression the president was for this thing was in January . . . and at that time it became very apparent to me that the cause I was supporting was lost, and that the president was for it.[12]

By January 17, 1986, a revised Covert Action Finding was submitted to the president. The revised draft was almost exactly the same as the previous one, but the cover memorandum proposed a major change, which would establish the United States as a direct arms supplier to Iran. In contrast with the Nir proposal (presented within the Finding), the cover memo suggested that the CIA buy 4,000 TOWs from the Department of Defense and, upon receiving payment, make a direct transfer to Iran (again with Israel making the "necessary arrangements"). Shultz, Weinberger, and Casey were not present at the meeting at which this decision was made. Furthermore, the January 17 Finding was neither given nor shown to certain key NSC principals, including Shultz and Weinberger, who testified that they did not see the signed Finding until after the Iran initiative became public knowledge on November 10, 1986.[13]

On May 3, 1986, Secretary Shultz received a cable from Under Secretary Michael Armacost suggesting that the Iran initiative was still on. This cable contained a report from Ambassador Charles Price in London describing meetings between Iranian representatives Khashoggi, Nir, and Ghorbanifar and British entrepreneur Tiny Rowlands, during which arms shipments to Iran allegedly were discussed. According to the cable, "The scheme, moreover, was okay with the Americans. It had been cleared with the White House. Poindexter allegedly is the point man. Only four people in the U.S. government are knowledgeable about the plan. The State Department has been cut out."[14]

Unable to find Poindexter, Shultz confronted Don Regan about this matter instead.

> I told Mr. Regan, and I showed him this— I said that he should go to the president and get him to end this matter once and for all. I opposed dealing with people such as those identified in the message and said it would harm the president if actively continued. Mr. Regan, I felt, shared my concern, said he was alarmed and would talk to the president. I later learned that Vice Admiral Poindexter reportedly told Ambassador Price that there was no more than a smidgen of reality to the story. . . . Soon thereafter I recall being told by both Vice Admiral Poindexter and Mr. Casey that the operation had ended, and the people involved had been told to 'stand down.'[15]

On May 6, 1986, the State Department issued a policy statement on terrorism, proclaiming in part: "The U.S. Government will make no concessions to terrorists. It will not pay ransoms, release prisoners, change its policies, or agree to other acts that might encourage additional terrorism. . . . The policy of the U.S. Government is, therefore, to reject categorically demands for ransom, prisoner exchanges, and deals with terrorists in exchange for hostage release." Meanwhile, with Poindexter's approval, Lieutenant Colonel North was busily planning a trip with McFarlane to Tehran to negotiate arms and spare parts shipments in exchange for the release of more hostages.[16]

By November 1986, arms transfers to Iran were proceeding at full throttle. During this time, two additional hostages—Reverend Lawrence Jenco and David Jacobsen—were released. The key operatives had also begun diverting funds from the arms transfers to the Contras. With the release of Jacobsen in November, however, the first public news of the Iran initiative began to spread. The Islamic Jihad claimed that the release of Jacobsen was *quid pro quo* for "overtures" from the U.S. government; on November 3, the

Lebanese magazine *Al Shiraa* reported on McFarlane's visits to Tehran and noted U.S. supply of arms to Iran.[17]

Upon learning of the public revelations, Secretary Shultz expressed concern to Poindexter that the arms deal might be viewed as a violation of the existing U.S. counterterrorism policy. Shultz proposed public disclosure of the NSC initiative to clarify "that this was a special one-time operation based on humanitarian grounds and decided by the president within his constitutional responsibility to act in the service of the national interest."[18]

On November 16, 1986, unable to convince President Reagan to declare a cessation of arms deals with Iran and to place the State Department in charge of Iran policy, Shultz appeared on television to state his opposition to any such further deals. Shultz also publicly contradicted the president's earlier claims that Iran had suspended its terrorist acts in recent months, maintaining that "Iran has and continues to pursue a policy of terrorism."[19]

On November 18, 1986, two State Department officials were permitted to view a copy of Director Casey's prepared testimony for his upcoming (November 21) appearance before Congress. This draft stated that all U.S. officials involved "believed that the November 1985 shipment of arms was actually oil drilling equipment." Two days later, Shultz confronted Reagan about the accuracy of Casey's prepared testimony. Casey's testimony—which was coordinated by Poindexter—was altered to reflect Shultz's and other officials' concerns. (However, congressional sources still doubted the full candor of Casey's written remarks.)[20]

On November 22, 1986, the president reportedly relayed a message telling Shultz, "Support me or get off the team." On November 25, the president met with Shultz and Regan, and reportedly put the State Department in charge of Iran policy and asked Shultz to remain in his post.[21]

On December 8, 1986, Secretary Shultz appeared before the House Foreign Affairs Committee. In his testimony, he distanced himself from the NSC actions in Iran-Contra. "I learned not as a result of being involved in the development of the plan, but, so to speak, as a plan was about to be implemented. I learned in various ways of two proposed transfers during 1985, but I was never informed and had the impression that they were not consummated. . . . I did not learn about any transfers of arms during 1986 in a direct way. But, as is always the case, you have bits and pieces of evidence float in. And so I weighed in on the basis of that, restating my views. What I heard was conflicting: at times that there was some sort of deal or signal in the works, and at other times that the operation was closed down. . . . So, again, there was this ambiguity from my standpoint. I would say to you that I did take the position . . . recognizing that if the president's initiative had any chance of success it would have to be a secret initiative for all the reasons that have been developed . . . whenever I would be called upon to do something to carry out those policies, I needed to know, but I didn't need to know things that were not in my sphere to do something about. . . . Now I believe that the conduct, the operational conduct of diplomatic activity, should be lodged in the State Department. And by and large it is. And if there is a lesson out of all of this, insofar as how things operate are concerned, I think that the lesson is that the—that operational activities, and a staff for conducting operational activities out of the National Security Council staff, is very questionable and shouldn't be done except in very rare circumstances.[22]

On March 14, 1987, President Reagan expressed regret for not having listened to Secretary Shultz and Secretary Weinberger's opposition to the Iran initiative in his weekly radio address. "As we now know, it turned out they were right and I was wrong."[23]

THE TOWER COMMISSION REPORT

[In December of 1986, President Reagan established a Special Review Board "to examine the proper role of the National Security Council Staff in national security operations, including the arms transfer to Iran."[24] Following are excerpts from the *Report of the President's Special Review Board,* more commonly known as *The Tower Commission Report,* released on February 26, 1987.]

Beyond the President, the other NSC principals and the National Security Advisor must share in the responsibility for the NSC system. President Reagan's personal management style places an especially heavy responsibility on his key advisors. Knowing his style, they should have been particularly mindful of the need for special attention to the manner in which this arms sales initiative developed and proceeded. On this score, neither the National Security Advisor nor the other NSC principals deserve high marks. . . . The principal subordinates to the President must not be deterred from urging the President not to proceed on a highly questionable course of action even in the face of his strong conviction to the contrary. . . . It does not appear that any of the NSC principals called for more frequent considerations of the Iran initiative by the NSC principals in the presence of the President. None of the principals called for a serious vetting of the initiative by even a restricted group of disinterested individuals. The intelligence questions do not appear to have been raised, and legal considerations, while raised, were not pressed. No one seemed to have complained about the informality of the process. No one called for a thorough reexamination once the initiative did not meet expectations or the manner of execution changed. While one or another of the NSC principals suspected that something was amiss, none vigorously pursued the issue.[25]

The NSC principals other than the President may be somewhat excused by the insufficient attention on the part of the National Security Advisor to the need to keep all the principals fully informed. Given the importance of the issue and the sharp policy divergences involved, however, Secretary Shultz and Secretary Weinberger in particular distanced themselves from the march of events. Secretary Shultz specifically requested to be informed only as necessary to perform his job. . . . Their obligation was to give the President their full support and continued advice with respect to the program or, if they could not in conscience do that, to so inform the President. Instead, they simply distanced themselves from the program. They protected their record as to their own positions on this issue. They were not energetic in attempting to protect the President from the consequences of his personal commitment to freeing the hostages.[26]

CRITICISM AND DEFENSE

[Following are excerpts from Shultz's testimony in Joint hearings on the Iran-Contra Investigation, July 23–24, 1987.]

REPRESENTATIVE MICHAEL DEWINE, Republican of Ohio: I think it is clear, that the facts are very plain, that you were right about a lot of this. With regard to the arms sale, you were right about the whole thing. In essence, you were a prophet. Just about everything you said was going to go wrong did go wrong. . . . I think the basic problem, at least in this Congressman's mind, was that neither you nor the President really know the essential facts. You gave Admiral Poindexter complete authority to decide what you needed to know. You took the risk, and it was a risk, that he would give you enough information about the Iran initiative for you to do your job. In essence, you left the fox to guard the chicken coop. . . . I am in basic agreement with what the Tower Commission said . . . in my opinion, you let Admiral Poindexter cut you out. You discussed your resignation

on three separate occasions, one of those occasions having to do with a polygraph. But you did not discuss it in regard to what has turned out to be the major foreign policy disaster of this Administration. You stated you did not want to know the operational details. In my opinion you purposefully cut yourself out from the facts. . . . It seems to me, Mr. Secretary, you permitted Admiral Poindexter to get between you and the President, just as he got between the President and the American people.

SECRETARY OF STATE SHULTZ: Well, I will just say that is one man's opinion and I don't share it.[27]

REPRESENTATIVE HENRY J. HYDE, Republican of Illinois: Now, Mr. Secretary, I can't escape the notion that had you opposed this flawed policy and were willing to resign over this . . . you could have stopped it dead in its track. And if you couldn't, you and Secretary Weinberger sure could. . . . I cannot believe, if you had been that forceful and that committed to opposing this flawed initiative, as much as Poindexter and North were committed to advancing it, you couldn't have stopped it dead in its tracks. And I ask you if that is not so?

SHULTZ: I doubt it very much. I will describe to you my own thinking and course of action. As I have thought about . . . what happened, there is a sense in which it falls into . . . three time periods. . . .

The first period was from some time in the middle of 1985 through, say, the middle of December 1985. During that period, I unearthed it; I opposed it; I thought I had taken part in killing it on more than one occasion. . . . [I]t was clear as it went on that the President had a desire to do it, and I didn't just say, "Well, you seem to be leaning against me, I'm going to resign." . . . The President listened to everything and he decided what he decided. . . . [W]ould you have said I should have sat there on December 7 in the White House and said "Mr. President, I see you are wavering, and if you should decide against me, goodbye?" That is not the way to play this game at all. . . .

The second episode goes, as I see it, between early January 1986 and late May, early June. . . . There we had a special proposal made, brought to us by the Israelis, which became the topic of a meeting, and I took a position in that meeting . . . and while there was no decision made at that meeting that I recall, I certainly did have the sense that Secretary Weinberger and I were on one side of the issue and everybody else, including the President, was on the other side, and that somehow or other this was going to move ahead. So again, I didn't say, "agree with me or goodbye." . . . [T]here is a lot more going on around the world than this particular set of events. . . . So always in the question of whether you resign or not is the question of the chance to help the President accomplish some positive things . . . nothing ever gets settled in this town, and you can say, "I will give up and leave," or "I will stay and fight." . . .

And then comes early June . . . when it became known to me . . . that there had been the mission to Tehran and it had fizzled. And Admiral Poindexter told me that the whole thing had been told to stand down. So at this point, I don't have anything to resign about. Subsequently, a couple of other things took place that gave me the feeling . . . that we were going forward with the effort with Iran which I thought was something worth doing . . . in a proper way. So I have no, no problem. . . .

I have never hesitated in my time in the Cabinet to speak up to Presidents, or to resign, if I felt the situation warranted. In this case, I looked at it the way I did.[28]

SENTOR DANIEL K. INOUYE, Democrat from Hawaii. Mr. Secretary: I have another question. And I ask this with great reluctance, because I realize that it is rather personal in nature, but I think it is relevant . . . I've been advised that in August of 1986 you tendered a letter of resignation to the President of the United States. Is that true? And if so, can you tell us something about it?

SHULTZ: . . . That is true. And I have asked the President to let me leave this office on a couple of other occasions, earlier.

INOUYE: Was that in any way related to the Iran-Contra affair?

SHULTZ: Well, in August of 1986 I thought that it was over. . . . [O]n the effort with Iran, I thought it was basically on a proper track.

But it was because I felt a sense of estrangement. I knew the White House was very uncomfortable with me. I was very uncomfortable with what I was getting from the intelligence community, and I knew they were uncomfortable with me, perhaps going back to the lie detector test business. I could feel it.

What I have learned about the various things that were being done, I suppose, explains why I was not in good odor with the NSC staff and some of the others in the White House. I had a terrible time. There was a kind of guerrilla warfare going on, on all kinds of little things. For example, as you know, the Congress doesn't treat the State Department very well when it comes to appropriated funds. And not only have we historically taken a beating but we've been cut brutally . . . and I think in a manner that it is not in the interests of the United States.

But anyway, one of the conventions that's grown up because we have no travel money to speak of . . . [is] the Air Force runs a White House Presidential Wing and when the Secretary of State has a mission, that gets approved, and then I get an airplane and the airplane, it's paid for out of this budget. If I had to pay for that airplane, I couldn't travel. So you have me grounded unless I can be approved.

Now it's not a problem. The system works all right and it's just assumed that that's the way it's supposed to be. But I started having trouble because some people on the White House staff decided that they were going to make my life unhappy and they stopped approving these airplane things. And we fought about this and so on. And finally— I hated to do this—I went to the President and I gave him little memorandums to check off "yes," or "no." That's no business for the Secretary of State to be taking up with the President of the United States. . . .

And so I told the President, "I'd like to leave and here's my letter." And he stuck it in his drawer. He said, "You're tired. It's about time you go on vacation, and let's talk about it after you get back from vacation." So I said, "OK," and I guess everybody knows what happened. . . .

At an earlier time, in the middle of 1983, I resigned. And that was because I discovered that Bud McFarlane, who was then the Deputy National Security Advisor, was sent on a secret trip to the Middle East . . . without my knowledge, while we were busy negotiating out there. And also, I found some things happened with respect to actions on Central America that I didn't know about beforehand.

So I went to the President and I said, "Mr. President, you don't need a guy like me for Secretary of State if this is the way things are going to be done, because when you send somebody out like that McFarlane trip, I'm done." . . . When the President hangs out his shingle and says, "You don't have to go through the State Department, just come right into the White House," he'll get all the business. That's a big signal to countries out there about how to deal with the U.S. Government. And it may have had something to do with how events transpired, for all I know. But it's wrong. You can't do it that way.

So the other time I resigned was after my big lie detector test flap, and again I could see that I was on the outs with everybody, so I said, "Mr. President, why don't you let me go home. I like it in California." And again, he wouldn't let that happen. That was late in 1985. Mr. McFarlane had resigned, and Mr. McFarlane and I, I think, worked very effectively together in . . . our efforts with the U.S.S.R. and . . . in the end, I didn't feel, with Mr. McFarlane having left, that it was fair to the President of the country for me to leave at the same time, so I didn't.

But I do think that in jobs like the job I have, where it is a real privilege to serve in this kind of job, or the others that you recounted, that you can't do the job well if you want it too much. You have to be willing to say goodbye, and I am.[29]

NOTES

1. The National Security Archive, *The Chronology* (New York: Warner, 1987), 114, 17.
2. Ibid., 118.
3. Ibid., 140–41.
4. Ibid., 177.
5. Ibid., 197, 200.
6. Ibid., 207.
7. Ibid., 208–11.
8. *Report of the President's Special Review Board* (Washington, D.C.: Feb. 26, 1987), 111–12.
9. *The Chronology,* 242.
10. Ibid., 247.
11. Ibid., 248.
12. Ibid., 249.
13. Ibid., 261–62.
14. Ibid., 356.
15. Ibid.
16. Ibid., 359.
17. Ibid., 535–37.
18. Ibid., 537.
19. Ibid., 559.
20. Ibid., 561, 574.
21. Ibid., 582, 592–93.
22. *New York Times,* Dec. 9, 1986, A12.
23. *The Chronology,* 654.
24. *Report,* I-1.
25. *Report,* IV-10, IV-11.
26. Ibid., IV-11.
27. *Iran-Contra Investigation,* Joint Hearings before the Senate Select Committee on Secret Military Assistance to Iran and the Nicaraguan Opposition and the House Select Committee to Investigate Covert Arms Transactions with Iran, 100 Cong. 1 Sess., 180–81.
28. Ibid., 131–34.
29. Ibid., 58–60.

Comment

Although the polygraph case and the Iran-Contra affair invite comparative analysis, it is best to begin by considering the polygraph case on its own. Had George Shultz followed the imperative "obey or resign," he would have quietly left office. By publicly threatening to resign, he succeeded in changing governmental policy. Should our judgment of Shultz's actions depend on whether he was acting according to his own conscience, whether his position on polygraph testing was morally correct, or both?

To clarify the moral basis of Shultz's objection, assume that polygraph tests can sometimes be effective for some purposes. (As Richard Nixon said: "I don't know how accurate the tests are, but I know they'll scare the hell out of people.") Shultz's moral objection seems to be expressed in personal terms, as a matter of personal honor: he is offended by the implication that he is not be to trusted. Are there ways of restating the objection that would make it less dependent on an official's own sense of honor? (Some other grounds include invasion of privacy, deception, self-incrimination, the chilling effect on legitimate dissent, and recruitment for government service.) More generally, consider whether in order to be justifiable the dissent must be based on principles that apply to all public officials, not just those who happen to be offended, as Shultz is. Would Shultz's objection still have been valid if the policy had exempted him? All members of the State Department? All who conscientiously opposed such tests?

In the same month that the polygraph test was proposed, Shultz began objecting to the arms-for-hostages plans. Although he continued to object throughout the fall and early winter, he "distanced [himself] from the march of events" (according to the Tower Commission). Contrast this low-keyed opposition with his angry protest in the polygraph case. Some critics of Shultz might state the contrast even more sharply: when his personal honor was at stake, the secretary threatened to resign; but when national blackmail and violations of democratic procedure occurred, he objected only privately and then mostly tried to disassociate himself from the plan.

What exactly is the difference between the two wrongs that would justify such different responses by Shultz? On the face of it, many of the differences (the seriousness of the consequences, the relevance to role) would seem to favor a stronger reaction against the hostage deal than the polygraph test. (A stronger reaction does not necessarily mean threatening to resign.) Perhaps Shultz really believed that he had stopped the plan ("strangled the baby in the cradle"), but he had plenty of signs that the operation was continuing (for example, the report from Ambassador Price in May). He may have believed that he was more likely to be able to stop the polygraph proposal but that belief would not itself justify his differential response.

It might be argued that Shultz saw the arms-for-hostages plan as a policy difference about which officials could legitimately disagree but viewed the polygraph proposal as a purely moral issue on which one should not compromise. Although this may partially explain Shultz's reactions (only partially, because dealing with terrorists, he seemed to believe, would be wrong even if successful), it does not justify them. A question persists: what is the ethical difference between legitimate policy disagreements and purely moral issues? And it is worth remembering that there may be ethically relevant differences among policy disagreements themselves: in some policy disputes officials may be obligated only to register their objections, but in others they may be required to resist the policy more vigorously.

Agent Rowley Blows the Whistle*

After the disaster of 9/11, Colleen Rowley, the chief counsel in the FBI's Minneapolis field office, made several attempts to inform her superiors about what she saw as serious problems in the organization that had prevented timely processing of intelligence about potential terrorist attacks. After she received no response and saw no changes underway, she wrote a long letter to the Director of the FBI. She gave the letter to a congressional committee, and after it was made public, she was considered a whistle-blower.

Rowley first became concerned during the investigation of Zaccarias Moussaoui, the alleged 20th hijacker, who had enrolled in a flight school in Minnesota. Officials at the school called authorities at the FBI's Minneapolis office when they grew suspicious of Moussaoui. Their suspicions were aroused by his eagerness to learn to fly a commercial jet (though he had training only on a single engine plane), his reluctance to talk about his background, and his payment of the $8,300 enrollment fee in cash. Immigration and Naturalization Service agents detained him on an immigration violation, but they and the FBI agents in Minneapolis (including Rowley) suspected that he might be involved in a terrorist plot. They wanted to search his computer, but officials in FBI headquarters refused to allow them to apply for the necessary search warrant. The officials did not believe the Minneapolis agents had shown "probable cause." Some independent observers later agreed that the case for a warrant was not as strong as the Minneapolis agents believed at the time. But when the agents obtained a warrant after September 11, they found the phone number of Moussaoui's roommate, who was one of the leaders of the hijackers.

Rowley believed that this failure was not an isolated episode. In 1998 an FBI special agent and chief pilot in Oklahoma City warned his supervisor that he had observed "large numbers of Middle Eastern males receiving flight training at Oklahoma airports in recent months." He wrote a memo that stated explicitly that this trend "may be related to terrorist activity." The agent based his information primarily on radio conversations he overheard during flight. Although the title of the memo was "Weapons of Mass Destruction," it was marked routine and never reached higher officials. In July 2001 Phoenix FBI Special Agent Kenneth J. Williams wrote a memo raising concerns about Islamic extremists training at U.S. flight schools. This warning was sent as an electronic computer message to roughly a dozen FBI officials for review. These midlevel supervisors in headquarters concluded that the information Williams provided was speculative. They did not send it to the acting director, Thomas J. Pickard. The new director, Robert Mueller, did see it after September 11.

In her letter, Rowley not only criticized these specific failures and the organizational culture that led to them, but also the failure of Mueller to deal with them after September 11. She accuses Mueller and senior aides of having "omitted, downplayed, glossed over and or/mischaracterized" her office's investigation of Moussaoui. Top FBI officials decided to "circle the wagons" and even tried to deny that the FBI had any knowledge that Islamic terrorists might be planning an attack involving hijacked airplanes. The FBI classified the letter, but the content was leaked before she testified to the Senate Intelligence Committee. Responding publicly to her letter, Mueller retracted that denial, and acknowledged the earlier failures. He said that he had initiated an internal investigation immediately after September 11, and now intended to carry out major reforms of the organization.

Fearing reprisals, Rowley asked the Senate Committee to give her whistle-blower protection. Employees of govern-

*Jaime Muehl wrote the introduction and selected the excerpts presented in this section.

ment intelligence agencies, such as the FBI and CIA, are excluded from the Whistle-blower Protection Act of 1989. It is a violation for an FBI employee to report problems to Congress. The concern is that employees of these agencies deal with sensitive and classified information that, if revealed, could potentially pose a threat to national security. FBI whistle-blowers are protected by internal Department of Justice regulations, and most whistle-blower cases are investigated internally by the FBI Office of Professional Responsibility.

The chair and ranking member of the Senate committee asked Mueller personally to guarantee that Rowley would not suffer any retaliation for coming forward. Mueller agreed, and in June 2002 extended this guarantee to all FBI employees. The Senate Judiciary Committee then unanimously adopted a bill that would provide enhanced protection for FBI whistle-blowers, but an anonymous member blocked it from coming to a vote in the Senate.

Not all whistleblowers have fared as well as Rowley. A prominent example is the case of Special Agent John Roberts, who was allegedly harassed after his interview on *60 Minutes* in which he criticized the FBI for practicing a double standard of discipline. A Justice Department Office of the Inspector General (OIG) report released in February 2003 confirmed many of Roberts' allegations. FBI Assistant Director Robert Jordan admitted that he passed over Roberts for the position of acting deputy because of his comments on the program, even though Roberts had seniority and had previously held the position.

Critics questioned both the content of Rowley's complaint and the way she made it. Vice President Dick Cheney characterized such inquiries as Rowley's about the possibility that the U.S. might have been able to prevent the 9/11 attacks as ludicrous, even "irresponsible" in times of war. Others said she should not have gone to Congress but stayed within the organization. Asked in an interview for *Time* magazine how she felt her FBI colleagues viewed her action, Rowley herself responded, "Even in my

office, with quite a bit of support, still a lot of people were looking at me like, what the heck?" Some saw her action as disloyal.

Rowley's letter gave congressional critics of the FBI new ammunition. Senators Grassley and Leahy reintroduced the FBI Reform Act in 2003 with the hope that, this time, it would be taken up by the Senate. The whistle-blower provisions in this act, like those in 2001, would give FBI whistle-blowers the same rights and protections enjoyed by almost all other federal employees. Opponents of the whistle-blower provisions argue that there are procedures already in place to address reports of wrongdoing in the FBI. Strengthened whistle-blower protections would prevent the Bureau from stripping away a whistle-blower's security clearances, even in cases where classified national security information had been improperly revealed.

In a speech in November 2003, Rowley offered the following advice to would-be dissenters: "Before blowing the whistle, make sure the matter is extremely significant, almost a matter of life or death. Be truthful and essentially right. Do not be motivated for yourself, and do it in the most constructive way possible."

EXCERPTS FROM COLLEEN ROWLEY'S MEMO TO FBI DIRECTOR ROBERT MUELLER

MAY 21, 2002

FBI Director Robert Mueller
FBI Headquarters Washington, D.C.

Dear Director Mueller:
I feel at this point that I have to put my concerns in writing concerning the important topic of the FBI's response to evidence of terrorist activity in the United States prior to September 11th. The issues are fundamentally ones of INTEGRITY and go to the heart of the FBI's law enforcement mission and mandate. Moreover, at this critical juncture in fashioning future policy to promote the most effective handling of ongoing and future threats to United States citizens' security, it is of absolute importance that

an unbiased, completely accurate picture emerge of the FBI's current investigative and management strengths and failures.

To get to the point, I have deep concerns that a delicate and subtle shading/skewing of facts by you and others at the highest levels of FBI management has occurred and is occurring. The term "cover up" would be too strong a characterization which is why I am attempting to carefully (and perhaps over laboriously) choose my words here. I base my concerns on my relatively small, peripheral but unique role in the Moussaoui investigation in the Minneapolis Division prior to, during and after September 11th and my analysis of the comments I have heard both inside the FBI (originating, I believe, from you and other high levels of management) as well as your Congressional testimony and public comments.

I feel that certain facts, including the following, have, up to now, been omitted, downplayed, glossed over and/or mischaracterized in an effort to avoid or minimize personal and/or institutional embarrassment on the part of the FBI and/or perhaps even for improper political reasons:

1) The Minneapolis agents who responded to the call about Moussaoui's flight training identified him as a terrorist threat from a very early point. The decision to take him into custody on August 15, 2001, on the INS "overstay" charge was a deliberate one to counter that threat and was based on the agents' reasonable suspicions. While it can be said that Moussaoui's overstay status was fortuitous, because it allowed for him to be taken into immediate custody and prevented him receiving any more flight training, it was certainly not something the INS coincidentally undertook of their own volition. I base this on the conversation I had when the agents called me at home late on the evening Moussaoui was taken into custody to confer and ask for legal advice about their next course of action. The INS agent was assigned to the FBI's Joint Terrorism Task Force and was therefore working in tandem with FBI agents.

2) As the Minneapolis agents' reasonable suspicions quickly ripened into probable cause, which, at the latest, occurred within days of Moussaoui's arrest when the French Intelligence Service confirmed his affiliations with radical fundamentalist Islamic groups and activities connected to Osama Bin Laden, they became desperate to search the computer laptop that had been taken from Moussaoui as well as conduct a more thorough search of his personal effects. The agents in particular believed that Moussaoui signaled he had something to hide in the way he refused to allow them to search his computer.

3) The Minneapolis agents' initial thought was to obtain a criminal search warrant, but in order to do so, they needed to get FBI Headquarters' (FBIHQ's) approval in order to ask for DOJ [Department of Justice] OIPR's [Office of Intelligence Policy Review] approval to contact the United States Attorney's Office in Minnesota. Prior to and even after receipt of information provided by the French, FBIHQ personnel disputed with the Minneapolis agents the existence of probable cause to believe that a criminal violation had occurred/was occurring. As such, FBIHQ personnel refused to contact OIPR to attempt to get the authority.... Notably also, the actual search warrant obtained on September 11th did not include the French intelligence information. Therefore, the only main difference between the information being submitted to FBIHQ from an early date which HQ personnel continued to deem insufficient and the actual criminal search warrant which a federal district judge signed and approved on September 11th, was the fact that, by the time the actual warrant was obtained, suspected terrorists were known to have hijacked planes which they then deliberately crashed into the World Trade Center and the Pentagon. To say then, as has been iterated numerous times, that probable cause did not exist until after the disastrous event occurred, is really to acknowledge that the missing piece of probable cause was only the FBI's (FBIHQ's) failure to appreciate that such an event could occur.... It is obvious, from my firsthand knowledge of the events and the detailed documentation that exists, that the agents in Minneapolis who were closest to the

action and in the best position to gauge the situation locally, did fully appreciate the terrorist risk/danger posed by Moussaoui and his possible co-conspirators even prior to September 11th. . . .

4) The fact is that key FBIHQ personnel whose job it was to assist and coordinate with field division agents on terrorism investigations and the obtaining and use of FISA [Foreign Intelligence Survey Act] searches (and who theoretically were privy to many more sources of intelligence information than field division agents), continued to, almost inexplicably[5] throw up roadblocks and undermine Minneapolis' by-now desperate efforts to obtain a FISA search warrant, long after the French intelligence service provided its information and probable cause became clear. HQ personnel brought up almost ridiculous questions in their apparent efforts to undermine the probable cause.[6] In all of their conversations and correspondence, HQ personnel never disclosed to the Minneapolis agents that the Phoenix Division had, only approximately three weeks earlier, warned of Al Qaeda operatives in flight schools seeking flight training for terrorist purposes!

Nor did FBIHQ personnel do much to disseminate the information about Moussaoui to other appropriate intelligence/law enforcement authorities. When, in a desperate 11th hour measure to bypass the FBIHQ roadblock, the Minneapolis Division undertook to directly notify the CIA's Counter Terrorist Center (CTC), FBIHQ personnel actually chastised the Minneapolis agents for making the direct notification without their approval!

5) Eventually on August 28, 2001, after a series of e-mails between Minneapolis and FBIHQ, which suggest that the FBIHQ SSA [Supervisory Special Agent] deliberately further undercut the FISA effort by not adding the further intelligence information which he had promised to add that supported Moussaoui's foreign power connection and making several changes in the wording of the information that had been provided by the Minneapolis Agent, the Minneapolis agents were notified that the NSLU [National Secu-

rity Law Unit] Chief did not think there was sufficient evidence of Moussaoui's connection to a foreign power. . . . Obviously verbal presentations are far more susceptible to mischaracterization and error. The e-mail communications between Minneapolis and FBIHQ, however, speak for themselves and there are far better witnesses than me who can provide their firsthand knowledge of these events characterized in one Minneapolis agent's e-mail as FBIHQ is "setting this up for failure." My only comment is that the process of allowing the FBI supervisors to make changes in affidavits is itself fundamentally wrong, just as, in the follow-up to FBI Laboratory Whistleblower Frederic Whitehurst's allegations, this process was revealed to be wrong in the context of writing up laboratory results. With the Whitehurst allegations, this process of allowing supervisors to re-write portions of laboratory reports, was found to provide opportunities for overzealous supervisors to skew the results in favor of the prosecution. In the Moussaoui case, it was the opposite—the process allowed the Headquarters Supervisor to downplay the significance of the information thus far collected in order to get out of the work of having to see the FISA application through or possibly to avoid taking what he may have perceived as an unnecessary career risk[7]. . . .

6) Although the last thing the FBI or the country needs now is a witch hunt, I do find it odd that (to my knowledge) no inquiry whatsoever was launched of the relevant FBIHQ personnel's actions a long time ago. Despite FBI leaders' full knowledge of all the items mentioned herein (and probably more that I'm unaware of), the SSA, his unit chief, and other involved HQ personnel were allowed to stay in their positions and, what's worse, occupy critical positions in the FBI's SIOC [Strategic Information and Operations Center] Command Center post-September 11th. (The SSA in question actually received a promotion some months afterward!) It's true we all make mistakes and I'm not suggesting that HQ personnel in question ought to be burned at the stake, but, we all need to be held

accountable for serious mistakes. I'm relatively certain that if it appeared that a lowly field office agent had committed such errors of judgment, the FBI's OPR [Office of Professional Responsibility] would have been notified to investigate and the agent would have, at the least, been quickly reassigned. I'm afraid the FBI's failure to submit this matter to OPR (and to the IOB [Intelligence Oversight Board]) gives further impetus to the notion (raised previously by many in the FBI) of a double standard which results in those of lower rank being investigated more aggressively and dealt with more harshly for misconduct while the misconduct of those at the top is often overlooked or results in minor disciplinary action. From all appearances, this double standard may also apply between those at FBIHQ and those in the field.

7) The last official "fact" that I take issue with is not really a fact, but an opinion, and a completely unsupported opinion at that. In the day or two following September 11th, you, Director Mueller, made the statement to the effect that if the FBI had only had any advance warning of the attacks, we (meaning the FBI), may have been able to take some action to prevent the tragedy. Fearing that this statement could easily come back to haunt the FBI upon revelation of the information that had been developed pre-September 11th about Moussaoui, I and others in the Minneapolis Office, immediately sought to reach your office through an assortment of higher level FBIHQ contacts, in order to quickly make you aware of the background of the Moussaoui investigation and forewarn you so that your public statements could be accordingly modified. When such statements from you and other FBI officials continued, we thought that somehow you had not received the message and we made further efforts. Finally when similar comments were made weeks later, in Assistant Director Caruso's congressional testimony in response to the first public leaks about Moussaoui we faced the sad realization that the remarks indicated someone, possibly with your approval, had decided to circle the wagons at FBIHQ in an apparent effort to protect the FBI from embarrassment and the relevant FBI officials from scrutiny. Everything I have seen and heard about the FBI's official stance and the FBI's internal preparations in anticipation of further congressional inquiry, had, unfortunately, confirmed my worst suspicions in this regard. After the details began to emerge concerning the pre-September 11th investigation of Moussaoui, and subsequently with the recent release of the information about the Phoenix EC, your statement has changed. The official statement is now to the effect that even if the FBI had followed up on the Phoenix lead to conduct checks of flight schools and the Minneapolis request to search Moussaoui's personal effects and laptop, nothing would have changed and such actions certainly could not have prevented the terrorist attacks and resulting loss of life. With all due respect, this statement is as bad as the first! It is also quite at odds with the earlier statement (which I'm surprised has not already been pointed out by those in the media!) I don't know how you or anyone at FBI Headquarters, no matter how much genius or prescience you may possess, could so blithely make this affirmation without anything to back the opinion up than your stature as FBI Director. The truth is, as with most predictions into the future, no one will ever know what impact, if any, the FBI's following up on those requests, would have had. Although I agree that it's very doubtful that the full scope of the tragedy could have been prevented, it's at least possible we could have gotten lucky and uncovered one or two more of the terrorists in flight training prior to September 11th, just as Moussaoui was discovered, after making contact with his flight instructors. . . . I think your statements demonstrate a rush to judgment to protect the FBI at all costs. I think the only fair response to this type of question would be that no one can pretend to know one way or another.

Mr. Director, I hope my observations can be taken in a constructive vein. They are from the heart and intended to be completely apolitical. Hopefully, with our nation's security on the line, you and our nation's other elected and appointed officials can rise above the petty politics that often plague other discussions and do the right thing. . . .

I have used the "we" term repeatedly herein to indicate facts about others in the Minneapolis Office at critical times, but none of the opinions expressed herein can be attributed to anyone but myself. I know that those who know me would probably describe me as, by nature, overly opinionated and sometimes not as discreet as I should be. . . . An honest acknowledgment of the FBI's mistakes in this and other cases should not lead to increasing the Headquarters bureaucracy and approval levels of investigative actions as the answer. Most often, field office agents and field office management on the scene will be better suited to the timely and effective solution of crimes and, in some lucky instances, to the effective prevention of crimes, including terrorism incidents. . . . Although FBIHQ personnel have, no doubt, been of immeasurable assistance to the field over the years, I'm hard pressed to think of any case which has been solved by FBIHQ personnel and I can name several that have been screwed up! Decision-making is inherently more effective and timely when decentralized instead of concentrated.

I have been an FBI agent for over 21 years and, for what it's worth, have never received any form of disciplinary action throughout my career. From the 5th grade, when I first wrote the FBI and received the "100 Facts about the FBI" pamphlet, this job has been my dream. I feel that my career in the FBI has been somewhat exemplary, having entered on duty at a time when there was only a small percentage of female Special Agents. I have also been lucky to have had four children during my time in the FBI and am the sole breadwinner of a family of six. Due to the frankness with which I have expressed myself and my deep feelings on these issues, (which is only because I feel I have a somewhat unique, inside perspective of the Moussaoui matter, the gravity of the events of September 11th and the current

seriousness of the FBI's and United States' ongoing efforts in the "war against terrorism"), I hope my continued employment with the FBI is not somehow placed in jeopardy. I have never written to an FBI Director in my life before on any topic. Although I would hope it is not necessary, I would therefore wish to take advantage of the federal "Whistleblower Protection" provisions by so characterizing my remarks.

Sincerely

Colleen M. Rowley

Special Agent and Minneapolis Chief Division Counsel

NOTES

5. During the early aftermath of September 11th, when I happened to be recounting the pre-September 11th events concerning the Moussaoui investigation to other FBI personnel in other divisions or in FBIHQ, almost everyone's first question was "Why?—Why would an FBI agent(s) deliberately sabotage a case? (I know I shouldn't be flippant about this, but jokes were actually made that the key FBIHQ personnel had to be spies or moles, like Robert Hansen, who were actually working for Osama Bin Laden to have so undercut Minneapolis' effort.) Our best real guess, however, is that, in most cases avoidance of all "unnecessary" actions/decisions by FBIHQ managers (and maybe to some extent field managers as well) has, in recent years, been seen as the safest FBI career course. Numerous high-ranking FBI officials who have made decisions or have taken actions which, in hindsight, turned out to be mistaken or just turned out badly (i.e., Ruby Ridge, Waco, etc.) have seen their careers plummet and end. This has in turn resulted in a climate of fear which has chilled aggressive FBI law enforcement action/decisions. In a large hierarchal bureaucracy such as the FBI, with the requirement for numerous superiors approvals/oversight, the premium on career-enhancement, and interjecting a chilling factor brought on by recent extreme public and congressional

criticism/oversight, and I think you will see at least the makings of the most likely explanation. . . . It's quite conceivable that many of the HQ personnel who so vigorously disputed Moussaoui's ability/predisposition to fly a plane into a building were simply unaware of all the various incidents and reports worldwide of Al Qaeda terrorists attempting or plotting to do so.

6. For example, at one point, the Supervisory Special Agent at FBIHQ posited that the French information could be worthless because it only identified Zaccarias Moussaoui by name and he, the SSA, didn't know how many people by that name existed in France. A Minneapolis agent attempted to surmount that problem by quickly phoning the FBI's legal Attache (Legat) in Paris, France, so that a check could be made of the French telephone directories. Although the Legat in France did not have access to all of the French telephone directories, he was able to quickly ascertain that there was only one listed in the Paris directory. It is not known if this sufficiently answered the question, for the SSA continued to find new reasons to stall.

7. Another factor that cannot be underestimated as to the HQ Supervisor's apparent reluctance to do anything was/is the ever present risk of being "written up" for an Intelligence Oversight Board (IOB) "error." In the year(s) preceding the September 11th acts of terrorism, numerous alleged IOB violations on the part of FBI personnel had to be submitted to the FBI's Office of Professional Responsibility (OPR) as well as the IOB. I believe the chilling effect upon all levels of FBI agents assigned to intelligence matters and their manager hampered us from aggressive investigation of terrorists. Since one generally only runs the risk of IOB violations when one does something, the safer course is to do nothing. Ironically, in this case, a potentially huge IOB violation arguably occurred due to FBIHQ's failure to act, that is, FBIHQ's failure to inform the Department of Justice Criminal Division of Moussaoui's potential criminal violations (which, as I've already said, were quickly identified in

Minneapolis as violations of Title 18 United States Code Section 2332b [Acts of terrorism transcending national boundaries] and Section 32 [Destruction of aircraft or aircraft facilities]). This failure would seem to run clearly afoul of the Attorney General directive contained in the "1995 Procedures for Contacts Between the FBI and the Criminal Division Concerning Foreign Intelligence and Foreign Counterintelligence Investigations" which mandatorily require the FBI to notify the Criminal Division when "facts or circumstances are developed" in an FI or FCI investigation "that reasonably indicate that a significant federal crime has been, is being, or may be committed." I believe that Minneapolis agents actually brought this point to FBIHQ's attention on August 22, 2001, but HQ personnel apparently ignored the directive, ostensibly due to their opinion of the lack of probable cause. But the issue of whether HQ personnel deliberately undercut the probable cause can be sidestepped at this point because the Directive does not require probable cause. It requires only a "reasonable indication" which is defined as "substantially lower than probable cause." Given that the Minneapolis Division had accumulated far more than "a mere hunch" (which the directive would deem as insufficient), the information ought to have, at least, been passed on to the "Core Group" created to assess whether the information needed to be further disseminated to the Criminal Division. . . .

EXCERPTS FROM DIRECTOR MUELLER'S BRIEFING

WEDNESDAY MAY 29, 2002

When I arrived at the FBI in September, it was already clear that there was a need for change at the bureau. . . .

But then came the events of September 11th, and the events of September 11th marked a turning point for the FBI. And I say that because I think it's fair to say that after 9/11, it became clearer than ever that we had to fundamentally change the way we do our business. . . .

In December, I described to you a new headquarters structure, one designed to support not hinder the critically important work of our employees stationed here and around the world. It is working, but quite obviously, there's a lot more work that needs to be done.

And today, I am presenting for congressional consideration the second, and I think clearly the most important part of what must be done. In the last few weeks, two separate matters have come to symbolize that which we must change. First is what did not happen with the memo from Phoenix, which points squarely at our analytical capacity. Our analytical capability is not where it should be. . . .

And second, the letter from Agent Rowley in Minneapolis points squarely to a need for a different approach, especially at headquarters. And with that proposition there really should be no debate.

And let me—let me just take a moment to thank Agent Rowley for her letter. It is critically important that I hear criticisms of the organization, including criticisms of me, in order to improve the organization, to improve the FBI. Because our focus is on preventing terrorist attacks, more so than in the past, we must be open to new ideas, to criticism from within and from without, and to admitting and learning from our mistakes. And I certainly do not have a monopoly—a monopoly on the right answers, and so I seek the input from those both within the organization as well as those without the organization.

Now, from new priorities, to new resources, to a new structure applying a new approach, I do believe that we are on the way to changing the FBI. And while we believe that these changes are relatively dramatic and a dramatic departure from the past, in the end, our culture must change with them. Long before me, the bureau had years of major successes, based on the efforts of the talented men and women who make up the FBI. It is a history we should not forget as we evolve to an agency centered on the prevention of any further terrorist attacks.

· · ·

It is critically important to our ability to address terrorism that we have a vibrant, active, aggressive headquarters and that it has the analytical capability to support that mission. And that's what I mean by—when I say up here, "Redefine the Relationship Between the Headquarters and Field."

And there's one other aspect in that—of that; is we cannot expect an office in the field to know what other offices are doing.

It's up to headquarters to make certain that, in the case of Moussaoui for instance, that the agents who were working on the Moussaoui case got the Phoenix memorandum that was put out in July by Agent Williams there. It is critically important that we have that connection of dots that will enable us to prevent the next attack. And to do that, headquarters has to assume a responsibility for assuring that information comes in, that information is analyzed, and that information is disseminated.

SENATORS CHARLES GRASSLEY AND PATRICK LEAHY REINTRODUCE THE FBI REFORM ACT OF 2003

CONGRESSIONAL RECORD–SENATE (TUESDAY, JULY 22, 2003) 108TH CONGRESS, 1ST SESSION, 149 CONG REC S 9710

Mr. GRASSLEY. . . .

First, title I of the bill contains much needed protections for FBI whistleblowers. As my colleagues know, I have long held that good government requires that the brave men and women who blow the whistle on wrongdoing be protected. It is my strong belief that disclosures of wrongdoing by whistleblowers are an integral part of our system of checks and balances. However, although whistleblowers play a critical role in ensuring that waste, fraud, and abuse are brought to light and that public health and safety problems are exposed, the same whistleblower protection laws that apply to almost all other Federal employees do not currently apply to the FBI. In fact, it is a violation for FBI agents to report problems to Congress. That restriction leaves patriotic, loyal FBI employees with little recourse. This bill will fix that problem.

I truly believe that reform at the FBI will only occur when FBI employees feel free to blow the whistle on wrongdoing. Without adequate whistleblower protections, I am concerned that agents, such as Colleen Rowley and others, who speak out about abuses and problems at the FBI will be subject to retaliation. Thus, this bill finally gives FBI whistleblowers the same rights and protections that other Federal employees currently possess. When this bill is passed, FBI employees who are retaliated against for blowing the whistle will be able to avail themselves of all the protections afforded by the Whistleblower Protection Act.

. . . Mr. President, I say to my fellow colleagues, it is time we acted on the reforms in this bill. It has been almost a year since this bill passed unanimously out of committee. Let's act to reform the FBI and help maintain America's trust and confidence in the Bureau. . . .

Mr. LEAHY. . . .

Mr. President, I am pleased to introduce today, with my friend the senior Senator from Iowa, the FBI Reform Act of 2003.

Our hearings and other oversight activities have highlighted tangible steps the Congress should take in an FBI Reform bill as part of this hands-on approach. Among other things, these hearings demonstrated the need to extend whistleblower protection [and] end the double standard for discipline of senior FBI executives.

Director Mueller once said it is "critically important" that he "hears criticisms of the organization . . . in order to improve the organization." I could not agree more. More than ever, the FBI must be open to new ideas, to criticism from within and without, and to facing up to and learning from past mistakes.

There are five key elements of our bill.

First, it strengthens whistleblower protection for FBI employees and protects them from retaliation for reporting wrongdoing.

Second, it addresses the issue of a double standard for discipline of senior executives by eliminating the disparity in authorized punishments between Senior Executive Service members and other Federal employees.

Third, it establishes an FBI Counterintelligence Polygraph Program for screening personnel in exceptionally sensitive positions with specific safeguards.

Fourth, it establishes an FBI Career Security Program, which would bring the FBI into line with other U.S. intelligence agencies that have strong career security professional cadres whose skills and leadership are dedicated to the protection of agency information, personnel, and facilities.

And fifth, it requires a set of reports that would enable Congress to engage the Executive branch in a constructive dialogue building a more effective FBI for the future.

Strengthening the FBI cannot be accomplished overnight, but with this legislation, we take an important step into the FBI's future.

Comment

Rowley criticized FBI officials for their actions both before and after September 11. But these criticisms provide different bases for the justification of whistle-blowing. To appreciate the ethical significance of the difference, consider whether Rowley would have been justified in going public with her criticism before September 11. She did not know about the Oklahoma city report or the Phoenix memo at that time, and had only suspicions about Moussaoui. Even if she had known more, she still had a strong obligation to work within the organization, unless she had compelling reasons to believe that her superiors would not take actions to correct the problems. In the months after September 11, she had stronger reasons for such a belief. Her most robust criticism was not of what can be called the first-order mistakes—failing to pursue the investigations before September 11—but the second-order mistakes—failing to take adequate steps to correct the first-order mistakes.

Two errors are commonly made in judging official dissent. One gives the dissenter too much moral credit by assessing the whistle-blowing mainly in light of later knowledge. We now know that a search of Moussaoui's computer would have revealed critical information relevant to the worst terrorist attack ever mounted in this country. But the question should be what Rowley or a reasonable person could or should have known at the time. The other error gives the dissenter too little credit by judging the whistle-blowing mostly in light of its effects. Assume that even if the pre-9/11 failures to which Rowley called attention could have been overcome, the attack still could not have been prevented. Grant also Mueller's claim that he was already undertaking reforms of the organization before Rowley's letter was made public. Even so, we may still want to argue that her whistle-blowing was justified. The focus should again be on what the dissenter could or should know at the time the decision is made to go public.

Rowley was one of three prominent whistle-blowers who appeared on the cover of *Time* as "persons of the year" in 2002. All were women. Some observers have suggested that women are more likely to dissent in organizations. They are not part of the old-boy networks of their organizations. They may be more willing to take risks with their careers and less willing to trust their colleagues who seem to be engaging in questionable conduct. Is this hypothesis plausible? If so, does it mean that as more women rise in the power structures of large organizations, there will be a higher proportion of whistle-blowers?

Like many whistle-blowers, Rowley is a sympathetic figure. We should also keep in mind that some dissenters are merely disgruntled employees with personal agendas and others have not exhausted all reasonable alternatives within the organization. Government organizations cannot serve their public purposes well if their leaders cannot count on a significant degree of loyalty from their subordinates. Consider whether the criticism of disloyalty some made against Rowley has any basis. If you do not think so, what facts in the case would need to be different in order to justify such a criticism? Evaluate Mueller's response in his May briefing.

Assess the legislative proposal that would give FBI whistle-blowers greater protection. Some might argue that although the rights of individual officials should be protected, the benefits of the practice for the democratic process are not great. Whistle-blowing is not particularly well suited to exposing patterns of abuse—systematic failures of an organization and its methods of oversight. Only people at relatively high levels of the organization can readily see the patterns and they are the least likely to blow the whistle. Moreover, whistle-blowing is not likely to occur as often as abuses occur because it will always be risky. Even if a whistle-blower does not suffer retaliation, his or her career almost always suffers. To what extent do these considerations limit the institutional value of whistle-blowing?

The Space Shuttle *Challenger*

Nicholas Carter

January 28, 1986. The space shuttle had already successfully flown twenty-four times and would that day attempt its twenty-fifth flight. To the outside observer, it seemed that NASA had, after more than a decade's work, successfully built a "space truck." After so many apparently flawless flights, there was little interest in this launch. For the first time, none of the networks was planning to show it live, despite the fact that this flight would mark the first time a civilian went to space.

At 11:30 A.M., the final countdown for lift-off had begun. It was a clear, crisp day. For those who had come to Cape Canaveral to watch, it looked like a beautiful day for flying. Many people were present but most conspicuous among the crowd gathered were the astronauts' families surrounded by photographers and NASA escorts. The astronauts' families were excited, yet nervous as well. They knew that, although the shuttle had successfully flown many times before, there were still dangers. After all, this launch had already been delayed three times. The adults had butterflies. The children, however, were full of enthusiasm. They were getting special treatment, and they knew that something very special was about to occur.[1]

In Brigham, Utah, in the shadows of the Wasatch Mountains, the engineers at Morton Thiokol who had designed the solid rocket boosters (SRBs) that lift the *Challenger* into

orbit gathered around a monitor to watch the lift-off. Bob Ebeling, one of the engineers, settled into his chair as Roger Boisjoly (pronounced "bo-zho-lay") walked by. Boisjoly was Morton Thiokol Inc.'s (MTI) most senior engineer on the SRB project. Ebeling went after his friend and asked him to come and watch. But Boisjoly had decided earlier he would not watch this launch attempt. In the last two days, it had grown unusually cold at Cape Canaveral. The freezing temperatures had alarmed Boisjoly and Arnie Thompson, one of the other senior Thiokol engineers. They felt that the O-rings might not be able to seal in such cold weather.

The O-rings are the bands designed to prevent pressure, heat, and flames from escaping through the SRB joints. (The SRB—there are two—provides the power to lift the Shuttle into orbit.) Upon ignition, the internal pressure in the SRB forces the walls to balloon out causing "joint rotation," and the gap the O-rings are supposed to fill becomes wider. It only takes a split second for this gap to grow too large for the O-rings to fill. After ignition, therefore, the O-rings must seal instantaneously (within the first three-fifths of a second). Otherwise, the O-rings do not seal properly, creating the likelihood of a shuttle explosion or crash.

Because the O-rings are rubber, the cold makes them less resilient and impairs their ability to move into the joints and fill them. One temperature test had been undertaken in March 1985 at Morton Thiokol to examine the effects of cold on the O-rings. Boisjoly conducted the tests, which involved compressing the O-rings with a metal plate and then drawing the metal plate away slightly to see how resilient the O-rings were at varying temperatures. At 100 degrees F., the O-rings never lost contact. At 75 degrees F., they lost contact for 2.4 seconds. And at 50 degrees F., the seals never regained contact. During ten minutes at 50 degrees F., the O-rings were unable to retake their original form. For Boisjoly, this was damning evidence that the O-rings were unreliable at low temperatures.[2]

The night before the launch, Boisjoly and Thompson had strenuously argued against launching. They believed it was too risky given the cold weather at the Cape. However, they had failed to convince either NASA or their own management at Thiokol. Angry and concerned, Boisjoly did not want to watch the take-off. But Ebeling was persistent, and Boisjoly finally relented.

Ebeling returned to his chair. Boisjoly found a place on the floor in front of Ebeling. On the screen was the gleaming Space Shuttle Challenger, cocked and ready for flight. Boisjoly hoped the flight would be successful. He hoped that the O-rings would seal. But he also hoped that when NASA recovered the SRBs they would find that the first of the two seals had failed.[3] This had happened before. He also hoped that the secondary seal would show more erosion than ever before. Then perhaps someone with authority would stop the launches until the O-ring problem was solved.[4]

The final seconds elapsed. The engines ignited. The mechanized arms holding the rocket upright moved away. The shuttle rose powerfully. Smoke and dust billowed out from underneath, creating enormous rolling clouds. The shuttle kept driving toward the sky. The critical stage for the O-rings had passed. The engineers breathed a sigh of relief. Ebeling turned to Boisjoly and told him that during the lift-off he had been praying that everything would go all right. The first minute of flight passed and everything looked good. Boisjoly kept watching. Suddenly an eruption of smoke engulfed the *Challenger.* And the rocket came apart. No one, not even NASA officials,

knew what had happened. Back at Cape Canaveral, the crowd was bewildered. The families drew together. The children cried uncontrollably. There was no hope that the seven astronauts had survived.

Without a word, Boisjoly got up and went back to his office to be alone. He spent the rest of the day unable to do anything. At one point, two engineers stopped in to see if he was O.K. Boisjoly could not speak. He just nodded that he was all right. After a long moment of silence, they left. Boisjoly knew what had gone wrong. His O-rings.[5]

. . .

The day before the *Challenger* disaster, a cold front had swept down the East Coast. The temperature hovered around 31 degrees F. Through tests NASA had determined that below 31 degrees F. the shuttle would not work.[6] The launch was scheduled for the next morning and a decision had to be made in time to start the twelve hour countdown. The cold weather had not been a factor in the previous launch delays, but the temperature was dropping now and was beginning to cause concerns, especially among Thiokol's engineers in Utah. Temperatures would be below freezing that night, and the engineers estimated that the temperature at the joint where the O-rings operated would be between 27 and 30 degrees F. by late morning the next day. The temperature in the air might be 31 degrees, passable by NASA rules but alarming to the Thiokol engineers. The coldest it had ever been for a launch, in January 1985, was 53 degrees F. During that launch, Flight 41-C, one of the SRB joints experienced the worst case of blow-by in the shuttle's brief history. (Blow-by occurs when the SRB's scalding gases have "blown by" the O-ring before it has sealed, burning the grease that dresses the O-rings.) Another flight later in 1985 (Flight 41-B) also gave the Thiokol engineers pause. On the day of that flight's launch, the temperature had been in the upper 50s. But the primary O-ring at one of the nozzle joints never sealed. Fortunately, the back-up seal did, but among Thiokol's engineers there was a growing suspicion that cold weather impaired the O-rings' sealing function.

These experiences of blow-by in cold weather led Thiokol to undertake tests to determine whether cold temperatures actually affected the O-rings. The O-rings are "activated" (i.e., pushed into the gap of the joint where they seal) by the initial pressure of the hot gases inside the SRB. When the force of the gas hits the O-ring it is so powerful that the O-ring is squashed. How long it stays squashed depends on its resiliency, its ability to bounce back and resume its original shape. And, in turn, the resiliency of the O-rings depends on the temperature. The tests showed that the O-rings, which are made of hard rubber (Viton), became less resilient when cold. The hot gases blowing past the O-ring will have enough time to burn away so much of it that it will lose its ability to seal altogether.

Tests and experience were revealing that cold definitely slowed the O-rings' sealing speed. Actual launch experience showed only that the O-rings worked at 53 degrees F., and even at that temperature there had been significant blow-by. No one knew how much colder it could be before the O-rings failed. In 1985, Thiokol began running tests on the joint design but they were proceeding slowly. Other than launch experience, there was no data to prove the O-rings' resistance to cold. The one temperature test that had been run showed that cold temperature *slowed* the sealing speed.

Even though the data base was small, it was the only evidence with which to make a decision. The Thiokol engineers did not feel it was safe to fly. On January 27, they communicated their concern to NASA officials at the Marshall Space Flight Center. Marshall was the NASA center responsible for the development of the SRBs; when Thiokol communicated with NASA, it was always through Marshall. They arranged to discuss the problem over a teleconference which they scheduled for that evening at 5:45 P.M. At this first teleconference, Thiokol engineers told Stanley Reinartz, manager of the Shuttle Projects Office at Marshall, and Judson Lovingood, his deputy, that they did not recommend launching until noon or later in the afternoon of the next day, the 28th. In order that Thiokol could "telefax" its data to Marshall officials at Marshall and at the Kennedy Space Center at Cape Canaveral, and in order to include other, responsible officials, they agreed to a second teleconference at 8:45 P.M.

At 8:45 P.M., the second teleconference began. The senior officials and key participants included, at Morton Thiokol, Utah: (1) Jerald Mason, senior vice president, Wasatch Operations; (2) Calvin Wiggins, vice president and general manager, Space Division, Wasatch; (3) Joe Kilminster, vice president, Space Booster Programs, Wasatch; (4) Bob Lund, vice president, Engineering; (5) Roger Boisjoly, member, Seal Task Force; and (6) Arnie Thompson, supervisor, Rocket Motor Cases; at Kennedy, Stanley Reinartz, and Lawrence Mulloy, manager, SRB Project (both Marshall officials); also at Kennedy, Allan McDonald, director of the Solid Rocket Motor (SRM) Project for Morton Thiokol; at Marshall, George Hardy, deputy director, Science and Engineering, and Judson Lovingood.

Essentially, there were three groups participating in the teleconference: NASA, the Thiokol management, and the Thiokol engineers. Reinartz was the senior NASA official at the teleconference. At this meeting, he had the ultimate say about whether or not to launch. He did have his superior at Marshall, the director, Dr. William Lucas. But NASA rules did not require Dr. Lucas to be present at this meeting. At Thiokol, the senior representative was Mason.

The teleconference began with Thiokol engineers explaining why they believed it unsafe to fly the next day. Their argument hinged on the evidence that the functioning of the O-rings was adversely affected by the cold. By the time preparations for the *Challenger* launch were underway, there had been several incidences of blow-by but not one on a launch where the temperature had been 67 degrees F. or higher. Boisjoly and his colleague, Arnie Thompson, presented this data and recommended not launching until the ambient temperature had reached at least 53 degrees F.

However, NASA officials challenged Thiokol's engineers and the connection they were making between O-ring failure and cold weather. Someone at NASA (and it is not known who) brought up Flight 61-A. That flight had experienced blow-by past the primary O-ring and it had been launched at *75 degrees F.* NASA could not square this evidence with that of Thiokol. Here after all was an instance where there had been an O-ring problem when it had been *warm.*

Boisjoly's explanation was that the blow-by on 61-A had been much less serious than on the colder flights. Moreover, although 61-A may have seemed an anomaly, compared to the total shuttle flight history it fit a pattern. Out of twenty flights at 66 degrees F. or higher only three showed evidence of O-ring malfunction. However, all four flights launched at temperatures below 66 degrees F. showed signs of O-ring malfunction.

Nevertheless, NASA's Marshall officials disagreed with the conclusions the Thiokol engineers were drawing. When asked by Stan Reinartz for his reaction to Thiokol's recommendation not to launch, George Hardy said he was "appalled" but that if that was their recommendation, he could not override it. As for Mulloy, NASA's SRB expert at Marshall, he stated that Thiokol's data was "inconclusive" and objected to the suggestion of Thiokol's engineers that all launches be postponed until the ambient temperature reached 53 degrees F. He pointedly asked, "My God, Thiokol, when do you want me to launch, next April?" This pressure on Thiokol to reconsider the engineers' recommendation was due to NASA's preflight review process that required, as a first step, contractor approval of shuttle readiness.

Since its first days, NASA had had a staff that made safety a priority, and the new willingness to launch at risk to human life surprised many of those who participated in the

teleconference. The attitude at NASA had always required proof that it was safe to fly, until January 27, when NASA officials were demanding rock-solid proof that it was *not* safe to fly. NASA's new attitude astounded Boisjoly. It had the same effect on Thiokol's vice president of engineering, Bob Lund, who reported to the presidential commission on the shuttle accident (the Rogers Commission), "I had never heard those kinds of things (i.e., the pressure to launch) come from people at Marshall."[7] Even some NASA officials were taken aback by the unprecedented relaxation of safety standards. Wilbur Riehl, a veteran NASA engineer involved in the teleconference, wrote a note to a colleague, "Did you ever expect to see MSFC [Marshall Space Flight Center] want to fly when MTI-Wasatch didn't?"[8]

After Boisjoly and Thompson had presented their view and Hardy and Mulloy had responded, Joe Kilminster, one of the four Thiokol managers involved in the teleconference, asked for a five minute "caucus" for Thiokol to discuss the situation among themselves. All agreed, and Thiokol went off the line. Mason, the senior vice president who had said nothing up to this point, took charge in the Thiokol-only discussion. Before anyone else spoke, he said in a soft voice, intending only the managers to hear, "We have to make a management decision."[9]

Boisjoly was furious. He and Thompson were sitting at the table with the managers and had overheard Mason's comment. They knew what Mason was driving at. By speaking of "a management decision," he meant overruling the engineers. Boisjoly and Thompson, alarmed, got to their feet and tried once again to show why Thiokol must uphold the recommendation not to launch. The mood was tense as they again presented their arguments and the data. Everyone knew what NASA wanted to hear: they wanted Thiokol to give them the go-ahead. As the two engineers struggled to convince the managers, Mason looked at them threateningly.[10] It did not take long before Boisjoly and Thompson recognized that the other managers were now impervious to their appeals. They sat down. Again, Mason said in a soft voice, "We have to make a management decision," then turned to Lund. Of the four managers present, Lund had the best understanding of the O-ring problem, since he had worked most closely with the engineers in designing and developing the SRB. That afternoon, when the engineers first heard about the projected cold weather for the next day's launch, they had gone to him and explained why they felt it was unsafe to fly. In the end, they had convinced him, and he in turn had supported their conclusion in the teleconference with NASA. Perhaps more than the engineers, the pressure was on him. Now, Mason turned to him and said, in words that became famous during the Rogers Commission hearings, "It's time to take off your engineer's cap and put on your manager's cap."[11] By the end of the managers' discussion, Lund had changed his mind. He would support the managers' conclusion that, though conditions for launching were not desirable, they were acceptable.[12]

Thiokol resumed its teleconference with NASA and told NASA officials of its final decision. As was required, Mulloy asked Kilminster to put in writing this recommendation to launch, sign it, and "telefax" it to NASA.

. . .

In the early 1970s, the shuttle program was sold to the president and Congress in a way that led inexorably to the arm-twisting in the teleconference and the shuttle disaster the following day. On January 27, only a few individuals, particularly Mulloy at NASA and Mason at Thiokol, were responsible for the reckless decision to launch. However, blame should not be restricted to them. A brief review of NASA's history shows that Nixon's space policy and his NASA administrator, Dr. James Fletcher, were responsible for developing the shuttle despite inadequate funding. It was a disastrous course on which to set NASA for the future.

Under President Kennedy, NASA had the political and financial support to work at a safe pace, never compelled to risk astronauts' lives. Kennedy saw the exploration of space as an important race between the United States and the Soviets. He ordered Vice President Johnson to determine how the United States could beat the Soviets in space. In his report, Johnson captures the Kennedy administration's attitude toward space. He writes, "In the crucial aspects of our Cold War world, in the eyes of the world, first in space is first, period. Second in space is second in everything."[13]

With a feeling that this was perhaps the most important undertaking of his administration, Kennedy poured money and support into space exploration. There would be no cutting corners. Things were going to be done right. Most importantly, safety was made a top priority, even at the expense of losing out to the Soviets in the short run. For example, in 1961, James Webb, NASA's administrator under Kennedy (and Johnson), was under tremendous pressure to attempt to send the first human being into suborbital flight. The Soviets were on the verge of accomplishing the feat themselves, and America was ready. But Webb, like T. Keith Glennan before him, knew that safety had to come first. There was still more testing necessary to guarantee the safety of the astronaut. Not only were these NASA officials deeply concerned for the safety of the astronauts, but they also realized that NASA's long-term interests would be best served by a safe space program. NASA could survive being beaten by the Soviets but could not if it killed astronauts. The essential tests were carried out, and the Soviets did beat the Americans in the race to launch a man into space, with the flight of Maj. Yuri Alexseyevich Gagarin on April 12, 1961. But the United States followed suit thirteen days later with the launching of Alan Shepard.

The Soviet successes continued, yet NASA officials proceeded only when they knew they were ready. In August 1961, the Soviets successfully completed a manned seventeen-orbit mission. Six months later, John Glenn became the first American to orbit Earth. With Kennedy's wholehearted support, NASA embarked on plans for a manned lunar mission.

With testing and the oversight of contractors' work a top priority, the moon mission proceeded cautiously. On Sunday, July 20, 1969, the lunar race ended when the United States successfully landed Apollo XI on the moon, thereby fulfilling Kennedy's promise of landing a man on the moon within the decade. Though the Apollo program spent more years under Johnson's watchful eye than under Kennedy's and the moon landing actually occurred under President Nixon, everyone knew that NASA belonged to JFK. It had been his leadership and support that had created the lunar attempt.

Nixon, more than anyone else, understood that NASA was still Kennedy's agency. Realizing he would get very little political mileage from another space program and recognizing that after the lunar landing the public's interest in space had at least been temporarily satisfied, Nixon did very little for the space agency.[14]

Three options were presented to his administration concerning America's future in space. Option A was presented by a team of NASA scientists perhaps most responsible for the success of the lunar landing. They wanted to develop (1) an economical shuttle to ferry people to and from (2) a space station from which (3) manned and unmanned flights to Mars would proceed. Option A would have cost about $10 billion a year. The idea of a manned flight to Mars appealed to many, and Spiro Agnew actually predicted that Nixon would opt for it. Option B called for an end to manned spaceflight by 1974 and provided a paltry $3 billion for research into possibilities for future manned or unmanned programs. Option C, presented by NASA Administrator Thomas Paine, was an enormous and totally reusable system. To develop this version of the shuttle would cost about $10–$12 billion. In the end, Nixon chose Option B. It was the least he could get away with politically without killing manned spaceflight completely. Paine resigned when he realized that he would not be able to win

from Nixon the kind of financial support he felt NASA should have.[15]

In response to the same budgetary constraints, George Low, acting as NASA administrator until another could be named, forwarded a cheaper plan than Paine's. Because Low cared so strongly about keeping the manned spaceflight programs alive, he went to all lengths to sell the shuttle to the Nixon administration. Though Paine's team had estimated that the cheapest shuttle system that could be developed was $10–$15 billion, Low said it could be done for $8 billion.[16]

Dr. James Fletcher was appointed NASA administrator in 1971. An ambitious man, Fletcher wanted another big, Apollo-like project for NASA to which he could attach his name. Option B did not give Fletcher the funds necessary to develop a manned space shuttle, but he decided to develop the shuttle anyway. Where former NASA administrators demanded the best, Fletcher was willing to proceed with whatever he could get. He continued to prune the shuttle budget, cutting costs that eroded safety margins.[17] Because it was less expensive, NASA agreed to use solid fuel rockets, not previously used by NASA in manned flight because, once ignited, they cannot be shut down. Thus in an emergency they leave the astronauts helpless. Another cost compromise was the elimination of an escape system for the astronauts.

In the end, Fletcher pared the shuttle cost projections down from $8 billion to $5.5 billion plus $1 billion for contingencies. The aggressive Office of Management and Budget (OMB), under the leadership of George Schultz, forced Fletcher back down to the $5.5 billion level.

But some former and current NASA officials recognized immediately the impossibility of putting the shuttle together on Fletcher's budget. John Naugle, who had been at NASA under Webb and was there under Fletcher, knew that the shuttle could never be self-financing as Fletcher predicted. He felt Fletcher was deceiving the public, and he believed that Fletcher should have told Nixon that the shuttle should operate as a purely public, R & D program and assume great costs, or that the United States should get out of manned spaceflight altogether.[18] Dr. Seamans, one of the top three NASA officials under Kennedy and secretary of the Air Force under Nixon, knew that NASA needed much more than Fletcher was projecting to develop the shuttle properly. He sensed that Fletcher was distorting the figures because he had a personal stake in the shuttle, wanting to oversee his own great space program.[19]

Fletcher sold the shuttle to Congress based on the idea that it would be "operational," that it would cover its costs by trucking satellites into space for the military and others. The promises he made in the early 70s were so unrealistic that the shuttle never approached being truly "operational." Much of Fletcher's sales pitch came from a study by Mathematica, a research firm commissioned by NASA to study the shuttle's cost effectiveness. Fletcher used the study to argue that the shuttle could pay for itself if it flew at least thirty times a year.[20] At that launch rate, Fletcher predicted that a pound of payload would only cost $100 and would be commercially competitive. But cost overruns were tremendous. According to the Congressional Budget Office, the cost per pound of payload, adjusted for inflation, is now $5,264 if all the development costs are included. If only the current per flight operational costs are considered, then the price per pound is $2,849.[21]

According to the General Accounting Office, Dr. Fletcher gave "misleading" and "overly optimistic" accounts of projected costs. He had predicted that the cost per launch would be $10.45 million. Not including all the construction costs, the cost today (adjusted for inflation) is $151 million ($279 million including construction costs).[22] Launch operations cost almost fifteen times more than originally predicted.

Boosting the launch rate was an ongoing demand at NASA. Officials at NASA understood that only a higher launch rate would quiet their critics in Congress and the Pentagon, and only a higher launch rate would enable the shuttle to compete with the unmanned Ariane, a French rocket able to send commercial satellites into space cheaply. In March 1985, James Beggs, administrator of NASA said, "The next eighteen months are very critical for the shuttle. If we are going to prove our mettle and demonstrate our capability, we have got to fly out that [flight] manifest."[23] The goal for 1986 was awesome, if not crazy— twenty-four flights.

The impossible promises that Fletcher made in the early 70s thoroughly affected NASA and the shuttle program. NASA had agreed to let economics be the measure of success. If it could produce a cost-efficient space craft, then and only then would the critics on Capitol Hill be silenced. Technological achievements, sending human beings to the moon, or building a reusable "space truck" were no longer enough to satisfy politicians or the public.

In order to succeed, the shuttle had to stay within budget, which meant that many corners had to be cut. Where money was saved, safety was spent. NASA cut back on the shuttle's design. In awarding contracts, NASA gave first priority to cost, not quality. For example, in choosing among design proposals for the SRB, NASA's Source Evaluation Board passed over the monolithic, unsegmented aerojet design that was judged to be safest. The monolithic SRB avoided the problems of joints where pressure and hot gas might escape, but it was too costly.

Moreover, there were cutbacks in testing and NASA oversight of contractors. Between 1974 and 1977, at least five studies found that NASA was shirking its responsibility to test shuttle parts under construction. One study, conducted by thirty-five aeronautical and space experts, found that testing was being "highly compressed"—from sixteen months to three—and called for more testing.[24] But NASA said that more testing would not be "cost effective." Over the course of the shuttle's development, more than half a billion dollars were cut from testing. Furthermore, the number of NASA officials responsible for checking the work of the contractors declined precipitously. NASA oversight of contractors practically stopped altogether. During the Apollo era, the Johnson Space Flight Center had twenty-eight contract monitors, whereas in 1980 it only had two.[25] Dangerously flawed parts went unnoticed. At one point, it was discovered that JetAir, a subcontractor of Rockwell, had doctored X-rays revealing cracks and faulty welding in the Orbiter.[26] Many hands were involved in putting the shuttle together, and NASA had lost control of them and the quality of their work.

Given the lack of funds, did NASA have any alternative to compromising its safety standards? Yes, NASA could have exited from manned spaceflight altogether or at least not committed to a completely manned space program like the shuttle. Except for the publicity that manned spaceflight receives and, consequently, the financial support that accrues to NASA from that favorable coverage, there is apparently very little that people can do in space that could not be done for much less by unmanned programs. Important groups outside NASA were, in fact, making this argument when the shuttle was still on the drawing board. Dr. Seamans, secretary of the Air Force at the time, did not support the idea of a manned shuttle. In his mind, it was unnecessary to have people aboard with all the requisite life support systems just to put satellites into orbit.[27] Even Mars and deeper space can be explored without human beings. Currently, in fact, the Voyager, an unmanned space vehicle, has far surpassed the shuttle in important discoveries.

But NASA officials, especially Fletcher and Low, wanted manned flight. And there were signs that the public wanted it too. Nixon apparently agreed to the shuttle idea primarily because he did not want to be remembered as the president who killed manned spaceflight. Therefore, it was

political obstacles and ambitions among NASA Administrators that brought about the decision to man the shuttle.

· · ·

With all the cost overruns and the shuttle delays, the pressure to live up to that "manifest" to which James Beggs had referred became intense. It was this pressure, constantly in the minds of every NASA manager, that led to risk-taking. With the goal set for twenty-four flights in 1986, the pressure had reached a new high. Even if no one talked explicitly about it, everyone felt it. The contractors, like Thiokol, knew that NASA did not want to hear the recommendations that a launch be delayed, especially if the delay were indefinite as it probably should have been with the O-rings.[28] And NASA managers knew that their superiors did not want to hear that recommendation from them either. In this kind of cover-your-eyes-and-go-for-it setting, loss of life was almost inevitable.

Because Fletcher had accepted an inadequate budget for the shuttle, he deserves much of the blame for risks taken later. However, he is not culpable alone. There were outside observers who were aware of potential dangers but remained silent. The General Accounting Office, a congressional watchdog agency, openly warned of safety compromises that NASA was allowing. But because of the success of the Apollo program, neither Congress nor the press paid much attention.[29] There were also NASA insiders who had access to reports disclosing mechanical flaws in the shuttle. At one time or another, engineers at NASA and at Morton Thiokol urgently warned about weaknesses in the O-rings' design. For several years, NASA engineers at Marshall expressed their concern over the O-ring design. In 1978, John Q. Miller, Marshall's chief of the SRB project, wrote George Hardy that the O-ring design might allow hot gas leaks that could result in "catastrophic failure." But Hardy did not respond to these warnings. He did not question Miller or the other engineers about their concerns, nor did he press Thiokol to address the design problems.[30] By 1981, NASA's engineers had stopped raising concerns about the O-rings even though no design changes were ever made.

And at Morton Thiokol, after flight 41-C where there had been substantial blow-by on one of the primary O-rings, the engineers began seriously to express their fears about the O-ring design. In the year preceding the *Challenger* disaster, the engineers' worries continued to escalate. A task force was established by Thiokol to improve the O-ring design. By midsummer 1985, some of Thiokol's engineers were deeply concerned. The management had been dragging its feet on the redesign effort and not assigning as many people to the task force as were needed. The engineers stopped mincing words. In one memo to the management, Bob Ebeling, one of the task force engineers, expressed how urgent it was that the task force become Thiokol's first priority. He wrote, "HELP! The seal task force is constantly being delayed by every possible means. We wish we could get action by verbal request [they had been frequently going to one of the managers, Joe Kilminster], but such is not the case. This is a red flag."[31]

Roger Boisjoly also wrote a memo: "This letter is written to insure that management is fully aware of the seriousness of the current O-ring erosion problem in the SRM joints from an engineering standpoint. . . . The mistakenly accepted position on the joint problem was to fly without fear of failure and to run a series of design evaluations which would ultimately lead to a solution or at least a significant reduction of the erosion problem. This position is now drastically changed as a result of the SRM 16A nozzle joint erosion [Flight 41-B] which eroded a secondary O-ring with the primary O-ring never sealing. If the same scenario should occur in a field joint (and it could), then it is a jump ball as to the success or failure of the joint because the secondary O-ring cannot respond to the clevis opening rate and may not be capable of pressurization. *The result*

would be a catastrophe of the highest order—loss of human life."[32]

Despite the engineers' appeal to Thiokol's management, the seal redesign effort continued to be neglected. After the accident, the redesign effort was finally made first priority at Thiokol. It went on day and night, and in two and a half months a solution had been found. Before the accident, only eight people out of an employee pool of two thousand had been assigned to the SRB redesign task force. With such a small task force, it would have taken two and a half years to come up with the same solution they found in two months of aggressive research.[33]

Knowledge of the dangers did exist. Still, the pressures to make the shuttle "operational" were such that both Marshall officials and Thiokol managers continued to recommend launching. Everyone knew that the lives of the astronauts and their families were being jeopardized, but the men in power pressed on, willing to take the risks. The end result was a tragedy that could have been avoided.

EPILOGUE

The official Rogers Commission report blamed NASA's system of communication for the shuttle accident. It concluded that sufficient information about the O-ring problem existed before the accident to have prompted an indefinite launch delay.[34] That the launches continued was due, the commission found, to mid-level NASA managers deciding independently that continuing the flights would not endanger the lives of the astronauts. Despite serious questions raised by Thiokol's engineers, these managers (such as Mulloy and Reinartz) never informed their superiors of the gravity of the engineer's concerns. The commission was "troubled by what appears to be a propensity of management at Marshall to contain potentially serious problems and to attempt to resolve them internally rather than communicate them forward."[35] The commission also concluded that NASA had made it clear that they did not welcome shuttle delays, thereby pressuring contractors to override internal dissent and approve flight readiness.[36]

However, due to the candid testimony of two Thiokol employees, Boisjoly and Allan McDonald, certain individuals were blamed, unofficially at least, for the accident. Mulloy seemed particularly responsible, especially after letting Morton Thiokol know how he was unhappy with the engineers' recommendation not to launch. He appeared to have pressured Thiokol into reversing that recommendation. Though NASA offered to continue his employ, he went into early retirement.[37] At Thiokol, the CEO blamed Mason for having "risked the company."[38] Mason also retired early. Kilminster was transferred out of all space programs but continued his job at Thiokol.

Boisjoly and McDonald were demoted for publicly speaking against the company's pro-launch decision. After Boisjoly testified before the Rogers Commission, a senior Thiokol official chastised him for having aired the company's dirty laundry. Sure, tell the truth, he was told, but put the company in a favorable light too. Boisjoly was kept on the payroll but was stripped of any responsibility in the SRB redesign effort.

After Chairman William Rogers vigorously protested the demotion of the two whistle-blowers, Thiokol quickly responded and promoted McDonald to head the SRB design effort. Boisjoly, however, was so stricken by a sense of responsibility for the lives of the astronauts that he could not continue to work and took a leave of absence. For months following the accident, he could not sleep and began to take medication. Finally, a year after the accident, he was well enough to speak publicly about his experience, which he has been doing now for over a year. He states that for personal reasons he will never be able to work on the shuttle again.

Four out of seven of the astronauts' families settled with the U.S. government for, unofficially, more than $750,000. Two of the families have filed suits against NASA,

one for $15 million. A third filed suit against Thiokol. As of August 1987, none of these suits had been settled.

NOTES

1. Malcolm McConnell, *Challenger: A Major Malfunction* (Garden City, N.Y.: Doubleday, 1987), 207–49.
2. Roger Boisjoly, "Company Loyalty and Whistle-blowing: Ethical Decisions and the Space Shuttle Disaster" (videotape), Jan. 7, 1987.
3. Each joint had a primary and a secondary seal.
4. Interview with Boisjoly, Fall 1987.
5. Boisjoly video and Boisjoly interview.
6. McConnell, 165.
7. *Report of the Presidential Commission on the Space Shuttle Challenger Accident* (Washington, DC, June 6,1986), Vol. 1, p. 94.
8. McConnell, 198.
9. Boisjoly interview, and McConnell, 199.
10. Boisjoly interview.
11. *Report of the Presidential Commission*, Vol. 1, 94.
12. *Report of the Presidential Commission*, Vol. 1, 97; and McConnell, 200.
13. Joseph J. Trento, *Prescription for Disaster* (New York: Crown, 1987), 36.
14. Trento, 84–87.
15. Ibid., 93–94.
16. Ibid., 102–3.
17. Fletcher's soft stand on safety is a point Trento makes throughout *Prescription for Disaster*.
18. Trento, 118–21.
19. Ibid., 112–13.
20. McConnell, 41.
21. Stuart Diamond, "NASA Wasted Billions, Federal Audits Disclose, *New York Times*, April 12, 1987, 1, 1:1.
22. Ibid.
23. McConnell, 62.
24. Ibid.
25. Ibid.
26. Ibid.
27. Trento, 112.
28. "The [Rogers] Commission concluded that the Thiokol management reversed its position and recommended the launch of 51-L [the *Challenger*], at the urging of Marshall and contrary to the views of its engineers in order to accommodate a major customer." *Report of the Presidential Commission*, Vol. 1, 104.
29. McConnell, Ch. 6, "The Spellbound Press."

30. *Report of the Presidential Commission,* Vol. 1, 123–24.
31. McConnell, 180.
32. *Report of the Presidential Commission,* Vol. 1, 139 (emphasis added).
33. Boisjoly interview.
34. *Report of the Presidential Commission,* Vol. 1, 148.
35. Ibid., 104.
36. Ibid.
37. The Associated Press, "Ex-Shuttle Rocket Chief Quits Space Agency," *New York Times,* July 17, 1986, V, 19:1.
38. Boisjoly interview.
39. Boisjoly video.

The Space Shuttle *Columbia**

On the morning of January 16th, 2003, the space shuttle *Columbia* took off from the Kennedy Space Center in Florida and reached orbit safely. The next day, as NASA technicians were reviewing video imagery of the liftoff, they noticed that a large piece of insulating foam had detached from an external tank and hit the shuttle's left wing at high speed. The size of the object raised immediate concerns about possible damage to the shuttle, but none of the available camera angles provided a clear view of the impact or of the wing. Over the next two weeks, while the shuttle was in orbit, NASA engineers and managers met and corresponded about the foam strike to decide what, if anything, should be done. Several engineers believed that the impact would expose the shuttle to severe danger as it tried to reenter the atmosphere. Some thought that NASA should request outside help to obtain in-orbit photographs of the shuttle's wing. Others were convinced that there was no real safety concern.

In the end, no steps were taken, either to obtain a clearer view of the shuttle's wing or to alert the crew to potential danger. As the *Columbia* entered the Earth's atmosphere on February 1st, ground controllers detected abnormal readings from some of the shuttle's temperature sensors. Data was then lost altogether from several sensors clustered on the shuttle's left wing. Within minutes, all contact with the *Columbia* was abruptly severed. At nine o'clock, the shuttle disintegrated as it was hurtling through the atmosphere at eighteen times the speed of sound. The seven astronauts onboard were killed.

Within days of the shuttle's destruction, a special committee was formed—the Columbia Accident Investigation Board (CAIB)—to investigate the causes of the accident. The board was asked not only to discover the immediate, technical causes of the shuttle's explosion, but also to give a broader assessment of NASA's institutional culture. The board therefore asked who should have done more to ensure that the danger was adequately recognized, and why those expressing concern were overruled. This second part of the investigation was especially important in light of the 1986 *Challenger* disaster, after which the Rogers Commission had issued broad recommendations for the overhaul of NASA safety, management, scheduling, and decision-making procedures. The CAIB was asked to assess whether these recommendations had been followed.

The CAIB report confirmed that the foam had damaged the shuttle's wing and caused its destruction. It singled out high-ranking managers by name and raised questions about their decision-making in the days (and years) before the shuttle's destruction. It also suggested that NASA had failed to fully implement the changes recommended years

---

*Alex Zakaras wrote the introduction and selected the excerpts presented in this section.

earlier by the Rogers Commission. Many of the problems that contributed to the *Challenger's* destruction had resurfaced—including intense schedule pressure and "inadequate concern over deviations from expected performance." In fact, the specific deviation in question here—the shedding of foam from the external tanks during the shuttle's ascent—had a long history. It had occurred on dozens of earlier flights, and had been recognized as a safety concern even before the *Challenger's* launch in 1986. Over time, however, since it had caused only minor damage, it came to seem a minor concern and an "accepted risk." The parallels to the *Challenger* are striking: Under pressure to stay on schedule, NASA engineers had once more ceased treating small deviations from the shuttle design as serious safety concerns.

The following excerpts from the report examine the two-week period during which the *Columbia* was in orbit and the several missed opportunities to recognize the full extent of the imminent danger. These excerpts highlight the decisions of two individuals in particular: Rodney Rocha, the chief engineer for the Thermal Protection System, and Linda Ham, the chair of the mission management team for this particular *Columbia* flight.

EXCERPTS FROM THE CAIB REPORT, AUGUST 2003

Note: Columbia's *final flight was numbered STS-107, and is sometimes described by that name in the report. The number 107 does not correspond to the total number of flights flown by NASA shuttles and does not designate this flight's location in a sequence of flights. (For instance, STS-112 was flown before STS-107). STS-107 was in fact the shuttle program's 113th flight, and* Columbia's *28th.*

FLIGHT DAY ONE–JANUARY 16, 2003

As soon as *Columbia* reached orbit, . . . NASA's Intercenter Photo Working Group began reviewing liftoff imagery by video

and film cameras on the launch pad and at other sites at and nearby the Kennedy Space Center. The debris strike was not seen during the first review of video imagery by tracking cameras, but it was noticed at 9:30A.M. EST the next day, Flight Day Two, by Intercenter Photo Working Group engineers at Marshall Space Flight Center. Within an hour, Intercenter Photo Working Group personnel at Kennedy also identified the strike on higher-resolution film images that had just been developed. The images revealed that a large piece of debris from the left bipod area of the External Tank had struck the Orbiter's left wing. . . .

First Imagery Request

Because they had no sufficiently resolved pictures with which to determine potential damage, and having never seen such a large piece of debris strike the Orbiter so late in ascent, Intercenter Photo Working Group members decided to ask for ground-based imagery of *Columbia*. . . .

To accomplish this, the Intercenter Photo Working Group's Chair, Bob Page, contacted Wayne Hale, the Shuttle Program Manager for Launch Integration at Kennedy Space Center, to request imagery of *Columbia's* left wing on-orbit. Hale, who agreed to explore the possibility, holds a Top Secret clearance and was familiar with the process for requesting military imaging from his experience as a Mission Control Flight Director. This would be the first of three discrete requests for imagery by a NASA engineer or manager. [All three were eventually thwarted, and no imagery was ever obtained.]. . .

Shortly after confirming the debris hit, Intercenter Photo Working Group members distributed an "L + 1" (Launch plus one day) report and digitized clips of the strike via e-mail throughout the NASA and contractor communities. This report provided an initial view of the foam strike and served as the basis for subsequent decisions and actions. . . .

FLIGHT DAY TWO–JANUARY 17, 2003

Already, by Friday afternoon (Flight Day Two), Shuttle Program managers and working engineers had different levels of concern about what the foam strike might have meant. After reviewing available film, Intercenter Photo Working Group engineers believed the Orbiter may have been damaged by the strike. They wanted on-orbit images of *Columbia*'s left wing to confirm their suspicions and initiated action to obtain them. Boeing and United Space Alliance engineers decided to work through the holiday weekend to analyze the strike. At the same time, high-level managers Ralph Roe, head of the Shuttle Program Office of Vehicle Engineering, and Bill Reeves, from United Space Alliance, voiced a lower level of concern. It was at this point, before any analysis had started, that Shuttle Program managers officially shared their belief that the strike posed no safety issues, and that there was no need for a review to be conducted over the weekend. The following is a 4:28 P.M. Mission Evaluation Room manager log entry:

> Bill Reeves called, after a meeting with Ralph Roe, it is confirmed that USA/Boeing will not work the debris issue over the weekend, but will wait till Monday when the films are released. . . . the energy/speed of impact at + 81 seconds, and the toughness of the RCC[1] are two main factors for the low concern. Also, analysis supports single mission safe re-entry for an impact that penetrates the system." [USA = United Space Alliance, LCC = Launch Commit Criteria]. . .

Shortly [thereafter], the deputy manager of Johnson Space Center Shuttle Engineering notified Rodney Rocha, NASA's designated chief engineer for the Thermal Protection System, of the strike and the approximate debris size. It was Rocha's responsibility to coordinate NASA engineering resources and work with contract engineers at United Space Alliance, who together would form a Debris Assessment Team. . . . Engineering signaled that the debris strike was initially classified as

"out-of-family"[2] and therefore of greater concern than . . . debris strikes [affecting previous shuttle flights]. At about the same time, the Intercenter Photo Working Group's L + 1 report, containing both video clips and still images of the debris strike, was e-mailed to engineers and technical managers both inside and outside of NASA. . . .

FLIGHT DAY FOUR–JANUARY 19, 2003

On Sunday, Rodney Rocha e-mailed a Johnson Space Center Engineering Directorate manager to ask if a Mission Action Request was in progress for *Columbia's* crew to visually inspect the left wing for damage. Rocha never received an answer. . . .

FLIGHT DAY SIX–JANUARY 21, 2003

At 7:00 A.M., the Debris Assessment Team briefed Don McCormack, the chief Mission Evaluation Room manager, that the foam's source and size was similar to what struck STS-112,[3] and that an analysis of measured versus predicted tile damage from STS-87[4] was being scrutinized by Boeing. An hour later, McCormack related this information to the Mission Management Team at its first meeting [held after the intervening Martin Luther King Day holiday]. . . . The transcript below is the first record of an official discussion of the debris impact at a Mission Management Team meeting.

> LINDA HAM: "Alright, I know you guys are looking at the debris."
> McCORMACK: "Yeah, as everybody knows, we took a hit on the, somewhere on the left wing leading edge and the photo TV guys have completed I think, pretty much their work although I'm sure they are reviewing their stuff and they've given us an approximate size for the debris and approximate area for where it came from and approximately where it hit, so we are talking about doing some sort of parametric type of analysis and also we're talking about what you can do in the event we have some damage there."
> HAM: ". . . I was thinking that the flight rationale . . . from STS-112. . . . I'm not sure that the

area is exactly the same where the foam came from but the carrier properties and density of the foam wouldn't do any damage. So we ought to pull that along with the 87 data where we had some damage, pull this data from 112 or whatever flight it was and make sure that . . . you know I hope that we had good flight rationale then."

McCormack: "Yeah, and we'll look at that, you mentioned 87, you know we saw some fairly significant damage in the area between RCC panels 8 and 9 and the main landing gear door on the bottom on STS-87 we did some analysis prior to STS-89 so uh . . ."

Ham: "And I'm really, I don't think there is much we can do so it's not really a factor during the flight because there is not much we can do about it. But what I'm really interested in is making sure our flight rationale to go was good, and maybe this is foam from a different area and I'm not sure and it may not be correlated, but you can try to see what we have."

McCormack: "Okay."

After the meeting, the rationale for continuing to fly after the STS-112 foam loss was sent to Ham for review.[5] She then exchanged e-mails with her boss, Space Shuttle Program Manager Ron Dittemore: . . .

-----*Original Message*-----

From: HAM, LINDA J. (JSC-MA2) (NASA)

Sent: Tuesday, January 21, 2003, 11:14 A.M.

To: DITTEMORE, RONALD D. (JSC-MA) (NASA)

Subject: FW: ET Briefing—STS-112 Foam Loss

You probably can't open the attachment. But, the ET rationale for flight for the STS-112 loss of foam was lousy. Rationale states we haven't changed anything, we haven't experienced any "safety of flight" damage in 112 flights, risk of loss of bi-pod ramp TPS is same as previous flights. . . . So ET is safe to fly with no added risk

Rationale was lousy then and still is. . .

[ET = External Tank]

Ham's focus on examining the rationale for continuing to fly after the foam problems with STS-87 and STS-112 indicates that her attention had already shifted from the [immediate] threat the foam posed [to the orbiting shuttle] to the downstream implications of the foam strike. Ham was due to serve . . . as the launch integration manager for the next mission, STS-114. If the Shuttle Program's rationale to fly with foam loss was found to be flawed, STS-114, due to be launched in about a month, would have to be delayed per NASA rules that require serious problems to be resolved before the next flight. An STS-114 delay could in turn delay completion of the International Space Station's Node 2, which was a high-priority goal for NASA managers. . . .

Second Imagery Request

Responding to concerns from his employees who were participating in the Debris Assessment Team, United Space Alliance manager Bob White called Lambert Austin [the head of the Space Shuttle Systems Integration at Johnson Space Center] on Flight Day Six to ask what it would take to get imagery of *Columbia* on orbit. They discussed the analytical debris damage work plan, as well as the belief of some integration team members that such imaging might be beneficial.

Austin subsequently telephoned the Department of Defense Manned Space Flight Support Office representative to ask about actions necessary to get imagery of *Columbia* on orbit. Austin emphasized that this was merely information gathering, not a request for action. This call indicates that Austin was unfamiliar with NASA/National Imagery and Mapping Agency imagery request procedures.

An e-mail that Lieutenant Colonel Timothy Lee sent to Don McCormack the following day shows that the Defense Department had begun to implement Austin's request. . . .

First Debris Assessment Team Meeting

On Flight Day Six, the Debris Assessment Team [co-chaired by Rodney Rocha] held its first formal meeting to finalize Orbiter damage estimates and their potential consequences. Some participants joined the proceedings via conference call. [Among the topics they discussed were the results of a mathematical modeling tool called "Crater," which a team of engineers at Boeing had used to estimate the damage that might have been caused by the foam strike.] Crater was normally used only to predict whether small debris, usually ice on the External Tank, would pose a threat to the Orbiter during launch. . . . [in this case,] engineers used Crater to analyze a piece of debris that was at maximum 640 times larger in volume than the pieces of debris used to calibrate and validate the Crater model. . . . Therefore, the use of Crater in this new and very different situation compromised NASA's ability to accurately predict debris damage. . . .

For the Thermal Protection System tile, Crater predicted damage deeper than the actual tile thickness. This seemingly alarming result suggested that the debris that struck *Columbia* would have exposed the Orbiter's underlying aluminum airframe to extreme temperatures, resulting in a possible burn-through during re-entry. Debris Assessment Team engineers discounted the possibility of burn-through for two reasons. First, the results of calibration tests with small projectiles showed that Crater predicted a deeper penetration than would actually occur. Second, the Crater equation does not take into account the increased density of a tile's lower "densified" layer, which is much stronger than tile's fragile outer layer. Therefore, engineers judged that the actual damage from the large piece of foam lost on STS-107 would not be as severe as Crater predicted, and assumed that the debris did not penetrate the Orbiter's skin. . . . The assumptions and uncertainty embedded in this analysis were never fully presented to the Mission Evaluation Room or the Mission Management Team.

Third Imagery Request

After two hours of discussing the Crater results and the need to learn precisely where the debris had hit *Columbia,* the Debris Assessment Team assigned its NASA Co-Chair, Rodney Rocha, to pursue a request for imagery of the vehicle on-orbit. Each team member supported the idea to seek imagery from an outside source. Rather than working the request up the usual mission chain of command through the Mission Evaluation Room to the Mission Management Team to the Flight Dynamics Officer, the Debris Assessment Team agreed, largely due to a lack of participation by Mission Management Team and Mission Evaluation Room managers, that Rocha would pursue the request through his division, the Engineering Directorate at Johnson Space Center. Rocha sent the following e-mail to Paul Shack shortly after the meeting adjourned.

-----*Original Message*-----

From: ROCHA, ALAN R. (RODNEY) (JSC-ES2) (NASA)

Sent: Tuesday, January 21, 2003 4:41 P.M.

To: SHACK, PAUL E. (JSC-EA) (NASA); HAMILTON, DAVID A. (DAVE) (JSC-EA) (NASA); MILLER, GLENN J. (JSC-EA) (NASA)

Cc: SERIALE-GRUSH, MOYCE M. (JSC-EA) (NASA); ROGERS, JOSEPH E. (JOE) (JSC-ES2) (NASA); GALBREATH, GREGORY F. (GREG) (JSC-ES2) (NASA)

Subject: STS-107 Wing Debris Impact, Request for Outside Photo-Imaging Help

Paul and Dave, The meeting participants (Boeing, USA, NASA ES2 and ES3, KSC) all agreed we will always have big uncertainties . . . until we get definitive, better, clearer photos of the wing and body underside. Without better images it will be very difficult to even bound the problem and initialize thermal, trajectory, and structural analyses. . . .

Can we petition (beg) for outside agency assistance? We are asking for Frank Benz with Ralph Roe or Ron Dittemore to ask for such. Some of the old timers here remember we got such help in the early 1980's when we had missing tile concerns.

Despite some nay-sayers, there are some options for the team to talk about: On-orbit thermal conditioning for the major structure, . . . limiting high cross-range de-orbit entries, constraining right or left hand turns during the Heading Alignment Circle (only if there is struc. damage to the RCC panels to the extent it affects flight control.

[USA = United Space Alliance, NASA ES2, ES3 = separate divisions of the Johnson Space Center Engineering Directorate, KSC = Kennedy Space Center]

Routing the request through the Engineering department led in part to it being viewed by Shuttle Program managers as a non-critical engineering desire rather than a critical operational need. . . .

FLIGHT DAY SEVEN–JANUARY 22, 2003

On the morning of Flight Day Seven, Wayne Hale responded to the earlier Flight Day Two request from Bob Page (See "First Imagery Request" above) and a call from Lambert Austin on Flight Day Five, during which Austin mentioned that "some analysts" from the Debris Assessment Team were interested in getting imagery. Hale called a Department of Defense representative at Kennedy Space . . . and asked that the military start the planning process for imaging *Columbia* on orbit.

Within an hour, the Defense Department representative at NASA contacted U.S. Strategic Command (USSTRATCOM) at Colorado's Cheyenne Mountain Air Force Station and asked what it would take to get imagery of Columbia on orbit. (This call was similar to Austin's call to the Department of Defense Manned Space Flight Support

Office in that the caller characterized it as "information gathering" rather than a request for action.) A representative from the USSTRATCOM Plans Office initiated actions to identify ground-based and other imaging assets that could execute the request.

Hale's earlier call to the Defense Department representative at Kennedy Space Center was placed without authorization from Mission Management Team Chair Linda Ham. Also, the call was made to a Department of Defense Representative who was not the designated liaison for handling such requests. In order to initiate the imagery request through official channels, Hale also called Phil Engelauf at the Mission Operations Directorate, told him he had started Defense Department action, and asked if Engelauf could have the Flight Dynamics Officer at Johnson Space Center make an official request to the Cheyenne Mountain Operations Center. Engelauf started to comply with Hale's request.

After the Department of Defense representatives were called, Lambert Austin telephoned Linda Ham to inform her about the imagery requests that he and Hale had initiated. Austin also told Wayne Hale that he had asked Lieutenant Colonel Lee at the Department of Defense Manned Space Flight Support Office about what actions were necessary to get on-orbit imagery.

Cancellation of the Request for Imagery

At 8:30 A.M., the NASA Department of Defense liaison officer called USSTRATCOM and cancelled the request for imagery. The reason given for the cancellation was that NASA had identified its own in-house resources and no longer needed the military's help. The NASA request to the Department of Defense to prepare to image *Columbia* on-orbit was both made and rescinded within 90 minutes.

The Board has determined that the following sequence of events likely occurred within that 90-minute period. Linda Ham asked Lambert Austin if he knew who was requesting the imagery. After admitting his participation in helping to make the imagery request outside the official chain of command and without first gaining Ham's permission, Austin referred to his conversation with United Space Alliance Shuttle Integration manager Bob White on Flight Day Six, in which White had asked Austin, in response to White's Debris Assessment Team employee concerns, what it would take to get Orbiter imagery. Even though Austin had already informed Ham of the request for imagery, Ham later called Mission Management Team members Ralph Roe, Manager of the Space Shuttle Vehicle Engineering Office, Loren Shriver, United Space Alliance Deputy Program Manager for Shuttle, and David Moyer, the on-duty Mission Evaluation Room manager, to determine the origin of the request and to confirm that there was a "requirement" for a request. Ham also asked Flight Director Phil Engelauf if he had a "requirement" for imagery of *Columbia*'s left wing. These individuals all stated that they had not requested imagery, were not aware of any "official" requests for imagery, and could not identify a "requirement" for imagery. Linda Ham later told several individuals that nobody had a requirement for imagery.

What started as a request by the Intercenter Photo Working Group to seek outside help in obtaining images on Flight Day Two in anticipation of analysts' needs had become by Flight Day Six an actual engineering request by members of the Debris Assessment Team, made informally through Bob White to Lambert Austin, and formally in Rodney Rocha's e-mail to Paul Shack. These requests had then caused Lambert Austin and Wayne Hale to contact Department of Defense representatives. When Ham officially terminated the actions that the Department of Defense had begun, she effectively terminated both the Intercenter Photo Working Group request and the Debris Assessment Team request. While Ham has publicly stated she did not know of the Debris Assessment Team members' desire

for imagery, she never asked them directly if the request was theirs, even though they were the team analyzing the foam strike.

Also on Flight Day Seven, Ham raised concerns that the extra time spent maneuvering *Columbia* to make the left wing visible for imaging would unduly impact the mission schedule; for example, science experiments would have to stop while the imagery was taken. According to personal notes obtained by the Board:

> Linda Ham said it was no longer being pursued since even if we saw something, we couldn't do anything about it. The Program didn't want to spend the resources.

Shuttle managers, including Ham, also said they were looking for very small areas on the Orbiter and that past imagery resolution was not very good. The Board notes that no individuals in the STS-107 operational chain of command had the security clearance necessary to know about National imaging capabilities. Additionally, no evidence has been uncovered that anyone from NASA, United Space Alliance, or Boeing sought to determine the expected quality of images and the difficulty and costs of obtaining Department of Defense assistance. Therefore, members of the Mission Management Team were making critical decisions about imagery capabilities based on little or no knowledge. . . .

After canceling the Department of Defense imagery request, Linda Ham continued to explore whether foam strikes posed a safety of flight issue. She sent an e-mail to Lambert Austin and Ralph Roe. . . .

-----*Original Message*-----

From: HAM, LINDA J. (JSC-MA2) (NASA)

Sent: Wednesday,   January   22,   2003 9:33 A.M.

To: AUSTIN, LAMBERT D. (JSC-MS) (NASA); ROE, RALPH R. (JSC-MV) (NASA)

Subject: ET Foam Loss

Can we say that for any ET foam lost, no "safety of flight" damage can occur to the Orbiter because of the density?

[ET = External Tank]

Responses included the following:

-----Original Message-----

From: AUSTIN, LAMBERT D. (JSC-MS) (NASA)

Sent: Wednesday, January 22, 2003, 3:22 P.M.

To: HAM, LINDA J. (JSC-MA2) (NASA)

Cc: WALLACE, RODNEY O. (ROD) (JSC-MS2) (NASA) ; NOAH, DONALD S. (DON) (JSC-MS) (NASA)

Subject: RE: ET Foam Loss

NO. I will cover some of the pertinent rationale. . . . there could be more if I spent more time thinking about it. . . . it is not possible to PRECLUDE a potential catastrophic event as a result of debris impact damage to the flight elements. As regards the Orbiter, both windows and tiles are areas of concern.

. . . While there is much tolerance to window and tile damage, ET foam loss can result in impact damage that under subsequent entry environments can lead to loss of structural integrity of the Orbiter area impacted or a penetration in a critical function area that results in loss of that function. . . .

-----Original Message-----

From: SCHOMBURG, CALVIN (JSC-EA) (NASA)

Sent: Wednesday, January 22, 2003, 10:53 A.M.

To: ROE, RALPH R. JSC-MV) (NASA)

Subject: RE: ET Foam Loss

No—the amount of damage ET foam can cause to the TPS material-tiles is based on the amount of impact energy—the size of the piece and its velocity (from just after pad clear until about 120 seconds—after that it will not hit or it will not have enough energy to cause any damage)—it is a pure kinetic problem—there is a size that can cause enough damage to a tile that enough of the material is lost that we could burn a hole through the skin and have a bad day—(loss of vehicle and crew—about 200–400 tile locations (out of the 23,000 on the lower surface)—the foam usually fails in small popcorn pieces—that is why it is vented—to make small hits—the two or three times we have been hit with a piece as large as the one this flight—we got a gouge about 8–10 inches long about 2 inches wide and 3/4 to an 1 inch deep across two or three tiles. That is what I expect this time—nothing worse. If that is all we get we have no problem—will have to replace a couple of tiles but nothing else.

[ET = External Tank, TPS = Thermal Protection System] . . .

The Board notes that these e-mail exchanges indicate that senior Mission Management Team managers, including the Shuttle Program Manager, Mission Management Team Chair, head of Space Shuttle Systems Integration, and a Shuttle tile expert, correctly identified the technical bounds of the foam strike problem and its potential seriousness. Mission managers understood that the relevant question was not whether foam posed a safety-of-flight issue—it did—but rather whether the observed foam strike contained sufficient kinetic energy to cause damage that could lead to a burn-through. Here, all the key managers were asking the right question and admitting the danger. . . . Yet little follow-through occurred with either the request for imagery or the Debris Assessment Team analysis. . . .

Second Debris Assessment Team Meeting

Some but not all of the engineers attending the Debris Assessment Team's second meeting had learned that the Shuttle Program was not pursuing imaging of potentially damaged areas. What team members did not realize was the Shuttle Program's decision not to seek on-orbit imagery was not necessarily a direct and final response to their request. Rather, the "no" was partly in response to the Kennedy Space Center action initiated by United Space Alliance engineers and managers and finally by Wayne Hale.

Not knowing that this was the case, Debris Assessment Team members speculated as to why their request was rejected and whether their analysis was worth pursuing without new imagery. Discussion then moved on to whether the Debris Assessment Team had a "mandatory need" for Department of Defense imaging. Most team members, when asked by the Board what "mandatory need" meant, replied with a shrug of their shoulders. They believed the need for imagery was obvious: without better pictures, engineers would be unable to make reliable predictions of the depth and area of damage caused by a foam strike that was outside of the experience base. However, team members concluded that although their need was important, they could not cite a "mandatory" requirement for the request. Analysts on the Debris Assessment Team were in the unenviable position of wanting images to more accurately assess damage while simultaneously needing to prove to Program managers, as a result of their assessment, that there was a need for images in the first place.

After the meeting adjourned, Rocha read the 11:45 A.M. e-mail from Paul Shack, which said that the Orbiter Project was not requesting any outside imaging help. Rocha called Shack to ask if Shack's boss, Johnson Space Center engineering director Frank Benz, knew about the request. Rocha then sent several e-mails consisting of questions about the ongoing analyses and details on the Shuttle Program's cancellation of the imaging request. An e-mail that he did not send but instead printed out and shared with a colleague follows.

"In my humble technical opinion, this is the wrong (and bordering on irresponsible) answer from the SSP and Orbiter not to request additional imaging help from any outside

source. I must emphasize (again) that severe enough damage (3 or 4 multiple tiles knocked out down to the densification layer) combined with the heating and resulting damage to the underlying structure at the most critical location (viz., MLG door/wheels/tires/hydraulics or the X1191 spar cap) could present potentially grave hazards. The engineering team will admit it might not achieve definitive high confidence answers without additional images, but, without action to request help to clarify the damage visually, we will guarantee it will not. Can we talk to Frank Benz before Friday's MMT? Remember the NASA safety posters everywhere around stating, "If it's not safe, say so"? Yes, it's that serious." [SSP = Space Shuttle Program, MLG = Main Landing Gear, MMT = Mission Management Team]

When asked why he did not send this e-mail, Rocha replied that he did not want to jump the chain of command. Having already raised the need to have the Orbiter imaged with Shack, he would defer to management's judgment on obtaining imagery.

Even after the imagery request had been cancelled by Program management, engineers in the Debris Assessment Team and Mission Control continued to analyze the foam strike. A structural engineer in the Mechanical, Maintenance, Arm and Crew Systems sent an e-mail to a flight dynamics engineer that stated:

> There is lots of speculation as to extent of the damage, and we could get a burn through into the wheel well upon entry. . . .

FLIGHT DAY EIGHT—JANUARY 23, 2003

Third Debris Assessment Team Meeting

The Debris Assessment Team met for the third time Thursday (Flight Day Eight) afternoon to review updated impact analyses. Engineers noted that there were no alternate re-entry trajectories that the Orbiter could fly to substantially reduce heating in the general area of the foam strike. Engineers also presented final debris trajectory data that included three debris size estimates to cover the continuing uncertainty about the size of the debris. Team members were told that imaging would not be forthcoming. In the face of this denial, the team discussed whether to include a presentation slide supporting their desire for images of the potentially damaged area. Many still felt it was a valid request and wanted their concerns aired at the upcoming Mission Evaluation Room brief and then at the Mission Management Team level. Eventually, the idea of including a presentation slide about the imaging request was dropped.

Just prior to attending the third assessment meeting, tile expert Calvin Schomburg and Rodney Rocha met to discuss foam impacts from other missions. Schomburg implied that the STS-107 foam impact was in the Orbiter's experience base and represented only a maintenance issue. Rocha disagreed and argued about the potential for burnthrough on re-entry. Calvin Schomburg stated a belief that if there was severe damage to the tiles, "nothing could be done." Both then joined the meeting already in progress. . . .

EPILOGUE

To put the decisions made during the flight of STS-107 into perspective, the Board asked NASA to determine if there were options for the safe return of the STS-107 crew. In this study, NASA was to assume that the extent of damage to the leading edge of the left wing was determined by national imaging assets or by a spacewalk. NASA was then asked to evaluate the possibility of:

1. Rescuing the STS-107 crew by launching *Atlantis*. *Atlantis* would be hurried to the pad, launched, rendezvous with *Columbia*, and take on *Columbia*'s crew for a return. It was assumed that NASA would be willing to expose *Atlantis* and its crew to the same possibility of External Tank bipod foam loss that damaged *Columbia*.

2. Repairing damage to *Columbia*'s wing on orbit. In the repair scenario, astronauts would use onboard materials to rig a temporary fix. Some of *Columbia*'s cargo might be jettisoned and a different re-entry profile would be flown to lessen heating on the left wing leading edge. The crew would be prepared to bail out if the wing structure was predicted to fail on landing.

[Both alternatives were ultimately found feasible, though risky.]

NOTES

1. Reinforced Carbon-Carbon (RCC) is a light gray, all-carbon composite. RCC, along with inconel foil (metal) insulators and quartz blankets, protect the orbiter's nose, chin, and wing leading edges from the highest expected temperatures and aerodynamic forces.

2. A problem is designated "in-family," according to the Board report, if it is "previously experienced, analyzed, and understood."

3. STS-112, flown in October 2002, was the most recent instance of foam debris causing damage to an orbiter. The impact left a crater that was approximately 4 inches wide and 3 inches deep.

4. During the launch of STS-87 *(Columbia)* on November 19, 1997, a "debris event" drew attention to the problem of debris-shedding and damage to the Shuttle. According to the CAIB report: "Post-landing inspection of the Orbiter noted 308 hits, with 244 on the lower surface and 109 larger than an inch. The foam loss from the External Tank thrust panels was suspected as the most probable cause of the Orbiter Thermal Protection System damage. . . . An investigation was conducted to determine the cause of the material loss and the actions required to prevent a recurrence."

5. Because the bipod ramp shedding on STS-112 was significant, both in size and in the damage it caused, and because it occurred only two flights before [the *Columbia*'s final flight (STS-107)], the Board investigated NASA's rationale to continue flying. [This decision was] among those most directly linked to the STS-107 accident. Had the foam loss during STS-112 been classified as a more serious threat, managers might have responded differently when they heard about the foam strike on STS-107. Alternately, in the face of the increased risk, STS-107 might not have flown at all.

Comment

Roger Boisjoly and Arnie Thompson argued long and hard, but failed to convince the managers of Morton Thiokol to recommend against launching the shuttle. We are not told whether Boisjoly and Thompson thought about threatening to resign or publicly protesting in other ways. But if they did, they might understandably have rejected public protest, expecting that it would lead to their dismissal and would leave no high-level defenders of safety standards at Thiokol or NASA. (They enjoyed neither the public prominence nor the career alternatives that George Shultz had.) In judging whether Boisjoly and Thompson should have done more (or less), keep in mind that they had to decide their own course of action when they had only rough estimates of the probabilities of a successful or disastrous launch. Also, by remaining on the job, their subsequent action (including their testimony) in defense of improved safety standards may have been more effective. However, it can be argued that had they publicly protested or threatened to resign before the launch, they might have actually stopped the launch and prevented the disaster.

Many discussions of official disobedience emphasize how much trouble officials get into by publicly protesting, leaking information, or otherwise employing unauthorized tactics in pursuit of a just cause. The *Challenger* case, in contrast, reveals the problems that officials can have simply by doing their jobs well, even if they do not disobey their superiors or violate any procedures. The case also suggests the need to look beyond the immediate decisions and decision makers to those policies and policy makers who create the conditions that lead to bad decisions. What practices at Thiokol and NASA hindered people like Boisjoly and Thompson from doing their jobs well? Who was responsible for those practices? How might the practices be changed so as to make official disobedience less necessary and internal criticism more effective?

Almost two decades later the shuttle failed again, disastrously, and the dissent that would have been appropriate failed to be expressed at all, also disastrously. Earlier, the dissent stood a reasonable chance of preventing the launch. Later, dissent offered little hope of saving the crew. The *Columbia* mission should have benefited from the lessons of the *Challenger*'s failure. Yet many of the same or similar problems of communication and decision-making remained. Many officials, including those in Congress and the executive branch, who failed to change the practices and procedures of NASA, and who put increasing pressure on the budget and the priorities of the agency, could be blamed. But this conclusion, taken alone, seems to let off the moral hook those immediately responsible for the *Columbia* disaster. Given that recommended changes should have been made and that the organizational culture should have been reformed, what should the officials have done once they recognized that the foam may have damaged the shuttle wing?

In the *Challenger* case, the whistle was blown and no one listened. (Or at least none of the key decision makers listened.) In the *Columbia* case, the whistle was not blown and no one thought he or she was the one to blow it. Those involved in the *Columbia* disaster lost at least three opportunities to find out that the risk of damage was higher than initially assumed: requesting photo imagery, questioning the "Crater" analysis, and asking the crew to conduct a visual inspection. Why were these opportunities lost and who was responsible for losing them? Rocha's unsent email (his "humble opinion") is the closest any of the officials in this case get to blowing the whistle. Is he to be faulted for not sending it?

Ham said that "what I'm really interested in is making sure our flight rationale to go was good. . . ." Some have suggested that she and other officials were more worried about defending their preparations for this launch and their plans for a future launch (which Ham was to direct) than in ensuring the safety of the crew in the current flight. Such considerations about policy are relevant for any official in a position of continuing responsibility. The question therefore is whether the right balance was struck in this situation.

Ham and others reassured themselves that, whatever the risk of damage, "it's not really a factor during the flight because there is not much we can do about it." They were right that neither the rescue nor the repair scenario had a high chance of success. Only afterward did NASA analysts conclude that both were feasible and even then they pronounced them risky. Should officials have confronted and debated that question more directly? If they had, they might have faced the dilemma of choosing between sending a rescue mission (with a high risk of losing its crew but some chance of bringing back both crews) or letting the current mission return as usual (with an even higher risk of losing its crew but no risk of sacrificing a rescue crew). Making the choice under the pressure of public scrutiny and debate would have intensified its difficulty.

Recommended Reading

A now classic statement of the theory of civil disobedience is John Rawls, *A Theory of Justice* (Cambridge, Mass.: Harvard University Press, 1971), pp. 363–91. Ronald Dworkin develops and applies some important distinctions in *A Matter of Principle* (Cambridge, Mass.: Harvard University Press, 1985), pp. 104–16.

General discussions of the concept of obligation that relate to civil disobedience are Michael Walzer, *Obligations* (New York: Simon and Schuster, 1971), chapters 1 and 2; A. John Simons, *Moral Principles and Political Obligations* (Princeton, N.J.: Princeton University Press, 1979); David Lyons, "Moral Judgment, Historical Reality, and Civil Disobedience," *Philosophy & Public Affairs,* 27 (Winter 1998), pp. 31–49; and Alec Walen, "Reasonable Illegal Force: Justice and Legitimacy in a Pluralistic, Liberal Society," *Ethics,* 111 (January 2001), pp. 344–73.

Specifically on the obligations of public officials, see the analysis by Arthur Applbaum, "Democratic Legitimacy and Official Discretion," *Philosophy & Public Affairs,* 21 (Summer 1992), pp. 240–74. On the political ethics of whistle-blowing, see Sissela Bok, *Secrets* (New York: Pantheon, 1982), pp. 210–29; C. Fred Alford, *Whistleblowers: Broken Lives and Organizational Power* (Ithaca, NY: Cornell

University Press, 2001); and Roberta Ann Johnson, *Whistleblowing: When It Works—and Why* (Boulder, Colorado: L. Rienner, 2003). On the value of dissent, see Cass Sunstein, *Why Societies Need Dissent* (Cambridge, Mass.: Harvard University Press, 2003) The practical and theoretical aspects of resignation are discussed in Edward Weisband and Thomas Franck, *Resignation in Protest* (New York: Penguin, 1975), and Albert Hirschman, *Exit, Voice and Loyalty* (Cambridge, Mass.: Harvard University Press, 1970). For discussion focused on the ethics of engineers like those featured in the *Challenger* case, see Michael Davis, "Thinking Like an Engineer: The Place of a Code of Ethics in the Practice of a Profession," *Philosophy & Public Affairs,* 20 (Spring, 1991), pp. 150–67.

For contending views on the problem of ascribing moral responsibility for government decisions to individual officials, see John Ladd, "Morality and the Ideal of Rationality in Formal Organizations," *Monist,* 54 (October 1970), pp. 488–516; Ronald Dworkin, *Law's Empire* (Cambridge, Mass.: Harvard University Press, 1986), pp. 167–75; and Dennis F. Thompson, *Restoring Responsibility* (Cambridge, England: Cambridge University Press, 2004), Part I.

Part Two

The Ethics of Policy

6   Policy Analysis

The question of means and ends—the focus of the first part of this book—speaks to only part of the moral world of politics. No less important is the question of the ends themselves: how should we choose among competing goals of policy? The most common framework for answering this question is some version of policy analysis, including cost-benefit, cost-effective, and risk-benefit analysis. All of these approaches draw on the moral framework of utilitarianism (insofar as they draw on any moral framework at all). They assume (1) that the ends or values of policies can be compared by a common measure of expected utility (also called happiness, satisfaction, or—most commonly—welfare) and (2) that the best policy or set of policies can be compared by a common measure of expected utility. The great appeal of this approach is that it appears to resolve conflicts among competing ends and seems to do so in a neutral way by simply adding up the preferences of all citizens. (Utility or welfare is typically defined as some form of the satisfaction of preferences.) The approach also appears democratic, since it purports to give the most people as much as possible of whatever they want.

Critics of policy analysis attack both of its assumptions. First, they point to problems of aggregation—the way the policy analyst adds preferences to arrive at total utility. Among criticisms of this kind are: (1) that individual utilities cannot be compared (How can we say whether a job for me is worth a slightly higher cancer risk for you? Or whether cheaper electric power for you is worth fewer fishing, hiking, and rafting opportunities for me?); (2) that ultimate values cannot be traded off against other goods (How can we put a price on life itself? Or even on the environment?); and (3) that individual preferences cannot be taken as given (How can we assume that public deliberations about policy will not significantly alter public perceptions of the value of environmental protection and economic development?)

The second set of criticisms concerns problems of distribution. Critics challenge the maximization principle because it ignores how utility is allocated among individuals. They object that for the sake of maximizing general utility, policy analysts will sacrifice (1) the rights of disadvantaged citizens in their own society; (2) the welfare of poorer nations; and (3) the welfare of future generations. Policy analysts try to take such groups into account, but the problem of distributive justice remains a formidable obstacle to the acceptance of their method.

The policy analysis undertaken in "Saving the Tuolumne" poses a classic choice between environmental protection (in California's beautiful Tuolumne Canyon) and economic development (in the form of new dams and reservoirs for more water and hydroelectric power). Many federal and state agencies—like the Federal Energy Regulatory Commission and the California State Water Resources Control Board in this case—operate under a legal mandate to approve new dams and reservoirs if and only if their public benefits are shown to exceed their costs. Critics of such legal mandates claim that policy analysis is biased in favor of economic development and against environmental protection. However, the policy analysis conducted by the Environmental Defense Fund in this case concludes in favor of protecting the Tuolumne Canyon instead of pursuing the Clavey-Wards Ferry Project.

To decide whether to preserve the Tuolumne Canyon or to build the dams and reservoirs, a policy analyst must quantify and compare many different values over time, including the values of water and hydroelectric power, whitewater rafting, fishing, boating, camping, and hiking. The Environmental Defense Fund's analysis uses sophisticated techniques of quantification, but even the most sophisticated techniques are subject to morally significant criticisms and often yield conflicting policy recommendations. Taken together, the Environmental Defense Fund's analysis and the critical review by the engineering consulting firm of R. W. Beck and Associates offer an opportunity to probe the moral strengths and weaknesses of policy analysis.

The aim of policy analysis is to estimate as many costs and benefits over time as are amenable to quantification. The controversy over saving the Tuolumne illustrates the value of quantifying even some of those values—such as hiking and whitewater rafting—that are often assumed to be unquantifiable. The controversy also illustrates the limits of such quantification. Policy analysts rarely if ever claim to have captured all the costs and benefits of alternative policies, but they attempt to capture as many as possible, as accurately as possible. Their quantification, even if completely accurate, is therefore only part of the broader analysis that would be necessary to determine whether the environmental protection in question is more or less valuable than the economic development.

Assigning utility to policy options and systematically assessing the quantifiable costs and benefits can help dispel some uncertainties and confusions regarding the policy decision of whether to preserve the environment or to develop energy resources. But the quantification is typically both controversial and incomplete. Although the controversy over the analysis in the Tuolumne case may seem merely technical, it reflects ethical differences about such questions as the value of noneconomic pursuits (such as hiking) versus economic pursuits (such as generating electrical power) and the obligation to future generations (to preserve natural beauty). Beyond the problem of adding up the costs and benefits, the problem of distributing them within a society and over time plays an important role in the controversy but a less than fully explicit role in the policy analysis. Although neither the report by the Environmental Defense Fund nor the critical review by Beck and Associates claims to deal with all the issues in the conflict between the values of environmental protection versus economic development, we should read them with as much attention to what they omit as to what they include.

Assigning value to human life is among the most controversial requirements of policy analysis, made all the more so when the value of different lives—those who are rich and poor, young and old, single and married, with and without dependent children—must be compared and a monetary value assigned to each for compensatory purposes. In the wake of the terrorist attacks of 9/11, Kenneth Feinberg—appointed as special master of the Victims Compensation Fund—accepted the unenviable task of determining how much compensation should be given to the many individuals who tragically lost family members or themselves were physically injured during the attacks and who filed a claim with the government. "The Calculator" shows not only the necessity of determining how much money to give to whom under these circumstances but also the difficulty faced by a committed calculator in publicly substantiating an "objective allocation formula," which assigned differential monetary values to the lives of individuals. A policy of providing monetary compensation to victims of a national tragedy seems to assume a common currency of publicly calculating the value of lives: money. Like policy analysts, Feinberg tried to find a way to compare very different values, and thus directly confronted the claim of incommensurability, which holds that there is not a single objective metric by which the various values of human life can be compared and assigned a single monetary value. Is there a single objective metric of comparison? If so, what is it? If not, how can monetary compensation best be allocated to victims of tragedies such as 9/11? The case invites consideration of whether there are better alternatives to the "objective qualification" formula, not only for the problem Feinberg confronted but also for similar problems that governments face in valuing life.

William Ruckelshaus, who was responsible for setting emissions standards in the Asarco case, was as sensitive to the weaknesses of policy analysis as he was to its strengths. Ruckelshaus held a series of public meetings with the people who would be most directly affected by his decision to discuss both the technical and moral dimensions of setting emissions standards for the Asarco smelting company. Some observers criticized Ruckelshaus for abdicating his responsibility to make policy on the basis of his own best technical and moral judgment. Others praised him for trying to educate the public about the difficulties of making decisions on the basis of imperfect and incomplete knowledge.

Like the Asarco case, "Listening to the City" does not provide a solution to the philosophical or technical problems of how to aggregate preferences to arrive at total utility or how to distribute risks and benefits among people. Instead, it suggests a political process by which resolution of these and other problems involving conflicts of values may be more fairly and fully considered. The political process, which takes place in many different forums with a wide variety of individuals who have a legitimate stake in decision-making, is called democratic deliberation. Among its several aims, democratic deliberation is said to help the democratic process express the value of mutual respect among citizens and better inform public decision-making by bringing a wider range of perspectives to bear on the process than public officials would otherwise be willing or able to consider. The July 2002 electronic town meeting sponsored by the Lower Manhattan Development Corporation and the Civic Alliance illustrates some of the risks and benefits of establishing deliberative forums on issues of public importance, perhaps none more emotionally charged than the city's plans for reconstructing Ground Zero.

Saving the Tuolumne
Linda Kincaid

From its origins high on Mount Lyell and Mount Dana in Yosemite National Park, the Tuolumne river flows 158 miles west to California's San Joaquin Valley. Despite hydroelectric developments at either end of the Tuolumne, the river still runs free in a 30-mile stretch through Tuolumne Canyon, between the O'Shaughnessy Dam in Yosemite and the headwaters of the New Don Pedro Reservoir. Here the Tuolumne hurtles down the western slope of the High Sierra, fed by four major tributaries—the Clavey River, Cherry Creek, and the Middle and South Forks. Only two roads wind into the isolated canyon, where the river courses between sheer granite cliffs and rugged slopes covered with digger pine, incense cedar, and oak. Mink, screech owl, river otter, and the endangered southern bald eagle share the canyon with large deer herds that travel there each winter from Yosemite. The cold water pools of the Tuolumne and Clavey Rivers harbor some of California's finest trout reserves—by one estimate two to three times more productive than the state's best flatwater fishing areas. Tuolumne Canyon also contains several historic and prehistoric sites, including ruins of abandoned gold mines and sites inhabited

by the Miwok Indians, who lived in the canyon until the mid-1800s.

The Tuolumne's continuous succession of rapids and cataracts make it one of the nation's finest and most popular whitewater rafting rivers. Each year between March and October, thousands of rafting enthusiasts travel a single-lane dirt road into Lumsden's Landing to make the 18-mile trip downriver to Wards Ferry. With twenty-five major rapids and a white-knuckle plunge over the eight-foot-high Clavey Falls, this stretch of the Tuolumne is considered comparable to the Colorado River in the Grand Canyon or Idaho's Salmon River. More than 15,000 rafters from all over the country made this run in one- to three-day trips in 1982, and a few hundred others braved the more treacherous stretch of the Tuolumne above Lumsden's Bridge. About 9,000 of those boaters ran the rapids on their own, while another 6,000 took trips arranged by one of ten commercial expedition firms. With government studies documenting an increasing demand over time for rafting on the Tuolumne, some expedition operators and environmental groups expect the number of Tuolumne rafters to double within the next decade.

While rafting is the Tuolumne's major attraction, others travel to the area to hunt, fish, hike, and camp. The U.S. Forest Service recorded 22,000 visitor-days at its campgrounds on the Tuolumne in 1983; and total recreational use is estimated at 35,000 user-days annually. Tuolumne River

Canyon is also home to three city-run family campgrounds, operated by the cities of Berkeley, San Jose, and San Francisco, which provide low-cost camping and recreation for city residents.

With its steep, narrow canyon walls and large volume of flowing water, the Tuolumne River Canyon is also an ideal site for hydroelectric development. In April 1983, the City and County of San Francisco and two irrigation districts in Merced and Stanislaus counties commissioned a feasibility study of their longstanding proposal to dam the Tuolumne for power and water. At the same time, a coalition of environmentalists, rafters, fishing enthusiasts, and California residents known as the Tuolumne River Preservation Trust was lobbying Congress to protect the river from further development under the federal Wild and Scenic Rivers Act. The dam proponents had already produced several favorable cost-benefit studies of their proposal; in June 1983, the trust asked economists at the Environmental Defense Fund to respond to those studies with an economic assessment of the proposed dam's environmental costs.

HYDROELECTRIC DEVELOPMENT ON THE TUOLUMNE

By 1983, existing hydroelectric developments on the Tuolumne captured 90 percent of its water and more than 70 percent of its power generating capacity—enough to supply drinking water to nearly 2 million Californians, irrigate 230,000 acres of farmland in California's Central Valley, and generate electricity to power some 400,000 homes. The City and County of San Francisco drew 300 million gallons of water a day from the Hetch Hetchy Reservoir, located inside Yosemite, and from two additional reservoirs on tributaries of the Tuolumne. The Hetch Hetchy System's three powerhouses provided nearly 300 megawatts (MW) of electrical capacity, which the San Francisco Public Utilities Commission sold to municipal departments of the city and to nearby

utility districts and industrial customers. Thirty miles downstream, the New Don Pedro Dam and Reservoir provided electricity and irrigation to the Modesto and Turlock Irrigation Districts (MID and TID).

The two irrigation districts distributed irrigation water and power to the city of Modesto, several smaller towns, and 230,000 acres of farmland in Stanislaus and Merced counties.[1] Located less than 100 miles east of San Francisco, in California's Central Valley, the two districts contained some of the richest farmland in the world, as well as a burgeoning population of professionals, industrial workers, and retirees. Electricity consumption in the MID-TID service area had increased more rapidly than in California as a whole from 1965–75, thanks to a dramatic increase in irrigated acreage and an influx of agricultural processors and other industries who had moved their plants from the metropolitan areas to Central Valley towns. A 1975 study by the consulting firm Arthur D. Little predicted that rapid economic growth would continue in the MID-TID service area through the year 2000. In 1979, a study of electricity demand in the MID service area by consultants Hittman and Associates found that the area's industrial growth had slowed somewhat, but predicted that electricity demand would still grow at an annual rate of 4.1 percent.

By 1983, the 150 MW power station at New Don Pedro Dam met only half the electricity demand in the two irrigation districts, forcing them to purchase additional power from the statewide utility, Pacific Gas and Electric Company (PG&E), and from San Francisco's Hetch Hetchy System. Using Hittman's 4.1 percent annual growth predictions, district planners projected that the gap between demand and generating capacity would continue to grow, to about 500 MW in 1995 and 600 MW in 2000 (Exhibit 1). Historically, MID and TID customers had enjoyed some of the lowest electricity rates in the nation, but rates began to rise in the early eighties as the districts invested in new sources and

EXHIBIT 1. COMBINED MID AND TID PROJECTED DEMAND REQUIREMENTS
VERSUS RESOURCES

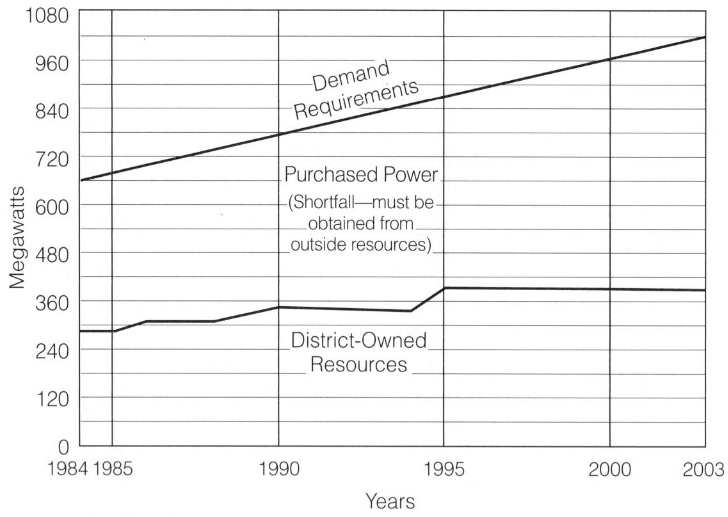

Source: R. W. Beck and Associates, *Clavey-Wards Ferry Projects, FERC Project No. 2774, Phase II Feasibility Evaluation,* for Modesto and Turlock Irrigation Districts.

bought more PG&E power to keep up with rising demand. District planners expected electricity prices to rise further after 1985, when they would have to renegotiate the price for power purchased from Hetch Hetchy.

Faced with rising demand for electricity and rising prices for outside sources, managers of both irrigation districts turned to the last undeveloped stretch of the Tuolumne and to a 1968 engineering study originally done for San Francisco, which recommended construction of two new hydroelectric facilities on the river—one at the mouth of the Clavey River and another at Wards Ferry, just above the New Don Pedro Dam. In 1976, San Francisco and the two irrigation districts had applied to the Federal Energy Regulatory Commission (FERC) for a preliminary permit to conduct a feasibility study of the so-called Clavey-Wards Ferry (CWF) proposal. But the year before, Congress had asked the U.S. Departments of Agriculture and Interior to study the Tuolumne's eligibil-

ity for preservation as a "wild and scenic" river, and FERC was forbidden to act on the permit application until the end of the three-year federal study period. The river study concluded that the entire 83 miles of river that flows through Yosemite National Park and the Stanislaus National Forest possessed "outstandingly remarkable scenic qualities" and should be included in the nation's wild and scenic rivers system. Although Congress never acted on President Carter's 1979 request to preserve the river, his request delayed FERC action on the permit application until 1982. San Francisco and the irrigation districts remained interested in the project, commissioning three updated economic reports on the project during this period. Finally, in April 1983, FERC granted the preliminary permit. MID, TID, and the City and County of San Francisco promptly hired the engineering consulting firm of R. W. Beck and Associates to perform a detailed three-year feasibility study of the Clavey-Wards Ferry proposal.

EXHIBIT 2. CLAVEY-WARDS FERRY ALTERNATIVE

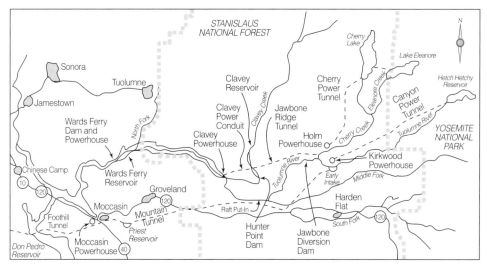

Source: R. W. Beck and Associates, *Clavey-Wards Ferry Project, FERC Project No. 2774, Phase II Feasibility Evaluation,* for Modesto and Turlock Irrigation Districts.

THE CLAVEY-WARDS FERRY PROJECT

As described in the FERC preliminary permit application, the CWF development would generate 980 gigawatt-hours (GWh) annually from two separate generating installations, the Clavey unit and the Wards Ferry unit (Exhibit 2). The Clavey unit would include two new dams and reservoirs and a 5.1-mile diversion tunnel. Jawbone Diversion Dam, 175 feet high and 255 feet long, would be located on the Tuolumne River just downstream from its confluence with Cherry Creek. The nearby Jawbone Creek Diversion Dam and Pipeline would divert Jawbone Creek flows into the new Jawbone Reservoir behind the Jawbone Diversion Dam. From Jawbone Reservoir, the Jawbone Ridge Tunnel would carry water to Clavey Reservoir. The Hunter Point Dam and Clavey Reservoir would be located on the Clavey River almost six miles upstream from its confluence with the Tuolumne. A 2.4 mile pressure tunnel would link the Clavey Reservoir to two 150-MW

generating units in the Clavey Powerhouse, to be located underground near the headwaters of the planned Wards Ferry Reservoir.

The Wards Ferry Unit would include a 450-foot-high, 1,060-foot-long rockfill Wards Ferry Dam, which would create the Wards Ferry Reservoir. The reservoir would have a usable storage of about 92,300 acre-feet[2]—providing an annual water supply of 12,000 acre-feet—and would store and regulate Tuolumne River flows for power generation and water supply. The Wards Ferry Powerhouse, which would be located underground in the dam's south abutment, would house two 50 MW generating units.

Beck estimated that construction of the CWF project could be completed in 1995, allowing for preparatory studies, FERC licensing, and a four-and-a-half-year construction period. Total capital costs were estimated at $860 million in 1995 dollars. The consultants estimated that by constructing CWF, the two irrigation districts would enjoy a net savings of $29 million in the first year of operation over the projected costs of purchasing power from PG&E; the CWF option would cost $18 million less in the first year than constructing or joining other utilities in new fossil-fuel plants.

Both proponents and opponents of the Clavey-Wards proposal agreed that its construction would substantially change existing conditions on the Tuolumne. The planned Wards Ferry Reservoir would inundate approximately 1,200 acres of the Tuolumne River Canyon, including traditional mule deer winter habitats and approximately 12 miles of trout spawning beds and stream habitat on the Tuolumne. Upriver, the Clavey unit was expected to reduce river flows in some 15 miles of the Tuolumne and 6 miles of the Clavey. Dam management would also cause abrupt changes in water-flows in these sections of the two rivers.

THE CASE FOR CLAVEY-WARDS FERRY

Proponents of the Clavey-Wards Ferry argued that the dams would provide a cheap, clean, renewable source of energy to help the districts keep pace with their steadily rising demands. "We needed a source of power," explained Turlock Irrigation District manager Ernest Geddes. "We needed a reliable and economical source. . . . If you look at what are the options, I could build a nuclear plant, or an oil-fired plant or a coal plant, or a hydro plant. . . . [Clavey-Wards Ferry] was the most economical alternative."

For Tuolumne County, which had endorsed the project, Clavey-Wards Ferry would help answer its desperate need for water. Distant communities like San Francisco had long ago appropriated most of the water which flowed through this sparsely populated county in the Sierra foothills, which is dominated by Yosemite National Park and Stanislaus National Forest. In the early eighties, Tuolumne County was one of the fastest growing in the state—its population was expected to grow from 40,000 to 60,000 between 1985 and 2000—and its small water supply was already strained.

Under an agreement with MID and TID, the county would get 12,000 acre-feet of water annually from Clavey-Wards Ferry, and a third of the revenue from the project's sales of excess power. (The county planned to dedicate those revenues to developing other water supplies.) The estimated 250 construction jobs and dozens of permanent jobs the project would require were also appealing in the county, where seasonal unemployment had reached 21 percent in the winter of 1983.

The project's proponents argued that the changes Clavey-Wards Ferry would bring to Tuolumne Canyon would increase recreational opportunities in the area (Exhibit 3). The development would bring new roads, opening the wilderness to tourists and permitting the development of more campsites. The new Wards Ferry Reservoir would offer opportunities for flatwater fishing, boating, and swimming. Proponents promised to maintain trout fishing opportunities by setting minimum flood levels at Jawbone Dam and Clavey Dam in consultation with state and federal fisheries agencies. And, they argued, the reduced flows between Jawbone Dam and Lumsden campground might improve fishing conditions, particularly for fly fishing.

Proponents conceded that the dams would reduce the Tuolumne's main whitewater run from 18 miles to 6.6 miles. But Geddes maintained that the dam at Jawbone Creek would increase raftable days by 20–25 percent by holding back the heavy spring runoff that sometimes made the river too wild to navigate in June and early July. (Dam proponents also pointed out that the Lumsden-Wards Ferry run would probably be too wild for rafting without the existing dams at Cherry Creek and Hetch Hetchy.) A more moderate, controlled flow, he said, would allow rafters to make the trip in their own small boats, rather than paying for professional river guides. Besides, they said, flatwater recreation was more popular and allowed a greater density of use than wilderness pursuits like rafting and hiking. "Rafting's

EXHIBIT 3. EFFECT OF CLAVEY-WARDS FERRY AND PONDEROSA ALTERNATIVES ON EXISTING ENVIRONMENT

Item	*Existing Baseline Conditions*	*Conditions with Clavey-Wards Ferry Alternative*
Lake recreation	• None on affected reach of the Tuolumne between Don Pedro and Hetch Hetchy Reservoir.	• Create opportunities at Wards Ferry Reservoir.
Whitewater Rafting	• 18-mile long, Class IV run below Lumden campground used by two commercial companies and individuals.	• Reduce Main run to 6.6 miles and reduce number of raftable days. Run will not support commercial operations.
	• Experts-only Cherry Creek run (kayaking and rafting).	• Eliminate Cherry Creek run because of flow diversions.
Fly Fishing	• Concentrated at and above Lumden campground.	• Minimum flow releases would preserve fly-fishing above Lumden campground.
Camping	• Limited to 3 developed campgrounds with 23 campsites; 14 undeveloped sites on Tuolumne used by river boaters.	• Lakeside campsites would be developed at Wards Ferry Reservoir. Some undeveloped sites would be inundated.
Hiking, Hunting, and Other Dispersed Activities	• Hiking and hunting concentrated in hills above Tuolumne Canyon.	• Same as existing conditions but improved access to canyon areas.
River Access	• Very limited.	• Improved.
Visual Character	• Flowing rivers, in rugged canyons. Tuolumne flows controlled by releases from Holm with limited evidence of recent human occupation.	• Considerable portions of canyon bottoms converted to lakes. Two dams on Tuolumne, access roads, and transmission line.
Water Supply	• None for Tuolumne County.	• Provide supply from Wards Ferry Reservoir.
Flood Control	• At Don Pedro Reservoir.	• Improve capability.
Cultural Resources	• Area contains known cultural sites.	• Potential for inundation of activity at sites.
Terrestrial Habitat	• Canyons include winter range of mule deer. Habitat of peregrine falcon and bald eagle, and possibly rare snail.	• Inundation causes loss of mule deer winter range and possible interruption of migration routes. Increased human access may make falcon and eagle habitat less favorable.
Aquatic Habitat	• Fish habitat limited by flow variability especially upstream of South Fork. No manmade barriers to fish migration between Don Pedro Reservoir and Early Intake.	• Habitat improvement upstream of South Fork due to more constant flow conditions. Below South Fork, Hunter Point and Wards Ferry dams would convert habitat from riverine to reservoir.

Source: R. W. Beck and Associates, *Clavey-Wards Phase II Feasibility Evaluation.*

a special interest thing," said Jerry Bellah, a member of the Tuolumne County Board of Supervisors. "I've lived here twenty-three years and I've never rafted the river. Not that many people do it."

THE OPPOSITION

In a sense, the modern environmental protection movement began with an earlier fight over the Tuolumne's future. In the early 1900s, naturalist John Muir led an impassioned campaign to prevent San Francisco from damming the Tuolumne and flooding the Hetch Hetchy Valley, which Muir and his followers felt was as beautiful as the neighboring Yosemite Valley. "Dam Hetch Hetchy!" he wrote, during the first nationwide letter-writing campaign to Congress on an environmental issue. "As well dam for water tanks the people's cathedrals and churches, for no holier temple has ever been consecrated by the heart of man."

Muir lost the battle when Congress passed the Raker Act of 1913, which permitted the City and County of San Francisco to build six dams and reservoirs in the Tuolumne watershed. He died before the dam was completed—of a broken heart, according to conservationist folklore—but from the Hetch Hetchy fight, the Sierra Club emerged as a strong voice for environmental protection.

By the early eighties, the fight to save the remaining 30 wild miles of the Tuolumne took on symbolic importance for environmentalists, who were frustrated by their agonizingly slow progress in protecting the nation's most spectacular rivers from development. When the Wild and Scenic Rivers Act was passed in 1968, conservationists hoped its protective system would include a hundred rivers by 1978 and 200 by 1990. But by 1978, only sixteen rivers had been added to the original eight, and by 1980, only a few more—most of them in Alaska—had won federal protection from Congress. The battle to save Tuolumne Canyon thus seemed to conservationists a test of the nation's commitment to the preservation of wild and scenic rivers. "If we can't win this one," John Amodio of the Tuolumne River Preservation Trust told *California* magazine, "you have to wonder, where can we win?"

THE CASE AGAINST CLAVEY-WARDS FERRY

Opponents of the CWF project believed it would decimate the Tuolumne and Clavey fisheries, eliminate all whitewater boating potential, adversely affect the canyon's wildlife population, and destroy forever the isolated, wilderness character that drew hikers and campers to the area. The Wards Ferry Reservoir would inundate two-thirds of the 18-mile whitewater run between Lumsden and Wards Ferry and virtually dry up the remaining section (minimum project flow releases there were scheduled at 35–75 cubic feet per second [cfs], just a fraction of the 1,000 cfs that professional river guides said were necessary for whitewater rafting). They argued that the Wards Ferry Reservoir would inundate 12 miles of prime trout spawning beds and stream habitat, while the Wards Ferry Dam would block spawning runs necessary to perpetuate the trout population downstream in the New Don Pedro Reservoir. The Clavey Reservoir would inundate more than a mile of stream habitat on the Clavey River and block the passage of fish. Average flows in the lower reach of the Clavey and in the Tuolumne below Jawbone Diversion would not meet U.S. Fish and Wildlife Service recommendations for maintaining the fish population. In addition, the fragile nontrout fish population in the lower Clavey would be threatened by flow changes and the encroachment of other species from the Wards Ferry Reservoir. The river fisheries also would be harmed by changes in seasonal flows, changes in water temperature and dissolved oxygen content from water releases from different levels of the reservoirs, and construction-related changes in turbidity and sediment transport. Construction activities, increased human presence in the area, and the erection of electrical transmission lines would destroy the canyon's scenic beauty and threaten several rare species of birds, particularly the endangered southern bald eagle. And a 1982 California Department of Water Resources report warned that the project would block several traditional migration routes used by Yosemite deer.

Opponents also argued that the new recreational opportunities created by Wards Ferry Reservoir would be extremely limited. The project consultants had acknowledged the reservoir would be a long, narrow, and deep lake which would be sunless most of the time. Furthermore, surface water levels would fluctuate by almost 100 feet, and access to the lake would be difficult given the canyon's steep, narrow sides. The fishing opportunities of the reservoir were equally uncertain, opponents argued, citing a former state Department of Fish and Game biologist's estimate that the reservoir would contain less than 10 pounds of fish per acre, compared to the free-flowing Tuolumne's 1,000 pounds of fish per acre. Even the project consultants had acknowledged area fishermen's preference for river fishing, and the federal wild and scenic rivers study had pointed out that "reservoir fisheries are in abundance in the Sierra foothills, whereas river trout fisheries of the quality of the Tuolumne are a rarity in the state."

The opponents complained that neither Beck nor the irrigation districts had adequately considered alternative sources of energy. They pointed out that the irrigation districts would be able to buy surplus off-peak energy from coal-fired power plants in the Southwest and Northwest, and from hydroelectric plants in the Pacific Northwest. They also argued that the districts had not adequately considered ways that conservation and load management could be used to meet the system's capacity needs.

ORGANIZING THE FIGHT

The Tuolumne River Preservation Trust was formed in 1981 to coordinate efforts of conservationists, rafting and fishing enthusiasts, and California residents who opposed further development on the Tuolumne. Led by two Bay-Area Sierra Club members, the trust helped to make the Tuolumne battle a cause célèbre in California, garnering widespread media coverage, celebrity attention and political support. By the summer of 1983, the campaign to save the Tuolumne had also picked up important support in San Francisco and the state capitol. Both the state Department of Fish and Game and Department of Water Resources opposed further development on the Tuolumne, as did San Francisco Mayor Dianne Feinstein, and the city's Board of Supervisors. (The city's Public Utilities Commission was still a nominal participant in the feasibility study, however.) At the same time, the trust was lobbying hard to persuade California's junior senator, Republican Pete Wilson, to include the Tuolumne River Canyon in his wilderness bill, S. 1515. The trust also hoped to win Wilson's endorsement for S. 142, a bill proposed by California's senior senator, Democrat Alan Cranston, to declare the Tuolumne a wild and scenic river.

In June of 1983, the trust asked economists at the Environmental Defense Fund (EDF) to prepare an economic evaluation of the Clavey-Wards Ferry project, including its environmental costs. The group intended to use the study in its lobbying efforts. But if its run at congressional protection for the Tuolumne failed, a comprehensive quantitative accounting of the project's private and environmental costs could help them fight the project before the Federal Energy Regulatory Commission and the California State Water Resources Control Board. The project proponents would have to obtain a construction license from FERC and a water rights permit from the state board; both agencies operated under legal mandates which allowed them to approve a project only if its benefits to the public exceeded its costs.

EDF had its own, wider interest in the trust's proposal for an economic evaluation of Clavey-Wards Ferry. With 7,000 members in California and nearly 50,000 nationwide, the group focused its research, lobbying, and organizing efforts on promoting long-run improvements in natural resource management. EDF had won a reputation for making economic arguments for environmental causes in the early 1970s, when the group had worked to convince utilities that marginal cost pricing would encourage energy conservation and save money. Early in 1983, EDF was searching for a way to deal with an unintended consequence of an earlier environmentalist triumph—the 1978 amendments to the Public Utilities Regulatory Policies Act (PURPA), which required utility companies to buy excess power produced by independent facilities. The new rules had been supported by environmentalists as an incentive for the development of cogeneration energy; in practice they also spawned a new boom in small hydroelectric development. Since 1978, hydro project applications to FERC had increased by 2,000 percent, and in the early 1980s, FERC was evaluating hundreds of applications to dam up rivers throughout the Sierras.

EDF felt that FERC's approval of hydro projects in the past had consistently undervalued their environmental costs, because of the agency's practice of weighing a qualitative judgment of environmental losses against the more easily quantified net economic benefits to the project developers. The trust's offer of funding for an economic assessment of the Clavey-Wards Ferry project's environmental costs gave EDF the chance to present FERC—and other environmental advocacy groups—with a method for quantifying the environmental effects of hydroelectric development. As Robert Stavins, the principal author of EDF's Tuolumne study recalled: "Rather than looking at it from a narrow, financial perspective, [we believed] we could look at it from a broader, social perspective by trying to internalize some of the environmental externalities."

While the techniques EDF would use were not new to economists, environmental advocacy groups had traditionally resisted the use of cost-benefit analysis in making decisions about environmental policy—the chairman of the Natural Resources Defense Council, for instance, has called the use of cost-benefit analysis in setting toxic standards "immoral," but most conservation advocates also recognized the power of economic arguments in the political world. "Environmentalists in general will support cost-benefit analysis when it confirms their preconceived position," explained EDF senior economist Zach Willey. "But when it doesn't, it's more controversial. I think, by and large, environmentalists are skeptical of cost-benefit analysis; they've seen how it's been used and will come up with all kinds of arguments about how it's not possible to quantify many environmental values. . . . [But EDF's Tuolumne study] was not inconsistent with the emotional view of many environmentalists that the environment is priceless. In fact, it was consistent in that it added some of the value of the environment to a particular decision."

COUNTING THE COSTS AND BENEFITS

Although Stavins drew much of his raw data from the Beck studies of the Clavey-Wards Ferry project, his analysis differed from theirs in two crucial ways. For one, his cost-benefit model was designed to add the project's environmental, or "external," costs and benefits onto the "internal," or financial, cost-benefit analysis that Beck had prepared. Stavins' estimate of environmental costs and benefits was admittedly incomplete. Although he recognized the project's environmental impacts could range from destruction of historic sites to threatening endangered bird species, he had to rest his calculations on the river's principal (and most easily quantified) existing recreational uses—trout fishing and whitewater rafting. As the CWF's "external" benefits, Stavins counted the value of the CWF's projected water supply and the flatwater fishing and boating opportunities that would be available at the planned Wards Ferry Reservoir.

Secondly, Stavins took issue with Beck's decision to estimate the project's benefits and costs for only its first year of operation, since such an approach did not account for the uneven streams of benefits and costs which would be spread out over fifty to one hundred years in such a project. Stavins elected instead to estimate the project's benefit/cost streams over the entire likely life of the project. His analysis produced estimates of the project's levelized annual costs and benefits by finding their present value of fifty years, inflated at 6 percent, discounted at 10.72 percent, and then levelized at 10.72 percent over fifty years. He chose the fifty-year planning period in keeping with FERC guidelines, and assumed the project would

come on line in 1994, adding three years to Beck's assumed four-year construction period. (Stavins believed that Beck's assumption was overly optimistic, given the U.S. Army Corps of Engineers estimate that hydroelectric projects even smaller than the Wards Ferry Dam required a six-year construction period.) The 10.72 discount rate was Stavin's estimation of the likely rate at which the districts would be able to float forty-year bonds, based on the Modesto Irrigation District's actual sales in 1983 of tax-exempt energy project revenue bonds. This choice was in keeping with FERC recommendations that for nonfederal projects the overall cost of money to the project developers should be used as the discount rate.

Stavins estimated the project's total levelized annual project benefits at slightly less than $188 million (Exhibit 4). The biggest

Exhibit 4. Social Benefits, Clavey-Wards Ferry Project

Benefit	Cost (dollars)
1. Levelized Annual Energy Benefit[a] (Table 4: $[(2) + (3) + (5) - (4)])$[b]	$146,720,000
2. Levelized Annual Capacity Benefit[c] (Table 4: $[(1) + (6)])$[b]	37,500,000
3. Annual Benefit of Increased Firm, Yield of Water for MID/TID (11,900 AF $\times$ $105/AF in 1990, 4 years at 6 % to 1994)	1,577,000
4. Levelized Annual Benefit of Increased Firm Yield $[(3) \times 2.148]$	3,388,000
5. Total Internal Levelized Annual Benefits $[(1) + (2) + (4)]$	187,608,000
6. Annual Flatwater Boating Benefit on Wards Ferry Reservoir (1,600 user-days $\times$ $20/day, 1994)	32,000
7. Annual Reservoir Fishing Benefit (4,000 user-days $\times$ $30/day, 1994)	120,000
8. Total External Levelized Annual Benefits $[(6) + (7) \times 2.148]$	327,000
9. Total Levelized Annual Project Benefits $[(5) + (8)]$	187,935,000

a. Annual Energy Benefit refers to the avoided cost of running the least expensive alternative to the project.
b. Table 4 not included here.
c. Annual Capacity Benefit refers to the avoided cost of constructing the capacity to provide the least expensive alternative.

share of that was the project's $184 million in electricity benefits, which he measured by using the standard industry practice of calculating the avoided cost of the least expensive alternative means of meeting an identical load. Beck, too, had used this method, but had based its analysis of benefits on a mix of coal and combustion turbine capacity and its associated energy. Stavins' least cost mix of alternative energy sources included purchase of coal energy off-peak from Southwest and Northwest utilities, purchase of off-peak hydro energy from the Northwest, with peak energy and capacity provided by the district's own combustion turbines and conservation and load management measures. He also counted the project's expected impact on fishing into the benefit side of the analysis

EXHIBIT 5. DATA USED IN TRAVEL COST MODEL (TCM) OF TUOLUMNE RIVER
WHITEWATER RECREATION

Region	Average Travel Costs[a] from Region to Site (dollars)	Per Capita Use from Region ($\times 10^{-6}$)
Humboldt	643.31	70.080
Butte	566.76	11.316
Santa Rosa	441.13	491.137
Yolo	456.09	2059.277
Tahoe-Reno	538.84	752.949
Sacramento	430.22	868.768
El Dorado	401.27	991.147
West Bay	485.56	1510.583
East Bay	470.34	1360.516
South Bay	468.03	716.121
Stockton	384.20	1200.421
Tuolumne	347.48	5315.727
Fresno	474.19	176.380
Los Angeles	629.28	271.885
San Diego	730.78	191.908
Pacific Northwest	1207.16	15.361
Nevada (less Washoe County)	660.27	65.049
West	894.24	33.340
Mountain	1443.66	38.310
Plains	1728.90	1.764
Great Lakes	1991.95	4.690
Atlantic	2065.78	4.492
New England	2102.11	2.752
Southeast	1920.41	0.992

a. Average travel cost for a representative user from a given region, i, consists of three principal components: actual transportation cost, opportunity cost of time spent traveling to and from the site, and opportunity cost of time spent on the site: $TC_i = TPC_i + OCT_i + OCS_i$

by estimating the project's energy generation at some 295 GWh less than Beck's projections, assuming the project operators preserved enough of the Tuolumne's original flows to protect the river's fish stock.[3]

Other benefits included water yield, which Stavins valued at $1.6 million, based on Beck's estimates that the water would be worth about $105/acre-foot in 1990. And he valued the project's "external" benefits—the 1,600 user-days of flatwater boating and 4,000 user-days of fishing that the Department of Interior had predicted for the Ward's Ferry Reservoir—at $327,000 a year. To place a dollar value on this benefit, Stavins chose the "unit-day" method, which relies on expert opinion to approximate the average willingness-to-pay of users for recreational resources.[4]

Valuing the project's costs was more complicated. Using Beck's 1980 estimate of the project's construction costs, Stavins produced an annual levelized "internal" cost estimate of $134 million. To estimate the project's "external costs," which he defined as the value of Tuolumne River whitewater

rafting opportunities to both users and nonusers, Stavins constructed a regional travel cost model. He began by estimating the willingness-to-pay, or consumer surplus, of users, using data on the river's current use to determine per capita visitation rates and costs from various geographic regions (Exhibits 5 and 6).

Then he econometrically estimated a so-called participation function, which would be used to derive the net per capita economic value of the river's recreational opportunities for each area. The per capita figures were then converted to regional total values and added together to produce an aggregate economic value. Stavins originally estimated the participation function using three alternative forms: linear, which produced a consumer surplus estimate of $16.6 million; double logarithmic, which estimated the consumer surplus at $2.1 million; and semilogarithmic, which produced an estimate of $3.1 million. In the final analysis, Stavins chose the semilog results, which produced a levelized annual consumer surplus estimate of $3 million.

EXHIBIT 6. COMMERCIAL WHITEWATER RECREATION TUOLUMNE RIVER, 1982

Outfitter	*Passenger Use Days*
A. A. Wet and Wild	440
American River Touring Association	1,162
Echo: The Wilderness Company	1,077
OARS	576
Outdoor Adventures	783
Outdoors Unlimited	804
Sierra Mac River Trips	377
Wilderness Waterways	585
All Outdoors	83
Sobek Expeditions	327
Zephyr River Expeditions	122
Total	6,336

Source: Environmental Defense Funds: *Tuolumne River: Preservation or Development?*, from Steve Cutwright, of the American River Touring Association.

EXHIBIT 7. SOCIAL COSTS, CLAVEY-WARDS FERRY PROJECT

Item	Cost (dollars)
1. Levelized Annual Internal Costs	$134,224,000
2. 1994 Consumers' Surplus of Users	3,099,000
3. 1994 User Fees (1983 Fee, $3 at 6%/year for 11 years)	128,000
4. 1994 Producers' Surplus (.125 profit × $350 at 6% for 11 years × 6,400)	532,000
5. 1994 Option Value (Consumer surplus/User × option-value × proxy population)	33,503,000
CA: $184.14 × 0.60 × 130,836 = $14,455,000 Other: $392.91 × 0.45 × 215,459/2 = $19,048,000	
6. 1994 Total Recreational Value [(2) + (3) + (4) + (5)]	37,261,000
7. Levelized Annual Cost of Recreational Value (Present value of 50 years, inflated at 6%, discounted at 10.72%, then levelized at 10.71 % over 50 years)	80,039,000
8. Total of Private and Recreational Annual Cost (item 1 + item 7)	214,263,000

EXHIBIT 8. USE AND INTRINSIC VALUES OF ENVIRONMENTAL RESOURCES FROM PREVIOUS EMPIRICAL STUDIES, 1974–1983

Study	Site	Estimates ($1994/ household/yr)[a]	Ratio of Nonuse to Use — Use	Nonuse
Meyer 1974	Fraser River, British Columbia	1,943	1,051	0.54
Horvath 1974	Southeastern United States	5,914	3,296	0.56
Dornbusch and Falcke 1974	Communities along seven U.S. bodies of water	—	—	1.39
Meyer 1978	Fraser River, British Columbia	601	754	1.25
Walsh, Greenley Young, McKean and Prato 1978	South Platte River, Colorado	264	138	0.52
Mitchell and Carson 1981	U.S. National	540	253	0.47
Cronin 1982	Potomac River	88	63	0.72
Desvouges, Smith and McGivney 1983	Mononganela River	109	71	0.65
Cronin (forthcoming)	Potomac River	92	73	0.79
Average Values		1,194	712	0.60[b]

a. inflated at CPI to 1982 and at 6%/year to 1994.
b. Does not include results from Dornbusch and Falcke 1974.

Source: Environmental Defense Fund, *Tuolumne River: Preservation or Development?* From Ann Fisher and Robert Raucher, "Intrinsic Benefits of Improved Water Quality: Conceptual and Empirical Perspectives." *Advances in Applied Microeconomics,* ed. V. Kerry Smith and Ann Dryden White (Greenwich, Conn., 1984), Vol. 3, pp. 37–66.

To that he added an estimate of user fees and producer surplus (Exhibit 7).

Stavins then turned to estimating rafting's "option value"—the amount interested nonusers would be willing to pay to insure access to rafting on the river at some future time. Stavins surveyed the economic literature and found nine studies that had quantified intrinsic recreational values as a positive fraction of user values (Exhibit 8). The nine studies used survey questions to elicit people's willingness to pay to preserve a recreational opportunity; they exhibited ratios of nonuse value to use value ranging from 0.47 to 1.39, with a weighted average of 0.60. Thus, on average, nonuser recreational value per household interested in the project was found to be approximately 60 percent of user recreational value per household. Stavins believed that he could multiply this number by his consumer surplus estimates to estimate the per capita option value for various geographic regions.

But then he had to identify the relevant population of interested nonusers. Stavins chose to use Sierra Club membership as a proxy for the population of interested nonusers. To be somewhat conservative, he estimated the total California option value as 60 percent of the total California per capita consumer surplus, multiplied by the full California Sierra Club membership; for other regions of the United States, he took 45 percent of the total consumer surplus, multiplied by half the non–California Sierra Club membership (Exhibit 9). All told, he produced an option value estimate of $33.5 million.

In the final analysis, Stavins estimated the annual social costs of the Clavey-Wards Ferry development at $214 million, outweighing its benefits by some $26 million. The calculations assigned the Clavey-Wards Ferry proposal a cost-benefit ratio of 0.877, indicating that the project would return about $.88 of benefits to society for each $1.00 invested in the project.

Exhibit 9. Estimating the Option Value Associated with Whitewater Boating on the Tuolumne River

California	
Consumer surplus per user from TCM model, based upon actual Tuolumne River rafting data	$184.14
Nonuser/user value ratio, based upon previous empirical research summarized by Fisher and Raucher	(1983) × 0.60
Estimated per capita California option value	$110.48
California membership of Sierra Club	× 130,836
Estimated 1994 total California option value	$14,455,000
Other regions of the United States	
Consumer surplus per user from TCM model, based upon actual Tuolumne River rafting data	$392.91
Nonuser/user value ratio, based upon previous empirical research summarized by Fisher and Raucher (1983) and reduced to account for effect of remoteness from site	×0.45
Estimated per capita non-California option value	$176.81
Non-California membership of Sierra Club, reduced by one-half to account for effect of remoteness from site	×107,730
Estimated 1994 total non-California option value	$19,048,000
Estimated total U.S. Option Value (1994)	$33,503,000

Environmentalists won their Tuolumne River protection crusade in September 1984, when Congress passed the California Wilderness Act and granted wild and scenic status to the entire 83 miles of the river above the New Don Pedro Reservoir. Pete Wilson, California's Republican senator, had declared his support for protecting the river a half a year earlier after intense lobbying from constituents and environmental groups. (Wilson's aides estimated that he received as many as 2,000 letters a week urging him to protect the Tuolumne.) But the victory wasn't clinched until June 1984, when Wilson and California's Democratic senator, Alan Cranston, agreed on a compromise between their two wilderness bills. In its final form, the act added fourteen new wilderness areas to the nine already designated in the Sierras—1.8 million acres on national forest lands, and another 1.4 million in Yosemite, Kings Canyon, and Sequoia National Parks.

The Environmental Defense Fund's (EDF) economic assessment of the Clavey-Wards Ferry dam proposal, released in summary form in October 1983, played an important role in the effort to win Wilson over. EDF economist Stavins believes that while politics, not economics, ultimately won Wilson over, the EDF study may have helped reduce his political risks in supporting wild and scenic protection for the Tuolumne. "Wilson wasn't going to read it, or his staff member wasn't going to read it and say, 'oh my God, we're wrong, this project is terrible for the socio-economy, let's change our vote,' " Stavins said. "What was likely to happen was that Pete Wilson, being the conservative southern California senator, would decide that this was a reasonable trade-off—that he ought to go for the wild and scenic (status) because he does have an environmentalist constituency in California. But he might need some sort of evidence to give to his conservative constituency of why he had done that. He couldn't say 'I did it because I love wild rivers and I don't like electricity,' but he

could do it by holding up the study, and saying, 'look, I changed my vote for solid economic reasons.' "

After the Tuolumne study was released, Stavins said, local conservation groups in Maine and New York used its analytic techniques to fight proposed hydroelectric developments in their states. In general, though, the major environmental organizations remained suspicious of the cost-benefit approach, and EDF recognized that the Tuolumne study's success couldn't hope to change that. "I didn't have globe-shaking hopes for the Tuolumne study," said Zach Willey, EDF's chief economist. "What is hoped was that it would influence a couple of senators and it did that."

The dam's proponents were predictably critical of the EDF study's methods and conclusions. R. W. Beck and Associates, the irrigation districts' engineering consultants, challenged Stavins' use of the controversial concept of "option value"—especially since option value accounted for some 90 percent of his estimates of the river's total recreation value.

Beck also maintained that social values could not really be quantified. "In order for a social benefit-cost analysis not to cloud such political decisions, it would have to provide definitive quantification of all externalities, not just a selected few," Beck associate Frank K. Dubar wrote to project manager Lawrence Klein. "The weighing of social values is best served by the political process during the Federal Energy Regulatory Commission licensing and the National Environmental Policy Act procedures for the Environmental Impact Statement using standard federal guidelines for economic determination."

Congress's decision to protect the Tuolumne forced the irrigation districts to look elsewhere for power and water. By 1986, the Turlock Irrigation District was moving ahead with plans to purchase surplus power from Pacific Northwest hydro plants and build more fossil-fuel generators. The district and Tuolumne County also were studying the potential for building a small hydroelectric development on the Clavey River.

Notes

1. Irrigation districts are governed by five-member boards elected to staggered four-year terms by the area residents.
2. An acre-foot equals 325,851 gallons—the amount of water required to flood one acre of land to a depth of one foot.
3. Stavins structured a monthly schedule of flows available for energy generation based on Beck's estimate of Tuolumne river flows minus flow releases recommended by the U.S. Fish and Wildlife Service as necessary to maintain river fisheries.
4. Stavins said he chose this method based on Water Resources Council guidelines, which suggest using the unit-day value method if the project meets the following three conditions: the site does not involve specialized highly skilled recreational activities for which opportunities are limited; the number of visits per year likely to be affected by the proposed project does not exceed 750,000; and the expected recreation costs do not exceed 25 percent of total project costs.

Review of EDF Analysis

January 27, 1984

Mr. Lawrence T. Klein
Project Director
Clavey-Wards Ferry Project
P.O. Box 5296
Modesto, California 95352–5296

Dear Larry:

As requested we have reviewed the publication: "The Tuolumne River: Preservation or Development? An Economic Assessment, Summary Report," by Environmental Defense Fund (EDF), October 1983. Principal author: Robert Stavins. The essence of the Report findings is that the R. W. Beck and Associates' assessment of the costs and benefits associated with the Clavey-Wards Ferry Project, failed to account for identifiable and quantifiable external costs and benefits. Accordingly, had such external effects been accounted for the benefit-cost ratio of the project would have been found to be less than one, and hence a finding would have been made that the project is not economically justified. This conclusion is based on the authors' finding that the benefits that would be lost (or alternatively costs incurred) in the form of foregone whitewater rafting and fishing, are sufficiently greater than any benefits gained as a result of flatwater recreational activities created. The Report introduces the concept of "option values" which applies a monetary value to the opportunity for anyone to go whitewater boating in the future, if they should decide to utilize that opportunity. Our comments on the Report follow: . . . The Report assumes elimination of whitewater boating by project construction. In the Clavey-Wards Ferry Alternative, the 6-mile reach upstream of Wards Ferry Reservoir would still be available for whitewater boating during the spring runoff period in average and wet years. No benefit credit from whitewater recreation was attached to this item by the authors. With the Ponderosa Alternative, however, the value of lost whitewater recreation would be zero; in fact, an annual benefit over the existing conditions would be attained since seven days of rafting would be possible during the summer months, versus five to six days presently.

The Report states that near-total degradation of the trout fishery would occur. This is not true, since minimum flow releases for fishery purposes at Jawbone Dam and Clavey Dam would be set in consultation with federal and state fisheries agencies.

Further, due to reduced flows between Jawbone Dam and Lumsden campground, it is considered that fishing conditions will improve, particularly for fly fishing.

The Report emphasizes that public policy decisions regarding the use of the nation's scarce natural resources are ultimately political decisions due to the conflicting social concerns. Yet the methodology proposed tries to quantify social values, particularly intrinsic values, which in reality cannot be definitively quantified. In order for a social benefit-cost analysis not to cloud such political decisions it would have to provide definitive quantification of all externalities, not just a selected few. The weighing of social values is best served by the political process during the FERC licensing and the NEPA procedures for the EIS using standard Federal guidelines for economic determination.

The authors have specified the recreation demand function by attempting to establish a casual relationship between number of visits to the recreational site from each of a number of discrete geographical origins and the travel and on-site costs associated with each such visit (this is what the author refers to as the "travel cost model"). The model appears oversimplified in that the demand for visitation to the site is presumed to be almost exclusively determined by price (travel cost), and completely ignores other important ingredients such as income, age, and other factors. The parameter estimates of such a simplified model are almost certain to be biased, which would result in overestimating the magnitude of the consumer surplus (benefits). . . .

Although intrinsic (option) values are not recognized by WRC in its recommended principles and guidelines, the option value shown in the EDF analysis for Clavey-Wards Ferry is some 90 percent of the total recreation value evaluated. If option values were to be quantified and included in an economic analysis, then all possible external social values should be included in order to present an unbiased analysis. For example, the whitewater boating option value could

well be balanced by the option value of having a renewable energy resource to counter the threat of Arab oil embargoes. Clearly, this is outside the scope of an economic analysis. Such varied option values are best evaluated by the NEPA-EIS process. Option values are at best controversial and mask any realistic analysis of recreation user values that might be presented.

In Table 1 of the Report, the total 1994 recreational value is $37,261,000 of which $33,503,000 is the option value (90%). Yet evaluation of the most significant portion of the recreation value is afforded essentially only a footnote stating that the option value is based upon a proportional relationship and that a value of 0.6 for the ratio of nonuse value/household to use-value/household was used. The evaluation of the proxy population, which significantly determines the total option value, is given no discussion in the Report.

On the other hand, the external benefits of flatwater recreational opportunities are based upon the normal unit-day value method in the analysis. This of course provides a substantial bias against the Clavey-Wards Ferry Project, since the option value of flatwater recreation lost if the project is not built has not been considered. For example, the estimated $37 million lost annually by whitewater rafting dwarfs the project recreation benefits (Clavey-Wards Ferry Alternative) of $327,000. Clearly, the cost of travel and value of time of the flatwater recreationists is not included on the same basis as that of the whitewater boaters.

Travel costs are estimated to be all out-of-pocket costs plus the opportunity costs of the travel time and the time spent at the recreational site. The value of such time is likely to be over-stated given that opportunity cost is measured as prevailing wage rates—certainly too high, especially for weekend visitors. Further, the authors seem to treat all whitewater rafters as commercial users, which results in an estimate of lost whitewater benefits of approximately $37 million annually or more than

$6,000 per rafter use, a completely unrealistic amount, commercial or not.

On the other hand, income and age are not considered in the evaluation of users' consumer surplus. This is important since rafting is expensive. Differences between weekday and weekend use are also not considered. This could also be significant since rafting flows are somewhat reduced on Saturdays and essentially nonexistent on Sundays under no-project conditions during summer months. The Report also assumes all users take two day trips and neglects the effect of one day trips.

For the whitewater user's opportunity cost of time, a "k" value of 0.6 times the average hourly wage rate of the region considered was used and stated to be conservative. The WRC, however, recommends a "k" value of .25–.33 times the wage rate since most people have free weekends and paid vacations and are not actually choosing between work and play. The analysis also does not consider the number of unemployed persons (students and nonworking family members) using the river. A weighted average reflecting the demographic makeup of visitors should be used. . . .

R. W. Beck and Associates conducted several analyses using the EDF method, but based on reasonable assumptions for various parameters. Calculations were made to determine the sensitivity of the benefit-cost ratio to variation in the proxy populations used, or to its elimination altogether. With the proxy population reduced by 50 percent (i.e., 50 percent fewer persons would be willing to pay to ensure that whitewater boating would be available in the future *if they should decide* to utilize the opportunity), the total 1994 recreational value is reduced to $20,511,000 rather than $37,261,000, and the benefit-cost ratio becomes 1.054 rather than 0.877, even using the less than satisfactory semi-log method. If the proxy population option value is eliminated, the total 1994 recreational value becomes $3,759,000 and the benefit-cost ratio 1.32. . . .

In summary the method proposed by the EDF analysis for the environmental economies of hydro power development is not used by the federal regulatory agencies. However, applying reasonable parameters to that method, with appropriate recognition of the environmental benefits of project development, results in substantiation of the benefit-cost ratio of about 1.3 calculated independently by Beck.

Very truly yours,
R. W. Beck and Associates

Comment

The EDF's cost-benefit analysis serves the cause of environmental protection and therefore casts doubt upon the claim that the method of policy analysis is biased against values that are not easily quantifiable. In serving the cause of environmental protection, however, the EDF analysis also diffuses criticisms that are often levied by environmentalists against techniques that quantify environmental values. Interestingly, it is the opponents of environmental protection who call such quantification into question.

Consider the various ways in which the EDF analysis quantifies environmental values and determine the extent to which it successfully establishes a "broader, social perspective by trying to internalize some of the environmental externalities." Setting aside the possible political advantages of invoking economic arguments to protect the environment, what can one say for and against putting monetary values on the recreational uses of the environment? Evaluate the following criticisms of EDF's analysis: (1) "the methodology proposed tries to quantify social values, particularly intrinsic values, which in reality cannot be definitively quantified"; (2) because it quantifies only some externalities, the analysis obscures the process of political decision making; (3) the analysis overstates the benefits of environmental protection by ignoring other "option values," such as "having a renewable energy resource to counter the threat of Arab oil embargoes" and "the option value of flatwater recreation lost if the project is not built"; and (4) the analysis takes preferences for recreation and energy resources as given even though these preferences typically can change over time.

Suppose that EDF's policy analysis is revised on the basis of new information and the updated analysis yields the opposite conclusion, that the net benefits of proceeding with the Clavey-Wards Ferry project now exceed the costs. Could proponents of environmental protection offer any morally defensible reasons to reject the analysis and to maintain their opposition to the Clavey-Wards Ferry project? Are there any considerations omitted from a cost-benefit analysis that are nonetheless relevant to the making of public policy? Are there any considerations included in cost-benefit analysis that should be excluded from consideration?

Policy analysis often seems inaccessible to citizens because of its technical vocabulary and quantitative techniques. Yet citizens should be able to evaluate such analyses in general terms by considering whether they address the right questions. Examine the EDF analysis and the Beck review in this spirit by asking: Are the basic assumptions plausible? Are any moral issues misconstrued as merely technical questions? What, if any, morally and politically relevant factors are ignored? If public officials believe that the economic analysis should not completely determine the outcome, can they say more than "I love wild rivers, and I don't like electricity"?

The conventional decision-making rule in policy analysis says to "choose the policy that maximizes the total expected utility," where the total expected utility is the sum of the benefits minus the costs, discounting for the uncertainty of each. Some critics of conventional policy analysis suggest that because future generations cannot participate in present decision-making and because people generally fear unchosen risk more than they desire unexpected benefits, we should adopt cautious decision-making rules, which minimize the risks to future generations. Assess the moral implications of the following rules: (1) Keep the options open (reject irreversible policies). (2) Protect the vulnerable (give special weight to future generations). (3) Maximize minimum payoff (make sure the worst outcome is as good as possible). (4) Avoid harm (give more weight to causing harms than to failing to produce benefits of the same size). Under what circumstances would these rules lead us to recommend environmental protection over energy development, or vice versa? How would you justify (or criticize) each of the rules?

The Risks of Asarco

Esther Scott

On July 12, 1983, William Ruckelshaus, administrator of the Environmental Protection Agency (EPA), announced in Washington proposed standards that would regulate arsenic emissions from copper smelting and glass manufacturing plants in the United States. Arsenic had increasingly been regarded as a dangerous air pollutant and as such fell within the purview of EPA. Issuing standards for pollutants was nothing new at the agency, but this announcement attracted more than usual interest: Ruckelshaus was proposing to involve the public in helping him decide just how stringent those regulations should be.

The arsenic standards were expected to have their greatest impact on Tacoma, Washington, because of its proximity to a copper smelter owned by the American Smelting and Refining Company (Asarco)—the only smelter in the nation that used ore with high arsenic content and a major source of arsenic emissions. The proposed standards applied the best available technology to reduce emissions; but even so, there would remain a residual risk factor that might, according to EPA calculations, result in roughly one additional cancer death per year among Tacoma area residents. However, imposing further requirements to eliminate that risk could drive up the plant's costs and make it uneconomical to run. The smelter employed more than five hundred people, in a state that was experiencing over 11 percent unemployment. "My view," Ruckelshaus later told a *Los Angeles Times* reporter, "is that these are the kinds of tough, balancing questions that we're involved in here in this country in trying to regulate all kinds of hazardous substances. I don't like these questions either, but the societal issue is what risks are we willing to take and for what benefits?" To get answers to that question, Ruckelshaus announced EPA's intention of actively soliciting the views and wishes of the people most affected by the proposed regulations: the residents who lived and worked near the Asarco smelter. "For me to sit here in Washington," Ruckelshaus told the assembled press, "and tell the people of Tacoma what is an acceptable risk would be at best arrogant and at worst inexcusable."

RUCKELSHAUS AT EPA

At the time the proposed arsenic regulations were announced, Ruckelshaus had only recently returned to the agency he had first headed in 1970, the year EPA was established. During the brief tenure of his predecessor, Anne Burford (formerly Gorsuch), EPA had become mired in scandal and controversy, and was frequently attacked for failure to enforce environmental laws and to carry out the agency's mission. The appointment of Ruckelshaus, who was highly regarded for his integrity and admired for his work as EPA's first administrator, had done much to restore credibility to the agency, but mistrust of the Reagan administration's commitment to environmental issues lingered in the public mind.

In Ruckelshaus' view, moreover, there were other troubling uncertainties facing his second EPA administration. In the 1980s, scientists were no longer assuming the existence of a threshold of safety from carcinogens: in theory, at least, adverse effects could occur from exposure to even one molecule of a carcinogenic substance. Ruckelshaus, in a June 1983 address to the National Academy of Sciences (NAS), put it this way: "[W]e must assume that life now takes place in a minefield of risks from hundreds, perhaps thousands, of substances. No more can we tell the public: You are home free with an adequate margin of safety." In this starker world, Ruckelshaus told the assembled scientists,

> We need more research on the health effects of the substances we regulate. . . . Given the necessity of acting in the face of enormous scientific uncertainties, it is more important than ever that our scientific analysis be rigorous and the quality of our data be high. We must take great pains not to mislead people regarding the risks to their health. We can help avoid confusion both by the quality of our science and the clarity of our language in exploring the hazards.

THE ASARCO SMELTER

The Asarco copper smelting plant on the edge of Tacoma was a model of the kind of wrenching choices the EPA administrator often faced in proposing regulations. Built in 1890, the Asarco smelter, whose 571-foot smokestack dominated the landscape around it, processed high arsenic content copper ore and produced commercial arsenic as a by-product from its smelter. (Arsenic is present as an impurity in certain ores, such as copper and lead, and can be produced either as a waste or as a by-product in the smelting of these ores. The arsenic was used in the manufacture of glass, herbicides, insecticides, and other products.) The Asarco plant—the only one in the nation that used high arsenic content ore—was also the only domestic producer of industrial arsenic, providing approximately one-third of the U.S. supply of arsenic.

In recent times, the smelter had been in shaky financial condition. World prices for copper had plummeted from $1.45/lb. in 1980 to $.60/lb. in 1982, and U.S. copper processors were facing intense competition from Japan. At the Asarco plant, the cost of producing copper was $.82/lb. The plant had for awhile been able to make a profit largely due to sales of residual metals—chiefly gold—from the copper smelting process; but as the price of gold dropped, so too did the plant's earnings and, according to Asarco officials, it had been losing money for several years.

For generations, the Asarco smelter had provided a livelihood to the families of Ruston, a small company town (population 636) that had sprung up around the big smokestack, and the surrounding area. In 1983, it employed roughly 575 workers on an annual payroll of about $23 million. (According to company estimates, it could cost the state of Washington as much as $5.5 million in unemployment benefits if the plant shut down.) The smelter also contributed to the economy of the area by spending approximately $12 million locally on supplies, indirectly supporting $13 million of auxiliary business, and paying $3 million in state and local taxes. Seventy-year-old Owen Gallagher, a former mayor of Ruston and an employee of Asarco for forty-three years, spoke for many town residents when he told reporters from the *Chicago Tribune:*

> I've worked in the plant all my life. So have my brothers, and so have my neighbors. We're not sick. This town was built around that plant. People came here looking for fire and smoke in the 1900s to find work. Now the government's complaining about that same smoke and trying to take our children's livelihood away.

But the fact was that Asarco had long been regarded as one of the major polluters in the Northwest, and held what one report called "the dubious distinction of being the worst arsenic polluter in the United States."[1] Commencement Bay, Tacoma's industrial harbor, had been designated a Superfund hazardous waste clean-up site partially because of accumulated arsenic both in the soil around the plant and in the bottom sand of the bay. Asarco was also one of the two major emitters of sulfur dioxide (SO_2, a by-product of burning carbon fuel) in the state of Washington.[2]

Area residents affected by this pollution made no bones about their feelings. Bill Tobin, a lawyer and resident of Vashon Island—a semi-rural, middle-income community two miles offshore from Ruston—pointed out that, because of the high smokestack and prevailing wind directions, "we are the dumping grounds for these pollutants without any benefits such as jobs or Asarco tax payments." Island residents were particularly concerned over high levels of arsenic found in urine samples of their children and in soil from local gardens. "I'm not for the loss of jobs," one homeowner told the *Tacoma News Tribune;* but he added, "Numerous people who staked their life savings on a place and a home are finding they can't enjoy the land because of the emissions of the Asarco plant." Vashon Island was by no means the only reluctant host to emissions from the smelter. Neighboring Tacoma received tons of air pollution from the plant, and little by way of taxes from the smelter to compensate. One member of the Tacoma city council described the effects of the smelter as "somebody standing on the other side of the city line with a thirty-ought-six and firing it into Tacoma."

Over the years, efforts to control pollution from the Asarco smelter came primarily from the regional level.[3] Since 1970, the Puget Sound Air Pollution Control Agency (PSAPCA), a regional air pollution authority, had issued a variety of orders aimed at reducing both SO_2 and arsenic emissions; but Asarco had either failed to comply and paid the relatively small penalties, or delayed action through litigation and variance proceedings.

However, despite the court battles and delays, PSAPCA had made some headway in getting Asarco to comply with its orders. As Asarco officials were quick to point out, the company had spent about $40 million over a ten-year period in equipment and practices designed to reduce pollution; it had also agreed to curtail operations when meteorological conditions would cause high ambient SO_2 levels. In the late 1970s, Asarco and PSAPCA negotiated a compromise agreement covering both SO_2 and arsenic emissions. For the latter, Asarco agreed to install, by 1984, secondary converter hoods, which would reduce "fugitive" arsenic emissions that were not funneled up the smokestack (and were considered more dangerous because they were less likely to disperse before reaching the public).[4] According to later EPA estimates, the cost of the converters would run to roughly $3.5 million in capital outlay (Asarco put the figure at $4.5 million), along with an estimated $1.5 million per year in operating and maintenance expenses. These costs were expected to result in an estimated product price increase of 0.5 to 0.8 percent.

While these local efforts were ongoing, EPA had been, more or less, out of the picture. Under the provisions of the Clean Air Act, the federal agency was required to identify, list, and promulgate National Emission Standards for Hazardous Air Pollutants (NESHAPs) for substances believed to be detrimental to human health. EPA had listed inorganic arsenic as a hazardous air pollutant in June 1980, but had decided the following year not to issue a NESHAP for it. This decision chagrined PSAPCA officials, who felt that a ruling from EPA would give them another tool to use in their dealings with Asarco. But, as it turned out, EPA was soon forced to take a stronger hand in the matter. In late 1982, the state of New York, concerned about arsenic emissions from a Corning Glass manufacturing plant in New Jersey, took EPA to court. The U.S. District Court subsequently ruled that the agency must publish proposed national standards by July 11, 1983, six months later. Thus was the stage set for Ruckelshaus' experiment in risk management.

TAKING IT TO THE PUBLIC

THE RISK ASSESSMENT

On July 12, 1983—the same day that Ruckelshaus announced the proposed regulations on arsenic emissions[5]—Ernesta Barnes, administrator of EPA's northwest regional office, appeared before the press in Tacoma. "We ask the public's help to consider the very difficult issues raised by arsenic air emissions," Barnes told the assembled reporters. "Together we must determine 'What is an "acceptable" or "reasonable" risk to public health from arsenic emissions.' " To aid in that process, she announced public hearings in Tacoma on August 30 and 31, to be preceded by "public workshops and other activities to inform you of the many technical issues involved."

The hearings—wherein the public had an opportunity to present testimony—would have been held anyway, because the proposed standards for the Tacoma smelter were part of a national rulemaking process. What was different, says Ernesta Barnes, were the workshops. The "underlying theory," she explains, was that the decision makers had a "moral responsibility" to provide "adequate information" and opportunity for discussion in advance of the hearings, "so that when the actual public hearing was held, those that had chosen to become especially well informed would have not only their own values on which to base their testimony, but also better information about what the facts actually were."

At the press conference, Barnes provided a brief sketch of some of the technical issues the workshops would cover, outlining the risk assessment EPA had performed as part of the standard-setting process. EPA analysts had used a dispersion model to calculate concentrations of arsenic at over one hundred locations within approximately twelve miles of the smelter, and combined those figures with "unit risk numbers"[6] derived from previous epidemiological studies of workers exposed to arsenic. The results of EPA's analyses yielded an estimate of some 310 tons of arsenic emissions spewed out each year by the Asarco smelter, and the risk of up to four related cancer deaths per year within twelve miles of the smelter.

Because EPA considered inorganic arsenic a non-threshold pollutant—i.e., even the most minute trace of it could not definitely be said to be harmless—it determined that the arsenic emissions from the Asarco smelter should be, in the language of the proposed standards, "controlled at least to the level that reflects best available technology (BAT), and to a more stringent level if, in the judgment of the administrator, it is necessary to prevent unreasonable risks." The appropriate BAT, Barnes explained at the press conference, was the converter hoods Asarco had already agreed to (and had in fact begun installing) in its negotiations with PSAPCA.[7] The hoods would, she said, reduce arsenic emissions from the smelter to 189 tons per year. "The number of related cancer cases within a twelve-mile radius of the plant," she added, "would drop from four per year to one a year."

Ruckelshaus was free to impose on his own a "more stringent level" of emission control. He could, for instance, set emissions standards that would require Asarco to use a lower arsenic content ore[8] or to convert to electric smelting. However, Asarco maintained that the added cost of shipping the low arsenic ore would force the company to close the smelter. Similarly, the expense of switching to electric smelting would amount to $150 million in capital outlays, and could also precipitate a shutdown. It was to consider such options and their implications that Ruckelshaus sought public involvement. "Should we interpret the legislative intent of the Clean Air Act to mandate a total shutdown to produce zero risk to public health?" Barnes asked at the

Tacoma press conference. " . . . Or is there a level of risk that is acceptable to the community and consistent with the law?"

REACTION

The workshops were not scheduled to start until mid-August, but debate on the issue began as soon as Barnes' press conference was over. Ruckelshaus' proposal to involve the public in the final decision making received, not surprisingly, intense coverage in the local media, but it was widely reported in the national press as well. Many of the headlines depicted Tacomans as facing a stark choice: "Smelter workers have choice: Keep their jobs or their health" (*Chicago Tribune*); "What Cost a Life? EPA Asks Tacoma" (*Los Angeles Times*); "Tacoma Gets Choice: Cancer Risk or Lost Jobs" (*New York Times*). Most articles quoted Tacoma area citizens who stood on opposite sides of the fence on the issue, citing their fears of ill health or unemployment. "I'm concerned about getting lung cancer," one resident told the *New York Times,* while the head of the local union representing the workers at the smelter countered, "Simply dying from cancer is not different from a man losing his job and then committing suicide."

Many observers were critical of Ruckelshaus for what one area resident called "copping out." "It is up to the EPA to protect public health," said Ruth Weiner, head of the Cascade Chapter of the Sierra Club, in an interview with the *New York Times,* "not to ask the public what it is willing to sacrifice not to die from cancer." Another local citizen told a *Los Angeles Times* reporter, "EPA came in recently and found that our drinking water was contaminated and just cleaned it up, saying they'd find out why later. Now, why aren't they just cleaning this mess up instead of asking people how much cancer they would like to have?"

On the day he announced the proposed regulations, Ruckelshaus had told the press that he was not seeking a referendum from the people, only seeing if a consensus emerged from the public meetings; however, he added, in a remark that was widely quoted, "I don't know what we'll do if there is a 50–50 split." Perhaps in part because of that remark, the notion persisted among the public and some of the press that Ruckelshaus was in fact taking a vote. This idea received its harshest expression in a July 16 *New York Times* editorial, titled "Mr. Ruckelshaus as Caesar," that compared the EPA administrator with a Roman emperor "who would ask the amphitheater crowd to signal with thumbs up or down whether a defeated gladiator should live or die." For Ruckelshaus to "impose such an impossible choice on Tacomans," the editorial stated, was "inexcusable."

Ruckelshaus responded to the editorial in a July 23 letter to the *Times* insisting that "no poll of Tacoma's citizens will be taken." The people of Tacoma were being asked for their "informed opinion," not a decision, he continued. "They know that the right to be heard is not the same thing as the right to be heeded. The final decision is mine." Ruckelshaus continued to defend his position despite the criticism. "Listen," he told the *Los Angeles Times,* "I know people don't like these kinds of decisions. Welcome to the world of regulation. People have demanded to be involved and now I have involved them and they say: 'Don't ask that question.' What's the alternative? Don't involve them? Then you're accused of doing something nefarious."

CONTROVERSY OVER NUMBERS

Disagreements with EPA over the proposed arsenic regulations were not limited to how the agency was handling the process. Even before the official round of workshops and hearings began, EPA's risk calculations were being called into question. Just days after Ruckelshaus announced the proposed regulations, Asarco officials noted that their own figures on arsenic concentrations in the vicinity of the smelter—based on routine monitoring on the site—were significantly lower than the estimates—based on a computer model provided by EPA; in a letter to EPA (later published in the *New York Times*), Asarco asserted that the agency had "overpredict[ed] maximum ambient concentrations of arsenic by a factor of 10." It soon turned up that EPA's model had some serious flaws—most notably the assumption that the smelter was on flat land, when in reality it was on the side of a steep hill. EPA quickly announced its intention of revising its estimates; and when they were published, the agency's new figures for overall arsenic emissions were indeed lower: 115 tons per year (instead of 310), to be lowered to 85 tons (instead of 189) with the installation of the converter hoods.[9] However, these new estimates were not available until late October—too late for the workshops but in time for the public hearings; in the meantime, there was uncertainty about what were the right figures and whom to trust. One leaflet distributed by the union at the time of the workshops asserted that the "figures used for the computer model were from 410 percent to 2267 percent higher than the actual figures."

Other questions about EPA's calculations arose around the time the workshops were to begin. Dr. Samuel Milham, Jr., of the Washington State Department of Social and Health Services, told the *Los Angeles Times* that EPA's projections of possible lung cancers were "baloney." Milham, who had conducted studies in the Tacoma area, found elevated lung cancer rates among retired Asarco workers, but, he added, "we have been looking for extra lung cancers in the community (among those who do not work at the smelter) and we haven't found them. Nothing."

THE WORKSHOPS

Against this backdrop of controversy, the northwest EPA office (Region 10) began conducting its workshops, aimed at acquainting residents with the details of the proposed regulations in preparation for the upcoming hearings. The first workshop was held on Vashon Island on August 10, 1983, followed soon after by two more in Tacoma itself. All three workshops (which were covered by local and national TV) were well attended, particularly the two in Tacoma, which drew environmental groups, local citizen organizations, and a large number of smelter workers, who had come at the urging of their union representative. (The importance of stacking the aisles with large numbers of supporters, one observer noted, might have stemmed from a lingering feeling that Ruckelshaus was going to make the decision by counting heads.)

The format of all three workshops was basically the same: after a formal presentation by EPA staff, the audience divided into smaller groups in order to encourage dialogue and permit more individual response to specific questions. EPA national headquarters sent two key policymakers—Robert Ajax, chief of the Standards Development Branch, and Betty Anderson, director of the Office of Health and Environmental Assessment—to assist in the process. They, along with Ernesta Barnes, rotated among the groups, answering questions. Each group had a "facilitator" (hired by EPA for the occasion), a recorder, and three EPA staff from the regional office. "Every comment [from the public] was recorded . . . and [later] typed up," says Barnes. To accompany discussion, staff from the Region 10 office prepared and distributed a number of handouts for the workshop, including illustrations of how hooding helped control emissions, excerpts from Ruckelshaus' NAS speech, and fact sheets on arsenic controls and risk calculations.

EPA had come prepared to discuss risk assessment figures and dispersion models and present graphs and charts, yet many of the questions they encountered had little to do with verifiable "facts." "The personal nature of the complaints and questions made a striking counterpoint to the presentations of meteorological models and health effect extrapolations," wrote Gilbert Omenn, dean of the School of Public Health at the University of Washington, in a letter to Ernesta Barnes. (Omenn had been hired by EPA to observe and help evaluate the workshops.) People asked about the symptoms of arsenic poisoning, about other health effects from arsenic, about the advisability of eating produce from Vashon Island gardens. One person asked whether it would be necessary to remove a foot of dirt from her garden to make it safe (and who would pay for it); another wanted to know what effect arsenic emissions would have on animals. Ruckelshaus, who had received a personal report on the Vashon Island workshop, later recounted that, after EPA health experts finished their presentation, "A woman got up in the audience and said, 'Last week, my dog ate some spinach and dropped over dead. Did he die of arsenic?' " There were more sobering moments as well, Ruckelshaus noted, as when "another woman got up and said, 'Will my child die of cancer?' "

Nevertheless, technical matters such as the risk figures and epidemiological studies formed the basis for the majority of questions. Several inquiries focused on EPA's dispersion model and the reliability of the proposed control equipment. One resident wanted to know if any studies had been done on birth defects or miscarriages in the area; another asked whether the risk posed by emissions from the smelter was greater than the risk from ambient carbon monoxide from cars. This last question highlighted EPA's difficulties in explaining adequately the risk numbers in a relative context. Although EPA had prepared a table illustrating comparative risk, it was described as "cluttered" and needing fuller explanation. One critic commented, "How can they expect a relatively unsophisticated public to understand what these risk figures mean when the environmental establishment in this state doesn't even understand them?"

Several questions betrayed a lingering hostility toward EPA for not resolving the issue on its own. "Seems like EPA is leaving the interpretation of the law up to the public," one resident commented. "Why has Asarco continued to obtain variances from complying with the law? What authority does EPA have to do this?" Another resident asked, "At this point in time is Asarco in violation of any clean air requirements? If so, why are they allowed to operate? Why is EPA spending taxpayers' money for this process if Asarco is not violating any laws?" "We elected people to run our government, we don't expect them to turn around and ask us to run it for them," said still another. "These issues are very complex and the public is not sophisticated enough to make these decisions. This is not to say that EPA doesn't have an obligation to inform the public, but information is one thing—defaulting its legal mandate is another."

In the end, the workshops got mixed, but generally favorable notices. "Many of the questioners were impressively well informed," Gilbert Omenn wrote. "I expect that some rethinking of elements of the *Federal Register* notice and the presentation of certain assumptions and facts will result from [the workshop]." "We also got educated," agrees Randy Smith, an EPA analyst from Region 10. "The questions raised at the workshops sent some people back to the drawing board."

CLOSING ARGUMENTS: THE HEARINGS

At the conclusion of the workshops, several groups asked EPA to postpone the formal hearing, slated for late August, to allow them more time to prepare the testimony. The agency agreed, and the hearings were rescheduled for early November. In the meantime, EPA participated in a few more workshops run by others—the city of Tacoma and the Steelworkers Union, where the comments and questions bordered on the openly hostile. ("I have seen studies which show that stress is the main source of cancer," one worker told an EPA representative. "The EPA is one main cause of stress.") By the end of the summer, all the interested parties were gearing up to present their arguments at the public hearing.

The hearings began on November 2, 1983. A panel of EPA officials (made up of representatives from the regional office, EPA headquarters, and EPA's research facility in North Carolina) presided over a three-day period, as roughly 150 people representing a variety of groups or just individual concerns offered their views on the proposed arsenic regulations. Their testimony ran the gamut from sophisticated technical arguments for more controls to anxious complaints that EPA was asking Tacoma residents to vote on a death sentence for one of their fellow citizens.[10]

PSAPCA'S TESTIMONY

Harvey Poll, chairman of PSAPCA, was first to speak at the hearings. The PSAPCA board had evaluated EPA's proposed standard, Poll told the hearing panel, and concluded that it had some serious shortcomings. The board's primary objection was that the proposal did not establish arsenic ambient air quality standards. (EPA was, however, constrained by statutory requirements, which directed the administrator to set technology-based, not ambient air, standards in issuing NESHAPS.) PSAPCA was also concerned that because the new hooding would reduce SO_2 emissions, Asarco would be able to operate the smelter more often (instead of curtailing operations during adverse meteorological conditions), thereby actually increasing the total volume of plant-wide arsenic emissions. PSAPCA wanted EPA to consider requiring Asarco to install a flue gas desulfurization system (at a cost several times higher than the $3.5 million for secondary hooding) or, more drastically, to force the company to convert to a new smelting technology at a projected cost of roughly $130–$150 million. PSAPCA had already issued a compliance order forcing the company to choose one of these options

by 1987 in order to reduce SO_2 emissions (and, of necessity, arsenic emissions) by 90 percent.

ASARCO'S TESTIMONY

Next to testify was Asarco, which had hired the public relations firm of Hill and Knowlton to organize and present its case at the hearings. In addition to Armand L. Labbe, an Asarco vice president and former manager of the Tacoma smelter, the company employed five expert witnesses to refute EPA's numbers and modeling assumptions and to assert that "there *now* exists an ample margin of safety" from arsenic emissions from the smelter [emphasis in original]. Most of the experts were affiliated with universities, and each boasted an impressive curriculum vitae with relevant experience.

"Epidemiological studies demonstrate that arsenic emissions from the Asarco Tacoma smelter are not at levels that pose a health risk to the public living in the vicinity of the plant," Labbe flatly stated. Tom Downs, a professor of biology at the University of Texas, disputed EPA's extrapolations of health effects: "[EPA's assumption about exposure to arsenic] is like saying that the effects of taking five aspirin tablets a day for a lifetime are the same as the effects of taking five-hundred aspirin tablets per day for 1 percent of a lifetime."

Despite its assertion, that, in the words of Asarco attorney C. John Newlands, "the Tacoma Smelter is now in compliance with Section 112 of the Federal Clean Air Act," the company stated its support for EPA's proposed arsenic standards—and at the same time outlined its opposition to ambient standards or to efforts to reduce emissions further. Asarco also detailed the projects—some of them voluntary—the firm had undertaken over the years to control SO_2 and arsenic pollution. Summing up the firm's position, Labbe reminded his listeners that a prolonged depression in the copper industry had hurt the Tacoma plant's ability to compete, and that the smelter had lost money in recent years. He concluded: "We are unable to commit additional expenditures beyond installation of BAT under present conditions."

ENVIRONMENTAL GROUPS

A host of environmental groups appeared at the hearings—ranging from long-established organizations like the American Lung Association of Washington (which, according to staff member Janet Chalupnick, played a key role in coordinating a coalition of clean air groups) to more recently formed groups like Tacomans for a Healthy Environment.[11] For the most part, the environmentalists' testimony was critical of EPA—arguing that its proposed regulation did not go far enough—and supportive of PSAPCA's more comprehensive recommendations. Several environmental organizations opposed EPA's "best available technology" approach, asserting that it effectively discouraged the development of new technology to improve emissions control. "By allowing a company to only install the available technology it says is affordable, the EPA is creating a situation in which the company is still allowed to emit substantial amounts of toxic substances but may be inclined for financial reasons to resist development of improved control technologies," said Brian Baird of Tacomans for a Healthy Environment. "If BAT standards are regularly used," he continued, "it seems reasonable to anticipate that the pace of technological development of all types of pollution control will be substantially slowed, because the market for Better Available Technologies will not only have been removed, it will have been significantly undermined."

In its testimony, the National-Audubon Society reiterated Baird's point: ". . . If EPA finds zero emissions of a pollutant to be impossible, they should set the standards at the lowest levels possible rather than at the levels achievable through pollution control technologies easily affordable by the polluting industries. In order to protect [the public] health, standards must be used to

force technological innovation to pollution control rather than to simply reinforce the status quo." Similarly, Nancy Ellison of the Washington Environmental Council chided EPA for proposing only the "absolute minimum" in regulation; nor did the council agree, she told the panel, "that the only choices available are hood installation or smelter shutdown. This is not a jobs-versus-the-environment issue."

THE SMELTER WORKERS

As Ellison's remark indicated, environmentalists in the area had been making an effort to reverse the longstanding pattern of labor vs. environmental interests, and to find common ground with the workers in resolving arsenic emissions problems. Further evidence of a fragile alliance between the two groups was observable in the testimony of Michael Wright, an industrial hygienist for the United Steelworkers union. "No one has to convince our union that arsenic at high levels is risky," said Wright. "We know what arsenic has done to many of our union brothers and sisters in the Tacoma Smelter and other copper smelters. It was the death of our members which provided the conclusive evidence that arsenic causes lung cancer." Wright went on to urge EPA to encourage the development of technology which would make the plant safer for workers and community residents by reducing pollution.[12] He supported the installation of secondary hooding and research to determine if further controls would be useful and economically feasible.

Not surprisingly, the union spoke out against requiring control equipment that was too costly, and would therefore force the plant to close. Referring to a study which he used to estimate the health risk of forcing the smelter to close, Wright claimed that the stress resulting from unemployment could cause eighty-four deaths in Pierce County over a six year period. "That," he asserted, "is a considerably greater risk of death than what EPA predicts from arsenic after the installation of secondary hooding."

Following Wright's testimony, individual smelter workers spoke before the panel. In what was often emotional testimony, several members of the "twenty-five year club"—people who had worked at the plant for more than a quarter of a century—made their case. "I'm eighty-eight years old and I ain't dead yet. I'm still breathing," said Ross Bridges. The workers reflected on the good life the smelter had made possible for them and their families. If the smelter closed, they maintained, it would leave them jobless. "No high-tech industry moving into Tacoma is going to hire me," one man lamented. "The smelter is all I've got."

VASHON ISLAND RESIDENTS

Residents of Vashon Island (which, except for Tacoma's North End, received the majority of emissions from Asarco) provided equally emotional testimony of the trauma that they had experienced as a result of the arsenic pollution. One man came to the hearing sporting a gas mask, several were clad in hospital patient garb, and some carried young children to the podium to make their point. One woman, who claimed to have been diagnosed by her doctors as ultra-sensitive to arsenic, tearfully told the panel that she and her husband had been forced to sell their small farm for a fraction of its worth—due to depressed real estate prices on the island—and leave the area. Michael Bradley, chairman of a group named Island Residents Against Toxic Emissions (IRATE), made note of a recent cautionary statement issued by a local health agency warning against eating vegetables grown in the arsenic-laced soil on the island. "If Asarco cannot clean up their act and prevent this kind of pollution then they should be forced to close," he stated angrily.

POSTMORTEMS

After three days of testimony, the hearings came to an end. Ruckelshaus was not expected to make a decision on the final standards for arsenic emissions until February or March of 1984. In the meanwhile, some assessment, at least of the process, had already begun. From an administrative point of view, the brunt of managing the tasks of informing and involving the public had fallen on Ernesta Barnes and EPA's Region 10 office. According to one source, roughly thirty people from the regional office had worked full-time for four months on the Asarco case. Randy Smith of the Region 10 office told one reporter that the "process proved terrifically costly and time-consuming."[13]

But the regional office did feel that there had been an internal payoff for them in a greater appreciation by EPA headquarters of what is meant to be "on the front lines." The regional staff felt that because of their frequent contact with area groups, they were better able to engage the public's participation. "After a while," remarked one regional staff member, "we realized we couldn't let [headquarters staff] do the spiel [in the public workshops]. The people from headquarters were just not enough in touch with the local level. . . . They were too scientific." Another regional office commented:

> At headquarters [in Washington, DC] they thought we were a bunch of bozos out here in the region. They could not understand why we were scrambling and bending over backwards to organize the workshops and put out easily digestible information for the public. When they arrived in Tacoma, however, and found themselves face-to-face with a well-informed and often angry public, they began to appreciate our problem a little better.

The process also proved beneficial to the regional office from the standpoint of image and public trust. A number of witnesses and observers agreed with Nancy Ellison of the Washington Environmental Council, who complimented the Region 10 office for its "openness and willingness to share information during this process." The office's cooperation and outreach efforts had, she continued, "gone a long way toward restoring trust and confidence in the agency here in the region."

Even Ruckelshaus' decision to involve the public received gentler treatment at some hands. Ruth Weiner of the Sierra Club, who had earlier criticized the EPA administrator for "copping out," stated at the conclusion of her testimony that the Clean Air Act "requires public involvement." She continued, "Moreover, in becoming involved, the public begins to appreciate the difficulty attendant on making regulatory decisions, the ease with which EPA can be made a scapegoat because the agency's blunders are so readily magnified, and the inadequacy of simply identifying 'heroes' and 'villains' in environmental protection. It may have been hard work and a headache for all of us, but the public involvement is most certainly worth it."

Ruckelshaus himself was largely in agreement with this last sentiment. Back in June, in his speech before the National Academy of Sciences, he had told his audience that, in managing risk, "we must seek new ways to involve the public in the decision-making process." He continued, "It is clear to me that in a society in which democratic principles so dominate, the perceptions of the public must be weighed." Later, as he looked back on the process he had kicked off when he announced the proposed arsenic regulations for the Asarco smelter, he found validation for these views. Ruckelshaus felt that local citizens had shown they were "capable of understanding [the problem of the smelter] in its complexities and dealing with it and coming back to us with rather sensible suggestions." In fact, he added, "the public—the nontechnical, unschooled public—came back with some very good suggestions as to how they could reduce the emissions of arsenic in the plant [and still keep it open]." But, perhaps, the final proof of the success of the venture would be in the decision that—as he had often repeated—Ruckelshaus alone would make. It was still an open question as to how Asarco might respond to citizens' suggestions, and whether it would feel as sanguine as Ruckelshaus about remaining

open. While he pondered his decision on the final standards, the debate on his risk management techniques continued.

NOTES

1. Barnett N. Kalikow, "Environmental Risk: Power to the People," *Technology Review* 87 (October 1984), p. 55. As a result of studies of workers exposed to arsenic in copper smelting and arsenic manufacturing plants, a number of widely respected groups, including the National Academy of Sciences and the National Cancer institute, concluded that inorganic arsenic was carcinogenic in humans. It has been linked to skin and lung cancer.

2. The other was a coal power plant in western Washington.

3. Under the provisions of the Clean Air Act, EPA routinely delegates many of its powers to regulate and enforce to the states, which in turn can delegate their powers to regional authorities.

4. The actual order from PSAPCA to install the hoods was not issued until 1981.

5. The standards actually comprised three sets of regulations—for copper smelting processing high arsenic content ore, for copper smelters processing low arsenic content ore, and for glass manufacturing plants. The Asarco smelter in Ruston was the only facility in the U.S. that fell into the first category. The risk assessment (and resulting standards) for high arsenic content copper smelters thus applied only to that one plant.

6. In its proposed regulations, EPA defined a unit risk number as its estimate of the lifetime cancer risk occurring in a hypothetical population which is exposed throughout their lifetime to a concentration of one microgram (1/28 millionths of an ounce) of a pollutant per cubic meter of air.

7. In fact, some critics felt that EPA's (albeit involuntary) entry into the regulatory scene delayed installation of the hoods, while Asarco waited to learn what EPA would propose as best available technology.

8. Asarco-Tacoma used ore that contained 4 percent arsenic; the remaining fourteen smelters in the United States used ores with 0.7 percent or lower arsenic content.

9. In announcing these lower figures on October 20, 1983, Ernesta Barnes did note that the amount of fugitive emissions released near ground level was higher than originally estimated.

10. According to one observer, a number of witnesses at the hearing were confused about the meaning of the term "risk," assuming that the risk of the one additional cancer death meant the certainty of the fatality—not the worst-case probability.

11. Tacoma is the Indian name for Mt. Rainier.

12. The Occupational Safety and Health Administration—not EPA—was responsible for setting safety standards in the workplace itself. According to Ernesta Barnes, OSHA had already issued regulations requiring workers to wear respirators in the smelter.

13. Kalikow, "Environmental Risk," p. 61.

Comment

William Ruckelshaus recognized that even the technically best policy analysis could not yield an answer to the question of what cancer risk should be borne by the residents of the Tacoma area, especially when a lower risk was likely to create higher unemployment. As an alternative or supplement to policy analysis, Ruckelshaus solicited the views of the people most affected by the proposed regulations. But he seemed to be uncertain about how best to use the results of this participatory process in making his final decision. In announcing his plan to hold public meetings, Ruckelshaus implied that he would let the people of Tacoma determine his decision: "For me to sit here in Washington and tell the people of Tacoma what is an acceptable risk would be at best arrogant and at worst inexcusable." Yet, in response to the *New York Times*'s charge that to impose such a choice on the citizens of Tacoma would itself be "inexcusable," Ruckelshaus said that he would not simply follow the opinion of the majority of Tacoma's citizens but would make his own decision, presumably on the basis of his own best judgment after taking into account the views expressed by the citizens of Tacoma. Is this a morally consistent position for the head of EPA to take? Is Ruckelshaus abdicating his official responsibility: (1) in giving (or appearing to give) so much weight to current public opinion; (2) in spending public funds on workshops rather than directly on environmental regulations; and (3) in raising levels of social stress among people who do not want to know the environmental risks under which they live?

Evaluate these reasons for involving the public in making regulatory decisions that require technical expertise: participation can (1) help restore (or create) confidence in a regulatory agency; (2) enable the public better "to appreciate the difficulty attendant on making regulatory decisions"; and (3) make the final decision fairer and wiser. Suppose that the workshops generated more criticism of the EPA and left the citizens of Tacoma more dissatisfied with Ruckelshaus' final decision than they otherwise would have been. How (if at all) would this outcome affect your judgment of whether the public should be included in the decision-making process?

Apart from the opinions of the citizens of Tacoma, what should Ruckelshaus take into account in making his final decision, and what importance should he accord to each relevant consideration? Consider how the following factors should be weighed in determining the regulatory standard: Asarco's level of wages and employment; cost to consumers of increased prices of Asarco products as a result of regulation; cost to the EPA of various levels of regulation; scientific uncertainty concerning cancer risk associated with various emission levels; best available technology (BAT); views of citizens who are not residents of the Tacoma area; harms and benefit of future generations; and the imputed value of life.

On the basis of information provided in the case, can you determine what Ruckelshaus' final decision should be? If not, what additional information does Ruckelshaus need in order to decide?

The Calculator
Elizabeth Kolbert

A little more than a year after September 11th, Kenneth Feinberg, who holds the title of special master of the Victim Compensation Fund, met with a group of firefighters in his midtown office. Feinberg, who is fifty-seven, has a long face, a prominent forehead, and an abrupt manner. Standing, he appears to be straining forward, and even when he is sitting down he leans in, as if about to get up again. That morning, Feinberg had taken off his jacket, and he greeted the firefighters in his shirtsleeves. His gold cufflinks—a gift to himself—were embossed with the scales of justice.

The first of the men to speak was a burly firefighter with a ruddy complexion. He had spent four weeks at the World Trade Center site, initially trying to rescue victims and then to recover remains. He told Feinberg that whatever he had breathed in during that time—pulverized glass, concrete, lead, traces of asbestos; "I call it a bunch of crap," he said—had reduced his lung capacity by more than fifty per cent. He coughed throughout the session.

"Sleeping's tough," he said. "When I'm getting depressed, my wife calls it 'the mood.' She takes the kids out." The fireman

This article was originally published by *The New Yorker Magazine,* November 22, 2002. It is reprinted with special permission from the author and publisher.

told Feinberg that he had recently had to quit the F.D.N.Y. and had taken a job monitoring security cameras at a school. "I can't play street hockey, can't play ball—my son, he can't understand why Daddy can't do nothing.

"This is what I take every day," he announced, holding up a freezer bag filled with medications. "There's a bunch of pills, there's nasal sprays, there's steroids, there's inhalers." He extracted some more medicines from a fanny pack. "This is what I keep on me all the time: albuterol, epinephrine—it's a self-stick. If it gets really bad, I've got to hit this and go to the hospital."

Eventually, a second firefighter—a slight man who sat slumped in his chair—spoke up. He explained that he had spent the afternoon of the attack sifting through the ruins of the World Trade Center concourse. "We were trying to dig this person out of the dirt and the debris and the dust and the smoke. You saw the astronauts on the moon, that dust surface? That was what was coming into your face. Three weeks later, I was coughing up blood, dirt, debris. Since then, I've been in the hospital three times. It's affecting my liver, my pancreas, my stomach, and nobody can really give me a definite answer why. My eleven-year-old son, he asks his mother, 'Is Daddy going to die now?' "

The Victim Compensation Fund, or V.C.F., as it is known, expires a year from next month. Between now and then, it is expected to issue checks to some three thousand families. The fund is the first of its kind, and, to the extent that it has a logic, Feinberg, as special master, has imposed it. It is Feinberg who drafted the rules for disbursing the fund, Feinberg who is determining how the rules are administered, and Feinberg who will hear appeals from people unhappy with the way the rules have been applied. In the case of victims like the firefighters, whose ailments did not manifest themselves until days, or even weeks, after the disaster, Feinberg has the authority to decide not just how much compensation they will receive but whether they will get any at all. By most estimates, the bill for the fund will eventually run to five billion dollars, though it is possible that it could be a good deal higher. How much higher is, once again, entirely up to Feinberg, who has been granted what amounts to a blank check on the federal Treasury.

Anyone in Feinberg's position would have found himself at odds with some of the victims' families; Feinberg has managed to infuriate just about all of them. "I've heard you say that you couldn't put yourselves in our shoes," a widow told him publicly a few months ago. "I think if you could feel our pain for one hour your tone and your mannerisms would be so drastically different than what they are." At the same meeting, a man who had lost his wife and niece said, "You have an arrogance about you that is so painful, you can't possibly believe." Feinberg, who is a lawyer by training, has spent most of his adult life immersed in disaster, and during that time has priced almost every imaginable form of human suffering, from birth defects and infertility to asbestosis and death. If the anger upsets him, he doesn't show it. "Everybody rants and raves," he told me.

The day Feinberg met with the firefighters, he listened, apparently unmoved. While they related their symptoms and fears, he jiggled his knee. He consumed two Halloween-size packages of Necco wafers, then stuffed the wrappers into a plastic cup. When the men were done, they asked him if he had any questions. He shook his head and showed them to the door.

Congress created the Victim Compensation Fund just ten days after September 11th. During the hurried negotiations, several candidates to manage it had been mentioned, including John Danforth, the former senator from Missouri, and George Mitchell, the former senator from Maine. Feinberg took a look at the legislation and decided, as he put it to me, "I've been trained for the last twenty years to do this." He rang up Senator Chuck Hagel, of Nebraska, an old friend of his. "The minute I called, he said, 'I know why you're calling,'" Feinberg told me. "'You're the man.' And he took it from there."

Feinberg grew up in Brockton, Massachusetts, where his father sold tires, and he still speaks—usually emphatically—in an unreconstructed Boston accent. As a kid, he performed in amateur theatricals, and even considered becoming an actor, but after attending the University of Massachusetts he decided, on the advice of his father, to go to N.Y.U. Law School instead. Feinberg clerked for the then chief judge of New York, Stanley Fuld, and later served as Edward Kennedy's chief of staff. He now lives in Bethesda, Maryland—he and his wife, Diane, have three grown children—in a house with a specially designed sound room where he keeps six thousand classical-music CDs. Before September 11th, he routinely got up at 5 A.M.; these days, he is often awake at three. He is in the office by six.

Oddly enough, Feinberg arrived at his current specialty in large part thanks to a talent for burlesque. In the early nineteen-seventies, at a birthday party for Fuld, Feinberg delivered a toast that impressed Judge Jack Weinstein, of the federal district court in Brooklyn. Weinstein and Feinberg became friendly, and a decade later, when Weinstein took over the Agent Orange case, he asked Feinberg if he would try to persuade the two sides to settle, so that the case wouldn't have to go to trial.

At the point that Weinstein brought Feinberg into it, the Agent Orange case was in its eighth year. It pitted hundreds of thousands of Vietnam veterans who had been exposed to the defoliant, and who had contracted diseases ranging from skin ailments to abdominal cancer, against the federal government and the herbicide's manufacturers, including Dow and Monsanto. Virtually no one on either side believed that an agreement could be reached. Nevertheless, Feinberg threw himself into the project, producing an eighty-page proposal in a few weeks. Both sides rejected it. They remained separated by a host of issues, most significantly money—the veterans were demanding a billion dollars, while the chemical companies refused to pay more than a few hundred thousand—and it appeared that a trial could not be avoided. At 3 A.M. on the day that jury selection was set to begin, they finally settled.

"Ken revealed himself as a superb negotiator," Judge Weinstein, who is eighty-one and still serving on the bench, told me. "He was very tough. He understood the case completely, better than either side's lawyers." The night the settlement was reached—the sum ultimately agreed upon was a hundred and eighty million dollars—Weinstein had taken a hotel room in Manhattan, and, just before dawn, he informed Feinberg that he could announce the deal. Weinstein recalls him bouncing on the bed: "He was very excited."

The Agent Orange case was precedent setting. It greatly expanded the possibilities of class-action lawsuits—some would argue disastrously so—and it was followed by a string of other so-called mass-tort cases. Rare was the large, high-profile settlement that Feinberg was not involved in. He was the special master in the DES case, which had a thousand plaintiffs, and he played a similar role in the case of the Dalkon Shield I.U.D., which had two hundred and fifty thousand. Feinberg served as the negotiator for Dow Corning when it was sued by four hundred and fifty thousand women over breast implants, and successfully negotiated the resolution to hundreds of asbestos cases. In the process, he earned a reputation of being highly effective and unusually abrasive.

"He had a style which conveyed a great sense of displeasure at your stubbornness or lack of understanding," Judith Vladeck, an attorney who represented Long Island Lighting Company ratepayers in another case that Feinberg mediated, told me. "It wasn't 'I don't agree with you.' It was 'What's wrong with you, how dumb can you be?' There was a firmness which I can appreciate now, but which I didn't enjoy being a victim of." In 1993, Feinberg left the law firm of Kaye, Scholer, Fierman, Hays & Handler, where he had been a partner, and formed his own firm, the Feinberg Group, with offices in New York and Washington.

Over the years, Feinberg has worked out a method for dealing with sprawling, complex cases, the key element of which he describes as stripping away the complexities. Under this method, individual circumstances are reduced to numbers, so that the whole settlement can be expressed in a set of tables. "The way you divvy up the money is to come up, to the extent you can, with an objective allocation formula," Feinberg told me. He offered the Dalkon Shield case as an example: "We had a matrix—here's what you get. A hysterectomy's worth this, pelvic inflammation's worth this, cervical cancer's worth this, migraine headaches are worth this. Demonstrate medically you've had any of this, and we'll pay you."

Numerically speaking, September 11th is much less daunting than most of the other cases Feinberg has been called upon to settle. "I mean, thirty-three hundred dead and injured is almost quantitatively not a mass tort," he observed. But the rawness of the emotion is something that Feinberg acknowledges he has never before experienced. "I made a very wise decision when I took this job," he told me. "I'm doing this for nothing. I love it when senators or congressmen come up to me and go, 'Ken, what a sacrifice that you're doing this for nothing, in the public interest, that's fabulous,' when of course the real reason I did it in the public interest—It *is* fabulous, if I do say so, it *is* a sacrifice. But, as a Machiavellian matter, can you imagine if these families knew I was getting paid for this, on the blood and bodies of the dead? 'You're only giving me three million, what did you make?' As a Machiavellian matter, I just completely undercut that whole line of criticism by telling people, 'I'm not getting paid for this, you know.' "

During the past year, Feinberg has held several dozen question-and-answer sessions with victims' families, mostly in the New York area but also in Boston, Washington, and Los Angeles. At these sessions, Feinberg explains the workings of the fund and listens to families' concerns, a process that often involves taking a good deal of abuse. On a recent sleety night, I drove out with him and his oldest son, Michael, to a session he was holding on Staten Island. Feinberg had already been out to Staten Island twice; the first time, a man had made what Feinberg, who is Jewish, considered to be an anti-Semitic remark. Michael, an N.Y.U. law student, was accompanying him to the third session to lend moral support.

"Staten Island, that's a Third World country," Feinberg told me, more than once, on the drive out. The meeting, at the Staten Island Hilton, was set for seven o'clock, and Feinberg hadn't had dinner, so before heading into the session he stopped at the hotel gift shop to buy a package of Chuckles for himself and a Snickers bar for Michael. In the lobby, he ran into several people he knew—there are some family members who follow him around from session to session—and he greeted them with wry heartiness. I sat down next to two men, both of whom had lost sons who were firefighters.

"You'll hear it said many times here that people don't care about the money, and it's true, we don't," one of them told me. "But somehow the higher the amount, the more value they put on your loved one's life, the more meaning it has. So I would like them

to say we all get a trillion dollars, just so I know my son was worth a trillion dollars, not that I would ever want it."

"That's right," the other man said. "You can't put a value on your son's life, but then they come out with these astronomical figures, and—well, you're not going to get that because of this, that, and the other reason. They kind of promise you something, but they don't deliver." A lot of families, the man added, "feel that this program is just a coverup to bail out the airlines, to bail out the Port Authority, to bail out New York City. It's for them, it's not really for us."

The Victim Compensation Fund was in fact created not for the victims' sake but for the airlines', and, more specifically, for protecting the airlines *from* the victims. In the days after September 11th, the country's major carriers were facing not just billions of dollars in immediate losses but tens of billions of dollars in potential legal claims, and lawmakers were worried that the nation's entire transportation system could collapse. They responded with the Air Transportation Safety and System Stabilization Act, which granted the carriers five billion dollars in cash and ten billion in loan guarantees. The act also limited the airlines' liability for the disaster to the amount of insurance that had been carried by the four hijacked flights. (This is generally believed to be a total of six billion dollars.) It was in a subsection of the bill that Congress created the V.C.F. Families who accept the payments from the fund relinquish the right to sue the airlines, the Port Authority, which owned the World Trade Center, and any other domestic entity; in return, they are supposed to receive from the government compensation for their pain and suffering and for their economic losses.

At the Staten Island meeting, the first few questions put to Feinberg were technical ones. Under the law, payments from the V.C.F. are supposed to be reduced by the amount of compensation that families have received from other sources, and one woman wanted to know whether a certain type of death benefit would count as an offset. (Feinberg has defined offsets to include life insurance and Social Security, but not the sums—in many cases, considerable— that families received from charity.) A man asked who should file a claim with the fund in the case of a family whose members were feuding.

Soon, however, the tenor of the questions shifted. A woman stood up at the microphone, holding a large photograph. "I'm the parent of a single firefighter," she said. "This is my son. Before he became a probationary firefighter, he served his country for five years in the United States Marine Corps, making sub-poverty-level wages. He then joined the Fire Department as a probationary firefighter and he graduated to making poverty-level wages. I would like to know why someone in his category is really being discriminated against regarding what you and the Victim Compensation Fund consider his life was worth?"

A few minutes later, a second woman, who had lost her sister, declared, "I just want to say that it's really a disgrace that a year and some months after the tragedy happened we're still all fighting." Addressing herself to Feinberg, she went on, "We've suffered enough. Why are you making our lives even more complicated? Make something easy, make everyone happy. I know you're all about the numbers, and the statute, and the regulations, and this computation, and this deduction, and 'This doesn't count,' and 'Please come to me and make your plea to me.' We don't need to make a plea. We're not begging for money. We want our people back."

Feinberg told the woman he could not bring people back, and he could not make them happy.

"Yes, you can," she insisted.

"No, I can't," he repeated. "I can't make you happy."

"But your children are alive and breathing, right?" someone called out.

"Thank God," Feinberg said, casting a glance in Michael's direction.

At first glance, the tables defy most notions of equity; the more needs a family is likely to have, the less well it fares. For example, the tables show that the widow of a twenty-five-year-old who had no children and was earning a hundred and twenty-five thousand dollars a year can anticipate a payment, before any offsets, of nearly four and a half million dollars. The widow of a man who was earning the same salary and was similarly childless but was forty can expect half that amount, while the widow of a forty-year-old who was making fifty thousand dollars and had one child can expect a quarter of it. Finally, the widow of a forty-year-old with two dependent children who was making twenty thousand dollars does worst of all. She can expect about a fifth, or slightly more than nine hundred thousand dollars.

When Feinberg is questioned about these sorts of inequities, he responds, invariably, that his hands are tied. "What you're really asking is: All lives are equal, why isn't everybody getting the same amount of money?" he told the mother with the photograph on Staten Island. "A very fair question, ladies and gentlemen. The answer is: Congress told me that is not the way to compute these awards. Congress said you must take into account the economic loss suffered by the victim's death." This claim is a useful one for Feinberg, and, up to a point, also accurate.

Aside from the inequities, what is most striking about Feinberg's tables is that a lot of numbers are missing. In those rows where the economic losses would be the greatest— low age crossed with high salary—instead of posting numbers Feinberg has put rows of "X"s. Moreover, he has declined to publish any figures at all for victims who earned more than two hundred and twenty-five thousand dollars a year.

It is unclear exactly how many victims Feinberg has left off his tables, but because the World Trade Center housed several large financial firms, where relatively young men and women routinely earned hundreds of thousands of dollars a year, the number is almost certainly a high one. Following a strict economic-loss calculation, some of these victims' families would be entitled to payments of ten, twenty, and, in a few cases, even thirty million dollars from the government. This, apparently, is what lawmakers mandated when they created the V.C.F., but it is not, it seems clear, what they—or just about anybody else—actually want to see happen now. Feinberg noted to me that both Senator Kennedy, a Democrat, and Senator Hagel, a Republican, had offered him the same advice on this point, which he summed up as "Don't let twenty percent of the people get eighty percent of the money." Exactly how Feinberg intends to treat what he calls the "high-end" families is not known—he keeps putting off resolving this issue—but he has indicated that, except in extremely rare cases, he is not going to give out awards of more than six million dollars.

Not surprisingly, Feinberg's position has infuriated the families of the most highly paid victims, who accuse him of acting arbitrarily, unfairly, and, finally, illegally. One day, I was sitting in Feinberg's office when a man whose wife had earned nearly four hundred thousand dollars a year came in to appeal his award. After several million dollars in offsets because of a life-insurance policy, the man was set to receive two million dollars. He felt he deserved at least another million. Feinberg asked the man whether he thought payments ought to be made solely on the basis of income, even if this meant that some already affluent families would receive ten million dollars in taxpayer money.

"Yes, absolutely," the man responded. "The idea is to compensate me so my lifestyle doesn't change, and my lifestyle is different from a guy washing dishes. I don't live in a two-hundred-and-fifty-dollar-a-month apartment. I live in a place that costs me five thousand dollars a month in mortgage payments."

Cantor Fitzgerald, the bond-trading firm that lost six hundred and fifty-eight people in the attack, has issued an eighty-page critique of Feinberg's handling of the fund, which notes that Congress instructed him "to determine economic loss—not to make value judgments about different groups of income earners." Stephen Merkel, the firm's general counsel, told me that Feinberg had sought "the power to make awards on whatever basis he feels like" and that his actions demonstrated "a complete disregard for the law itself." When confronted with criticism of this sort, Feinberg offers precisely the opposite defense from the one he gave the mother on Staten Island.

"The law gives me unbelievable discretion," he says. "It gives me discretion to do whatever I want. So I will."

Perhaps because of this discretion, a number of conspiracy theories swirl around Feinberg: that he has cut a nefarious deal with the Bush Administration, that he is secretly taking orders from Attorney General John Ashcroft, that—and this is really a subset of the first two—he is using the Victim Compensation Fund to advance the cause of tort reform. Although Feinberg is an outspoken, Teddy Kennedy-style Democrat, he was appointed special master by Ashcroft, a conservative Republican, who also—theoretically, at least—has the power to un-appoint him. At every opportunity, Feinberg praises Ashcroft, calling him his "No. 1 ally." When I asked him how he and the Attorney General had managed to bridge their not inconsiderable political differences, he smiled and said, "It's either a tribute to bipartisanship or very Machiavellian, or a little bit of both."

Feinberg uses the word "Machiavellian" to refer to his own actions surprisingly often. The first time I heard him do so, I was puzzled; by the third or fourth time, I realized that he didn't mean it as self-criticism. During the weeks that I followed Feinberg around, I attended half a dozen meetings at his conference table, at which a total of about thirty cases were discussed. Feinberg was by turns gentle and hostile, confiding and withholding, depending on what seemed most efficacious. With awards below the average—currently about $1.5 million—he was almost always willing to add a few hundred thousand; on one occasion, I heard him promise to give a widow an additional half million dollars for no other reason than that she had come in with her two small children and asked for it. As far as I could make it out, Feinberg's reasoning in these cases amounted to: Let's do what seems to work, and worry about how to justify it afterward. With awards in the very upper reaches, by contrast, he was staunchly, even theatrically, recalcitrant. One lawyer told Feinberg that he had calculated the proper payment for his client to be between sixteen and seventeen million dollars.

"You've lost your fucking mind!" Feinberg exclaimed. "This guy should file a suit."

"He might—you're giving him every reason to," the lawyer replied, calmly.

"I want him to!" Feinberg said. "And do me a favor—hold a press conference. Say I wouldn't give the guy sixteen million dollars—tax free!"

So far, only about eight hundred families, or a quarter of those eligible, have submitted claims to the fund, a proportion that is lower than Feinberg would like, but one that he maintains he is not, at this point, particularly concerned about. Feinberg's stated goal is to have ninety percent of the families accept payment from the fund, and so relinquish the right to sue the airlines, the Port Authority, or the City of New York. Accepting the payment doesn't necessarily mean being happy with it, or even feeling that it is fair; it just means recognizing that it is better than the alternative, which is years of litigation and a high risk of getting nothing. "Who's going to fight?" Feinberg told me. "No one's going to fight."

One evening after a series of meetings with victims' families, I stayed behind to talk to Feinberg. We sat in the empty conference room, which offered a view of several lanes of rush-hour traffic and a sliver of the East River. I asked him for his own views on the fund and whether it was structured fairly. Was it right for some families to receive huge payments while others, who needed help much more, received comparatively little? This was, he said, an "interesting and debatable" question, but by no means the most difficult one, which, in his opinion, was whether the fund should exist at all.

"I'll show you e-mails from people that'll break your heart," he told me. " 'Dear Mr. Feinberg, my son died in Oklahoma City. Why not me?' 'Dear Mr. Feinberg, my son died in the first World Trade Center bombing, in '93, why not me?' Anthrax—why not me? African Embassy bombing—why not me? U.S.S. Cole—why not me? And then you get even beyond terrorism. 'My husband died last year saving three little girls in a Mississippi flood—why not him?' " If there was an essential distinction between September 11th and these other tragedies, Feinberg didn't offer it. "Where do you stop?" he asked. We talked for a while longer, and then Feinberg told me, politely but firmly, that he had to leave. He was meeting Michael, and they were going to the opera.

Comment

The Victim Compensation Fund (VCF), established ten days after 9/11, exemplifies both how a public official can assess the differential monetary value of lives for the purposes of compensating families of victims of a national tragedy and how controversial such an assessment can be. A lawyer by training, Kenneth Feinberg accepted the congressional assignment of calculating differential monetary settlements with victims' families based on the economic losses suffered by the victim's death. He had earlier defended such calculations as a general practice in controversies where legal settlements depended on arriving at a mutually acceptable way of compensating the victims of medical malpractice and similar class action lawsuits. Calculations of compensation that put a price on life according to loss in expected future earnings (among other measurable factors) enable policy analysts to strip away complexities and reduce the vast array of individual circumstances to a number, which then can be assigned a monetary value. Critics argue that such calculations ignore what they call "incommensurability": the impossibility of reducing the variety of values within and across different lives to any single measure, money being no exception. Feinberg does not deny the validity of this argument. He acknowledges that it is "interesting and debatable" whether richer families should receive compensation payments far in excess of what poorer families receive. He goes a step further and questions whether a compensation fund should exist at all. What are the considerations that speak in favor of and against a victim compensation fund? In favor and against a national government being the source of the fund?

Absent the practical purpose of protecting the airlines from legal suits that could send some of them into bankruptcy, are there defensible ethical aims of victims' compensation? Does the source of the victimization—terrorism versus a natural disaster—make a difference? Is there any justification for compensating families of victims of 9/11 but not the victims of the Oklahoma City bombing? Families of victims of 9/11 but not families of fallen soldiers in Iraq?

Assuming that a victim compensation fund can be justified, how should the compensation be calculated? One alternative suggested by many of the families is that all should receive the same payment since "all lives are equal." Was Congress right or wrong in mandating that economic loss be taken into account in making the compensatory payments? Does your answer depend on whether the congressional mandate was necessary in order to protect the airlines, the Port Authority, and other institutions from being sued by the richer families of victims? Is protecting public institutions from legal suit more or less justified than similarly protecting private institutions?

Defenders of policy analysis apparently reject the claim of incommensurability when they reduce various values to the single metric of money and calculate differential payments to individuals. One of the strongest claims made by policy analysts is that no better alternative exists. Can the alternative of paying all families equally for similar loss of life be justified on the basis of policy analysis? Feinberg makes a very different argument in favor of differential payments to families: that his hands are tied by congressional mandate. Evaluate this argument in light of another fact acknowledged by Feinberg, his vast discretion in this case. Although Congress said that economic loss must be taken into account, Feinberg did not follow a strict economic-loss calculation, especially when he determined payments to those victims' families who would otherwise have been entitled to payments over six million dollars. Is there a way of justifying on the basis of a strict cost-benefit calculation this use of discretion? If so, on what basis is the value of life then determined? If not, is policy analysis committed to compensating rich families more than poor ones for the loss of their loved ones? Suppose that Feinberg's discretion in this instance was justified.

Would other uses of discretion have been even more justifiable? Could a calculator take economic loss into account and still pay poor families as much (or more) than rich families?

Feinberg also had considerable discretion in the way in which he met with the victims' families, responded to their perspectives on the VCF, and defended his decisions. In light of Feinberg's goal of arriving at an "objective allocation formula," what is the ethical value, if any, of his meeting with the families, responding to their criticisms, and defending (or revising) his decisions in light of their comments? Can you suggest a better process than the one Feinberg employed? Would a process that relied on more than a single person have been more justifiable or just more cumbersome?

Listening to the City: What Should Be Built at Ground Zero?

Archon Fung and Susan Rosegrant

When the twin towers of New York City's World Trade Center collapsed after terrorists crashed hijacked airplanes into the two buildings on September 11, 2001, the city, the state, and the nation immediately launched an unprecedented rescue and recovery operation. Behind the scenes, officials also began planning to reconstruct the key 16-acre site at the tip of Lower Manhattan—a job that promised to be the largest urban development project in U.S. history. Two public agencies shared responsibility for redeveloping the World Trade Center site: the Port Authority of New York and New Jersey and a newly created Lower Manhattan Development Corporation.

*This is a condensed and edited version of a case written under the supervision of Archon Fung by Susan Rosegrant for the John F. Kennedy School of Government Case Program (KSG 1687.0 and 1687.1.2003). Funding was provided by the William and Flora Hewlett Foundation and by the Harvard University Center for Ethics and the Professions. Copyright by the President and Fellows of Harvard College.

The Port Authority of New York and New Jersey was a financially self-supporting public agency that owned the World Trade Center site and managed many of the region's airports, tunnels, and bridges. The governors of New York and New Jersey each appointed six members to its board. The Port Authority completed the World Trade Center in 1973, and managed it until July 2001, when it leased the complex to a group led by developer Larry Silverstein for a period of 99 years. Insiders say the Authority's agenda was clear: to rebuild all of the World Trade Center's lost commercial space, both out of a sense of institutional pride and in order to continue collecting $120 million in annual rent from its tenants.

Because the rebuilding task in Lower Manhattan was so immense, officials decided to form a new reconstruction entity. New York Governor George Pataki and New York City Mayor Rudolph Giuliani jointly announced the creation of the Lower Manhattan Development Corporation (LMDC) in November 2001 to oversee the rebuilding of Downtown, south of Houston Street. Although it was understood that

LMDC and the Port Authority would both work together, Pataki didn't define a division of responsibilities. Observers generally applauded Pataki's choice of John Whitehead to chair LMDC. The former State Department official and Goldman Sachs co-chairman was seen as a principled public figure without a personal agenda in the redevelopment. From his appointment, Whitehead insisted that the rebuilding process would be deliberate, transparent, and open to public input.

THE PROGRAM

When the Lower Manhattan Development Corporation (LMDC) began to look at what would rise from the ruins in Lower Manhattan, staff "realized, and the board agreed, that since everything was so new and the mandate was very broad and extremely important, we'd better do a lot of listening before we did a lot of talking and decision-making," said Whitehead. In this unprecedented task, it was unclear to them which public goals and values their expertise in planning and development ought to serve. LMDC thus announced that it would set up eight advisory councils to represent key constituencies—families; residents; restaurants, retailers, and small businesses; arts, education and tourism; financial services firms; professional firms; commuters and transportation; and development.

At the end of March, LMDC issued a request for proposals (RFP), based in part upon ideas from these councils, for a land use design for the World Trade Center site. According to RFP author and LMDC Vice President Alexander Garvin, LMDC hoped to attract proposals not just from established corporate design firms, but also from a number of small, cutting-edge architects who might produce innovative and unconventional solutions. That intent, however, was never tested. As soon as the RFP went out, the Port Authority protested, claiming that it had not been consulted. LMDC pulled the RFP days later.

On April 19, the Port Authority issued a new RFP "in cooperation with" LMDC for an urban design and transportation study for Lower Manhattan and the World Trade Center site. The more conservative hand of the Port Authority was clear in the document, observers say. With decades of experience in building and managing enormous public works in the region, the Port Authority was more confident than LMDC in its professional view of what should be rebuilt, and how it should be done. They favored time-tested design principles and proven expertise. Those submitting proposals had to have a minimum of ten years' experience in urban planning, a strong regional presence in the greater New York/New Jersey area, and either planning experience with large urban mixed-use complexes or been the prime consultant on three or more public works projects valued at more than $100 million.

There thus appeared to be a fundamental disparity between the two agencies with regard both to the decision-making process that should guide reconstruction and substantive priorities. In early April, LMDC had published draft Principles for Action and a 14-point Preliminary Blueprint for Renewal. These documents drew upon and reflected suggestions from LMDC's own advisory councils and ideas that had surfaced in the public debate, including a pledge to adhere to an inclusive and open public process, and recommendations to expand residential development and reintegrate the site with surrounding neighborhoods by restoring at least part of the street grid.

While the Port Authority didn't reject those ideas, it had a different vision of the reconstruction process and therefore different objectives. Since the World Trade Center fell, insiders say, the Authority had been committed to what was known internally as the Program—the requirement that all the commercial space that had been lost would be rebuilt on the site, thus sustaining the $120 million annual revenue stream from the lease on the twin towers. Specifically, that meant rebuilding 11 million square feet of office space, and 600,000 square feet of retail, as well as a 600,000-square-foot hotel. Without the lease revenue, officials said, the authority might have been forced to cut its $9.5 billion five-year capital plan by as much as $1.5 billion. Planned capital projects included improvements in regional airports, bridges, tunnels, and the PATH transit system, as well as a program to deepen channels to the authority's maritime ports.

But the Port Authority and LMDC did their best to present a united front. On May 22, a design group headed by Beyer Blinder Belle Architects & Planners won the urban planning contract for the World Trade Center site. Port Authority instructed them to abide by the constraints of the Program.

A GROWING PUBLIC RESPONSE

During these months, non-governmental groups such as the Civic Alliance sought to create a public debate about the World Trade Center site redevelopment. They retained AmericaSpeaks, a Washington, D.C.-based organizer of "21st Century Town Meetings," to help design and facilitate events. (AmericaSpeaks didn't agree to stage the meeting until the Civic Alliance promised to invite representatives from LMDC, the city's Economic Development Corporation, and other official policy-making agencies.)

AmericaSpeaks had developed an approach to public deliberation that attempted to combine the depth and intimacy of small group discussions with the power of large group consensus. Participants—carefully recruited to be inclusive and diverse—divide into small groups to deliberate over policy concerns and vote on discussion questions. After the groups send their ideas and input via computers to a team of analysts to synthesize and tabulate for the larger assembly's approval, AmericaSpeaks delivers the results to sponsoring officials. Prior AmericaSpeaks projects included engaging citizens in creating the strategic plan and budget for Mayor Anthony Williams of Washington, D.C., and orchestrating a national dialogue on Social Security reform.

According to AmericaSpeaks leaders, these electronic town meetings allowed a wide range of citizens to contribute to important public debates, and so improved policy-making.

On February 7, more than 600 participants, representing a broad cross-section of the region, gathered at the South Street Seaport on the eastern side of Lower Manhattan for "Listening to the City," as the meeting was named. Civic Alliance leader and co-founder Robert Yaro notes that the session was the first opportunity for officials from the LMDC to meet at one time with Port Authority leaders, representatives of recently elected Mayor Michael Bloomberg, as well as small business owners, relatives of victims, members of the various civic groups hoping to influence the process, and the general public. "There had been smaller meetings of neighborhood residents and of families, but it was the first time that all of the stakeholders had a chance to be there and to listen to each other," said Yaro.

According to organizers, the goal of the meeting was not to make hard decisions nor to debate issues like how many towers Silverstein should rebuild, but to develop a vision for how Lower Manhattan should look in a decade. Participants sat in groups of ten or twelve, with a trained facilitator for each table. Each participant had a simple numbered keypad for polling, and each table had a laptop computer, with one person designated as the scribe. As tables discussed questions about the future of the World Trade Center site and Lower Manhattan, the scribes captured the essence of conversations—including both consensus ideas and strongly-held individual views—and sent that information to a group known as the "theme team." The theme team then identified the key concepts that emerged from all the discussions, and presented them to the entire room for corrections and additions, rejections and endorsements.

The "visions" that ultimately emerged from Listening to the City echoed many of the recommendations articulated by groups like New York New Visions and the Civic Alliance. According to participants, planners should redevelop the World Trade Center site and Lower Manhattan as a 24-hour, mixed-use community; construct low- and moderate-income housing; increase services and amenities; build a new transportation hub and improve connections to other parts of Manhattan and the region; create more open space and access to the waterfront; and make sure that the memorial and the events of September 11 informed future development in the area. These priorities departed strikingly from the concern with financial stability and revenue in the Port Authority's program.

Afterward, Louis Tomson, LMDC's president and executive director, told America-Speaks President Carolyn Lukensmeyer that LMDC would co-sponsor a second Listening to the City meeting in the summer, as soon as concrete land use plans could be put before the public.

PLANNING THE SECOND TOWN MEETING

Organizers dramatically raised their hopes and expectations for that second meeting. By May, AmericaSpeaks had already decided to invite 4,000 to 5,000 participants, primarily to accommodate widespread interest and to collect a large amount of information, but also to gain media attention. "The New York media market is very competitive," says project manager Ashley Boyd, "and a 1,000-person meeting doesn't make headline news."

While public meetings can draw quite unrepresentative participants, America-Speaks "aimed to create a universe that would reflect people who had worked in the Trade Center, who lived in the area, and who were impacted economically, which included all the boroughs and the closest suburbs of Connecticut and New Jersey," says Boyd. AmericaSpeaks took demographic data from those locations as a starting point, but tried to draw extra participants from Lower Manhattan, as well as from groups such as rescue workers, and family members of those killed in the attacks. "Part of the reason why traditional public participation processes have not been as effective as they might have been is because they draw the usual suspects," explains Boyd.

For the first Listening to the City meeting in February, the Civic Alliance had been the primary sponsor and had controlled the meeting's content. This time, however, LMDC and the Port Authority were funding about half of the $2 million event, and expected substantial control. Corporate and foundation sponsors donated the other $1 million. The $2 million total covered all aspects, including planning; participant recruitment; computer rentals; lunch; child care; and translation services. Bringing these diverse sponsors together proved extremely taxing. AmericaSpeaks, Port Authority, and the Civic Alliance differed regarding the substance of material that would be included in a common discussion guide for participants. It was more difficult still for these groups to agree upon a common agenda for the day. "I've never gone through a design process that was so politicized and where there were so many battles over things like sequence of activities," says Daniel Stone. Of particular concern was the question of who would set the agenda and what the bounds of discussion would be. LMDC was determined to present the site plans in the morning when attendance was likely to be highest, and before reporters left to file their stories after lunch. The Civic Alliance, however, insisted that site decisions couldn't be made outside of the context of the larger goals of redevelopment, and that those macro issues had to go first. After a number of testy meetings, LMDC finally claimed the prime morning spot, but with the compromise that the day would begin with an open-ended question about the values that should influence development at the site and in Lower Manhattan, thus allowing discussion of the Civic Alliance's central concerns.

PUBLIC AGENCIES MEET THE PUBLIC

On July 20, some 4,300 people gathered at the Jacob Javits Convention Center in Lower Manhattan for the second Listening to the City electronic town meeting. (Another, much smaller meeting two days later attracted about 200 participants, and about 800 people took part in an online dialogue over the following two weeks.) As LMDC and the Civic Alliance had agreed, Robert Yaro launched the meeting with a presentation about social equity issues in Lower Manhattan, and then invited participants to discuss hopes and concerns about rebuilding and remembering. Following presentations on urban planning, the six site options, and requirements of the Program, participants discussed criticisms and recommendations, first, with the Program in place, and, second, without those constraints. (In addition to the commercial space obligations, the Program mandated a memorial; new open space; cultural and civic institutions; a permanent PATH terminal and Downtown concourse; a bus facility; service and loading areas; and power and other utilities.) "If you didn't give people a chance to comment about that," says Stone, "people who were upset about the Program were going to use all their time talking about what they didn't like about the Program, and not talking about the site options within the Program."

Participants expressed broad approval of some aspects of each of the plans. Many liked the expansion of open green space that all provided. Many also endorsed the long pedestrian promenade featured in three of the plans connecting the Trade Center site to Battery Park. In a straw poll taken with the wireless keypads, over 80 percent of respondents thought that it was "very important" or "important" to reconnect the east and west sections of Lower Manhattan through pedestrian access.

However, the symbolic stakes of reconstruction quickly became clear in divisions among discussants. Many participants approved of plans that preserved the footprints of the two towers as open space because building there would desecrate sacred ground. Participants at one table, for example, hoped to "convince people not to build on the footprint" because "some people will never be recovered." But given the scarcity of land in lower Manhattan, and the difficulty of constructing a memorial and reconnecting the street grid while leaving the footprints clear, others argued that a blanket prohibition against building on the large areas was unwise. One participant pointed out that the reconstruction of cities such as London after World War II did not disrespect the fallen, and that "it's not practical to leave the footprints untouched." At the extreme, several argued that the two towers should be rebuilt to their original specifications, and that to do less would be to concede a kind of defeat to the attackers.

As conversations developed through the day, however, a surprising level of agreement emerged regarding priorities and values that should have guided the reconstruction effort. Many rejected the very premises of the Port Authority's Program. Those seated at one table said that they "felt constrained by the prerequisite criteria of the 'plan,'" and that the six plans as presented are largely six versions of one way of looking at the problem, rather than six discrete, visionary proposals to set our minds working." Another wrote more simply that "current leases [and] owners should not dictate future development possibilities! Should not be a business-driven project—public interests come first."

Beyond excessive commercial space, many participants also felt that the six plans lacked architectural verve. One table complained, "all six current plans are unacceptable because they are uninspiring [and have] no significant skyline." Separate tables converged in their opinion of both the plans and the quality of upstate architecture when they wrote that the plans were "boring, dull, bland—too much like the Albany South Mall;" that they looked "too much like Albany state government buildings—bland;" and that "they all look like Albany (no offense)."

A significant number of those attending also felt that the plans, and the planning process, did not sufficiently emphasize the importance of building a memorial to those killed on September 11. One table wrote that the "memorial structure should be planned first [and] all other building subsequent to those decisions." Because concrete preparation for the memorial had not yet begun, however, many participants were puzzled by the connection between a yet-to-be-planned memorial and the site plans they had reviewed in the morning. Criticizing the existing process, almost 80 percent of participants responded that it was "very important" or "important" that the planning of the memorial be linked to the planning of the rest of the site. While both the LMDA and Port Authority had focused upon the alternative commercial, residential, transport, and other practical uses of the area, the priority of the memorial emerged as a significant theme in the public discussion.

Toward the end of the day, in the Civic Alliance-led segment, titled "Rebuilding Lives," the conversation expanded to issues beyond physical reconstruction. When participants were asked to discuss the alternative goals and courses of action that should guide the revitalization of Lower Manhattan, many stressed the importance of building a robust, mixed-used

neighborhood. New York should "create a 24/7 community that did not previously exist in order to invigorate Lower Manhattan and create a more dynamic environment for all inhabitants and visitors," one table wrote. That around-the-clock community, many added, ought to include people of all classes: "middle income people who work in the city should be able to actually LIVE in the city [so] affordable housing is a must." Most participants also agreed that the reconstructed area should include many more amenities—grocery stores, restaurants, schools, libraries, laundromats, and parks—than existed before September 11.

Before the meeting began, some observers had worried that extreme opinions would dominate the day. But while differences plainly existed, most observers say the debate remained productive. "To me the extraordinary thing was [that] there were 4,000 to 5,000 people debating urban design," recalls Alexander Garvin. "Never in the history of planning had that happened before." Moreover, what ultimately emerged from the hundreds of intense discussions was a clear and unambiguous consensus: None of the site plans provided a satisfactory setting for the memorial, and, says Carolyn Lukensmeyer, "it was a unanimous rejection of the Program." She adds: "LMDC wanted to learn as much as they could about the public's evaluation of the elements that made up those concept plans, and they got that information."

John Whitehead, who observed the meeting carefully, describes the day as "wonderful," despite the stinging dismissal. "In spite of the fact that they were criticizing our plans," he says, "I've never seen an expression of true democracy as good as that represented." But the across-the-board condemnation of the six site plans, and the repudiation of the Program, took the Port Authority by surprise, observers say. "They saw it as a setup," says one LMDC official. "They saw it as LMDC using the Port Authority as a lightning rod for all the opposition, and they felt betrayed." For the historically isolated authority officials to be exposed to that kind of public scrutiny, the official says, was like "bats flying around in the daytime."

Still, despite the group's strong consensus, and officials' apparent willingness to listen, many participants doubted that anything had been accomplished. When asked at the end of the meeting whether they believed decision makers would take their input seriously, only one-third of voters said they were confident or very confident they would do so. (Forty-five percent said they were somewhat confident and 22 percent had little confidence. When Robert Yaro of the Civic Alliance summed up the results by saying that more than 80 percent of participants believed their voices would be heard, the shouting crowd set him straight.) "One of the people at the table I was sitting at was saying, 'They're never going to listen, they're going through the motions,' " one said.

EPILOGUE

The barrage of press coverage following the July 2002 Listening to the City meeting forced officials to heed the priorities that emerged from that public discussion. Within a week, Governor George Pataki declared that some of the lost commercial space should be rebuilt off-site, saying he would "urge the Port Authority and Lower Manhattan Development Corporation (LMDC) to look beyond just the 16 acres." (*New York Times*, July 27, 2002). In August, LMDC officials announced the schedule for a new design study that emphasized creativity and risk-taking on the part of firms.

In October, LMDC, the Port Authority, and the city jointly announced a new program that revised the previous commercial space requirements. The program, which Robert Yaro of the Civic Alliance dubbed "World Trade Center Lite," cut mandated

office space by one million square feet, and allowed designers to reduce the amount of office space that had to be on site by about 40 percent, to 6.5 million square feet. (Retail and hotel requirements remained the same, but included the option of expanding them to one million square feet each.) Designers were also asked to include an underground transit hub, to add visual interest to the skyline with at least one tall tower, and to plan for depressing West Street under a promenade. The guidelines noted a "strong preference" for keeping the footprints of the towers free for a memorial. "Very seldom do you see big public authorities, number one, engage in a process like this, and number two, pay attention to the results," says Yaro. "It's an extraordinary achievement."

On December 18, LMDC and the Port Authority presented nine new land use plans. "Unlike the initial group of proposals released by the agency last July," wrote *New York Times* architecture critic Herbert Muschamp in the paper the next day, "these plans throb with energy, imagination, intelligence and the sheer thrill of contributing to a battered city's rebirth."

Some critics, including Eva Hanhardt of Imagine New York and Ronald Shiffman of the Civic Alliance, still believed that officials were moving forward precipitously on land use plans before developing an overall vision for Lower Manhattan. Although the Libeskind plan had responded powerfully to many of the architectural issues raised by Listening to the City, the design didn't address the social issues—such as affordable housing and an increase in neighborhood services—that emerged from Listening to the City.

Although AmericaSpeaks and some civic groups had lobbied for another Listening to the City meeting, LMDC and Port Authority officials said there would not be a third event. However, according to John Whitehead, LMDC chairman, the agency would continue to find ways to reach out to the public. Alexander Garvin concurs, claiming that the events of September 11 had underlined the importance of involving citizens in public policy decisions. "This was an attack on democracy, and we need to demonstrate to the world how a democracy functions," he says. "There's no choice here."

Comment

In November 2001, the governor of New York and mayor of New York City created the Lower Manhattan Development Corporation (LMDC) to oversee the rebuilding at the site of ground zero, the former World Trade Center. No specific decision-making process had been politically mandated. However, John Whitehead, chosen by Governor Pataki to chair the LMDC, made it clear from the outset that he was committed to what political theorists call a deliberative democratic process, one that engages the public in discussion with decision makers in open and transparent ways before decisions are finalized. The Port Authority, which shared responsibility for developing plans for ground zero, did not share Whitehead's enthusiasm for this kind of process. From the perspective of policy analysis and from a deliberative democratic perspective, what can be said for and against Whitehead's commitment to "a lot of listening before we did a lot of talking and decision making"? For and against the Port Authority's "Program"?

While eight advisory councils appointed by the LMDC did their work, a much larger and more technologically advanced deliberative forum—an electronic town meeting designed by AmericaSpeaks—enlisted the participation of many more citizens than even eight advisory councils could accommodate. On what grounds might these electronic town meetings be said to improve policy making or contribute something important to public debates? On what grounds might policy makers oppose them? If the organizers thought that the goal of the town meetings was not to make hard decisions but rather to create a "vision," how could an impartial observer or open-minded citizen assess the success of the town meetings? Can the success of such deliberative forums be measured? If so, by what metrics? If not, is success or failure merely in the eyes of the participants and/or policy makers? Consider whether the case study provides sufficient evidence for judging the success or failure of the first town meeting. Does it provide evidence for judging whether either the LMDC or Port Authority policy makers had reason to support the second town meeting? A third one?

The debate among the four groups over when and how during the second town meeting to present the site plans for redevelopment shows how disputes about agendas can be as value-laden as those about the larger goals of redevelopment. But some observers argued that the time spent in wrangling over the agenda should be considered a cost of any deliberative process and must be weighed against the benefits. If so, how can it be so weighed and with what practical effect? What are the other factors that might be considered in such a cost-benefit calculation—or is such a calculation an inappropriate way to assess the process of deliberation?

Whitehead concluded that he had "never seen an expression of true democracy as good as that [second town meeting] represented." Yet the broad public condemnation of the six site plans and the repudiation of the Port Authority's Program were not universally applauded. Many of the participants—who themselves formed part of the consensus that rejected the Program—thought that nothing important had been accomplished because they doubted whether the public officials had taken their views seriously. How can this disagreement about the value of the deliberation be best assessed? Did the new design study with guidelines that expressed a "strong preference" for keeping the footprints of the towers free for a memorial provide support for the success of the deliberation? Were the nine new land use plans, which were favorably reviewed by the *New York Times* architecture critic, evidence of success? Some would argue that involving citizens in a decision-making process is valuable regardless of the results. But others would insist that there must be some tangible evidence of results to justify such time-consuming involvement. Consider what various democratic theories—and critics of democracy—have to say about the values that are at stake here, and how they relate to a policy analysis that measures the costs and benefits, and chooses the process that calculably maximizes net benefits.

Recommended Reading

An introduction to how advocates of policy analysis intend it to be used is Edith Stokey and Richard Zeckhauser, *A Primer for Policy Analysis* (New York: Norton, 1978). More recent discussions are Matthew D. Adler and Eric A. Posner, *Cost-Benefit Analysis: Legal, Economic, and Philosophical Perspectives* (Chicago: University of Chicago Press, 2001); and Anthony E. Boardman et al., *Cost-Benefit Analysis: Concepts and Practice*, 2nd ed. (New York: Prentice Hall Pearson Learning, 2000). For a broader approach, see Deborah Stone, *Policy Paradox: The Art of Political Decision Making*, rev. ed. (New York: Norton, 2001). A well-informed critique is Peter Dorman, *Markets and Mortality: Economics, Dangerous Work, and the Value of Human Life* (Cambridge: Cambridge University Press, Cambridge, UK, 1996). For a flavor of the ethical controversy over policy analysis, see Alasdair MacIntyre, "Utilitarianism and Cost/Benefit Analysis," in Tom Beauchamp and Norman Bowie (eds.), *Ethical Theory and Business* (New York: Prentice Hall, 2000), pp. 266–76; and Tom Beauchamp, "A Reply to MacIntyre," in Beauchamp and Bowie, pp. 276–82.

David T. Wasserman and Alan Strudler defend the moral relevance of counting lives without recourse to consequentialist reasoning in "Can a Nonconsequentialist Count Lives?" *Philosophy & Public Affairs*, 31 (2003), pp. 71–94.

An exchange of opposing perspectives on utilitarianism, the ethical foundation of most policy analysis, appears in John Smart and Bernard Williams, *Utilitarianism: For and Against* (Cambridge: Cambridge University Press 1973). For a useful collection on consequentialism (the broader philosophical conception of which utilitarianism is one form), see Stephen Darwall (ed.), *Consequentialism* (Oxford: Blackwell, 2002).

A sophisticated version of utilitarianism as a foundational moral theory is James Griffin, *Well-Being: Its Meaning, Measurement, and Moral Importance* (Oxford: Oxford University Press, 1986).

For critiques of utilitarianism as a political morality, see Amy Gutmann and Dennis Thompson, *Democracy and Disagreement* (Cambridge, Mass.: Harvard University Press, 1996), ch. 5; and Will Kymlicka, *Contemporary Political Philosophy* (Oxford: Clarendon Press, 1990), pp. 9–49. Two contemporary defenses of utilitarianism as a political morality are Russell Hardin, *Morality within the Limits of Reason* (Chicago: University of Chicago Press, 1988); and Robert Goodin, *Utilitarianism as a Public Philosophy* (New York: Cambridge University Press, 1995). For a critique of economic approaches to value, see Elizabeth Anderson, *Value in Ethics and Economics* (Cambridge, Mass.: Harvard University Press, 1993).

On the issue of justice for future generations, see Peter Laslett and James Fishkin, (eds.), *Justice Between Age Groups and Generations* (New Haven, Conn.: Yale University Press, 1991); and Brian Barry, "Intergenerational Justice in Energy Policy," in Milton Fisk (ed.), *Justice* (Atlantic Highlands, N.J.: Humanities Press, 1993), pp. 223–37.

Different approaches to environmental ethics can be found in: Andrew Light and Avner De-Shalit (eds.), *Moral and Political Reasoning in Environmental Practice* (Cambridge, MA.: MIT Press, 2003); Kristin S. Shrader-Frechette, *Environmental Justice: Creating Equality, Reclaiming Democracy* (New York: Oxford University Press, 2002); and Cass R. Sunstein, *Risk and Reason: Safety, Law, and the Environment* (Cambridge, UK: Cambridge University Press, 2002). A useful collection is Andrew Light and Holmes Rolston (eds.), *Environmental Ethics: An Anthology* (Oxford: Blackwell, 2002). Economists, philosophers, and other scholars analyze ways of measuring the quality of life in Martha Nussbaum and Amartya Sen (eds.), *The Quality of Life* (Oxford: Oxford University Press, 1993). A broad ethical discussion of utilitarianism and its application to environmental policy appears in Peter Singer, *One World* (New Haven, Conn.: Yale University Press, 2002), chapters 1, 2.

On the importance of public deliberation, see Amy Gutmann and Dennis Thompson, *Why Deliberative Democracy?* (Princeton, N.J.: Princeton University Press, 2004), pp. 63–67. A critical appraisal of public deliberation appears in Lynn Sanders, "Against Deliberation" *Political Theory*, 25:3 (1997), pp. 347–77. A wide array of perspectives on deliberation and its political and ethical value can be found in Stephen Macedo (ed.), *Deliberative Politics: Essays on Democracy and Disagreement* (Oxford: Oxford University Press, 1999); and David Estlund (ed.), *Democracy* (Oxford: Blackwell, 2001).

7   Distributive Justice

On what principles should government control the distribution of goods to citizens? Utilitarians and their progeny do not believe that any special theory of justice is necessary. The right distribution is the one that maximizes the total welfare of most citizens, even if this entails sacrificing the liberty and opportunity of the few to the many. While utilitarianism is widely criticized for ignoring claims of individuals that even the welfare of the whole society should not override, critics do not agree on what theory of distributive justice to put in its place.

Libertarians argue that governments should secure only liberty, not distribute goods such as income, health care, or education. Goods, in this view, come into the world attached to specific people who have earned, inherited, or received them by free exchange, and for the state to redistribute their property without their consent is a violation of their fundamental right to liberty. Because "taxation is on a par with forced labor" (Robert Nozick), even a democratic government may not tax the rich to provide welfare for the poor. Nor may it protect the rich from competition by sheltering their industries or licensing their professions. Individual liberty, understood as noninterference, trumps both social welfare and democracy.

Egalitarian critics argue that, just as utilitarianism can be faulted for submerging individuals beneath all social purposes, so libertarianism can be criticized for elevating them above all social responsibility. For egalitarians, our social interdependence creates certain duties of mutual aid or reciprocity.

Most egalitarian theories of distributive justice also give priority to basic liberty over social welfare. But their list of basic liberties differs from that of libertarians. It includes political liberty, freedom of religion, speech, and assembly, and the right to hold personal property. But it does not include an absolute right to commercial property or unqualified freedom of contract. According to egalitarians, although basic liberty has priority, not all liberty is basic, and even basic liberty is not the only good that governments should distribute or safeguard for all individuals. Other primary goods include income and wealth, the distributions of which are just (according to John Rawls' difference principle) only if they maximize the welfare of the least advantaged citizens.

Egalitarians are commonly criticized for subordinating individual liberty to equality. This criticism is compelling only if one accepts the absolute value of the libertarians' expansive understanding of liberty. A more general problem is that the maximization of some primary goods (such as health care, security, and education)

313

might require an egalitarian government to neglect other primary goods, since there is virtually no limit to the resources that can be spent on making people healthy, secure, and well educated.

Democratic theories of distributive justice build upon this criticism. The people, constituted by democratic majorities at various levels of government, should have the right to determine priorities among goods according to what they deem most important to their collective ways of life. Most democratic theorists recognize that majorities should have the right only when the procedures by which they make decisions are fair. But the requirements of this standard of procedural fairness are controversial. Some democrats argue that it requires governments only to secure certain basic liberties, such as freedom of speech, association, and the right to vote. Others claim that it also requires governments to guarantee the distribution of a basic level of opportunity—in the form of income, education, food, housing, and health care—for all citizens. The first position has been criticized for permitting majority tyranny over disadvantaged minorities, the second, for smuggling egalitarian values into democratic theory and thereby encroaching on the rights of democratic majorities who may not favor so much equality.

The political controversies over the distribution of health care and welfare in the United States are instructive problems in distributive justice. Good health care is necessary for pursuing most other things in life. Yet equal access to health care would require the government not only to redistribute resources from the rich and healthy to the poor and infirm but also to restrict the freedom of doctors and other health care providers. Such redistribution and restrictions may be warranted, but on what principles and to what extent? The first case—the Arizona state legislature's decision in 1987 to eliminate funding for most organ transplants—is part of this continuing controversy over whether government has a right or a responsibility to provide citizens with the preconditions of a decent life. The second case, which describes the controversy over rationing health care services to low-income Oregonians, highlights the very expansive role of government in regulating access to health care for millions of low-income citizens. By evaluating these political decisions that in different ways importantly affect the distribution of medical care, we can clarify our understanding of the relative strengths and weaknesses of competing theories of distributive justice.

The third case—a controversy over welfare reform in Wisconsin—focuses on an increasingly important set of moral issues that are often neglected by conventional theories of distributive justice. Should a minimal level of economic welfare be guaranteed unconditionally to all citizens? Or should welfare be made conditional on a citizen's willingness to work? If welfare is to be unconditional, how can government justify paying citizens not to work? If welfare is to be conditional, how can a citizen's willingness to work be fairly assessed in an economy where not enough jobs are available? In assessing the controversy over welfare reform in Wisconsin, we must consider not only the principled relation between the rights of citizens and their responsibilities but also the practical requirements of any welfare policy that seeks to enforce the responsibilities as well as the rights of citizens.

The final case takes us beyond the inevitability of death and taxes to the discretionary ethics of imposing taxes on large estates after the death of their proprietors.

For what purposes, if any, does distributive justice demand (or permit) taxing large estates of affluent individuals upon their death? Both sides in the 2003 congressional debate over a proposed repeal of the federal estate tax emphasize issues of fairness, although they sharply disagree over which of two competing tax proposals fairness favors.

Defunding Organ Transplants in Arizona
Pamela Varley

Dianna Brown, who will be buried this morning in Yuma, was the first person to die under Arizona's newest death penalty law. She was forty-three years old. She had committed no murder. No conspiracy. No theft. No parking violation. No crime. Dianna Brown's only offense was to be poor and sick. Under Arizona law, that's now punishable by death.

E. J. Montini, Arizona Republic

September 18, 1987

In the spring of 1987, the Arizona state legislature voted to eliminate funding for most organ transplants from the state's health care program for the indigent, the Arizona Health Care Cost Containment System (AHCCCS—pronounced "access"). At the same time, however, the legislature voted to increase other kinds of health coverage provided by AHCCCS. The most controversial item was the extension of basic health service to pregnant women and to children between the ages of six and thirteen[1] in the so-called "notch group"— families that earn too much to qualify for AHCCCS automatically, but still earn less than the federal poverty level.[2]

Although the decision to extend health coverage to these women and children was debated extensively, the decision to defund organ transplants slipped through the legislature with relatively little notice or attention. A few months later, however, the legislators had to confront the effect of their decision in the person of forty-three-year-old Dianna Brown, a Yuma woman suffering from terminal liver disease. In accordance with the new state policy, AHCCCS denied Brown's request for a liver transplant in August 1987. A few weeks later, she died. In the flurry of news coverage attending her death, several legislators publicly questioned their decision to defund the transplants and called for reconsideration of the matter in the 1988 legislative session.

BACKGROUND

In a brief characterization of Arizona's political landscape, the 1988 *Almanac of American Politics* states, "Arizona citizens face squarely first questions—government or free enterprise, development or environment, regulation or freedom—and tend to come out squarely on one side or the other." More often than not, the Almanac adds, they come out squarely on the conservative side. Arizona is the only state to have voted Republican in every presidential election since 1948, and Republicans heavily dominate both chambers of the state legislature. The Grand Canyon State also prides itself on a certain independent spirit. For instance, Arizona is the only one of the forty-eight contiguous states to have steadfastly resisted the convention of daylight savings

Reprinted by permission of the Case Program, Kennedy School of Government, Harvard University. Copyright. 1988 by the President and Fellows of Harvard College.

time.[3] It was the last state to develop a state park system. And from 1972 to 1981, it was the only state in the country which had not accepted the federal Medicaid program.

Although the Dianna Brown case may have taken the public and even some legislators by surprise, it did not spring from nowhere. It grew out of a several-year struggle within AHCCCS to establish and enforce an organ transplant policy. More broadly, the case arose in the context of long-standing controversy over the type and cost of health care provided to Arizona's poor.

THE BIRTH OF AHCCCS

Medicaid was created at the national level in 1966 as an optional program: if a state met the federal standards established for health care of the poor, the federal government would pay a share of the costs (the percentage varied depending on the relative wealth of the state). Many states were quick to sign on, but Arizona legislators steered clear of the program. "State policymakers feared intrusive federal intervention, as well as the potential for fraud and abuse and the uncontrolled cost to the state," according to a June 1987 report on the program prepared by the federal Health Care Financing Administration (HCFA).[4] For the next fifteen years, each county in Arizona continued to provide some measure of health care to the poor with its own dollars. Over time, however, the county system resulted in "unequal eligibility, uneven services [across the state], and, most important, an increasing cost burden on the counties," according to the HCFA report. In the seventies, as elsewhere in the country, health care began escalating dramatically in Arizona—from $49 million in 1974 to $106 million in 1979—until they consumed, on average, a quarter of each county's annual revenues, drawn primarily from property taxes. In 1980, when Arizonans passed a referendum limiting the property tax levy, the counties' budget squeeze became a flat-out crisis: "The counties faced the possibility of a complete fiscal breakdown in 1981," HCFA wrote.

It was under this kind of financial pressure that the state legislature began to talk of ushering in a Medicaid program as a way to tap into federal funds. But many legislators remained reluctant, and during the summer of 1981, they bargained with HCFA to set up a program significantly different from a conventional Medicaid system. The Arizona program would be "experimental," designed "to contain cost by encouraging cost competition among prepaid plans and discouraging overutilization of health care," according to HCFA. In each county, different health maintenance organizations (HMOs) would bid to provide an agreed-upon health care package to AHCCCS-eligible residents in return for a fixed payment per person per month from AHCCCS.[5] The goal was to create within each HMO an incentive to keep medical costs low for routine health care. Similarly, the federal government would pay a fixed "capitation rate" per month to the state for each Medicaid-eligible person in the program (a departure from the usual method of reimbursement: paying a share of the actual medical costs incurred.[6]) For this reason, the state had an incentive to keep its own costs low and to push for low bids from HMOs.

The set-up of the AHCCCS program was also to be different from conventional Medicaid in several respects. For one thing, the entire program was to be administered by a private firm. For another, AHCCCS would not cover the full array of Medicaid services (the state received a special waiver so that it would not have to provide skilled nursing facilities for long-term care,[7] home health care, family planning, or nurse mid-wife services). Within the state, the program was never even called "Medicaid." In fact, according to AHCCCS Deputy Director David Lowenberg:

> When we submit a budget (to the legislature], or make presentations, or talk about policy issues, it's in terms of "AHCCCS" or—the closest we'll get is "Title IX programs." I've been asked not to put the word "Medicaid" in, because Medicaid brings up all the bad that

[the legislators] have either heard personally or read about in other states. There is a high level of concern of the abuse, the fraud. They did not want to be a party to such a system in this state.

The legislature and governor approved the creation of AHCCCS in November of 1981, and the program took effect eleven months later. In retrospect, health care professionals tend to think this speedy implementation allowed too little time for program planning and development. In any event, in its first eighteen months, AHCCCS was "beset with administrative and budgetary problems," according to the HCFA report. The agency was criticized by the public for the lengthy, cumbersome process for determining eligibility. (In some cases, people reportedly died for lack of medical treatment before their eligibility was determined.) Due to financial irregularities, the legislature decided to shift administrative control of AHCCCS from the private firm to the state in March of 1984, and hired Dr. Donald F. Schaller to head the program. Schaller had had extensive administrative experience with health maintenance organizations ever since 1972, when he had left fifteen years of work in private practice to co-found the Arizona Health Plan—one of the oldest HMOs in the state. When he came to AHCCCS, Schaller had also spent a year as senior vice president and medical director of the CIGNA Healthplan, and a year as consultant to a consortium of four HMOs working with AHCCCS.

Although AHCCCS remained controversial within the state under Schaller's leadership, he is widely credited with bringing the agency under fiscal and administrative control. By early 1987, 200,469 people were covered by AHCCCS,[8] and the program had a year-long budget of $294 million. More than two-thirds of Arizona's licensed physicians participated in the program directly or through an HMO, and fourteen different private HMOs were contracted to provide health care for the program.

During its first shaky year and a half of operation, AHCCCS had no policy about funding transplants per se, partly because the agency received few transplant requests. Before his arrival, Schallar says, "I'm not sure how many transplants were paid for or what happened. There may have been one or two."

THE STATE OF THE ART IN TRANSPLANTATION

The practice of transplanting organs to treat patients began to emerge in the United States in the 1950s and early 1960s— initially with dismal survival rates, which steadily improved. During the 1980s, transplantation became a more viable method of treatment and was used for an increasing number of organs. By 1987, the simplest and most routine transplants available were cornea and bone transplants, followed by kidney transplants. Heart, liver, and bone marrow transplants were increasingly common, and pancreas, heart-and-lung, and other organ combinations, while rarer, were actively being developed.

But there was no question that these organ transplants were costly. According to a 1984 study,[9] the fully-allocated one-year cost of a liver transplant averaged between $230,000 and $340,000, and of a heart transplant, between $170,000 and $200,000. "This is in the range of four to ten times the cost of the other most expensive currently employed medical technologies," the task force reported:

> The costs of doing the transplant operation itself are relatively minor, whether the operation lasts three hours or twenty-three hours. The real costs come from the post-operative hospitalization and the frequent need to rehospitalize transplant patients to treat various complications. These are very common (averaging more than one per case in most reports on the literature). They include rejection episodes, complications from the operation itself, and infections that develop because such patients take drugs to suppress their immune systems to fight organ rejection, making them more vulnerable to other infections. There are also significant costs in pre-operative work-ups, routine postoperative hospitalization, organ procurement, etc.

THE HISTORY OF TRANSPLANT FUNDING IN ARIZONA

Arizona was home to one of the pioneers of the heart transplant field—a much-celebrated young surgeon named Jack Copeland, who built a nationally recognized heart transplant program at the University of Arizona Medical Center in Tucson. Dr. Timothy Icenogle, a surgeon on Copeland's team, says that progress in the heart transplant arena was swift and dramatic in the 1980s. "Back in 1981, there were very dark days and nights of trying to take care of transplants. Survivorship wasn't very good back then. It was back in the days when there were just a few brave souls venturing into this."

It was also back in the days when transplants were covered by virtually no private insurers. "What happened back in 1981, before anyone was paying for this, [the patients] all had to go out and fundraise. And if they had the money, then they came to the 'active' list."[10] If they couldn't come up with the money, he adds, "they died fundraising." By 1986, however, Icenogle said that "almost all private insurers paid for it and if they didn't want to pay for it, we [encouraged the patient] to sue them, [with] nearly 100 percent success."[11]

> Really, the insurers don't have a choice, because heart transplantation now is not experimental. It is an accepted therapeutic modality, and it is the treatment of choice. It is just as therapeutic as getting penicillin for your pneumonia.

Icenogle adds that some companies—especially HMOs competing for business—have been persuaded that the "public embarrassment" of a protracted battle over payment of a transplant is not worth the fight. "One of them we coerced into paying for a patient, because they realized that the fallout from the lawsuit—and having to go in front of the television cameras and say what schmucks they were—was going to cost them a great deal of money."

"We play a sort of an advocacy role," Icenogle adds. "I think society demands something more from physicians than [to be] just a glob of bureaucrats, and I think we have to take a stand now and then. Our role, essentially, as patient advocate, is to tell them, well, just because the insurance company says they're not going to pay, that is not the end of all the resources. We can help show them other resources that are available."

IN THE CONTEXT OF DEREGULATION

The increasing number of organ transplants, and the growing costs associated with them, coincided with another development in the state's health care system: the deregulation of medical facilities in March 1985. Before deregulation, hospitals were required to seek permission to make capital investments in their facilities. Regulation proponents argued that without such a process, hospitals would begin to perform more and more glamorous high tech, high-dollar medical procedures—like transplants—and that costs would escalate while quality of care would decline.[12] Says Rep. Cindy Resnick (D-Tucson), a member of the House Health Committee, the transplant units "get a great deal of PR and they get a great deal of money."

> It is a money-making system. If it was just pure concern about the [medical] needs out there, we'd have far more burn units than we have transplant units. The reality is they make money on those units. You can bring in anywhere from a million to three million dollars on that service alone to a hospital a year.

"There's also a prestige factor," adds Phil Lopes, a regional director of the regulatory Health Systems Agency before it was dismantled. "You do all these fancy high tech things with somebody's ticker, and there's something sexy about that. Everybody wants to have one of those, wants to have that service. You're in the Big Time."

DON SCHALLER'S VIEW

Right from the start, Schaller was uncomfortable about AHCCCS funding of transplants for several reasons. For one, he questioned whether a program with tight resources should be spending its money on high-dollar, high-risk procedures. After all, AHCCCS was intended as a general health program for the genuinely poor. By contrast, many of AHCCCS's transplant recipients did not start out poor enough to qualify for the program, but—due to their illnesses or to the failure of their private insurance companies to cover their medical expenses—they had "spent down" their assets and become AHCCCS-eligible. Schaller worried that AHCCCS might, *de facto,* be swallowed up by such heavy dollar expenses and turn into a catastrophic health program for the general public. AHCCCS should provide "basic health care to poor people, not just cater to people who have real expensive health problems," he said in an interview aired May 29, 1986, on KAET-TVs "Horizon" program.

Schaller also had several fundamental concerns about the ethics and equity of the complex organ transplant system. For one, he questioned the fairness of the system by which scarce organs were allocated—namely, to those with money, media-appeal, or political support. For another, he objected to the high rates doctors and hospitals were charging for the procedures. When an organ was rejected, for instance, the doctors might re-transplant, substantially increasing the patient's cost: "The way things are set up, when the doctor reoperates, guess what? He gets another fee."

> The charges, I think, are excessive. Most of the funding for these procedures goes to private individuals that charge full bore and excessive fees. I would have less objection if the money went to the University of Arizona, and the University of Arizona had on its staff a physician that got only a salary for performing procedures, not a fee for each service. You could almost say that, since the surgeons charge a fee for service, they might even have a financial incentive to do more and more procedures.

Does Schaller think organ transplants have become a racket? "It's not a racket," he says, "but the financial part of it has come close to that."

Surgeons disagree with Schaller's characterization of the costs. In a September 15, 1987, television interview during KAET-TV's "Horizon" program, Dr. Lawrence Koep, a liver transplant surgeon in Phoenix, said:

> The vast majority of the cost is hospital-incurred cost. Personnel, drugs, beds, those are where we spend the lion's share of the money. Time in the operating room—these are long operations—that's horribly expensive. The kind of technology available, particularly in the OR [operating room] and the intensive care unit, is just mind-boggling.

According to Icenogle, the University of Arizona actually provides one of the least expensive heart transplants in the country, but the basic truth, he says, is that "some health care is just more expensive than other health care."

> If penicillin were more expensive, then the state legislature would not approve penicillin for pneumonias. Outpatient health care is less expensive than inpatient health care. But what it really comes down to is—is the health care proven, effective, and therapeutic?

In a few rare instances, he says, the University Medical Center has waived costs for patients, but he adds,

> I don't think the University Medical Center can make it a policy to absorb the state's responsibility to take on transplantation. Those kind of dollars do not exist. The hospital is a small hospital, it's only three hundred beds. This place does not have money to throw away.

AHCCCS'S TRANSPLANT POLICY UNDER SCHALLER

When Schaller came on board, there was an established procedure for handling organ transplant requests. The patient would submit a request to AHCCCS which would eventually end up on the director's desk. The director would make the final decision either to grant or deny the request. Such decisions had been so infrequent before the mid-1980s that they had not caused much consternation within AHCCCS. But when Schaller became director, the number of transplants—and the amount of money spent on them—began to climb.

In 1984, AHCCCS paid for one heart, one liver, and four kidney transplants. In 1985, the program paid for two heart and sixteen liver transplants. The following year, it was one heart, one liver, seven bone marrow, and twelve kidney transplants.[13] Aggregate costs for heart, liver, bone marrow, and kidney transplants rose from $451,012 in 1984 to $1,060,954 in 1985 to $2,141,663 in 1986. In addition, transplant patients' medical expenses after surgery— even when successful—were chronically high as they needed to take immunosuppressant drugs, at an average cost of $500 per month, for the rest of their lives.

Schaller began to take a hard look at the transplant requests coming to AHCCCS, and to consider the merits of each. Rep. Resnick recalls:

> [There was] one instance—perhaps a rumor— that one of our patients, who ultimately had a liver transplant, needed a new liver because they'd used up the last one with alcohol. And they're quickly on the road to using up the second one. That's difficult for physicians in Dr. Schaller's position to see. First, the transplant is imposed on him, and then he's paying for something [and] perhaps—as he said before—the money could have been used much more wisely someplace else.

Schaller soon discovered, however, that he did not always have clear authority to make decisions about transplant requests. "You've got the legislature pushing on one end, the governor says something else, then you've got a judge that says, 'You've got to do this,'" says Schaller. "You know, we tried to have a policy, but it was hard to implement a single policy and apply it the same across every case." The reality was that AHCCCS made its decisions on a case-by-case basis. Before the state legislature took action on the matter—and before the Dianna

Brown case surfaced—AHCCCS confronted several controversial transplant cases. Two, in particular, contributed to the development of the legislature's policy.

SHARON BRIERLEY: A CASE OF POLITICAL PRESSURE

Whenever he did deny a transplant request, Schaller found himself engulfed in a whirlwind of political pressure, sometimes from the legislature, sometimes from the governor, and sometimes even from the White House. In 1984, for example, Schaller ran into trouble when he initially refused the request of forty-one-year-old Sharon Brierley for a liver transplant. Brierley had moved to Tucson four years earlier from Vermont after an unhappy marriage, and before she had established a new career, she began to suffer from cirrhosis of the liver, reportedly caused by a previous bout with hepatitis. When Brierley learned she needed a liver transplant, she appealed to AHCCCS. After reviewing the particulars of her case, Schaller refused Brierley's request. (In the interest of patient confidentiality, Schaller declined to talk about any specific transplant decisions.) Two state legislators intervened on Brierley's behalf. At first Schaller stood firm, but in the end, after "much wrangling and political intercession from the State House to the White House," Brierley's transplant costs were shared by the hospital, AHCCCS, and the federal government.[14]

After the Brierley case, Schaller decided to formalize his transplant policy. Following the lead of the Medicare system,[15] Schaller decided that AHCCCS—again, using its own administrative discretion to determine appropriateness—would cover heart and bone marrow transplants, but would cover liver transplants only for patients under the age of eighteen, for whom survival rates were higher. For patients eighteen and older, Schaller argued, liver transplants were still "experimental" procedures, and thus AHCCCS was under no obligation to provide them.

BARBARA BRILLO: A CASE OF JUDICIAL PRESSURE

This policy soon received a legal challenge, however. Barbara Brillo, a forty-six-year-old woman, requested a liver transplant early in 1986 and was denied by AHCCCS on grounds that she was too old. Brillo's husband, Jerome, frantically tried to reverse the decision—an effort which ended with several state legislators and a White House aide exerting pressure on AHCCCS. At the same time, he tried to fundraise for his wife. By April, still without the requisite $50,000 needed for preliminary tests at the liver transplant center at Phoenix's Good Samaritan Hospital, and with Barbara Brillo's life expectancy down to one or two months, Jerome Brillo arranged for his wife to travel to a Pittsburgh center. "Down deep, I really thought they would come through for us eventually," he told the *Arizona Star* (April 11, 1986). "But, as the weeks went by, my hopes got dimmer. Yes, I'm bitter, because you know what? This could happen to anyone. And believe me, if you don't have the $50,000 (down payment), you're nowhere."

Schaller continued to defend his decision, and to feel the heat for it. In a July 7, 1986, interview on KAET-TV's "Horizon" program, Brillo's attorney, Howard Baldwin, asked, "Why should we pay $110,000 for Don Schaller's salary when we could use that money to provide medical care? Or why should we have a PR man for AHCCCS? It always troubles me to find people fighting for principles over other people's bodies."

After a rancorous court battle, Brillo won her case in the summer of 1986 on grounds that the surgery was medically necessary and was not properly considered experimental. AHCCCS was forced to fund her liver transplant, which had been carried out in Pittsburgh in the interim. Within AHCCCS, "the [Brillo] court decision really precipitated a lot of discussion," says Lowenberg.

> I think what that did is showed us how vulnerable we were going to be to make policy on what's covered and not—and just from the

real practical standpoint, as an agency—how do you budget that? What you soon learn is that you really don't have control, because [if you deny patients], they're going to take it to court, and you don't know how the judge is going to rule. In this case, we lost.

In fact, as AHCCCS would write in a report to the legislature the following spring:

> Although the courts, including the Supreme Court, have stated that the states have wide discretion in determining the scope of benefits that they will provide under Medicaid,[16] several courts have held that a particular organ transplant must be covered, since it was determined to be medically necessary under the circumstances.

The report also stated that although no state policy would be "foolproof in the absence of federal law," AHCCCS's counsel advised that at the least, "a statutory amendment will be required to effectively exclude coverage of organ transplants for medically needy persons, indigent persons, and eligible children." Thus, AHCCCS decided to ask the legislature to enact a state transplant policy into law. The next question: exactly what kind of law did AHCCCS want to recommend to the legislature?

CREATING THE NEW POLICY

During the summer of 1986, Schaller and a group of his top administrators began to discuss various policy options. These discussions were fairly freewheeling, according to Lowenberg, with administrators tossing out a number of possibilities. He recalls:

> We started to get into [ideas like], "Well, we'll cover *one* heart transplant, but we won't cover *two* heart transplants"—in other words, if the [first transplant fails and the] person needs another one. [But] what's the rationale for drawing the line [there]?

So early on, the AHCCCS team began to consider a blanket policy: no transplants, period, a position also favored initially by the governor's staff. But, Lowenberg says, the AHCCCS administrators soon convinced themselves that this approach did not really make any sense either:

> Initially it was—either you have transplants or you don't—because when you start making exceptions, then it becomes more and more difficult to draw the line. . . . Then, of course, we began to look at the kidney and say, "Well, wait a minute, that doesn't make sense for the kidney or the cornea."

So Schaller and the AHCCCS team began to consider a policy to fund kidney, cornea, and bone transplants, but no other kind of organ transplants. This, they argued, was easily defensible, because kidney, cornea, and bone transplants were significantly different medically and economically from transplant of heart, liver, and bone marrow. In the case of corneas and bone transplants, the procedures were simple, there was no tissue match, and they could be performed at many health care establishments.

In addition, these procedures seemed to meet the "cost-benefit" test: "For the eye implant, it was [a question:] do we allow the person to be on [the] SSI Disabled [list]? Is that in the best interests of the public, that the person becomes blind and cannot work and must be supported by either the state or the federal government?" says Lowenberg.

Kidneys were different from other major organs in that they did not require the donor's death, and were, in fact, often donated by relatives of the patients. Questions of speed, timing, and tissue match were therefore removed from the equation. What's more, though not cheap, kidney transplants were less expensive over time than the alternative—dialysis treatment. AHCCCS discovered that on average, dialysis cost $2,500 per month while the average kidney transplant cost $68,000. Thus, "the 'break-even point' economically justifying kidney transplants may be after two years and three months," AHCCCS wrote in a report to the legislature. Heart, liver, and bone marrow transplants were in a whole different league, however,

in terms of cost and complexity as were new transplant procedures for the pancreas or heart-and-lung.

After some consideration, AHCCCS did recommend, in the form of its budget request, that the legislature fund only kidney, cornea, and bone transplants—but, cautions Lowenberg, "I think it's real important to understand that we didn't present necessarily a 'policy.' We presented [that] this is an issue that you at the legislature and governor's office need to decide."

LEONARD KIRSCHNER'S VIEW

Schaller left AHCCCS to become a private consultant in January of 1987 and was succeeded the following month by Leonard Kirschner, a physician who, most recently, had served as the medical director of an HMO in Phoenix that treated AHCCCS patients.

Although Kirschner came to AHCCCS after the agency had already submitted a recommendation to the legislature, he quickly got behind the proposal: "Philosophically, I was already in agreement with them," he says. Kirschner's reasoning about the issue, however, was somewhat different from Schaller's. To the incoming director, "aggregate costs" were the major concern, and spending dollars where they would do the most good. A physician with twenty-two years of service in the military, Kirschner believed that—like the triage practiced on the battlefield—a public program with limited resources must establish clear priorities for treatment. Thus, he favored broad-based health care for the poor over organ transplant coverage. "You take a high risk population that gets no prenatal care—the teenage pregnancy out of the barrio, doesn't want anybody to know she's pregnant, doesn't take care of herself, is on alcohol, and tobacco, or maybe drugs—the risk of low birth weight is up to about 18 percent," he says.

> What's the cost to society for that bad baby? Neonatal intensive care unit costs for that baby are probably going to be in the range of

$40,000. And to boot, what you are met with on the outside as that child grows up frequently is residual damage from that premature birth: low IQ, low lifetime learning expectancy, won't be able to function, mental retardation, seizures—all the bad things that happen from low birth weight.

So where do you want to spend your money? Do I want to spend my money on doing eight heart transplants at a million and a half dollars? Or go out and get more of these poor people who are not getting prenatal care, and give them some prenatal care? That's about $2,000 a case. What's $2,000 into a million five? 700 cases? What about 700 deliveries for eight heart transplants?

"This is probably going to make me sound like Attila the Hun," Kirschner adds, but "when I have limited resources, it's women and children first. The *Titanic* concept of medicine."

More broadly, Kirschner believes that the trend toward high-tech medicine is a bad one, not just from a financial point of view but also from a human one. "A young man I was peripherally involved with a year ago had a bone marrow transplant and then went into bone marrow rejection, which is a horrible experience. He died a horrible death," he says. "Obviously spending all those resources and causing him a death far worse than he would have had from the disease makes one sit there and say, 'Well, why in the world did I do that to that person?' "

Every time we bring a new person into the world, we accept the fact that that person's going to die, and we're almost reaching the point in society where we want to repeal that biological fact.

Now if there's an individual who does have those resources and wants to purchase that, we live in a capitalist society. So be it. But in a public program, that has the widest range of responsibilities, and limited resources to handle those responsibilities, I think it's unacceptable to use those limited resources in a way that really doesn't further the public good.

LEGISLATIVE ACTION IN THE SPRING OF 1987

The legislature—which meets in regular session for only one hundred days a year in Arizona—confronted major budget difficulties during its 1987 session. Conservative Republican Governor Evan Mecham had just taken office and had come to the legislature with an extremely lean budget. At the same time, the state was dealing with a budget overrun from the preceding year, and the legislature was making some midyear corrections to make up the difference. "So agencies, including ourselves, had to accept serious cutbacks," says AHCCCS's Lowenberg.

What's more, the legislature had to make a number of major budgetary decisions about the AHCCCS program in 1987. The whole program, enacted for five years as a "demonstration," was scheduled to end in October unless the legislature voted to extend it. In addition, the legislature was considering proposals to add services to AHCCCS, including long-term health care, provided at that time by county governments, and service to pregnant women and children between the ages of six and thirteen in the notch group—at that time, not offered at all.

Health care committees in both the House and Senate came up with versions of the omnibus AHCCCS bill. In the Senate discussion, the chair of the Health and Welfare Committee—Senator Greg Lunn (R-Tucson)—played a significant role. Lunn was a moderate young Republican, especially interested in environmental matters, who had come to office in 1981 from a career in broadcast journalism. He was known as an articulate rising young star whose district included the University of Arizona and its Medical Center. Upon learning that the legislature might defund organ transplants, the Medical Center urged its state senator to preserve funding for heart transplants. Lunn found the university's arguments convincing, and, likewise, convinced his colleagues in the Senate to include funding for heart transplants—but not for liver or bone marrow transplants—in the AHCCCS budget. His reason, he says, was "basically twofold":

> I thought that relative to the other major categories of transplantation that we were, in essence, precluding payment for in the future—liver transplants and bone marrow transplants—that heart had shown a greater rate of success in terms of the success of the procedure itself, longevity, and the quality of life associated after a successful procedure was done.[17] Additionally, I was certainly persuaded by the fact that I believe we have one of the preeminent centers for heart transplantation here in the state at the University of Arizona Medical Center, and I thought it was in the interests of that facility and the research they were doing that AHCCCS continue to be a payer.

When the bill moved to the House Health Committee, the question of organ transplants received little consideration, however, and the committee opted for the recommendation of AHCCCS's administration. The two versions of the AHCCCS bill, with assorted differences, then went to the House-Senate conference committee on health care, also chaired by Lunn, for final negotiations.

THE CONFERENCE COMMITTEE RESOLUTION

When the AHCCCS bills reached the conference committee, the Senate bill included coverage for heart transplantation and also for psychotropic drugs, another expensive item. The House bill included neither of these items, but did include a significant expansion of coverage for the notch group.[18] "As in any conference committee procedure, you end up assuming that those elements that are consistent are in the bill, and then you argue about the differences," says Lunn. Within the conference committee, therefore, the transplant debate was narrowed to the question of whether or not to fund heart transplants.

Dr. Jack Copeland, the head of the U of A's heart transplant center, weighed in with a letter to the committee. The U of A had performed a total of 125 heart transplants, he wrote. During the past three years, AHCCCS had funded five heart transplants and one artificial heart ("bridge-to-transplant") procedure. "Five of these patients are doing well and living a high quality of life, and the bridge-to-transplant patient has returned to full-time employment. We currently have two AHCCCS patients needing heart transplants who are being evaluated and we project there will be five or six AHCCCS patients per year." Copeland then offered some economic arguments for funding heart transplants:

> For most of our patients (married males, less than fifty years of age with pre-school or teenage children), the major reasons for undergoing cardiac transplantation were to maintain some semblance of family stability and to resume competitive employment. Our patients are generally referred for vocational rehabilitation and one third have returned to work within six months of transplantation.

Copeland argued that even if AHCCCS refused a patient a transplant, it would have to continue to provide some health care to the person while s/he continued to deteriorate and die. Heart transplants were only performed in dire cases—where the patient's life expectancy was less than twelve months—but those health care costs could still run quite high. He wrote that on average, "according to the National Heart Transplant Study, the cost difference between a patient who is transplanted and one who is not is approximately $6,100"—not much money in the scheme of things. Copeland added:

> Should the nontransplanted patient die leaving a wife and three children (aged five, ten, and fifteen), the family becomes eligible for monthly Social Security benefits approximating $1,036 which payments continue until the youngest child reaches the age of eighteen or until age twenty-one for all three children should they pursue college educations.

Copeland also included cost estimates for heart transplants ($65,000 to $80,000) in his letter, and mentioned that his center was likely to become one of ten approved transplant centers across the country designated by Medicare and therefore approved treatment facilities for Medicare patients.

These last two points aroused the anger and concern of AHCCCS administrators. For one, they felt Copeland had vastly underestimated the true cost of an average heart transplant (which they calculated to be $165,000).[19] In addition, they saw the emergence of the U of A as a nationally recognized transplant center to be a double-edged sword: in increasing numbers, patients would move to the state to receive medical treatment, and if they established residency and were income eligible, AHCCCS would have to pay for them. Already, two such patients had surfaced, according to Schaller, who appeared before the conference committee as a consultant to the committee:

> We're finding ourselves as a state paying for patients who move in from Idaho and California with no ability to go back to those states and collect from their Medicaid agencies our costs. That's one of the reasons I don't think we ought to pay for this, because if we're going to be attracting people from all over the country who are so impressed with Dr. Copeland's ability, I'm wondering who's going to pay for 'em. If he wants to be a regional center, let him go out and collect his money from everybody in the region—not AHCCCS.

Furthermore, AHCCCS warned that if the program began to cover each transplant requested, it would not be long before most health insurance carriers would cease to consider transplants as a covered benefit on the theory that AHCCCS (and the taxpayers) is the paying alternative.

AHCCCS also confronted the committee with another problem: The Health Care Financing Administration. While HCFA had been willing in the past to provide extra funding for transplants on a case-by-case basis, the federal agency decided in 1986 that this arrangement was not in keeping with the spirit of the ground rules of the AHCCCS-Medicaid experiment. Thus,

HCFA wanted the costs of the transplants to be covered the way any other medical costs were covered—out of the basic capitation rate given to the state. In a letter to AHCCCS dated October 17, 1986, HCFA wrote that "the state will include all organ transplant costs in the base computations used to determine capitation rates for categorically eligible AHCCCS recipients, and HCFA will not provide a regular federal match based on actual organ transplant costs for these procedures on an individual basis." Paul Lichtenstein, federal project officer for AHCCCS under HCFA's Office of Research and Development, says that HCFA would have been more than willing to increase the capitation rate to reflect the cost of transplants for Medicaid-eligible people. But according to Lowenberg, it is not reasonable to try to work such changeable and erratic costs into a standard formula: "It's our viewpoint that with such a low-volume, high price type of incident, i.e., transplant, it doesn't make sense to attempt to include it in a capitation. . . . Capitation is never going to cover all the costs. Never."

This legislative tug-of-war over funding for heart transplants ended with a decision that heart transplants *might* be funded in part, but only if HCFA relented and agreed to share the costs on a case-by-case basis. Says Lunn:

> It ended in a compromise. A lot of people would have just as soon not had [heart transplants] in there at all. I would have just as soon had [them] in there [unconditionally] as an AHCCCS-covered service. So—just tire people out, that's the way—we never finished the bill. When we *abandoned* the bill, that's what it looked like.
>
> Ultimately, everything [in dispute between House and Senate committees] went in the bill, but modified. The way hearts got modified was squirrelly language about "if HCFA agrees to paying for it the way we would like them to participate, then we'll go ahead and do it." Psychotropics got modified by saying, "subject to legislative appropriation," so it wasn't an entitlement—it was, we'll fight that out when we come to the Appropriations Committee next year. And the notch group

stuff was modified by putting it off a year, to a later effective date. It was like trying to fit an elephant through a keyhole. You had to push it in different places to get it to fit.

My recollection is that [the heart transplant compromise] was proposed by AHCCCS itself. I think they probably were much more aware than I at the time of the chances of convincing Health Care Financing Administration to go along on that basis were pretty damned small, because that seems to be the case now. So I think, in retrospect, I may have been snookered.

Another member of the conference committee—Rep. Resnick—characterizes the legislature's negotiations over AHCCCS as "raw politics," primarily focused on the question of funding for pregnant women and children in the notch group. Resnick, who had been in the legislature since 1983, was a liberal Democrat from Tucson who had become active in health policy matters in 1980, when she joined a coalition working to bring Medicaid to Arizona. Like most Democrats, Resnick had initially opposed establishment of AHCCCS in favor of a more comprehensive, conventional Medicaid program. Once the AHCCCS program was in place, however, she and other Democrats had worked to make it as comprehensive as possible. During the 1987 session, the Democrats drew a line in the sand: without the notch group extension, they would vote against extending AHCCCS beyond October. The strategy, says Resnick, ultimately worked; the notch group expansion was included.

The legislative vote on the final omnibus AHCCCS bill—including both the notch group coverage and the transplant policy—was overwhelming: 44 to 6, with 10 not voting in the House; 23 to 2 with 5 not voting in the Senate. But, with so much emphasis on the notch group coverage and the general extension of AHCCCS, this vote did not reflect legislative opinion on the transplant issue per se, according to Resnick:

There is such a select group in the legislature that actually dealt with the AHCCCS issues— there were probably eight of us at the most,

and then probably only three to four of us who were intimately involved with the discussion. I don't think [the others] considered [transplants one way or the other]. In the broad scheme of things, the bill looked okay.

In any event, under the terms of the AHCCCS bill, the new transplant policy took effect August 18, 1987. Within the month, the case of Dianna Brown surfaced.

DIANNA BROWN'S STORY

Dianna Brown, forty-three, was a woman from the city of Yuma with lupoid hepatitis, an ailment which had shrunk her liver so that she could not process liquids properly. She had been nearly incapacitated since January of 1985, when her illness forced her to quit her job as manager of a doughnut shop. "I noticed I couldn't pick up anything from the counters," she told the *Arizona Republic*.[20] At one point, she remembers, "I nearly fell into the fryer."

"I said, 'I'm going to have to take a leave of absence until I get better.' But then I never got better. I only got worse."

Born in Texas, Brown had quit school at a young age to support her family, and by the summer of 1987, virtually everyone in her immediate family had serious health problems. Her mother was living in a nursing home. Brown had been caring for her niece's two children ever since her niece had suffered brain damage in a car accident. Her sister had recently suffered a heart attack.

"If a transplant isn't necessary, I don't want it," Brown told the *Arizona Republic* in an interview printed September 7, 1987. "But if it is the only solution, I would like a chance for a chance." She said that she hoped "to work again": "That is a dream off in the future. Surely there is something I can do. I might not be able to work with my hands like I used to, but I'm sure I still could do something.

"I can understand that you have to look at the overall picture. I always try to understand. I can't say I always do—Lord knows I don't—but I try."

Four days later, the *Republic* reported that the husband of a woman who had undergone a successful liver transplant had started a transplant fund for Brown with $35,000 left over from their family's fundraising effort. A radio talk-show host joined the effort, and within a few days had increased the sum to $37,000. But it was too little too late. On September 11, Brown's kidneys began to fail, preventing her body from eliminating toxins. This led to brain damage, coma, and eventual liver failure. On September 14, she died. "I don't think her death was unreasonably painful or prolonged," her personal physician, Dr. George Burdick, told the *Republic* the next day, "but in my mind it was unnecessary."

Brown's family did not even have enough money for her funeral.

THE AFTERMATH OF DIANNA BROWN'S DEATH

When Dianna Brown died, the press began to reconstruct the legislature's policy decision of the previous spring, and in general, reporters and some legislators characterized it as a conscious "tradeoff" between transplants and the notch group expansion. Some observers and participants, however, believe this represents a rewriting of history. "That argument is just a whitewash," says Icenogle. "What we're talking about here is a legislature that just doesn't want to come up with money, period. And this is their way of trying to defuse the issue."

Rep. Resnick agrees that the legislature was not really trading services. "That's how the press perceived it, and maybe they were not totally wrong, but from my perspective, we weren't making a trade." Instead, she says, dropping funding for transplants was a quick way to respond to Schaller's concern "that the thing was out of control." Other legislators agreed that they relied heavily on AHCCCS's recommendation in making their

transplant policy. Says Lunn, "You try to listen to medical experts in terms of what is reasonable and what is cost-effective and what makes sense from a medical standpoint."

"Our legislative session is only one hundred days," adds Resnick, "so it's difficult to say, 'Let's talk about it during the session.' It was easier just to say, 'Let's drop authority for AHCCCS to provide these transplants and then let's re-look at the issue.' No one ever thought that we would just drop it and never deal with transplants."

Resnick saw the transplant debate as part of a larger set of issues. Rather than make an "up" or "down" decision on funding organ transplants under AHCCCS, she believed the legislature should stand back, take a broader view, and "deal with the issue of catastrophic health care."

> We ought to make the health system responsive to those kinds of needs, but it isn't necessarily the AHCCCS system. It isn't necessarily a program for the poor that ought to be responding to that.
>
> What I don't want to see is that we change state policy, allowing more flexibility in the AHCCCS program, without addressing all the other issues related to that decision, without discussing the ramifications of having too many hospitals doing heart transplants, without discussing ramifications related to the insurance industry, which will—if there's somebody out there who's going to pay for these services—back down real quick in providing those for their own clients. So my preference would be that we discuss it all at the same time. Otherwise you get a really bad decision.

Other legislators focused primarily on the financial aspect of the question, and the issue of fairness to individuals in need of transplants. AHCCCS's refusal to fund Brown's transplant was "asinine," "grossly discriminating," and "embarrassing," according to Rep. Earl Wilcox (D-Phoenix), a member of the House Health Committee. "If we don't make taking care of this problem a priority in our next session, we'll be remiss as legislators."[21]

EXHIBIT 1. ARIZONA HEALTH CARE COST CONTAINMENT SYSTEM ADMINISTRATION

Human Organ Transplants	Fiscal 1986–1987			Program Change			Fiscal 1987–1988 Request		
	Number	Cost Per	Amount	Number	Cost Per	Amount	Number	Cost Per	Amount
Heart Transplants	0	0	0	8	164,000	1,312,000	8	164,000	1,312,000
Liver Transplants	1	134,000	134,000	5	134,000	670,000	6	268,000	804,000
Bone Marrow Transplants	1	230,000	230,000	7	230,000	1,610,000	8	460,000	1,840,000
Totals	2		364,000	20		3,592,000	22		3,956,000

a. For fiscal 1986–1987, transplants are paid as inpatient hospital in the Fee-for-Service category. Number and costs are estimated as transplant bills have not been submitted at the date of this budget request.

EXHIBIT 2. ARIZONA HEALTH CARE COST CONTAINMENT SYSTEM

Memorandum

TO:	Leonard J. Kirchner, M.S., M.P.H. Director
FROM:	Bill Merrick, Assistant Director Division of Financial Management
SUBJECT:	Expansion of the Children's Program to Include Age Six (6) through Thirteen (13)
DATE:	March 23, 1987

Before going on to the numbers, I calculated the fiscal impact for nine (9) months beginning October 1, 1987, and six (6) months beginning on January 1, 1988. These breaks logically follow our contracting cycle. In my opinion, it would not be cost effective to start the program on July 1, 1987 as AHCCCS would need to bid this population for the period July 1, 1987 to September 30, 1987.

Now the numbers:

	Number of Children	Total	State	Federal
Nine (9) months beginning October 1, 1987	27,000	$10,304,400	$8,449,800	$1,854,600
Six (6) months beginning January 1, 1988	26,200	$6,800,500	$5,576,400	$1,224,100

For the purpose of comparison, I also calculated the fiscal impact of just adding the six (6) year olds by the nine (9) and six (6) month breaks.

	Number of Children	Total	State	Federal
Nine (9) months beginning October 1, 1987	4,250	$ 1,708,628	$1,401,075	$307,553
Six (6) months beginning January 1, 1988	4,023	$ 1,078,155	$ 895,009	$183,146

Should you have any questions, just give me a buzz.

"It's not a comfortable decision that we had to make," says Senate Minority Leader Alan Stephens (D-Phoenix). "Unfortunately, you have to look at it in the context of Arizona state government."

It's been a battle in this state, in a conservative era, to increase services. And we do it on a piecemeal basis. If you want to look at people's deaths, and the case of Mrs. Brown obviously comes to mind in this situation, but if you went back, I'm sure you could find a lot of people that died in this state as a result of not getting care that's routinely given in other states, because we didn't provide the service that other states provide.

But other legislators stood by their decision. "None of us can live forever," said Sen. Doug Todd (R-Tempe). "I think it was a decision that was made by the legislative body to benefit the most residents of the state of Arizona."[22]

"The public generally is not willing to, say, double the taxes in this state to insure that everyone got the maximum possible health care—the public isn't willing to accept that," stated Rep. Bill English (R-Sierra Vista) in an interview aired September 15, 1987 on KAET-TV's "Horizon" program. While he defended the legislature's decision to defund transplants, however, he left open the possibility of changing the decision in the future:

> I'm going to say that next year, the decision may very appropriately be a different decision, with progress in the state of the art [of transplantation]. What is the right decision for today may not be the right decision for tomorrow.

NOTES

1. The legislature had already voted to cover notch group children under age six the year before.

2. In January 1987, AHCCCS's income eligibility cut-off for a family of four was $5,354, while the federal poverty level for a family of four was $13,750. Advocates for the poor estimated that fully two-thirds of Arizona's poor were not eligible for the AHCCCS program.

3. More recently, parts of Indiana have also chosen to exempt themselves from the law.

4. *Evaluation of the Arizona Health Care Cost Containment System,* by Nelda McCall, project director, and Paul Lichtenstein, federal project officer, Office of Research and Demonstrations, HCFA, Department of Health and Human Services, June 1987.

5. HMOs were not expected to finance catastrophic health care, however; thus the relatively exorbitant costs were assumed by AHCCCS. For instance, if any individual's costs exceeded a set amount per year—typically $20,000—then the HMO would be responsible for only a small percentage of the excess; the bulk of the cost would be paid by AHCCCS.

6. This "capitation rate" was to be 95 percent of what HCFA projected it would have paid the state under a conventional Medicaid program (which would have been 60 percent of costs for all Medicaid-eligible residents).

7. Long-term care was still to be provided county-by-county.

8. Of those people, 127,983 were either AFDC or SSI recipients, and thus automatically eligible for federal reimbursement. Another 51,770 were in roughly the same income range, but were not ADFC or SSI recipients; these people were not eligible for federal reimbursement. In addition, 20,716 AHCCCS recipients were children under age six from notch group families.

9. *Report of the Massachusetts Task Force on Organ Transplantation,* presented to the Massachusetts Commissioner of Public Health and the state's Secretary of Human Services in October 1984.

10. Those waiting in line for a suitable donor organ and ready for surgery at any time.

11. AHCCCS did its own informal survey of some twelve HMOs and insurance companies in the state, and found that while many offered some kind of coverage for transplants, they sometimes imposed limits on them as well. For instance, eight of the companies surveyed offered coverage for heart transplants, but one of the eight had a "cap" on the total amount it would spend and one said its decisions would be based on its own assessment of the individual's case. Thus, in reality, half the companies offered unlimited coverage and half offered limited coverage or none at all.

12. By fall of 1987, no one had traced the impact of deregulation of transplants per se, but a *Phoenix Gazette* reporter, Brad Patten, did a survey of hospitals performing by-pass surgery published on August 26, 1987, and found that: ten hospitals had begun performing by-pass surgery since deregulation; the number of open heart surgeries was up 36 percent from 1983 to 1986, but the number performed per hospital was down 85 percent; hospitals performing a relatively low volume of by-pass operations had a death rate twice that of hospitals performing a high volume of such procedures; and that overall, the death rate for Medicaid patients in by-pass procedures had increased 35 percent in Arizona between 1984 and 1986.

13. Of the forty-five patients to receive these transplants between 1984 and 1986, nine died within a few months of surgery.

14. *Arizona Daily Star,* May 29, 1986.

15. Medicare tends to be a standard-bearer for states in determining which procedures are considered "experimental" and which are regarded as standard medical care. Health care providers and insurers are under no obligation to provide "experimental" care to patients.

16. AHCCCS administrators found that, by 1986, thirty-three states were paying for liver transplants, twenty-four for hearts, thirteen for hearts-and-lungs, and three for pancreases.

17. This view of transplants was not uniformly held. Leonard Kirschner, for instance, argued that on purely medical grounds, he found liver and bone marrow transplants for children to be the most successful and defensible procedures.

18. According to Bill Merrick, assistant director of AHCCCS's Division of Financial Management, health care for some 26,200 notch group children under six between January 1, 1987, and

June 30, 1987, was expected to total $6.8 million (with HCFA paying $1.2 million). He estimated that to serve 27,000 children aged six to thirteen from October 1, 1987, to June 30, 1988, would cost $10 million—with HCFA picking up about $1.9 million. (See Exhibit 2.)

19. In fact, the AHCCCS administrators showed the committee that in another context, the university itself had estimated the cost of a heart transplant

at $153 million. That cost-estimate included hospitalization as well as twenty-four months of drugs and follow-up care, however.

20. "Patient doomed by policy; AHCCCS refuses to fund transplant," by Martin Van Der Werf, *Arizona Republic,* September 7, 1987.

21. *Arizona Republic,* Sept. 16, 1987.

22. Ibid.

Comment

Did the Arizona legislature make a moral mistake in defunding most organ transplants? To answer this question, we need to consider the practical alternatives open to the legislature: no funding of transplants at all, partial funding (of all transplants), full funding (of some or all transplants), or funding of a more comprehensive health insurance program. We also need to distinguish between the choices available to individual representatives and those available to the legislature as a whole. How should an individual legislator view the alternative suggested by Representative Resnick— extend the funding of AHCCCS with greater "notch group coverage" but postpone the decision to fund organ transplants until the legislature can consider a catastrophic health care policy? How should one assess, from the perspective of the legislature as a whole, Dr. Schaller's worry that a decision to fund transplants might convert AHCCCS from a program for poor people into a catastrophic health program for the general public?

Try to identify the moral principles that underlie the arguments made by various physicians and legislators, and then consider objections to them. What principle, for example, supports Dr. Kirschner's "Titanic" concept of medicine, which favors broad-based health care for the poor over organ transplant coverage? Assess the conception of the public good in Kirschner's argument that it is "unacceptable [for government] to use . . . limited resources in a way that really doesn't further the public good." Can a vote against funding heart transplants be morally defended on grounds that funding will encourage too many heart patients to move to Arizona? Can a vote in favor of funding be defended partly on the grounds that funding will benefit a state medical school that excels in heart transplantation?

Schafer and the AHCCCS team claim that a decision to fund kidney, cornea, and bone transplants but not heart, liver, and bone marrow transplants is "easily defensible" because of the medical and economic differences between the two sets of services. What (if any) is the moral relevance of these differences?

Part of the controversy focused on whether the legislature was deliberately trading off transplant funding for notch group expansion (as the press suggested) or whether they simply did not want to appropriate the funds necessary to fund both (as Dr. Icenogle claimed). How would you decide whether a legislature is trading one health need for another or declining to spend more on total health care? What is the moral difference between these approaches? How should a legislator decide how much money the government should spend on health care? Representative English suggests that the criterion is what the public is willing to pay for health care. Is this a sufficient standard? A necessary one? For what reasons is health care properly considered a more important good than some other goods funded by government? Which others? How much access to health care is enough?

Assess Representative Wilcox's claim that the refusal to fund Dianna Brown's transplant was "grossly discriminating." Is the differential treatment people receive by virtue of their state residence equally troubling, as Senator Stephens suggests? Or are differences in treatment acceptable as long as they "benefit most residents of the state of Arizona," as Senator Todd argues? Explain how we should (and should not) distinguish between those health care services that must be funded and those that need not be funded to satisfy the principle of distributive justice. Compare and contrast the justice of the following: (1) funding treatment for different diseases on the basis of total cost; (2) funding treatment for different diseases on the basis of cost-effectiveness; (3) funding treatment for people suffering from the same disease on the basis of survival rates; (4) funding treatment for people suffering from the same disease on the basis of future productivity; (5) funding basic health care for poor citizens; (6) funding basic health care for all citizens; (7) funding basic and catastrophic health care for all citizens. Before you conclude that only the last avoids injustice, you need to answer the argument that it too is likely to be discriminatory by reducing funds available for other basic human services, such as welfare, education, and police protection.

Should the Arizona legislature be faulted for the process by which it made the decision to defund organ transplants? What might have been gained and lost had the legislative debate (or the committee deliberations) been more extensive and more public?

Rationing in Public: The Oregon Health Plan
Paul Safier

In 1989, the Oregon legislature passed a controversial program that sought to ensure that all state residents would be guaranteed at least minimal health insurance. The centerpiece of the Oregon Health Plan (OHP) was Senate Bill 27, which made provisions for converting the state's Medicaid program. The current system provided public health insurance only to residents living in families with incomes at or below 58 percent of the federal poverty level; the new one would provide coverage to all residents living in poverty. The controversy surrounding the plan revolved around one particular feature: it proposed to expand access to Medicaid as part of an explicit exercise in medical rationing. Under the plan, Medicaid recipients would receive health coverage on the basis of a "priorities list." This list would rank all medical procedures from the most to the least important. At each new legislative session, the Oregon legislature would determine how far down the list it was willing to fund. All procedures above the funding line would be paid for by Medicaid. All procedures below the line would not. As a result, more people would receive Medicaid coverage, but Medicaid would cover fewer procedures.

The proposal provoked intense national debate. Supporters of the plan hailed Oregon's effort as a bold attempt to face up to what its chief sponsor called an "era of limits," one which would allow the state to do the most good for the greatest number of people on its limited health care budget. Critics of the plan described it as an unconscionable exercise in using cost considerations to determine what persons with which medical conditions deserve which treatments. One of the plan's most prominent national opponents, Senator Al Gore Jr. (D-TN), called it "playing God with spreadsheets."

THE TRANSPLANT CONTROVERSY

The decision to develop the Oregon Health Plan had come in the wake of the perceived failures of Oregon's first attempt to allocate health care resources based on judgments about which type of medical services should have highest priority, given limited state resources. Faced with over $48 million in social program needs and only $21 million available in the budget, the Oregon state legislature voted in July 1987 to discontinue Medicaid funding for heart, liver, pancreas, and bone marrow transplants—services that were considered optional under federal Medicaid rules. This decision was justified on the grounds that such procedures have low rates of success,[1] and, even when successful, benefit only a few people relative to the amount of the budget they consume. Between 1985 and 1987, Oregon had funded transplant operations for 19 people at a price of $1.2 million. Of those 19, only nine had survived. During the same 1987 session, the

legislature voted to allocate additional funds to its health care budget to provide pre-natal care to approximately 1,200 pregnant women whose families were unable to obtain private health insurance, but had incomes too high for them to qualify for Medicaid.

Although these decisions were not widely noted when they were made, they became subject to intense scrutiny in November of that year when Coby Howard, a 7-year-old boy suffering from leukemia, was denied funding for a bone-marrow transplant, funding that he would have received had his case come up only six months earlier. Without help from the state's Medicaid program, Coby's mother was forced to engage in an extensive campaign for donations, hoping to raise the $100,000 required for the surgery that she had been told stood a 50 percent chance of saving her son's life. (The doctor at the hospital where the operation was to be performed estimated its chance of success to be more in the range of 20 percent.) On December 2, 1987, Coby Howard died, having spent many hours of his last weeks of life in front of cameras as part of his family's efforts to raise the needed money. At the time of his death, his family had managed to come up with all but $30,000 of the required total.

Coby Howard's saga received considerable attention, both in Oregon and nationwide. The state's actions were denounced on television news programs and in editorials throughout the country. In light of the public uproar over the boy's death, some members of the legislature proposed reviving funding for transplants. In a January 28, 1988, meeting of the Legislative Emergency Board—the Oregon legislature only meets in regular session during odd-numbered years—Representative Tom Mason (D-Portland) introduced a motion before the six-member Ways and Means Committee to appropriate $220,000 from the state's general fund to pay for transplant operations for the eight remaining Medicaid recipients whose requests had been denied under the new policy. In the nearly two months since Coby Howard's death, public attention had increasingly shifted from the boy's fate to the fate of those eight individuals. The $220,000 was to be a stopgap measure until March, by which time it was anticipated that the Joint Interim Subcommittee on Human Resources would have had time to review the issue of state funding for organ transplants more thoroughly.

As presented by Representative Mason, the issue before the legislature was exceedingly simple: there were eight state residents who needed money for transplant operations and there was money in the budget to pay for them. Although it was too late to do anything for Coby Howard, it was not, he urged, too late for the state to ensure that these Medicaid recipients got the chance at life that Coby Howard had been denied.

Mason's proposal drew the opposition of then Senate President John Kitzhaber (D-Roseburg), an emergency-room physician who still practiced in his home city when the legislature was not in session. Kitzhaber argued that if the legislature did appropriate the money for organ transplants it would be doing so because the initial decision not to fund them had become controversial, not because paying for organ transplants was the best way for the state to use its health care dollars. Kitzhaber readily acknowledged that there were serious problems with the state's health care delivery system. But, he argued, the proper way to address those problems was to come up with a comprehensive policy on spending priorities that would ensure that the money the state did spend on health care was spent in the most beneficial ways. It was not, he urged, to make what he considered an essentially reactive decision.

"Everybody dies," Kitzhaber said. "You can't keep people alive forever, but what you can do is save as many as you can. It's not a lack of compassion, but sooner or later we have to come to grips with an era of limits."[2] Noting that some of the money that was taken away from the organ transplant program had been used to provide prenatal care for uninsured mothers, Kitzhaber told his colleagues that infants who die from lack of prenatal care "die just as dead [as more publicized deaths], but they die quietly and we won't know about them. They don't have names and faces that we can relate to, but I assure you that they have names and faces that their parents relate to."[3]

Before a crowd of 75 onlookers, including the families of some of the patients in need of transplant operations, and with Mason pleading with his colleagues not to let Oregon "become known as the state that lets children die,"[4] the motion failed on a tie vote.

Representative Mason reintroduced the motion the next day when the full 17-member Emergency Board met. In his remarks, Mason tried to defend the position that it is acceptable to formulate policy in direct response to high profile cases. "Once we know someone's life is in danger," he said, "we have a moral duty to do what is in our power to save that life." In addition, he insisted that it was misleading to present the underlying issue as a choice between funding organ transplants and addressing other health care needs, since, he argued, cuts could always be made in non-health care related spending. Doing this, he admitted, would not allow the state to do everything for everyone. There would still be residents whose medical needs the state was unable to meet. But, he added, "it is not good public policy not to do what you can simply because you cannot do more."[5]

When it was Senator Kitzhaber's turn to speak, he tried to counter Mason's arguments by insisting that the fundamental problem was not with how much money was spent on health care. Even if the state went ahead and budgeted more money to Medicaid, its resources, he argued, would still ultimately be limited, meaning that a decision would still have to be made about which health care programs deserved funding. "We cannot," he said, "avoid making rationing decisions by incrementally increasing expenditures in the health care area without any clear or comprehensive policy to guide us. When we spend money on one set of expenditures, we are not spending it on other things." Concluding his remarks, he said: "I just want to close by saying that we are going to have to ration health care. I believe we already do it. We can either do it in the context of conscious social policy or we can do it by default."[6]

Once again, Mason's motion was defeated, this time by a 9 to 6 vote (with two abstentions). Kitzhaber's efforts against the refunding of the organ transplant program had earned him the opportunity to attempt to restructure the state's health care system. They had also earned him the nickname "Dr. Death" from his critics.

UNINSURED OREGONIANS

The controversy over the funding of organ transplants had provided the Oregon Health Plan with the political momentum it needed to get started. According to the Plan's chief architect, Senator Kitzhaber, however, what made the issue of health care spending priorities so crucial in the first place was a more general problem facing the state—that of uninsured Oregonians. Kitzhaber traced the genesis of the Oregon Health Plan back to a legislative decision that had preceded the transplant controversy, one having to do not with *what* was covered by Medicaid, but with *whom* the program covered.

According to Kitzhaber, Oregon's large number of uninsured residents could be attributed both to rising health care costs and to what he saw as flaws in the structure of the existing Medicaid system. By 1989, the United States had experienced nearly two decades of unprecedented growth in overall health care spending. Throughout the 1980s, health care costs had risen at twice the rate of inflation. States facing skyrocketing Medicaid expenditures often chose to control program costs by restricting access to the program, taking advantage of federal Medicaid rules which allowed states wide latitude in determining Medicaid eligibility. Under Medicaid rules, participating states were required to cover all "medically necessary" services for persons designated as

"categorically needy"—a group that at the time consisted almost exclusively of those receiving Social Security Insurance (SSI) (primarily the elderly and the disabled) and women and children eligible for cash assistance under Aid to Families with Dependent Children (AFDC).[7] Eligibility for AFDC was determined by individual states, while eligibility for SSI was set at the federal level. In addition to restricting access to the program through altering AFDC eligibility rates, states could address the problem of rising Medicaid costs in three ways: by raising taxes, by taking resources away from other social programs, or by cutting reimbursement rates to health care providers who participated in the Medicaid program.

In 1989, the cut-off point for Medicaid in Oregon was at 58 percent of the federal poverty level, or roughly $387 dollars a month for a family of two. In addition, because of Medicaid's links to SSI and AFDC, whole categories of poor persons were automatically excluded from the program. Non-disabled adults without dependent children were ineligible for Medicaid no matter what their income status. Uninsured residents who could not afford to pay out-of-pocket medical expenses often ended up addressing their medical needs through emergency room visits, frequently delaying seeking medical attention until their ailments became both more serious and more expensive to treat. A large portion of the costs for this unfunded care was being shifted to those who could pay in the form of higher medical bills and higher insurance premiums, leading many employers within the state to stop providing health insurance to their employees.

Together, these various factors contributed to a situation in which many less well off Oregonians were without health insurance. In 1989, the state estimated that there were between 400,000 and 450,000 uninsured residents, or roughly 16 percent of the state's population. Of that group, at least a third were thought to be living in poverty.

What struck Kitzhaber most about this situation was how poorly equipped, in his estimation, the existing Medicaid system was to deal with the pressures created by surging health care costs. For the most part, individual states were prevented from responding to rising health care costs by cutting less important health services out of the package of Medicaid benefits. But states were allowed to make their own decisions about who was eligible for the program—decisions, according to Kitzhaber, that were typically made as last-ditch efforts to balance state budgets. Moreover, Kitzhaber argued, none of this "looked like" rationing. At no point in the process were legislators required to directly decide what care would *not* be provided. All they determined was who would receive benefits.

To Kitzhaber, proposing that Oregon institute medical rationing amounted to nothing more than proposing that the state reverse the order of its Medicaid decision-making process. Under the system he wanted to develop, the state would first define the population for which it was responsible, and only then define the level of care to be provided to that population. That way, he argued:

> the state can no longer arbitrarily change eligibility for reasons of budgetary expediency. Everyone retains coverage. The debate centers on the level of that coverage—on what we as a society feel is "adequate," on what level of health care we as a society are willing to actually fund, and thus guarantee to all of our citizens. Because ultimately the socially acceptable minimum level of care is what society is willing to pay for.[8]

According to Kitzhaber, shifting the Medicaid debate from *whom* to cover to *what* to cover would have two primary advantages. It would force the state to use the money it did spend on Medicaid more efficiently. And, because under the new system the state would know exactly who was going to be denied which services as a result of its funding decisions, it would force the legislature to confront the consequences of its decisions in a more honest fashion.

THE BASIC HEALTH BENEFITS ACT

In winter of 1989, the Oregon legislature introduced the Oregon Basic Health Services Act (OBHSA). The centerpiece of OBHSA was "The Basic Health Benefits Act," or Senate Bill 27 (S.B. 27),[9] which made provisions for expanding the state's Medicaid program to cover all Oregonians, regardless of category, in households at or below 100 percent of the federal poverty level.[10] (In 1989, this level was set at $840 per month for a family of three). This expansion in coverage was to be paid for, in part, through a combination of two mechanisms—the explicit prioritization of health care services, and the delivery of covered services through managed care systems. Because S.B. 27 involved altering the state's Medicaid program in ways that ran afoul of federal Medicaid rules, a waiver from the federal government had to be obtained before the program could be implemented.

Under the proposed bill, Oregon's Medicaid system would operate in the following manner. First, S.B. 27 called for the creation of the Oregon Health Services Commission (HSC)—an eleven member organization, made up of both health care providers and consumers, that would be charged with the task of compiling "a list of health services ranked by priority, from the most important to the least important, representing the comparative benefits of each service to the population served."[11] The Health Services Commission would prepare a new list of rankings every two years to be submitted to the legislature at the start of each biennial session.[12] It would then be the legislature's job to determine how far down the list to fund. An item-by-item actuarial analysis would be conducted in order to provide the legislature with information about the estimated costs of placing the funding level at each particular line on the list. In years in which the legislature found that its previous Medicaid budget would not be enough to continue the program at the existing level of benefits, it would have two options—(1) allocate more money to the

Medicaid budget, or (2) deny more services by moving the cut-off point higher up the list. The legislature would not have the option of cutting program costs by creating new eligibility restrictions or by reducing reimbursement rates to providers. Nor could it move any particular services up or down the list. Once the funding point was set by the legislature, then, for the next two-year period, all treatments above that point would constitute the "basic" health care package to be automatically covered for all recipients of Medicaid.

Next, the state would purchase health insurance from participating health maintenance organizations (HMOs) for Medicaid recipients at the estimated per-person costs of funding all services above the cut-off point. Hospitals and doctors working with participating HMOs would then use the list to determine which medical procedures they were going to be reimbursed for providing to Medicaid patients. Health providers would be paid for performing any service above the cut-off point. All services needed to establish a diagnosis would automatically be funded, even in cases where treatment for the condition eventually identified turned out to fall below the funding line. A provider who determined that a particular patient required an unfunded service would have three options: (1) perform the treatment without reimbursement; (2) petition the state to fund the treatment for that particular patient; or (3) deny the patient the treatment. Providers choosing the third option would be shielded from any malpractice lawsuits relating to health problems experienced by Medicaid patients as a consequence of being denied treatments below the cut-off point.

THE FLOOR DEBATE

From January through March of 1989, Senate Bill 27 was subjected to extensive debate in the Oregon legislature. Throughout the debate, Senator Kitzhaber tried his best to characterize the program as nothing more than "an attempt to impose some logic and clinical rationale" on the way the state went about allocating its health care resources.[13] It was simply a fact, he argued, that the state could do more good by providing medically prioritized "basic" care to everyone in poverty than by providing a larger, but unevaluated, set of benefits to a portion of that population, while leaving the rest excluded from all but emergency care.

Many Oregonians expressed reservations about the proposed move to explicit medical rationing for the Medicaid population. Within the legislature, S.B. 27's most vocal opponent was Representative Mason, who had clashed with Kitzhaber over the funding of organ transplants in the previous year. To him, the state was using a genuine problem with the existing system (rising medical costs leading to declining access to health care) as an excuse to take what he considered an entirely unwarranted step (allowing cost considerations to determine what medical care the poor would receive). The most equitable way to address the problems created by medical inflation, he argued, was to regulate doctors' fees and hospital purchases of expensive technology, not to ask Medicaid recipients to make do with less coverage. "You can measure a society's real concern," he said, "by how we treat the most unfortunate of us. The intent [of the bill] is to spread our health care resources as thinly as possible to the poor and allow people who don't get enough to die."[14] Mason warned that while the program might sound benign when described in the abstract, the true nature of cost-conscious medicine would become apparent once the Health Services Commission put together its priorities list. "[T]here will be surprises on that list that will curl your hair," he predicted.[15]

A different objection to providing Medicaid coverage on the basis of a priorities list was presented by state Representative Rodger Wehage (R-Oregon City). Wehage argued that the program would force Oregon doctors to violate the Hippocratic Oath which requires doctors to consider only the potential benefits to the patient when making treatment decisions. If the bill passed, such treatment decisions would, he said, be made by "an elitist commission composed of Government appointees," instead of doctors and patients. "No government commission," he said, "should have the authority to pre-empt a health care decision because the decision does not conform to political consensus."[16]

Kitzhaber's response to objections of this type was to insist that rationing medical services was the only politically feasible way to control the costs of providing public health insurance. Regulating Medicaid fees, he argued, would only work if it was done as part of a comprehensive move toward a single-payer health care system like the one found in Canada—a move that most observers considered highly unlikely, not to mention something that could not be accomplished by the state of Oregon acting alone. In Oregon's past experience, when Medicaid fees were reduced in the context of a health care system in which the government was *not* the dominant purchaser of health care, then doctors responded by simply refusing to treat Medicaid patients. Using a priorities list to set Medicaid coverage would, Kitzhaber argued, at least get at the heart of one factor driving the rise in overall health care spending. It would introduce fiscal discipline into a system in which doctors and their patients had no incentives to avoid unnecessary costs.

Another objection to S.B. 27 that was raised during the debate in the legislature was the claim that the bill would have the effect of legitimizing inequalities in the quality of health care being received by state residents. Representative Dick Springer (D-Portland) objected to the proposal on the grounds that it would "create two classes of citizens, based upon wealth, and that the poor [would be forced] to accept a lower standard of care."[17] Senator Bill Kennemer (R-Clackamas County), arguing along similar lines, complained that the "bill sets a precedent for inferior care for the poor."[18]

Kitzhaber conceded that instituting the proposed changes would mean that the state would be creating a system in which those with public health insurance were not guaranteed the level of care received by those with private health insurance. But, he argued, discrepancies of that kind were inevitable, and not necessarily cause for public concern. "[T]he rich," he said,

> will always have access to more health care than the poor. That is difficult for most of us to accept, although we readily accept this income-based discrepancy in other cases. No one, for example, argues that food stamps be redeemable at Oregon's finest restaurants as long as the purchase of adequate food is possible. What we are saying is that the discrepancy between rich and poor is an acceptable part of our system as long as what the poor are getting is adequate and that they are *all* getting it.[19]

Perhaps the strongest opinions about the proposed rationing scheme came from outside the legislature. Lon Christensen, director of the Northwest Seasonal Worker's Association, claimed that Oregon's willingness to consider not funding certain medically beneficial procedures would make it "the first state in the union to practice death squad medicine."[20] Most of the major consumer groups in the state took a more ambivalent position about the bill. In general, they expressed support for the idea of expanding access to Medicaid. Many, however, were unwilling to come out strongly in favor of the proposed legislation until they were given a more concrete picture of what health benefits were actually going to be provided under the plan. While most of the groups agreed that it would be better to provide all residents living in poverty with genuinely adequate health care than to provide more generous benefits to a smaller segment of that population, many nevertheless insisted that expanded access would only represent an improvement over the existing system if the level of provided benefits did not decline too much.

Despite the many concerns that were raised about the move to explicit medical rationing, Kitzhaber and his legislative allies managed to build up an extensive coalition of support for the bill. In March of 1989, S.B. 27 was approved by a 19 to 3 margin in the Senate and 58 to 2 margin in the House. The next step was for the Health Services Commission to devise the priorities list.

PUBLIC PARTICIPATION

The heart of the Oregon Health Plan was to be the so-called priorities list: the list ranking all health services from first to last in order of importance. It was the list that would guide the legislature in determining how much money it needed to allocate to Medicaid in order to provide "adequate" care. Once that decision was made, the list would serve as the basis for determining who would receive what care. The program's designers therefore considered it absolutely crucial that the rankings be compiled in a manner that would inspire public confidence and trust.

One way in which the Oregon legislature proposed to do that was by encouraging public participation in the ranking process. S.B. 27 explicitly required the Health Services Commission to keep all of its meetings open to the public and to sponsor a variety of forums providing residents with opportunities to express their views about the best way to rank the health services. This emphasis on public involvement was in part a reflection of the continuing fallout from the 1987 controversy over Medicaid funding for organ transplants. Even Senator Kitzhaber, who never wavered in his support for the initial decision to cut the funding, conceded during the ensuing controversy that the decision had been made in the wrong way—as part of a routine end-of-session effort to make budget by the Human Resources Subcommittee. No attempt was made to solicit input about the decision from either the general public or from health care professionals, nor was much of an effort made to publicly connect the decision on transplants to the decision to fund additional prenatal care. Later that year, when people started to lose access to life-saving treatments as a result of the legislature's actions, outraged Oregonians had no clear understanding of why the legislature had made the choice that it had. One concrete lesson that Kitzhaber and the other developers of the Oregon Health Plan took from that experience was that any attempt to make hard choices in a sensitive policy area such as health care would likely fail if the public considered itself entirely cut off from the decision-making process.

S.B. 27 made provisions for two different types of citizen involvement. First, it required the Health Services Commission to "[c]onduct public hearings prior to making [its] report solicit[ing] testimony and information from advocates for seniors; handicapped persons; mental health services consumers; low-income Oregonians; and providers of health care."[21] Second, S.B. 27 required the Commission "to actively solicit public involvement by a community meeting process for consensus on the values to be used to guide health allocation decisions."[22]

The "community meetings" were designed and presided over by Oregon Health Decisions (OHD), a local advocacy group dedicated to encouraging public debate on bioethical issues that had worked with Senator Kitzhaber during the developmental stages of the Oregon Health Plan. While the public hearings were understood as opportunities for different groups in the state to express their interests as they related to prioritization, the community meetings had a different focus. They were intended to provide individual state residents with a forum in which to express their opinions about what values should guide the priority-setting process. This was viewed as the proper role for citizen input. Decisions about the actual order of health services on the list—as opposed to the values that the order ought to reflect—were considered the province of health care experts. According to the Health Services Commission's report on priority setting: "the purpose [of the meetings] was to learn which health care values were seen as important to the community."[23]

In the winter of 1990, 47 community meetings were held. Meeting times and locations were publicized in local newspapers and on radio and television stations. Despite the efforts of OHD coordinators to recruit representative members of the state population, attendance at the meetings was skewed toward the health care profession and the well off. Of the 1,048 who participated in the 47 meetings, more than two-thirds were employed in the health care industry in some capacity. Only 9.4 percent of participants were without health insurance (compared to 16 percent of the state's population), and only 4.4 percent were recipients of Medicaid (compared to 6.8 percent of the state's population).

The format for each meeting was as follows.[24] Participants were shown a demonstration explaining how the Oregon Health Plan would work, the reasons why it was developed, and the role that their discussion would play in the ultimate formation of the priorities list. Following the demonstration, participants were split up into groups. Each group member was then asked to complete an exercise that required making prioritizing decisions. In the standard exercise, participants were told to assign rankings of "essential," "very important" or "important" to nine different types of health care with the stipulation that each ranking could be used only three times. Examples of types of health care included: "Treatment for conditions which are fatal and can't be cured. The treatment will not extend the person's life for more than five years"; "Preventative care which definitely can prevent early death or a reduction of quality of life"; and "Treatment for chronic ongoing conditions where health care will improve quality of life for the person's remaining years." (Some participants were uncomfortable with the exercise. One group at a meeting in Portland—Oregon's largest urban area—reportedly refused "to play the 'prioritization game,' " claiming that the issue that should be discussed was *whether* to prioritize, not how to prioritize. The leader of that group, a person receiving public assistance, expressed the view "that the entire process was unjust because it targeted the poor.")

After completing the exercise, participants were then asked to justify the prioritizing decisions that they had made to the other members of their group. Each group was encouraged to try to reach a consensus on the values that they thought should inform decisions like the ones that they had been asked to make, before submitting the matter to a vote. Each group then appointed a representative to present and defend its "findings" to the other groups, with that process then serving as a springboard for a more general discussion of health care priorities.

OHD prepared a report summarizing the meeting discussions and submitted it to the Health Services Commission. The report organized the views expressed in the meetings into 13 "themes," each intended to represent a value that members of the public thought should guide the ranking process (e.g., "personal responsibility" or "community compassion") or a concern that should be emphasized (e.g., "quality of life" or "cost effectiveness"). (See Appendix 1.) The "themes" were primarily meant to serve as a "checklist" to aid the Health Services Commission in compiling its rankings, providing it "with a perspective for testing the authenticity of the values that will guide" the priority-setting process.

According to the report, the most heavily emphasized themes were "prevention" and "quality of life," which were both mentioned at every meeting. Preventative services were said to be worthy of being "prioritized high on the list" because such services are "highly cost-effective," "benefit large numbers of people," and allow individuals to take control of their own health. "Quality of life" was identified as one of, if not the sole, goal of medical care, with services aimed at improving "quality of life" understood to be those that "enhance a person's productivity and emotional well being, restore an individual's health, reduce pain and suffering, or allow one to function independently." According to the report: "It was generally agreed that measures that do not improve quality of life or do not allow one to die with dignity should not be given high priority." Other notable views summarized in the report were: "Services with high success rates should be available while services or procedures which have limited effectiveness should be placed lower on the list of priorities." And: "Available funds should be used for routine care that will help more [people], not on transplants or life support when funds are limited."

The report served as the Commission's only source of information about "community values."

COST-BENEFIT ANALYSIS

The public hearings and community meetings were intended to play a role in the ultimate formation of the priorities list. The task of actually compiling the rankings, however, fell exclusively to the Health Services Commission (HSC). To produce the list, HSC had to find a way to rank, in order of importance, approximately 1,600 different health services. Each health service consisted of a single "condition-treatment" pair matching a particular condition (e.g., appendicitis) with a particular treatment for that condition (an appendectomy). Although the statute establishing the Commission had stated that it was supposed to rank services according to "the comparative benefits of each service to the population served," the Commission had been given very little explicit guidance about how to go about generating its rankings. Nothing like what they were being asked to do had ever been attempted before—at least not on the scale of Oregon's initiative. There was no clear consensus, either among the members of the Commission or the medical community at large, on what the basis for setting priorities ought to be.

What was clear was the purpose that the priorities list was intended to serve. It was intended as a tool to aid the state legislature in making the most effective allocation decisions with the finite resources it allocated to Medicaid. With that in mind, the Commission decided to use a cost-benefit formula, one that would rank the different health services according to the amount of benefit they provide for each dollar spent. This would allow the rankings to take into account not only how beneficial a particular health service was believed to be, but also the volume of that service that could be purchased for each dollar spent, thus ensuring that highly beneficial, but very expensive, health services would not be allowed to consume the entire pool of resources indiscriminately. Instead, a service's position on the list would be determined both by how valuable the service it provides was judged to be, and by how much of the overall pool of resources it left to be devoted to other health services.

Taking a cost-benefit approach to prioritization presented one major challenge, however—how to compare the "benefits" produced by very different types of health care services. For services that are intended to perform similar functions, comparing benefits is fairly simple. A treatment for a particular type of cancer that can be expected to prolong its recipient's life by 10 years produces exactly twice as much benefit as one that can be expected to prolong life for only 5 years (assuming that the two treatments have the same side effects). The difficulty arises when attempting to compare medical procedures that are each valued by health care consumers, but are valued for performing quite different functions. An appendectomy performs one function, hip-replacement surgery another, and a vasectomy yet another—all, however, perform a service that health care consumers want. Using a cost-benefit formula as a basis for ranking all available health services required a method to convert the benefits provided by different health services to a common unit of measurement.

To address this difficulty, the Commission decided to use a formula devised by Robert Kaplan, a professor at the University of San Diego School of Medicine, called the Quality of Well-Being (QWB) Scale. Kaplan's formula rates the health benefit of medical treatments according to their expected impact on quality of life. Because Kaplan's formula takes into account both a service's impact on quality of life and the duration of that impact, it was thought to provide a basis for comparing such different medical treatments as those which improve quality of life but do not prolong life (e.g., hip replacements), those which prevent death and provide a recovery to pre-condition quality of life (e.g., appendectomies), those which prevent death but do not provide a recovery to pre-condition quality of life (e.g., surgical treatment for severe head injuries), as well as those which prolong life but do not improve quality of life (e.g. life support for the terminally ill). An additional advantage of using the QWB scale was that it allowed the Commission to incorporate the view expressed at many of the community meetings that the primary goal of medical care should be to improve the quality of life.

In order to get data about the quality of life impact of different health services, the Commission conducted a telephone survey of 1,000 randomly selected Oregonians. Survey respondents were asked to rank different states of impaired health (e.g., inability to walk or chronic shortness of breath) according to the anticipated effect of that state on a person's quality of life. Rankings were given on a scale of 0 (as bad as death) to 100 (no health problems), with ratings falling between those two poles corresponding to the percentage of a normal quality of life expected to be experienced by a person in that particular state of health. Examples of impaired health states that respondents were asked to consider include: "You can be taken anywhere, but have to be in bed or in a wheelchair controlled by someone else. Otherwise, you have no health restrictions"; or "You can go anywhere and have no limitations on your physical or other activity, but you have headaches or dizziness." In addition to being a way to generate data for the quality of life measurements, the survey was viewed as another method for tying the rankings to the views of the public.

Once the survey was completed, the average survey rating for each of the states of health that respondents had been asked to evaluate was divided by one hundred, with the resulting number being taken to represent the QWB score of that state, or its position on the Quality of Well-Being Scale (from 0.0 to 1.0). In order to use these numbers to measure the benefit provided by the different health services, the Commission then matched the health states that had been assigned different survey-based QWB scores with the expected results of treating, or not treating, each of the different medical conditions. This provided the Commission with enough information to determine the costs and the benefits of each of the 1,600 health services, and then ultimately to rank them, from lowest to highest, according to cost per unit of health benefit. (See Appendix 2.)

By the spring of 1990, the Commission had collected enough data to produce an initial draft of the list using the cost-benefit formula. The data was plugged into a computer and, on May 2, the Commission released its draft of the priorities list. The result was a public-relations disaster. Treatments for thumb-sucking and acute headaches ranked much higher than treatments for cystic fibrosis or AIDS. Outpatient visits for minor problems were at the very top of the list. Appendectomies, a treatment almost certain to prevent death without side effects in every case, were ranked below tooth-cappings, a procedure designed to stave off tooth decay.

Almost from the moment the list was made public, the plan's critics began touting it as an indication of what life under medical rationing could be expected to look like. Some of the consumer groups that had expressed tentative support for the plan when it was being debated in the legislature threatened to start actively campaigning against it. The goodwill and enthusiasm that the project had managed to inspire throughout the state up to this point looked to be evaporating.

There were a number of different theories among the Commissioners about what went wrong with the initial list. Everyone conceded that one problem was in the accuracy of data. Many of the cost estimates, for instance, were overly crude. In addition, there were problems with the duration of benefit data. Other problems, however, were attributed to the cost-benefit approach itself. Much of the critical reaction to the initial priorities list centered on the fact that low-cost/low-benefit services such as tooth-cappings were assigned similar priority ratings as high-cost/high-benefit services such as appendectomies—an inevitable result of using a cost-benefit formula. Tooth-capping procedures ended up ranked higher than appendectomies because, while a single appendectomy was determined to produce 144 times as much long-term health benefit as a single tooth-capping, tooth-cappings were estimated to be 150 times cheaper, resulting in their having the lower cost-benefit ratio of the two. (See Appendix 3.) To work effectively, the cost-benefit formula required the ability to assign accurate numerical values to the relative importance to society of very different health services, something that the results of the first list led some members of the Commission to doubt could ever be done. Could it really be said that 144 tooth-cappings produce *exactly* as much benefit to society as one appendectomy?

One prominent observer likened the overwhelmingly negative reaction to the first list to the public uproar that had followed the death of Coby Howard in 1987.[25] Once again, the state of Oregon was being accused of placing too much emphasis on the costs of medical care and of neglecting the special importance the public places on saving life whenever possible.

A New Approach

Whether or not the problems with the cost-benefit formula were ultimately correctable, the initial list seemed to confirm the worst fears that many had about medical rationing. It was clear to the Commission that any priorities list that looked anything remotely like it would cause public support for the program to wither. Senator Kitzhaber, who had originally hoped to have the program ready to be submitted for federal approval by late summer of 1990 in order to best take advantage of its initial political momentum, now urged the Commission to take as much time as it needed to produce a list in which it had confidence. Commission-member Rick Wopat summed-up HSC's thinking at the time this way: "We realized that the initial formula did not take into account a lot of what people were telling us in public hearings and polls."[26]

A new ranking system was developed, one which allowed Commission-members to rely more directly on their own priority judgments, and on the input they had received from the public. The new system ranked health services primarily according to *type* of health care, rather than costs per unit of health benefit. This eliminated the need to directly compare the benefits of very different health services. Under the new ranking system, a service belonging to a category of health care considered inherently important, such as life-saving care with high rates of success, would automatically have priority over a service belonging to a category of care considered less beneficial, regardless of the relative costs of the two procedures. Commission-member Tina Castanares defended this move away from a formula-driven ranking system to one driven by category assignment. "Maybe we're not applying science," she said, "but we're applying fairness."[27]

The new list was compiled in the following manner. First, the number of health services was reduced from 1600 to 709.[28] Next, the 709 health services were sorted into 17 different categories of health care. Services were placed in particular categories according to the area of health care (e.g., maternity care), the seriousness of the medical conditions (e.g., acute, fatal), or the degree of medical effectiveness (e.g., treatments which provide minimal or no improvement in quality of life) with which they were associated. The Commissioners then ranked the 17 different categories by assigning each of them scores across three dimensions: (1) "Value to Society"; (2) "Value to an Individual at Risk of Needing the Service"; and (3) "Whether the Service should be considered Essential to Basic Health Care." Ranked first were treatments with a high chance of preventing death with a full recovery. Ranked last were treatments for fatal or nonfatal conditions that provide minimal or no improvement in quality of life. (See Appendix 4.) Next, services within each category were ranked according to impact on quality of life. Services within the same category that had been assigned the same net benefit score were ranked according to cost, with the less expensive service ranked first.

Once all the services had been ranked using the new methodology, the Commissioners conducted a line-by-line examination of the list. Items that appeared "out of position" were then moved up or down the list "by hand." These movements were justified by appealing to the different "themes" from the community meetings (e.g., "prevention" or "quality of life"). In all, approximately 33 percent to 50 percent of the items on the list were moved by hand, though only 5 percent to 10 percent were moved more than 50 positions from where they had been assigned on the basis of category and net benefit alone. Once the rankings were finalized, the Commission labeled the services in the first 9 categories "essential," the services in the next 4 "very important," and the services falling in the final 4 categories "services that are valuable to certain individuals, but are of minimal gain or high cost."

The new category-driven ranking system brought about a number of significant changes in the order of the list. Appendectomy operations were moved from line 396 (out of 1,600) to line 5 (out of 709). Mastectomies for breast cancer went from 683 (out of 1,600) to 172 (out of 709). In perhaps the most revealing change, liver, bone marrow and cardiac transplants for patients diagnosed as having a good chance of recovery were moved from the bottom third of the original list to the upper-third of the new one.

According to the Commission's report on the prioritization process, the values expressed in the community meetings ended up affecting the second set of rankings in a number of ways. A heavy emphasis was placed on preventative medicine and comfort care, as well as on family planning services— heavier, according to some medical professionals who served on the Commission, than they would have received if the decisions had been made by health care experts alone.[29] As a result, active medical or surgical treatments for the terminally ill, defined as those with less than a 10 percent chance of survival, fell into the last category (lines 672–708, depending on the specific condition), while hospice care and pain medication for the terminally ill was ranked at 164. Similarly, the category of "family planning services" ended up ranked 6 out of 17, leading to such results as vasectomy operations being judged of higher priority than hip replacement surgeries.

In May of 1991, the list was finally completed to the satisfaction of the Health Services Commission and presented to the Oregon legislature with the recommendation that it be funded through line 640 (medical therapy for testicular and polyglandular dysfunction). In the debate in the legislature over where to set the funding line, both Senator Kitzhaber and Governor Barbara Roberts stressed the need to use the initial funding decision to demonstrate the level of Oregon's commitment to its poor. The state still needed federal approval before it could institute the plan, and it was widely believed that the level at which the program was initially funded would have a large impact on how the plan was perceived in Washington. Ultimately, the legislature chose to set the cut off point at line 587 (medical therapy for esophagitis), which required the state to increase its Medicaid budget by $33 million. This was enough to cover 98 percent of the "essential" services, 82 percent of the "very important" services and 7 percent of the services that were judged to be of minimal gain and/or high cost despite the demand for them.[30]

Among the services that were not going to be funded were medical therapy for post-mastectomy breast reconstruction (600), medical therapy for post-concussion syndrome (638), and medical therapy for chronic bronchitis (643). Active medical or surgical therapy for the terminally ill was not going to be covered. Liver transplants for non-alcoholic cirrhosis were well above the cut-off point (366), while liver transplants for cancer of the liver, which have a much lower rate of success, fell below it (610).

By summer of 1991, the Oregon legislature had accomplished all that it could on the program without a waiver from the federal government. The next step was to appeal to Washington.

THE NATIONAL DEBATE

Because Medicaid is a federal program, jointly funded by participating states and the federal government, Oregon had to obtain permission from the federal government in order to alter its Medicaid system. Two features of the proposed plan in particular required the waiving of federal Medicaid rules: (1) the move from providing all "medically necessary" health services to providing only those services above the funding point, and (2) the expansion of the numbers of persons made eligible for Medicaid through the severing of the program's links with AFDC and SSI. The waiver could come either from the Health Care Financing Administration (HCFA), under the demonstration authority conferred by Section 1115 of the Social Security Act, or from Congress in the form of special legislation.

Oregon officials were well aware that federal approval for the plan might be difficult to get. From the plan's earliest developmental stages, there had been no shortage of critics nationwide who were eager to express their disapproval of Oregon's intention to explicitly ration health care. Two particularly passionate and noteworthy critics were Senator Gore of Tennessee and Representative Henry Waxman (D-Calif.), who was chair of the house subcommittee that oversees Medicaid. In the summer of 1989, Waxman and Gore had successfully blocked the efforts of two senior members of Oregon's Congressional delegation, Senator Bob Packwood (R) and Representative Ron Wyden (D), to get Congress to include a waiver grant for the plan as part of that year's federal budget bill. Gore, who had been sharply critical of Oregon's activities ever since the 1987 decision to discontinue funding for some organ transplants, then vowed to filibuster any subsequent bill that included a Medicaid waiver, circulating a letter to his congressional colleagues urging them not to support any plan that would, he said, take health services away from "the poor women and children who use Medicaid."[31] An unusually diverse assortment of advocacy organizations joined Waxman and Gore in the fight against federal approval of the plan, including the Children's Defense Fund, the National Council of Senior Citizens, the National Right to Life Committee, the U.S. Catholic Conference and the United Cerebral Palsy Association.

In August of 1991, Oregon formally submitted a waiver application to the HCFA, kicking off a debate over the Oregon Health Plan that Gore called "the single most important debate on the future of health care in the United States."[32]

On September 16, 1991, Waxman convened a special hearing of the Congressional Subcommittee on Health and the Environment to discuss whether the plan merited federal approval. Although much of the discussion was focused on specific details of the plan, the most heated exchanges centered on the issue of whether it was acceptable, as a matter of public policy, to allow the package of health benefits received through Medicaid to fluctuate in response to budgetary pressures. Waxman testified that, even if the package of benefits provided by the program was acceptable at the level that the Oregon legislature was initially willing to fund it, the logic of the program's design seemed to encourage an erosion of benefits as the state's budget tightened. "There is no end-point," he argued, "no line below which conditions could not be dropped. . . . [T]here is no basic benefits package, just a guarantee that everyone who is poor will remain eligible for treatment of whatever conditions are still above the line."

Governor Roberts of Oregon tried to address Waxman's concerns by promising that she would not let funding for the program lapse below what was required in order to keep the benefits package at roughly the level that would be provided with the funding line set at 587 (in 2003 the funding line was 558—see below). She refused, however, to commit to a particular line on the list, maintaining that to do so would impair the plan's flexibility in ways that would go against its fundamental purpose.

Others who spoke at the hearing, however, expressed concerns about what Oregon was proposing to do that were not as easy to address. A number of speakers went so far as to insist that the federal government had a responsibility not to lend its official seal of approval to the ideas behind the Oregon Health Plan, no matter how generously the program ended up being funded. More specifically, Oregon was accused of breaking dangerous new ground in explicitly embracing each of the following views: (1) it is acceptable for standards regarding an individual's basic entitlement to health care to be altered for budgetary reasons; (2) it is acceptable for those with public health insurance to receive coverage not equal to that provided by private insurers; and (3) it is acceptable for a system of health care priorities not to be committed to doing everything possible to prolong life.

Debra Blankenship, a member of Oregon Fair Share, a group representing the interests of low-income Oregonians, who herself stood to be added to Medicaid if the program received approval, declared: "I am appalled that my medical care would ultimately be decided by a list of covered procedures that would fluctuate with state funding."

To those who had worked on putting together the Oregon Plan, the focus of the debate in Washington seemed entirely misplaced. The debate seemed to be more about comparing Oregon's proposal to an ideal health care system than examining politically feasible ways to address the flaws in the existing one. Jean Thorne, the state Medicaid director, said: "To those who say it's not the perfect plan, I say we are not in the business of philosophy. We are trying to increase access to health care for the poor."[33] Senator Kitzhaber contended that Oregon was being blamed for problems inherent to a situation in which the medical needs of the poor outstripped society's willingness to pay for public health insurance, rather than being credited for coming up with a system that would, he anticipated, make those problems more manageable. It was particularly disingenuous, he argued, to accuse Oregon of breaking new ground in accepting that the poor will receive less health coverage than the non-poor, and that what coverage they do receive may change in response to fiscal pressures, given the number of people living in poverty that the existing system left without any coverage at all.

With the efforts of Oregon's Congressional delegation to push approval of the plan through Congress effectively blocked by Waxman and Gore, the fate of the Oregon Plan rested with the Health Care Financing Administration, which was under presidential control through the supervision of the Department of Health and Human Services. One source of optimism for Oregon officials was that President George Bush was already on record in support of the plan, having cited it as an example of the state-led health care reform that he preferred to reform at the federal level. Prospects for a waiver further improved in April of 1992, when the Office of Technology Assessment (OTA), a nonpartisan congressional research agency from which Waxman and Representative John Dingle (D-Mich.) had requested an evaluation of the plan, released its findings. While the OTA expressed reservations about "the lack of a guaranteed minimum set of benefits below which coverage would not be allowed to fall," it concluded that with the plan funded through line 587, "health care access would be improved for newly eligible participants and would not be clearly either better or worse for most current beneficiaries."[34] This provided supporters of the plan with important ammunition for their claims that it at least merited approval on a trial basis.

By the spring of 1992, officials in the Bush administration were predicting that approval from Health and Human Services was imminent. The plan's opponents began preparing for disappointment. Then, a new wrinkle emerged.

THE AMERICANS WITH DISABILITIES ACT

The initial debate over whether the federal government should allow Oregon to go ahead with the Oregon Health Plan was dominated by concerns about the program's lack of a guaranteed minimum, and about the acceptability of asking poor women and children to bear the burden of expanding access to Medicaid. In late spring of 1992, however, the Bush administration began to focus its attention on an issue that had played only a relatively minor role in the debate up to that point—the issue of whether the plan would discriminate against persons with disabilities.

In October of 1991, shortly after congressional hearings on the plan had concluded, Representative Christopher Smith (R-NJ), one of Congress' most outspoken opponents of abortion and euthanasia, requested a legal analysis of the plan from the National Legal Center for the Medically Dependent and Disabled, Inc. (Legal Center). The Legal Center concluded that, if enacted, the Oregon Plan would violate the recently enacted Americans with Disabilities Act (ADA). The Legal Center's analysis provided impetus for advocates of the disabled, many of whom had already expressed concerns about the plan. In July of 1992, 20 national organizations representing persons with disabilities publicly urged President Bush to reject Oregon's waiver request.

On August 3, 1992, Louis Sullivan, then secretary of the Department of Health and Human Services (DHHS), informed Governor Roberts by letter that he was returning the state's proposal back to Oregon "for further work." On the basis of an analysis substantially similar to the one provided by the Legal Center, Sullivan contended that because the plan proposed to deny Medicaid funding for the treatment of certain conditions associated with diminished quality of life, the plan was in violation of the ADA's mandate that all persons be given equal access to government services, regardless of disability. "The record regarding the manner in which the list of condition/treatment pairs was compiled," he wrote,

contains considerable evidence that it was based in substantial part on the premise that the value of the life of a person with a disability is less than the value of the life of a person without a disability. Any methodology that would intentionally ration services by associating quality of life considerations with disabilities does not comport with the mandate of the ADA.[35]

The specific ADA-based objections to Oregon's ranking system centered on the use of information gleaned from the community meetings about the importance of quality-of-life considerations to medical prioritization, as well as from the telephone survey about the quality of life associated with different states of disability. Advocates for the disabled presented three specific objections to setting health care priorities based, at least in part, on the judgments of the general public about the negative impact of disabilities on quality of life. First, there was the concern that such a ranking system might end up judging health care expenditures on disabled persons, or persons whose conditions, even if successfully treated, made them susceptible to disabilities, to be of relatively low priority. In a letter to President Bush, the Consortium of Citizens with Disabilities argued that the methodology underlying the priority list would potentially justify the choice to save a non-disabled person's life over that of a disabled person's on the grounds that saving the former's life would produce a higher net benefit (from 0 to 1.0) than saving that of the latter (from 0 to whatever health state the person was left by his or her disability).[36] This, according to the Consortium's analysis, raised the specter that persons would be denied potentially life-saving care because the general public judged their lives not to be worth saving.

Second, there was the concern that a ranking system that accommodated the priority judgments of predominately non-disabled persons would end up systematically undervaluing treatments for conditions only experienced by persons with disabilities. One example that was cited was the Commission's decision to place treatments for "infertility"—considered a disability under the ADA—in category 15 out of 17. This placement constituted discrimination, it was argued, because it was justified on the grounds that infertility services were not highly valued by members of the Oregon public, rather than for medical or economic reasons. This, said critics, amounted to giving infertility services low priority for the sole reason that people without infertility problems did not consider them particularly important.

Third, it was argued that by using the public's judgments about the quality of life of persons with disabilities to formulate policy, the state of Oregon was lending its authority to what disability-rights advocates contended were essentially prejudicial assumptions about the life-prospects of the disabled. According to the Legal Center's analysis: "the Oregon Plan would serve to perpetuate, rather than eliminate, societal and individual prejudices about the value of living with disabilities."[37]

Defenders of Oregon's methods maintained that the ADA-based objections rested on a misunderstanding of how the quality-of-life data was being used. In particular, the concerns about the disabled being denied treatment that would not be denied to non-disabled persons were said to be unfounded. Because the priorities list focused on the net impact brought about by *particular* treatments for *particular* conditions, information about other conditions a patient might be suffering from would not be considered in determining whether to fund a specific treatment. Two patients suffering from appendicitis would be treated in exactly the same fashion regardless of whether one of them suffered from some unrelated condition that affected his or her quality of life as defined by the data used to generate the list (e.g., confinement to a wheel chair).

But incorporating quality of life judgments did affect how the rankings would allocate health care in other ways. Services that were likely to leave their recipients without any impairments were ranked higher than ones that were not. Incorporating quality of life judgments in the ranking system also meant that patients suffering from different *conditions* would have their treatments prioritized according to whether or not they were likely to experience a complete recovery.

The Legal Center's analysis dramatized this aspect of the Oregon Plan in the following way:

> [I]magine [this] scenario. Patient A and Patient B are both injured in an accident. Treatment A is recommended for Patient A, while Treatment B is recommended for Patient B. Both treatments cost the same. However, Treatment A will sustain Patient A's life but will not restore the abilities A lost after the accident (such as the ability to walk), while Treatment B will sustain B's life and restore his ability to walk. If the basis of funding B but not A is a quality of life judgment that being able to walk is of greater benefit than not being able to walk, for example, then a decision to deny treatment for A would be discrimination based on A's resulting level of disability. In effect, B's life would be considered more valuable than A's life because B will regain an additional function, while A would not. [A] distinction between two effective treatments would be based not on treatment effectiveness, because both treatments would sustain life, but on an inappropriate assessment of the underlying quality of life each patient will have after treatment. This scenario describes the Oregon Plan.[38]

Defenders of the program pointed out that while such a scenario was technically possible under the Oregon Health Plan, it was highly unlikely to arise.[39] Since all treatments with a significant chance of saving life had been placed in one of the three highest ranked categories, it was considered extremely unlikely that treatments similar to either of the ones described in the Legal Center's hypothetical would fall below the funding point. However, the proposed priority rankings did mandate one coverage decision not entirely unlike the one described above. While life-saving procedures for most premature infants received a high ranking on the list (line 22), life-saving procedures for those in the category of "extremely premature" (defined as infants who weigh less than 500 grams and are at less than 23 weeks of gestation) ranked next to last, just ahead of life-saving treatment for infants born with only partial brains. While this ranking difference was based in part on the fact that life-saving techniques have a relatively small chance of being successful in cases of extremely low birth weight, it was also based on quality of life considerations. Infants in such a state who do survive stand a very good chance of being extremely disabled, suffering both from severe mental retardation and cerebral palsy. Because of this fact, life-saving measures for such infants had been placed in the last of the list's 17 categories ("Fatal or nonfatal conditions for which treatment provides minimal or no improvement in quality of life"). Under the proposed plan, Medicaid would pay for comfort care for infants in that state, but would not fund any potentially life-saving measures—exactly the reverse of the funding decision that would be made under the existing Medicaid system. According to Secretary Sullivan, denying life-saving care to extremely premature infants on the grounds that their condition renders them more likely to be severely disabled than other premature infants constituted discrimination under the ADA.[40]

Oregon officials tried to defend the use of quality-of-life measurements by pointing to the need for the rankings to reflect the importance of medical services designed to improve function or quality of life (e.g., hip replacement surgery), rather than prolong life. Lynn Read, director of the Oregon Health Plan, maintained that using quality-of-life data to set priorities would benefit the disabled, since it would provide a basis for justifying treatments to improve conditions for people with permanent disabilities. This would especially be the case, she emphasized, if the quality of life data came from people who judged disabling conditions to be very serious, as any service capable of improving those conditions would end up meriting a high net-benefit score.[41]

In late August of 1992, Michael Astrue, general counsel for the Department of Health and Human Services, flew out to Oregon to clarify DHHS's decision. He explained that the rankings "were not necessarily objectionable in themselves. It was the methodology." If the influence of the data from the telephone polling was eliminated and references

to "quality of life" were removed from the list then, he said, there would be "a very high likelihood of approval." When pressed by Commission members about how medical services could be ranked without using information about the relative value health care consumers place on different medical outcomes, Astrue replied that priority judgments of that kind were for physicians and other health experts to make, not the potentially biased general public.[42] The Health Services Commission interpreted DHHS's overall stance to be that "the involvement of the public resulted in the waiver denial even though the product (the prioritized health services list) was generally acceptable."[43] Members of the Commission found this conclusion particularly discouraging. They took pride in their efforts to ensure that priorities had been set in a manner that gave effective representation to community values.[44]

APPROVAL

Although Oregon officials refused to concede that the method they had used to devise the priorities list had discriminated against the disabled, they agreed to revise the list in accordance with DHHS recommendations. A new draft of the list was produced, using a ranking system that eliminated the influence of the quality of life data. The plan was resubmitted for federal approval on November 13, 1992, less than two weeks after Bill Clinton had defeated George Bush in the 1992 presidential election. The day before Clinton was to take office, Bush's Justice Department wrote a letter to DHHS claiming that the plan "continues to have features that violate the ADA." Noting that in completing this latest version of the list "commissioners [had] made adjustments to the list on the basis of certain community or social values, including 'quality of life' and 'ability to function,' as expressed by Oregonians in public meetings," the Justice Department once again advised that to achieve compliance with the ADA "the rankings should be redone without taking such community values into account."[45] Over

70 advocacy groups for the disabled urged Clinton to reject the plan, citing the Justice Department's most recent evaluation. Al Gore, Clinton's selection for vice-president, was reported to be trying to persuade Clinton to deny Oregon's waiver application.

On March 19 the newly appointed Secretary of the Department of Health and Human Services Donna Shalala officially granted Oregon permission to implement the plan on a five-year trial basis, subject to a number of conditions. The Health Services Commission was asked to revise the list one last time to bring it into compliance with the ADA, removing steps 2 and 3—the steps referring to a treatment's effectiveness in eliminating residual symptoms—from the four-step method that had been used to compile the latest rankings. An additional condition of approval was that Oregon would have to seek permission from DHHS any time that it wanted to eliminate more services by moving the cut-off point any higher.

In March and April of 1993, the Health Services Commission reranked the list, using the following two-step method:

1. Health services were ranked according to their effectiveness in preventing death.

2. Tied services were ranked according to the average cost of treatment, with the less expensive service ranked higher.

The Commission then reviewed the list. Services whose initial placement did not seem to reflect their importance to health care were moved either up or down in the rankings in accordance with a list of "subjective criteria" that was "developed using the values expressed at the public hearings and the community meetings."[46] HSC received preapproval of the list of subjective criteria from the Department of Health and Human Services for use in making adjustments to the rankings. The effect of employing the subjective criteria was to make the order of the rankings very similar to what it had been under the category-driven ranking system submitted for federal approval back in 1991, only without explicitly using any of the methods that had proved objectionable to DHHS. The new priorities list included 696 services and

was slated to be funded through line 565. Unfunded services included post-mastectomy breast reconstruction (566), liver transplants for cancer of the liver (582), medical therapy for sprains of the Achilles tendon (635) and medical or surgical treatment for cancer with a less than 5 percent five-year survival rate (672).

On February 1, 1994, the Medicaid portion of the Oregon Health Plan went into effect. In the first year of the program, 120,000 new eligibles joined up, an enrollment figure that the program had not been expected to meet until between its third or fourth year. In November of 1994, John Kitzhaber was elected governor of Oregon.

AFTERWORD

Between February 1994 and January 1999, the Medicaid portion of the Oregon Health Plan had an average of 370,000 clients enrolled in it at any given time. Of that group, more than 100,000 were persons who would not have qualified under previous Medicaid eligibility standards. The percentage of uninsured adults declined in the state from 18 percent to 12 percent, while the number of uninsured children declined from 21 percent to 10 percent.[47] This occurred during a period when the ranks of the uninsured continued to increase in other parts of the United States. The final figures of 2002 show that 12.2 percent (roughly 420,000) of the Oregon population, and 8.5 percent (72,400) of the children in Oregon, were uninsured.[48]

The benefits package provided by the plan remained relatively constant throughout this period. In 1995, the Health Services Commission integrated mental health and chemical dependency services into the list. That year, the legislature chose to fund the 745-item integrated list through line 581. In 1996, the Legislative Emergency Board attempted to move the funding line from 581 to 573, but the Health Care Financing Administration only approved a move to 578. In December of 1996, HCFA notified the state of Oregon that it is "unlikely to approve any further requests to move the funding line for the OHP benefit package." However, in 2003 the funding line was 558 (pterygium)—excluding among many other illnesses chronic bronchitis, infertility, and liver cancer.

With little or no movement in the funding line, costs for the program rose steadily. Total state funds invested in Medicaid and related programs increased from $786.4 million in 1991–93 (the last legislative budgeting period before the plan was implemented) to nearly $2.4 billion in the Governor's Recommended Budget for 1999–01. As a percentage of Gross State Product (GSP), Medicaid expenditures grew from .64 percent of GSP in 1991–93 to 1.1 percent of GSP in 1997–99. In 1999, an assessment of the program prepared by the Office for Oregon Health Plan Policy and Research (OHPPR) said this about the Medicaid portion of the Oregon Health Plan: "By any measure, the Medicaid Demonstration's total direct costs are more than the pre-Demonstration Medicaid program." The OHPPR also concluded, however, that some of the increased state spending was being offset by declining rates of growth in overall state health care costs, a trend it linked to reductions in the amount of medically uninsured residents forced to rely on charity care.[49]

Because the Oregon Health Plan proved more expensive than the previous Medicaid system, the program's political viability came into question almost from the moment it was first put into effect. In 1995, the legislature voted to begin charging monthly premiums, ranging from $4 to $28, to Medicaid recipients who were made newly eligible by the program. In 1996, in what was viewed by proponents of the plan as a clear indication of its public support, Oregon voters overwhelmingly approved a measure to help fund the program through an additional tax on tobacco products (roughly, 30 cents per pack of cigarettes). In 1997 and 1999, the Republican-dominated state legislature attempted to significantly reduce program costs by moving the eligibility criteria to a number below 100 percent of the federal poverty level, only to be rebuffed by Governor Kitzhaber's veto. Kitzhaber, who was elected to a second term

as Oregon's governor in November of 1998, vowed that during his time as governor he would block any fundamental changes to the Oregon Health Plan.

APPENDIX 1

REPORT OF THE OREGON HEALTH DECISION COMMUNITY MEETINGS PROCESS

Themes from Community Meetings (The frequency of discussion of each theme is shown in parenthesis.)

1. Prevention (all community meetings)—"is cost effective"; "improves quality of life"; "benefits many."

2. Quality of life (all community meetings)—"services with the goal of enhancing a person's productivity and emotional well-being, reducing pain and suffering, and allowing one to function independently should be given highest priority."

3. Cost effectiveness (more than 3/4 of community meetings)—"maximizes dollar for dollar effectiveness of care."

4. Ability to function (3/4 of community meetings)—"a service's benefits can be measured by how successful an individual is at functioning properly."

5. Equity (3/4 of the community meetings)—"no person should be excluded from receiving health care when they need it."

6. Effectiveness of treatment (more than 1/2 of community meetings)—"the higher the likelihood of success for a treatment, the higher its placement should be."

7. Benefits many (1/2 of community meetings)—"health services that benefit many with the dollars that are available should have higher priority than those which help only a few."

8. Mental health and chemical dependency (1/2 of community meetings)—"mental health is an important component of overall health"; "chemical dependency problems have a large negative impact on society as a whole."

9. Personal choice (1/2 of community meetings)—"being an active part in one's

own health care"; "preserves autonomy and human dignity."

10. Community compassion (less than 1/2 of community meetings)—"a concern for life, preserving the integrity of an individual and a family, and compassion for the vulnerable such as children and the elderly"; "also referred to in the context of relieving pain and death with dignity."

11. Impact on society (less than 1/2 of community meetings)—"conditions that have a great ripple effect on society (e.g., child abuse, alcoholism) should be given priority over those that have more limited effects."

12. Length of life (less than 1/2 of community meetings)—"length of life is felt to be valuable when it incorporates the number of years of future functioning and quality of life."

13. Personal responsibility (less than 1/2 of community meetings)—"individuals should not be completely absolved of personal responsibility for their own health, especially if lifestyles are leading to bad health."

APPENDIX 2

THE COST-BENEFIT FORMULA

1. Cost-benefit ratio: Cost/(Duration of benefit × Net benefit)

A. Cost: Cost is calculated by taking all the charges associated with the service, including medication and ancillary services.

B. Duration of benefit: Duration of benefit is calculated from the median onset of the condition onward, based on an average life expectancy of 75 years.

C. Net benefit: QWB score (with treatment)—QWB score (without treatment)

D. QWB score (with and without treatment): QWB score (with treatment) is calculated by taking each potential with treatment outcome, multiplying its QWB score by the probability of its occurring, and then taking the results for each of the potential outcomes and adding them together. QWB score (without treatment) is calculated in the same way, only using each possible without treatment outcome.

2. Example: medical & surgical treatment for acute myocardial infarction (heart attack).

A. Possible Outcomes With Treatment:

1. 0% will die despite treatment (QWB score = 0)

2. 30% will experience residual chest pain (QWB score = 0.747)

3. 30% will have residual shortness of breath (QWB score = 0.682)

4. 30% will recover completely (QWB score = 1.0)

B. Possible Outcomes Without Treatment:

1. 0% will die (QWB score = 0)

2. 30% will experience frequent chest pains (QWB score = 0.747)

3. 20% will experience shortness of breath (QWB score = 0.682)

4. 20% will recover completely (QWB score = 1.0)

C. Estimated QWB With Treatment:

Outcome	Probability	QWB	Probability × QWB
1	.10	0	0.0000
2	.30	0.747	0.2241
3	.30	0.682	0.2046
4	.30	1	0.3000
			0.7287 (estimated QWB)

D. Estimated QWB Without Treatment:

Outcome	Probability	QWB	Probability × QWB
1	.30	0	0.0000
2	.30	0.747	0.2241
3	.20	0.682	0.1364
4	.20	1	0.2000
			0.5605 (estimated QWB)

E. Net Benefit:
Net benefit = 0.7287 − 0.5605 = 0.1682.

F. Duration of Benefit:

Median age at onset of diagnosis = 46 years.

Treated patient will benefit for the remainder of his or her life.

Duration of Benefit = 75 (average life expectancy) − 46 = 29 years.

G. Cost:

Average total costs for treating one heart attack sufferer = $32, 500.

H. Cost-Benefit Ratio:

32,500 / (29 × 0.1682) = 6662.84.

APPENDIX 3

APPENDECTOMIES VS. TOOTH-CAPPING ACCORDING TO THE COST-BENEFIT FORMULA

Appendectomies	*Tooth-Cappings*
Net Benefit (NB) = .97 QWB	Net Benefit (NB) = .08 QWB
Duration of Benefit (D) = 48 yrs	Duration of Benefit (D) = 4 yrs
Cost (C) = $5744	Cost (C) = $38.10
C/(NB × D) = 5744/46.56	C/(NB × D) = 38.10/.32
Cost/Benefit = 123.3	Cost/Benefit = 119.1
(These numbers are approximate.)	

APPENDIX 4

CATEGORIES USED IN 1991 PRIORITIES LIST

"ESSENTIAL" SERVICES.

1. Acute, fatal—treatment prevents death with full recovery.

Examples: Appendectomy for appendicitis; repair of deep, open wound in neck area.

2. Maternity care—including most newborn disorders.

Examples: Obstetrical care for pregnancy; medical therapy for low birth weight babies.

3. Acute, fatal conditions—treatment prevents death without a full recovery.

Examples: Medical therapy for acute bacterial meningitis; surgical treatment for head injury with prolonged loss of consciousness.

4. Preventative care for children.

Example: Immunizations.

5. Chronic, fatal—improves life span and/or quality of life.

Examples: Medical therapy for asthma; medical therapy for type 1 Diabetes Mellitus.

6. Reproductive services—excludes maternity and infertility services.

Examples: Contraceptive management; vasectomy.

7. Comfort care for conditions in which death is imminent.

Example: Hospice care.

8. Preventative dental care for adults and children.

Example: Teeth-cleaning.

9. Effective preventative care for adults.

Examples: Mammograms; blood pressure screening.

"VERY IMPORTANT" SERVICES.

10. Acute, nonfatal conditions—treatment causes return to previous health state.

Example: Medical therapy for acute thyroiditis; restorative dental services for dental caries.

11. Chronic, nonfatal—one-time treatment improves quality of life.

Example: Hip replacement surgery; laser surgery for diabetic retinopathy.

12. Acute, nonfatal conditions—treatment can improve condition, but not restore to previous health state.

Example: Arthroscopic knee surgery; relocation of dislocated elbow.

13. Chronic, nonfatal—repetitive treatment improves quality of life.

Examples: Medical therapy for chronic sinusitis or migraine headaches.

SERVICES THAT ARE VALUABLE TO CERTAIN INDIVIDUALS, BUT ARE OF MINIMAL GAIN OR HIGH COST.

14. Acute, nonfatal—self-limited conditions for which treatment expedites recovery.

Examples: Medical therapy for diaper rash or acute conjunctivitis.

15. Infertility services.

Example: In-vitro fertilization.

16. Less effective preventative services for adults.

Example: Screening of non-pregnant adults for diabetes.

17. Fatal or nonfatal conditions—treatment provides minimal or no improvement in quality of life

Example: Medical therapy for viral warts; medical therapy for end stage HIV disease.

Notes

1. In the years since 1987, new technologies have been developed that have given soft organ transplants a much higher rate of success.
2. *The Oregonian,* Jan. 31, 1988.
3. *The Oregonian,* Jan. 29, 1988.
4. *The Salem Statesman-Journal,* Jan. 29, 1988.
5. Transcript of the Oregon Legislature Emergency Board, Jan. 29, 1988.
6. Ibid.
7. In 1989, Congress instituted new rules adding to the ranks of the "categorically needy" pregnant women and children up to the age of six in families with incomes up to 133% of the federal poverty level, and children between the ages of six and eight in families with incomes up to 100% of the federal poverty level.
8. John Kitzhaber, "The Oregon Basic Health Services Act," 1990: Salem, Oregon State Senate, 9.
9. The other components of OBHSA were "The Health Insurance Partnership Act" (S.B. 935), which would create incentives for employers to provide health insurance for their employees, and "The State Health Insurance Pool" (S.B. 534), which would establish a "high risk" insurance pool for persons who do not qualify for Medicaid, but whose preexisting medical conditions prevented them from obtaining private health insurance.
10. Pregnant women and young children were still to be covered up to 133% of the federal poverty level, as required by federal Medicaid rules.
11. Senate Bill 27, Section 4a, lines 11–13.
12. The Health Service Commission would be allowed to alter its rankings in response to changes in the field of medicine that took place in the two-year period between legislative sessions.
13. John Kitzhaber, testimony before the Senate Health Insurance and Bio-Ethics Committee, Jan.12, 1989.
14. *HealthWeek,* March 17, 1989.
15. *The Oregonian,* Nov. 26, 1989.
16. Rodger Wehage, "Vote explanation—SB 27," March 6, 1989. Official Bill File, Senate Bill 27: Oregon State Archives, Salem, Oregon.
17. Dick Springer, "Vote explanation—SB 27," March 6, 1989. Official Bill File, Senate Bill 27: Oregon State Archives, Salem, Oregon.
18. Bill Kennemer, "Vote explanation—SB 27," March 6, 1989. Official Bill File, Senate Bill 27: Oregon State Archives, Salem, Oregon.
19. John Kitzhaber, testimony before the Senate Health Insurance and Bio-Ethics Committee, Jan. 12, 1989.
20. *American Medical News,* March 11, 1991.
21. Senate Bill 27, section 4a, lines 2–5.
22. Senate Bill 27, Section 4a, lines 8–10.
23. Oregon Health Services Commission, "Prioritization of Health Services: A Report to the Governor and Legislature," 1991, 21.
24. Unless otherwise noted all the information in the next three paragraphs comes from Romana Hasnain and Michael Garland "Health Care in Common: Report of the Oregon Health Decisions Community Meeting Process," April 1990: Portland, Oregon.
25. David Hadorn, "Setting Health Care Priorities in Oregon: Cost-Effectiveness Meets the Rule of Rescue," *JAMA,* May 1, 1991—vol. 265, no. 17.
26. *New York Times,* Feb. 22, 1991.
27. *Associated Press,* May 15, 1990.
28. The reduction in ranked services from 1,600 to 709 was brought about by merging many different treatments for the same condition and deleting outmoded procedures.
29. Personal communication with Paige Sipes-Metzler, July 15, 1999. This was also reported in "Assessment of the Oregon Health Plan Medicaid Demonstration," Office for Oregon Health Plan Policy and Research, Feb.1999: Salem, Oregon, p. 13.
30. The 2% of "essential" services that ended up being uncovered were services that had been moved "by hand" to positions lower on the list than the other services in their category because they were judged to be less important than their categorization would suggest. The same was the case with the 8% of unfunded "very important" services.
31. *Congressional Quarterly Weekly Report,* May 18, 1991.
32. *The Oregonian,* Feb. 25, 1992.
33. *Washington Post,* July 1, 1991.
34. U.S. Congress, Office of Technology Assessment, Evaluation of the Oregon Medicaid Proposal, OTA-H-531 (Washington, D.C.: U.S. Government Printing Office, May 1992), p. 22.
35. Letter of Aug. 3, 1992, from Louis Sullivan, Secretary of Health and Human Services, to Oregon Governor Barbara Roberts, with accompanying

"Analysis under the Americans with Disabilities Act ('ADA') of the Oregon Reform Demonstration."

36. *Congressional Quarterly Weekly Report,* Aug. 8, 1992.

37. Letter of Dec.17, 1991, from Thomas J. Marzen, lead counsel for the National Legal Center for the Medically Dependent and Disabled, Inc., to Representative Christopher Smith (R-NJ).

38. Ibid.

39. David Hadorn, M.D. "The Problem of Discrimination in Health Care Priority Setting," *JAMA,* Sept. 16, 1992—vol. 268, no. 11, p. 1454–1459.

40. Sullivan also contended that the different rankings given to liver transplants for non-alcoholic cirrhosis of the liver (line 366) and alcoholic cirrhosis of the liver (690—well below the proposed cut-off point) constituted discrimination under the ADA, since alcoholism is defined as a disability. Oregon was told that it could continue to rank treatments for the two types of cirrhosis differently so long as what was ranked low was not transplants for everyone suffering from alcoholic cirrhosis, but only transplants for non-recovering alcoholics. Treating transplants for non-recovering alcoholics differently has a medical basis, since continued drinking might cause the benefits of the transplant to be of shorter duration. HSC's initial decision to rank alcoholic and non-alcoholic cirrhosis differently had been based on ideas that came out of the "community meetings"—namely, that "personal responsibility" should be a factor to consider when setting priorities. This was deemed discriminatory.

41. Gail McBride, "Bush Vetoes Health Care Rationing in Oregon," *British Medical Journal,* Aug. 22, 1992, p. 437.

42. *The Oregonian,* Aug. 27, 1992.

43. Oregon Health Services Commission, "Prioritization of Health Services Report to the Governor and Legislature," 1993, p. 8.

44. Personal communication with Paige Sipes-Metzler, July 15, 1999.

45. Letter of January 19, 1993, from Timothy Flanagan, assistant attorney general, Office of Legal Counsel, Department of Justice, to Suzanne Zagame, acting general counsel, Department of Health and Human Services.

46. Oregon Health Services Commission, "Prioritization of Health Services Report to the Governor and Legislature," 1999, p. 19.

47. These facts come from Oregon Health Service Commission's "Prioritization of Health Services Report to the Governor and Legislature" 1999.

48. From the final report for 2002 released by OHPPR. See http://www.ohppr.state.or.us/data/ops/summary_ops_2000.xls

49. "Assessment of the Oregon Health Plan Medicaid Demonstration," Office for Oregon Health Plan Policy and Research, Feb. 1999: Salem, Oregon, p. 95–99.

Comment

The philosopher David Hume argues that scarcity is a background condition of distributive justice. There would be no need for justice, Hume suggests, if all humanly available resources were infinite. Supporters of Oregon's rationing program argue that in an "era of limits" when the state's budget cannot afford to support universal health care, there is no choice other than to ration. Rationing in public rather than out of public view, they further argue, makes the process and its outcomes more democratically justifiable. In addition to judging whether they are generally right about rationing in public, we also need to evaluate the justice of Oregon's specific health plan and the process by which it was promulgated.

Begin by considering whether the rationing of health care is a necessity. Is it feasible to offer everyone as many health care goods and services as they both want and need? Many have suggested a distributive principle based on need but not on want: to each according to his or her health care needs. To interpret this principle, you will need to articulate and defend the distinction between needs and wants. Does the principle "to each according to health care needs" avoid the need to ration health care or would it still be necessary, and if so why? Are there any plausible social conditions under which health care rationing of some sort would not be necessary?

Next ask whether the sort of rationing recommended by the Oregon plan is the most morally defensible. To answer this question, you will need to evaluate a set of moral standards applied to the Oregon plan and its feasible alternatives. Evaluate the following utilitarian, libertarian, and egalitarian standards, and any other that you find more defensible, in their application to the Oregon plan and its alternatives: (1) the state should do the greatest good for the largest number of people under its budgetary limits; (2) the state should maximally protect the freedoms of every citizen, which include market freedoms from taxation; (3) the state should offer equal access to health care to all persons within its jurisdiction. How does the Oregon plan measure up to the standard you deem most defensible? Is there an alternative plan that better satisfies the most defensible standard?

Evaluate the difference between two health care plans of similar public expense (1) one that covers the costs of all the health care prescribed by most physicians to everyone covered by the plan with a greater restriction on the number of people covered by the plan, and (2) the other that covers the cost of only a subset of medical procedures that most physicians would prescribe but with far less restriction on the number of people covered by the plan. Is there no ethical difference, on balance, between the two plans, or does your assessment depend on comparing who is covered by each of the plans?

Before you assess the process by which the state of Oregon decided on its rationing plan, you should pause to consider whether and why any state should attend to people's health care needs. One representative argued from individual obligation that "Once we know someone's life is in danger, we have a moral duty to do what is in our power to save that life." What might support such a moral duty, and does it apply more or less robustly to public institutions than to individuals? What, if any, are its inherent and discretionary limitations? For example, how should the state respond to the skyrocketing costs of neonatal care for infants born on the (ever-changing) verge of viability? To the ever-increasing (and very costly) possibilities of organ transplants? To the improved (and also very costly) care for cancer patients? Are there desirable results of treatments beyond saving or extending life that should be considered in the justification of devoting large public resources to health care?

Now turn to the way in which the Oregon plan was formulated, a multilevel process of public deliberation designed to encourage participants "to think and express themselves in the first person plural . . . as members of a statewide community for whom health care has a shared value." Consider whether and why such public deliberation makes the plan more justifiable than it would be in its absence. Assume that less publicly visible ways (for example, anonymous public opinion polls) were available to obtain the input of citizens, and these would have attracted less opposition or minimized public objection to the plan. Why would these have been more or less desirable?

One of the most serious criticisms of the deliberative process in Oregon over health care is that it applied only to rationing for low-income citizens. Critics point to the injustice in making some poor citizens sacrifice health care that they need so that other poor citizens can receive what they need even more urgently, while at the same time better-off citizens can get whatever treatment they need. This basic injustice, critics continue, distorts the deliberative process. The surveys and the community meetings are asking a morally skewed question: how best to ration health care only for the poor? When Oregon legislators saw what treatments would need to be eliminated from the list because of the financial constraints, they pushed for a larger budget, thereby partially responding to the problem. But the general problem still remained, raising the question of whether a deliberative process has more or less potential than a nondeliberative process to move in a direction that addresses this basic criticism of the Oregon plan. What modifications to the Oregon process would aid in realizing its potential?

Deliberative processes raise the twin issues of who should be included in the deliberations and how much weight the views of each of those included should be given in decision-making. How would you recommend resolving the dispute between the priorities that were endorsed through Oregon's public deliberations and those endorsed by advocates of the Americans with Disabilities Act (ADA)? Consider how the deliberative process within Oregon might have been modified to respond to these criticisms before the plan was finalized and sent to Washington for approval.

Finally, imagine that you are hired by a subcommittee of the Oregon legislature as an ethical consultant to recommend a revised process that would be employed in the future to determine how Oregon would distribute health care. What is your recommendation and on what basis would you defend it? Do you ask that your recommendation be made public or be kept confidential?

Welfare Reform in Wisconsin

Jonathan Goldberg

Russell and Sheryl Harvey lived in a poor neighborhood in Milwaukee, Wisconsin, with their five children. Neither Russell nor Sheryl had worked for a long time, and the family subsisted on welfare. Because the children had been physically abused by someone outside the family, the entire family was in counseling and on medication. The Harveys had decided Sheryl should remain at home (rather than work) to raise their children, who Russell described as having personal problems. Under the welfare system at that time, Aid to Families with Dependent Children (AFDC), the government provided Medicaid health insurance benefits for the Harvey family, so long as Russell Harvey's

income was very low. Harvey applied for every available job that included health care benefits for his family, but was rejected by the few he could find.[1] Harvey did not apply for other jobs, fearing his family would lose their Medicaid benefits.

The Harveys' situation took a turn for the worse when Wisconsin instituted work requirements in an early form of Temporary Assistance to Needy Families (TANF— which would replace AFDC throughout the nation in 1996). Russell Harvey had to work to receive a basic income under Wisconsin's new welfare policy, but he could not find a job. "I was going out everywhere, even out in the boondocks, putting in applications.

Nothing was coming up," he said. Harvey wanted to work—employment would mean independence from the welfare system, which he felt was degrading and limited his and his family's opportunities to enjoy life. He worried about the effect of welfare on his children, saying it "gave them a negative outlook on things." Harvey was not unwilling to work; he simply was unwilling to accept a job that would leave his family without health insurance.

In 1994, the Harveys sought help from the New Hope Project, an experimental program designed to provide an escape from poverty through employment. The New Hope Project resolved their dilemma, providing Harvey with a community service job, personal counseling, and health care subsidies contingent upon his employment. Four years later, with his children receiving adequate health care, Harvey was employed in the private sector as a security guard, owned a car, and was in the process of buying his first house.

. . .

Debate over welfare raged throughout the 1980's, as states and private organizations experimented with various alternatives to the status quo. Conservatives argued that welfare was doing more harm than good: it encouraged poverty and dependency by creating disincentives to work while increasing the incentive to be poor by providing poor families with an income and health care. Liberals attacked the status quo as well. They argued that racial and gender discrimination, the absence of affordable child care and health care, and a lack of education and training prevented the poor from escaping poverty through employment. They also claimed that low-income individuals and families could not overcome poverty on their own because of a lack of jobs.[2]

The Harveys' story can be seen to reflect both conservative and liberal criticisms of welfare. Like many others, the Harveys had encountered two problems under AFDC: (1) disincentives to work in the form of Medicaid and a guaranteed basic income

provided by AFDC, and (2) a shortage of employment opportunities providing either health insurance or a large enough income to purchase coverage privately.

ORIGINS OF THE NEW HOPE PROJECT

Brought about by conversations in the 1980's between Julie Kerksick, John Gardner, David Riemer, and Charlie Dee, the New Hope Project incorporated both conservative and liberal perspectives on welfare into its design. Kerksick and Gardner were liberal husband-and-wife union organizers working for the United Farm Workers. Riemer, a conservative Harvard-educated bureaucrat and activist, was on the national board of directors of Congress for a Working America. Dee, a liberal activist who had just bowed out of the Democratic primary for Congress, wanted to use the knowledge about welfare he gained while running for office to inform the debate over poverty policy. Meeting occasionally over breakfast and lunch, the four found much common ground in their experiences dealing with low-income individuals and families despite their political differences. They devised a poverty-reduction plan they felt would, given time and funding, achieve the ideal of eliminating poverty.

The solution to poverty seemed simple to New Hope's organizers: financially rewarding work. They were convinced that poor people want the opportunity to work to support themselves and their families. In order to take advantage of such an opportunity, however, poor workers would need help, in the form of child care, health care, and a sufficient wage.[3]

New Hope was incorporated in 1990. Kerksick stayed on board to become the executive director of the program and Dee became a governing board member, while Gardner joined the Milwaukee school board and Riemer signed on with the administration of Republican Mayor John Norquist. New Hope benefited from the oversight of an academic advisory board, a team of prominent poverty experts, including Larry Mead, a New York University professor who advocated work requirements; and Deborah Weinstein, a respected advocate of children's causes at the Children's Defense Fund. New Hope was governed by another board, consisting of local professionals and business leaders, and some of the low-income Milwaukee residents who participated in the program. The two boards raised $17 million from corporations and the government to fund New Hope. The Manpower Development Research Corporation, a welfare policy think tank, was hired to evaluate the experiment.

WORK, AND YOU WILL NOT BE POOR

New Hope offered 1,362 low-income Milwaukee volunteers an escape route from poverty.[4] Designed to correct the incentive structure of the existing welfare system, its goal was to encourage, rather than discourage work. Volunteers would have access to New Hope's benefits for three years.

Welfare As It Was:
- Aid to Families with Dependent Children (AFDC) provided a basic income to custodial parents whose income fell below a specified level. In 1996, the average welfare grant for a parent with one child was $287 per month, about one-quarter of the poverty line.[5]
- Supplemental Security Income (SSI) provided cash payments to elderly, blind or disabled people whose income fell below a specified level.
- Medicaid paid the medical expenses of people qualifying for AFDC or SSI.
- Earned Income Tax Credit (EITC, or EIC) was a small tax credit, identical to a cash subsidy, granted to the working poor.
- AFDC was replaced by Temporary Assistance to Needy Families (TANF) in 1996. SSI, Medicaid, and the EIC continue to operate.

The New Hope Offer:
- Access to employment. Caseworkers would help participants find private-sector employment. If private-sector employment could not be found, participants could work in a community service job (CSJ). Each CSJ had a six-month time limit. Each participant was limited to two CSJs.
- Work would pay. An earnings supplement would guarantee an income above the poverty line to each New Hope participant who worked a minimum of 30 hours a week.
- Health care and child care. New Hope would offer a subsidy for health insurance and child care to participants who met the 30-hour minimum. Wage, child care, and health care benefits would be withdrawn slowly with increases in income.
- Work requirement. New Hope participants who did not work at least 30 hours a week would not receive the earnings supplement, health care subsidy, and child care subsidy.
- Government benefits. Because New Hope billed itself only as a foundation for, but not a complete, poverty policy, New Hope participants could access any government benefits—such as AFDC, EIC, Medicaid, or subsidized housing— to which they were entitled.

New Hope's board and staff also intended New Hope to avoid problems they detected in the existing *administration* of welfare, under both Aid to Families with Dependent Children (AFDC) and Temporary Assistance to Needy Families (TANF). First, New Hope welcomed all low-income adults, whereas AFDC and TANF, the mainstays of public welfare policy, were offered only to custodial parents: "We need to look beyond, 'Who is on AFDC?' and ask, 'Who is poor?' " said Sharon Shulz, a New Hope board member.

Second, New Hope solicited and incorporated the input of participants throughout its design and operation, which staff and board members said improved New Hope and gave participants a sense of empowerment.

Interviews with participants confirmed that New Hope, unlike government and other private programs they had used, sought and responded to their feedback. Participants also appreciated the respect New Hope's caseworkers showed them, especially in light of their experiences with government programs, which they regarded as depressing and degrading. "[My rep] was cool," said one. "Because he not only treated us [right] because we're New Hope people, he treated us [right] just 'cause we were people."[6]

NEW HOPE AND POVERTY POLICY

Participation in New Hope was voluntary and did not require the surrender of any government benefits or relief options. Its strongest sanction, denial of New Hope benefits to those who did not work the 30-hour minimum each week, was really no punishment: Without New Hope, participants would not have enjoyed these benefits at all. Inasmuch as New Hope was meant to inform future policy and programs (which would likely *not* be voluntary), however, disagreements about the fairness of work requirements, among other questions, would need to be faced.

WORK

New Hope declared the importance of work to be its guiding principle. "We believe the single most important lesson that the New Hope Project can impart to American public policy is that a work-based system should be the foundation for U.S. policy towards the poor as we enter the 21st century."[7] New Hope required participants to work in order to access its benefits because New Hope's architects believed low-income adults wanted to support themselves and their families without dependence on government support.

The "self-esteem of the individual and the individual's family" is the most important reason to require work, said one New Hope board member. "Almost everyone

needs to think they are contributing to something." Larry Mead contended that work is a common obligation that this democratic society places on all its citizens and is the "price of admission" to equality and community.[8] David Riemer offered still another justification, which focused on the unfairness to taxpayers of entitlements to people who are able to work. "People have a right to not work," he said, "but people do not have a right to receive money if they don't."

PERSONAL OBSTACLES

Although most people involved with New Hope believed work requirements to be desirable and fair, some were concerned that personal barriers to employment—mental health problems, lack of transportation, addiction, domestic violence, lack of basic skills or training, arrest records, developmental disorders, and the like—would result in New Hope unfairly denying its benefits at times.

New Hope caseworkers confirmed that they were hard pressed to help participants facing personal obstacles to employment. "Clearly there are some people with significant barriers," board member Sharon Shulz said. "These are people with significant life issues. Does this mean we need a safety net? In my opinion, yes." Shulz said she supports programs that would help poor individuals overcome their personal obstacles, like substance abuse treatment programs. She would even support, she said, a system of ongoing grants to low-income people, which would conflict with a work requirement and likely antagonize New Hope's conservatives.[9]

Like the majority of people involved with New Hope, Riemer dismissed this objection to the work requirement. He argued that people are often responsible for their personal barriers to employment because the barriers are usually the result of an individual's bad choice, like the choice to use drugs. Furthermore, the programs that help people deal with their personal problems already exist. Reimer said he would welcome reforms of existing support programs in order to deal more effectively with personal barriers to employment, but would be unwilling to consider creating new programs to deal with personal barriers or an entitlement for poor adults with personal barriers.

"You're not going to get 100 percent [to work and escape poverty]. You're not going to get 90 percent. You might not even get 75 percent. You will always have low-income people who engage in self-destructive behavior," Riemer said. "My goal is not to eradicate poverty per se but to give the poor access to a system that would [raise you out of poverty] if you were a responsible worker." If people suffer because they do not work, according to Riemer, so be it. Except for the disabled and the elderly, people should shoulder the responsibility of employment.

CHILDREN AND FAIR WORKFARE

Although conservatives and liberals clashed over who is responsible for adult unemployment, all agreed that poor children bear no moral responsibility for their parents' failure to earn a living or comply with employment rules. But if work is required and adults forfeit their right to income or health care by being unemployed, what should society do for their children?

Supposing work requirements were fair to adults, some liberals argued, it would still be unfair to deny basic necessities to a child because her parent does not work. Therefore, because of the impact on children, requiring parents to work is not fair. The argument was so prevalent that conservative policy expert Charles Murray labeled it INFTC, or "It's not fair to the children," dismissing it as an empty and overused slogan of the left.

Several people involved with New Hope agreed that a work obligation is unfair to children, yet still supported requiring work. Associate Director Tom Back said the harm done to children by work requirements is less grave than the damage caused by providing low-income adults with an entitlement, thereby discouraging them from work. No one at New Hope challenged this view. "At the end of the day, you could look back at New Hope and say there are ways to have more safety-net health care and child care provisions for the children," Back said. "But we know from the old system [AFDC] that when you make it an entitlement, it takes away the incentive to work, the reward to work." Denying benefits to children because their parents are unemployed, Back said, "is part of moving to a work-based offer. You've got to be willing to move that responsibility to the parent."

Deborah Weinstein and other liberals at New Hope argued that if work requirements were to be made fair to children, more help in securing and keeping a job would be necessary. Poor "families with children need a set of work supports," Weinstein said. New Hope provided some of those supports, she explained, but still more were needed to help parents with problems that prevented, or greatly increased the difficulty of, working. Weinstein believed the reason some parents would not work despite a work requirement is the presence of problems they cannot handle, such as a drug addiction, a transportation problem, or a mental health problem. She offered a plausible explanation of why one parent would not work: "If you have an ancient car you are using to get back and forth to work, and the car breaks down . . . what can you do?"

In order to make work obligations morally acceptable, social policy should at least provide child care, health care for children, transportation assistance, a child support collection system, education, training, and job counseling, according to Weinstein. She said caseworkers should pursue an individualized and flexible approach tailored to each poor person's needs. For example, a mother who suffers from substance abuse could be considered to be working during the ten hours each week she attends a substance abuse workshop. Weinstein presented evidence recently collected about TANF showing that the "people who have been sanctioned [i.e., have had their benefits withdrawn because they are not working] tend to be the people who have one or more severe barriers to employment." Society needs to help parents "who may need help getting to the point that they can comply" with work requirements. Workfare can be fair to children only if it is fair to their parents. On the other hand, she said, "if all you do is wait for them [the parents] to fail, then that is just a recipe for putting more children into destitution."

New Hope's conservatives, especially Riemer and Mead, advocated a different solution to the moral dilemma posed by children sanctioned for a parent's unemployment: remove the children from their parents and place them in foster care. Riemer believes that the benefits of requiring parents to work outweigh the moral cost of slighting the children. "Some people may find that to be a harsh policy, but I think giving money to people on the condition that they exist is more damaging," he said. Riemer acknowledged that taking a child away from her parent can be harmful to the child and upsetting to all involved. Nonetheless, taking children away from their parents is a necessary evil, according to Riemer. Mead, however, had no reservations about removing children from their parents. "It really isn't about the children," he said. "Needy children do not have a claim on public resources. When you eliminate entitlement, children don't get aid unless they leave their parents. That is a cost."

Others disagreed, arguing that removing children from their parents causes them great and irreparable harm. "I'm so hesitant to say, 'Take the kids away.' That is the worst thing you can do to the family," said one New Hope participant. "Splitting up families is a catastrophic last resort." Weinstein argued that taking children from their parents "would be really devastating to children."

She cited the case of a mother who was unable to comply with a work requirement because of her substance abuse problem, but was nonetheless providing basic necessities for her children. The woman was able to find someone to care for her children while she underwent treatment, and was later able to support her children independently. "It would have been terrible to simply take the children away on a long-term basis," Weinstein said. "There was love there." Eileen Sweeney, a poverty expert at the Center for Budget and Policy Priorities, argued against removing children from their parents because foster care is very poor. "The systems in place for taking children away are disastrous," she said.

WORK OBLIGATIONS AND THE UNAVAILABILITY OF WORK

In order to prevent participants willing to work from being sanctioned for unemployment caused by a lack of jobs, New Hope provided each participant with two community service job opportunities. Each community service job (CSJ) was limited to six months. "If you are going to require people to work, I do believe you must provide public jobs as employment of last resort," Julie Kerksick argued. America's economy is a non-full employment economy, she noted. Guaranteed jobs and work requirements should go hand-in-hand. Kerksick added that CSJs are effective in helping people with no job history or skills make the transition to independence and unsubsidized employment. In the New Hope Project, "CSJs played a special role for people who, for whatever reason, were unable to get and keep a job," she said.

New Hope's creators had wanted to extend the CSJ time limit to further alleviate the problem of poor people willing, but unable, to find work. The need for funding from Governor Thompson, however, prevented New Hope from providing more ample community service employment, Charlie Dee said. According to Dee, Thompson's job creation efforts in Wisconsin strictly limited subsidized employment opportunities to avoid dependency on government-created employment and the state would not fund long-term guaranteed jobs at New Hope.

The time restriction on CSJ use, while not a problem for the majority of CSJ users, caused difficulties for a significant minority of them. Thus, 20.5 percent of CSJ users returned to unemployment when their CSJ ended, according to Manpower Development Research Corporation (MDRC). An additional 12.5 percent of CSJ users "moved from unsubsidized employment, through a CSJ, to unemployment."[10] It is likely that a significant portion of CSJ users were denied New Hope's benefits, even though they wanted to work, when their CSJ ended.

Kerksick said that denying a job and employment benefits to someone who wanted to work but could not find employment was "of course unfair." Kerksick insisted, however, that the unfair denial of employment and benefits was uncommon at New Hope. Scarcity of jobs was not the cause of the unemployment of the 30 percent of CSJ users who were unemployed when their CSJs ended, Kerksick argued. The boom in Wisconsin's economy during the operation of New Hope made employment readily available, she maintained. Kerksick did not know the reasons for their unemployment, but suggested health, family, and personal discipline problems may have been common causes.

Kerksick acknowledged that Governor Thompson's reasons for vetoing the original design of New Hope, which included no time limits, were proved valid by New Hope. Each CSJ should be limited to six months, Kerksick said, to avoid the displacement of permanent workers and the exploitation of CSJ workers. If a CSJ worker, after six months, was productive and useful to the employer, the employer should and would hire the worker permanently, she said. If the CSJ worker was unproductive, there would be no reason for the worker or employer to continue participating in the CSJ.

She also argued for a limit on the number of six-month CSJs available to a low-income person during a given period of, for example, three years. The limit would decrease the cost of a community service employment policy and make CSJs politically palatable. The limit would also prevent CSJs from becoming a new form of dependency by giving CSJ workers an incentive and a mandate to secure unsubsidized employment.

CSJS: PRODUCTIVE EMPLOYMENT OR MAKE-WORK?

Some New Hope board members said there were drawbacks to community service jobs, regardless of their duration. "Subsidized employment can be. . . make-work, it can be unreal, it can be a burden on the taxpayer," said Joan Moore, a University of Wisconsin–Milwaukee professor and member of New Hope's academic advisory board. She accused some past community service employment programs of providing jobs more similar to welfare than to actual private-sector employment, at the expense of the taxpayer or sponsoring foundation.

Dee contended that New Hope CSJs were similar to real employment, both demanding and productive. "We always knew as we designed it, that it would not be make-work," he said. Even though New Hope participants were guaranteed two CSJs, they had to apply for each particular job and could be fired if they did not fulfill their responsibilities, Dee explained. His argument was supported by an MDRC report published during New Hope's operation indicating that "both site sponsors and participants described the CSJs as 'real' jobs that involved productive activities."[11]

Nevertheless, some observers, like poverty expert Eileen Sweeney were unsure whether such results could be reproduced on a larger scale. Sweeney doubted whether CSJ employment would be available, productive, and demanding if New Hope, a demonstration with self-imposed time and size limitations, were to be expanded. Even

MDRC's very positive report on CSJs acknowledged that "although it was a relatively small program, New Hope did have to wrestle with the problem of obtaining the appropriate number and variety of slots during CSJ implementation."[12] Would CSJs be available, productive, and demanding if New Hope were expanded?

"CONTINUING TO MAKE WORK PAY"

In order to get poor people to work, work must pay a living wage, argued New Hope associate director Tom Back. In 1997, nearly nine million people in the U.S. between the ages of 18 and 64 were poor even though they worked, over two million of them full-time and year-round.[13] These nine million working poor constituted 60 percent of the working age, non-disabled poor.[14] If one included as working those who were studying or keeping house, the percentage rose to approximately 87 percent.[15] "The entire design of the Project is based on experience and data that for many people the best they can do in the market is not enough to get them connected to the labor force in a permanent way," Back explained. New Hope called its employment benefits a necessary incentive to work.

Michael Tanner, an expert on welfare issues at the Cato Institute, a conservative Washington think tank, argued that the earnings supplement and child care and health care subsidies would create a disincentive to work, "particularly . . . in the phase-out range," when higher earnings would be tempered by the phasing out of benefits. According to Tanner, providing an earnings supplement does not eliminate the prison of welfare, but rather creates a new entitlement that merely moves the prison up the income scale. He cited studies that showed reductions, ranging from 7 percent to 15 percent, in working hours in the phase-out range of earnings supplements.

New Hope tried to minimize the phase-out problem by reducing the benefits slowly as a participant's income rose, what the

program called "continuing to make work pay." But, by its own admission, New Hope failed in continuing to make work pay for some participants. The program blamed the incentive structure of state and federal anti-poverty programs, but acknowledged its own culpability as well:

> Increases in earnings [only for participants with dependent children who make more than $6 or $7 per hour] were largely offset by (a) a sharp reduction in the New Hope earnings supplement, (b) equally sharp reduction in the federal and state EITC, (c) loss of Food Stamps, (d) federal and state taxation, and (e) the introduction of co-pays for child care and health care. In most cases, at these earnings levels the implicit marginal tax rate exceeded 50 percent; in some cases, it exceeded 100 percent.[16]

METHODS OF ASSESSING NEW HOPE

Most at New Hope acknowledged that a cost-benefit analysis could provide a useful comparison between the price of New Hope and the improvements it effected. While no one disputed that a cost-benefit analysis should be prepared and discussed, many questioned the ultimate importance of the cost-benefit analysis. They echoed Back's warning: "you cannot quantify all the things involved." Critics of the cost-benefit analysis maintained that certain nonquantitative improvements and advantages—like parents having more time to spend with their children or the difference between earning an income and receiving an entitlement—could not be fairly included in the analysis. Instead of emphasizing measurable costs and benefits, they offered other criteria by which to measure New Hope's achievements, such as whether the program promoted independence, social justice, and work.

"We have to consider what the value is to society of having a work-based, participant-supported system, even if you have, on some level, additional costs here," Back said. "Welfare reform is costly." He expressed his conviction that New Hope would be shown to be cost-effective in reducing poverty in comparison with other programs and that, even if it were not as cost-effective as other programs, New Hope would warrant additional spending because it "matches the values of society."

New Hope's success should be measured by the achievement of its original goals, according to Mark Greenberg, a researcher at the Center for Law and Social Policy who would help analyze New Hope. "New Hope partly hoped to change behavior and partly was seen as a matter of social justice," he said. New Hope should be judged not only by its ability to increase income and employment, which would prominently figure in the cost-benefit analysis, but by its ability to achieve its moral purpose, Greenberg argued. If New Hope achieved its vision—that people who work should not be poor and that those who want to work should have access to it—then New Hope succeeded to a significant degree, regardless of income and employment changes, he said.

That New Hope encouraged, rather than discouraged, work was the indicator of New Hope's success, according to New Hope participant Colleen Hammernick. She said welfare recipients, both New Hope participants and people familiar with the program, realized employment was an alternative to welfare and dependency. "I know people who have been on the welfare system. . . . It makes them think they can't work or they don't want to work." New Hope encouraged work and was therefore "definitely" a success, she said.

Tom Schrader, a New Hope board member, was critical of cost-benefit analysis, asserting that the creation of a program like New Hope was a moral imperative. Questioned about the cost and efficacy of New Hope, he replied, "If there is any hope of getting people to have greater responsibility for themselves and their families, a greater degree of self-sufficiency, there has to be a change in policy to something resembling New Hope—that I absolutely believe." But

Schrader did not overlook cost entirely, adding that he thinks a policy similar to New Hope would cost less in the long run than alternative policies.

MDRC indicated in its 1999 executive summary of New Hope's results that "the New Hope vision is not easily summarized in any traditional benefit-cost framework, since many of its key goals and achievements cannot be captured in dollar terms. New Hope sought to reduce poverty, improve family functioning, and improve the well-being of children."[17]

Nonetheless, MDRC included an initial cost-benefit analysis in its assessment of New Hope's first two years. "Through two years, it cost, on average, approximately $9,000 per participant to provide the New Hope package of services and benefits. Offsetting reductions in public assistance and the value of the work produced in CSJs reduce the costs to about $7,200 per participant. In return, New Hope produced clear impacts on children, moved families out of poverty, and provided participants with about $4,600 in cash or in-kind benefits."

The two-year cost-benefit analysis did not include nonquantitative benefits in a monetary form. After several pages of monetary costs and benefits, nonquantitative benefits such as "increased work effort/self-sufficiency" and "improved child outcomes" are noted by the presence or absence of a plus sign. (See Figure A.) The explanation notes:

An important aspect of any program that redistributes income from taxpayers to low-income workers is that it increases equity in society. This has value above and beyond the value of the added income to the low-income workers who benefit directly. A different way of looking at this is to give different weight to a dollar gain for participants versus a dollar loss for other taxpayers. Right now, New Hope would break even financially if a dollar gained by participants would be worth $1.57 to taxpayers.[18]

However, beyond this explanation, "non-monetary costs (for example, increased

FIGURE A. COST-BENEFIT ANALYSIS OF NEW HOPE PER PARTICIPANT
(TWO-YEAR TOTALS)

All participants

| | | Perspective | |
| | | | |
Component	Participants	Program Founders and Non-participants	Society
Cash income and food stamps			
Earnings, excluding CSJ	−306		−306
CSJ earnings	945	−945	
Wage subsidies from program and government	1072	−1072	
Taxes	−96	96	
Income from cash welfare	−142	142	
Income from food stamps	17	−17	
Total cash income and food stamps	1490	−1796	−306
Health and child care benefits			
New Hope health care subsidy	1464	−1464	
Medicaid	−58	58	
New Hope child care subsidy	2376	−2376	
Milwaukee county child care subsidy	−659	659	
Total health insurance and child care	3123	−3123	
Value of CSJ work		945	945
Administrative costs		−906	−906
Case management, benefit administration, development and management of CSJs		−2352	−2352
Total net financial benefits	4613	−7232	−2619
Other benefits and costs			
Increased work effort/self-sufficiency	+	+	+
Reduced stress/worries	+		+
Improved child outcomes	+	+	+
Improved health outcomes	+	+	+
Increased equity in society	+	+	+

time pressure) and benefits (for example, reduced worries) are not quantified and therefore not included in the bottom line benefit-cost comparison."

MDRC planned to reassess both New Hope's mixed impacts and costs in a future cost-benefit analysis. To answer criticisms of the limitations of cost-benefit analysis, Hans Bos, who was to conduct the new analysis at MDRC, said he would put monetary values on the nonquantitative benefits produced by New Hope, such as improvements in children's lives and decreases in the anxieties of participants.

The cost-benefit analysis should not be treated as a simple-minded yes-or-no verdict where a net gain is required to judge New Hope a success, Bos said. Policymakers, in analyzing the cost-benefit analysis, should consider that "one dollar for a poor person is worth more than one dollar for taxpayers." Many social programs, like Medicare, which provides health insurance for the elderly, are politically popular even though costs consistently exceed benefits, according to Bos. Even if New Hope shows a net loss, expanding New Hope might be a good idea, he said. Suppose that New Hope resulted in a net $1,500 loss per family involved. One should then ask, "Is it worth $1,500 per family to achieve this social goal? Is the redistribution worth it?"

The cost-benefit analysis should be used as a starting point for public debate about New Hope and poverty policy, Bos and Kerksick agreed. Bos said the debate over the cost-benefit analysis would bring to the surface moral issues that normally underlie different political positions. People should realize they put a premium on redistribution and discuss what that premium should be, he said. Society needs to think about what its social programs should achieve and how much it is willing to spend to attain those moral goals, Bos argued. Furthermore, the discussion of the cost-benefit analysis should not be limited to the moral aspects of policymaking. Bos said he hoped that the new analysis would make clearer which aspects of New Hope were effective and how the New Hope offer should be changed, if it is expanded.

Kerksick expressed the hope that discussing the results and effectiveness of New Hope would brush away polemic and partisan arguments and create a common ground about the future of poverty policy. New Hope and the cost-benefit analysis of its performance force society to think about what can be done for low-income people and how much society is willing to pay for it, she said.

CONCLUSION

New Hope's staff, boards, and participants disagreed about whether New Hope should serve as a model for poverty policy, but they all concurred that as an experiment to learn about poverty, the $17 million budget that brought New Hope to life was well spent. New Hope, which has been studied by academics, the British government, and the Clinton Administration, among others, yielded valuable lessons about poverty reduction, they said.

"I don't have any doubt that this program is worth the money. It is the only job guarantee program that has ever been tested," Larry Mead said. For Mead, the value of New Hope lay in the refutation of its underlying presumption that the opportunity to escape poverty does not exist in the free market. Mead disagreed with New Hope's underlying assumption from the start of the project and felt the report vindicated his views.

Although New Hope board member David Meissner did not share Mead's conclusions about the lessons learned from New Hope, he agreed that the knowledge gained justified spending $17 million on the experiment. "I think it was spent well. It was worth the investment. Would I do it again? I would do it again." Nonetheless, he was unsure if New Hope should be replicated as public policy. "Should the whole country turn to this program? That has yet to be determined," he said. Policymakers have to "look at what it has accomplished and what are its limitations."

As far as New Hope participant Russell Harvey was concerned, New Hope was a success and should be expanded. "Before New Hope," Harvey explained, "I had a real down look at finding a job. No matter who I turned to for help, there was nobody to give me any help, let alone treat me like a human being." New Hope, he said, was different. "Man, they would do anything and everything to help you get a job. . . . They were there, they were behind you," he said. "They were there to help you, like a mother, like a father."

APPENDIX A

INITIAL FINDINGS

PERSONAL TESTIMONY

In discussions held by MDRC, New Hope participants explained how New Hope improved their lives. One woman said:

> I spend more time with my kids. A lot. It just helps me out because they're at an age now where there's so many things going on here in the world. . . . I was working a lot of hours and I was paying for child care, never seeing my kids. . . . Now, I don't have to pay [as much] for child care anymore. I work less hours, spend more time with my children, go to field trips with them.[19]

Participants also indicated the earnings supplements were more important than the statistics would later reflect.

> The wage supplement was important financially, but it also gave participants some extra confidence because it allowed them to be "normal." What did they mean by normal? The focus group discussants indicated that they wanted to act like middle-income people. They wanted to be able to provide for their families and occasionally treat themselves and/or their families along the way. One participant expressed it well: "I could go to Northwood [mall] and say, oh I want them shoes, and I can get them shoes. I ain't got to wait a whole month."[20]

New Hope also seemed to improve participants' lives more generally, enabling some to get off welfare and make ends meet for the first time. The participants discussed their lives before New Hope:

> Many of the participants said that, when hearing of the New Hope offer, a feeling of "*Finally!*" and "*It's about time!*" came over them. They felt that, at long last, someone was going to make it easier for them to do what they have always wanted to do: support their families and themselves. For once, someone was supporting their efforts to

succeed. Lois described her initial thoughts about New Hope:

> I had already made the decision that it was time for me to start working my way off AFDC. My youngest child was out. Three, I think she was about to turn four and . . . I planned to work my way off it. To me New Hope was, it was a security net. You could make that step without having to be afraid. . . .

These feelings were echoed throughout all of the sessions regardless of which component of the New Hope program was discussed. Participants described how poverty limited their life choices, from the quality of child care they chose to their ability to provide their children with family entertainment (e.g., a movie on the weekend). These participants expressed a feeling of intense daily pressure just to provide the bare essentials for themselves and their families. They felt that, all too often, they came up short.[21]

Earl Kilgore, one of six New Hope participants on New Hope's governing board, said he was grateful for the emotional support and community service job New Hope gave him. Kilgore, who was released from prison in 1991, said, "I appreciate what New Hope has done for me. I'd be back in prison otherwise."[22] A woman struggling with two health problems said that without New Hope, "I'd probably would have gone back to the county now, just to get the medical part, signing over my house and my car and other things just to get some type of medical coverage."[23]

Of course, many stories were not ones of success. Caseworkers said many participants were unable to escape poverty through employment because of personal problems. They also noted that some participants were unable to secure private sector employment.

DATA

MDRC planned to publish the results of their research on New Hope as the Project continued, as well as after it was completed. In its 1999 report, MDRC's numerical analysis divided New Hope's participants into two subgroups, those employed full-time when they became New Hope participants and those not employed full-time when they entered the program. Each subgroup was compared to a control group composed of adults who applied to be New Hope participants but were randomly assigned to the control group. (See Figure B.)

Those not employed full-time when they entered New Hope earned $695 more per year than their control group peers earned.

FIGURE B. WAS NEW HOPE SUCCESSFUL? THE OUTCOME, STATISTICALLY[24]

For participants not employed full-time upon entering New Hope

	New Hope Participants	Control Group	Difference
Earnings	$5,949	$5,254	$695
Earnings subsidies from New Hope and government	$1,297	$760	$537
Earnings-related income	$7,246	$6,014	$1,232
Cash welfare	$2,334	$2,326	$8
Food stamps	$1,623	$1,540	$83
Total income	$11,203	$9,880	$1,323
Earnings-related income above the Poverty line	21.6%	14.7%	6.9%
Total hours worked	1320	1178	142

For participants employed full-time upon entering New Hope

	New Hope Participants	Control Group	Difference
Earnings	$10,445	$11,015	($570)
Earnings subsidies from New Hope and government	$1,898	$1,380	$518
Earnings-related income	$12,343	$12,395	($52)
Cash welfare	$1,039	$1,289	($250)
Food stamps	$1,066	$1,190	($124)
Total income	$14,448	$14,874	($426)
Earnings-related income above the Poverty line	48.7%	42.7%	6.0%
Total hours worked	3411	3598	−187

For the sons of participants

	New Hope Participants	Control Group	Difference
Teacher report			
Academic rating	3.3	2.9	0.4
Social skills rating	3.7	3.3	0.4
Total positive behavior	3.6	3.3	0.3
Total negative behavior	2.3	2.6	−0.3

(continued)

FIGURE B. WAS NEW HOPE SUCCESSFUL? THE OUTCOME,
STATISTICALLY   (*CONTINUED*)

	New Hope Participants	Control Group	Difference
Child Report(%)			
Expects to finish high school	4.6	4.3	0.3
Expects to attend college	4.3	3.7	0.6
Expects to finish college	4.1	3.5	0.6
Occupational prestige expectations	58.3	54.1	4.2
Children who were ever in: (%)			
Formal care	59.7	52.3	7.4
Home-based care	62.9	66.3	−3.3
For the daughters of participants			
Teacher report			
Academic rating	3.4	3.3	0.1
Social skills rating	4.1	4.1	0
Total positive behavior	3.8	3.7	0.1
Total negative behavior	2.2	2.1	0.1
Child Report (%)			
Expects to finish high school	4.1	4.3	−0.2
Expects to attend college	4.0	4.2	−0.2
Expects to finish college	3.9	3.9	0
Occupational prestige expectations	57.2	56.4	0.8
Children who were ever in: (%)			
Formal care	57.2	44.7	12.5
Home-based care	63.7	60.4	−6.7

When combined with the earnings supplements provided by New Hope and the state and federal Earned Income Credits (EIC), the earnings-related income of these New Hope participants was $1,232 more per year than the earnings-related income of the control group members. This earnings increase allowed 21.6 percent of these participants to live above the poverty line. Of the control group participants, 14.7 percent lived above the poverty line. Despite the earnings supplements, access to community service jobs, counseling, and child care and health care incentives, 78.4 percent of the New Hope participants who were not employed full-time when the program began continued to live below the poverty standard. Surveys showed that participants originally not employed full-time worried less about medical care, affordable housing, and general financial health, although New Hope did not improve their feelings of depression, self-esteem, or mastery.

The results were mixed for those employed full-time when they entered New Hope: participants' average earnings and earnings-related income was lower than control group members' average earnings and earning-related income, but more participants escaped poverty than control group members did. Participants earned $570 *less* than control group members. When EIC and the New Hope earnings supplement was included, participants' earnings-related income rose to $52 *less* than the earnings-related income of the control group members. Kerksick argued that the decline in earnings "may have been positive" because the decline reflects a reduction of work hours by participants who "entered the program frazzled by 50-hour work-weeks and second jobs." During the first two years, New Hope participants originally employed full-time worked more than 50 hours per week for two months while the control group members logged more than 50 hours per week for four months.

Furthermore, although the average income of participants was lower than the average income of control group members, more participants enjoyed an earnings-related income above the poverty line than control group members did. Thus, 48.7 percent of participants originally employed full-time had earnings-related incomes above the poverty line. In comparison, 42.7 percent of control group members originally employed full-time had earnings-related incomes above the poverty standard. That more participants originally employed full-time had earnings-related incomes above the poverty line despite participants' lower average income is logical, MDRC researcher Hans Bos said. New Hope made working one's way out of poverty easier; working 30 hours a week guaranteed participants an income above the poverty standard, but also discouraged earning much more than the poverty line by working two or more jobs—New Hope's employment benefits gave participants who had one job a living wage.

New Hope participants originally employed full-time did not report being less pressed for time, having fewer worries about bills or paying for food, or enjoying higher self-esteem than their control group peers. They did, however, report receiving more social support and having more time to spend with their children.

IMPACT ON CHILDREN

Both statistical and anecdotal evidence suggested that New Hope improved the lives of children. (See Figure B.) In particular, New Hope had a very positive effect on boys: teachers' ratings of the academic performance, study skills, social competence, and behavior of sons of New Hope participants showed statistically significant improvements; in addition, the boys themselves reported significant improvements in their occupational and educational expectations.

"These are much bigger differences than most people would have expected," said Aletha Huston, a University of Texas psychologist who participated in the evaluation of New Hope. She attributed the improvements to the variety of child care options New Hope made available, which allowed for more formal supervision and tutoring. Boys and girls whose parents were New Hope participants were more likely to receive center-based care and school-based extended care. Furthermore, children of New Hope participants were more likely to participate in structured out-of-school activities, such as lessons, organized sports, and religious classes than children of parents in the control group.

Although the improvements noted in MDRC's first report were statistically significant, New Hope was not a panacea. The percentage of New Hope boys between the ages of nine and twelve who expected to finish college, 4.1 percent, was 17 percent higher than the percentage for control group boys. The percentage of New Hope girls who were ever in formal child care, 57.2 percent, was 28 percent higher than the percentage for control group girls. Yet, 95.9 percent of New Hope boys did not expect to finish college and 42.8 percent of New Hope girls were never in formal child care. "It's certainly not an unqualified, 'Oh wow, we've solved all the problems,' " Huston said. "But these are striking findings for the children."[25] Evaluators of New Hope indicated the statistical magnitude of the improvement in boys' academic performance was approximately equivalent to adding 100 points to an S.A.T. score.[26]

Toby Herr, director of Project Match, a Chicago employment program, said she worried that a rush to measure the improvement in children's lives would eclipse the search for explanations of the improvement. But MDRC might have stumbled upon the cause in its interviews with New Hope participants: the example their parents set by working.

> All parents in the focus groups felt that their children had higher regard for them now that they were working. Their being employed also seemed to bolster their children's self-pride. Several participants felt that this heightened self-esteem and their increased contact with their children resulted in their children's better school performance. One woman discussed how her working made her teenage daughter want to go out and get a job and instilled a sense of family and responsibility she had never seen before in her daughter. . . . This sense of pride instilled by the parent's working was especially prevalent if the parent had moved off the welfare rolls, as one parent discussed:
>
>> Welfare is a big stigma for kids, and even though we had been on welfare a lot of years, I mean my children were very ashamed to go to school . . . use food stamps and use the medical coverage at the doctor's office. . . . Just the act that you're working means a lot to children. All those things fed into their esteem and it helps to build up their esteem.[27]

Although New Hope's gains were modest, they were also encouraging. Keith Bradley, the undersecretary of state in Great Britain, said he was inspired by New Hope's results. Mead said New Hope

made "moderate" gains, but was cautious not to overstate them. "They're clearly not enormous," Mead said of the impacts of New Hope. "They didn't overcome poverty." Kerksick, on the other hand, emphasized that there were measurable, statistically significant improvements. "You can look at all this and say, 'Oh my God, look at all those people in poverty,'" she said. "Or we can look at this and say, 'Can you see any difference?' And you can see a difference."[28]

APPENDIX B

SUBSEQUENT EVALUATIONS

As for the longer-term results of the New Hope project, the most striking effect was on the recipients' children's well-being. The debate continues about whether this should be considered an insignificant side effect, overshadowed by the little impact New Hope had on work and poverty in the lives of its participants, or whether it is in fact a consensual, long-deferred national goal. Along with it continues the debate on the possibility of a cost-effective calculation of such factors.

I: A JUNE 2003 REPORT FROM MDRC

The principle guiding the New Hope Project was that anyone who works full-time should not be poor. The program was designed to increase employment and income as well as use of health insurance and licensed child care, and it was hoped that children would be the ultimate beneficiaries of these changes.

A team of researchers at MDRC and the University of Texas at Austin examined New Hope's effects in a large-scale random assignment study. This interim report from the study focuses on the families and children of the 745 sample members who had at least one child between the ages of 1 and 10 when they entered the study. The new findings draw on administrative records and survey data covering the period up to five years after study entry (Year 5), that is, two years after the program ended. A final report will examine New Hope's effects after eight years.

Key Findings

Employment and Income.   Parents in the New Hope group worked more and earned more than did parents in the control group. Although the effects diminished after Year 3, when the program ended, they did persist for some parents. The provision of community service jobs was important to increasing employment: 30 percent of program group members worked in a community service job while in New Hope. The program reduced poverty rates through Year 5.

Parents' Well-Being.   Although New Hope had few effects on levels of material and financial hardship, it did increase parents' instrumental and coping skills. Program group members were more aware of "helping" resources in the community, such as where to find assistance with energy costs or housing problems, and more of them knew about the Earned Income Tax Credit (EITC). They also reported better physical health and fewer signs of depression than did control group members.

Parenting and Children's Activities. Although New Hope had few effects on parenting, it did increase children's time in formal center-based child care and after-school programs. Even in Year 5, after eligibility for New Hope's child care subsidies had ended, children in New Hope families spent more time than their control group counterparts in center-based child care and after-school programs and correspondingly less time in home-based and unsupervised care. New Hope also increased adolescents' participation in structured out-of-school activities, such as youth groups and clubs.

Children's Outcomes.   At the end of both Year 2 and Year 5, children in the New Hope group performed better than control group children on several measures of academic achievement, and their parents reported that the children got higher grades in reading

and literacy skills. New Hope also improved children's positive social behavior. All these effects were more pronounced for boys than for girls.

The New Hope findings support the wisdom of recent expansions in work supports for poor families, including increases in the value of the EITC and greater eligibility for Medicaid and child care subsidies. The program's lasting effects on children also have special relevance to the redesign of the nation's income support system. Language proposed in the 2003 reauthorization of the 1996 federal welfare reform legislation would establish improving the well-being of poor children as the law's overarching purpose. The present findings show that fulfilling this purpose need not be at odds with the goal of moving parents to work.

Source: New Hope for Families and Children: Five Year Results of a Program to Reduce Poverty and Reform Welfare. Danielle Crosby, Greg Duncan, Carolyn Eldred, Aletha Huston, Edward D. Lowe, Vonnie McLoyd, Cynthia Miller, Cindy Redcross, Lashawn Richburg-Hayes, Marika N. Ripke, Thomas S. Weisner

II: NEW HOPE IN COMPARISON TO THE W-2 PROGRAM THAT REPLACED IT

In 1997, Wisconsin Works (W-2) began and New Hope ended. W-2 set out to correct some flaws of New Hope:

- In New Hope there were no significant reductions in the amounts paid to clients in cash welfare and food stamps.
- Those participants of New Hope who were working more than 40 hours a week before they joined the plan reduced their hours and average wages fell by $0.46 an hour.
- W-2 had stricter work requirements (far fewer exceptions to the work quota were made).
- It expanded the number of hours required (from 30 to 40), limited benefits to a certain

length of time, and distributed benefits on an individual rather than family basis.

• It opened welfare administration to competition by different non-profit groups.

W-2 preliminary Results: Wisconsin saved $10.25 million in W-2's first 28 months and still spent 45 percent more per family according to the Wisconsin Policy Research Institute.

Source: Amy Sherman, "Lessons of W-2," Public Interest, Summer 2000; Lawrence Mead, "The Twilight of Liberal Welfare Reform," *Public Interest,* Spring 2000.

NOTES

1. Quotations and information were gathered from telephone interviews between June and September, 1999, unless otherwise noted. Russell Harvey, Larry Mead, Julie Kerksick, David Riemer, Charlie Dee, Deborah Weinstein, Tom Back, Lois Quin, Tom Ver-Hage, Colleen Hammernick, Joan Moore, David Meissner, Tom Schrader, Bill Schambra, Michael Tanner, Eileen Sweeney, Patricia Fernandez-Kelly, Aletha Huston, Toby Herr, Marc Greenberg, and Hans Bos were interviewed.

2. Conservative experts include Charles Murray, George Gilder, and Larry Mead. Liberal experts include William Julius Wilson, David Ellwood, and Daniel Patrick Moynihan.

3. In his 1988 book, *The Prisoners of Welfare,* Riemer argued that the United States lacked a true safety net: access to employment, the guarantee that employment meant above-poverty wages, and child care and health care to make employment possible. Although Riemer's book was not an official blueprint for New Hope, the Project was clearly designed to rectify many of the problems in the welfare system that Riemer had identified. David Raphael Riemer, *The Prisoners of Welfare* (New York: Praeger, 1988).

4. What does the word "poor" mean? The poverty threshold of the Census Bureau, in 1997, was $16,400 for a family of four or $12,931 for a single householder with two children.

5. "Characteristics and Financial Circumstances of AFDC Recipients," Administration for Children and Families, 1996.

6. Dudley Benoit, "The New Hope Offer: Participants in the New Hope Demonstration Discuss Work, Family, and Self-Sufficiency" (Manpower Development Research Corporation, 1996), p. 15.

7. "The New Hope Project's Lessons for American Public Policy" (Milwaukee, Wisconsin: New Hope, 1999), p. 12.

8. Larry Mead, *Beyond Entitlement: The Social Obligations of Welfare* (New York: Free Press, 1986), p. 243.

9. Indeed, for participants not originally employed full time, people with two or more personal barriers earned about $2,000 less on average than people without any personal barriers during the first two years of New Hope's operation. This compares favorably, however, with the control group members not originally employed full time, for whom the average income differential between people with two or more personal barriers and people without personal barriers was about $3000. "The New Hope Project's Lessons," p. 12.

10. Some participants quit unsubsidized higher-paying jobs to take a CSJ because they wanted to reduce work hours, change careers, or work closer to home. A portion of these participants found themselves unemployed when their CSJ expired. Susan M. Poglinco, Julian Brash, and Robert C. Granger, "An Early Look at Community Service Jobs in the New Hope Demonstration" (Manpower Development Research Corporation, July, 1998), pp. 26–27.

11. Poglinco, Brash, and Granger, "Community Service Jobs," p. 1.

12. Ibid., p. 3.

13. The value of means-tested non-cash transfers is not included as income. Joseph Dalaker and Mary Naifeh, U.S. Bureau of the Census, Current Population Reports, Series P60–201, "Poverty in the United States: 1997" (Washington: U.S. Government Printing Office, 1998), p. 15.

14. Survey of Income and Program Participation, 1997.

15. *Current Population Survey* (Washington: U.S. Bureau of Labor Statistics and U.S. Bureau of the Census, 1997), Table 12.

16. "The New Hope Project's Lessons," p. 15.

17. Johannes M. Bos, Aletha C. Huston, et. al., *New Hope for People with Low Incomes* (New York: Manpower Development Research Corporation, 1999), p. ES-31.

18. Ibid., p. 259.

19. Benoit, "Work, Family, and Self-Sufficiency," p. 27.

20. Ibid., p. 24.

21. Ibid., pp. 11–12.

22. *Milwaukee Journal Sentinel,* March, 19, 1998, p. 3.

23. Benoit, "Work, Family, and Self-Sufficiency," p. 15.

24. All statistics represent yearly averages based on the first two years of data, the most recent years for which data is available.

25. *New York Times,* May 15, 1999, p. A11.

26. Ibid.

27. Benoit, "Work, Family, and Self-Sufficiency," p. 27.

28. Julie Kerksick, quoted in *New York Times,* May 15, 1999, p. A11.

Comment

Central to the controversy over welfare reform is the question vividly raised by the New Hope Project in Wisconsin: Should welfare be made conditional on work? Evaluate David Riemer's answer: "people have a right to not work, but people do not have a right to receive money if they don't." First, identify the moral principle implicit in that argument. Then, consider the practical implications of the principle for welfare reform in Wisconsin. What difference, if any, would the availability of work make to the claim that able-bodied people should do something in exchange for support by society? Evaluate Julie Kerksick's alternative answer: "If you are going to require people to work . . . you must provide public jobs as employment of last resort." If work is unavailable, what demands, if any, may a state make on unemployed citizens? What demands, if any, may unemployed citizens make on the state?

Assess Sharon Shulz's argument that most people would work if only they could but many face personal barriers to employment: "Clearly there are some people with significant barriers . . . with significant life issues. Does this mean we need a safety net? In my opinion, yes." The safety net supported by Shulz includes substance abuse treatment programs and ongoing grants to low-income people who fail to find employment whether due to the barrier of drug addiction, mental health, domestic violence, lack of basic skills and education, arrest record, developmental disorder, or transportation problems. This is a diverse list of disadvantages, and some might argue that they should be treated differently in welfare policy. All disadvantages are not ethically equal. But on what basis should we distinguish among the disadvantages, and with what implications for policy?

Welfare recipients have responsibilities to society as well as rights. But controversy surrounds what those responsibilities should be and what the consequences of a failure to meet them should be. Consider specifically whether all able-bodied citizens have a responsibility to work, or whether the government should support even the surfers at Malibu.

What difference should considerations of fairness to children make in designing and evaluating a workfare program? Critics of work requirements say that even if they are fair to adults, it still is unfair to deny basic necessities to children because their parents do not work. In assessing this criticism, be sure to take into account claims that: (1) the benefits of requiring parents to work outweigh the cost to children; (2) the benefits to children outweigh the costs of providing welfare to parents; (3) children should be taken away from parents who cannot afford to support them; (4) "[s]plitting up families is a catastrophic last resort"; (5) "[i]t really isn't about the children. Needy children do not have a claim on public resources"; and (6) needy children have the greatest claim on public resources. On what basis and to what extent can either side in this debate substantiate its cost-benefit claims? Try to formulate a consistent set of values or principles that would support each of the opposing positions vis-à-vis children in this debate.

To what extent should our assessment of workfare in programs such as the New Hope Project depend on empirical data? Which data, if any, are most determinative and why? How comprehensive and convincing is the cost-benefit analysis? On what empirical grounds would you be willing to rest your case for or against workfare? What more would you need to add to those grounds to make your case as solid as you think it can and should be?

Evaluate the moral case for and against these features of a welfare reform or workfare program: (1) creating jobs for welfare recipients; (2) assigning welfare recipients to jobs; (3) penalizing welfare recipients who fail to find a job; (4) saving money on welfare in order to lower taxes or reduce the deficit; (5) providing direct income subsidies for poor parents who have child-rearing responsibilities; (6) providing child care for poor parents with the expectation that they will work outside the home; and (7) raising the minimum wage and/or changing tax policy to make a full-time job pay enough to support a small family.

Although welfare reform programs continue to be controversial, they are also widely considered an important priority in American politics. Are there any principled grounds on which citizens might mutually agree to support some form of welfare reform? Evaluate the following as possible grounds for a mutually acceptable justification for welfare reform: (1) the right to work; (2) the right to live a good life; (3) the right to live one's own life; (4) the responsibility to work; (5) the responsibility to support one's dependents; (6) the obligation to give something back to society in return for support; (7) society's duty to support the basic needs of children and individuals who are disabled through no fault of their own.

Death and Taxes*

One of the oldest and most common forms of taxation in the United States is a levy on property held by individuals at the time of their death. An estate tax assesses the entire estate, regardless of how it is disbursed (spousal inheritance is usually exempt). Because taxes imposed at death provide incentive to transfer assets earlier, gift tax laws are generally necessary to prevent wealthy individuals from avoiding the estate tax. The federal estate tax is integrated with the federal gift tax so that large estates cannot be shielded from taxa-tion by lifetime giving. Many states also impose estate taxes. The rationale for such taxation is that of equalizing opportunities across generations.

The first estate tax in the United States was enacted July 6, 1797, to help pay for naval rearmament. It required the purchase of federal stamps for wills and estates, and was terminated four years later. In 1862, during the Civil War, a direct tax on inheritances ranging from 0.75 percent to 5 percent was imposed. In 1916, a new 10 percent tax on estates over $5 million was imposed. It was raised to 25 percent in 1917, but this rate applied only to estates over $10 million. Under President Franklin Roosevelt, the top rate was raised to 60 percent in 1934, and to

---

*Sigal Ben-Porath wrote the introduction and selected the excerpts presented in this section.

70 percent in 1935. Until 2001, the estate tax remained essentially unchanged, apart from rate adjustments and periodic increases in the amount of money exempt from tax.

To be subject to the tax, the size of an estate had to exceed $675,000 in 2001. The estate tax exemption was scheduled to rise to $1 million by 2006. An estate of any size may be bequeathed to a spouse free of estate tax.

For many years the tax has been sharply criticized as unfair—some called it the "death tax"—but the critics never won a majority. After the election of George W. Bush, who had promised tax cuts as part of his economic plan, and with the Republicans in the majority, Congress began considering in 2001 a bill to repeal the estate tax. Congress passed and President Bush signed a tax cut bill that slowly phases out the estate tax, repealing it entirely in 2010, and then renewing it in 2011. In June 2003 Congress debated H.R.8, a bill introduced by Jennifer Dunn (R-Washington) to make the repeal of the estate tax permanent (hence continuing the phasing out process, but withdrawing the scheduled renewal).

Senator Earl Pomeroy (D-North Dakota) introduced a substitute bill that kept the tax for large estates, but gave immediate and permanent relief to smaller estates. It set the estate tax exemption at $3 million for an individual and $6 million for a couple, thus exempting many more individuals from the tax. The debate in the Congress was thus between the Majority's H.R.8 bill, which offered a gradual repeal beginning with exempting higher-income individuals, and Pomeroy's bill, which offered an immediate repeal for smaller estates. The debate included opinions supporting each of these perspectives, in addition to those voicing opposition to the tax cut altogether (and thus opposing both H.R.8 and the Pomeroy substitute).

Excerpts from the June 2003 debate follow.

For H.R.8 — Supporting a Gradual Repeal of the Estate Tax

STATEMENT OF HECTOR V. BARRETO, ADMINISTRATOR OF U.S. SMALL BUSINESS ADMINISTRATION

Good Morning, Chairman Manzullo and distinguished Members of the [House Small Business] Committee. I am pleased to be here this morning to participate with all of you in this roundtable discussion on the small business provisions of the President's economic growth package. . . .

Small businesses are the backbone of our economy—they employ more than half the private work force, generate about 50 percent of the nation's gross domestic product, and create two-thirds to three-fourths of the net new jobs. . . .

Through a combination of income tax rate reductions, an increase in allowable deductions for expenses and the permanent repeal of the estate tax, American small business owners and their families will get to keep more of what they earn.

．．．

The President has also proposed the permanent repeal of the estate tax so small business owners will no longer be faced with the prospect of leaving their family an insurmountable tax bill along with the family business—and the difficult decision of whether or not to sell the business to pay the tax. Instead of forcing their heirs to sell the business to pay the government, the repeal will provide certainty for family-owned small businesses that want to transfer the business to the next generation of entrepreneurs. And finally, the President's plan to abolish the double tax on dividends will help businesses to grow and create jobs by reducing the cost of capital.

MR. RYUN (R-KANSAS)

Mr. Speaker, my constituent Mary Ann wrote me about the effect of the estate tax on her family's farm. Her mother's family owned that farm for five generations. Mary Ann promised her mother it would stay in the family for generations to come. After her parents passed away, Mary Ann was faced with the high cost of the estate tax on the valuable family land she had inherited. Sadly, the family had to part with the farm in part due to the death tax.

Examples such as this have become far too common in my district and across this great Nation. The estate tax has devastated numerous family farms and businesses. It discourages entrepreneurship, thrift, and diligence.

We should not penalize an individual's efforts to make life better for their children. I am opposed to the government taxing anyone's property simply because the owner has died. The time has come to permanently repeal the estate tax.

I urge my colleagues on both sides of the aisle to join me in ending the death tax once and for all.

MR. WILSON (R-SOUTH CAROLINA)

Mr. Speaker, I cannot think of a more unfair and immoral tax than the death tax.

It is fundamentally wrong to tax a person their entire life and then, upon death, have the IRS take up to 60 percent of what they have saved. This is a cruel tax that punishes people for working hard and saving enough to pass something on to their children.

This tax has hit the Palmetto State very hard, as in South Carolina, 1,518 death tax returns were filed in 2001. As a former probate attorney, I have seen firsthand where those who inherit family businesses or farms are forced to lay off workers, cut salaries, liquidate assets, or even take out loans to keep the doors open.

Thanks to President Bush's leadership, we have passed legislation that would end the death tax, but only temporarily. I urge my colleagues to support . . . H.R.8, the Death Tax Repeal Permanency Act of 2003.

We must make this repeal permanent and end this unfair tax.

AGAINST H.R.8, FOR PRESERVING THE ESTATE TAX

MR. PASCRELL (D-NEW JERSEY)

. . . The recent CBO study found that between 1979 and 1997, the after-tax incomes of the top 1 percent of the families rose 157 percent. The wealthiest 5 percent went up 81 percent compared with only a 10 percent gain of the people in the middle of the income distribution.

Mr. Speaker, during that period of time, incomes in the bottom fifth of the population actually fell. That is what is unfair. I want to examine tonight the five myths, I call them lies, that the Republicans have put forth on the estate tax.

The first myth: Many Americans will benefit from the repeal of the estate tax. It is in all of their literature. Well, let me see what the case is. Because the estate tax only falls on estates worth over a million, it only affects the richest of the 1.4 percent of American families. Two-thirds of the estate tax revenues comes from the wealthiest 0.2 percent. When the higher exemptions are fully implemented so a two-parent family could transfer $7 million to their children without any estate tax, only 0.05 percent would be subject to the estate tax.

So in myth number 1, a study by the Center on Budget and Policy Priorities found that after all repeal of the estate tax, and that is where the other side is headed, the largest 4,500 estates, therefore the wealthiest 0.003 percent of all the taxpayers will receive as much relief from the repeal as 142 million Americans.

Myth number 2: The estate tax is forcing family farmers to lose their farms. We could not find one farmer who was losing their farm, and then they try to quote from the American Farm Bureau Federation, and they could not find one farmer who lost their farm either. And as far as

I am concerned, the American Farm Bureau Federation is just like the National Association of Manufacturers, they talk, do no good, and we continue to export jobs overseas. They are both worthless. Tell a lie enough times, and folks might believe it. The small farmers are not represented by the American Farm Bureau Federation.

Myth number 3: The estate tax stifles creativity and innovation by punishing the successful. Listen to what Andrew Carnegie said about that myth, that each generation should "have to start anew with equal opportunities. Their struggles to achieve would, generation after generation, bring the best and the brightest to the top."

. . . Myth number 4: Taking 55 percent of someone's life earning is unfair. That is a myth. Conservatives, particularly on the other side, do not let facts get in the way of political ideology. The effective tax rate, which is the percentage of an estate, which is actually taxed, does not even come close to 55 percent, Mr. Speaker, and they know it.

In 1999, the effective tax rate on all estates was only 24 percent, less than half of the 55 percent reported. The 24 percent effective rate leaves heirs 76 percent of the value of the estates.

Mr. Speaker, do not let Americans think you are going to help them on this estate tax when we are talking about a tiny percent of the population. The other side of the aisle is trying to create that myth.

Finally, Mr. Speaker, the estate tax is double taxation. Do you want a list of those poor people in the middle class that we double tax on issues? There are a lot of ways that we tax beside the income tax. This is a myth and they have quoted from folks that do not even support the position. This vote that we will take on Thursday is one that everybody should look at the facts, not how things are perceived, not at how things look, look at who is being helped and look at the redistribution of wealth in this country, and we will see who is guilty of class warfare.

Without the estate tax, these assets would never be taxed. But that is exactly the point.

Conservatives who argue that it is unfair to tax them twice are really trying to get out of having them taxed at all. Repeal of the estate tax means that huge amounts of capital gains would be passed on to children without ever having been taxed.

The fact that the estate tax also falls on a part of an estate made up of previously taxed income is not problematic because it is no different than how any other income is treated. Under our tax system, the same dollar is taxed multiple times as it moves through the economy from employer to employee to a gas station and then on to the next employee, ad infinitum. It is unfair and inconsistent to single out the estate tax for exemption from this system.

SUPPORTING THE POMEROY SUBSTITUTE BILL — REFORM OF THE ESTATE TAX

MR. UDALL (D-NEW MEXICO)

Mr. Speaker, today, we are once again debating a tax bill that hopefully will never see the light of day in the other body. Here in the House, we have repeatedly cut taxes for the wealthiest few, while our deficit has exploded and we have ignored the countless priorities that our nation currently faces.

That's what this debate is really about. It's about priorities. Their priority is to help the wealthiest few. I am proud to say that I do not share the Majority's priorities.

My priorities include our disabled veterans. If we didn't pass this bill, we could possibly pass the concurrent receipt legislation.

My priorities include a fair Child Tax Credit to help the working poor who make between $10,000 and $27,000.

My priorities include providing decent housing and a quality education for our military families.

My priorities include a fiscally sound economic growth plan that creates more jobs by building more roads, bridges and updating our crumbling schools.

Unfortunately, by passing H.R.8, we cannot begin to address the nation's real priorities.

Mr. Speaker, while I support reducing the tax burden on working families whenever possible, I believe H.R.8 badly misses the mark. As written, H.R.8 would add $80 billion per year to the ever-growing federal deficit. While we are permanently eliminating the tax paid on the largest 2 percent of estates, we are contributing yet again to the exploding national debt—a debt our children and grandchildren must pay. In essence, H.R.8 is a stealth tax on future generations.

The federal estate tax should be reformed, not repealed. I support the plan offered by Mr. Pomeroy of North Dakota that would have provided immediate estate tax relief in a responsible manner. I support Mr. Pomeroy's attempt to exempt estates up to $3 million (and $6 million for couples) from all federal estate taxes. This plan would exempt 99.6 percent of all estates in the country. In fact, only 400 estates nationwide would pay the estate tax under the Pomeroy plan. Not only is this plan fairer, it would be fully paid for by eliminating unnecessary corporate tax shelters.

Although supporters of H.R.8 use family farmers and small business owners as the rationale for the bill, this claim is just a myth. There already are special provisions in the tax code to ease the burden on small businesses and family farms. In 1998, only 1.4 percent of all returns that paid the estate tax had farm assets that were taxed. Even with the changes made to the estate tax during the 107th Congress, the Congressional Research Service has estimated that less than one percent of small businesses and farms would be forced to liquidate assets to pay the tax. Our plan would have helped these families. Sadly, H.R.8 will not.

I urge my colleagues to vote yes on the Pomeroy substitute and no on final passage.

MS. SCHAKOWSKY (D-ILLINOIS)

Mr. Speaker, I rise in strong opposition to H.R.8 and in support of the Pomeroy substitute. The House Republican leadership and President Bush are once again putting the interests of the Bush class ahead of the needs of working families and our future well being. They are once again demonstrating that they have the wrong priorities.

Providing tax relief for low wage hard working families remains a low priority for House Republicans and the Bush Administration. Instead, they want to once again provide even more tax breaks for people who need it the least by eliminating that inheritance tax. Republicans are denying immediate assistance to 12 million children who come from families that earn between $10,500 to $26,000 a year, and where one million of the children have parents that currently serve or have served in the military. Nearly 674,000 children or one in four children back in my home state of Illinois would have qualified for this aid. This is an outrage. Talk about having your priorities backwards!

Proponents of this legislation make baseless claims that it will help small businesses, farmers and working families. The claim that the estate tax puts small family farms out of business. The National Farmers Union disputes this assertion, "There is no evidence that the estate tax has forced the liquidation of any farms, and existing estate tax already exempt 98 percent of all farms and ranches." The fact is that the estate tax currently affects only the richest 2 percent of estates, and the number dramatically shrinks as the exemption rises to $3.5 million in 2009. H.R.8 eliminates the tax on the wealthiest 2 percent of all Americans—people like Bill Gates and Ken Lay. In my home state of Illinois less than 2,500 families would benefit from the repeal of the estate tax. The rest of the public would not benefit from it at all. In fact, it will hurt their future and further damage our struggling Bush economy, where 2.7 million private sector jobs have been lost.

H.R.8 will hurt our economic future because it would add at least an additional trillion dollars to the federal deficit over the next twenty years. The vast majority of Americans will have to make sacrifices to pay for this tax cut for millionaires. If this bill is enacted into law there will be less money available for Social Security, Medicare, and prescription drugs for seniors, not to mention homeland security and education. Mr. Speaker, how can it be that we do not have money to fund the Leave No Child Behind Act but we do have money to give more tax cuts for the super rich? How can this be?

Let me be clear. I am a strong supporter of small businesses and family farms and I am not against reforming the estate tax. I believe that families with modest assets should be exempt from the estate tax. That is why I support the Pomeroy substitute which exempts estates worth less than $3 million for an individual and $6 million for families from the estate taxes. The substitute would exempt 99.65 percent of all estates.

The Bush Administration and their Republican colleagues have a one track mind. They are once again attempting to lower taxes for the richest 1 percent. Just last month the Bush Administration and leaders in Congress passed tax cuts for millionaires and tax dodging corporations. President Bush made it a top priority and Vice President Cheney personally negotiated the final bill language with the Republican Congressional leadership. The tax bill passed last month will provide a $604,000 tax break for Vice President Cheney and $332,000 to Treasury Secretary John Snow. In total, it could provide up to $3.2 million in total tax savings for President Bush, Vice President Cheney, and the Cabinet. I wonder how much the families of President Bush, Vice President Cheney, and the Cabinet would benefit from repeal of the estate tax?

H.R.8 undermines our basic sense of fairness. The legislation undermines progressive aspects of our tax code. It replaces it with a regressive tax code that puts more of a burden on middle and low wage families. A regressive tax code restricts opportunities for those who are not born into wealthy families. William Gates Sr., a supporter of the estate tax recently said, "What makes America great is the broad ownership of property and enterprise. We all succeed to the extent that children are born without vast disparities in access to education, health care, and opportunity. We are weakened when our policy makers are more concerned with preserving existing wealth and power than creating avenues for new asset creation and opportunity." I couldn't agree with him more.

Finally, the estate tax gives wealthy individuals an incentive to contribute to charity. Charitable organizations are very concerned about efforts to repeal the estate tax. According to the Joint Economic Committee Democrats, eliminating the estate tax could reduce contributions by 6 to 12 percent. This would reduce revenues for soup kitchens, AIDS prevention programs, and other vital community organizations that rely on charitable contributions to stay afloat.

Support America's families. Oppose the underlying bill and support the Pomeroy substitute.

Comment

"Two things are certain in life," the expression goes: "death and taxes." But not every tax is certain, as President George W. Bush reminded us when he signed a bill that would phase out the estate tax by 2010. Even if taxes of some sort are certain, their level varies significantly with the vagaries of democratic politics, and the principles presented to defend them. The most prominent principles in the 2003 congressional debate over whether to abolish the estate tax were overwhelmingly those of distributive justice. Is it fair to tax estates after death? Is it fair to exempt large estates from such taxes?

Before attending to the specific arguments offered in the congressional debate over abolishing the estate tax, try to answer a basic question of distributive justice as it applies to taxation more generally. Assuming that tax monies are directed toward publicly justifiable purposes, how should a government distribute the burdens of taxation among citizens? (If tax monies are not used for publicly justifiable purposes, then the question of distributing the burden should not arise, and taxes should be abolished. But not even libertarians argue that all taxes should be abolished. They too think that taxes can and should serve publicly justifiable purposes.)

Evaluate the fairness of four of the most commonly discussed ways of distributing tax burdens: citizens should contribute (1) an equal amount regardless of their income and wealth (a regressive tax); (2) an equal proportion of their income and wealth (a flat tax); (3) an increasingly greater proportion as their income and wealth increases (a progressive tax); or (4) in proportion to their consumption of goods and services (a consumption tax). What conception of distributive justice is most defensible with regard to taxation? To what extent does your answer depend on knowing how the benefits of taxes are distributed?

Now turn to the question of what distributive justice permits or demands with respect to taxing the estates of individuals, the subject of the 2003 congressional debate. Drawing on the conception of distributive justice that you deem most defensible with regard to taxation generally, assess the following arguments offered in the debate and any others that you think are morally relevant to determining whether to support abolishing the estate tax:

1. Taxation should seek to equalize opportunity across generations.
2. Taxation should not penalize "people for working hard and saving enough to pass something on to their children."
3. It is unfair to force family farmers and other small businesses out of business after the proprietor's death.
4. Abolishing the estate tax "is a stealth tax on future generations" because the deficit will increase.
5. The estate tax is unfair because it doubly taxes the same assets, first when they are earned and then when they are inherited.
6. "It is unfair and inconsistent to single out the estate tax for exemption from this system [of taxing the same dollar multiple times as it moves through the economy]."
7. The estate tax is an economic disincentive for more wealthy individuals.
8. "The estate tax gives wealthy individuals an incentive to contribute to charity."

Which of these arguments rely on factual claims, and to what extent are the validity of those claims ascertainable?

The opponents to abolishing the estate tax supported a substitute bill (the "Pomeroy Plan") that would also decrease the estate tax but only on estates below a threshold of $3 million for an individual (and $6 million for a married couple). To what extent should the monetary threshold set for taxing estates make a moral difference, and why?

Finally, ask whether you took into account any considerations in assessing the particular issue of taxing estates that you did not apply in considering the justice of taxation more generally. Is taxation of inheritance different from other forms of taxation? If so, in what ways do the differences make an estate tax more or less justifiable?

Recommended Reading

The most consistent statement of libertarian theory is still Robert Nozick's *Anarchy, State and Utopia* (New York: Basic Books, 1974), especially pp. 149–231. For the libertarian case against government subsidies for medical care, see Loren E. Lomasky, "Medical Progress and National Health Care," in Marshall Cohen et al. (eds.), *Medicine and Moral Philosophy* (Princeton, N.J.: Princeton University Press, 1981), pp. 115–38.

John Rawls' *A Theory of Justice* (Cambridge, Mass.: Harvard University Press, 1971) is the most systematic statement of egalitarianism. See especially pp. 90–108 and 221–34. See also Brian Barry, *Justice as Impartiality* (Oxford: Clarendon Press, 1995); and T. M. Scanlon, "The Diversity of Objections to Inequality," in *The Difficulty of Tolerance: Essays in Political Philosophy* (Cambridge: Cambridge University Press, 2003). Even Rawls, however, can be criticized on egalitarian grounds: see G. A. Cohen, *If You're an Egalitarian, How Come You're So Rich?* (Cambridge, Mass.: Harvard University Press, 2000). John Roemer brings together the perspectives of philosophy and economics in his *Theories of Distributive Justice* (Cambridge, Mass.: Harvard University Press, 1998).

The Arizona case is discussed in Amy Gutmann and Dennis Thompson, *Democracy and Disagreement* (Cambridge, Mass.: Harvard University Press, 1996). For a Rawlsian defense of distributing health care based on need, see Norman Daniels, *Just Health Care* (Cambridge: Cambridge University Press, 1985). More recently Daniels has developed an approach that emphasizes a deliberative process much like that proposed by Gutmann and Thompson: Norman Daniels and James E. Sabin, *Setting Limits Fairly: Can We Learn to Share Medical Resources?* (Oxford: Oxford University Press, 2002). For another egalitarian perspective and a discussion of rationing, see Ronald Dworkin, "Justice and the High Cost of Health," *Sovereign Virtue: The Theory and Practice of Equality* (Cambridge, Mass.: Harvard University Press, 2000). For an assessment of egalitarian principles applied to health care policy, see Amy Gutmann, "For and Against Equal Access to Health Care," in Ronald Bayer et al. (eds.), *In Search of Equity: Health Care Need and the Health Care System* (New York: Plenum Press, 1983), pp. 43–68. A very good collection on justice of health care is Rosamond Rhodes, et al (eds.), *Medicine and Social Justice* (Oxford: Oxford University Press, 2002).

For the role of reciprocity in welfare reform, see Amy Gutmann and Dennis Thompson, *Democracy and Disagreement*, ch. 8. For other philosophical perspectives on welfare, see Robert Goodin, *Reasons for Welfare: The Political Theory of the*

Welfare State (Princeton, N.J.: Princeton University Press, 1988); David Schmidtz and Robert Goodin, *Social Welfare and Individual Responsibility (For and Against)* (Cambridge: Cambridge University Press, 1998); and Philippe Van Parijs (ed.), *Arguing for Basic Income: Ethical Foundations for a Radical Reform* (London: Verso, 1992). An introduction to welfare policy is Joel Blau and Mimi Abramovitz, *The Dynamics of Social Welfare Policy* (New York: Oxford University Press, 2003).

On the moral importance of employment, see Judith N. Shklar, *American Citizenship: The Quest for Inclusion* (Cambridge, Mass.: Harvard University Press, 1991), ch. 2; Russell Muirhead, *Just Work* (Cambridge, Mass.: Harvard University Press, 2004); Richard J. Arneson, "Is Work Special? Justice and the Distribution of Employment," *American Political Science Review,* 84 (1990), pp. 1127–48; and Jon Elster, "Is There (or Should There Be) a Right to Work?" in Amy Gutmann (ed.), *Democracy and the Welfare State* (Princeton, N.J.: Princeton University Press, 1988), pp. 53–78.

For a discussion of taxation and inheritance from an egalitarian perspective, see Thomas Nagel and Liam Murphy, "Inheritance," in *The Myth of Ownership* (Oxford: Oxford University Press, 2002). Contrast Nagel and Murphy's arguments to Nozick's in *Anarchy, State, and Utopia* (see above).

8 Equal Opportunity

Imagine a hundred yard dash in which one of the two runners had his legs shackled together. He has progressed ten yards, while the unshackled runner has gone fifty yards. How do they rectify the situation? Do they merely remove the shackles and allow the race to proceed? They could say that equal opportunity now prevailed. But one of the runners would still be forty yards ahead of the other. Would it not be the better part of justice to allow the previously shackled runner to make up the forty-yard gap; or to start the race all over again?

—*Lyndon B. Johnson*

Deciding what is the better part of justice in a footrace is easy. The social problem that President Johnson intended his analogy to address is as difficult as it is enduring: What educational and employment policies does justice require in a society with a history of discrimination that has yet to be overcome? The problem is hard in part because the stakes are so high. Higher education and jobs are a means to self-fulfillment, income, power, prestige, and self-respect. Yet the race for university admissions and employment cannot be started over again, and university administrators and employers may not be obliged to help those who have been shackled by discrimination make up the distance in the ongoing race.

The most widely accepted principle governing university admissions and jobs in our society is nondiscrimination. The nondiscrimination principle has two parts. The first stipulates that the qualifications be relevant to the social function of the position. The second specifies that all qualified candidates be given equal consideration.

This simple statement of the principle masks the complexity of its application in particular cases. What qualifications are relevant, for example, to the job of teaching mathematics in a public high school? Knowledge of mathematics clearly is relevant, but the job should not necessarily go to the candidate who knows the most mathematics. Just as relevant to the job but much harder to measure is teaching ability. Certain personality traits—ability to get along with other teachers or to win the respect of students—also predict success on the job. But it would be unfair to refuse to hire blacks or women because other teachers cannot get along with them or because some students have less respect for them. We must therefore add a proviso to the principle of relevance: Candidates should not be disqualified on grounds of prejudice.

Equal consideration certainly prohibits employers from refusing to look at a candidate just because the person is a woman or black. But it may also require employers to actively seek applications from women and blacks if they are not

385

applying for jobs because of past discrimination. Equal consideration therefore may require different treatment for different categories of people: more active recruitment for blacks and women than for white males and more active recruitment for blacks than for women.

Although interpreting nondiscrimination becomes still more complex with regard to college and university admissions, the two parts of the principle—relevant qualifications and equal consideration of all qualified candidates—also provide general guidance. Universities should set admission qualifications that are relevant to their legitimate educational and social purposes. These purposes vary among institutions of higher education but they always include educating groups of talented students in order to contribute to society and improve their own lives. One complexity of applying nondiscrimination to admissions in higher education is that many selective colleges and universities believe that a diverse student body is necessary to achieve their educational purposes; they count on students learning from the perspectives of their peers who bring different talents and come from diverse geographic, economic, ethnic, racial, and national backgrounds. The relevant qualifications of an applicant therefore depend on assessing the potential contribution of that applicant to creating an educationally vibrant class rather than only on discrete measures of merit. Another complexity of applying nondiscrimination in universities lies in interpreting how admissions should take into account the social goal of educating professionals who serve all sectors of society, not primarily the most privileged.

As in the realm of employment, equal consideration of all qualified applicants prohibits universities from refusing to consider students just because they are black or Hispanic. It also permits—and may even require—actively seeking applications from members of underrepresented groups when they are not applying because of past discrimination. When universities consider every applicant on the basis of his or her qualifications—and admit students from diverse backgrounds in order to create both an educationally vibrant class and more equal opportunity in society—they are engaging in a form of affirmative action that is consistent with the principle of nondiscrimination. But equal consideration of all qualified applicants does not permit universities to admit students in groups—even disadvantaged groups—without regard to their individual qualifications.

Affirmative action takes a different form in both employment and admissions when it becomes what has been called preferential hiring and admissions—or preferential treatment. Proponents of preferential treatment—the selection of basically qualified persons of a disadvantaged group over more qualified persons of an advantaged group—reject the requirements of relevant qualifications and equal consideration now in order to overcome the effects of past discrimination and to achieve a society of fair opportunity for all in the future. They correctly point out that the requirement of equal consideration does not permit employers or university admission officers to choose less qualified candidates because they are underrepresented in the workforce or have been discriminated against in the past. Although they concede that equal consideration would be justified in a just society, they argue that only preferential treatment can satisfy the principles of fair equality of opportunity in a society still burdened by a history of injustice.

There are three distinct interpretations of how preferential treatment remedies past discrimination. The first is that preferential treatment makes up the distance that women and minorities have lost in the race for higher education and employment by giving them the positions they would have had if they had not been discriminated against. Critics argue that preferential treatment is at best an imperfect means of achieving this goal because the most qualified women and minorities often have suffered the least past discrimination. On the second interpretation, preferential treatment provides compensation or restitution for past injuries. Critics of this view question whether university admissions and jobs are the most effective or fairest means of compensation. They suggest that the costs of preferential treatment are inequitably distributed and the benefits are rarely directed toward those who have suffered the most. On the third interpretation, preferential treatment breaks down the racial or sexual stereotyping of highly visible social positions—a stereotyping that makes it presently impossible to engage in truly nondiscriminatory admissions and hiring practices. Proponents of preferential treatment therefore argue that it establishes the social conditions for nondiscrimination in the future. But critics claim that passing over more-qualified candidates for valuable social positions is too high a price to pay.

The first case, one of the earliest and now a classic in employment policy, in this chapter illustrates a set of hiring practices designed to remedy a private company's history of discrimination. In judging the AT&T settlement, which affected the jobs of thousands of people, we can draw on statistical generalization about the past employment practices and future goals of the employer. We also can distinguish affirmative action policies that are and are not consistent with nondiscrimination. Even when we are concerned with justice to individuals in assessing these policies, we must attend to social goals of policies such as overcoming the effects of past discrimination and creating a society of more equal opportunity.

The second case—the 2003 Supreme Court decision of *Grutter* v. *Bollinger et al.*—features affirmative action in admissions to the Law School of the University of Michigan. The arguments contained in the 5–4 majority decision by Justice Sandra Day O'Connor and the amicus curiae (friend of the court) briefs on both sides of this controversy bring out many of the most salient arguments for and against affirmative action in higher education, based on rival interpretations of nondiscrimination in educational opportunity. The third case in this chapter raises the question of what equal opportunity permits or demands in elementary and secondary schooling. On what grounds should we decide whether educational vouchers—such as those in the plan for low-income families in Milwaukee, Wisconsin, the first such major plan in the United States—increase or decrease equal educational opportunity? Are there other grounds—such as a right to parental choice or separation of church and state— on which we should assess voucher plans in education?

The final case in this chapter—which pits handicapped golfer Casey Martin against the PGA Tour, Inc.—highlights how extensive the realm of equal opportunity has become not only in theory but also in practice. The handicapped golfer case also raises the question of what constitutes equal opportunity to take part in a competition in which the rules cannot be free from a substantial degree of arbitrariness. Almost no one who defends governmental regulation in the interests of equal opportunity doubts that the principle centrally applies to education and employment. Many more question whether and how it applies to other realms, which are often included under the legal rubric of "public accommodations," such as golf tournaments and other recreational and social activities. This case illustrates how lines may be drawn to distinguish between discrimination and nondiscrimination in such realms at the same time as the lines are subject to reasonable disagreement.

Affirmative Action at AT&T

Robert K. Fullinwider

INTRODUCTION

On January 18, 1973, American Telephone and Telegraph Company (AT&T) entered into an agreement with several agencies of the federal government to implement what was called by the judge who approved it the "largest and most impressive civil rights settlement in the history of this nation."[1] Over a six-year period AT&T spent millions of dollars and undertook extensive overhaul of its personnel policies to carry out the terms of the agreement.

Several pieces of litigation flowed directly from the agreement itself. Moreover, the government used its "victory" over AT&T as the springboard for further successes, gaining affirmative action agreements with Delta Airlines later in 1973 and with the Bank of America and several trucking companies in 1974. Also in the same year it won an agreement with nine steel companies, representing 73 percent of the steel industry, which resulted in a back-pay settlement of $31,000,000 and extensive changes in the employment practices of the companies.[2]

The case began in late 1970 when AT&T applied to the Federal Communications Commission (FCC) for an increase in long

distance rates. In December of 1970, the Equal Employment Opportunity Commission (EEOC) asked to intervene in the proceedings. The EEOC had been created by Title VII of the Civil Rights Act of 1964 to enforce the Title's prohibition of employment discrimination. At the time EEOC sought to intervene in the FCC hearings it had received more than 2,000 individual charges of illegal discrimination against AT&T.[3] Because the FCC's own rules prohibited discrimination in the industries it regulated, the EEOC decided to take advantage of the pending rate hearing to press a case against AT&T on many grounds, accusing it of violating equal pay and antidiscrimination legislation as well as FCC rules.

In January 1971, the FCC decided to establish a separate set of hearings on the employment practices of AT&T and to allow the intervention of EEOC. The hearings were to determine if AT&T's practices violated equal employment opportunity policies and to "determine . . . what order, or requirements, if any, should be adopted by the Commission."[4] During the sixty days of hearings, involving 150 witnesses and hundreds of exhibits, a voluminous record of AT&T employment practices was created.[5]

EEOC charged that AT&T engaged in widespread sex segregation of jobs. Males were consistently channeled away from "female" jobs and females away from "male" jobs; transfers and promotion policies maintained the segregation; most of the lowest paying jobs were "female" jobs; and women were paid less than men when they did comparable work.

Of AT&T's 800,000 employees in 1970 (encompassing those employed by AT&T and its Bell System companies but excluding Western Electric and Bell Labs), more than half were women. Yet women comprised only 1 percent of career management personnel. Those women who held career management positions were generally limited to staff positions, without supervisory functions. Upper management personnel were drawn from two sources. On one hand, they were recruited into management training courses from colleges and universities. Company policy limited or excluded women from these courses. Secondly, management personnel were also recruited from within the Bell companies, primarily from craft positions. These were "male" occupations.[6]

At the nonmanagement level, operator, clerical, and inside sales jobs were considered "female" jobs; craft and outside sales jobs were considered "male." Men and women applicants were given different tests and channeled into different divisions.

> Since women were not allowed to take the tests, they could not qualify for craft jobs in the Plant Department. When openings arose in the Plant Department, women employees with seniority were not permitted to bid on them.[7]

Of the more than 400,000 women employed by AT&T in 1971, 80 percent were in three job categories: operator, clerical, and administrative (secretarial). Each of these was an overwhelmingly "female" job. Sex-segregation of jobs was in fact more extensive within the Bell Companies than within the nation as a whole.[8]

The jobs that women worked in were lower paying than the jobs men worked in even when they did the same work. The inside craft job of "frameman" was a male job in all companies except Michigan

Bell, where it was called, "switchroom helper" and was a female job. When it finally concluded its affirmative action agreement with the government, AT&T had to give $500,000 in pay raises to the switchroom helpers at Michigan Bell to bring their wages to the level they would have been paid had they been male framemen.[9]

The EEOC also accused AT&T of discriminating against blacks and other minorities. Of the 72,000 blacks employed in 1970, 80 percent were female. Black males were few and held the lowest-paying "male" nonmanagement jobs. There were extremely few blacks in management positions. Hispanics were likewise poorly represented in the workforce of those Bell companies located in areas of the country with high Hispanic populations.[10]

In 1971, as the EEOC and the company prepared for the hearings, they also began informal negotiations, encouraged by the administrative law judge, to find a basis for settling the case without formal proceedings. The negotiations continued on an intermittent basis throughout 1971 and 1972 as the hearings were conducted. During this period the Department of Labor issued Revised Order #4. This was a set of rules to implement Executive Order 11246, issued by President Johnson in 1965. It required all federal contractors as a condition for retaining or acquiring federal contracts to take "affirmative action" to assure nondiscrimination in employment practices. The Executive Order assigned to the Secretary of Labor the responsibility of designing and enforcing rules to implement the Order. Revised Order #4 contained rules which required contractors to create affirmative action plans containing goals and timetables for the hiring and upgrading of "underutilized" groups—minorities and women. The Department of Labor assigned to General Services Administration (GSA) the authority to administer Revised Order #4 in the telephone industry.

In the winter of 1972, AT&T submitted an affirmative action plan to GSA. Six months later, without consulting EEOC, GSA approved the plan. EEOC protested to the Solicitor of the Department of Labor, who set aside the GSA approval and joined EEOC in its negotiation with AT&T.[11]

EEOC had by this time filed charges against AT&T in three different federal courts. The hearings before the FCC still held open the possibility it would take regulatory action against AT&T. Moreover, the new participation of the Labor Department meant that AT&T's status as a federal contractor could be jeopardized unless it produced a satisfactory affirmative action plan. Faced with dim prospects of resisting successfully on three fronts, AT&T agreed to a consent decree in January, 1973, which was approved by the federal District Court in Philadelphia, one of the jurisdictions in which EEOC had filed charges. Without formally admitting any wrongdoing, AT&T agreed to undertake to increase the representation of women and minorities in job categories in which they were underrepresented and to compensate through back-pay and wage increases those who were putatively victims of its past discriminatory practices. In return, the government agreed to suspend its legal and administrative actions.

II.   THE CONSENT DECREE

There were two elements to the agreement embodied in the January, 1973 consent decree. AT&T would first pay $15,000,000 in back-pay to 13,000 women and 2,000 minority men, and would make additional wage adjustments for 36,000 women and minorities.[12] As it worked out, the wage adjustment amounted to $30,000,000 the first year, for a total outlay of $45,000,000. (On March 30, 1974, AT&T and the government signed a second consent decree, which covered management personnel, calling for an additional $30,000,000 in back-pay and wage adjustments for 25,000 persons.)

Second, the company formulated a Model Affirmative Action Plan which altered its recruiting, transfer, and promotion policies, and which set hiring and promotion "targets" or "goals" for fifteen job classifications. The ultimate minority goals for each Bell company were set in accordance with the minority ratio in the local labor force. The ultimate female goals were set at 38 percent for most job classifications in which they were underrepresented.[13] Accomplishment of these ultimate goals would result in proportional representation of minorities and women in all the job classifications in which they were underrepresented—that is, would result in minorities and women being employed in the same proportions to their numbers in the relevant labor force. The objective was "statistical parity."

To move toward the ultimate goals yearly intermediate "targets" were formulated for each Bell company and each job classification by means of an elaborate formula. Based on estimations of yearly hiring and promotion opportunities in a classification, the current percentage of minorities or women in that classification, and the ultimate goal for that classification, yearly goals could be formulated.[14]

For example, suppose in job X at Central Bell 10 percent of the workers were female. Since the ultimate goal for females in X is approximately 40 percent (this is the level of female participation in the nation's workforce), the company was only at 25 percent of "full utilization" (proportional representation). By a special formula, this percentage was to be multiplied by a factor of 2 and the resulting percentage would be the goal for female new hires for the year. If, for example, there were ten openings anticipated for the coming year in X, five of those hired would have to be women.

The hiring and promotion goals, consequently, required hiring and promotions at rates proportionately greater than the availability of women and minorities in the relevant labor pools or promotion pools. This was clearly expressed in the Model Affirmative Action Plan:

> The Equal Employment objective for the Bell System is to achieve, within a reasonable period of time, an employee profile, with respect to race and sex in each major job classification, which is an approximate reflection of proper utilization. . . .
>
>   This objective calls for achieving full utilization of minorities and women at all levels of management and nonmanagement and by job classification *at a pace beyond that which would occur normally.* . . .[15]

An important feature of the Model Plan, which facilitated this accelerated hiring and upgrading, was provision for an "affirmative action override." In accord with its union contract, the company's promotion criteria called for "selection of the best qualified employee and for consideration of net credited service. . . ."[16]

Where employees were equally qualified, length of service was supposed to be decisive. The "affirmative action override" permitted (and required) both criteria—"best qualifications" and "longest service"—to be defeated whenever adhering to them did not allow the company to meet its goals (targets). In a supplemental order signed in 1976, the obligation of AT&T in regard to its affirmative action goals was expressed thus:

> . . . to the extent any Bell System operating company is unable to meet its intermediate targets in [non-management] job classification 5–15 using these criteria [i.e., best qualified, most senior], the Decree requires that . . . selections be made from any at least basically qualified candidates for promotion and hiring of the group or groups for which the target is not being met. . . .[17]

Thus, the consent decree and the Model Plan quite clearly envisaged the use of racial and sexual preferences. The intermediate targets or goals of the operating companies in the Bell System were mandatory; and the companies could and must hire or promote less qualified and less senior persons over more qualified and more senior persons if this was what it took to achieve the intermediate targets.

Since the consent decree applied to 800,000 employees for six years, it is not hard to imagine that there were numerous instances in which employees or applicants were preferred over others because of their race or sex. It is difficult to establish exactly how frequently AT&T resorted to racial or sexual preferences. The company changed the way it defined "affirmative action overrides" during the duration of the decree, it avoided careful counting, and it never classified as overrides any preferences given in management jobs (classification 1–4).[18]

Two observers report 28,850 overrides in 1973–74, although they differ on how many there were in 1975–76. The first claims there were about 12,000, the second that there were approximately 6,600.[19] A third observer reports 70,000 overrides during the four-year period.[20] It would probably be a reasonably conservative conjecture that over the full 1973–79 life of the consent decree, and counting both nonmanagement and management jobs, at least 50,000 times AT&T gave a racial or sexual preference in hiring or promoting someone. AT&T achieved 90 percent of its intermediate goals in 1974, 97 percent in 1975, and 99 percent thereafter.[21]

In January 1979, the consent decree expired. AT&T retained most features of its program, aiming in the future to continue efforts toward the long-range goal of approximate proportional representation. It did, however, drop the affirmative action override from its repertoire of affirmative action tools.

III.   RESULTS

As a consequence of the implementation of the Model Plan, considerable progress was made in increasing the representation of women and minorities in jobs from which they had been largely excluded in the past. For example, between 1973 and 1979 there was a 38 percent increase in the number of women employed in the top three job classifications (officials and mangers), while there was only a 5.3 percent increase in the number of men. Women made significant strides in sales positions, increasing in numbers by 53 percent (a growth rate seven times faster than that of white males), and in inside crafts, increasing by 68 percent (white males were decreasing by 10 percent).[22] In the outside crafts, the number of women grew by 5,300 while the number of men declined by 6,700. Only in clerical positions did the number of women grow at a lesser rate than men.[23]

Black and Hispanic males also made gains in management and sales positions and inside crafts. In each case their growth rate exceeded the rate of total growth in these jobs.

Although women made important strides in status and mobility at AT&T, the total number of women employed actually declined between 1973 and 1979. At the end of 1972, AT&T employed 415,725 women (52.4 percent of all employees); at the beginning of 1979, it employed 408,671 women (50.8 percent of all employees). This overall decline was not inconsistent with the consent decree. The decree had two aims in regard to women. One was to move women in significant numbers into previously "male" jobs. The other was related: to break down the stereotype of "male" and "female" jobs at AT&T. Both aims were promoted by acting to increase the number of men in the administrative (i.e., secretarial), clerical, and operator jobs. This both worked against the stereotyping and allowed the company to significantly increase the share of women in other job categories without at the same time raising even higher their share of the total workforce.[24]

Two examples illustrate the steps AT&T took to break down the sex-segregation of earlier years. For one thing, the company made clerical positions entry level jobs for men. In 1973, 17 percent of men hired in the Bell companies entered through clerical positions, while 83 percent entered through craft positions. In 1979, 43.7 percent of men hired entered through clerical positions, while only 56.3 percent entered through crafts. Overall, the percentage of men in clerical roles grew from 5.9 percent to 11.1 percent.[25]

Secondly, the company made valiant efforts to increase the number of women in outside crafts. As a result of its efforts, by 1979, 4.7 percent of outside craft workers were women, a 550 percent increase from 1973. This achievement was not without its difficulties or costs. The company inaugurated new pole-climbing courses, instituted new safety procedures, modified equipment for use by women, and recruited aggressively. Even so, the company was never faced with a superfluity of female applicants for outside jobs. There were high rates of female failure in the pole-climbing course, and high rates of attrition among those females who worked in the outside jobs. Accident rates for women were two to three times those of men.[26] In its new affirmative action program after the consent decree expired in 1979, AT&T decided to slow its integration of women into outside crafts.

IV.   COSTS AND BENEFITS

The affirmative action program with its override provision generated unhappiness and lowered morale among white male employees, who viewed themselves as victims of "reverse discrimination and blocked opportunity." One survey indicated most white male employees were antagonistic toward the program.[27] It is easy enough to understand how perceptions of "reverse discrimination" could occur. In 1976, for example, fully two-thirds of all promotions went to women.[28] Instances in which the override resulted in very qualified and senior men being passed over in favor of inexperienced women doubtlessly occurred often enough to provide ample gripe material on the male grapevine. Thousands of grievances were filed within the company and there were two dozen reverse discrimination law suits.[29]

The most important law suits were by the major Bell union, the Communications Workers of America (CWA), which attempted without success to overthrow the affirmative action override.[30] In an unusual case, one AT&T worker, Daniel McAleer, did manage to win $7,500 in damages from the company as a result of his being passed over for promotion in favor of a woman. The court, which upheld his claim of reverse discrimination, explained:

> This is a sex discrimination case. Plaintiff . . . was denied promotion by American Telephone & Telegraph Co. (AT&T). He was entitled to promotion under the provisions of a collective bargaining agreement but the job was given to a less qualified, less senior female solely because of her sex.[31]

The disgruntlement of male employees was not the only negative effect of the affirmative action program. One observer reported in *Fortune* that "two different telephone consultants . . . believe the consent decree had done some damage to AT&T's efficiency."[32] The decree resulted in some promotions of inexperienced and inadequately trained persons. There was some lowering of quality standards and the development of "double standards of discipline and performance."[33] Minorities and women were able to air grievances outside of regular channels, and supervisors were more reluctant to discipline or complain about women and minority workers. The supervisors' authority and power were eroded in other ways too, especially by

the centralization of personnel decisions in the personnel offices. Previously, supervisors had considerable say about who got promoted.

The policy of forcing men to enter through clerical positions resulted in increased turnover, as did the efforts to increase the number of women in the outside crafts. There, the high attrition and accident rate of women probably resulted in some general decline in performance. However, overall turnover for all employees at AT&T appeared to have actually declined between 1973–1979.[34]

The affirmative action override, requiring the use of racial and sexual preferences, certainly contained the potential of pitting white against black, male against female. Racial and sexual hostility could have been inflamed. However, despite the widespread disgruntlement of white males with the affirmative action program, there appears to have been little adverse impact on employee relations.[35]

On the other hand, AT&T has reaped benefits from the consent decree. A company that employs 800,000 people has a voracious need for labor; and by virtually doubling its pool from which to fill its crafts, sales, and management jobs, the company has a richer source of talent to draw upon than before. Large numbers of qualified and ambitious minorities and women are now able to compete with white males for jobs, often with a resulting increase in the quality of those who win the competition.

Personnel departments, as a result of the need to monitor and manage the achievement of the affirmative action goals, have taken over much of the role in promoting and upgrading workers. Although a negative effect of this is erosion of the authority of supervisors, a positive effect is the greater objectivity and rationality that has been brought to the promotion process. The affirmative action plan and its goals have forced AT&T to be very much clearer about qualification and

training standards for career advancement, and this has benefitted both company and workers.[36]

V. THE ISSUE POSED

That white male employees suffered lowered morale under the AT&T affirmative
action program is not by itself morally
significant. People can be disgruntled by
changes which are perfectly legitimate or
even morally mandatory. Whites, for
example, might resist being supervised by
blacks out of prejudice and hatred; or
males might resent being bossed by perfectly qualified females. The disgruntlement of employees is more than just a
management problem if it is based on
legitimate grievances. In the case of the
AT&T affirmative action program, there is
no question that direct and explicit sexual
and racial preferences were given in order
to fill hiring and promotion goals. The
representational aims of the affirmative
action program could not otherwise have
been accomplished. As a result, the expectations of achievement and advancement
were frustrated for many persons because
they turned out to be the wrong color
or sex.

Is it reasonable or permissible to advance
such representational aims by policies
which select by race or sex? Aren't such
policies unfair to some individuals? In an
attitudinal survey taken in 1978, one AT&T
worker offered this lament:

> One thing that really bothers me is moving up
> in the company. I am white, male, twenty-five.
> I am not a brain, but average. I have a lot of
> drive and want to get ahead. I have just been
> notified there is some kind of freeze which
> will last three or four months.
> (Note: frequently, when a goal couldn't
> be met, all promotions would be frozen until
> a person of the right sex or race could be
> found for the next slot.) In that time, if I am
> passed over, the company will go to the

street. *This is not fair. I work for the company but my chances are less than someone
on the street.*"[37]

One irony of the AT&T program was that
this "unfairness" was not always confined
to white males. As we have noted, a central
feature of the consent decree was the aim
that male participation in "female" jobs
would increase just as female participation
in "male" jobs increased. Thus, the Model
Plan called for male hiring quotas in clerical
jobs, with the ultimate goal of having
25 percent males in this category of jobs.
(An informal goal called for 10 percent
male operators.[38]) Affirmative action override thus was not applied only against white
males; it was actually on occasion applied
against women as well.

One AT&T employee, Bertha Biel, went
to court when she was passed over for
advancement so that a man could be selected.
The court record tells the story:

> The employee, a female records clerk, on
> March 29, 1973 applied for a promotion to
> the position of operations clerk, a higher-paid
> job, when it became available. In January of
> 1973, however, the Company had conducted
> a work force analysis, required by the terms
> of the Title VII decree, and determined that
> males were underutilized in clerical posi-
> tions. Under the decree the position of opera-
> tions clerk falls into job class 11, a clerical
> job title which had traditionally been filled by
> females. The decree required the establish-
> ment of male hiring goals for this job class.
> In October 1973 the Company had one job
> class 11 opening to be filled for the remainder
> of the year. It had not met its intermediate
> goals for that year since no males had sought
> the opening. Accordingly, it filled its last
> opening for the year by hiring a male not
> previously employed by the Company.[39]

The court held against Bertha Biel and
for the company. Thus, Bertha Biel could
join the twenty-five-year-old male worker's
lament: "This is not fair. I work for the

company but my chances are less than someone on the street."

On one level, it may seem a legal puzzle that a program like AT&T's which used sexual preferences against both men and women, as the occasion dictated, could be held by courts to be an appropriate expression of a law which says that it is an unlawful practice for an employer "to discriminate against any individual with respect to his compensation, term, conditions, or privileges of employment, because of such individual's race, color, sex, or national origin . . ." (Title VII, Civil Rights Act of 1964, 42 U.S.C. 20002[2]). On another level, we are confronted with the question whether—judicial approval aside—the AT&T program was morally acceptable and an expression of a just social policy. Questions of fairness and justice were central to many of the complaints by AT&T workers and to the litigation by the unions. Likewise, decisions about the moral rightness (or at least moral tolerability) of the affirmative action program were made by management, judges, and government officials involved in its implementation. Moreover, the AT&T consent decree occurred in the midst of an ongoing public debate about the morality of "reverse discrimination."

NOTES

1. *EEOC v. AT&T*, 365 F. Supp. 1105 (1973), at 1108.

2. See *United States v. Allegheny-Ludlum Industries,* 11 FEP Cases 167 (1975); Phyllis A. Wallace, "What Did We Learn?" in Phyllis A. Wallace, ed., *Equal Employment Opportunity and the AT&T Case* (Cambridge, Mass.: MIT Press, 1976), p. 278.

3. Phyllis A. Wallace and Jack E. Nelson, "Legal Processes and Strategies of Intervention," in Wallace, ed., *Equal Employment Opportunity,* p. 243.

4. Ibid., p. 246.

5. 365 F. Supp. at 1109.

6. Wallace, *Equal Employment Opportunity,* p. 4; Judith Long Laws, "The Bell Telephone System: A Case Study," in Wallace, ed., *Equal Employment Opportunity,* pp. 160–61.

7. Laws, "Bell System," p. 154

8. Ibid., p. 157.

9. Wallace and Nelson, "Legal Processes," p. 252; and Wallace, "The Consent Decree," in Wallace, ed., *Equal Employment Opportunity,* pp. 273–74.

10. Wallace, "Equal Employment Opportunity," in Wallace, ed., *Equal Employment Opportunity,* p. 258; Herbert R. Northrup and John A. Larson, *The Impact of the AT&T-EEO Consent Decree* (Philadelphia: The Wharton School, University of Pennsylvania, 1979), pp. 6–7 and tables pp. 41–65.

11. Wallace and Nelson, "Legal Processes," pp. 243–51.

12. Wallace, "Consent Decree," p. 272. The text of the decree is given on pp. 283–96.

13. Carol Loomis, "AT&T in the Throes of 'Equal Employment,'" *Fortune* 99 (Jan. 15, 1979), p. 47. The ultimate female goal for the outside crafts was set at 19 percent.

14. For details, see Northrup and Larson, "Impact," pp. 19–22.

15. FEP 431: 82. Emphasis added.

16. *EEOC v. AT&T,* 13 FEP Cases 392 (1976), at 402.

17. 13 FEP Cases at 402.

18. Loomis, "AT&T," p. 54. "All personnel executives interviewed testified that it [giving preference] has been both regular and often has been the only way the targets could be met." Northrup and Larson, "Impact," p. 57.

19. Loomis, "AT&T," p. 54; Northrup and Larson, "Impact," p. 14.

20. Jerry Flint, "In Bell System's Minority Plan, Women Get Better Jobs, But Total Number of Female Workers Drops," *New York Times,* July 5, 1977, C13.

21. "Loomis, "AT&T," p. 50; Northrup and Larson, "Impact," p. 12.

22. Northrup and Larson, "'Impact," pp. 25, 53, 55, 65.

23. Ibid., pp. 59, 61.

24. Since women compose about 40 percent of the U.S. labor force, they were already overrepresented—in gross numbers—at AT&T. The problem was not the lack of women employees, but the segregating of them.

25. Northrup and Larson, "Impact," pp. 59, 64.

26. Ibid., pp. 60–62; Loomis, "AT&T," p. 50.

27. Northrup and Larson, "Impact," p. 78.

28. Ibid., p. 80; Loomis, "AT&T,'" p. 54; Flint, "Bell System's Plan," p. C13.

29. 13 FEP Cases at 418; Loomis, "AT&T," p. 54.

30. See *EEOC v. AT&T,* 365 F. Supp. 1105 (1973); *EEOC v. AT&T,* 506 F. 2d 735 (1974); *EEOC v. AT&T,* 13 FEP Cases 392 (1976).

31. McAleer v. AT&T, 416 F. Supp. 435 (1976), at 436.

32. Loomis, "AT&T," p. 57.

33. Northrup and Larson, "Impact," p. 76.

34. Loomis, "AT&T," p. 57; Northrup and Larson, "Impact," p. 68.

35. Northrup and Larson, "Impact," p. 79.

36. Ibid., pp. 68, 232; Loomis, "AT&T," p. 57.

37. Northrup and Larson, "Impact," p. 78. Emphasis added.

38. Loomis, "AT&T," p. 47; Northrup and Larson, "Impact," p. 58.

39. *Telephone Workers Union v. N.J. Bell Tel.,* 584 F. 2d 31 (1978), at 32.

Comment

Consider the evidence that critics of AT&T could present when they first made their charges of discrimination by the company. The statistics on the numbers of women and blacks in various job categories are an important part of the evidence, but they prove nothing by themselves. What additional information makes, or would make, the charge of discrimination against AT&T morally compelling?

Consider separately the justification for the two elements of the consent decree of January 1973: (1) back-pay and wage adjustments and (2) the model affirmative action plan. Was the government right to require both elements, or would only one have been preferable?

An advocate of nondiscrimination might criticize the consent decree for requiring AT&T to institute preferential hiring rather than to pursue a policy of nondiscrimination in the future. What would a policy of nondiscrimination require of AT&T? Try to specify in as much detail as possible nondiscriminatory qualifications for the various job categories. Consider, for example, whether length of service with the company is a discriminatory standard. Also, try to specify what a nondiscriminatory policy of recruitment would be.

What are the best reasons for rejecting a policy of hiring the most qualified candidates? Would the fact that such a policy takes a long time to break sexual and racial stereotypes and to achieve a balanced workforce be a good reason? How do we decide how long is too long?

Next consider what is morally questionable about the affirmative action override instituted by AT&T. Which, if any, of the following effects of the override can you justify: (1) bypassing more qualified men from outside the company; (2) bypassing more qualified men for promotion from inside the company; (3) discriminating against women for clerical jobs; or (4) decreasing efficiency of service and increasing prices to consumers?

Some critics of preferential hiring argue that justice permits using affirmative action goals (employment targets based on predictions of how many women and minorities will be hired if practices are nondiscriminatory) but prohibits using quotas (places reserved for women and minorities regardless of their relative qualifications). Is there a clear distinction between goals and quotas in the AT&T plan? Is the use of either, or both, morally justifiable?

Affirmative Action at the Michigan Law School*

Affirmative action in the United States began in March 1961, when President Kennedy established the President's Committee on Equal Employment Opportunity. Its purpose was to end discrimination in employment by the government and its contractors, and it required that every federal contract include the following pledge: "The Contractor will not discriminate against any employee or applicant for employment because of race, creed, color, or national origin. The Contractor will take affirmative action, to ensure that applicants are employed, and that employees are treated during employment, without regard to their race, creed, color, or national origin." The term *affirmative action* was used here for the first time to describe the active effort to overcome racial discrimination.

The effects of such discrimination were especially evident in the composition of America's top professional and corporate ranks. In the 1960s, few African Americans could be found in positions of corporate power, government, law, medicine, and throughout higher education. In 1965, less than 5 percent of college students nationwide were black (compared to 11 percent of the total population of the United States). At highly selective colleges and graduate schools, whose graduates became leaders in business and government, the percentage was even lower. African American students made up only 2.3 percent of the student body at Ivy League colleges in 1967 (Bowen and Bok, p. 4—see Recommended Reading at the end of this chapter). In the mid-1960s, selective colleges and universities began recruiting black students with

grade point averages (GPAs) and test scores lower than the averages of their white classmates (similar to their long-standing recruitment of varsity athletes). This practice also became associated with the idea of affirmative action.

Although public justifications of affirmative action in education vary widely, three kinds of argument are most common: (1) affirmative action helps compensate for historical injustices against citizens belonging to particular ethnic minorities, (2) affirmative action provides equal opportunities for members of minority groups who still encounter discrimination, and (3) affirmative action promotes the values served by diversity in education (and those values serve all students, not just those who suffer the injustices or inequalities of unequal opportunity). These arguments were put to the constitutional test in 1978, in the landmark *Regents of University of California v. Bakke,* when a divided Supreme Court upheld the rights of colleges and universities to use race and ethnicity as criteria in student admissions. The case produced six separate opinions from the Supreme Court. Justice Powell wrote the deciding opinion, which subsequently guided selective colleges and universities throughout the United States in designing their admissions policies.

Justice Powell framed his opinion within the constitutional requirements of strict scrutiny: the use of race as a factor in any governmental decision had to be "narrowly tailored" to achieve a compelling state interest. When a state university's admissions decisions "touch upon an individual's race or ethnic background," wrote Powell, "he is entitled to a judicial determination that the burden he is asked to bear on that basis is precisely tailored to serve a compelling government interest" (*Bakke*, 438 U.S., at 299). (Because all selective private universities in

---

*Alex Zakaras wrote the introduction and selected the excerpts presented in this section.

the United States accept substantial amounts of state funding, Powell's opinion was broadly recognized as relevant to private as well as public universities.) The relevant government interest, Powell wrote, was "the attainment of a diverse student body" (*Bakke*, 311). Powell argued that nothing less than the "nation's future" hangs on its ability to train leaders "through wide exposure to the ideas and mores of students as diverse as this Nation of many peoples" (*Bakke*, 313). The state, then, had a strong interest in securing diversity in education—strong enough to justify the use of race as one factor among many in university admissions criteria. Powell was careful, however, to clearly state that the state's interest in such diversity could never be used to override the rights of individuals guaranteed by the Constitution.

Powell rejected a number of other rationales for affirmative action. First, he rejected the claim that, in its regulation of admissions policies, the state has a strong interest in redressing historical injustice. In Powell's view, the correction of some general historical injustice of society at large would lead to efforts at racial balancing that are far too broad to be respectful of individual rights. He also dismissed the claim that the state could sanction affirmative action in order to counteract the effects of current discrimination: "The purpose of helping certain groups whom the faculty of the Davis Medical School perceived as victims of 'societal discrimination' does not justify a classification that imposes disadvantages upon persons . . . who bear no responsibility" for this discrimination. Powell is here referring to qualified students of other races who would find it more difficult to be admitted to university because of affirmative action. Just as many conservative critics rejected his arguments on the value of diversity, many of his more liberal critics took issue with these latter positions. The *Bakke* opinion therefore remained controversial, although the law of the land, into the late 1990s.

In December 1997, Barbara Grutter, a white applicant who had recently been denied admission to the University of Michigan Law School, filed a lawsuit against the school. Grutter alleged that she had been the victim of racial discrimination, and that her application had therefore been unfairly rejected. Grutter had applied with a 3.8 GPA and a 161 LSAT score (in the same year, all three minority applicants with comparable scores were admitted). Her lawyers argued that the University of Michigan's admissions policy, which in their view allowed race to be used as a "predominant" factor in assessing applications, violated the Equal Protection Clause of the Fourteenth Amendment, and Title VI of the Civil Rights Act.

Grutter's lawsuit was intended as a direct challenge to the *Bakke* decision, and was taken up by the Supreme Court in 2002. The case, *Grutter v. Bollinger*, quickly became the focus of vigorous public debate. President George W. Bush's administration submitted a brief recommending that affirmative action be abolished (see "Brief for the United States" later), whereas several important American businesses, as well as high-ranking, retired military officers, submitted briefs defending affirmative action (see "Consolidated Amici Curiae Brief"). On June 23, 2003, *Grutter* was decided by a 5–4 margin with a majority opinion that, unlike in *Bakke*, all five justices in the majority signed. Justice Sandra Day O'Connor, who was widely considered the "swing" justice in the case, wrote the majority opinion. The court ruled in favor of the University of Michigan, reaffirming its commitment to the practice of affirmative action (Justice O'Connor's "syllabus" follows later).

O'Connor's decision cites, among many other things, the persistence of racial disparities in higher education. By the turn of the millennium, though the number of black students enrolled in four-year colleges had increased substantially, black adults were still much less likely than white adults to have achieved a college degree. While 34 percent of white adults (over the age of twenty-five) had completed four or more years of college, only 17.8 percent of black adults had done the same (U.S. Bureau of the Census, cited in the *Journal of Blacks in Higher Education,* Issue no. 36, Summer 2002).

The *Grutter* decision marked an important victory for defenders of affirmative action, although the shape of affirmative action policies—in practice or in theory—cannot be settled exclusively in the courts. The court, in its practical role, can pave the way for colleges and universities to engage in affirmative action if they so choose but it certainly cannot force college and universities to do so nor can it prevent legislatures and voters from making affirmative action illegal. The court, in its theoretical role, can articulate a case for the constitutional legitimacy and justice of affirmative action, but it cannot prevent citizens from offering up their own interpretations of constitutional legitimacy and justice. Even in the wake of *Grutter,* affirmative action therefore remains a live political issue—in state legislatures, election campaigns, and public referenda.

In fact, resolutions to end affirmative action were introduced to the legislatures of six states in 2003, including New York and Massachusetts. Activists were also collecting signatures for ballot initiatives to this effect in several other states, including Michigan. If approved by voters, these initiatives would prevent public schools from using race in admissions. Successful initiatives to this effect were passed in California in 1996 and the state of Washington in 1998. In part because of such initiatives, the issue remains a point of contention and debate during election campaigns, local and national.

BRIEF FOR THE UNITED STATES (AMICUS CURIAE SUPPORTING PETITIONER)

THEODORE B. OLSON, SOLICITOR GENERAL

January 16, 2003

The Equal Protection Clause of the Fourteenth Amendment provides that no state shall "deny to any person within its jurisdiction the equal protection of the laws."[1] Its central purpose is to guarantee "racial neutrality in governmental decision-making."[2] Thus, the Amendment seeks to "do away with all governmentally imposed discriminations based on race" and create "a Nation of equal citizens . . . where race is irrelevant to personal opportunity and achievement."[3] That is particularly true in the context of public educational institutions, which have a duty to "act in accordance with a 'core purpose of the Fourteenth Amendment.' "[4] In light of the critical role of education, public institutions must make educational opportunity "available to all on equal terms."[5]

· · ·

The Law School contends that its interest in enrolling a "diverse" student body is sufficiently compelling to justify its admitted use of racially discriminatory admissions standards (emphasizing that "racial and ethnic diversity in legal education is important both to a law school's mission in training effective lawyers, and to the perception that our legal system is able to administer equal justice"; citing evidence that "students learn more effectively when they are educated in racially and ethnically diverse environments," and "given our racial separation, Americans ordinarily have little contact with members of different racial groups, such that exposure to a diverse student body provides unique educational opportunities"). The Law School's interest in "diversity," however, cannot, as a matter of law, justify racial discrimination in admissions in light of the ample race-neutral alternatives.

Public Universities Have Ample Means to Ensure That Their Services Are Open and Available to All Americans

Ensuring that public institutions are open and available to all segments of American society, including people of all races and ethnicities, represents a paramount government objective. No segment of society should be denied an opportunity to obtain access to government services and public institutions. Nowhere is the importance of such openness more acute than in the context of higher education. A university degree opens the doors to the finest jobs and top professional schools, and a professional degree, in turn, makes it possible to practice law, medicine, and other professions. If undergraduate and graduate institutions are not open to all individuals and broadly inclusive to our diverse national community, then the top jobs, graduate schools, and the professions will be closed to some.

Nothing in the Constitution requires public universities and governments to close their eyes to this reality or to tolerate artificial obstacles to educational opportunity. Public universities have substantial latitude to tackle such problems and ensure that universities and other public institutions are open to all and that student bodies are experientially diverse and broadly representative of the public. Schools may identify and discard [apparently] neutral criteria that, in practice, tend to skew admissions in a manner that detracts from educational diversity. They may also adopt admissions policies that seek to promote experiential, geographical, political, or economic diversity in the student body, which are entirely appropriate race-neutral governmental objectives. The adoption of such policies, moreover, has led to racially diverse student bodies in other States. And public universities can address the desire for broad representation directly by opening educational institutions to the best students from throughout the State or Nation and easing admissions requirements for all students.

For example, in Texas, which has operated without race-based admissions policies since they were invalidated by the Fifth Circuit in 1996, the undergraduate admissions program focuses on attracting the top graduating students from throughout the State, including students from underrepresented areas. By attacking the problems of openness and educational opportunity directly, the Texas program has enhanced opportunity and promoted educational diversity by any measure. . . . Under this race-neutral admissions policy, "pre-Hopwood diversity levels were restored by 1998 or 1999 in the admitted and enrolled populations and have held steady."[6] Thus, in 1996, the last year race was used in University of Texas admissions decisions, four percent of enrolled freshmen were African Americans, 14 percent were Hispanic, and less than one percent were Native Americans. In 2002, three percent of enrolled freshmen were African American (this figure has fluctuated between four and three percent since 1997), 14 percent were Hispanic, and less than 1 percent were Native American. . . . Similar race-neutral programs are now in place in California and Florida and have had similar results.

· · ·

These Ample Race-Neutral Alternatives Render Respondents' Race-Based Policy Both Unnecessary and Unconstitutional

. . . Although respondents have not been clear about what they mean by diversity, we assume that they are not pursuing racial diversity for its own sake.[7] In any event, respondents' race-based policy is not necessary to ensure that minorities have access to and are represented in institutions of higher learning. The ability of race-neutral alternatives, such as those adopted in Texas, Florida, and California, to achieve diversity by any measure and however defined make clear that respondents' policy fails this fundamental tenet of the Court's narrow-tailoring decisions.[8]

In addition, to the extent the Law School seeks candidates with diverse backgrounds and experiences and viewpoints or "achievements in light of the barriers [an applicant has] had to overcome,"[9] it can focus on numerous race-neutral factors including a history of overcoming disadvantage, geographic origin, socioeconomic status, challenging living or family situations, reputation and location of high school, volunteer and work experiences, exceptional personal talents, leadership potential, communication skills, commitment and dedication to particular causes, extra-curricular activities, extraordinary expertise in a particular area, and individual outlook as reflected by essays. Such a system of seeking experiential diversity directly would lead to the admission of a more diverse student body than the Law School's current race-based admissions policy. Such programs have pro-duced school systems to which minorities have meaningful access and are represented in significant numbers, as the experience in Texas, Florida, and California demonstrates. Such a system would also avoid running afoul of the principle this Court has stressed in a wide variety of contexts that the Equal Protection Clause does not allow govern-mental decision-makers to presume that individuals, because of their race, gender, or ethnicity think alike or have common life experiences.

Indeed, such a race-neutral policy would be superior to race-based policies in numerous ways. It would treat all appli-cants as individuals. It would also focus on "a far broader array of qualifications and characteristics."[10] It would apply to minorities beyond those belonging to the currently preferred groups who have extraordinary life experiences, unusual motivation, or the ability to succeed in the face of significant obstacles. The Law School, however, has not sought to imple-ment its goals through race-neutral means. Instead, respondents have adopted a sys-tem that both applies substantial race-based preferences and ensures that a "critical mass" of particular minority groups are admitted. This failure to consider and implement efficacious race-neutral alternatives is sufficient to render the program unconstitutional. . . .

Other Requirements of This Court's
Narrow Tailoring[11] Analysis Reinforce
the Unconstitutionality of Respondents'
Race-Based Admissions Policy

. . . The Law School's admissions policy . . . "has no logical stopping point" and would permit racially discriminatory admissions standards in perpetuity.[12] The Law School's policy "provides no guidance . . . [as to] the . . . scope of the . . . [preference]" or how long race must be relied upon to attain it.[13] Indeed, the logic and inevitable outcome of the Law School's "critical mass" rationale would permit the univer-sity to rely on racial and ethnic admissions preferences indefinitely to obtain and sustain any racial balance, including proportional representation or "outright racial balancing," it believes contributes to its educational mission.[14]

Unlike remedial programs that, by design, aim for obsolescence by seeking to remedy the discrimination that justifies a race-based remedy, the pursuit of a critical mass of minority students has no logical stopping point. That pursuit would justify race-based measures that are "ageless in their reach . . . and timeless in their ability to affect the future,"[15] and would "assure that race will always be relevant in Ameri-can life, and that the 'ultimate goal' of 'eliminating entirely from governmental decision-making such irrelevant factors as a human being's race,' will never be achieved."[16] This Court has never found such an open-ended and potentially unlim-ited racial preference narrowly tailored.

The Law School's race-based admissions policy [also] unfairly burdens innocent third parties. The Court has recognized that "[t]he American people have always regarded edu-cation and [the] acquisition of knowledge as matters of supreme importance" in part because "education provides the basic tools by which individuals . . . lead economically productive lives to the benefit of us all."[17] It has also explained that government should not impose "barriers presenting unreason-able obstacles to advancement on the basis of individual merit" since "[t]he promise of equality under the law [ensures] that all citi-zens, regardless of race, ethnicity, or gender, have the chance to take part."[18] The Law School's discriminatory admissions criteria unfairly burden qualified applicants not subject to its preference by accepting favored minority candidates who have lesser objective qualifications. As the Court has explained, "[t]he exclusion of even one [person] ... for impermissible reasons harms that [individual] and undermines public confidence in the fairness of the system."[19]

In the final analysis, this case does not require this Court to break any new ground to hold that respondents' race-based admissions policy is unconstitutional. . . .

CONSOLIDATED *AMICI CURIAE* BRIEF

FROM RETIRED MILITARY LEADERS

February 19, 2003

Amici are former high ranking officers and civilian leaders of the Army, Navy, Air Force, and Marine Corps including former military academy superintendents, Secretaries of Defense and present and former members of the U.S. Senate. They are deeply interested in this case because its outcome could affect the diversity of our nation's officer corps and in turn the military's ability to fulfill its missions. Amici's judgment is based on decades of experience and accomplishment at the very highest positions in our nation's military leadership.

Based on decades of experience, *amici* have concluded that a highly qualified, racially diverse officer corps educated and trained to command our nation's racially diverse enlisted ranks is essential to the military's ability to fulfill its principal mission to provide national security. The primary sources for the nation's officer corps are the service academies and the ROTC, the latter comprised of students already admitted to participating colleges and universities. At present, the military cannot achieve an officer corps that is *both* highly qualified *and* racially diverse unless the service academies and the ROTC use limited race-conscious recruiting and admissions policies. . . .

More than 50 years ago, President Truman issued an executive order ending segregation in the United States armed services. That decision, and the resulting integration of the military, resulted not only from a principled recognition that segregation is unjust and incompatible with American values, but also from a practical recognition that the military's need for manpower and its efficient, effective deployment required integration. Since that time, men and women of all races have trained and fought together in our armed services, from Korea to Vietnam to Afghanistan. Today, almost 40 percent of servicemen and women are minorities; 61.7 percent are white, and the remaining almost 40 percent are minorities, including 21.7 percent African-American, 9.6 percent Hispanic, 4 percent Asian-American and 1.2 percent Native American.[20]

In the 1960s and 1970s, however, while integration increased the percentage of African-Americans in the enlisted ranks, the percentage of minority officers remained extremely low, and perceptions of discrimination were pervasive. This deficiency in the officer corps and the discrimination perceived to be its cause led to low morale and heightened racial tension. The danger this created was not theoretical, as the Vietnam era demonstrates. As that war continued, the armed forces suffered increased racial polarization, pervasive disciplinary problems, and racially motivated incidents in Vietnam and on posts around the world. "In Vietnam, racial tensions reached a point where there was an inability to fight."[21] By the early 1970s, racial strife in the ranks was entirely commonplace.[22] The lack of minority officers substantially exacerbated the problems throughout the armed services. For example, at the end of the Vietnam War, only three percent of Army officers were African-American.[23] The military's leadership "recognized that its racial problem was so critical that it was on the verge of self-destruction. That realization set in motion the policies and initiatives that have led to today's relatively positive state of affairs."[24]

"It is obvious and unarguable that no governmental interest is more compelling than the security of the Nation."[25] The absence of minority officers seriously threatened the military's ability to function effectively and fulfill its mission to defend the nation. To eliminate that threat, the armed services moved aggressively to increase the number of minority officers and to train officers in diverse educational environments. In full accord with *Bakke* and with the Department of Defense Affirmative Action Program, the service academies and the ROTC have set goals for minority officer candidates and worked hard to achieve those goals. They use financial and tutorial assistance, as well as recruiting programs, to expand the pool of highly qualified minority candidates in a variety of explicitly race-conscious ways. They also employ race as a factor in recruiting and admissions policies and decisions.

These efforts have substantially increased the percentage of minority officers. Moreover, increasing numbers of officer candidates are trained and educated in racially diverse educational settings, which provides them with invaluable experience for their future command of our nation's highly diverse enlisted ranks. Today, among active duty officers, 81 percent are white, and the remaining 19 percent are minority, including 8.8 percent African-American, four percent Hispanic, 3.2 percent Asian American, and .6 percent Native American. A substantial difference between the percentage of African-American enlisted personnel (21.7 percent) and African-American officers (8.8 percent) remains. The officer corps must continue to be diverse or the cohesiveness essential to the military mission will be critically undermined. . . .

Amici submit that the government's compelling interest in promoting racial diversity in higher education is buttressed by its compelling national security interest in a cohesive military. That requires both a diverse officer corps and substantial numbers of officers educated and trained in diverse educational settings, including the military academies and ROTC programs.[26] President George Washington eloquently underscored the vital importance of direct association among diverse individuals in education and in the profession of arms:

> [T]he Juvenal period of life, when friendships are formed, & habits established that will stick by one; the Youth, or young men from different parts of the United States would be assembled together, & would by degrees discover that there was not that cause for those jealousies & prejudices which one part of the Union had imbibed against another part. . . . What, but the mixing of people from different parts of the United States during the War rubbed off these impressions? A century in the ordinary intercourse, would not have accomplished what the Seven years association in Arms did.[27]

The crisis that resulted in integration of the officer corps is but a magnified reflection of circumstances in our nation's highly diverse society. In the 1960s and 1970s, the stark disparity between the racial composition of the rank and file and that of the officer corps fueled a breakdown of order that endangered the military's ability to fulfill its mission. That threat was so dangerous and unacceptable that it resulted in immediate and dramatic changes intended to restore minority enlisted ranks' confidence in the fairness and integrity of the institution. In a highly diverse society, the public, including minority citizens, must have confidence in the integrity of public institutions, particularly those educational institutions that provide the training, education and status necessary to achieve prosperity and power in America.

There is presently no workable alternative to limited, race-conscious programs to increase the pool of qualified minority officer candidates and establish diverse educational settings for officer candidates. Plainly, as respondents' briefs show, the alternative proposed by the United States—admission of students who achieve a specified class rank—is no alternative for private universities and colleges or for graduate schools or for any public institution with a national student body.

Equally to the point, the armed services must have racially diverse officer candidates who *also* satisfy the rigorous academic, physical, and personal prerequisites for officer training and future leadership. It is no answer to tell selective institutions, such as the service academies or the ROTC, automatically to admit students with a specified class rank, even if such a system were administratively workable. This lone criterion mandates the admission of students unable to satisfy the academic, physical, and character-related demands of the service academies or the officer training curriculum. Moreover, even if the pool of minority ROTC candidates remains quantitatively stable, such a policy will reduce the number of high quality minority candidates for ROTC scholarships. Minority candidates are not fungible in the way the government's proposed alternative suggests. In the interest of national security, the military must be selective in admissions for training and education for the officer corps, *and* it must train and educate a highly qualified, racially diverse officer corps in a racially diverse educational setting.

It requires only a small step from this analysis to conclude that our country's other most selective institutions must remain both diverse and selective. Like our military security, our economic security and international competitiveness depend upon it. An alternative that does not preserve both diversity and selectivity is no alternative at all. Nor does telling the military to work harder to recruit high quality minority candidates make sense. Each service already has numerous aggressive minority recruiting programs and expends significant funds and human resources on service preparatory academies and other programs in efforts to increase the pool of qualified minority candidates. As the growing percentage of minority officers reveals, the military services are making substantial progress toward diverse, highly qualified leadership—progress envied by other institutions in our society. That progress must be protected and must continue. The admissions policies of the service academies and the ROTC reflect a collective military judgment—that the carefully tailored consideration of race in the admission and training of officer candidates is essential to an integrated officer corps and hence to our fighting force. Today, there is no race-neutral alternative that will fulfill the military's and the nation's compelling need for a diverse officer corps of the highest quality to serve the country.

"SYLLABUS" (SUMMARY OF DECISION), *GRUTTER V. BOLLINGER et al.*

SANDRA DAY O'CONNOR

June 23, 2003

The Law School's narrowly tailored use of race in admissions decisions to further a compelling interest in obtaining the educational benefits that flow from a diverse student body is not prohibited by the Equal Protection Clause, Title VI, or § 1981.

A. In the landmark *Bakke* case, this Court reviewed a medical school's racial set-aside program that reserved 16 out of 100 seats for members of certain minority groups. The decision produced six separate opinions, none of which commanded a majority. Four Justices would have upheld the program on the ground that the government can use race to remedy disadvantages cast on minorities by past racial prejudice. Four other Justices would have struck the program down on statutory grounds. Justice Powell, announcing the Court's judgment, provided a fifth vote not only for invalidating the program, but also for reversing the state court's injunction against any use of race whatsoever. In a part of his opinion that was joined by no other Justice, Justice Powell expressed his view that attaining a diverse student body was the only interest asserted by the university that survived scrutiny. Grounding his analysis in the academic freedom that "long has been viewed as a special concern of the First Amendment,"[28] Justice Powell emphasized that the " 'nation's future depends upon leaders trained through wide exposure' to the ideas and mores of students as diverse as this Nation."[29] However, he also emphasized that "[i]t is not an interest in simple ethnic diversity, in which a specified percentage of the student body is in effect guaranteed to be members of selected ethnic groups," that can justify using race.[30] Rather, "[t]he diversity that furthers a compelling state interest encompasses a far broader array of qualifications and characteristics of which racial or ethnic origin is but a single though important element."[31]

Since *Bakke,* Justice Powell's opinion has been the touchstone for constitutional analysis of race-conscious admissions policies. Public and private universities across the Nation have modeled their own admissions programs on Justice Powell's views. Courts, however, have struggled to discern whether Justice Powell's diversity rationale is binding precedent. The Court finds it unnecessary to decide this issue because the Court endorses Justice Powell's view that student body diversity is a compelling state interest in the context of university admissions.

B. All government racial classifications must be analyzed by a reviewing court under strict scrutiny.[32] But not all such uses are invalidated by strict scrutiny. Race-based action necessary to further a compelling governmental interest does not violate the Equal Protection Clause so long as it is narrowly tailored to further that interest.[33] Context matters when reviewing such action.[34] Not every decision influenced by race is equally objectionable, and strict scrutiny is designed to provide a framework for carefully examining the importance and the sincerity of the government's reasons for using race in a particular context.

C. The Court endorses Justice Powell's view that student body diversity is a compelling state interest that can justify using race in university admissions. The Court defers to the Law School's educational judgment that diversity is essential to its educational mission. The Court's scrutiny of that interest is no less strict for taking into account complex educational judgments in an area that lies primarily within the university's expertise. Attaining a diverse student body is at the heart of the Law School's proper institutional mission, and its "good faith" is "presumed" absent "a showing to the contrary."[35] Enrolling a "critical mass" of minority students simply to assure some specified percentage of a particular group merely because of its race or ethnic origin would be patently unconstitutional. But the Law School defines its critical mass concept by reference to the substantial, important, and laudable educational benefits that diversity is designed to produce, including cross-racial understanding and the breaking down of racial stereotypes.

The Law School's claim is further bolstered by numerous expert studies and reports showing that such diversity promotes learning outcomes and better prepares students for an increasingly diverse workforce, for society, and for the legal profession. Major American businesses have made clear that the skills needed in today's increasingly global marketplace can only be developed through exposure to widely diverse people, cultures, ideas, and viewpoints. High-ranking retired officers and civilian military leaders assert that a highly qualified, racially diverse officer corps is essential to national security. Moreover, because universities, and in particular, law schools, represent the training ground for a large number of the Nation's leaders, the path to leadership must be visibly open to talented and qualified individuals of every race and ethnicity. Thus, the Law School has a compelling interest in attaining a diverse student body.

D. The Law School's admissions program bears the hallmarks of a narrowly tailored plan. To be narrowly tailored, a race-conscious admissions program cannot "insulat[e] each category of applicants with certain desired qualifications from competition with all other applicants."[36] Instead, it may consider race or ethnicity only as a " 'plus' in a particular applicant's file"; *i.e.,* it must be "flexible enough to consider all pertinent elements of diversity in light of the particular qualifications of each applicant, and to place them on the same footing for consideration, although not necessarily according them the same weight."[37] It follows that universities cannot establish quotas for members of certain racial or ethnic groups or put them on separate admissions tracks. The Law School's admissions program, like the Harvard plan approved by Justice Powell, satisfies these requirements. Moreover, the program is flexible enough to ensure that each applicant is evaluated as an individual and not in a way that makes race or ethnicity the defining feature of the application.

The Law School engages in a highly individualized, holistic review of each applicant's file, giving serious consideration to all the ways an applicant might contribute to a diverse educational environment. There is no policy, either *de jure* or *de facto,* of automatic acceptance or rejection based on any single "soft" variable. Also, the program adequately ensures that all factors that may contribute to diversity are meaningfully considered alongside race. Moreover, the Law School frequently accepts nonminority applicants with grades and test scores lower than underrepresented minority applicants (and other nonminority applicants) who are rejected. The Court rejects the argument that the Law School should have used other race-neutral means to obtain the educational benefits of student body diversity, *e.g.,* a lottery system or decreasing the emphasis on GPA and LSAT scores. Narrow tailoring does not require exhaustion of every conceivable race-neutral alternative or mandate that a

university choose between maintaining a reputation for excellence or fulfilling a commitment to provide educational opportunities to members of all racial groups.

The Court is satisfied that the Law School adequately considered the available alternatives. The Court is also satisfied that, in the context of individualized consideration of the possible diversity contributions of each applicant, the Law School's race-conscious admissions program does not unduly harm nonminority applicants. Finally, race-conscious admissions policies must be limited in time. The Court takes the Law School at its word that it would like nothing better than to find a race-neutral admissions formula and will terminate its use of racial preferences as soon as practicable. The Court expects that 25 years from now, the use of racial preferences will no longer be necessary to further the interest approved today.

NOTES

1. U.S. Const. Amend. XIV.
2. *Miller v. Johnson, 515 U.S. 900, 904 (1995).* Accord *Washington v. Davis, 426 U.S. 229, 239 (1976).*
3. *Wygant v. Jackson Bd. of Educ., 476 U.S. 267, 277 (1986)* (quoting *Palmore v. Sidoti, 466 U.S. 429, 432 (1984));* *Croson, 488 U.S. at 505–506.*
4. *Wygant, 476 U.S. at 277 (plurality opinion) (quoting Palmore, 466 U.S. at 432);* see *Brown v. Board of Educ., 347 U.S. 483 (1954); Sweatt v. Painter, 339 U.S. 629 (1950).*
5. *Plyer v. Doe, 457 U.S. 202, 223 (1982).*
6. Gary M. Lavergne & Dr. Bruce Walker, *Implementation and Results of the Texas Automatic Admissions Law (HB 588) at the University of Texas at Austin* 3 (last modified Jan. 13, 2003) <http://www.utexas.edu/student/research/reports/ admissions HB588-Report5.pdf>.
7. See *Bakke, 438 U.S. at 307* (opinion of Powell, J.) ("[p]referring members of any one group for no reason other than race or ethnic origin is discrimination for its own sake").
8. The justices offer the following explanation of the "narrow tailoring" requirement in a headnote to *Grutter* (Thomas dissenting): "(1) To be narrowly tailored, a race-conscious admissions program cannot (a) use a quota system; (b) put members of certain racial groups on separate admissions tracks; or (c) insulate applicants who belong to certain racial or ethnic groups from the competition for

admission. (2) Instead, a university may consider race or ethnicity only as a "plus" in a particular applicant's file, without insulating the applicant from comparison with all other applicants for the available seats. (3) An admissions program must be flexible enough to (a) consider all pertinent elements of diversity in light of the particular qualifications of each applicant, and (b) place the elements on the same footing for consideration, although not necessarily according them the same weight" [footnote not in original brief].

9. *DeFunis v. Odegaard, 416 U.S. 312, 331 (1974)* (Douglas, J., dissenting).

10. *Bakke, 438 U.S. at 315* (opinion of Powell, J.).

11. *See note 8 above.*

12. *Croson, 488 U.S. at 498*; see *Wygant, 476 U.S. at 275* (plurality opinion); *Metro Broad., 497 U.S. at 613, 614* (O'Connor, J., dissenting).

13. *Croson, 488 U.S. at 498* (quoting *Wygant, 476 U.S. at 275*).

14. *Metro Broad., 497 U.S. at 625* (O'Connor, J., dissenting) (quoting *Croson, 488 U.S. at 507*).

15. *Wygant, 476 U.S. at 276; accord Croson, 488 U.S. at 497–498.*

16. *Croson, 488 U.S. at 495* (quoting *Wygant, 476 U.S. at 320* (Stevens, J., dissenting) (footnote omitted)).

17. *Plyler, 457 U.S. at 221* (quoting *Meyer v. Nebraska, 262 U.S. 390, 400 (1923)*).

18. *Plyler, 457 U.S. at 222; J.E.B. v. Alabama ex rel. T.B., 511 U.S. 127, 146 (1994); Georgia v. McCollum, 505 U.S. 42, 59 (1992)* (quoting *Ristaino v. Ross, 424 U.S. 589, 596 n.8 (1976)*).

19. *J.E.B., 511 U.S. at 142 n.13; see Bakke, 438 U.S. at 361* (opinion of Brennan, White, Marshall & Blackmun, JJ.) (noting that "advancement sanctioned, sponsored, or approved by the State should ideally be based on individual merit or achievement, or at least on factors within the control of an individual").

20. Dep't of Def. ("DoD"), Statistical Series Pamphlet No. 02–5, *Semiannual Race/Ethnic/Gender Profile by Service/Rank of the Department of*

Defense & Coast Guard 4 (Mar. 2002) ("*DoD Report*").

21. D. Maraniss, "United States Military Struggles to Make Equality Work," *Washington Post,* Mar. 6, 1990, at A01 (quoting Lt. Gen. Frank Petersen, Jr.).

22. B. Nalty, *Strength For The Fight: A History Of Black Americans In the Military* (1986) 308–10.

23. Office of the Undersecretary of Def. Personnel & Readiness, *Career Progression of Minority and Women Officers* v (1999) ("*Career Progression*"). Research Project, *Diversity: 2015 and the Afro-American Army Officer* (1998) 2–3.

24. *Ibid.,* at 3.

25. *Haig* v. *Agee,* 453 U. S. 280, 307 (1981) (internal quotations omitted).

26. See *Haig,* 453 U. S. at 307; *Sweatt* v. *Painter,* 339 U. S. 629, 634 (1950) (students in racially-homogenous classrooms are ill-prepared for productive lives in our diverse society).

27. Letter from Pres. George Washington to Alexander Hamilton (Sept. 1, 1796), *reproduced in* J. Ellis, *Founding Brothers: The Revolutionary Generation* 960–61 (2001).

28. 438 U.S., at 312, 314, 98 S.Ct. 2733,

29. *Id.,* at 313, 98 S.Ct. 2733.

30. *Id.,* at 315, 98 S.Ct. 2733.

31. *Ibid.*

32. Justice O'Connor later defines this standard as follows: "this means that such classifications are constitutional only if they are narrowly tailored to further compelling governmental interests."

33. *E.g., Shaw v. Hunt, 517 U.S. 899, 908, 116 S.Ct. 1894, 135 L.Ed.2d 207.*

34. See *Gomillion v. Lightfoot,* 364 U.S. 339, 343–344, 81 S.Ct. 125, 5 L.Ed.2d 110.

35. 438 U.S., at 318–319, 98 S.Ct. 2733.

36. *Bakke, supra,* at 315, 98 S.Ct. 2733 (opinion of Powell, J.).

37. *Id.,* at 317, 98 S.Ct. 2733.

Comment

The principle of equal opportunity requires that admissions to selective colleges and universities be done on a nondiscriminatory basis, but what does nondiscrimination mean in this context? The Fourteenth Amendment to the U.S. Constitution prohibits denying any person within its jurisdiction "the equal protection of the laws." Equal protection of the laws is the constitutional language of nondiscrimination, but it is no more self-interpreting than its sister principle of nondiscrimination in specific contexts such as the admissions decisions of selective universities.

The briefs in this case along with Justice O'Connor's majority opinion articulate many of the moral arguments for and against the admissions policy of Michigan Law School, which considers identification as a member of a disadvantaged racial group as one among many applicable characteristics of an applicant relevant to its admission decisions. On what moral grounds should a law school consider race as one among many relevant characteristics? In the earlier *Bakke* decision, Justice Powell wrote that securing racial diversity in a university student body is a compelling state interest. Writing for the majority in the *Grutter* case, Justice O'Connor affirms Powell's earlier opinion. What does it mean in moral terms, as distinct from constitutional terms, to say that racial diversity in a university student body is a compelling state interest? Consider both the educational and the societal benefits that can be a consequence of racial diversity in universities and professional schools. Does racial diversity in a student body necessarily bring such benefits or must universities take additional steps to ensure that they will be forthcoming?

What are the strongest arguments made by those who would deny universities the right to aim for racial diversity in their admission policies? Evaluate the arguments offered in favor of color-blindness in admissions and against taking race into account even as one among many qualifications for admission. Does it make any moral difference whether race is considered one among many qualifications of applicants as distinct from a preponderant qualification? If not, does the ideal of equal opportunity in higher education support or prohibit the use of race in admissions? What are the other moral perspectives from which affirmative action can be assessed? If it is defensible depending on the circumstances, what are the relevant circumstances?

In the government's amicus brief, Solicitor General Olson argues that color-blindness or racial neutrality in governmental decisions must be a basic commitment of any society committed to the principle of equal protection of the law. At the same time, Olson recommends that colleges use racially neutral admissions criteria that select students partly on the basis of their "geographical, political, or economic" characteristics. Is there any moral principle that would treat race differently from these other characteristics? Is discrimination in favor of members of a disadvantaged racial group different either in kind or in its social consequences from discrimination in favor of a disadvantaged class or regional identity?

Critics of affirmative action based on race have argued that it advantages students of color who have otherwise privileged backgrounds. These critics argue that affirmative action at selective universities thereby perpetuates exclusion of the truly disadvantaged students, those who come from poor families. What evidence would be needed to evaluate this argument? Is an argument in favor of affirmative action based on class consistent with the arguments presented by opponents to race-based affirmative action in the Michigan case? Assess the meaning of the term "diversity" as it is used by the various participants in the Michigan admissions debate. Are certain kinds of diversity more educationally and socially important than others, and if so why?

In concluding her opinion affirming the constitutionality of using race as one among many factors in law school admissions, Justice O'Connor expresses the expectation that affirmative action policies will become obsolete in twenty-five years. What might a defender of affirmative action today expect to change in the next twenty-five years? If conditions do not change as O'Connor expects, should her successors revise their assessment of the legitimate term of affirmative action policies? Consider why affirmative action policies might be considered defensible only as temporary remedies on the way to a society of equal opportunity for all. Is there any argument for considering affirmative action policies of some kind—whether based on race, class, or some other social marker of disadvantage—to be a more permanent feature of the political landscape of a diverse democracy?

The race-neutral admissions policy that Olson describes was adopted by Texas universities in the wake of the *Hopwood* decision. The brief by retired military leaders suggests that the Texas model is unworkable for private institutions, or for public institutions that aim at attracting a national pool of students. What would "workable" mean if the moral premise is that race cannot be a consideration in university admissions? Are there other race-neutral alternatives that could work for such institutions?

The authors of the military leaders' brief offer an argument grounded in equality: in a society of equal opportunity, the proportion of black officers as well as black enlisted men and women in the military should match that of society as a whole. They argue that most soldiers themselves believe in the importance of this kind of equality, and that its violation adversely affects troop morale.

Consider, more generally with regard to other kinds of social policy, whether taking race into account is (1) wrong in principle, (2) wrong because of its societal effects, (3) wrong because of its impact on individuals, or (4) defensible depending on the circumstances? If wrong in principle, does your principle admit any exceptions? If wrong because of its societal effects, what effects make taking race into account wrong? If wrong because of its impact on individuals, what effects make it wrong? If defensible depending on what circumstances, which circumstances and why?

The Vouchers That Made Milwaukee Famous*

Educational vouchers are tuition subsidies for students in public schools to attend private schools. They were first introduced in the 1950s as a method of improving the quality of elementary and secondary education. Publicly funded voucher programs have been instituted in Milwaukee, Wisconsin, and Cleveland, Ohio, with many other states preparing pilot programs of publicly or privately funded vouchers.

The Milwaukee Parental Choice Program (MPCP) is the nation's oldest program giving low-income families vouchers of up to $5,882 to enroll their children in private schools of their choice. It has grown from 341 students at seven schools in 1990–1991 to more than 13,000 students at some 100 schools in 2003–2004.

The Milwaukee plan is a means-tested voucher plan: MPCP students come from

*Sigal Ben-Porath wrote the introduction and selected the excerpts presented in this section.

Milwaukee families with incomes at or below 175 percent of the federal poverty level ($32,532 for a family of four in 2003–2004). Private schools participating in the program must admit all eligible choice students and use a random selection process when applications exceed available space.

When it began in 1990 the Milwaukee voucher program included only nonreligious schools that agreed to participate in the program. In 1995 the program was expanded to provide vouchers for children attending religious schools, but it stipulates that any such school must excuse a student from participation in any religious instruction or activity at the request of the child's parent or guardian. This expansion of the program was challenged by a number of interested parties, and hence did not go into affect until 1998–1999.

When religious schools were finally allowed to be included in the program, the number of voucher-funded students quadrupled to 6,050. Prior to the inclusion of religious schools, only Milwaukee taxpayers paid for the voucher program. However, when expansion to religious schools quadrupled the costs, the legislature spread the cost statewide, charging taxpayers from every school district outside of Milwaukee for half of the $28 million price tag. Participating schools could receive a payment for each voucher student equal to a school's per-student expenditure, up to a maximum of $4,894. Participating private and religious schools were required to submit audited financial data to the state to qualify for this funding.

After adjusting for services that private schools do not provide (e.g., special education), on average, private schools participating in the program spent about the same per pupil as the city's public schools. Total charges in high-cost religious schools were almost the same as the costs in the public system. Low-cost religious schools spent about $4,000 per pupil, while nonreligious schools spent about $6,300 per pupil. A report published in 2001 claimed that the taxpayer cost of a voucher student is almost double the tuition that nonvoucher parents paid in the same private school.[1]

The program was endorsed and supported by national groups, among them religious organizations of various denominations, the Bradley Foundation, the Milton and Rose Friedman Foundation, and the Black Alliance for Educational Options (BAEO). The program was prominently opposed by, among other organizations, the National Education Association, the American Federation of Teachers, and the American Civil Liberties Union.

The controversy over the Milwaukee voucher plan encapsulates ongoing debates about the moral purposes of public education, the meaning of equal educational opportunity, and the proper understanding of the separation of church and State.

I. PURPOSES OF PUBLIC EDUCATION

SUPPORTING VOUCHERS

Excerpts from the Wisconsin Supreme Court Opinion
(*Davis v. Grover,* 166 Wis. 2d 501)

III.   The Public Purpose Doctrine

. . . In considering questions of "public purpose," a legislative determination of public purpose should be given great weight because " 'the hierarchy of community values is best determined by the will of the electorate' and that 'legislative decisions are more representative of popular opinion because individuals have greater access to their legislative representatives." (Citations omitted). Without clear evidence of unconstitutionality, "the court cannot further weigh the adequacy of the need or the wisdom of the method" chosen by the legislature to satisfy the public purpose. . . . No party disputes that education constitutes a valid public purpose, nor that private schools may be employed to further that purpose. Rather, the parties

dispute whether the private schools participating in the MPCP are under proper
government control and supervision
. . .

[The opponents of vouchers] contend
the controls in the MPCP over participating private schools are woefully inadequate and insist that these schools be
subject to the stricter requirements of sec.
121.02, Stats. MPCP advocates, on the
other hand, believe the statutory controls
applicable to private schools coupled with
parental involvement suffice to ensure the
public purpose is met. The circuit court
agreed with the MPCP advocates' contention, as we do . . .
Under sec. 118.165, Stats., a private school
must:

(1) Be organized to primarily provide
private or religious-based education;

(2) Be privately controlled;

(3) Provide at least 875 hours of instruction each school year;

(4) Provide a sequentially progressive
curriculum of fundamental instructions in
reading, language arts, mathematics, social
studies, science, and health;

(5) Not be operated or instituted for the
purpose of avoiding or circumventing com-
pulsory school attendance;

(6) Have pupils return home not less
than two months of each year unless the
institution is also licensed as a child welfare agency.

Even though private schools are not subject to the same amount of controls that are
applicable to public schools, they are subject
to a significant amount of regulation, which is
geared toward providing a sequentially progressive curriculum. This issue is uniquely
complicated, however, by the underlying
thesis of the MPCP that less bureaucracy
coupled with parental choice improves educational quality.

Keenly aware of this potential problem,
the legislature included within the MPCP
sufficient supervision and control measures.
The State Superintendent is required to
annually report to the legislature comparing
the students participating in the MPCP with
students in the MPS. The report includes
data on academic achievement, daily attendance, percentage of dropouts, and percentage of pupils suspended and expelled. The
State Superintendent is authorized to conduct financial and performance audits on
the program, and the Legislative Audit
Bureau is mandated to perform financial
and performance evaluation.

We believe that these detailed reports and
evaluations in conjunction with the private
school requirements . . . provide sufficient
and reasonable control under the circumstances to attain the public purpose to which
this legislation is directed.

Control is also fashioned within the
MPCP in the form of parental choice. Parents generally know their children better
than anyone. The program allows participating parents to choose a school with an
environment that matches their child's personality, with a curriculum that matches
their child's interest and needs, and with a
location that is convenient. If the private
school does not meet the parents' expectations, the parents may remove the child
from the school and go elsewhere. In this
way, parental choice preserves accountability for the best interests of the children.

In *Wisconsin v. Yoder,* 406 U.S. 205
(1972), the United States Supreme Court
also recognized the importance and the
strong tradition of parental choice in education. Using a balancing of interests test, the
Yoder Court held that the First and Fourteenth amendments prevent the state from
compelling Amish parents to cause their
children to attend formal high school to age
sixteen. In so deciding, it stated:

> Providing public schools ranks at the very
> apex of the function of a State. Yet even this
> paramount responsibility . . . yield[s] to the
> right of parents to provide an equivalent
> education in a privately operated system.

Yoder involved the protection of the Religion Clauses, whereas the present case
involves purely secular considerations.

However, the *Yoder* Court declared that purely secular considerations "may not be interposed as a barrier to reasonable state regulation of education." We have determined in this case that the reporting and private school requirements applicable to the MPCP provide sufficient and reasonable state control under the circumstances.

Further, the cost of education and the funds available for education are dependent upon the taxpayers' ability to fund an intensive public educational program. The amount of money allocated to a private school participating in the MPCP to educate a participating student is less than 40 percent of the full cost of educating that same student in the MPS. . . . This amount is inconsequential compared to the more than $6.4 billion that is annually expended for public education in Wisconsin. The amount of money to fund the MPCP represents only about four one-hundredths of one percent (.04 percent) of the public money allocated for public education throughout the state. Therefore, we hold that the MPCP does not violate the public purpose doctrine because the MPCP contains sufficient and reasonable controls to attain its public purpose.

CONCUR: LOUIS J. CECI, J. (concurring).

Let's give choice a chance!

Literally thousands of school children in the Milwaukee public school system have been doomed because of those in government who insist upon maintaining the status quo . . .

The Wisconsin legislature, attuned and attentive to the appalling and seemingly insurmountable problems confronting socioeconomically deprived children, has attempted to throw a life preserver to those Milwaukee children caught in the cruel riptide of a school system floundering upon the shoals of poverty, status-quo thinking, and despair. . . . The reason why the legislature adopted the classification of private schools specifically located in the city of Milwaukee is that the Milwaukee public school system evidently is viewed by the legislature as a failure despite the dedicated labors of its hundreds of teachers and administrators. Perhaps this experimental program will point the way for improvements that can be utilized throughout the public schools of this state.

. . . The fashioning of a constitutional system of public education is not only the legislature's constitutional prerogative, it is far better equipped than any court to do it. I am not unaware of the terrible political complexities involved in fashioning such legislation, but I have full confidence in the legislature's ability to resolve it.

. . . Apparently the legislature has decided in this constitutionally proper experimental program to give choice a chance. I believe that the legislature has fashioned a constitutionally correct experimental program to deal with the terrible problems it is attempting to resolve. I join the majority opinion, with which I am in full accord.

Let's give choice a chance!

OPPOSING VOUCHERS

White Paper Prepared for U.S. Secretary of Education Richard W. Riley for a Speech at the National Press Club, Washington, D.C. (September 23, 1997)

Vouchers Threaten the Fundamental Mission of Public Education

Using public tax dollars for private school vouchers fundamentally undermines 200 years of public education in America. As Neil Postman has suggested in his book *The End of Education,* ". . . public education does not serve the public. It creates the public. And in creating the right kind of public, the schools contribute toward strengthening the spiritual basis of the American Creed. That is how Jefferson understood it, how Horace Mann understood it, how John Dewey understood it." Private school vouchers strike at this ideal because they would:

- **Divert attention from the need to improve the public schools.** Providing private school vouchers for a few children will not help to improve the quality of education for most of America's children. Expanded choice in public schools through magnet schools and charter schools, coupled with a focus on the basics, increased parent involvement, improved teaching, and high standards for achievement and discipline, can do far more to improve the education of *all* children than private school vouchers for a few. The purpose of any school improvement idea should be to invite effective innovation in more schools, particularly those schools that are lagging behind.

- **Add to the public cost of education.** A voucher system would substantially increase the public cost of education by providing public funds to pay private school tuition for children who are already enrolled in private schools. If a voucher program open to all students were implemented today, it would cost American taxpayers over $15 billion to pay the tuitions of the 5 million students already enrolled in private schools. . . .

- **Reduce accountability.** Vouchers could create a situation at the elementary/secondary school level analogous to that at the postsecondary level; in the last four years, 700 for-profit schools in our nation's higher education system were removed from the federal loan program by the U.S. Department of Education because of their misuse of federal tax dollars. Private schools operate outside of the scope of public authority, and therefore have no public accountability for providing a quality education to all students.

- **Force private and parochial schools to become less private and less parochial.** If a system-wide voucher program were adopted, the influx of public dollars into these unregulated schools would result in increased pressure for greater public scrutiny and accountability for these public expenditures. Quality private and parochial schools are valuable parts of the educational variety in our democracy, and these pressures would ultimately interfere with their unique missions and curricula.

Expanding the options available to students and families is a worthy goal, as long as this is not done in a way that undermines a quality education for all children. But private school vouchers are too small, too costly, and too divisive to have any potential for improving the public school system.

II. EQUAL EDUCATIONAL OPPORTUNITY

SUPPORTING VOUCHERS

Annette "Polly" Williams[2]

In 1988, Governor Tommy Thompson (Republican) submitted a budget which included the Parental Choice Bill: a voucher program for up to 1 percent of Milwaukee's children. The poorest children would receive a $1,000 grant to attend any private nonsectarian school in the Milwaukee area.

The Republican bill found an unexpected supporter in State Representative Annette "Polly" Williams, a black activist and former welfare mother. When Williams failed to enlist support for some revisions she favored in the Parental Choice Bill, she introduced her own bill. She refined the proposal through a series of community meetings during 1989–1990. At a hearing on the topic which the Urban Education Committee called, a large crowd of school choice supporters gathered, among them many black parents. At the hearing, Williams said:

> This is a step in the right direction toward dealing with the problem of education in our city. . . . [The bill] empowers parents to make the ultimate decision for their children. None of the other things [legislators can do] will make a difference unless they empower parents.

Williams rejected committee members' contentions that some low-income parents do not have the aptitude to choose alternatives to the public school system, or that the proposed bill would pull out the top students from the public school system. She charged that such objections were racist:

> I've heard the excuse: if you are poor, you're stupid. Until you have parents as part of

everything, until you incorporate them, nothing will change . . . are you concerned about the 70% White flight from MPS [Milwaukee public schools] or Black students who leave MPS for suburban schools? It's ironic that the only time concern is raised is when poor people talk about educational alternatives. Why penalize poor parents, saying you have to stay and keep the system alive. The state is spending a lot of money to help middle-class families make more choices, but when it comes to poor people, it's a different standard.

Among the poor, predominantly black community of Milwaukee's inner city, parental choice began to emerge as the favored solution to the problems of the system of public education. In a city where many public schools were failing, many parents felt that the opportunity to choose a private school for their children would help overcome the educational and social disadvantages they faced. Some black organizations, most notably the Black Alliance for Educational Options (BAEO), continued to support the Choice program in Milwaukee as well as in other areas around the United States, even as more moderate groups such as the NAACP opposed it.

OPPOSING VOUCHERS

The American Teachers Federation and American Educational Association

The American Teachers Federation has long held that the voucher system is a waste of taxpayers' money. They maintain that smaller class sizes and other investments in existing programs could serve all students in the underachieving Milwaukee public school system, rather than the small proportion that would benefit from vouchers. Along with the National Education Organization and other oppositional groups it sponsored a number of legal challenges to the Milwaukee vouchers plan.

In July 1997 AFT released the position paper that follows.

Milwaukee Voucher Program a Poor Investment
At What Price to Public School Students?

In 1996–97, about 1,650 students received vouchers worth $4,400, at a cost to taxpayers of over $7 million. By contrast, 100,000 students attended MPS in 1996–97. How could the $7 million spent on vouchers have otherwise been spent to help public school students? Here are a couple of examples:

- **Higher Academic Standards.** Two years ago, MPS scrapped a multiple-choice math test they had used since the late 1970s in favor of a much more rigorous test. The test also came with a new rule: Students who don't pass won't graduate. Of the first Milwaukee high school students who took the test, 79 percent failed. School leaders, teachers, parents and students banded together to improve achievement. High schools started after- school and Saturday tutoring sessions in math. The city shifted funds to help. Churches and businesses donated supplies and volunteered tutors. After a lot of hard work, more than 80 percent of the first Milwaukee high school class to take the test passed it. If MPS had had an additional $7 million to spend on professional development, smaller class sizes and more tutoring programs, the evidence suggests the number could have been even higher.

- **Investing in What Works.** Researchers have focused a lot of attention on identifying effective academic programs for elementary school students. One such program is called Success for All. Extensive long-term research in Success for All schools throughout the U.S. shows that Success for All fifth graders read a full grade level higher than their non-Success for All counterparts, with results even more dramatic for at-risk children. Program designer Robert Slavin estimates that it costs between $40,000 and $55,000 to cover the total cost of materials and training for a Success for All school of 500 students.

What this means is that, for $7 million (the money spent on vouchers), Success for All could have been implemented in every public elementary school in Milwaukee (there are 113 total), serving 56,665 kids—with more than $1 million to spare. . . .

- **Education dollars are scarce.** Taxpayers in Wisconsin have already spent millions of dollars (not counting court costs) on a voucher program that has yielded no discernible academic benefits to students. Instead of being distracted by promises to save a handful of students with unproven fads like vouchers, we could be saving the overwhelming majority of youngsters by investing in proven public school reforms: high standards of conduct and academic achievement. Americans of all backgrounds are deeply committed to public education, not vouchers. Americans want high standards of conduct and achievement in our public schools, not vouchers. And high standards of conduct and achievement work. This nation's schoolchildren—90 percent of whom attend public schools—deserve no less.

The National Education Association's Official Position on Vouchers

The Educational Case against Vouchers

Student achievement ought to be the driving force behind any education reform initiative. . . .

Americans want consistent standards for students. Where vouchers are in place—Milwaukee, Cleveland, and Florida—a two-tiered system has been set up that holds students in public and private schools to different standards.

NEA and its affiliates support direct efforts to improve public schools. There is no need to set up new threats to schools for not performing. What is needed is help for the students, teachers, and schools who are struggling. A voucher lottery is a terrible way to determine access to an education. True equity means the ability for every child to attend a good school in the neighborhood.

Vouchers were not designed to help low-income children. Milton Friedman, the "grandfather" of vouchers, dismissed the notion that vouchers could help low-income families, saying "it is essential that no conditions be attached to the acceptance of vouchers that interfere with the freedom of private enterprises to experiment." A pure voucher system would only encourage economic, racial, ethnic, and religious stratification in our society. America's success has been built on our ability to unify our diverse populations.

III.   Church-State Relations

A large proportion of private schools in the United States have a religious affiliation and provides some amount of religious instruction. Opponents of a voucher system argue that aid to religious schools violates the proper separation of church and state by providing public funding to religious schools, while threatening both religious liberty and nonsectarian public education. Voucher advocates respond that the support for religious schools through publicly funded vouchers does not undermine the separation of church and state, because the schools remain private; it merely allows all parents—not only the wealthy—to choose a desirable education for their children.

Four years after the MPCP began operating, the Wisconsin legislature decided to expand the program to include religious schools. This increased public controversy as both proponents and opponents enlisted further support for their causes. The charge that the program blurred the constitutional separation of church and state generated a surge of legal challenges and public contests. The fact that the amended bill included an "opt-out" provision, which allowed a parent or guardian to withdraw their children from religious instruction in the school of their choice, did not solve the matter. Many claimed that because the whole school day was infused with religious instruction, the partial exemption did not avoid the entanglement of church and state. In addition, the demand that students be selected randomly was apparently violated by many parochial schools who gave precedence to parishioners. In 1999, an alliance of voucher opponents—the NAACP and the People for the American Way Foundation—complained in a letter to Wisconsin State Superintendent of Public Instruction John Benson that thirty-five schools appeared to violate the choice law's requirement that participating schools use random selection in choosing which choice students they enrolled. Some failed to submit a random selection plan; others, including several Catholic schools, improperly gave preference to parish members or sought to exempt them from the random selection process.

OPPOSING VOUCHERS

When the MPCP was expanded to include private religious schools, it lost one of its most ardent supporters—State Representative Polly Williams. In 1997, Polly Williams introduced her own revision of Wisconsin's voucher legislation, which among other changes excluded religious schools. She was immediately opposed by the Metropolitan Milwaukee Association of Commerce, the Wisconsin Catholic Conference, and the Bradley Foundation-funded Partners Advancing Values in Education.

Polly Williams explained:

> When I formed a coalition with Tim Sheehy [the president of the Metropolitan Milwaukee Association of Commerce] and the Catholic archdiocese, and those people who say they supported us, I did so because it was a way of helping my parents. I knew all along they didn't care about my children. They cared about their agenda . . . If they really cared about our community the way they say, we would not be in such dire need right now. They have all the power and money in their hands. They could help make the conditions better in our community. But they don't."[3]

In a later interview Williams said:

> The conservatives made me their poster girl as long as it appeared I was supporting their case. And now I am the odd person out. They want

the religious schools to be tax-supported. Blacks and poor are being used to help legitimize them as the power group.

The 1999 school board elections in Milwaukee drew the attention of the national media and a host of national organizations. The teachers unions, the NAACP, People for the American Way (PFAW) and other prominent groups launched a campaign to elect board members who opposed the voucher program, mostly on the basis of its alleged violation of church-state separation. In spite of their efforts, all five candidates who opposed school choice were defeated at the polls.

The PFAW released the following statement regarding the general debate about vouchers.

How Do Vouchers Affect Religious Liberty?

Voucher programs are not only unsound as a matter of education policy, but they also violate the separation of church and state and threaten students' religious liberty. Most schools participating in voucher programs are pervasively sectarian; therefore, the provision of public funds to these schools forces taxpayers to subsidize religion. This forced subsidization of religion violates freedom of conscience and is, we believe, completely contrary to the intent of the Founders and the core principles behind the constitutional separation of church and state. Thomas Jefferson, for example, viewed freedom of conscience as the idea that no one "shall be compelled to . . . support any religious worship, place, or ministry whatsoever." And in his famous "Memorial and Remonstrance Against Religious Assessments," James Madison explained his objection to such assessments by noting: "The Religion then of every man must be left to the conviction and conscience of every man. . . . Who does not see that . . . the same authority which can force a citizen to contribute three pence only of his property for the support of only one establishment, may force him to conform to any other establishment, in all cases whatsoever?"

In addition to requiring compelled support of religion, voucher programs also result in the public funding of religious discrimination. Unless voucher statutes provide to the contrary, the evidence shows that private religious schools will use religious affiliation to decide which students to accept. Private religious school administrators surveyed around the country have stated that they would not accept voucher students if forced to allow students to opt out of religious services. Further, even where "opt-out" provisions are allowed, the religious instruction in many religious schools permeates all academic subjects, making "opting out" impracticable and threatening the quality of voucher students' academic experience.

SUPPORTING VOUCHERS

Governor Tommy Thompson

In his January 1995 State of the State Address, Governor Thompson defended the inclusion of religious schools in the program.

We created the first private school choice program in the country. . . . We have good schools in Wisconsin. We have excellent students . . . and have some of the best teachers in the world. But we still have some work to do. Tonight, I am asking teachers, principles, parents and entire communities to join me in creating a new system of public education for the 21st century. This will mean challenging the status quo. . . . We are going to put education back where it belongs . . . back in the hands of our parents, our teachers, and our students. . . . Our students, our parents, and our taxpayers will get what they want. If you saw the state spending millions of dollars to bus children to schools far from home when there are openings in good schools in their own backyards . . . you'd start making some changes. If you saw that less than half of Milwaukee high school freshmen actually graduate . . . and graduate with a D+ average . . . you'd start making some changes.

If you saw that only 79% of our students actually go to school on a regular basis, you'd start making some radical changes. Our first step in changing education is a complete redefinition of public education in Wisconsin. From now on in Wisconsin, a public school will mean a school that is serving the public. School choice is part of this new public education. School choice is more than a program . . . it is a philosophy.

It is the belief that parents know best when it comes to their own children. . . .

It is the belief that poor parents have the same right to choose that other parents do. . . .

It is the belief that parents will choose the best school for their child. That's education serving the public. We are expanding our Milwaukee private school choice program to include more children and all private schools. If a mother in Milwaukee wants her child to walk to the private school across the street instead of being bused to a public school across town, she's going to have that choice. If that private school across the street has a religious affiliation she is still going to have that choice.

Religious values are not our problem. Drop-out rates are.

Government is allowed to pay for whatever pre-school a parent chooses. It is allowed to pitch in for whatever college they choose. It is only for K–12 that we assume bureaucrats know best and parents have no say. Not anymore.

· · ·

In *Jackson v. Benson*, 218 Wis. 2d 835 (1998), the Wisconsin Supreme Court ruled in a 4–2 decision that permitting religious schools to participate in the voucher program did not violate the Wisconsin's constitutional provision against spending state funds for religious purposes. The court also held that the voucher program did not violate the U.S. Constitution's First Amendment guarantees of separation of church and state because it met the three-pronged test set down by the U.S. Supreme Court that: (1) the government's expenditure must have a legitimate secular purpose; (2) it must not have the primary effect of advancing religion; and (3) it must not lead to excessive entanglement between the state and participating private, religious schools.

AFTERWORD: CONTROVERSY OVER THE EFFECTS OF THE PROGRAM

The debate over the justice of the voucher program has not been resolved by the studies of its effects.[4] At the request of the Wisconsin legislature, John Witte of the University of Wisconsin–Madison undertook a study of all students and schools participating in the program in 1990–1995. He compared voucher students to a control group of randomly selected public school students, and found that there were no differences in reading and math achievement in any year.

His study was criticized by voucher advocates, among them Paul Peterson, Jay Greene, and Jiangtao Du of Harvard University.[5] In a study funded by the Olin Foundation, these researchers reported large test gains in math and reading for students who have been in private schools for at least three years.

The controversy prompted the two additional efforts. Witte's 1997 reanalysis of data collected in his earlier evaluation compared vouchers students to various samples of MPS students and unsuccessful voucher applicants. Witte concluded that there were no math or reading advantages for the voucher students. A third study by Cecilia Rouse compared voucher students to both MPS sample and unsuccessful voucher applicants. Rouse found no effect for reading, but indicated evidence of a positive math effect to voucher students.[6]

Although controversy over the effects continues, the program continues to grow. Currently the program is enrolling students for the 2004–2005 year, with an anticipated participation of about 15,000 low-income students.

NOTES

1. The average amount of the voucher received by participating schools ($4,545) exceeded their average published tuition fees ($2,281) by 99 percent. "Revenues, Expenditures and Taxpayer Subsidies in Milwaukee's Voucher Schools" (paper presented March 23 to the 2001 annual meeting of the American Education Finance Association, Cincinnati, Ohio) by F. Howard Nelson, Rachel Egen, and Dwight Holmes.

2. The description of Williams's perspectives and her quotes in this section are from Mikel Holt, *Not Yet "Free at Last"* (Oakland, CA.: Institute for Contemporary Studies Press, 2000), chapter 4.

3. Quoted in *Educational Week* Aug.6, 1997.

4. The studies referred to in this section are available online: Witte, John F., and Christopher A. Thorn. The Milwaukee Parental Choice Program, 1990/1991–1994/1995 [computer file] Witte's findings, with discussions and yearly update since 1991: http://dpls.dacc.wisc.edu/choice Greene, Peterson and Du secondary (and contrasting) analysis of Witte's findings: http://hdc-www.harvard.edu/pepg/op/evaluate.htm.

5. Greene, Jay P., Peterson, Paul E., and Jiangtao Du et al., "The Effectiveness of School Choice in Milwaukee: A Secondary Analysis of Data from the Program's Evaluation," Program on Education Policy and Governance: Occasional Paper, Department of Government and Kennedy School of Government, Harvard University, March 1997.

6. Rouse, Cecilia. "Private School Vouchers and Student Achievement: An Evaluation of the Milwaukee Parental Choice Program," *The Quarterly Journal of Economics*. Vol. 113, No. 2, 1998.

Comment

What does equal opportunity imply for the question of who should decide which elementary and secondary schools children attend? Voucher plans like Milwaukee's give low-income parents a choice of sending their children to a school beyond those in their residential public school districts. The amount of added choice varies with parental means, the monetary worth of the voucher, and the private schools that opt into the voucher program. Does such choice increase or decrease equal opportunity for disadvantaged children? An answer to this question requires specifying the relevant alternatives. First, compare the Milwaukee voucher plan to the status quo ante of public and private schooling in the city. Is the plan an improvement in equal opportunity (for whom?) over what existed in Milwaukee before it was instituted? Second, compare the plan to alternatives that would spend as much or more to improve Milwaukee public schools. Some observers suggest that there are alternative ways of investing in elementary and secondary education that would be more promising from the perspective of equalizing educational opportunity for elementary and secondary school children in Milwaukee. Specify what more you would need to know to evaluate the justifiability of this plan—and what would be required to make that knowledge more publicly available.

Does the justification of publicly funded voucher plans depend on whether and how private schools are regulated by government? Some voucher advocates argue that the key to the success of voucher schools is that they are far less regulated than public schools. The opinion of the Wisconsin Supreme Court, however, emphasizes the "public purpose doctrine": the importance of a substantial degree of public control to ensure that even private schools realize the public purposes of elementary and secondary schooling. Both advocates and opponents of Milwaukee's voucher plan believe that schools have public purposes, but they disagree about what those purposes are or how to interpret them in practice. Which, if any, of the following aims of publicly funded schooling can be defended from a public perspective, and why: (1) preparing children for equal democratic citizenship; (2) cultivating individual autonomy, the ability reflectively to choose a good life for oneself; (3) socializing children into a communal way of life; and (4) conveying to children the fundamental religious or secular values of their parents.

Some proponents of voucher programs rest their case not on equalizing educational opportunity but on a right of parents to choose for themselves how and where their children are schooled. First, consider the arguments that are made for the right of parents to choose the schools their children attend. If schools continue to be publicly funded, how limited or unlimited should that right be, and why? Second, what is the strongest argument against such a parental right? The right of children to equal educational opportunity is sometimes set against this parental right. What would such a right entail? Is it publicly defensible? Is it necessarily in conflict with parental rights?

Many arguments made for and against parental choice depend on the educational consequences for children who are enrolled in voucher schools and those who are enrolled in nonvoucher schools. How can the consequences of various voucher and nonvoucher systems best be compared? To date, all assessments of consequences have been either indeterminate or reasonably contested. As long as this continues to be the case, on what grounds can parents, democratically elected officials, and judges claim the authority either to choose schools for children or regulate how they operate? Consider the following possible grounds and any others you find defensible: (1) educational quality; (2) equal opportunity; (3) democratic decision making; (4) judicial decision making; (5) parental choice; (6) freedom of religion; and (7) separation of church and state.

Some opponents of the Milwaukee program claim that "vouchers threaten the fundamental mission of public education," which they define not as serving but as creating the public by bringing diverse groups of children together within public schools during formative years of their life. Is this ideal defensible? To what extent is it realizable? Consider how other defensible interpretations of the fundamental mission of public education would undermine or support voucher plans.

A Golfer's Handicap?

Simone Sandy

In January 1998, professional golfer Casey Martin won the Lakeland Classic, a tournament governed by PGA Tour, Inc. Although a Tour rule required competitors to walk the course, Martin used a motorized cart, armed with an injunction from a federal judge.

Martin has a rare and serious circulatory disorder (Klippel-Trenaunay-Weber syndrome), which reduces blood flow in his right leg. Walking aggravates the condition of his leg, causing him severe pain and putting him at risk for fracturing his tibia, and possibly amputation. Wearing a stocking that aids circulation and inhibits swelling helps him walk, but "just getting from his cart to the ball and around the greens takes considerable effort."[1] Martin could not continue to play golf without a cart.

Martin had made it through PGA Tour's first two 1997 qualifying events, where carts were allowed. When Martin requested permission to use a cart in the final December 1997 qualifying event, the Tour refused. PGA Tour, Inc. had a no-cart rule—which it insisted on maintaining—for its final qualifying events, as well as for tournaments on its PGA and its Nike Tours. Martin believed he had a right to use a cart under the Americans with Disabilities Act (ADA), and sued PGA Tour. The ADA prohibits discrimination against the disabled in employment and access to government services, programs, and activities; public transportation; public

accommodations; and telecommunications. It requires operators of "public accommodations," such as golf courses, to make "reasonable modifications" to accommodate people with disabilities, unless the changes would "fundamentally alter the nature" of the activity.[2] "I don't want to miss the chance to be a professional golfer because I can't use a cart," said Martin. "I could live with not making it because I wasn't good enough. I want the chance."[3]

A federal judge issued a temporary injunction that would ultimately let Martin ride until his case was decided. PGA Tour released the following statement in response: "Casey Martin is a courageous young man and a fine golfer, and we appreciate his desire to play on the PGA Tour; however, everyone who plays on the PGA Tour should be subject to the same rules and regulations."[4] In a January 17, 1998 statement, the Tour elaborated on its position: "Professional golf is an athletic competition and the ability to walk five miles each day for consecutive competitive rounds, week after week, often under adverse conditions and over challenging terrain, is part of the endurance and stamina required to play golf at its highest level." The Tour also said it did not believe the ADA was meant to apply to professional sports.[5] Indeed, Martin was the first professional athlete to invoke the ADA in order to compete in a sport.

Public response to Martin's Lakeland win was mixed. One journalist speculated that the cart gave Martin an edge and lamented the dilemma: "Martin wants the courts to level a playing field that cannot be leveled. Without a cart, he's at a severe disadvantage. With a cart, Martin has a significant advantage. . . . Nobody is allowed a head start in sports. It violates the core of athletics."[6] Another sportswriter countered, "[T]he cart didn't hit any of Martin's winning shots."[7] PGA Tour Commissioner Tom Finchem issued a statement, congratulating Martin "as we do the victor in all events. . . . The fact remains that Mr. Martin participated and won using a golf cart under terms of a court order."[8] Tiger Woods, who was Martin's teammate at Stanford, spoke in mixed support. "As a friend, I'd love to see him have a cart," Woods said, but a cart might be an advantage "if it's 100 degrees in Memphis."[9]

District Court Trial

During the February 1998 District Court trial, Martin showed a videotape in court of what his right leg was like: He removed his stocking to reveal an atrophied leg. When he stood his leg immediately swelled and discolored as it filled with blood that could not return easily to his heart. When he lay down, the symptoms slowly subsided. Martin said that when he used a cart he still experienced pain but it was not as severe. Martin's orthopedist, Donald C. Jones, testified that Martin is at risk—even using a cart—of fracturing his shinbone, which has been eroded by the disorder. "Walking across the street is a serious risk," Dr. Jones said. "His leg is at risk for fracture with virtually any activity."[10] Martin said he would prefer to walk the courses if he could.

PGA Tour did not dispute that Martin has a disability that prevents him from walking the course, but its attorneys distinguished the PGA and Nike Tours from recreational golf. "The walking rule is a substantial rule, expressly designed to inject stress and fatigue, and impact the outcome of the game," said Tour attorney Andrew Hurwitz. "In an elite competition, certain rules must apply equally to everyone."[11] PGA Tour argued that to waive the rule for Martin would fundamentally alter their tournaments.

Several golf champions testified in favor of the Tour's position. Ken Venturi recounted walking in 100-degree heat on the final 36-hole day of the 1964 U.S. Open. Although he was severely dehydrated and a doctor warned him to quit, Venturi persevered and won without a cart. The last year during which the U.S. Open was played with a 36-hole final day was 1964, but Venturi maintained that walking was essential. "By taking away walking, we're taking away what everybody else has to do. It's changing the level of competition," he said. "I'm not here to go against Casey Martin. I have the greatest admiration for him. But the idea is changing the rules. Where do you draw the line?" Tour lawyers also presented videotaped testimony from Arnold Palmer and Jack Nicklaus, each of whom said walking is a fundamental part of tournament golf.[12]

Decision and Response

On February 12, 1998, the District Court decided in Martin's favor. In his written decision, Judge Thomas M. Coffin thus summarized the questions of the case:

> This case presents profound questions regarding the application of the Americans with Disabilities Act (ADA). Does the ADA apply to athletic events or sports organizations? If so, are the most elite events and organizations, such as those at the professional level, somehow exempt from coverage? If the ADA is applicable, may a rule of competition be modified to accommodate a disabled competitor, or are the rules untouchable because any alteration of any rule would fundamentally alter the nature of the competitions?[13]

Coffin stated that PGA Tour was not exempt from the ADA: "The disabled have just as much interest in being free from discrimination in the athletic world as they do in other aspects of everyday life."[14] He found that Martin's use of a cart would not be an "unreasonable modification," particularly since "the PGA tour permits cart use at two of the four types of tournaments it stages."[15] Coffin accepted the Tour's stated purpose of the walking rule, that it adds an element of fatigue to the shot-making competition. But he found that the fatigue associated with walking five miles in five hours was not significant and that Ken Venturi's fatigue was caused by dehydration and heat exhaustion, not walking. "Many spectators at the 1964 U.S. Open had to be treated for exhaustion as well, and they were not walking," Coffin wrote. Coffin also found that Martin walked approximately 25 percent of the course getting between his cart and shots, and that the fatigue Martin would experience doing this, with his disability, would be greater than the fatigue of an able-bodied peer walking from shot to shot. He called the suggestion that Martin would have a competitive advantage with a cart "a gross distortion of reality."[16]

Fred Couples, a PGA Tour golfer with a bad back, was one of many who disagreed with the decision. "I don't understand how anyone can say . . . you don't expend any energy playing [golf]," Couples argued. "It's much easier to play golf riding a cart."[17]

Other golfers with physical disabilities agreed with the court. Sonny Ackerman, who has twice been the senior national amputee golf champion, said that if golf were about endurance, "we'd all be out running laps." Edward Eckenhoff, president of the National Rehabilitation Hospital and a paraplegic golfer said that a golf cart gives no more advantage to a golfer with a physical disability than glasses give an advantage to a golfer with poor vision.[18]

APPEALS

PGA Tour appealed the District Court's ruling. On March 6, 2000, the Ninth Circuit U.S. Court of Appeals unanimously upheld the ruling. The court opinion said a golf course is a public accommodation even "behind the ropes" during a tournament and that a golf cart was a reasonable accommodation for Martin's disability that would not fundamentally alter PGA tournaments.[19] "All that the cart does," wrote Judge William C. Canby, Jr., "is permit Martin access to a type of competition which he otherwise could not engage in because of his disability. That is precisely the purpose of the ADA."[20]

The day after the Ninth Circuit upheld the District Court's decision, the Seventh Circuit U.S. Court of Appeals issued a contradictory ruling. Ford Olinger, a professional golfer with a degenerative hip disorder, was denied use of a cart for qualifying events for the U.S. Open tournament. The court said to grant Olinger a cart would fundamentally alter the nature of the competition. Because they held tournaments in various states where these seemingly contradictory rulings applied, PGA Tour and the U.S. Golf Association faced a particularly difficult position with regard to their rules of the game. Such a split in circuit court decisions increases the likelihood that the Supreme Court will accept a case upon appeal.[21]

PGA Tour filed an appeal with the Supreme Court in July 2000, arguing that it was "unprecedented for a federal court to order that a professional athlete be allowed to compete without adhering to the full set of substantive rules applicable to other competitors."[22] Martin's lawyers countered: "If no rule of competition, regardless of its purpose, can be modified to permit participation by people with disabilities, then—ironically—sport would become the only industry in America permitted to construct barriers to access that are unrelated to performance."[23] In September 2000, the Supreme Court decided to take the case on appeal.

In the months before the highest court in the land decided the case, amicus briefs were submitted on each party's behalf.

The ATP Tour (men's professional tennis) and Ladies Professional Golf Association submitted a brief in support of PGA Tour, which argued in part:

> [T]he Ninth Circuit ignored the most essential nature of all athletic competition—and especially professional level competition: athletic competition is based on nothing more than an agreed-upon set of uniform rules. . . . Athletic competition is supposed to favor the more skilled and physically able. It is a test of who is the "best" at mastering the game as defined by its rules, and it is this characteristic that makes it compelling to both competitors and spectators. When courts begin to change the rules of how the game is played to assist a particular individual with a disability, this essential characteristic is vitiated. A competition judicially managed to eliminate this or that "unfairness" may appear more "fair" in the view of a court because less skilled or less able-bodied individuals may be able to compete, but it is not the same athletic competition envisioned by the creators and fans of the game. The fundamental fairness of the game—i.e., that all the rules apply equally to all competitors—has changed, and we no longer have a competition that tests who is the "best" at that particular game.[24]

Several of the Congressmen who led the effort to pass the ADA in the first place submitted a brief on Martin's behalf, which argued that the language and legislative history of the ADA "unequivocally support the decision of the Ninth Circuit," and PGA Tour's "efforts to carve out exceptions or limitations to the broad scope of [the ADA], e.g., for participants in professional sports, are ill conceived." The brief concluded:

> Petitioner's contentions that it should be excepted from the reasonable modification obligation because it conducts high-level sports competitions, the uniformity of its rules should be inviolate, and individualized modifications would be burdensome, have no basis in the statutory language or legislative history of the ADA.[25]

THE SUPREME COURT RULES

On May 29, 2001, in a 7–2 ruling, the Supreme Court upheld the decision of the Court of Appeals. The majority opinion, written by Justice Stevens, rejected PGA Tour's argument that competing golfers are not covered by the ADA. The Court's opinion found the walking rule to be peripheral. Even if the walking rule does subject players to fatigue, Steven's wrote:

> [I]t is an uncontested finding of the District Court that Martin "easily endures greater fatigue with a cart than his able-bodied competitors do by walking." The purpose of the walking rule is therefore not compromised in the slightest by allowing Martin to use a cart. A modification that provides an exception to a peripheral tournament rule without impairing its purpose cannot be said to "fundamentally alter" the tournament. What it can be said to do . . . is allow Martin the chance to qualify for and compete in the athletic events petitioner offers to those members of the public who have the skill and desire to enter. That is exactly what the ADA requires. Martin's request for a waiver of the walking rule should have been granted.[26]

The dissenting opinion, written by Justice Scalia, argued that it was not for the Court but rather for PGA Tour itself to declare walking either essential or non-essential to its tournaments. Invoking no less a golf authority than Mark Twain, Scalia emphasized:

> Nowhere is it writ that PGA Tour golf must be classic "essential" golf. Why cannot the PGA Tour, if it wishes, promote a new game, with distinctive rules (much as the American League promotes a game of baseball in which the pitcher's turn at the plate can be taken by a "designated hitter")? . . . [The rules] are (as in all games) entirely arbitrary, and there is no basis on which anyone . . . can pronounce one or another of them to be "nonessential" if the rulemaker (here the PGA Tour) deems it to be essential. . . . [I]t is [also] quite impossible to say

that any of a game's arbitrary rules is "essential." Eighteen-hole golf courses, 10-foot-high basketball hoops, 90-foot baselines, 100-yard football fields—all are arbitrary and none is essential. The only support for any of them is tradition and (in more modern times) insistence by what has come to be regarded as the ruling body of the sport—both of which factors support the PGA Tour's position in the present case. (Many, indeed, consider walking to be the central feature of the game of golf—hence Mark Twain's classic criticism of the sport: "a good walk spoiled.")[27]

AFTER THE DECISION: EVERYONE WINS?

Tour Commissioner Tom Finchem called Martin on May 30, 2001, to share the Court's decision and congratulate him. Martin was pleasantly surprised. Under the circumstances, so was Finchem.

The ruling's language encouraged Finchem that PGA Tour would be able to keep its tournaments much the same as they had been. "The court clearly focused its decision on Casey Martin and Casey Martin only," Finchem said. "They go so far as to say that Casey Martin may be the only person in the world that has the ability to play on the PGA Tour with a condition that precludes him from walking the course."[28]

Most of Martin's peers were happy for him. "I don't think this is hurtful for the game," said former PGA Championship winner Paul Azinger. "Casey Martin is a unique individual, and his is a unique situation."[29] Still, some worried that the ruling would leave the Tour open to future problems, fearing that many others with less debilitating conditions would try to benefit from the ruling. Hal Sutton, a member of the Tour's Policy Board and veteran PGA Tour golfer said, "The next person's disability, it might not be as clear. I think it's going to create a big problem. We're in

a real gray area now."[30] Many say there is not room in the law for the abuse some anticipated. Stephen F. Gold, an expert on the disabilities act who closely followed the case since Martin filed suit in 1997, said, "This is a narrow fact-based opinion, and I believe it will have zero impact on the game."[31]

EPILOGUE

In January 2004, the anticipated flood of professional golfers requesting accommodations under the ADA had yet to come. Martin continued to play on satellite tours but had not claimed a PGA Tour card since 2000. "I know, deep down, I'm capable, but it's been a struggle," Martin said in a January 2004 press conference. "I'd love to be busy again, and hectic and controversial," he said, "and all the stuff I took for granted."[32]

NOTES

1. Bob Harig, "Disabled Golfer Drives for Dough," *Washington Post,* Jan. 12, 1998, final edition, http://www.lexis-nexis.com/.

2. Linda Greenhouse, "Disabled Golfer May Use a Cart on the PGA Tour, Justices Affirm," *New York Times,* May 30, 2001, late edition, http://www.lexis-nexis.com/.

3. William Gildea, "The Cart Before the Course," *Washington Post,* Jan. 9, 1998, final edition, http://www.lexis-nexis.com/.

4. Steve Harrison, "Disabled Pro Golfer Fights No-Cart Rule," *Washington Post,* Dec. 19, 1997, final edition, http://www.lexis-nexis.com/.

5. Steve Harrison, "Martin Moves from Course to Court," *Washington Post,* Jan. 17, 1998, final edition, http://www.lexis-nexis.com/.

6. See Thomas Boswell, "The Rules are Still the Rules," *Washington Post,* Jan. 14, 1998, final edition, http://www.lexis-nexis.com/.

7. Dave Anderson, "Give Martin a Ticket to Ride," *New York Times,* Jan. 15, 1998, late edition, http://www.lexis-nexis.com/.

8. Harig, "Disabled Golfer Drives for Dough."

9. Anderson, "Give Martin a Ticket to Ride."

10. Richard Sandomir, "Martin Gives the Court a Look at Disfigured Leg," *New York Times*, Feb. 3, 1998, late edition, http://www.lexis-nexis.com/.

11. "Casey Martin Case Heads Back Into Court," *Washington Post*, May 5, 1999, final edition, http://www.lexis-nexis.com/.

12. Thomas Heath, "Golf's Greats Testify Against Martin," *Washington Post*, Feb. 6, 1998, final edition, http://www.lexis-nexis.com/.

13. *Casey Martin v. PGA Tour, Inc.*, 994 F. Supp 1242, 1243 (1998).

14. Ibid., 1246.

15. Ibid., 1248.

16. Ibid., 1251–52.

17. Clifton Brown, "Martin Decision Could Increase Course Traffic," *New York Times*, Feb. 12, 1998, late edition, http://www.lexis-nexis.com/.

18. Ibid.

19. *Casey Martin v. PGA Tour, Inc*, 204 F.3d 994, 1002 (9th Cir. 2000).

20. Ibid., 1000.

21. Marcia Chambers, "PGA Seeks a Review of Cart Suit," *New York Times*, June 4, 2000, late edition, http://www.lexis-nexis.com/; and Marcia Chambers, "Conflicting Rulings Keep Cart Issue in Courts," *New York Times*, Apr. 18, 2000, late edition, http://www.lexis-nexis.com/.

22. Linda Greenhouse, "Case on Use of Carts Goes to High Court," *New York Times*, Sept. 27, 2000, late edition, http://www.lexis-nexis.com/.

23. Ibid.

24. *Brief for ATP Tour, Inc. and the Ladies Professional Golf Association, Amici Curiae, in Support of the Petitioner*, Nov. 13, 2000.

25. *Brief Amici Curiae of the Honorable Robert J. Dole, Tom Harkin, Steny H. Hoyer, James M. Jeffords and Edward M. Kennedy in Support of Respondent*, Dec. 13, 2000.

26. *PGA Tour, Inc. v. Casey Martin*, 532 U.S. 661, 690 (2001).

27. Ibid., 699–701.

28. Clifton Brown, "Martin's Case Ends, but Debate Goes on Among Tour Players," *New York Times*, late edition, http://www.lexis-nexis.com/.

29. Ibid.

30. Leonard Shapiro, "Martin's Victory Produces Various Views," *Washington Post*, May 30, 2001, final edition, Http://www.lexis-nexis.com/.

31. Marcia Chambers, "Martin Case Raises Issues on Its Impact," *New York Times*, June 3, 2001, late edition, http://www.lexis-nexis.com/.

32. Ron Agostini, "Martin's Resolve as Strong as Ever," *Modesto Bee*, Jan. 21, 2004, all editions, http://www.lexis-nexis.com/.

Comment

Casey Martin's challenge to PGA Tour, Inc. to permit him to use a motorized cart even though the Tour had instituted a "no-cart rule" vividly raises two ethical questions that are central to understanding the implications of the equal opportunity principle applied to contemporary social life. What constitutes equal opportunity to compete in professional sports? To what extent should government be involved in regulating professional sports in the interests of equalizing opportunity? But also keep in mind that the issue is more general: it involves the meaning of equal opportunity in any competitive activity that has its own goals and rules.

Were Martin not handicapped in some significant way, his challenge to the PGA Tour rules would have been denied with little or no public debate. But Martin's physical disability renders suspect the PGA Tour's refusal to make any exception to its "no-cart rule." At the same time it raises the question of what exceptions must be made to rules of the game, for whom, and why.

In this case, the principle of equal opportunity gains both public visibility and legal legitimacy through the Americans with Disabilities Act (ADA), which requires operators of "public accommodations" such as golf courses to make "reasonable modifications" to accommodate people with disabilities unless the changes "fundamentally alter the nature" of the activity. Consider how you would interpret and defend your interpretation of three basic parts of the ADA in response to Martin's challenge:

1. Should the PGA Tour be considered a public accommodation for this purpose?
2. Is a judicial requirement that the PGA Tour permit Martin to use a cart in its golf tournament within the scope of a "reasonable modification" of the rules?
3. Does this modification fundamentally alter the nature of the tournament?

Defenders of the PGA Tour's policy of no exceptions argue that professional sports are based on a set of conventional rules whose uniform application—no exceptions—is essential to the "fundamental fairness" of the game. Note that this is a moral argument: "The rules must be equally applied to all competitors or else the game is unfair." On what understanding of nondiscrimination does this argument depend? Compare the understanding of nondiscrimination that underlies the opposing argument in favor of allowing Martin to use the cart: that the fatigue he would experience would be at least as great as that of an able-bodied golfer walking from hole to hole. If true, is this claim sufficient to decide this case? Consider the broader implications for sports and other competitive activities if one accepts or rejects that such a claim is sufficient. If you reject its sufficiency, what further arguments would you have to make to justify a clearly nondiscriminatory decision?

Is there any moral basis on which to disagree with the claim that "the disabled have just as much interest in being free from discrimination in the athletic world as they do in other aspects of everyday life"? Consider whether someone who accepts the following fairness claim (made by a journalist who defended the PGA Tour's position) could also consistently defend Martin's side in this case: "Nobody is allowed a head start in sports. It violates the core of athletics."

The arbiters of this controversy were public officials—legislators who passed the ADA and judges who interpreted its application, rather than the PGA Tour commissioner working with other officials of the organization. Some would argue that even if the best interpretation of equal opportunity favors the Supreme Court's decision in this case, governments should not be so intimately involved in regulating a professional sports tournament as were the courts in this case. What is the strongest case to be made that a court should not impose its opinion against the judgment of the PGA Tour, regardless of whether that judgment is consistent with fairness or equal opportunity? Compare the strongest case that can be made in favor of judicial imposition in this realm. To what extent does your comparison depend on determining the social function of a sports tournament and the social interest of disabled individuals in being free from discrimination in this athletic realm? Can one consistently claim that the court's decision is defensible yet "will have zero impact on the game"?

Recommended Reading

For philosophical background, see William Galston, "A Liberal Defense of Equal Opportunity," and other selections in Louis Pojman, ed., *Equality: A Reader* (Oxford: Oxford University Press, 1996). An analysis that blends economic and philosophical perspectives is John E. Roemer, *Equality of Opportunity* (Cambridge, Mass.: Harvard University Press, 2000). A useful collection, which includes some classic authors, is David Johnston (ed.), *Equality* (Indianapolis: Hackett, 2000). Also see this valuable collection, which features more contemporary authors: Mathew Clayton and Andrew Williams (ed.), *Social Justice* (Basingstoke, Hampshire, England: Palgrave MacMillan, 2002).

Only a few contemporary theories of justice specifically discuss the principles governing distribution of jobs. They include Michael Walzer, *Spheres of Justice* (New York: Basic Books, 1983), pp. 129–64; Ronald Dworkin, *A Matter of Principle* (Cambridge, Mass.: Harvard University Press, 1985), Part 5; and Amy Gutmann and Dennis Thompson, *Democracy and Disagreement* (Cambridge, Mass.: Harvard University Press, 1996), ch. 9.

Judith Jarvis Thomson defends preferential hiring when candidates are equally qualified in "Preferential Hiring," in Marshall Cohen et al. (eds.), *Equality and Preferential Treatment* (Princeton, N.J.: Princeton University Press, 1977), pp. 19–39. Robert Simon criticizes Thomson's limited defense in "Preferential Hiring: A Reply to Judith Jarvis Thomson," in *Equality and Preferential Treatment, pp.* 40–48. George Sher considers whether preference may be given to a candidate who is less than the best qualified person for a job in "Justifying Reverse Discrimination in Employment," in *Equality and Preferential Treatment,* pp. 49–60.

For broader discussions of affirmative action and equality, see Anthony Appiah and Amy Gutmann, *Color Conscious: The Political Morality of Race* (Princeton, N.J.: Princeton University Press, 1998); Glenn C. Loury, *The Anatomy of Racial Inequality* (Cambridge, Mass.: Harvard University Press, 2001); Ronald Dworkin, "Affirmative Action: Does it Work?" and "Affirmative Action: Is it Fair?" *Sovereign Virtue: The Theory and Practice of Equality* (Cambridge, Mass.: Harvard University Press, 2000); and George Sher, "Diversity," in *The Affirmative Action Debate* (see below). Michael Rosenfeld combines the perspectives of law and philosophy in *Affirmative Action and Justice: A Philosophical and Constitutional Inquiry* (New Haven, Conn.: Yale University Press, 1991).

Four of the most useful collections of essays on affirmative action and preferential treatment are George E. Curry and Cornel West (eds.), *The Affirmative Action Debate* (Reading, Mass.: Addison Wesley, 1996); Francis J. Beckwith and Todd E. Jones, *Affirmative Action: Social Justice or Reverse Discrimination?* (Buffalo, N.Y.: Prometheus, 1997); Russell Nieli, *Racial Preference and Racial Justice: The New Affirmative Action Controversy* (Washington, D.C.: Ethics and Public Policy Center, 1991); and Steven M. Cahn (ed.), *The Affirmative Action Debates* (New York: Routledge, 2002). For the most careful empirical study of the effects of affirmative action policies in American higher education, see William Bowen and Derek Bok, *The Shape of the River: Long-Term Consequences of Considering Race in College and University Admissions* (Princeton, N.J.: Princeton University Press, 1998). For a critical view of affirmative action policies, see John McWorter, *Losing the Race: Self-Sabotage in Black America* (New York: Free Press, 2000).

For a variety of perspectives on the ethics of school vouchers and school choice, see Alan Wolfe, ed., *School Choice: The Moral Debate* (Princeton, N.J.: Princeton University Press, 2002). For a perspective on vouchers rooted in a democratic theory of education, see Amy Gutmann, *Democratic Education* (Princeton, N.J.: Princeton University Press, 1999). On ethical issues in athletics, see Robert L. Simon, *Fair Play: The Ethics of Sport* (Boulder Colo.: Westview Press, 2003); and Jan Boxill (ed.), *Sports Ethics: An Anthology* (Oxford: Blackwell, 2002).

9 Liberty and Morality

"Over himself, over his own body and mind, the individual is sovereign," concludes John Stuart Mill in a classic statement of the principle of individual liberty. Yet a vast number of public policies apparently violate this principle, some for paternalistic and others for moralistic reasons. Paternalism is interference with a person's liberty with the aim of promoting his or her own good. Moralism is interference with a person's liberty with the aim of enforcing social morality (or preventing immorality). John Stuart Mill rejected paternalism and moralism absolutely: "because it will be better for him to do so" or "because it will make him happier" or because it violates social morality (but does not otherwise cause harm) never justifies restricting the liberty of a sane adult.

Yet there is much morally to be said about both paternalism and moralism. Most people value other goods, such as health and happiness, along with liberty. And sometimes they can secure these goods, or their future liberty, only if society restricts their present freedom of choice. When Mill considers specific examples in which important interests other than liberty are at stake, he abandons his absolutist prohibition against paternalism. He defends preventing someone from crossing an unsafe bridge and approves outlawing slavery based on voluntary contract.

Recognizing that some people always and all people sometimes are incapable of exercising liberty, many contemporary political theorists accept an even broader range of paternalistic restrictions on adult behavior than Mill did. They would favor, for example, banning the use of harmful drugs and requiring the use of seat belts and motorcycle helmets. Others, condemning the rapidly growing intrusion of government into the lives of citizens, defend Mill's explicit absolutism or something as close to absolutism as possible. The controversy in political theory parallels the challenge of paternalism in contemporary politics: Can government protect the welfare of its citizens without denying their claims to freedom?

We might begin to meet this challenge by justifying paternalistic intervention only if it satisfies these criteria: (1) the decisions it restricts are already unfree or seriously impaired; (2) the intervention is minimally restrictive in time and effect; and (3) the person whose freedom is restricted could accept the goal of the intervention were his or her decisions unimpaired. But to state these criteria is not to solve the problems of paternalism, especially as they arise in public policies that affect many people and have uncertain consequences. When are the decisions of a group of people unfree or seriously impaired (compared to what standard of normalcy)?

How limited must an intervention be (and how limited can it be while still being effective)? In what sense must the affected individuals accept its purposes? Must they all accept it or only a majority? Which majority?

"Decriminalizing Marijuana for Medical Use" illustrates each of these problems that arise in deciding whether a paternalistic policy is justifiable. Federal and state officials, as well as ordinary citizens, disagree about whether the decisions of individuals with life-threatening diseases such as cancer are so unfree as to justify paternalistic intervention. How unfree must a decision be to justify paternalistic intervention, and how could it be shown that cancer patients are not exercising free choice in deciding to use marijuana? Citizens and officials also differ about what is the least restrictive yet effective means of protecting patients against medical fraud: requiring a prescription to obtain the FDA-approved pill that contains marijuana's medicinal ingredient THC, decriminalizing marijuana for medical purposes without a prescription, or decriminalizing marijuana for adults to be used at their discretion. The parties to the dispute also offered competing accounts of what people really want when they use marijuana: an effective medical cure or therapy, pain relief, psychic comfort, or all of the above. The case should prompt you to ask what goal of a paternalistic prohibition or restriction could be accepted by those who would want to use marijuana for medical purposes? Many of the same issues posed by the controversy over decriminalizing marijuana arise in even more heightened form in the disputes over the regulation of a large number of new drugs, which, after extensive testing, may turn out to be either effective or dangerous for individuals suffering from AIDS, but which in the meantime seem to many AIDS patients their only hope.

Moralism rather than paternalism is at issue both in the practice of dwarf-tossing and in legalizing gay marriage. Unlike paternalism, moralism does not rest on a showing of harm in the usual sense, but rather on a claim that an action or practice is morally wrong, independently of any harm it may cause. All the people who participate in gay marriages and in dwarf-tossing consent to the practices, and there is no showing of harm to anyone other than the claim that the immorality of the practices itself constitutes a harm. The harm is usually understood as an indignity or degradation of the individuals who engage in the practice. Or, from some religious perspectives in the case of gay marriage, the alleged harm is dependent on the belief that "homosexuality" is sinful or that sanctifying a same-sex union is offensive.

This view of moralism—that the claimed harm is inherent in the practice itself—is controversial. The case of gay marriage brings out in full force the controversy over the very nature of moralism. Many opponents of gay marriage not only condemn "homosexual" activity in itself, they also make the consequentialist argument that the institution of same-sex marriage will undermine the sanctity of marriage and erode the moral fabric of American society. Strictly speaking, this opposition to same-sex marriage counts as moralism to the extent that the consequentialist harms are all dependent on the moralist view that same-sex relations are themselves morally wrong or sinful, quite apart from any harm that they inflict on others. To test whether the fundamental case against a practice is moralism, we can ask: If little or no plausible empirical evidence of harm to self or others of the practice can be produced, are the critics of the practice still prepared to prohibit or restrict it? If the answer is yes, the case is one of moralism.

Although strict liberals claim that morality should never be enforced and tend to see moralism as a conservative doctrine of the moral majority, most liberals along with conservatives support some moralistic laws, such as those against public nudity. But, absent a showing of harm to self or others, liberals generally are far more reluctant to support the public enforcement of morality than are conservatives. Both liberal and conservative perspectives on moralism, however, raise the same question of when, if ever, can government enforce morality without violating the legitimate claims of individuals to liberty.

Consider three criteria for justified moralism: (1) the action or practice is wrong, independent of any harm it causes; (2) the wrong is of sufficient relevance to public purposes to warrant the enactment of a public policy; and (3) the legal regulation or prohibition is not itself likely to cause greater harms or wrongs than those it is seeking to prevent. Each of these criteria is open to revision or rejection in the course of evaluating whether the legalization of gay marriage or the ban on dwarf-tossing in bars is justified.

"The Controversial Curriculum" centers on the religious objections of some fundamentalist Christian parents to exposing their children to the reading curriculum prescribed by the school board of Hawkins County, Tennessee. Although nobody in the case challenges the sincerity of the parents' religious claims, many people disagree about the extent to which the religious claims of parents should be given weight within the curriculum in the public school, even when the claims are made only on behalf of the parents' own children. At stake in such disputes are the morality and liberty of parents, the future liberty and democratic citizenship of children, and the legitimacy of parental authority versus that of a democratically elected school board to determine the curriculum of a public school.

Both paternalism and moralism in public policy raise not only the problem of a hard choice among competing goods but also a dilemma of process: Who has the authority to make paternalistic or moralistic decisions and by what procedures should they make them? We may agree that the policy is correct but criticize the way it was made. In "The Controversial Curriculum," a democratically elected school board discussed the parents' objection but not publicly and in the end rejected their request to exempt their children from reading the textbooks. The quality of the process by which public policies are made—for example, whether there are adequate and open deliberations—may be relevant to judging the legitimacy of the outcome. The issue of legalizing gay marriage highlights the controversial role of courts in overriding popular majorities at the legislative level. When is the defense of individual rights sufficient to legitimize judicial intervention at the state or federal level (or both)? Would a constitutional amendment be sufficient to legitimize a ban on gay marriage?

In the California marijuana case, answering the question of whether citizens should be free to use marijuana also leaves open a series of questions concerning the process by which paternalistic decisions should be made. Where should the authoritative majority reside—at the local, state, or federal level? What are the comparative advantages of deciding the issue by a referendum rather than by a representative legislative body? State officials and federal officials had to determine how to react to the results of a state referendum that conflicted with a federal law. Should their action be based on (1) purely procedural considerations—who has the authority to decide; (2) purely substantive considerations—which law is right; or (3) some other specified combination of considerations?

To answer these questions, we must consider the moral duties of citizens, legislators, bureaucrats, and judges in a democracy. In one theory of democracy, attributed to Joseph Schumpeter, the only moral duty of politicians is to preserve the institutional arrangements that make possible the ongoing "competitive struggle for the people's vote." A different democratic theory, associated with Mill, offers a more demanding ideal of representation, which would hold legislators, bureaucrats, and judges who have broad discretion accountable for particular policies. Because legislators and high-level public officials wield so much power over so many people, we can insist that they give citizens sufficient information to assess their decisions, especially on salient and controversial issues such as legalizing marijuana and instituting a controversial curriculum.

Decriminalizing Marijuana for Medical Use

Simone Sandy

Ever since 1937 in the United States, it has been a federal crime to cultivate, possess, or distribute marijuana. The 1970 Controlled Substances Act categorizes marijuana along with heroin and LSD as a Schedule I substance. Schedule I substances are so categorized for having a high potential for abuse and no accepted medical value.

In a 1996 ballot initiative in California, 56 percent of voters supported decriminalizing the possession and cultivation of marijuana for medical purposes. The aims of the Compassionate Use Act of 1996 (also called Proposition 215) are:

(A) To ensure that seriously ill Californians have the right to obtain and use marijuana for medical purposes where that medical use is deemed appropriate and has been recommended by a physician who has determined that the person's health would benefit from the use of marijuana in the treatment of cancer, anorexia, AIDS, chronic pain, spasticity, glaucoma, arthritis, migraine, or any other illness for which marijuana provides relief;

(B) To ensure that patients and their primary caregivers who obtain and use marijuana for medical purposes upon the recommendation of a physician are not subject to criminal prosecution or sanction; and

(C) To encourage the federal and state governments to implement a plan to provide for the safe and affordable distribution of marijuana to all patients in medical need of marijuana.[1]

COMPASSIONATE USE

In California's ballot pamphlet for the November 1996 election, physicians and nurses presented evidence in support of Proposition 215. On the basis of both medical research and their own firsthand experiences, they claimed that marijuana had medical benefits.

"When standard anti-nausea drugs fail," they stated, "marijuana often eases patients' nausea and permits continued treatment. . . . University doctors and researchers have found that marijuana is also effective in: lowering internal eye pressure associated with glaucoma, slowing the onset of blindness; reducing the pain of AIDS patients, and stimulating the appetites of those suffering malnutrition because of AIDS 'wasting syndrome'; and alleviating muscle spasticity and chronic pain due to multiple sclerosis, epilepsy, and spinal cord injuries."[2]

Those who argued against Proposition 215 in the ballot pamphlet (including a physician) did not claim that marijuana was an ineffective treatment. Rather, they stated that marijuana was neither safe nor more effective than FDA-approved drugs for people with AIDS, glaucoma, or cancer.[3]

News accounts of the enactment of Proposition 215, and the subsequent conflicts between Californians and federal enforcement agents, were sprinkled with stories of seriously ill Californians who used marijuana as a last resort. One such story, which appeared in the Sunday magazine section of the *New York Times,* featured a San Francisco district attorney who was slowly dying from AIDS-related wasting syndrome. His doctor prescribed Marinol—an FDA-approved pill with a synthetic form of THC (an active ingredient of marijuana and an appetite stimulant) as its active ingredient. When that didn't work, she suggested that inhaled marijuana had worked better than Marinol for many of her other patients. The attorney tried that and it worked. "It's against the law, yes, but I'm not thinking of myself as a prosecutor. I'm a man fighting for his life," he said.[4]

Since 1996, popular support for the medical use of marijuana has grown. A 2004 survey of 500 registered voters in California found that 74 percent favored legal protections for those who use marijuana to cope with illnesses, compared with 56 percent

who approved it on the ballot. The poll also showed that a majority of Californians from all major political, ideological, and age groups supported the Compassionate Use Act.[5]

For some very ill Californians, there is no question that they will continue to smoke marijuana for relief—and most Californians do not want to punish them for doing so. The question remains whether the law will be on their side.

WAR ON DRUGS

"Because people say something makes them feel better doesn't make it medicine. That's a definition of snake oil," said John Walters, director of the Office of National Drug Control Policy (also known as the federal drug czar).[6]

The U.S. Drug Enforcement Administration (DEA) and Office of National Drug Control Policy have stated unequivocally that marijuana remains a dangerous and illegal substance and have denounced California's law. The government has never "approved medicine by popular referendum" and "would be ill-advised to start now," said DEA Director Asa Hutchinson.[7]

The DEA has argued that all medications must undergo the Food and Drug Administration's (FDA) approval process and that an FDA-approved medication (Marinol) containing a synthetic version of marijuana's medicinal ingredient (THC) is available. The DEA also has claimed that the campaign for the medical use of marijuana is fueled by organizations that favor legalization of marijuana for all uses, which would be opposed by most Americans. (In a 2004 survey, 56 percent of Californians surveyed opposed the legalization of marijuana for general use.[8]) The DEA also has noted the difficulties presented by California's law in distinguishing between illegal and medical marijuana providers:

The DEA and its local and state counterparts routinely report that large-scale drug traffickers invoke Proposition 215, even when no evidence exists of any medical claim. In fact, many large-scale marijuana cultivators and traffickers escape state prosecution because of bogus medical marijuana claims. Prosecutors are reluctant to charge these individuals because of the legal confusion in California. Therefore, high-level traffickers posing as "care givers" are able to sell illegal drugs with impunity.[9]

"As much as [proponents of medical use] seek to focus on people suffering with illnesses," the DEA's fact sheet on medical marijuana argues, "we must keep the debate properly centered on the safety of our kids. In a time where drug use among kids has increased 78 percent in the last four years, this country cannot afford to undermine drug prevention efforts with these pro-marijuana ballot initiatives."[10]

ENFORCEMENT OF THE CONTROLLED SUBSTANCES ACT

The federal government has stated that the Controlled Substance Act trumps any ballot initiative. It therefore has been active in law enforcement in California. Its early responses to California's enactment of Proposition 215 included filing lawsuits against several "marijuana buyers' clubs" and threatening doctors with prosecution if they recommended marijuana to patients for medical purposes.

In January 1998, the office of the U.S. Attorney for Northern California filed civil lawsuits against six marijuana-selling clubs and their operators, accusing them of distribution of marijuana. Michael Yamaguchi, the U.S. Attorney, said the suits were intended to "send a clear message regarding the illegality of marijuana cultivation and distribution."[11] According to Yamaguchi, DEA agents made undercover buys at the six clubs and found them to be lax in their scrutiny of people's medical claims. He also stressed that even if the clubs were rigorous in checking

buyers' claims, the clubs would still be violating federal law.[12]

Later that year, U.S. District Judge Charles Breyer issued an injunction barring marijuana distribution. Three clubs closed and two remained open for lack of evidence against them. The sixth club, the Oakland Cannabis Buyers Cooperative (OCBC), ignored the injunction, declaring that medical necessity required its remaining open. The city of Oakland designated club officials as city agents.[13] OCBC was held in contempt of court, which they appealed as well as Breyer's injunction.

In 1999, the Ninth U.S. Circuit Court of Appeals reversed the District Court decision, instructing Breyer to modify his injunction to allow for the distribution of marijuana for medical purposes.[14] In 2001, however, a U.S. Supreme Court majority held that because the Controlled Substances Act says marijuana has no medical value, "medical necessity" could not be used as a legal defense. In the Court's majority opinion Justice Clarence Thomas noted that several "underlying constitutional issues" remained undecided, including whether the Controlled Substances Act "exceeds Congress' Commerce Clause powers, violates the substantive due process rights of patients, and offends the fundamental liberties of the people under the Fifth, Ninth, and Tenth Amendments."[15] These issues would be addressed in future cases.

Knowing that California's Compassionate Use Act allows the medical use of marijuana only with a doctor's recommendation, the federal government declared in December 1996 that doctors who recommend marijuana to patients could face federal prosecution and lose their power to write prescriptions. One month later, California physicians, patients, and others responded with a class-action suit saying such punishment would violate their First Amendment free speech rights.[16]

A district judge issued an injunction preventing the government from taking action against physicians simply for recommending marijuana, which the Ninth U.S. Circuit Court of Appeals affirmed in an October 2002 ruling. Ninth Circuit Chief Judge Mary Schroeder wrote that the government's policy "does not merely prohibit the discussion of marijuana; it condemns expression of a particular viewpoint, i.e., that medical marijuana would likely help a specific patient. Such condemnation of particular views is especially troubling in the First Amendment context." Schroeder stated that physicians could be prosecuted: "If in making the recommendation, the physician intends for the patient to use it as the means for obtaining marijuana, as a prescription is used as a means for a patient to obtain a controlled substance, then a physician would be guilty of aiding and abetting the violation of federal law."[17]

The government appealed the case to the Supreme Court, which let the Ninth Circuit decision stand.

FEDERAL ENFORCEMENT EFFORTS CONTINUE

In 2001 and 2002 the federal government escalated its efforts to enforce the Controlled Substances Act in California by raiding high-profile medical marijuana facilities operating with the support of local law enforcement, confiscating plants, and arresting growers. In September 2002, the DEA raid of the farm of the Santa Cruz County's Wo/Men's Alliance for Medical Marijuana (WAMM) sparked protests throughout Northern California. The protests included a public distribution by Santa Cruz officials in front of city hall of marijuana to approved patients.[18] Federal agents confiscated 167 marijuana plants from the WAMM farm and arrested director Valerie Corral and her husband. No charges were filed against the Corrals.[19]

Santa Cruz Mayor Chris Krohn was angered by the Santa Cruz county raid. He added that he would appreciate the DEA's help with managing the city's heroin problem.[20] The raid also prompted California Attorney General Bill Lockyer to write a letter to U.S. Attorney General John Ashcroft. "A medicinal marijuana provider such as the Santa Cruz collective represents little danger to the public," he wrote, "and it is certainly not a concern which would warrant diverting scarce federal resources away from the fight against domestic methamphetamine production, heroin distribution or international terrorism, to cite just a few far more worthy priorities."[21]

CHARGES AGAINST A MARIJUANA SUPPLIER

Edward Rosenthal, columnist and author of several books on growing marijuana, was arrested in February 2002 during one of several federal raids on medical marijuana growing operations. He was charged with marijuana cultivation, conspiracy to cultivate marijuana, and maintaining a place for its cultivation. In the wake of the injunction against the Oakland Cannabis Buyers' Cooperative, Rosenthal had been deputized by the city of Oakland as an official medical marijuana supplier.

During Rosenthal's trial, U.S. District Judge Breyer blocked the jury from hearing information on Rosenthal's official role as a medical marijuana provider on grounds that the federal laws against marijuana cultivation do not take purported medical use into account. "You are not to consider the purpose for which marijuana is grown," Breyer told the jury, "You cannot substitute your sense of justice, whatever that is, for your duty to follow the law."[22]

In February 2003, the jury convicted Rosenthal, but many jurors asked Breyer for leniency in Rosenthal's sentence. California's attorney general also requested leniency. "[The jury] didn't have the whole truth. They didn't have nothing but the truth. They had lies and deceptions and half-truths," Rosenthal said. "This was not a trial. This was a kangaroo trial."[23]

Inspired by Rosenthal's conviction, thirty members of Congress introduced HR 1717, the Truth in Trials Act, which would provide individuals charged with federal marijuana offenses with "medical marijuana defense" in federal court, on the basis of their state's laws. "This is an issue of states' rights, plain and simple," said California Representative Sam Farr, lead sponsor of the bill. "The voters of California have passed a medical marijuana initiative, but the federal government has exhibited little respect for our state's laws."[24]

In June 2003, Judge Breyer sentenced Rosenthal to a day in jail, which Rosenthal had already served after his arrest. Breyer said that because Rosenthal had reason to believe he was following the law, an atypical sentence was called for. Breyer also fined Rosenthal $1,300 and put him on supervised release for three years. A federal prosecutor had asked that Rosenthal be sentenced to 6.5 years in prison.[25]

Rosenthal appealed his conviction and prosecutors appealed his sentence.

CALIFORNIANS PUSH THE ENVELOPE

Californians have in recent years initiated litigation preemptively seeking protection from federal prosecution for growing and using marijuana for medical purposes. The district and appeals courts have been divided over the questions these suits raise. The U.S. Supreme Court may yet be called on to decide on some of the questions it openly left unresolved in *U.S. v. Oakland Cannabis Buyers' Cooperative.*

In 2003, two seriously ill California women sued U.S. Attorney General John Ashcroft, seeking an injunction that would allow them to obtain and use marijuana without fear of prosecution. They filed the suit out of concern that future federal raids would deprive them of the marijuana they felt they acutely needed (*Raich v. Ashcroft*).

U.S. District Judge Martin Jenkins ruled that the court was "constrained [by federal law] from granting their request."[26] In a 2–1

ruling, the Ninth Circuit reversed the District Court's decision. The majority opinion invoked the Commerce Clause of the Constitution, stating that federal prosecution of medical marijuana users under the Controlled Substances Act is unconstitutional if the marijuana is not sold, transported across state lines, or used for nonmedicinal purposes.[27] The Justice Department appealed the decision to the Supreme Court, which was expected to decide in summer 2004 whether to take the case.

Several months after the DEA raided their marijuana farm, WAMM and several of its patients—joined by the city and County of Santa Cruz—sued for damages and requested an injunction protecting them from further raids. Referencing the Ninth Circuit *Raich v. Ashcroft* decision as a precedent, U.S. District Judge Jeremy Fogel enjoined the Justice Department from raiding or prosecuting the members of WAMM. According to Fogel, applying the Controlled Substances Act to WAMM "is an unconstitutional exercise" of federal intervention.[28]

NOTES

1. Cal Health & Saf Code § 11362.5 (2004).

2. California Secretary of State, "Argument in Favor of Proposition 215," *Ballet Pamphlet for November 5, 1996 General Election,* http://vote96.ss.ca.gov/Vote96/html/BP/215yesarg.htm.

3. California Secretary of State, "Argument Against Proposition 215," *Ballet Pamphlet for November 5, 1996 General Election,* http://vote96.ss.ca.gov/Vote96/html/BP/215noarg.htm.

4. Michael Pollen, "The Pot Proposition: Living With Medical Marijuana," *New York Times,* July 20, 1997, late edition, http://www.lexis-nexis.com/.

5. Bob Egelko, "Medical Pot Law Gains Acceptance," *San Francisco Chronicle,* Jan. 30, 2004, final edition, http://www.lexis-nexis.com/.

6. John Blackstone (reporting), "Just What the Doctor Ordered," *Sunday Morning,* CBS News Transcripts, Oct. 20, 2002, http://www.lexis-nexis.com/.

7. Rich Ehisen, "The Battle Over Medical Marijuana," *California Journal* 51, no. 7 (July 1, 2003), 36, http://www.lexis-nexis.com/.

8. Bob Egelko, "Medical Pot Law Gains Acceptance."

9. U.S. Drug Enforcement Administration, "California Medical Marijuana Information," http://www.dea.gov/ongoing/calimarijuanap.html

10. "Pot Movement Seeks Sympathetic Juries," *United Press International,* June 4, 2003, http://www.lexis-nexis.com/.

11. Mary Curtius and Maria L. LaGanga, "U.S. Launches Drive to Close Marijuana Clubs," *Los Angeles Times,* Jan. 10, 1998, http://www.lexis-nexis.com/.

12. Ibid.

13. Jordan Lite, "Justice Department Asks For Re-hearing of Medical Necessity Defense," *Associated Press State & Local Wire,* Oct. 27, 1999, AM cycle, http://www.lexis-nexis.com/.

14. *U.S. v. Oakland Cannabis Buyers' Cooperative,* 190 F.3d 1109 (1999).

15. *U.S. v. Oakland Cannabis Buyers' Cooperative,* 532 U.S. 483, 494 (2001).

16. Jennifer Warren, "Suit Seeks to Bar U.S. Sanctions for Prescribing Pot," *Los Angeles Times,* Jan. 15, 1997, http://www.lexis-nexis.com/.

17. *Conant v. Walters,* 309 F.3d 629, 637, 635, (2002) quoted in Jason Hoppin, "9th Circuit Backs Doctors' Right to Discuss Marijuana," *The Recorder,* Oct. 30, 2002, http://www.lexis-nexis.com/.

18. John Blackstone (reporting), "Just What the Doctor Ordered."

19. Jason Hoppin, "9th Circuit Backs Doctors' Right to Discuss Marijuana," *The Recorder,* Oct. 30, 2002, http://www.lexis-nexis.com/.

20. John Blackstone (reporting), "Just What the Doctor Ordered."

21. Rich Ehisen, "The Battle Over Medical Marijuana."

22. Bob Egelko, "Judge Keeps Tight Rein on Pot Trial," *San Francisco Chronicle,* Jan. 31, 2003, final edition, http://www.lexis-nexis.com/.

23. Jason Hoppin, "Marijuana Guru Found Guilty by Reluctant Jury," *The Recorder,* Feb. 3, 2003. http://www.lexis-nexis.com/.

24. Rich Ehisen, "The Battle Over Medical Marijuana."

25. Bob Egelko, "Convicted Pot Grower Rosenthal Is Spared Jail Time," *San Francisco Chronicle,* June 5, 2003, final edition, http://www.lexis-nexis.com/.

26. *Raich v. Ashcroft,* 248 F.Supp.2d 918, 931 (2003).

27. David Kravets, "Judge Tells Feds to Back Off From Medical Pot Group," *Associated Press State & Local Wire,* April 22, 2004, http://www.lexis-nexis.com/.

28. Ibid.

Comment

"Decriminalizing Marijuana for Medical Use" may be analyzed, first, by deciding whether California voters endorsed the best policy and, second, by judging the process by which they decriminalized marijuana and how public officials (at both state and federal levels) responded to state decriminalization in the face of a conflicting federal law.

The first step in judging California voters' decision to decriminalize marijuana is to decide whether the federal prohibition on the medical use of marijuana is paternalistic. There is a common tendency, which needs to be resisted, to describe any case of justified paternalism as nonpaternalistic. Mill, for example, denies that intervention in the case of the person crossing the unsafe bridge is paternalistic: "for liberty consists in doing what one desires, and he does not desire to fall into the river." But if the person wants to cross the bridge and if we thwart his desire in order to save his life, then our intervention is paternalistic. Determining whether a restriction on freedom is paternalistic, therefore, must be separated from the question of whether the restriction is justified (as it is in Mill's example).

Another common tendency is to conflate the problems of paternalism and democracy by labeling any democratic decision paternalistic simply because its effect is to limit the freedom and protect the interests of a minority. A law devised to satisfy the preferences of a democratic majority may not be paternalistic if, for example, its purpose is to restrict the majority's own freedom. If, however, the legal ban on marijuana at the federal level is an example of a majority voting to restrict the freedom of a minority, then it is properly considered paternalistic. Calling a law paternalistic, we must remember, does not in itself determine whether it is justified.

The law endorsed by a sizable majority of California voters—"Proposition 215: The Compassionate Use Act of 1996"—flew in the face of the more blanket federal ban on marijuana. Yet Prop 215 does not establish an entirely nonpaternalistic policy with respect to marijuana use. People are not entirely free to use marijuana as they see fit; instead, they are free to use marijuana only for medical purposes. In order to assess the substance of the California law, it is essential to distinguish between its nonpaternalistic features and the paternalism that it shares with the federal law: its overlapping ban on recreational (or nonmedicinal) marijuana use. Consider alternative ways in which California voters could have made marijuana available for medicinal purposes, and their paternalistic and nonpaternalistic features: permitting its sale over the counter, with or without mandatory labeling; and legalizing its use by prescription only, with or without limitations as to the specific medical conditions for which it may be legally prescribed.

The next step to consider in judging the content of the California law is to ask what would count as the least restrictive means of protecting individuals from the potential dangers of using marijuana while still gaining the benefits individual users seek. People who disagree about whether to decriminalize marijuana are likely to disagree about its benefits. What benefits do people seek when they use marijuana for medical purposes, and how should those benefits be evaluated? Consider alternative ways of describing the benefits of using marijuana: an effective medical cure or therapy, pain relief, psychic comfort, or a simple preference to sample its benefits by using it. On what empirical or ethical basis should these benefits along with dangers of using marijuana be judged for the purposes of making public policy?

The final step in assessing the content of the California law is to ask whether reasonable adults can accept the public goal of whatever paternalistic features remain in governmental regulation of marijuana. Consider what (if any) public goals could lead reasonable adults to accept restrictions on using marijuana for nonmedicinal purposes. Is it plausible to maintain that those whose freedom is restricted by the remaining ban nevertheless accept the goal of governmental intervention or would accept it if their decision-making faculties were not impaired? Evaluate the claim in support of the remaining prohibition on use of marijuana that reasonable adults would not want to use marijuana for nonmedical purposes.

Even if the content of a law can be justified, questions still should be asked about the process by which the law is enacted and enforced. Taking into account the comparative advantages of direct versus representative democracy, we should consider whether the legalization of marijuana for medicinal purposes should have been decided by a referendum rather than by legislative deliberation and decision making. To what extent does your judgment depend on how many citizens were directly involved in the decision? On the extent and quality of the deliberation afforded by referenda versus legislative decision making? On the public accountability and expertise of the decision makers?

It is not entirely clear under existing law whether the citizens of California and their accountable representatives in the state legislature have the authority to determine the state's policy on marijuana—or only the federal government (by virtue of the 1970 Controlled Substances Act). But from the perspective of political ethics and democratic theory the question is what is the most justifiable assignment of authority for such decisions. In evaluating the level of government (local, state, federal) that should make a decision of this sort, we need to determine the relevance of each of the following considerations and its practical implications: (1) the political freedom of citizens to be governed by laws of their own making; (2) the market freedom of citizens; (3) the quality of political deliberation; (4) the quantity of political participation; (5) equal protection of all persons under the law; and (6) local experimentation within the several states that could provide greater knowledge of the effects of different policies.

After the state referendum passed by a substantial majority, on what grounds should the state and federal attorneys general have decided how to react to the conflicting laws? Determine which of the following considerations should make a difference in how they react: (1) the requirements of their official role; (2) their judgment of the justice of the competing laws; (3) the size of the state majority opposing the federal law; (4) the popularity of the federal law within the state or in the nation; and (5) their judgment of the likely result of a judicial challenge to either the state or federal law.

Tossing Dwarfs in Illinois
Simone Sandy

Deja Vu, a nightclub in Springfield, Illinois, which routinely featured semi-nude dancing, planned more novel entertainment for August 16, 1989. The club had booked a four-foot, eight-inch, 120-pound man known as "Danger Dwarf" to appear in what was billed as a dwarf-tossing competition. Offering a prize of $100 for the person able to throw Danger Dwarf the farthest and highest, Deja Vu intended to charge patrons $5 each to watch or participate in the tournament.[1]

The Springfield City Council, the Illinois District Attorney's Office, Springfield members of the Little People of America (LPA), and other concerned residents expressed their opposition to the upcoming event. Bob Church, executive director of Springfield Mayor Ossie Langfelder's office, regretted that the city was "unable through a licensing process to do anything about it."[2] In similar cases elsewhere, city and state officials had prevented dwarf-tossing competitions by threatening to revoke the liquor licenses of offending taverns. Deja Vu, however, did not have a liquor license. Although Springfield could do nothing, legally, to prevent the contest, the city council passed a resolution denouncing events "such as dwarf tossing, which represent conduct that is both demeaning and insensitive to human values."[3] Deja Vu management canceled the competition without explanation.[4]

A month later, the city council passed an ordinance that imposed a series of fees and restrictions upon dwarf-tossing events, including the requirement for special permits. According to one critic of the ordinance, "Springfield, Illinois, did not ban the practice outright, but made dwarf tossing such a burdensome activity that promoters no longer find Springfield an attractive place to toss dwarfs. . . . The cumulative effect of all these requirements is to wipe out whatever profit margin a promoter otherwise would have."[5]

The managers of Deja Vu were neither the only nor the first club owners to promote a dwarf-tossing event. During the mid to late 1980s, tavern owners in several states, eager to attract more business, held competitions in the event, which originated in Australia as a contest among bouncers. Typically, several contestants vie to throw a dwarf the farthest, and the winner is awarded a cash prize. The dwarfs wear protective gear, including padding, neck braces, and helmets, and are usually thrown into piles of mattresses. They also wear harnesses with handles for the convenience of the tossers. In one variation of dwarf-tossing, commonly known as "dwarf bowling," a dwarf is strapped to a skateboard and rolled head-first toward plastic bowling pins.

Many of the dwarfs who are tossed apparently find the work easy, lucrative, and even enjoyable, especially compared to their former jobs or their daytime employment. Israel Torres, a dwarf who tours bars and clubs as "Little Mr. T," earns up to $2,000 a night being tossed in various contests. Torres states, "I've never been hurt. . . . Before this I was a professional wrestler for seventeen years. Here I make better money and it's a lot easier. . . . I like doing it."[6] "Lenny the Giant," a dwarf who was thrown a winning distance of eleven feet, five inches in British Dwarf-Throwing Championships, comments, "I used to work on an assembly line at an electronics factory—that's where I really felt degraded."[7] David "Midge" Wilson, a dwarf who tours Florida bars, asserts, "I like what I'm doing. I know what I'm doing. And it pays."[8]

Like the Springfield City Council and LPA, many officials and citizens object that the practice is dangerous for the dwarfs who are tossed, offensive and demeaning for all dwarfs, and degrading for our society as a whole. They point out that dwarfs have more fragile skeletal systems and extremely sensitive spinal cords, the injury of which could easily cause paralysis or death.[9] After he learned of an upcoming dwarf toss in his city, Mayor Harold Washington of Chicago responded, "This alleged contest is degrading and mean-spirited, endangers its participants, and is repugnant to everyone truly committed to eliminating prejudice against any group."[10] For many critics of dwarf-tossing, the most important issue is human dignity. Paul Steven Miller, a dwarf who is on the board of directors of the Billy Barty Foundation (a national dwarf advocacy organization), wrote:

> Dwarf-tossing is not a joke. It ridicules and demeans dwarfs. It causes people to view dwarfs as objects and freaks to gawk at. Dwarf-tossing affects not just the dwarfs who are thrown, but such exploitation hurts all dwarfs by eroding our self-esteem and by perpetuating stereotypes and misconceptions. Very few dwarfs work in circuses or as actors. Dwarfs are successfully employed in almost every possible occupation, for example, as teachers, engineers, lawyers, accountants, medical technicians.[11]

Some public officials have also denounced dwarf-tossing as a practice that debases not only dwarfs but all citizens of the cities and states where such contests are held. After signing legislation penalizing New York bars that sponsor the sport by revoking their liquor licenses, Governor Mario Cuomo said, "Any activity that dehumanizes and humiliates these people is degrading to us all."[12]

Many others, including the dwarfs who are tossed, defend the rights of consenting adults to make a living by being thrown in dwarf-tossing competitions. They say that policies banning such competitions infringe upon dwarfs' rights. Wilson asserts that his decision to earn his livelihood this way doesn't hurt anyone,[13] and that he doesn't think that others, particularly the Little People of America, ought to prescribe how he should handle his dwarfism.[14] Another defender of the activity argues, "The groups and individuals who claim to be harmed . . . do not have any rights violated. Dwarfs who do not get tossed, do-gooders, and a large segment of the general public may find the practice offensive, but that does not mean they have any right to do anything about it, just like no one has a right to prevent Jane from burning an American flag (if she owns it)."[15]

Defenders of the practice also emphasize the safety precautions that the promoters and dwarfs take. They point out that "dwarfs who wish to be tossed assume the risks of their activity," and that many take out insurance.[16] Some of those who believe it wrong to ban dwarf-tossing argue that many widely accepted sports are much more dangerous. "Midge" Wilson comments, "I think it's much milder than two people being in a ring beating each other. They don't protest that."[17]

Florida and New York have enacted laws that make it impossible for bars to sponsor dwarf-tossing but do not directly prohibit the practice in all cases. In both states, tavern owners can lose their alcoholic beverage licenses if they sponsor dwarf-tossing events. In Florida, they may also be compelled to pay fines up to $1,000. There are no penalties for participation in the competitions. Nor are there penalties for taking part in dwarf-tossing outside of bars.[18]

Notes

1. Rick Pearson, "Dwarf-Tossing Game Sounds Sour Note for Springfield Officials," *Chicago Tribune,* Aug. 16, 1989; Daniel Egler, "'Dwarf Tossing' Contests Goes Out the Window," *Chicago Tribune,* Aug. 17, 1989.

2. Pearson, "Dwarf-Tossing Game."

3. Egler, "'Dwarf Tossing' Contest."

4. Ibid.

5. Robert W. McGee, "If Dwarf Tossing Is Outlawed, Only Outlaws Will Toss Dwarfs: Is Dwarf Tossing a Victimless Crime?" *American Journal of Jurisprudence,* 38, 335–58.

6. Ibid.

7. Ibid.

8. Amy Wilson, "Short Story: It's a Tall Order Being the Only Dwarf Tossed These Days, But 'Midge' Wilson Fills It Well," *Chicago Tribune,* Jan. 11, 1989.

9. Letta Tayler, "Latest Bar Sport Called Dehumanizing to Dwarfs," *Newsday,* June 27,1989; Ann Landers, "We Haven't Scraped the Barrel's Bottom Yet," *Chicago Tribune,* July 9, 1989.

10. Mike Royko, "Dwarf-Tossing Thrown for a Loss," *Chicago Tribune,* Nov. 18, 1985.

11. "On Being Little But Not Belittled," *New York Times,* Dec. 10, 1989.

12. Associated Press, "New York Dwarf-Tossing Ban Signed by Cuomo," *Chicago Tribune,* July 25, 1990.

13. Wilson, "Short Story."

14. Anne V. Hull, "Dwarf-Tossing a Controversial Sport," *St. Petersburg Times,* Sept. 16, 1988.

15. McGee, "If Dwarf Tossing Is Outlawed."

16. Ibid.

17. Hull, "Dwarf-Tossing a Controversial Sport."

18. McGee, "If Dwarf Tossing Is Outlawed"; Associated Press, "New York Dwarf-Tossing Ban."

Comment

Evaluate the strongest case for banning the practice of dwarf-tossing in bars and the strongest case for permitting it, considering all the reasons that were given by dwarfs and public officials for and against the practice, and any other reasons that are relevant to resolving the controversy. First, identify the paternalistic reasons and consider the extent to which they are relevant to the case against dwarf-tossing. Is the danger of physical injury to dwarfs, for example, a necessary or sufficient reason for banning the activity? Second, examine the reasons that are based on moral considerations independent of the harm that the practice may cause dwarfs. Third, assess the nature and moral force of the argument that the activity "hurts all dwarfs by . . . perpetuating stereotypes and misconceptions." Is this a paternalistic argument or a moralistic argument, or neither?

To what extent is empirical evidence relevant to assessing the following criticisms of dwarf-tossing: (1) the activity is demeaning to dwarfs; (2) the activity is harmful to the self-esteem of dwarfs; (3) the activity perpetuates prejudicial stereotypes of dwarfs; and (4) the activity exploits dwarfs? What weight, if any, should we give to the fact that the major organized associations of dwarfs oppose the activity for all the reasons stated above? Does the consent of individual dwarfs to the activity make any difference in whether any of these critical claims should lead to banning or discouraging the practice?

Are there any significant moral differences between (1) banning the practice entirely in any public place; (2) banning bars from engaging in the practice by denying them liquor licenses; (3) levying a fine against bars if they engage in the practice; and (4) passing a public resolution that opposes events "such as dwarf tossing, which represent conduct that is both demeaning and insensitive to human values"? Which, if any, of these responses to dwarf-tossing are justified, and why? What additional information about dwarf-tossing, if any, do you need to answer this question?

What are the implications of your evaluation of dwarf-tossing for any other restrictions on individual liberty that aim to enforce social morality? Consider the ways in which regulating one or more of the following activities would differ in morally relevant ways from regulating dwarf-tossing: (1) public nudity, (2) sodomy, (3) incest, (4) pornography, (5) desecration of shrines and sacred symbols, (6) cruelty to animals, (7) mistreatment of corpses, and (8) commercial sale of bodily organs.

Making Marriage Gay*

On November 18th, 2003, the Massachusetts State Supreme Court ruled that same-sex couples could not be prohibited from marrying. In a split, 4–3 decision, the court reported that it had "failed to identify any constitutionally adequate reason" for such a prohibition.

The controversial ruling was followed up by another on February 4th, 2004, which asserted that nothing short of full marriage rights would pass constitutional muster—legislators could not create a separate legal category of "civil unions" for gay couples.

Before these rulings, gay marriage was not legally recognized anywhere in the United States. The only other state with comparable legislation was Vermont, which as of 2000 allows gay couples to obtain legally recognized "civil unions." The Massachusetts rulings were therefore the first of their kind, and they touched off a vigorous national debate about the public significance of marriage.

President George W. Bush promptly condemned the ruling, as did Massachusetts Governor Mitt Romney and a host of conservative and Christian organizations devoted to the preservation of traditional values. Legislators in several other states—including Arizona, Georgia, Virginia, Oklahoma, Kentucky, and Michigan—moved quickly to introduce state constitutional amendments reinforcing the ban on gay marriage in their own states. Many of these same lawmakers also began to push for a federal constitutional amendment.

Conservatives offered up a number of arguments against the "four robed individuals" of the Massachusetts bench: same-sex marriage, they charged, would undermine the sanctity of the institution of marriage itself and erode the moral fabric of American society; marriage is an institution structured around procreation and child rearing, and is therefore inappropriate for same-sex couples. Most of these arguments rested on the fundamental conviction that the traditional family is vital to the perpetuation of a moral and orderly society, and the state therefore has a powerful interest in protecting the traditional understanding that marriage can happen only "between a man and a woman."

For the decision's supporters, however, it marked an historic turning point in the struggle for equal rights. They argued that gay and lesbian couples had long been victims of legal discrimination which had resulted in their exclusion from one of the most important social institutions of modern society and such exclusion was not merely symbolic: marriage has far-reaching legal implications in domains as diverse as health care, property and inheritance, child care and visitation, and criminal law. They compared laws prohibiting gay marriage to miscegenation laws (prohibiting interracial marriages), and noted that these, too, were once defended as pillars of the moral integrity of American society. Some took the argument onto conservative ground and argued that the ruling marked an important and more inclusive reaffirmation of family values.

Defenders of gay marriage argue on grounds of equal protection that marriage must be equally available to all citizens. Even civil unions would therefore relegate gay and lesbian individuals to the status of second-class citizens. The court's critics claim, however, that marriage—defined as the union of one man and one woman—is in fact already available to everyone equally. Homosexuals, like heterosexuals, are free to marry a person of the opposite sex. They argue that the issue should therefore remain in the hands of state legislatures, who must choose whether to create a *new* right to same-sex unions. This conflict reveals a deep disagreement about the content and justification of the right to marry (the conflict is highlighted in the Massachusetts court opinions that follow).

The Massachusetts court decision was only one phase of a political contest that will be fought in many different political arenas. Massachusetts legislators addressed the issue at a constitutional convention held in February and March 2004 (see excerpts later). Several amendments were introduced which would have limited marriage to "one man and one woman." Eventually, the legislature approved a constitutional amendment that would ban gay marriage but establish "civil unions" with identical legal rights and benefits. The amendment will have to be approved by popular vote in 2006 before it can become law.

---

*Alex Zakaras wrote the introduction and selected the excerpts presented in this section.

On February 24th, President Bush officially endorsed an amendment to the federal Constitution prohibiting same-sex marriage. He argued that marriage was "the most enduring human institution," and should not be tampered with by a small group of liberal judges. Because it would require two-thirds of the vote in both legislative houses, as well as support from three-fourths of the states, such an amendment would very likely be defeated. The president's endorsement nonetheless contributed to the conservatives' attempt to move the issue into the foreground of the 2004 elections. Public opinion polls conducted in the fall and winter of 2003–2004 have consistently shown that a majority of Americans oppose same-sex marriage.[1]

THE MASSACHUSETTS SUPREME COURT SPEAKS

EXCERPTS FROM GOODRIDGE V.
MASSACHUSETTS DEPT. OF PUBLIC
HEALTH, NOVEMBER 18, 2003

Marriage is a vital social institution. The exclusive commitment of two individuals to each other nurtures love and mutual support; it brings stability to our society. For those who choose to marry, and for their children, marriage provides an abundance of legal, financial, and social benefits. In return it imposes weighty legal, financial, and social obligations. The question before us is whether, consistent with the Massachusetts Constitution, the Commonwealth may deny the protections, benefits, and obligations conferred by civil marriage to two individuals of the same sex who wish to marry. We conclude that it may not. The Massachusetts Constitution affirms the dignity and equality of all individuals. It forbids the creation of second-class citizens. In reaching our conclusion we have given full deference to the arguments made by the Commonwealth. But it has failed to identify any constitutionally adequate reason for denying civil marriage to same-sex couples. . . .

Barred access to the protections, benefits, and obligations of civil marriage, a person who enters into an intimate, exclusive union with another of the same sex is arbitrarily deprived of membership in one of our community's most rewarding and cherished institutions. That exclusion is incompatible with the constitutional principles of respect for individual autonomy and equality under law.

.   .   .

The . . . question is whether, as the department claims, government action that bars same-sex couples from civil marriage constitutes a legitimate exercise of the State's authority to regulate conduct, or whether, as the plaintiffs claim, this categorical marriage exclusion violates the Massachusetts Constitution. We have recognized the long-standing statutory understanding, derived from the common law, that "marriage" means the lawful union of a woman and a man. But that history cannot and does not foreclose the constitutional question. . . .

We begin by considering the nature of civil marriage itself. Simply put, the government creates civil marriage. In Massachusetts, civil marriage is, and since pre-Colonial days has been, precisely what its name implies: a wholly secular institution. No religious ceremony has ever been required to validate a Massachusetts marriage. . . .

Without question, civil marriage enhances the "welfare of the community." It is a "social institution of the highest importance."[2] Civil marriage anchors an ordered society by encouraging stable relationships over transient ones. It is central to the way the Commonwealth identifies individuals, provides for the orderly distribution of property, ensures that children and adults are cared for and supported whenever possible from private rather than public funds, and tracks important epidemiological and demographic data. Marriage also bestows enormous private and social advantages on those who choose to marry. Civil marriage is at once a deeply personal commitment to another human being and a highly public celebration of the ideals of mutuality, companionship, intimacy, fidelity, and family. "It is an association that promotes a way of life, not causes; a harmony in living, not political faiths; a bilateral loyalty, not commercial or social projects."[3] Because it fulfils yearnings for security, safe haven, and connection that express our common humanity, civil marriage is an esteemed institution, and the decision whether and whom to marry is among life's momentous acts of self-definition.

Tangible as well as intangible benefits flow from marriage. The marriage license grants valuable property rights to those who meet the entry requirements, and who agree to what might otherwise be a burdensome degree of government regulation of their activities. . . . The Legislature has conferred on "each party [in a civil marriage] substantial rights concerning the assets of the other which unmarried cohabitants do not have."[4]

The benefits accessible only by way of a marriage license are enormous, touching nearly every aspect of life and death. The department states that "hundreds of statutes" are related to marriage and to marital benefits. With no attempt to be comprehensive, we note that some of the statutory benefits conferred by the Legislature on those who enter into civil marriage include, as to property: joint Massachusetts income tax filing; tenancy by the entirety (a form of ownership that provides certain protections against creditors and allows for the automatic descent of property to the surviving spouse without probate); extension of the benefit of the homestead protection (securing up to $300,000 in equity from creditors) to one's spouse and children; automatic rights to inherit the property of a deceased spouse who does not leave a will; the rights of elective share and of dower (which allow surviving spouses certain property rights where the decedent spouse has not made adequate provision for the survivor in a will); entitlement to wages owed to a deceased employee; eligibility to continue certain businesses of a deceased spouse; the right to share the medical policy of one's spouse; thirty-nine week continuation of health coverage for the spouse of a person who is laid off or dies; preferential options under the Commonwealth's pension system; preferential benefits in the Commonwealth's medical program, MassHealth; access to veterans' spousal benefits and preferences; financial protections for spouses of certain Commonwealth employees (fire fighters, police officers, and prosecutors, among others) killed in the performance of duty; the equitable division of marital property on divorce; temporary and permanent alimony rights; the right to separate support on separation of the parties that does not result in divorce; and the right to bring claims for wrongful death and loss of consortium, and for funeral and burial expenses and punitive damages resulting from tort actions.

Exclusive marital benefits that are not directly tied to property rights include the presumptions of legitimacy and parentage of children born to a married couple; and evidentiary rights, such as the prohibition against spouses testifying against one another about their private conversations, applicable in both civil and criminal cases. Other statutory benefits of a personal nature available only to married individuals include qualification for bereavement or medical leave to care for individuals related by blood or marriage; an automatic "family member" preference to make medical decisions for an incompetent or disabled spouse who does not have a contrary health care proxy; the application of predictable rules of child custody, visitation, support, and removal out-of-State when married parents divorce; priority rights to administer the estate of a deceased spouse who dies without a will, and the requirement that a surviving spouse must consent to the appointment of any other person as administrator; and the right to interment in the lot or tomb owned by one's deceased spouse.

Where a married couple has children, their children are also directly or indirectly, but no less auspiciously, the recipients of the special legal and economic protections obtained by civil marriage. Notwithstanding the Commonwealth's strong public policy to abolish legal distinctions between marital and nonmarital children in providing for the support and care of minors, the fact remains that marital children reap a measure of family stability and economic security based on their parents' legally privileged status that is largely inaccessible, or not as readily accessible, to nonmarital children. Some of these benefits are social, such as the enhanced approval that still attends the status of being a marital child. Others are material, such as the greater ease of access to family-based State and Federal benefits that attend the presumptions of one's parentage.

It is undoubtedly for these concrete reasons, as well as for its intimately personal significance, that civil marriage has long been termed a "civil right." . . . Without the right to marry—or more properly, the right to choose to marry—one is excluded from the full range of human experience and denied full protection of the laws for one's "avowed commitment to an intimate and lasting human relationship."[5] Because civil marriage is central to the lives of individuals and the welfare of the community, our laws assiduously protect the individual's right to marry against undue government incursion. Laws may not "interfere directly and substantially with the right to marry."[6] . . .

. . .

The Massachusetts Constitution protects matters of personal liberty against government incursion as zealously, and often more so, than does the Federal Constitution, even where both Constitutions employ essentially the same language. . . . The individual liberty and equality safeguards of the Massachusetts Constitution protect both "freedom from" unwarranted government intrusion into protected spheres of life and "freedom to" partake in benefits created by the State for the common good. Both freedoms are involved here. Whether and whom to marry, how to express sexual intimacy, and whether and how to establish a family—these are among the most basic of every individual's liberty and due process rights. And central to personal freedom and security is the assurance that the laws will apply equally to persons in similar situations. "Absolute equality before the law is a fundamental principle of our own Constitution."[7] The liberty interest in choosing whether and whom to marry would be hollow if the Commonwealth could, without sufficient justification, foreclose an individual from freely choosing the person with whom to share an exclusive commitment in the unique institution of civil marriage. . . .

The department posits three legislative rationales for prohibiting same-sex couples from marrying: (1) providing a "favorable setting for procreation"; (2) ensuring the optimal setting for child rearing, which the department defines as "a two-parent family with one parent of each sex"; and (3) preserving scarce State and private financial resources. We consider each in turn.

The judge in the Superior Court endorsed the first rationale, holding that "the state's interest in regulating marriage is based on the traditional concept that marriage's primary purpose is procreation." This is incorrect. Our laws of civil marriage do not privilege procreative heterosexual intercourse between married people above every other form of adult intimacy and every other means of creating a family. General Laws c. 207 contains no requirement that the applicants for a marriage license attest to their ability or intention to conceive children by coitus. Fertility is not a condition of marriage, nor is it grounds for divorce. People who have never consummated their marriage, and never plan to, may be and stay married. People who cannot stir from their deathbed may marry. While it is certainly true that many, perhaps most, married couples have children together (assisted or unassisted), it is the exclusive and permanent commitment of the marriage partners to one another, not the begetting of children, that is the sine qua non of civil marriage.[8]

Moreover, the Commonwealth affirmatively facilitates bringing children into a family regardless of whether the intended parent is married or unmarried, whether the child is adopted or born into a family, whether assistive technology was used to conceive the child, and whether the parent or her partner is heterosexual, homosexual, or bisexual. If procreation were a necessary component of civil marriage, our statutes would draw a tighter circle around the permissible bounds of nonmarital child bearing and the creation of families by noncoital means. The attempt to isolate procreation as "the source of a fundamental right to marry," overlooks the integrated way in which courts have examined the complex and overlapping realms of personal autonomy, marriage, family life, and child rearing. Our jurisprudence recognizes that, in these nuanced and fundamentally private areas of life, such a narrow focus is inappropriate.

The "marriage is procreation" argument singles out the one unbridgeable difference between same-sex and opposite-sex couples, and transforms that difference into the essence of legal marriage. . . . In so doing, the State's action confers an official stamp of approval on the destructive stereotype that same-sex relationships are inherently unstable and inferior to opposite-sex relationships and are not worthy of respect.

The department's first stated rationale, equating marriage with unassisted heterosexual procreation, shades imperceptibly into its second: that confining marriage to opposite-sex couples ensures that children are raised in the "optimal" setting. Protecting the welfare of children is a paramount State policy. Restricting marriage to opposite-sex couples, however, cannot plausibly further this policy. "The demographic changes of the past century make it difficult

to speak of an average American family. The composition of families varies greatly from household to household."[9] Massachusetts has responded supportively to "the changing realities of the American family,"[10] and has moved vigorously to strengthen the modern family in its many variations. . . . The "best interests of the child" standard does not turn on a parent's sexual orientation or marital status.

The department has offered no evidence that forbidding marriage to people of the same sex will increase the number of couples choosing to enter into opposite-sex marriages in order to have and raise children. There is thus no rational relationship between the marriage statute and the Commonwealth's proffered goal of protecting the "optimal" child rearing unit. Moreover, the department readily concedes that people in same-sex couples may be "excellent" parents. These couples (including four of the plaintiff couples) have children for the reasons others do—to love them, to care for them, to nurture them. But the task of child rearing for same-sex couples is made infinitely harder by their status as outliers to the marriage laws. While establishing the parentage of children as soon as possible is crucial to the safety and welfare of children, same-sex couples must undergo the sometimes lengthy and intrusive process of second-parent adoption to establish their joint parentage. While the enhanced income provided by marital benefits is an important source of security and stability for married couples and their children, those benefits are denied to families headed by same-sex couples. While the laws of divorce provide clear and reasonably predictable guidelines for child support, child custody, and property division on dissolution of a marriage, same-sex couples who dissolve their relationships find themselves and their children in the highly unpredictable terrain of equity jurisdiction. Given the wide range of public benefits reserved only for married couples, we do not credit the department's contention that the absence of access to civil marriage amounts to little more than an inconvenience to same-sex couples and their children. Excluding same-sex couples from civil marriage will not make children of opposite-sex marriages more secure, but it does prevent children of same-sex couples from enjoying the immeasurable advantages that flow from the assurance of "a stable family structure in which children will be reared, educated, and socialized."[11] . . .

In this case, we are confronted with an entire, sizeable class of parents raising children who have absolutely no access to civil marriage and its protections because they are forbidden from procuring a marriage license. It cannot be rational under our laws, and indeed it is not permitted, to penalize children by depriving them of State benefits because the State disapproves of their parents' sexual orientation. . . .

The department suggests additional rationales for prohibiting same-sex couples from marrying, which are developed by some *amici.* It argues that broadening civil marriage to include same-sex couples will trivialize or destroy the institution of marriage as it has historically been fashioned. Certainly our decision today marks a significant change in the definition of marriage as it has been inherited from the common law, and understood by many societies for centuries. But it does not disturb the fundamental value of marriage in our society.

Here, the plaintiffs seek only to be married, not to undermine the institution of civil marriage. They do not want marriage abolished. They do not attack the binary nature of marriage, the consanguinity provisions, or any of the other gate-keeping provisions of the marriage licensing law. Recognizing the right of an individual to marry a person of the same sex will not diminish the validity or dignity of opposite-sex marriage, any more than recognizing the right of an individual to marry a person of a different race devalues the marriage of a person who marries someone of her own race. If anything, extending civil marriage to same-sex couples reinforces the importance of marriage to individuals and communities. That same-sex couples are willing to embrace marriage's solemn obligations of exclusivity, mutual support, and commitment to one another is a testament to the enduring place of marriage in our laws and in the human spirit. . . .

The marriage ban works a deep and scarring hardship on a very real segment of the community for no rational reason. The absence of any reasonable relationship between, on the one hand, an absolute disqualification of same-sex couples who wish to enter into civil marriage and, on the other, protection of public health, safety, or general welfare, suggests that the marriage restriction is rooted in persistent prejudices against persons who are (or who are believed to be) homosexual. "The Constitution cannot control such prejudices but neither can it tolerate them. Private biases may be outside the reach of the law, but the law cannot, directly or indirectly, give them effect."[12] Limiting the protections, benefits, and obligations of civil marriage to opposite-sex couples violates the basic premises of individual liberty and equality under law protected by the Massachusetts Constitution.

CORDY, J. (DISSENTING, WITH WHOM SPINA AND SOSMAN, JJ., JOIN)

Limiting marriage to the union of one man and one woman does not impair the exercise of a fundamental right. Civil marriage is an institution created by the State. In Massachusetts, the marriage statutes are derived from English common law, and were first enacted in colonial times. They were enacted to secure public interests and not for religious purposes or to promote personal interests or aspirations. As the court notes in its opinion, the institution of marriage is "the legal union of a man and woman as husband and wife," and it has always been so under Massachusetts law, colonial or otherwise. . . .

Civil marriage is the institutional mechanism by which societies have sanctioned and recognized particular family structures, and the institution of marriage has existed as one of the fundamental organizing principles of human society. Marriage has not been merely a contractual arrangement for legally defining the private relationship between two individuals (although that is certainly part of any marriage). Rather, on an institutional level, marriage is the "very basis of the whole fabric of civilized society,"[13] and it serves many important political, economic, social, educational, procreational, and personal functions. . . .

The institution of marriage provides the important legal and normative link between heterosexual intercourse and procreation on the one hand and family responsibilities on the other. The partners in a marriage are expected to engage in exclusive sexual relations, with children the probable result and paternity presumed. Whereas the relationship between mother and child is demonstratively and predictably created and recognizable through the biological process of pregnancy and childbirth, there is no corresponding process for creating a relationship between father and child. Similarly, aside from an act of heterosexual intercourse nine months prior to childbirth, there is no process for creating a relationship between a man and a woman as the parents of a particular child. The institution of marriage fills this void by formally binding the husband-father to his wife and child, and imposing on him the responsibilities of fatherhood. The alternative, a society without the institution of marriage, in which heterosexual intercourse, procreation, and child care are largely disconnected processes, would be chaotic.

The marital family is also the foremost setting for the education and socialization of children. Children learn about the world and their place in it primarily from those who raise them, and those children eventually grow up to exert some influence, great or small, positive or negative, on society. The institution of marriage encourages parents to remain committed to each other and to their children as they grow, thereby encouraging a stable venue for the education and socialization of children. More macroscopically, construction of a family through marriage also formalizes the bonds between people in an ordered and institutional manner, thereby facilitating a foundation of interconnectedness and interdependency on which more intricate stabilizing social structures might be built. . . .

It is undeniably true that dramatic historical shifts in our cultural, political, and economic landscape have altered some of our traditional notions about marriage, including the interpersonal dynamics within it, the range of responsibilities required of it as an institution, and the legal environment in which it exists. Nevertheless, the institution of marriage remains the principal weave of our social fabric. A family defined by heterosexual marriage continues to be the most prevalent social structure into which the vast majority of children are born, nurtured, and prepared for productive participation in civil society.[14] It is difficult to imagine a State purpose more important and legitimate than ensuring, promoting, and supporting an optimal social structure within which to bear and raise children. At the very least, the marriage statute continues to serve this important State purpose. . . .

The question we must turn to next is whether the statute, construed as limiting marriage to couples of the opposite sex, remains a rational way to further that purpose. Stated differently, we ask whether a conceivable rational basis exists on which the Legislature could conclude that continuing to limit the institution of civil marriage to members of the opposite sex furthers the legitimate purpose of ensuring, promoting, and supporting an optimal social structure for the bearing and raising of children.

In considering whether such a rational basis exists, we defer to the decision-making process of the Legislature, and must make deferential assumptions about the information that it might consider and on which it may rely. We must assume that the Legislature (1) might conclude that the institution of civil marriage has successfully and continually provided this structure over several centuries; (2) might consider and credit studies that document negative consequences that too often follow children either born outside of marriage or raised in households lacking either a father or a mother figure,[15] and scholarly commentary contending that children and families develop best when mothers and fathers are partners in their parenting;[16] and (3) would be familiar with many recent studies that variously support the proposition that children raised in intact families headed by same-sex couples fare as well on many measures as children raised in similar families headed by opposite-sex couples;[17] support the proposition that children of same-sex couples fare worse on some measures;[18] or reveal notable differences between the two groups of children that warrant further study.[19]

We must also assume that the Legislature would be aware of the critiques of the methodologies used in virtually all of the comparative studies of children raised in these different environments, cautioning that the sampling populations are not representative, that the observation periods are too limited in time, that the empirical data are unreliable, and that the hypotheses are too infused with political or agenda driven bias.[20]

Taking all of this available information into account, the Legislature could rationally conclude that a family environment with married opposite-sex parents remains the optimal social structure in which to bear children, and that the raising of children by same-sex couples, who by definition cannot be the two sole biological parents of a child and cannot provide children with a parental authority figure of each gender, presents an alternative structure for child rearing that has not yet proved itself beyond reasonable

scientific dispute to be as optimal as the biologically based marriage norm. Working from the assumption that a recognition of same-sex marriages will increase the number of children experiencing this alternative, the Legislature could conceivably conclude that declining to recognize same-sex marriages remains prudent until empirical questions about its impact on the upbringing of children are resolved.

The fact that the Commonwealth currently allows same-sex couples to adopt, does not affect the rationality of this conclusion. The eligibility of a child for adoption presupposes that at least one of the child's biological parents is unable or unwilling, for some reason, to participate in raising the child. In that sense, society has "lost" the optimal setting in which to raise that child—it is simply not available. In these circumstances, the principal and overriding consideration is the "best interests of the child," considering his or her unique circumstances and the options that are available for that child. . . .

That the State does not preclude different types of families from raising children does not mean that it must view them all as equally optimal and equally deserving of State endorsement and support. For example, single persons are allowed to adopt children, but the fact that the Legislature permits single-parent adoption does not mean that it has endorsed single parenthood as an optimal setting in which to raise children or views it as the equivalent of being raised by both of one's biological parents. The same holds true with respect to same-sex couples—the fact that they may adopt children means only that the Legislature has concluded that they may provide an acceptable setting in which to raise children who cannot be raised by both of their biological parents. The Legislature may rationally permit adoption by same-sex couples yet harbor reservations as to whether parenthood by same-sex couples should be affirmatively encouraged to the same extent as parenthood by the heterosexual couple whose union produced the child.

Similarly, while the fact that our laws have evolved to include a strong affirmative policy against discrimination on the basis of sexual orientation, have decriminalized intimate adult conduct, and have abolished the legal distinctions between marital and non-marital children, may well be a reason to celebrate a more open and humane society, they ought not be the basis on which to conclude that there is no longer a rational basis for the current marriage law. To conclude the latter based on the former threatens the process of social reform in a democratic society. States must be free to experiment in the realm of social and civil relations, incrementally and without concern that a step or two in one direction will determine the outcome of the experiment as a matter of law. If they are not, those who argue "slippery slope" will have more ammunition than ever to resist any effort at progressive change or social experimentation, and will be able to put the lie to the arguments of the proponents of such efforts, that an incremental step forward does not preordain a result which neither the people nor their elected representatives may yet be prepared to accept.

In addition, the Legislature could conclude that redefining the institution of marriage to permit same-sex couples to marry would impair the State's interest in promoting and supporting heterosexual marriage as the social institution that it has determined best normalizes, stabilizes, and links the acts of procreation and child rearing. While the plaintiffs argue that they only want to take part in the same stabilizing institution, the Legislature conceivably could conclude that permitting their participation would have the unintended effect of undermining to some degree marriage's ability to serve its social purpose.

As long as marriage is limited to opposite-sex couples who can at least theoretically procreate, society is able to communicate a consistent message to its citizens that marriage is a (normatively) necessary part of their procreative endeavor; that if they are to procreate, then society has endorsed the institution of marriage as the environment for it and for the subsequent rearing of their children; and that benefits are available explicitly to create a supportive and conducive atmosphere for those purposes. If society proceeds similarly to recognize marriages between same-sex couples who cannot procreate, it could be perceived as an abandonment of this claim, and might result in the mistaken view that civil marriage has little to do with procreation: just as the potential of procreation would not be necessary for a marriage to be valid, marriage would not be necessary for optimal procreation and child rearing to occur.[21] In essence, the Legislature could conclude that the consequence of such a policy shift would be a diminution in society's ability to steer the acts of procreation and child rearing into their most optimal setting. . . .

Concerns about . . . unintended consequences cannot be dismissed as fanciful or far-fetched. Legislative actions taken in the 1950's and 1960's in areas as widely arrayed as domestic relations law and welfare legislation have had significant unintended adverse consequences in subsequent decades including the dramatic increase in children born out of wedlock, and the destabilization of the institution of marriage.[22]

There is no question that many same-sex couples are capable of being good parents, and should be (and are) permitted to be so. The policy question that a legislator must resolve is a different one, and turns on an assessment of whether the marriage structure proposed by the plaintiffs will, over time, if endorsed and supported by the State, prove to be as stable and successful a model as the one that has formed a cornerstone of our society since colonial times, or prove to be less than optimal, and result in consequences, perhaps now unforeseen, adverse to the State's legitimate interest in promoting and supporting the best possible social structure in which children should be born and raised. Given the critical importance of civil marriage as an organizing and stabilizing institution of society, it is eminently rational for the Legislature to postpone making fundamental changes to it until such time as there is unanimous scientific evidence, or popular consensus, or both, that such changes can safely be made. . . .

THE MASSACHUSETTS CONSTITUTIONAL CONVENTION CONVENES

EXCERPTS FROM FEBRUARY 11–12, 2004

SPEAKER FINNERAN:

[The recent] 4–3 decision has caused extraordinary division and controversy. Everybody I have spoken to has commented on the vituperative language of the decision. I have read and re-read the decision. In the majority opinion was a statement that I would describe as libelous and defamatory of this institution. The libel spoke to the definition of marriage that has come to us from custom, tradition, every society, every culture, every nation in all of recorded history as one man and one woman. The defamatory statement stated this: in light of that extraordinary history, the [court] said this about you and the citizens of Massachusetts: they said that definition was rooted in animus and bigotry. That libel has not only been uttered against you and your predecessor[s]. It was also . . . aimed at the three judges in the minority. . . .

I would try to rebut with facts the libel and slur uttered against us. The court may have, when reviewing papers, . . . wanted to avail themselves to the history of this place, going back to the early 1980s. Some of you passed bills prohibiting discrimination against gay and lesbian neighbors and friends in housing, employment, credit and a whole host of things long before it became politically fashionable. That was a statutory prohibition and there has been no attempt to repeal or modify them. The court may have studied our support for adoption of children by gay and lesbian couples. The court may have availed themselves to your support for programs for gay and lesbian youth. The court might have noted that 38 states have enacted [Defense of Marriage Act] statutes and there has been no effort to do so here. We thought [it] not necessary, we can continue to move forward.

Last but not least, the Commonwealth may have noticed that it's been reported there has been almost a three-year active effort to effectuate and implement a civil union bill. . . . The court could have only concluded that the Legislature, on its own initiative and desire to make sure our gay and lesbian family and friends feel welcome in this wonderful place, the court would have had to take notice that it has been steady, sustainable and astounding progress on gay and lesbian issues. The notion of having this progress be sustainable is important. The progress on gay and lesbian issues has occurred all across the board, more notably in Massachusetts than other jurisdictions.

The [proposed] amendment addresses four things. It would define marriage as one man and one woman and for the first time present to the court rational bases—plural—for our adoption of that definition of marriage. . . . The second thing the amendment does is by specific reference to civil unions and to the House and Senate would make crystal clear our desire and intention to move forward and adopt some form of civil unions. The debate is occurring in the midst of the tumult and full consideration is being given to that. . . . Third, this amendment, if adopted would begin the course of correction of the [court's] intrusion into an area where they are not to operate, the area of policy. That is your jurisdiction and domain. That is the reason you ran for office, to shape and speak out and fight for public policy. It is emphatically not the domain of the [court]. It is the citizens who hold the penultimate power in this matter. They are the only ones who can amend the constitution. People on both sides talk about the sacred nature and text of our constitution. The people must be given an opportunity to be heard. . . .

REP. SMIZIK

My political and formative years took place during the civil rights struggles of the 60s.

The judges in the heart of the south were at risk of impeachment, life and limb, and of being ostracized. Still they upheld the equal protection law of the constitution. They challenged the separate but equal doctrine of the south. They made decisions not popular with the majority but to fulfill their role and uphold provisions in the constitution that protect the minority from the oppression of the majority. Thurgood Marshall helped champion equal protection. We face an equal protection decision. Gay couples cannot get marriage licenses. In *Goodridge,* 78 couples sought equal rights to marry. They argued the constitution of Massachusetts calls for equal protection under the law. Our [court] concluded the plaintiffs were correct. The court exercised its judgment as the court is required to do. If we push with one of these amendments today, we will be trying to usurp the court's decision. I can't go that route. Courts have a long history of providing civil rights to our citizens. I appreciate the special role decisions have made regarding constitutional rights. The courts have eliminated the doctrine of separate but equal. I have heard that god has made us all. The beauty of our constitution is it makes it easy to solve the problem. All god's children should be equal under the eyes of the law. In 1968, I attended law school when MLK and Bobby Kennedy were assassinated. They railed against the denial of equal protection. I was inspired by their words and convinced by their conviction and courage. Dr. King said now is the time to make justice a reality for all of god's children. Kennedy and King called on us to take action. Kennedy said each time a person stands up for an ideal, he sends forth a tiny ripple of hope. These ripples build a current that can sweep down the mightiest walls of oppression and resistance. Extend that ripple of hope for those who have not been given equal rights in our state.

REP. PARENTE

. . . Mother nature left her blueprint behind, the DNA of a man and a woman. . . . The statute of marriage was created to give statutory protection to the family unit, the man and woman and the children they create. Mother nature used the pattern to populate the world. People say how can you talk like that? We have all kinds of family units. Don't give me examples of bad behavior to support this argument. . . . We have heard talk today about religion. . . . I just want to say to those who say we should never discuss religion and we should throw god out of our lives, you know the mind that goes to church on Sunday is the same mind that comes to work on Monday. . . . That is just part of who we are. I look to the constitution to support my right to say that. One senator said there is no mention of religion in the constitution. They have deleted sections, but the preamble refers to god, everybody's god. They refer to him as the divine legislator. Harvard was founded in 1636 and is protected by this constitution. It's okay to mention god in this section. When you talk about the constitution, make sure you read it first. What's next if we show our disdain for religion here?. . . . I believe that the family unit that Mother Nature created, a man and woman and children, there are unique qualities that the man and women bring to the relationship. . . .

REP. ST. FLEUR

This is difficult for me on a number of levels. I have come to . . . anger for the first time since coming to this House. And I want to explain to you why I feel this way. You can't compromise on discrimination. You can't color it another way. Let's start with race. You have to deal with it. We had to deal with it in the Constitution, with women and immigrants. I, my friends, fit all those categories and but for the equal protections of the laws, I would not enjoy the position and freedom I enjoy today. I cannot compromise on the Constitution. I can't compromise on discrimination. I am also Catholic. But . . . my role as a legislator is [separate] from my role in a parish. . . . We are seeking . . . state action— not private action, not religious action. And if the state is involved in marriage, we ought to do it equally. That's one of the fundamental protections of government. This is one of those times when we are called to rise above the personal and establish fundamental principles for which we ought to live. . . . What is special about this American democracy is we are willing to put aside the power of the majority to respect the power of the minority. This is not simply about gay rights. This is about who we are as an American democracy. . . . This court speaks about a population that we are not quite comfortable with. Isn't that what this is about? So we cling to history and tradition. . . . We should look to our fundamental principles.

REP. FAGAN

I believe we are really voting on not changing the constitution at all. The actions of this body will preserve and protect rights of all citizens to vote themselves. Our constitution in 1788 in the first part says all power residing in the people derived from them, legislative or executive and judicial, are at all times accountable to the people. I grew up Catholic and have a traditional view of marriage. My view does not supercede those of others. I am not smarter than the people who chose to vote for me. I have confidence in the citizens of my city. I agree with the previous speaker. Our constitution should not be changed. I will support this amendment not because I believe the constitution should be changed, but the contrary. The right of every citizen to be heard should be protected. Ben Franklin said a government of the people derives its power from the people. We are a government of laws so long as we adhere to the will of the people so governed. We have come a long way. If we do not let our constituents vote, there will be no resurrection of the constitutional rights we hold so dear.

SEN. JOYCE

[The court] has said the constitution protects all and does not allow for a separate but unequal class of citizens. . . . I am sworn as you are to uphold the constitution. I will vote to allow gays and lesbians the right to share in medical decisions, health care for their partners and children. . . . Polls show the argument to let the people decide has great

appeal. That may influence our governor's statements. [But] we are charged with exercising our judgment. It is our responsibility to cast votes, even when the matter is controversial. . . . I am unconvinced that civil rights should be decided at the ballot box when emotions are so inflamed. Had the ban on interracial marriage or the decision segregating schools been put on the ballot, each may have been overturned. That does not mean those decisions were wrong. Marriage will allow same-sex couples to have the unquestioned right to hospital visitation and to leave pension and Social Security benefits to one another and their children. They will be expected to support one another and their children. As Justice Greaney wrote, we share a common humanity and participate together in the social contract. Simple principles of decency dictate that we extend full acceptance, tolerance and respect. We should reject the Speaker's amendment, which would deny civil marriage, civil rights and this convention even the right to vote on civil unions.

SEN. PACHECO

We have a compromise proposal that does three things: first, it preserves the definition of marriage as one man and one woman. Second, it takes care of the interests of existing people who already have rights accrued to them and affords them in the future. Third, it gives the citizens a voice and a vote. In my district, I met with members of the Roman Catholic Church in my district. They told me they wanted marriage defined as the union of one man and one woman. What do I say to [same-sex couples] who already have benefits from their employers? They said, "I have no problem with the individuals having those benefits." They said they were fine with that, so long as it was not defined as marriage. . . . We know those on the far left and right will not embrace this issue. But if one applies common sense and good listening skills, the mainstream average citizen is saying to us marriage should be one man and one woman, but we want to take care of the average rights of our citizens.

SEN. BARRIOS

[This is] a historic event. . . . What is special about today and what has attracted all of us to prepare speeches and listen to our colleagues, is an unprecedented event in history should it be successful. For the first time since 1780, we would amend our constitution to set up a two-tiered structure. On May 17 all of us will have the same rights, and protections and benefits of marriage. What this constitution will do is take away rights, benefits and protections. We are denying protections to a certain class of citizens. I am biased—you are all thinking that. He is up there because he is gay. I am the first person to speak on this who is directly affected by it. We will lose inheritance benefits, health care as a state employee and numerous financial benefits. My two children are also affected by this, Nathaniel and Javier, as well as my partner Doug. . . . Don't fool yourself about what you are voting for. This will deny basic rights that many of you might not understand are rights which you have. . . . If I were to die tomorrow . . . my partner would be ineligible for Social Security survivor benefits. I am currently barred from designating my partner as my pension beneficiary. How am I to make sure my children are taken care of.

NOTES

1. A Jan. 9–11 CNN/*USA Today*/Gallup poll asked Americans if they would favor or oppose a law that would allow same-sex couples to legally get married, or if they have no opinion on the issue at all. The results show that a majority of Americans, 53 percent, oppose such a law, and 44 percent of respondents oppose it strongly. Twenty-four percent of Americans say they would favor such a law, and 23 percent do not have an opinion about gay marriage.

2. *French v. McAnarney,* 290 Mass. 544, 546, 195 N.E. 714 (1935).

3. *Griswold v. Connecticut,* 381 U.S. 479, 486, 85 S.Ct. 1678, 14 L.Ed.2d 510 (1965).

4. *Wilcox v. Trautz,* 427 Mass. 326, 334, 693 N.E.2d 141 (1998).

5. *Baker v. State, supra* at 229, 744 A.2d 864.

6. *Zablocki v. Redhail, supra* at 387, 98 S.Ct. 673.

7. Opinion of the Justices, 211 Mass. 618, 619, 98 N.E. 337 (1912).

8. It is hardly surprising that civil marriage developed historically as a means to regulate heterosexual conduct and to promote child rearing, because until very recently unassisted heterosexual relations were the only means short of adoption by which children could come into the world, and the absence of widely available and effective contraceptives made the link between heterosexual sex and procreation very strong indeed.

9. *Troxel v. Granville,* 530 U.S. 57, 63, 147 L. Ed. 2d 49, 120 S. Ct. 2054 (2000).

10. *id.* at 64.

11. Post at (Cordy, J., dissenting).

12. *Palmore v. Sidoti,* 466 U.S. 429, 433, 80 L. Ed. 2d 421, 104 S. Ct. 1879 (1984) (construing Fourteenth Amendment).

13. J. P. Bishop, *Commentaries on the Law of Marriage and Divorce, and Evidence in Matrimonial Suits* § 32 (1852).

14. See *Children's Living Arrangements and Characteristics:* March, [*385] 2002, *United States Census Bureau Current Population Reports* at 3 (June 2003) (in 2002, 69 percent of children lived with two married parents, 23 percent lived with their mother, 5 percent lived with their father, and 4 percent lived in households with neither parent present).

15. See Rodney, *Behavioral Differences between African American Male Adolescents with Biological Fathers and Those without Biological Fathers in the Home,* 30 J. Black Stud. 45, 53 (1999) (African-American juveniles who lived with their biological fathers displayed fewer behavioral problems than those whose biological fathers were absent from home); Chilton, *Family Disruption, Delinquent Conduct and the Effect of Subclassification,* 37 Am. Soc. Rev. 93, 95 (1972) (proportion of youth charged with juvenile offenses who were not living in husband-wife family was larger than comparable proportion of youth charged with juvenile offenses who were living in husband-wife family); Hoffmann, *A National Portrait of Family Structure and Adolescent Drug Use,* 60 J. Marriage & Fam. 633 (1998) (children from households with both mother and father reported relatively low use of drugs, whereas children from households without their natural mothers and from other family type households had highest prevalence of drug use). See also D. Blankenhorn, *Fatherless America: Confronting Our Most Urgent Social Problem* 25 (1995).

16. H. B. Biller & J. L. Kimpton, *The Father and the School-Aged Child,* in *The Role of the Father in Child Development* 143 (3d ed. 1997); H.B. Biller, *Fathers and Families: Paternal Factors in Child Development* 1–3 (1993); Lynne Marie Kohm, *The Homosexual "Union": Should Gay and Lesbian Partnerships be Granted the Same Status as Marriage?* 22 J. Contemp. L. 51, 61 & nn. 53, 54 (1996) ("statistics continue to show that the

most stable family for children to grow up in is that consisting of a father and a mother").

17. See, e.g., Patterson, *Family Relationships of Lesbians and Gay Men,* 62 J. Marriage & Fam. 1052, 1060, 1064–1065 (2000) (concluding that there are no significant differences between children of same-sex parents and children of heterosexual parents in aspects of personal development).

18. See, e.g., Cameron, *Homosexual Parents,* 31 Adolescence 757, 770–774 (1996) (concluding results of limited study consonant with notion that children raised by homosexuals disproportionately experience emotional disturbance and sexual victimization).

19. See, e.g., Stacey, *(How) Does the Sexual Orientation of Parents Matter?,* 66 Amer. Soc. Rev. 159, 172, 176–179 (2001) (finding significant statistical differences in parenting practices, gender roles, sexual behavior but noting that "heterosexism" and political implications have constrained research). See also Coleman, *Reinvestigating Remarriage: Another Decade of Progress,* 62 J. Marriage & Fam. 1288 (2000) (concluding that future studies of impact of divorce and remarriage on children should focus on "nontraditional" stepfamilies, particularly same-sex couples with children, because impact of such arrangements have been overlooked in other studies).

20. See, e.g., R. Lerner & A. K. Nagai, *No Basis: What the Studies Don't Tell Us About Same-Sex Parenting,* Marriage Law Project (Jan. 2001) (criticizing forty-nine studies on same-sex parenting—at least twenty-six of which were cited by *amici* in this case—as suffering from flaws in formulation of hypotheses, use of experimental controls, use of measurements, sampling and statistical testing, and

finding false negatives); Stacey, *(How) Does the Sexual Orientation of Parents Matter,* 66 Am. Soc. Rev. 159, 159–166 (2001) (highlighting problems with sampling pools, lack of longitudinal studies, and political hypotheses).

21. The court contends that the exclusive and permanent commitment of the marriage partnership rather than the begetting of children is the *sine qua non* of civil marriage, . . . and that "the 'marriage is procreation' argument singles out the one unbridgeable difference between same-sex and opposite-sex couples, and transforms that difference into the essence of legal marriage." . . . The court has it backward. Civil marriage is the product of society's critical need to manage procreation as the inevitable consequence of intercourse between members of the opposite sex. Procreation has always been at the root of marriage and the reasons for its existence as a social institution. Its structure, one man and one woman committed for life, reflects society's judgment as how optimally to manage procreation and the resultant child rearing. The court, in attempting to divorce procreation from marriage, transforms the form of the structure into its purpose. In doing so, it turns history on its head.

22. See *Nonmarital Childbearing in the United States 1940–99, National Center for Health Statistics,* 48 Nat'l Vital Stat. Reps. at 2 (Oct. 2000) (*nonmarital childbirths increased from 3.8 percent of annual births in 1940 to 33 percent in 1999); M.D. Bramlett, Cohabitation, Marriage, Divorce, and Remarriage in the United States,* National Center for Health Statistics, Vital & Health Stat. at 4–5 (July 2002) (due to higher divorce rates and postponement of marriage, proportion of people's lives spent in marriage declined significantly during later half of twentieth century).

Comment

Evaluate the strongest case for and against extending marriage as a civil institution to same-sex couples, considering all the reasons offered by public officials in Massachusetts and any other reasons that are relevant to resolving the controversy.

Examine whether and how opponents of gay marriage address the three criteria (outlined in the introduction to this chapter) that might justify a moralistic prohibition. First, what do they think makes the institution of same-sex marriage wrong in itself? Second, do they show how this wrong is sufficiently relevant to a public purpose to warrant prohibition? Third, do they provide evidence or offer reasons to think that prohibiting gay marriage will not cause greater wrong than what it is seeking to prevent (the official recognition of civil union between same-sex couples)?

Advocates claim that legalizing same-sex marriage avoids the injustice of violating the equal civil rights of individuals—constitutionally guaranteed by equal protection of the laws. Denying same-sex couples who are willing to make a lifelong commitment to one another the right to marry violates equal protection of the laws. Justice Marshall goes so far as to suggest that the prohibition would perpetuate the status of gays as "second-class citizens." How should a public official compare this kind of injustice—which could also be called a "wrong"—with the wrongs that opponents associate with same-sex marriage? Are the wrongs claimed by advocates and opponents of the same kind, which can be weighed against one another, or are they distinguishable in some way?

Opponents of same-sex marriage offer reasons that go significantly beyond the moralistic claim that gay marriage is wrong. They also point to its harmful consequences. Justice Cordy's dissent appeals to the damaging social consequences of legalizing gay marriage. He warns of unintended consequences for society at large, for the institution of marriage, and also specifically of the effects of gay parenting on children. The majority decision by Justice Marshall, by contrast, emphasizes the equal benefits to gay and heterosexual couples that accompany civil marriage and the absence of any evidence to support claims about the harmful consequences. No evidence, she writes, has been offered "that forbidding marriage to people of the same sex will increase the number of couples choosing to enter into opposite-sex marriages in order to have and raise children." Similarly, no evidence has been offered that gay couples are or would be worse parents than heterosexual couples. She concludes that the arguments based on bad social consequences are themselves bad. Consider whether refuting any or all of these arguments is necessary to justify extending marriage as a civil union to same-sex couples.

Some of the dispute in this case turns on disagreements about the fundamental purpose of marriage and its relationship to parenting. Justice Cordy's dissent suggests that marriage serves the function of educating and socializing children and of creating stable social structures. He believes that the state endorses it precisely (and exclusively) for these reasons. In this view, marriage is a state interest because of the broader social function it serves. Justice Marshall's majority opinion, however, argues that long-standing laws endorse many marriages that never involve (nor are necessarily intended to involve) child rearing. Her opinion focuses instead on a host of other benefits, legal as well as emotional, that accrue to the two individuals who decide to marry. On what basis should marriage, understood in one or another of these ways, be publicly endorsed by the law in a constitutional democracy? Should marriage be a state interest at all? If so, why? Many people argue that the institution of "civil union" rather than "marriage" for specified public purposes should be a satisfactory substitute. Should this alternative be regarded as a reasonable compromise?

Assuming that civil marriage is here to stay for the foreseeable future in American constitutional democracy, consider whether equal treatment of same-sex couples under the law is a state interest. If so, what does it require? Opponents of same-sex marriage do not deny equal protection under the law. They argue that marriage is the union of one man and one woman, and is therefore available to everyone for whom the institution is legally and legitimately designed. Are defenders of gay marriage really pushing for something other than equal protection under the law—for an entirely new civil institution—the union of two people of the same sex? Or are they justified in using the term *marriage* to describe what they want? Who has the authority to define marriage? If a constitutional amendment were passed that declared "civil marriage to be a union between one man and one woman," would prohibiting gay marriage be just?

Several state legislators draw explicit analogies between sexuality and race. In defense of gay marriage, they argue that forbidding it is like forbidding interracial marriage. And defining "marriage" as the union exclusively of one man and one woman is no different from defining marriage as the union of a man and a woman exclusively of the same race. To what extent is this analogy between sexuality and race accurate? In what ways, if any, is the issue of gay marriage different from the issue of racial discrimination?

As the debate in the state legislature demonstrates, the public controversy in this case focused not only on the issue of whether to legalize gay marriage but also on the question of whether judges should be making this decision against the will of a legislative majority, and whether a legislative majority should make the decision against the will of a majority of the citizens whom they represent. Consider whether the fact that most legislators and most citizens in Massachusetts (or in the United States) oppose gay marriage should be relevant to the court's decision. If so, relevant for what reasons? If not, what considerations negate its relevance?

Finally, this case raises the more general question of whether instituting legal rights of which majorities do not approve is consistent with the idea of democracy. One does not have to assume a conception of democracy as strict majority rule to raise doubts about the democratic legitimacy of new rights created by unelected and unaccountable authorities. But neither does one have to assume a conception of democracy that insulates all rights from the challenge of majorities. In this case, and others you think comparable, evaluate the arguments for and against the creation of rights that are unpopular with the majority of the people. In any constitutional democracy, some rights should certainly be protected against the will of majorities. Is civil marriage for same-sex as well as opposite-sex couples among those rights?

The Controversial Curriculum

Gregory M. Stankiewicz

In January 1983, the Hawkins County school district appointed a textbook selection committee in accordance with Tennessee state law to consider what textbooks should be purchased for the following school year. After examining several basic reading series, the committee recommended the Holt, Rinehart, and Winston series for students from kindergarten to the eighth grade.[1] The Holt series was used by approximately 15,000 school districts in all fifty states.[2]

On May 12, 1983, during a regularly scheduled meeting, the elected members of the Hawkins County Board of Education unanimously approved the committee's recommendation.[3] The books were selected as a means of teaching reading skills as well as citizenship. According to Tennessee state law, education must:

> help each student develop positive values and . . . improve student conduct as students learn to act in harmony with their positive

values and learn to become good citizens in their school, community, and society.[4]

The board hoped that the new Holt series would do just that.

Mrs. Frost's Discovery

Vicki Frost vividly remembers the day when she opened her sixth-grade daughter's reading textbook. The textbook was brand new, one in the series of readers that the Hawkins County School Board had just purchased for the 1983–84 school year. What Frost read shocked and dismayed her.

The fictional story her daughter was assigned, "A Visit to Mars," tells about children communicating with aliens through thought transfer, or telepathy. Frost was immediately troubled. She considers herself a born-again Christian, and her belief is that supernatural powers can be the prerogative only of God. She sincerely believes it to be against her faith for her children to read stories like "A Visit to Mars."[5]

Frost continued reading, discovering that the problem was not limited to just one, or even a few, of the stories in the basic readers. She also examined her second-grade daughter's textbook and found that textbook no less offensive. In all, she discovered seventeen categories of offensive material, including issues of evolution, "secular humanism," "futuristic supernaturalism," pacifism, feminism, the occult, and false views of death. After more than two hundred hours of reading, Frost concluded that the entire Holt series was filled with statements and topics that were incompatible with her religious beliefs.[6]

Frost criticized the series for promoting a belief in the importance of mankind that eclipses the glory of God, a belief that she associates with "secular humanism."[7] Frost therefore objected to the claim made by one textbook in discussing the Renaissance that "a central idea of the renaissance was a belief in the dignity and worth of human beings."[8] Since Frost defines "futuristic supernaturalism" as the teaching of "man as God," she was offended by the description of Leonardo da Vinci as having a creative mind that "came closest to the divine touch." She also objected to a passage from a story, "Seeing Beneath the Surface," that describes using one's imagination to see things not visible to one's eyes. According to Frost, it is an occult practice for children to imagine beyond the bounds of scriptural authority. And, although the textbooks that discuss evolution contain a disclaimer that evolution is a theory, not a proven fact, Frost also objected to the factual manner in which the theory is nevertheless presented, as well as the pervasive number of times the topic is mentioned.[9]

Moreover, the Holt series portrays situations that Frost associated with feminism and role reversal, points of view offensive to her religious beliefs. One Holt textbook, for example, shows a young boy cooking alongside a young girl who is reading to him from a cookbook. The objectionable passage reads: "Pat reads to Jim. Jim cooks. The big book helps Jim. Jim has fun."[10]

Frost was troubled by the way some of these stories encourage children to make moral judgments, such as whether it is right or wrong to kill animals. Her view is that these textbooks should teach reading, good English, and grammar and not secular humanism or any other moral values.[11]

Frost also objected to stories dealing with the beliefs of other religions. The story "Hunchback Madonna," for example, includes this passage:

> They came to see and pray before the stoop-shouldered Virgin, people from as far south as Belen who from some accident or some spinal or heart affliction are shoulder-bent and want to walk straight again. Others, whose faith is not so simple or who have no faith at all, have come from many parts of the country and asked the way to El Tordo, not only to see the curiously painted Madonna in which the natives put so much faith, but to visit a single grave in a corner of the *campo santo* that, they have heard, is covered in spring with a profusion of wild flowers, whereas the other sunken ones are bare altogether, or at the most sprinkled only with sagebrush and tumbleweed.[12]

Frost could not condone exposure of her children to other religious perspectives (such as the one portrayed by the "Hunchback Madonna") or to values that conflict with her beliefs without a statement that her religious beliefs are correct and the others are incorrect.[13]

The Hawkins County Board of Education had selected the new Holt textbooks partly because the materials *would* expose children to diverse cultural and religious views. For Frost, however, "Jesus Christ being the only means of salvation, . . . we cannot be tolerant of religious views on the basis of accepting other religious views as equal to our own."[14] Frost believes that her religion requires that she shield her children from the many ideas conveyed in the new readers. Nothing short of complete exemption for her children from reading the Holt series would do.

ORGANIZED PROTEST

On September 1, 1983, Frost and Jennie Wilson, the grandmother of two elementary school children, organized a parents' meeting in the middle school to discuss ways of protesting the textbooks. As a result of the meeting, a small group of Hawkins County residents formed a new group, called Citizens Organized for Better Schools (COBS).[15]

The members of COBS, along with some other protesting parents who never joined the organization, were all fundamentalist Christians from various denominations. The group never gained the support of the majority of Hawkins County residents.[16] Some of the leaders and other members of the various fundamentalist congregations disagreed with Frost's view of the requirements of their religion.[17] The mayor of Frost's town would comment, "I think the people support their teachers and school officials, that [the Holt series] is good material, that it is not extreme, that it is not brainwashing the children."[18] A nationwide poll of adult Americans found that 75 percent agreed that students should be

exposed to religious beliefs which differ from those of their parents.[19]

Although COBS represented only a small minority of Hawkins county residents, they made themselves heard. Members of COBS attended the September and October meetings of the Board of Education, protesting the Holt series and petitioning the board to remove the series from the schools and return to the older textbooks. At the same time, Frost and seven other families individually approached their children's principals, asking that some alternative arrangement be worked out so that their children would not have to read the Holt textbooks. The principal of one elementary school refused; the principals of the middle school and the other two elementary schools decided to allow alternative arrangements. These arrangements consisted mostly in excusing the individual students from class during reading periods and allowing them to read instead from older textbooks in other rooms or offices. The exempted children seemed to be doing well academically under these arrangements. All of them continued to receive above-average grades.[20]

THE BOARD OF EDUCATION VOTES

In its November meeting, the Hawkins County Board of Education was once more confronted by angry COBS members. The board felt it was time to clarify the situation regarding the new Holt series. With no public discussion, the board members unanimously approved a resolution requiring teachers to "use only textbooks adopted by the Board of Education as regular classroom textbooks."[21] The board vote reversed the decision of those principals who had authorized alternative arrangements. All students now would be required to attend regular reading classes.

Shortly after the board's decision, several middle school students who continued to refuse to read the new Holt series were suspended for three days. Upon their return, the students again refused to attend reading classes and/or read the Holt textbooks and were suspended an additional ten days.[22]

After this second suspension, most of the protesting families removed their children from the Hawkins County public schools and enrolled them in religious or other area public schools, or taught them at home. Two of the students who did remain, however, were eventually given some accommodation: individual teachers, apparently against the board's ruling, quietly excused these students from reading the Holt series or noted on the students' worksheets that the students were not required to believe the stories that they read.[23]

THE SCHOOL BOARD'S VIEW

Board members and their supporters acknowledge that COBS members' religious beliefs are genuine, but they argued that the board's decision was necessary to ensure that all public school children be exposed to different cultural and religious ideas. The elected superintendent of the Hawkins County School District pointed out that "while it is true that these textbooks expose the student to varying values and religious backgrounds, neither the textbooks nor the teachers teach, indoctrinate, oppose, or promote any particular value or religion."[24] According to their critics, COBS and the protesting parents were attempting to impose censorship on the public school curriculum. The People for the American Way, a nationwide civil liberties group, would argue that the parents and their supporters were attempting to establish "a right to a sectarian education in the public schools."[25] A lawyer for the Board of Education noted, "There is no way [Vicki Frost] could attend public schools and not be offended," given all of her objections to the textbooks.[26]

Other supporters of the school board's decision emphasized that replacing the Holt series would have been a very expensive option. If the board had chosen the option of allowing some schools to continue providing alternative services, these individual exemptions also would be costly, especially of teachers' time and effort. The exemption could prove disruptive for the other students,

leading them to believe that they too could be exempt from their required classes if only they and their parents protested. The Tennessee commissioner of education would argue that:

> [Permitting] individual teachers, students, parents or ministers to choose the textbook of their liking would inescapably result in widespread chaos not only within the Hawkins County School System but also every public school system within the State of Tennessee.[27]

Alternatively, to avoid disruption, schools would teach from materials so bland as not to offend anybody. Such a response, according to a lawyer for the school board, would lead to the "formation of lowest common denominator education."[28]

THE PROTESTORS' VIEWS

COBS and its supporters denied that they were defending censorship. They argued that they were only trying to protect their right to the free exercise of their religion. The parents had given up on their early attempts to have the Board of Education withdraw the textbooks and now wanted only to exempt their children from reading material that they considered incompatible with their religious convictions.[29]

Concerned Women for America, a national group, would characterize COBS's aim as the establishment of "the right of Christians to refuse to read material which offends their religious convictions."[30] Requiring the children to read the Holt textbooks, the group would argue, is similar to requiring Jewish children to sing Christmas carols or black children to read racially offensive literature.[31]

Others defending COBS also argued that the case revolved around the rights of *any* minority not to be forced by the state to act against its religious beliefs. If protesting parents would not allow their children to read the Holt textbooks, the only alternative the school board left open to them would be to pull their children out of the Hawkins County school system. The school board's actions thereby denied children of the protesting parents a public school education. Michael Farris, a lawyer who would defend the parents, likened this situation to the one faced by black children before the Supreme Court's *Brown v. Board of Education* decision that outlawed "separate but equal" black schools: "What the state is trying to do is force Christian kids out of public schools. Black kids didn't use to have any choice, either. In this case it's doubly discriminatory because black schools were paid for by the Government."[32] Many of the Hawkins County parents, Farris argued, would have to pay tuition to send their children to private religious schools that did not assign offensive material.

Some observers viewed the conflict as one over who should control the public school curriculum—the state, the county school board, the local community, or parents of enrolled children. Defenders of the protesting parents argued that they—not the state of Tennessee, the county school board, or the local community—should determine their children's education.

NOTES

1. See *Mozert v. Hawkins County Public Schools,* 647 F. Supp. 1194 (E.D. Tenn. 1986), at 1196.

2. Alain L. Sanders, "Tilting at 'Secular Humanism': In Tennessee, A Modern Replay of the Celebrated 'Monkey Trial,'" *Time,* July 28, 1986, p. 68.

3. 647 F. Supp. at 119 6. On the school board being elected, see Stephen Bates, *Battleground: One Mother's Crusade, the Religious Right, and the Struggle for Our Schools* (Las Cruces, N.M.: Poseidon, 1993), pp. 163–64.

4. Tennessee Code Annotated (TCA) 49–6–1007 (1986 Supp.), cited in *Mozert v. Hawkins County Board of Education,* 827 F. 2d 1058 (6th Cir. 1987), at 1060.

5. Dudley Clendinen, "Fundamentalist Parents Put Textbooks on Trial," *New York Times,* July 15, 1986, p. A14.

6. 827 F. 2d at 1061–62.

7. Sanders, "Tilting at 'Secular Humanism.' "

8. Clendinen, "Fundamentalist Parents," p. A14.

9. This description is taken from the summary of Vicki Frost's testimony, in 827 F. 2d at 1062.

10. The passage and illustration is reprinted in Sanders, "Tilting at 'Secular Humanism.' "

11. 827 F. 2d at 1062.

12. Fray Angelico Chavez, "The Hunchback Madonna," in *Great Waves Breaking* (New York: Holt, Rinehart, and Winston, 1983). Reprinted, in the *New York Times,* "2 Examples of Textbook Material Called Objectionable in Suit," Oct. 25, 1986, p. 8.

13. 827 F. 2d at 1062.

14. Vicki Frost's testimony, as quoted in Clendinen "Fundamentalist Parents," p. A14.

15. 647 F. Supp. at 1196.

16. See Bates, *Battleground,* pp. 136–37.

17. 827 F. 2d at 1061.

18. Randall Housewright, mayor of Church Hill, Tennessee, quoted in Clendinen, "Fundamentalist Parents," p. A14.

19. Poll results are from a nationwide Media General/ Associated Press poll of 1,464 adult Americans, who were interviewed by telephone, September 8–17, 1986. The results have a margin of error of plus-or-minus 3 percentage points. Quoted in Associated Press, "Textbook Pool Finds Diversity Is Favored in Treating Religion," *New York Times,* Oct. 22, 1986, p. A23.

20. 647 F. Supp. at 1196, at 1201.

21. Ibid., at 1196.

22. Ibid., at 1196–97, at 1201–02 (fn. 13).

23. 827 F. 2d at 1060.

24. Superintendent Bill Snodgrass, quoted in 827 F. 2d at 1063; on the superintendent being elected, see Bates, *Battleground,* 163–64.

25. Anthony Podesta, president of People for the American Way, quoted in Sanders, "Tilting at 'Secular Humanism.' "

26. Timothy Dyk, quoted in Sanders, "Tilting at 'Secular Humanism.' "

27. Robert McElrath, Commissioner of Education of the State of Tennessee, quoted in 647 F. Supp. at 1202.

28. Timothy Dyk, quoted in Dudley Clendinen, "Fundamentalists Win a Federal Suit over Schoolbooks," *New York Times,* Oct. 25, 1986, p. 1.

29. 647 F. Supp. at 1195.

30. Beverly LaHaye, founder of Concerned Women for America, writing in a fundraising letter, quoted in Sanders "Tilting at 'Secular Humanism.' "

31. LaHaye, quoted in Stuart Taylor, Jr., "Supreme, Court Roundup; Justices Refuse to Hear Tennessee Case on Bible and Textbooks," *New York Times,* Feb. 23, 1988, p. D29.

32. Michael Farris, quoted in Associated Press, "7 Tennessee Families and Schools Nearing End of Battle over Books," *New York Times,* July 28, 1986, p. A10.

Comment

Citizens disagree about what morality should guide the education of children, yet education cannot be morally neutral. Tennessee state law mandates that schools help children "develop positive values" and "learn to become good citizens in their school, community, and society." Even if the citizens of Tennessee can agree that teaching positive values and educating good citizens are justifiable ends of public education, they disagree about what constitutes positive values, good citizenship, and an education adequate for these ends. May a public school try to educate all its students "to become good citizens" even if some parents object to the kind of citizenship education mandated by the school? If there are multiple ways of educating good citizens, what are the strongest arguments for authorizing an elected school board rather than individual parents to decide which way to educate for citizenship in public schools? Would your answer differ if a controversy like this took place in a private school?

Is respect for the religious freedom of parents a compelling reason to exempt children from a prescribed curriculum in public schools? What about respect for the religious convictions of the students themselves? Assess the analogies suggested by Concerned Women for America: exempting Jewish children from singing Christmas carols and exempting black children from reading racially offensive literature.

Does the existence of the option of sending their children to private schools provide a response to the objections of the dissenting parents? Evaluate the argument that it is doubly discriminatory to require the dissenting parents to pay for a private education for their children. Is this a fair price to ask parents to pay if they disagree with the public school curriculum? Is accommodating the religious convictions of parents a fair price to ask public schools to pay? To what extent do answers to these questions depend on the content of the religious convictions of parents and their compatibility with the aims of education in a democracy? Which of the following claims about the curriculum, if correct, would support the position of the parents or that of the school board: the curriculum (1) indoctrinates children; (2) promotes feminism; (3) promotes a belief in the dignity and worth of human beings; (4) encourages children to make their own moral judgments; (5) offends the religious convictions of some parents; (6) exposes children to cultural and religious ideas that are unacceptable to their parents; or (7) increases the chances that children will question their parents' religious convictions.

Consider which of the religious convictions expressed by Vicki Frost and COBS are compatible, first, with citizenship education in general and, second, with the reading curriculum of the Hawkins County school in particular. What kind of education for citizenship would be compatible with the religious convictions of dissenting parents?

What should the Hawkins County School Board have decided in the face of the parental protest? Evaluate the various arguments presented for and against the position of the protesting parents and any others that should carry moral weight in this case. Consider the options open to the Hawkins County School Board, including, (1) altering their reading curriculum for all children, (2) not altering it for any children, and (3) altering it only for the children of dissenting parents. Should the school board have any moral discretion in deciding what to do?

Also central to this controversy is the question of who should have the authority to determine the content of education for citizenship in Tennessee. Consider the alternative sources of authority over education in Tennessee and their legitimate claims to influence the outcome of this controversy: parents, teachers, principals, textbook selection committees, school boards, legislatures, and courts. Are there moral limits to the legitimate authority of any or all of these educational agents?

Finally, evaluate the process by which the Hawkins County School Board resolved to require teachers to use only textbooks adopted by the board and to deny any exemption to children of the dissenting parents. Can you recommend a more defensible process by which such controversies should be resolved?

Recommended Reading

The classic source on paternalism and moralism is Mill's *On Liberty,* Introductory, ch. 4 and 5. For modern discussions of paternalism, see Gerald Dworkin, "Paternalism," *Monist,* 56 (1972), pp. 64–84, reprinted in R. Wasserstrom (ed.), *Morality and the Law* (Belmont, Calif.: Wadsworth, 1971); Joel Feinberg, *The Moral Limits of the Criminal Law,* vol. 3, *Harm to Self* (New York: Oxford University Press, 1986); John Kleinig, *Paternalism* (Totowa, N.J.: Littlefield and Adams, 1984); Dennis F. Thompson, "Paternalistic Power," in *Political Ethics and Public Office* (Cambridge, Mass.: Harvard University Press, 1987), ch. 6; and Cass R. Sunstein and Richard H. Thaler, "Libertarian Paternalism Is Not an Oxymoron," *University of Chicago Law Review,* 70 (Fall 2003), pp. 1159–1202. For contemporary discussions of moralism, see Gerald Dworkin (ed.), *Morality, Harm, and the Law* (Boulder, Colo.: Westview Press, 1994); Joel Feinberg, *The Moral Limits of the Criminal Law,* vol. 4, *Harmless Wrongdoing* (New York: Oxford University Press, 1988); Elizabeth Anderson, *Value in Ethics and Economics* (Cambridge, Mass.: Harvard University Press, 1993); and Martha C. Nussbaum, *Hiding from Humanity: Disgust, Shame, and the Law* (Princeton, N.J.: Princeton University Press, 2004).

More generally, on liberty, moralism, and paternalism, see Amy Gutmann and Dennis Thompson, *Democracy and Disagreement* (Cambridge, Mass.: Harvard University Press, 1996), ch. 7; and Gerald Dworkin, *The Theory and Practice of Autonomy* (New York: Cambridge University Press, 1988).

On the ethics of gay marriage, consult Andrew Sullivan's *Same-Sex Marriage: Pro & Con—A Reader* (Vintage Books, 1997) Another compilation of varied perspectives can be found in Lynn Doyle, Mark Strasser, William Duncan, and David Coolidge (eds.) *Marriage and Same-Sex Unions: A Debate* (Westport, Conn.: Praeger, 2003). Also see Carlos Ball, *The Morality of Gay Rights: An Exploration in Political Philosophy* (Oxford, UK: Routledge, 2002).

On the political morality of education, see Amy Gutmann, *Democratic Education* (Princeton, N.J.: Princeton University Press, 1999); "Symposium on Citizenship, Democracy, and Education," *Ethics,* 105 (April 1995); Amy Gutmann, "Undemocratic Education," in Nancy L. Rosenblum, *Liberalism and the Moral Life* (Cambridge, Mass.: Harvard University Press, 1989), pp. 71–88; and William Galston, "Civic Education in the Liberal State," in *Liberalism and the Moral Life,* pp. 89–102.

10   Liberty and Life

The idea that all persons have a right to life as well as liberty commands widespread support. But what beings possess the right to life is one of the most divisive questions of our recent political history. The "pro-life" movement defends a fetus's right to life, while "pro-choice" groups defend a woman's right to abortion. They disagree on questions of both personal morality (whether having an abortion is moral) and political morality (whether abortion should be legal and the right to an abortion constitutionally protected).

The structure of the pro-life argument is:

The fetus is a person in the generic sense.
It is wrong to kill a person (except in self-defense).
Abortion is therefore wrong (unless a mother's life is at stake). It should therefore be illegal.

The typical pro-choice argument has a parallel logic supporting the opposite conclusion:

The fetus is not a person in the generic sense but part of a woman's body that significantly affects her life.
A woman has a right to control her own body and life. Abortion therefore is a woman's right.
It should therefore be legal.

The two sides are divided by fundamentally different perceptions of what a fetus is, perceptions that seem impervious to change by rational argument. Many people on each side view the perception of the other side as "not simply false, but wildly, madly false—nonsense, totally unintelligible, and literally unbelievable" (Roger Wertheimer). While philosophers may not even in principle succeed in resolving this controversy, they have made more modest contributions that are morally and politically significant. They have shown that the premises of each side support less extreme conclusions on the level of both personal and political morality. And they have offered reasons for both sides to recognize and respect some degree of genuine moral disagreement in the abortion debate without forsaking their own fundamental premises.

Some philosophers have argued that even if the fetus is a person, its death may be justifiable. Self-defense is not the only justification for letting an innocent person die. One is not obligated to save an innocent person at great personal sacrifice if one is not otherwise responsible for the person's situation. On this view, the basic premise of the pro-life position leads to a less absolutist stance against abortion: abortion is permissible in cases of rape and incest. Other writers have suggested that even if abortion is arguably wrong at the level of personal morality, it may still be right for a liberal state to legalize it when the public is so divided about its morality, and its wrongness depends on sustaining a rationally contestable claim about the constitutional personhood of the fetus.

Philosophers also have criticized the logic of the extreme pro-choice position. They have argued that the right of a woman to control her body is not absolute: it does not include the right to destroy for trivial reasons what is admittedly a potential life. And the pro-choice position is not, as some proponents assume, neutral as a political morality. Giving all women a choice between having or not having an abortion is still, for those who believe that the fetus is a person, giving women the right to kill innocent people. To those who believe in the personhood of the fetus, this choice is immoral, just as for those who do not believe that the fetus is a person, outlawing abortion is immoral because it restricts a woman's right to control her own body and her freedom more generally.

The political morality of abortion is complex because no policy can be morally neutral, and neither side has reasons adequate to convince the other of the moral superiority of its position. Political philosophers have suggested several ways of dealing with situations of this kind. One is to consider a compromise that is fair to both sides, though not fully satisfying the moral claims of either. Another is to find a method of decision-making that is procedurally fair, even if its results favor one side of the moral controversy. Yet a third is to accommodate the moral convictions of one side to the extent possible without ceding any ground from the side that all things considered has the best reasons on its side. Despite the vast literature on abortion, none of these alternatives has yet to be exhaustively examined.

The cases on abortion in this chapter add moral complications to an already difficult political issue and political complications to an already difficult moral issue. Joseph Califano's involvement in the abortion controversy when he was secretary of the Department of Health, Education, and Welfare raises the question of whether, once abortion is legal, the government should subsidize the procedure for poor women. Most people who believe that abortion is a woman's right also argue that the government should subsidize it for poor women. This is the position taken by Senator Packwood when he criticized Joseph Califano's opposition to funding abortion for poor women as essentially (and unjustifiably) saying to them: "tough luck." But critics point out that having a right to free speech, for example, does not obligate the state to provide anyone with a subvention for publication. Most pro-life advocates, agreeing with Califano's position on this issue, argue that, even if the law permits some women to obtain abortions, there is no reason for the government to subsidize the taking of innocent lives. Yet some who believe that abortion is morally wrong dissent from this view on grounds that the exercise of legal rights should not be effectively withheld from the poor. In Califano's memoir, these and other moral positions are passionately represented. Califano's position while he was in public office raises yet another issue in political ethics: What should a public official do when the policy he may be instructed to enforce violates his own moral principles?

The conflict faced by Senator Scott Heidepriem in South Dakota concerned his dual responsibility as a state representative: on the one hand, to ensure a fair legislative hearing for a potentially popular antiabortion bill, and on the other hand, to act consistently with his strong convictions regarding a woman's legal right to abortion. Although Heidepriem prided himself on following fair procedures, the question of what constitutes procedural fairness in such a case is almost as controversial as the legalization of abortion itself.

Ever since its 1973 decision in *Roe v. Wade,* the Supreme Court has affirmed a woman's right to abortion and "invalidated statutes that, in the process of regulating the methods of abortion, imposed significant health risks" (*Stenberg v. Carhart,* 530 U.S. 914 2000). But the "Partial-Birth Abortion Ban Act" that Congress passed in 2003 placed a new limit on that right. While banning the use of a dilation and extraction (D&X) method of abortion, it allowed no exception for a woman's health. The debate about the bill raised once again the issue of when, if ever, the right to life of a fetus can justify restricting a woman's right to abortion. The ban applied even when a doctor certifies that a woman's health is at stake. Many defenders of the federal ban took the occasion to challenge the assumption that the Supreme Court should be the final authority in determining whether the right of a woman or a fetus takes precedence in cases involving "partial-birth" abortions.

As technology produces new possibilities for improving human welfare, it also creates new conflicts in making decisions about human values. In the debate over the use of human embryos to conduct stem cell research, a salient conflict is between liberty and life. On the one hand, stem cell research is widely supported because it may have the potential for ameliorating and even possibly curing debilitating congenital diseases such as diabetes, Parkinson's disease, and Alzheimer's. On the other hand, because there is no known way of extracting stem cells from an embryo without destroying it, stem cell research is criticized by those who believe that it destroys life. They argue that it is immoral to use embryos for medical research and still worse to destroy them simply for the sake of engaging in such research. The uncertain potential of saving human lives is thus pitted against the controversial claim that it degrades human life to destroy (or for some, even to use) embryos to save human life. In addition to congressional hearings, a special commission, the President's Council on Bioethics, held extensive public deliberations on stem cell research. This case therefore also affords an opportunity to consider the merits of a deliberative process of decision making at the national level.

The final case raises another important issue at the intersection of political ethics and bioethics. To what extent (if at all) should the government permit the standards that govern the protection of subjects who enroll in drug-testing regimes in poorer societies to be lower than would be allowed in the United States? The controversy within the worldwide medical community over the use of a placebo-controlled trial in sub-Saharan Africa for a shorter (and therefore less expensive) regime of AZT raises the question of the extent to which the standards of health care should be universal or local. It invites us to ask how the value of liberty (manifested here by the requirement of informed consent) and the value of life (protected here by providing at least standard care to all subjects) should be interpreted and applied in radically different social and economic contexts. The competing ethical considerations raised in this controversy show just how difficult it can be to find a satisfying resolution to the conflicts created by the extreme deprivation that devastates not only individuals but also entire societies.

Administering Abortion Policy
Joseph A. Califano, Jr.

The abortion issue marked my initiation by public controversy as Secretary of Health, Education, and Welfare.

It was certainly not the issue I would have chosen to confront first. The abortion dispute was sure to make enemies at the beginning of my tenure when I particularly needed friends; guaranteed to divide supporters of social programs when it was especially important to unite them; and likely to spark latent and perhaps lasting suspicions about my ability to separate my private beliefs as a Roman Catholic from my public duties as the nation's chief health, education, and social service official.

The issue whether Medicaid should fund abortions for poor women was more searing than many I faced, but it was quintessentially characteristic of the problems confronting HEW. The abortion dispute summoned taproot convictions and religious beliefs, sincerely held and strenuously put forth by each side, about the rights of poor people, the use of tax dollars, the role of government in the most intimate personal decisions. The pro- and anti-abortion forces each claimed that the Constitution and the American people were on its side, and each truly believed that it was protecting human life. Wherever those forces struggled to prevail—in the courts, the

Congress, the executive regulatory process, the state legislatures, and city councils—there were HEW and its Medicaid program. And there was no neutral ground on which HEW or its Secretary could comfortably stand, for any decision—to fund all, or none, or some abortions—would disappoint and enrage millions of Americans who were convinced that theirs was the only humane position.

The controversy exposed me to the world of difference between being a White House staffer—however powerful—and being a Cabinet officer, out front, responsible not only to the President as an advisor but also to the Congress and the American people. It was one thing to be Lyndon Johnson's top domestic policy advisor crafting Great Society programs, but not accountable to the Congress and not ultimately responsible. It was quite another to be the public point man on an issue as controversial as federal financing of abortions for poor people.

Lyndon Johnson had held his White House staff on a particularly short leash. We spoke only in his name—explaining what he thought, how he felt, what his hopes and objectives for America were. "The only reason Hugh Sidey [of Time] talks to you is to find out about me, what I think, what I want. He doesn't give a damn about you," Johnson so often told us, "so make sure you know what I think before you tell him what you think I think." Indeed, during my lengthy press briefings

Reprinted with the permission of Simon and Schuster from *Governing America* by Joseph A. Califano, Jr. Copyright © 1981 by Joseph A. Califano, Jr.

on new legislative programs, as Johnson read early pages of the instantly typed transcript in his office, he sometimes sent messages to me to correct statements or misimpressions before the briefing ended.

Cabinet officers, of necessity, function with less detailed and immediate presidential guidance. It goes with the territory for a Cabinet officer to put a little distance between himself and the President, particularly on such controversial issues as abortion. Presidents expect, as they should, that their Cabinet officers will shield them from as much controversy as possible so that precious presidential capital can be spent only for overriding national objectives the President selects.

Jimmy Carter first talked to me about abortion when we lunched alone in Manchester, New Hampshire, in early August 1976. He expressed his unyielding opposition to abortion and his determination to stop federal funding of abortions. He asked me to work with Fritz Mondale to make his views known to the Catholic hierarchy and influential lay Catholics. Mondale was using his Minnesota friend Bishop James Rausch, who was then the general secretary of the National Conference of Catholic Bishops, to get Carter's view across, and Charlie Kirbo would be quietly communicating with Terence Cardinal Cooke in New York, but Carter said he wanted a "good Catholic" to spread the word of his strong opposition to abortion. I was impressed by the sincerity and depth of Carter's views on abortion and I found his determination to get credit for those views politically prudent in view of the inevitable opposition his position would incite. It later struck me that Carter never asked my views on the subject, and I never expressed them. Our conversation simply assumed complete agreement.

The assumption was well grounded. I consider abortion morally wrong unless the life of the mother would be at stake if the fetus were carried to term. Under such tragic and wrenching circumstances, no human being could be faulted for making either choice, between the life of the mother and the life of the unborn child. Those are the only circumstances under which I considered federal financing of abortion appropriate.

During the 1976 presidential campaign, I never had to reconcile my beliefs as a Catholic about abortion with any potential duty to obey and execute the law as a public servant. In promulgating Carter's view, like any proponent of a presidential candidate, I took as a given his ability to translate that view into law or public policy. Since my conversations were with those who opposed abortion, no one asked me what Carter would do if the Congress enacted a different position into law.

In talks with Monsignors George Higgins and Francis Lally, and others at the Catholic Conference, I sought to convince them that Carter shared their view. Higgins was an old friend from the Johnson years and he helped get Carter's position better known in the Catholic community. But Higgins confided that nothing short of a firm commitment to a constitutional amendment outlawing abortion would satisfy the conservative elements of the Catholic hierarchy. When I reported this to Mondale, he expressed doubt that Carter would—or should—go that far, particularly since in January 1976 he had said he did "not favor a constitutional amendment abolishing abortion." I agreed.

Eventually, in response to the numerous questions on abortion during the campaign and after a meeting with Catholic bishops in Washington on August 31, 1976, Carter said that he had not yet seen any constitutional amendment he would support, but he "would never try to block . . . an amendment" prohibiting abortions. He added pointedly that any citizen had the right to seek an amendment to overturn the Supreme Court's 1973 *Roe v. Wade* decision, which established a woman's constitutional right to have an abortion, at least in the first trimester of pregnancy.

In November 1976, after the election, as Mondale, Tip O'Neill, and other friends reported conversations in which Carter or his close advisors such as Jordan and Kirbo were checking on my qualifications, it became clear that I was a leading candidate for the HEW post. Then, for the first time, I had to focus on the depth of my personal religious belief about abortion: As Secretary of Health, Education, and Welfare, would I be able, in good conscience, to carry out the law of the land, even if that law provided for federal funding of all abortions? I asked myself that question many times before others began asking it of me.

Both my parents are devoutly religious Catholics. Their influence and my education at St. Gregory's elementary school in Brooklyn, at the Jesuit high school Brooklyn Prep, and at the College of the Holy Cross had provided me not only with some intellectual sextants but with a moral compass as well. Like many Catholic students and young lawyers in the 1950s, I had read the works of John Courtney Murray, a leading Jesuit scholar and philosopher. His writings on the rights and duties of American Catholics in a pluralistic society and the need to accommodate private belief and public policy were guides for liberal Catholics of my generation. But even with this background, it was an exacting task in modern America to get clarity and peace in my private conscience while satisfying the legitimate demands of public service and leadership.

The abortion issue never came up in the Johnson administration. But family planning, even the aggressive promotion of the use of contraceptives to prevent pregnancy as a government policy, was an issue I had confronted in those years. President Johnson was an ardent proponent of birth control at home and abroad. He repeatedly rejected the unanimous pleas of his advisors from Secretary of State Dean Rusk to National Security Advisor Walt Rostow to ship wheat to the starving Indians during their 1966 famine. He demanded that the Indian government first agree to mount a massive birth control program. The Indians finally moved and Johnson released the wheat over

a sufficiently extended period to make certain the birth control program was off the ground.

Johnson spoke so often and forcefully about birth control that the Catholic bishops denounced him publicly. He sent me to try to cool them off. Working discreetly with Monsignor Frank Hurley, then the chief lobbyist for the Catholic Conference in Washington, we reached an uneasy off-the-record truce: If LBJ would stop using the term "birth control" and refer instead to the "population problem," which allowed increased food production as a possible solution, the bishops would refrain from public attacks on him. Johnson agreed, and spoke thereafter of "the population problem"—but with equal if not greater vigor.

During my years with Lyndon Johnson, and the legislative fights to fund family planning services through the Public Health Service and the War on Poverty, I had to relate my private conscience to public policy on family planning. The alternatives of teenage pregnancy, abortion, mental retardation, poverty, and the like were far worse than providing access to contraceptives; to expect all citizens to practice premarital celibacy or all married couples to use the rhythm method was unrealistic in America's increasingly sexually permissive society. I was able to reconcile my private conscience with public policy. I concluded that it made sense for government to fund family planning programs that offered and even encouraged artificial birth control. I had no moral qualms about such a policy in a pluralistic society so long as it respected individual dignity and religious belief. The Catholic bishops disagreed with Johnson. But among theologians there was a great diversity of opinion about the moral propriety of birth control in various personal situations; I inclined to the more liberal position.

Abortion was a far more difficult issue. Here I faced my own conviction that abortion was morally wrong except to save the life of the mother, that medically unnecessary abortions offended fundamental standards of respect for human life. It is one thing temporarily to prevent the creation of a human life; quite another level of moral values is involved in discarding a human life once created. With abortion, I had to face direct conflict, between personal religious conviction and public responsibility.

I was to learn how difficult it would be to preserve the precious distinction between public duty and private belief. Setting forth my own and the President's view of appropriate public policy on federal funding of abortion, putting the issue in perspective, relating it to considerations of fairness, and striving to separate my own personal views from my responsibilities as a public official once the Congress decisively acted on the legislation were to be matters of enormous complexity and lonely personal strain. Whatever inner strength I mustered from my own religious faith, the public anguish would not be eased by the fact that I was the only Catholic in the Carter Cabinet.

The anti-abortion, right to life groups and the pro-abortion, freedom of choice organizations had turned the annual HEW appropriations bill into the national battleground over abortion. The issue was whether, and under what circumstances, HEW's Medicaid program to finance health care for poor people should pay for abortions. It would be debated and resolved in the language of the HEW appropriations law, and the regulations implementing the law. This made the Secretary of HEW an especially imposing and exposed figure on the abortion battlefield.

With the Supreme Court's *Roe v. Wade* decision in 1973, HEW's Medicaid program promptly began funding abortions for poor women as routinely as any other medical procedure. By 1976, estimates of the number of HEW-funded abortions ranged as high as 300,000 per year. The furies that the *Roe* decision and its impact on HEW's Medicaid program set loose turned abortion into a legal and political controversy that the courts and the Congress would toss at each other for years. The federal financing

of an estimated 300,000 abortions set off an emotional stampede in the House of Representatives in 1976, led by Republican Representative Henry Hyde of Illinois, and reluctantly followed by the Senate, to attach a restriction to the 1977 HEW appropriations bill prohibiting the use of HEW funds "to perform abortions except where the life of the mother would be endangered if the fetus were carried to term."

Before the restriction took effect, pro-abortion groups obtained an injunction from Federal District Judge John F. Dooling in Brooklyn, blocking its enforcement until he could decide whether the Supreme Court decision in *Roe v. Wade* established an obligation of the federal government to fund abortions, as a corollary to the right to have them performed.

Whatever the courts ultimately ruled; the abortion issue would continue to be a volatile inhabitant of the political arena. Sincerely held as I believe it was, Carter's stand was also a critical part of his election victory. Betty Ford's strong pro-abortion views and Gerald Ford's ambivalence were thought by Carter to have hurt the Republican candidate.

But Carter's appointment of pro-abortionist Midge Costanza as a senior White House aide and his strong support of the Equal Rights Amendment and other feminist causes gave women's groups some hope that his position would be softened. The pro-lifers were suspicious because Carter's colors blurred on the litmus test of supporting a constitutional amendment outlawing abortion. With pro- and anti-abortion advocates poised to battle for the mind of the administration, I prepared for my confirmation hearings on January 13, 1977.

From my religious and moral convictions, I knew my conscience. From my training at Harvard Law School and my life as a lawyer and public servant, I knew my obligation to enforce the law. But on the eve of becoming a public spokesman for myself and the administration, I sought the reassurance of double-checking my moral and intellectual foundation. I consulted an extraordinary Jesuit priest, James English, my pastor at Holy Trinity Church in Georgetown. He came by my law office on the Saturday morning before the confirmation hearing. He sat on the couch against the wall; I sat across the coffee table from him. I told him I wanted to make one final assessment of my ability to deal with the abortion issue before going forward with the nomination. If I could not enforce whatever law the Congress passes, then I should not become Secretary of Health, Education, and Welfare.

Father English spoke softly about the pluralistic society and the democratic system, in which each of us has an opportunity to express his views. Most statutory law codifies morality, he noted, whether prohibiting stealing or assault, or promoting equal rights, and the arguments of citizens over what the law should be are founded in individual moral values. He said that my obligation to my personal conscience was satisfied if I expressed those views forcefully.

I postulated a law that any abortion could be funded by the federal government, simply upon the request of the woman. He said that so long as I tried to pursue the public policy I believed correct, then I was free—indeed, obliged if I stayed in the job—to enforce that permissive law. I was relieved, comforted by his quiet assurance. As I thanked him for coming by, he mentioned an expert in this field, Father Richard McCormick, a Jesuit at the Kennedy Institute of Bioethics at Georgetown, whose advice I might find helpful.

On the following Monday evening, January 10, representatives of the National Women's Political Caucus sat on the same red couch Father English had occupied. It was the most intense of a series of meetings with various special interest groups.

As the women filed through the door to my office, I shook hands with each one. Their eyes seemed cold and skeptical, and reflected deep concern, even when they smiled. The warm welcome with which I greeted them masked my own foreboding about the imminence of the clash on abortion.

The discussion began on common ground: the failure of the Nixon and Ford administrations to enforce laws prohibiting sex discrimination. One after another, the representatives of each group in the women's political caucus attacked the enemy: discrimination in the Social Security system (in terms far more forceful than Jimmy Carter's quaint accusation that the benefit structure encouraged senior citizens to "live in sin"), in the federal income tax system, and on the nation's campuses. Most mentioned female appointments at HEW, but since they knew I was searching for qualified women, they did not linger on the personnel issue. Margot Polivy, a tough and talented attorney litigating to eliminate discrimination in women's athletics, pressed her case for HEW enforcement of Title IX, the law prohibiting sex discrimination at educational institutions that receive federal funds.

I shared most of the views the women expressed on these subjects and they knew it. When are they going to stop circling their prey, I thought, and ask about abortion?

Dorothy Ross, a committed feminist who had been helping me recruit for HEW jobs, was seated at my left. She had told me abortion would be the key topic and I wanted to get it over with. Then one of the women put the question: "What's your view on abortion?"

I had decided to make my view unmistakably clear. It was important to state my position on abortion before the Senate confirmation hearings. No senator should be able to claim that his vote was cast for my confirmation without knowing my view on this subject. But in the tension of the moment, it was not easy or pleasant to get the words out.

"I believe abortion is morally wrong," I said softly and firmly. "That is my personal belief."

There was a brief moment of breathtaking at the depth of conviction in my voice. Then the women responded.

"Would you deny federal funds for abortion?" one woman angrily asked.

"I oppose federal funding for abortion." The circling was over. The questions were accusations called out like counts in an indictment.

"The Supreme Court gives a woman a right to an abortion. You would deny that right to poor women?"

"You'd deny a woman her constitutional right?"

"How can you be a liberal and hold such a view?"

"Suppose the woman's life is at stake?"

"What about rape or incest?"

"Suppose the child would be retarded, a vegetable?"

"Are you going to impose your religious views on HEW?"

The questions came with such furious vehemence that I had to interrupt to respond.

"Look," I said, "I have no intention of imposing my personal view on anybody. I am prepared to enforce the law, whatever it is."

"But how could you possibly," one of the women asked, "when you have such strong personal views, such religious commitment?"

"There's nothing wrong with religious commitment," I fired back, "and nothing about it prevents me from enforcing the law."

The women made no attempt to disguise their anger or their suspicion. I wanted to end the meeting before it further deteriorated. The subject was even more volatile than I had anticipated. I was shaken by the obvious depth and genuineness of their emotional and intellectual conviction, and the difficulty of some of the questions they had raised. But there was nothing to be gained by heated exchanges. If there were no other matters on their minds, I suggested we conclude the meeting. They were just as anxious as I to cut off discussion: they, out of a desire to report to their colleagues and plan strategy; I, out of relief.

The parting was superficially amicable, but the battle lines had been drawn. Washington's feminist network buzzed with reports of the meeting throughout that evening and the next day. Late that Tuesday afternoon I was told that the women's groups would attack my nomination on the basis of my stand on abortion.

By Wednesday, the day before my confirmation hearing, the National Abortion Rights Action League had asked to appear, on behalf of fourteen groups which supported federal funds for abortion, before both Senate committees scheduled to hear me testify on my nomination.

As I drove to my office early on Thursday morning, the radio news broadcasts were announcing that Senator Robert Packwood of Oregon, a staunch proponent of Medicaid-funded abortions and member of the Finance Committee which had jurisdiction over my nomination, would question me closely on abortion and might well oppose my nomination unless I changed my reported views.

I needed a much more sophisticated grasp of the political code words on abortion. I knew my own position, but the Senate hearing rooms of Washington were paneled and carpeted with good intentions and clear views ineptly expressed by well-meaning witnesses. I wanted to be sure I could maneuver through the verbal and emotional minefield of pro- and anti-abortionists. It was imperative for those in the abortion controversy, from Cardinal Cooke to National Abortion Rights Action League Executive Director Karen Mulhauser, to understand the words I spoke as I meant them, and I wanted to be confident that I knew what they would hear when I spoke. Far more careers have been shattered in Washington because of what people say than because of what they do—and far more often through words spoken by inadvertence or ignorance than by design.

As I parked my car, I recalled Father English's recommendation of Father Richard McCormick as an ethicist well versed in the abortion controversy. I called him as soon as I got to the office. I told him I had only a few minutes before leaving for the Senate hearing. I quickly reviewed the old ground with him, the obligation to enforce a law contrary to my personal view. Then I moved to some of the harder questions, about pursuing a public policy for our pluralistic country that differed from my personal beliefs.

"What about rape and incest? In terms of public policy, it seems to me that when a woman has been the victim of rape or incest, a case can be made to permit an immediate abortion."

"First of all," McCormick responded, "the woman may be able to solve the problem, if she acts fast enough without even getting to an abortion. Even after fertilization but before implantation in the uterus, there are things like twinning and possible recombination of fertilized eggs. These things create doubt about how we ought to evaluate life at this stage. It may take as long as fourteen days for the implantation process to end."

"Do you mean that from an ethical point of view, you don't see any abortion problem for up to two weeks?" I asked.

"I mean there are sufficient doubts at this stage to lead me to believe it may not be wrong to do a dilation and curettage after rape. It's very doubtful that we ought to call this interruption an abortion. Absolutist right to life groups will still complain. But serious studies support this. The pro-abortionists feel very strongly about rape and incest."

"Suppose the doctor says the child will be retarded, or severely handicapped physically?"

"That is a much more difficult question. The Church would not permit an abortion, and the right to life and pro-abortion groups feel deeply here," McCormick replied.

"And what about some severe or permanent damage to the mother's health short of death?"

"That's another tough question in public policy terms. The Church would oppose abortion."

"Well, it's going to be an interesting morning," I mused aloud.

McCormick summed up rapidly. "You should always keep in mind three levels of distinction here. First, there is the personal conscience and belief thing. Second, there is what the appropriate public policy should be in a pluralistic democracy, which could be more liberal on funding abortions than one would personally approve as a matter of conscience or religious conviction. Actual abortion for rape and incest victims might be an example here. And third, there is the obligation of the public official to carry out the law the nation enacts."

"So I could pursue a policy for the country that funded abortion for rape and incest victims even though the Church—and I as a matter of personal and religious conviction—opposed abortion under those circumstances."

"Yes, you could."

I thanked him and rushed out of the office to my confirmation hearing.

I had to walk past a long line of people waiting to get into the standing-room-only Senate Finance Committee room in the Dirksen Building. Inside the door I had to weave through spectators and climb over legs to get to the witness table. The lights of all three networks were on me, sporadically augmented by clicking cameras and flashing bulbs from photographers sitting and kneeling on the floor in front of me. Seated behind their elevated and curved paneled rostrum, the committee members and staff looked down at me.

The hearing began promptly at 10:00 A.M. After fifteen minutes in which I made a brief opening statement and received some generous praise from Chairman Russell Long, Senator Packwood began:

"Mr. Califano, you know I have some strong feelings about abortion. . . . What is your personal view on abortion?"

The cameras turned on me.

I began by expressing my recognition of the difficulty of the abortion issue and the sincerity and depth of feeling on all sides. I noted that Carter and I shared identical views on the subject, although we came from quite different religious, cultural, and social backgrounds. I then set forth my views:

"First, I personally believe that abortion is wrong.

"Second, I believe that federal funds should not be used for the purpose of providing abortions.

"Third, I believe that it is imperative that the alternatives to abortion be made available as widely as possible. Those alternatives include everything from foster care to day care, family planning programs to sex education, and especially measures to reduce teen-age pregnancies.

"Finally, we live in a democratic society where every citizen is free to make his views known, to the Congress or to the courts. If the courts decide that there is a constitutional right in this country to have an abortion with federal funds, I will enforce that court order. If the Congress changes its mind and amends the statute which it has passed, or passes other laws which direct that funds be provided for abortion, I will enforce those laws. I will enforce those laws as vigorously as I intend to enforce the other laws that I am charged with enforcing if I am confirmed, including laws against discrimination against women on the basis of sex in Title IX, the Title VI laws."

Packwood pressed: "You are opposed and would be opposed to federal funds for abortions under any circumstances . . . if the life of the woman is jeopardized, if the fetus is carrying a genetic disease?" I testified I did not oppose federal funding of abortion where carrying the fetus to term endangered the life of the mother. That was not as far as Packwood wanted me to go.

Packwood continued: "What I am really interested in, Mr. Califano, what I would hope is that your feelings as a person would not interfere with the law, the enforcement of the laws." I assured him that my personal views would not interfere with my enforcement of the law.

Packwood asked what my recommendation would be for legislation in the future.

The same as Carter's, I responded. "We would recommend that federal funds not be used to provide abortions" in Medicaid or any other program.

Packwood's first-round time was up. The tension in the room eased a little as other senators asked questions on Social Security, balancing the budget, eliminating paperwork, busing, race discrimination, a separate department of education, Medicare and Medicaid management, handicapped rehabilitation programs, fraud and abuse in the welfare program, older Americans, alcoholism, and other matters prompted by special interest constituencies and the concerns of Americans that HEW intruded too deeply in their lives. The ever-present staffers whispered in senators' ears and passed their slips of paper from which senators read questions.

Texas Senator Lloyd Bentsen tried to lighten the atmosphere as he began: "Mr. Chairman, I am very pleased to see Mr. Califano here. I have known him for many years and have a great respect for his ability, intelligence, integrity, and judgment—until he took this job." The room burst into laughter.

At about noon, it was Packwood's turn again. When our eyes engaged, it was a signal for all the buzzing and rustling in the room to stop. As I expected, he went right to abortion, asking how I would change the law if I had the power to do so. I told him that President Carter and I would support the ban on the use of federal funds for abortions except where the mother's life was at stake. "That is the position . . . of the Carter administration," I concluded, quoting from one of the President-elect's campaign statements.

Packwood felt so strongly about the issue his face went florid with anger.

I thought for an instant about raising the issue of rape and incest, but immediately decided against it. This abortion controversy would be with me and the President for a long time and I didn't want to go any further than absolutely necessary without careful thought.

With his blue eyes blinking in disbelief, Packwood's voice rose: "If you had a choice . . . your recommendation would be that no federal funds will be used for those two hundred and fifty or three hundred thousand poor women, medically indigent, mostly minorities, who could not otherwise afford abortions?"

I reiterated: that would be my recommendation and the position of the administration. When I expressed the need to provide alternatives to abortion, Packwood interrupted: "How do you deal with teen-age pregnancies once the teen-ager is pregnant?" I said we needed more sensitive, decent human alternatives, treating the pregnant teen-ager as a person, letting her remain in school or continue her education in a home. I also recognized the need for better sex education and more effective family planning programs.

Packwood expressed support for all such programs. Then, his voice again rising, he said, "What we are saying, as far as the Carter program goes, with all the planned parenthood facilities, all the homes for unwed mothers, all the decent facilities to take care of them, if that woman wants to have an abortion and is poor and cannot afford it, tough luck." The last two words came out in angry disgust.

I could hear the whir of the television cameras.

"Senator, what I am saying is that we should reduce these cases to the greatest extent possible."

Packwood repeated for the television evening news: "Still, tough luck, as far as federal help is concerned."

I noted that "the federal government is not the only source of all funds," and private organizations were free to finance abortions. I then reminded Packwood that the administration position "is what the Congress has said in the Hyde amendment. The Senate and the House . . . voted for that amendment last year."

He asked whether the administration would oppose funding abortions in a national health insurance program. I said it would.

Packwood shook his head in apparent despair. We come to this issue from such different premises, I thought. To him, it is unfair for the government not to fund abortions for poor women when the Supreme Court has established a constitutional right to an abortion in the first trimester. To me, there is no question of equity. I thought abortion was wrong for women who could afford it unless the life of the mother was at stake, so I had no misgivings on grounds of equity in opposing the use of public funds to pay for abortions for poor women, as a matter of statutory law. Where the life of the mother was endangered, I favored public funding of abortions for the poor. The constitutional right to an abortion in the first trimester did not, in my mind, carry with it the right to public funding. The Constitution guarantees many precious rights—to speak and publish, to travel, to worship— but it does not require that the exercise of those rights be publicly funded.

Packwood cited Carter's hedging during the campaign and asked about a constitutional amendment to reverse the Supreme Court decision striking down state abortion laws. I responded that I opposed any constitutional amendment on abortion. "We run to the Constitution to stop busing, we run there on prayers in schools. We have to stop running to the Constitution to solve all of our problems." Packwood, still unsatisfied, had no further questions.

As the television crews disassembled their cameras, Senator Harry Byrd launched an attack on HEW's interference in local schools with excessively detailed civil rights questionnaires, and asked me about my support for voluntary charitable organizations.

The hearing before the Senate Finance Committee lasted so long that I had less than an hour before the Senate Committee on Labor and Public Welfare session began early in the same afternoon. Within fifteen minutes of its start, Senator Jacob Javits of New York asked about my ability to carry out the law, in view of my personal beliefs. I told Javits I had no qualms of conscience about my ability to enforce the law, "whatever the law is."

After a two-and-one-half-hour interlude of questions on civil rights enforcement, the isolation of HEW from the rest of the nation, welfare reform, busing, museums, education funding, biomedical research, national health insurance, conflicts of interest, animal testing of drugs, lack of coordination among Cabinet departments, and HEW's unresponsiveness to state and local government, Maine Democratic Senator William Hathaway returned to abortion. He characterized my position as being "morally and unalterably opposed to abortion," and then asked: "Does this mean that your convictions are so strong that if Congress should enact a law, whether it is national health insurance or whatever, that did provide federal funds for abortion, that you would recommend to President Carter that he veto such legislation?"

I hedged to get time to answer this unexpected question. I had never discussed this situation with Carter and I did not want to box the President in by simply saying I would or would not recommend a veto. "I do not think President Carter, in terms of his own views, needs my advice on whether to veto that legislation."

As Hathaway pressed, asking what I would recommend if Carter sought my advice and how active a role I would take, I decided to finesse the question. "I cannot answer that question. Laws come over with lots . . . of provisions in them, and whether one provision is of such overriding importance in terms of the national administration's policy that the bill ought to be vetoed . . . is something very difficult to judge in the abstract." There was no way I would judge this issue now.

Hathaway sensed what I was thinking and helped out by noting the difference between a national health insurance program that the administration wanted with abortion funding being the only unwelcome provision and a bill that simply provided federal funds for abortion.

He then asked whether I would lobby the Congress against legislation which permitted federal funds to be spent for abortion. I told him that the administration would lobby against such legislation.

Hathaway expressed concern about anyone forcing his religious or other beliefs on the public, citing as examples a Christian Scientist HEW Secretary who did not believe in modern medicine, or a vegetarian Secretary of Agriculture who did not believe food stamps should be spent for meat. I responded firmly that if I had the slightest hesitation about enforcing whatever law the Congress passed, I would not be sitting in front of him.

Hathaway didn't question that. His concern was that no individual "should enforce his particular religious or moral beliefs into the policy-making area." I responded that "the Congress had made a judgment last year that restricting federal funds for abortions was a matter appropriate for legislation." As to my personal views, I was expressing them so every senator who had to vote on my confirmation would know them.

Unlike the exchange with Packwood, the exchange with Hathaway ended on a conciliatory note. He appreciated my candor and hoped that I would maintain an open mind during the course of the debate on abortion.

But neither the press nor the American public was prepared for any conciliation on this issue. Before I had departed the hearing room the first of some 6,473 letters and telegrams and hundreds of phone calls, unyielding on one side or the other, began arriving at my office. That evening, the *Washington Star*'s front page headlined: ANGRY SENATOR BLASTS CALIFANO ON ABORTION. The story featured Packwood's questioning and his "tough luck" comment. It did report my commitment to enforce the law vigorously, and it questioned an assumption that Packwood and Hathaway had made— that the woman's right to an abortion established in *Roe v. Wade* implied a right to federal funds to pay for the procedure. Earlier in the week, during oral arguments before the Supreme Court on pending abortion cases, several Justices had questioned any such right to funds. There were indications that the Court would throw the scalding issue back into the legislative-executive political process. That possibility only enhanced the significance of my views—and President Carter's.

That evening Carter telephoned me: "How did the testimony go today?"

"All right, I think, Mr. President," I responded hesitantly. "I hope I didn't create any problems for you."

"What did they ask you about?"

"Most of the questions were on your campaign promises, like welfare reform and national health insurance, and then typical special interest questions about HEW's constituencies and busing. I testified for seven hours. But the fireworks came in the thirty minutes of questioning about abortion."

"I saw what you said in the paper and on television. You hang tough. You're saying the right things."

"Thank you, Mr. President."

In public comments outside the hearing, Packwood expressed deep concern and anger. Javits predicted a long and contentious struggle over the issue. And Karen Mulhauser of the National Abortion Rights Action League said it was "unthinkable" that a leading civil rights attorney "would openly discriminate" against indigent women. "We really didn't know until this week how extreme Califano's views were," she added. The lead editorial in the *Washington Post,* my former law client, was headed "Mr. Califano on Abortion," and took after me and my new boss: "The fact that each man reached this conclusion as a matter of personal conviction makes the conclusion itself no less troubling. For, personal or not, the effect of their common position would be to deny the poor what is available to the rich and not-so-rich. To argue as they do, that the emphasis should be on other medical services and/or pregnancy services does not address this inequity."

On Inauguration Day, January 20, 1977, the new President sent the nominations of the nine Cabinet members-designate whose hearings were completed to the Senate for confirmation. Eight were swiftly confirmed. Senator Packwood denied the Senate the necessary unanimous consent to consider my nomination that day.

Majority Leader Bob Byrd called my nomination to the Senate floor on January 24. Packwood was vehement. He said I held my views so passionately, so vigorously, that "I think it is impossible that Mr. Califano will be able to fairly administer the laws involving abortion, assuming that the Supreme Court says women . . . continue to have a right to an abortion, and that they continue to have a right to federal funds to help them."

Javits shared Packwood's view favoring federal funds for abortion, but he felt my qualifications in other areas merited my being confirmed. Other Republicans, from Senate Minority Leader Howard Baker to arch-conservative Carl Curtis, the ranking minority member of the Finance Committee, supported the nomination. The debate was brief, the vote 95 to Packwood's 1. Strom Thurmond was the first to phone to tell me of the Senate confirmation and congratulate me.

I called to thank each senator who had spoken on my behalf. Then I thought about Packwood. I felt that he had been petty in holding my nomination up four days, and that there had been an element of grandstanding in it. However, I had to accept the fact that his beliefs on abortion were as sincerely held as mine. From his point of view, putting that extra spotlight on me may have provided a little insurance that I would be careful to enforce a law that funded abortions more widely than I considered appropriate. I had been confirmed overwhelmingly, and I had to deal with him as a member of the Senate Finance Committee that had jurisdiction over such key HEW programs as Social Security, Medicare, Medicaid, and welfare. I swallowed a little hard and called him: "Bob, I understand your view on abortion. But I'm now Secretary and you and I agree on virtually every other social issue. I hope our differences on abortion won't prevent us from working together." Packwood, clearly surprised, thanked me for the call.

In a *New York Times* editorial on January 31 condemning my position on abortion, one element struck me as amusing: "Mr. Califano's statement in one sense represents his personal opposition to abortion. In another sense, it is a free political ride, earning credit for the administration from abortion foes without his having any real decision to make. It was Congress, though sharply split, which last fall decreed the ban on Medicaid funds for abortions. It is the courts, now scrutinizing that ban, which will decide. And Mr. Califano has pledged, as he must, to carry out the orders of the courts." I could understand the point of the editorial, but I hardly considered my experience before the Senate committees a free ride.

The abortion issue would track me for most of my term as HEW Secretary. I shortly discovered that, like Champion and Shanahan, few, if any, of my colleagues at HEW shared my view or the President's on abortion. Everyone in the top HEW management who expressed his opinion disagreed with mine. Only at the Christmas open house, when they streamed through my office to shake hands and have a picture taken, would HEW employees—mostly the blacks or Catholics—whisper, "Don't let them kill those black babies," or "God bless you for your stand against abortion."

The same was true at the White House. A few staff members, such as Midge Costanza, were publicly outspoken in favor of federal funding for abortion. Shanahan called me on July 15, 1977, and said she was going to a meeting at the White House, set up by Midge Costanza to organize the women in the administration to urge Carter to change his position on abortion. Shanahan said they might draft a petition asking to see Carter and setting forth their views. I was incredulous that a White House staffer would organize such

a meeting. I had no question about Shanahan's loyalty, but was appalled at Costanza's judgment and seriously questioned her loyalty to Carter. Two of the other top appointees at HEW, Assistant Secretary for Human Development Services Arabella Martinez and Assistant Secretary for Education Mary Berry, also went to the meeting.

A story was in the *Washington Post* on the morning following the Friday afternoon meeting. Jody Powell called Shanahan at about 11:00 A.M. "I just wanted to find out what right you all think you had to have a meeting like that in the White House?" Before Shanahan could respond, he answered, "No right, none at all."

"We have a right to express our views," Shanahan began.

Powell snapped, "At least General Singlaub [who disagreed with the President's policy in Korea] resigned. I can respect him."

"I did not give up my First Amendment rights when I joined the administration," Shanahan shot back.

Powell was incensed. "Most of these turkeys wouldn't have a job if it weren't for the President."

Shanahan spoke firmly, in the tense, modulated tone her voice often assumed when all her energy was devoted to maintaining her composure: "These women left damn good jobs to join the administration. Most are better qualified than men who got jobs of the same rank."

"Not you, Eileen, I don't include you," Powell responded defensively to the former economic correspondent for the *New York Times,* "but these turkeys would not have jobs if the President hadn't given them one."

When Shanahan told me about this conversation later that afternoon, she was still trembling with indignation and rage. Fortunately, she found great satisfaction in her work and she and I had developed a relationship of sufficient respect that she decided not to resign.

I assumed Carter would be enraged when he heard about the women's meeting—and he was, privately, and at the Cabinet meeting on Monday, July 18: "I don't mind vigorous debate in the administration. As a matter of fact, I welcome it," Carter said, "but I do not want leaks to the press or attacks on positions we've already established. If the forty women had listened to my campaign statements, they should know my position." Carter then contrasted Commerce Secretary Juanita Kreps and HUD Secretary Pat Harris with the group of women who met with Midge Costanza. Kreps raised her hand to speak. The President recognized her. In her soft-spoken, polite, and respectful manner, she said: "Mr. President, I appreciate the intent of your comment about me and I, of course, am loyal to you as we all are." What well-chosen words, I thought. "But"—Kreps paused to make certain we were all appropriately postured on the edge of our Cabinet chairs—"you should not take my absence from the meeting of the women as an indication of support for the administration's position on abortion."

Carter seemed somewhat surprised, not at Kreps's position, but at the quiet firmness with which she expressed her view in front of the Cabinet and the "barber shop" patrons (as I sometimes thought of the crew of aides and note-takers that sat against the wall in the Cabinet Room). From across the Cabinet table, Pat Harris promptly agreed with Kreps, but promised to keep her views within the official family. The President, so uncomfortable that he almost sounded defensive, indicated he was of course not talking about "Juanita and Pat," and reiterated his desire for "full debate," but he insisted on "complete loyalty" once an administration decision was made.

When the President walked in to begin the Cabinet meeting two weeks later, on August 1, the first Costanza had attended after her women's meeting, he put his arm around her, kissed her, and said, "Nice to see ya, darlin."

Whatever distance the President wanted from me on other policies, like school integration, the anti-smoking campaign, or Social Security cuts, he held me at his side whenever he spoke of abortion: during a March 1977 Clinton, Massachusetts, town meeting and on a Los Angeles television show in May 1977 ("Joe Califano, who is Secretary of HEW, feels the same way I do against abortions'); in Yazoo City, Mississippi, in July 1977 (". . . the Secretary of HEW agrees with me completely on this issue . . ."); at a Bangor, Maine, town meeting in February 1978 ("Joe Califano, who is head of HEW, is a very devout Catholic. . . . I happen to be a Baptist, and his views on abortion are the same as mine"); with college and regional editors and at general press conferences.

There were demonstrations, first in front of the building where my law office was located, then at the corner of Independence Avenue and Third Street, S.W., where the HEW headquarters and my offices were. The demonstrations, always peaceful but with increasingly sensational placards during 1977, were, as I looked out my window, a constant reminder of the potential of this issue to consume my energies to the detriment of other programs. A week after my confirmation, on January 31, 1977, Karen Mulhauser led a contingent of marchers from the National Abortion Rights Action League, carrying signs ("Califano Will Enslave Poor Women") that, however overdrawn they seemed to me, conveyed how many Americans felt. Coupled with the personal turmoil the issue stirred in several key managers I had recruited, both men and women, I decided it was imperative to set an overall tone and strategy from the beginning.

I was a bureaucratic child of the 1960s, acutely sensitive to the potential of an issue that touches on human life to kindle a consuming movement—as the military draft fueled the anti-Vietnam War movement. On abortion, the issue was life itself. If we all believed that life began at the same time, there would be no debate on abortion. If all citizens believed life begins at the moment of conception, then they would consider it intolerable for their national government to permit, much less fund, abortion because it involves the elimination of life. If, however, the body politic unanimously believed that life does not begin until the second or third trimester, or that there is no life until the fetus can be viable separate from the mother's body, then it would offend social justice for the government of such a single-minded people not to fund abortions for the poor when rich and middle-class women could easily obtain them to avoid serious illness or the later creation of retarded or physically handicapped life. However, the American people are far from unanimous in their view of when life begins; indeed, disagreement on that issue has been so strong it spawned as bitter a social and political dispute as the 1970s produced.

I concluded that it was not sufficient simply to express my view clearly and consistently, but that it was also essential to communicate the certainty with which I held it. Any hedging would only encourage those who disagreed to hope for a change that would not be forthcoming, and those who agreed to take steps to stiffen my resolve. By repeatedly and clearly setting forth my position, I could perhaps deflect the resources of some of the pro- and anti-abortion partisans to other targets they felt they had the opportunity to influence or the need to bolster.

My second conclusion was that I must do all I could to avoid unnecessary provocation. My obligation was to keep some measure of political decorum in this emotional debate. I did not have the luxury of an outside antagonist to be flip or hyperbolic. I refused to see or speak before pro-life groups who wanted to give me awards or roses, and I tried (not always with success) to avoid crossing picket lines or confronting demonstrators directly. In 1977, this involved going to a lot of places through the back door.

I had to display a calm and reasoned approach because of my obligation to enforce whatever law the Congress ultimately passed or the courts eventually declared constitutional. On this issue, above all, it was not enough for me to be fair; it was critical for the interested people to perceive they were being fairly treated.

Maintaining a sense of integrity was important not only to the public, but to the professionals in the department. HEW's Center for Disease Control was charged with the surveillance of communicable diseases. Most commonly identified with monitoring and reporting on influenza or other communicable diseases, the center was also responsible for surveillance of abortions and abortion-related deaths in the United States. In October 1977, at the peak of the legislative debate over Medicaid funding for abortion, there were reports that an Hispanic-American woman had checked into a McAllen, Texas, hospital with complications from an abortion improperly performed in Mexico. There were allegations that the woman was covered by Medicaid and had been told by a Texas doctor that if she had only come a few weeks earlier, she would have been eligible for Medicaid funding for an abortion, but now the law prohibited it. The woman died within a few days of being admitted to the hospital.

I called Bill Foege, whom I had recently appointed director of the center, and asked him to check out the reports. He came to Washington and nervously told me that while it was difficult to establish the facts because the woman might have gone to Mexico to keep the abortion secret, she had received two Medicaid-funded abortions before the Hyde amendment took effect. "So we may have a confirmed death from an abortion improperly performed on an otherwise Medicaid-eligible woman," Foege said, resting his paper on his lap as though trying to produce relief from a tension that still persisted.

I studied him silently for a moment and then realized that he was concerned about my view of the center's role in keeping abortion statistics.

"Look," I said, "You must understand this: I want you to keep statistics as accurately as you can, to investigate as meticulously as you can. Our obligation—whatever my views—is to set the facts before the Congress and the people. Particularly on an issue like this, we must maintain the integrity of HEW's data. The only way to deal with an issue this hot is to be accurate."

His face brightened in relief. "That's just the way I feel," he said.

While I could not predict the route or timetable, I sensed that the abortion issue was inexorably headed for my desk. On June 20, 1977, the Supreme Court decided in *Beal v. Doe* and *Maher v. Roe* that the federal government had no constitutional obligation to fund discretionary abortions that were not medically necessary. Like so many ardently awaited Supreme Court decisions, this one created as much controversy as it resolved. The Court had cleared the way to having the Hyde amendment go into effect, thus restricting Medicaid funding to abortions where the life of the mother would be endangered if the fetus were carried to term. The Court had also moved the debate back into the political arena, to the floors of the House and Senate and the HEW regulatory process.

I asked my staff to prepare a guideline to implement the Hyde amendment. Judge Dooling in Brooklyn would now have to withdraw his order blocking enforcement of that amendment and I wanted to be ready to issue the necessary instructions the same day the judge acted. Any delay would only give the pro- and anti-abortionists more time to demonstrate. If I could act immediately, there would be only one day of newspaper and television coverage.

As we planned to move as quickly and quietly as possible, the President was hit with a question about the Supreme Court decision at his July 12 press conference. I was signing routine mail, casually watching the televised conference, when Judy Woodruff of NBC News caught my attention with a question asking how "comfortable" the President was

with the recent Supreme Court decision "which said the federal government was not obligated to provide money for abortions for women who cannot afford to pay for them." The President reiterated his view that "I would like to prevent the federal government financing abortion."

Woodruff followed up: "Mr. President, how fair do you believe it is then that women who can afford to get an abortion can go ahead and have one and women who cannot afford to are precluded?"

In an echo of a statement by John Kennedy, the President answered, "Well, as you know, there are many things in life that are not fair, that wealthy people can afford and poor people can't. But I don't believe that the federal government should act to try to make these opportunities exactly equal, particularly when there is a moral factor involved."

I had been leaning back in my chair and almost went over backward. I was stunned at the President's response. It was clear to me that he had no idea of the bitter reaction his comment would incite. It couldn't have been deliberate. At worst, it was an on-the-spot, clumsy attempt to appeal to fiscal conservatives and right-to-lifers; at best it was an inept, off-the-top-of-his-head answer to a question for which he was not prepared. Within an hour Eileen Shanahan was in my office, tears of anger welling in her eyes, to tell me that the press wanted my comment on the President's "life is unfair" remark. "None, none, none," I said.

The only person who told me she agreed with the comment of the President was Eunice Kennedy Shriver, who wrote me on July 15: "In terms of the equity argument, I think the President's answer is satisfactory." It was one of the few times I can recall disagreeing with the political judgment of this extraordinary woman. She had become and remained a dedicated and politically persistent participant in the abortion controversy, an energetic opponent of federal funding.

In July, unknown to the public, to most of the antagonists prowling the halls of

Congress with roses and hangers and, indeed, to most congressmen and senators, a secret compromise remarkably close to the agreement the House and Senate would reach in December was beginning to take shape in the mind of Eunice Kennedy Shriver. She called me, as she was undoubtedly calling others, in the middle of the month, three weeks after the Supreme Court tossed the issue back to the Congress. She had "some language that might be acceptable to both the House and Senate" and end the widespread access to abortion. "We've got to face the rape and incest argument, don't you think?" And, spraying words in her staccato Massachusetts accent, she added: "We also have to deal with serious damage to the mother—physical damage, not this fuzzy psychological stuff."

Eunice read me some language and concluded, "I'm sending this over to you, personally and confidentially, and you can use it as your own."

Just as I was about to hang up, she added, "And Joseph, when we get over this, we need a teen-age pregnancy bill. I'm getting Teddy to introduce it and I want the two of you to work together on it." Eunice was working on a bill to fund centers to help teen-agers who were pregnant (she was so well connected within HEW that I got her revision of my draft testimony in support of the bill before I even received the draft from the departmental staff). Impressed by a Johns Hopkins program that helped teenagers deal with their babies and avoid having more, she wanted to duplicate it around the nation. But even there she stood firmly on abortion. When the teen-age pregnancy bill was being considered in 1978 and HEW Deputy Assistant Secretary Peter Schuck was quoted as saying states might give funds to clinics providing abortions if they were providing services to pregnant teen-agers, Eunice sent me a strong letter: "I certainly have not worked on this bill for three years under the assumption that abortion services would be provided under the bill. . . . I will not continue, quite frankly,

if abortion services are permitted under this legislation." Due in large measure to her lobbying on the Hill, when the bill was eventually enacted, no abortion services were funded under it.

The confidential proposal Eunice Shriver sent me suggested modifying the Hyde amendment to prohibit the use of funds to perform an abortion, except in cases of rape and incest, where necessary to save the life of the mother, or where the mother has an organic disease that would cause grave damage to her body if the pregnancy were continued to term. Under her proposal, she estimated that only a thousand to fifteen hundred abortions per year would be performed under Medicaid, mainly involving mothers with severe heart or kidney disease or severe diabetic conditions. "I am told," her letter concluded, "that 80 percent of the abortions performed under Medicaid would be eliminated by this language."

There were few takers for the Shriver compromise in July, but before the abortion legislation saga ended in December 1977, the House and Senate would agree on language reflecting her influence and access to key members.

On August 4, 1977, Judge Dooling reluctantly lifted his injunction against enforcing the Hyde amendment. Within hours, I announced that HEW would no longer fund abortions as a matter of course, but would provide funds "only where the attending physician, on the basis of his or her professional judgment, had certified that the abortion was necessary because the life of the mother would be endangered if the fetus were carried to term."

The House and Senate Conferees' report on the Hyde amendment approved funding for termination of an ectopic (fallopian tube) pregnancy, for drugs or devices to prevent implantation of the fertilized ovum on the uterus wall, and for "medical procedures for the treatment of rape or incest victims." I had asked Attorney General Griffin Bell to interpret that language. His opinion concluded that the Hyde amendment and the quoted language prohibited funding abortion for rape or incest (unless the life of the mother was threatened), but permitted funding for prompt treatment before the fact of pregnancy was established.

On the same day Judge Dooling lifted his injunction and I issued my guidelines under the Hyde amendment to the 1977 HEW Appropriations Act, the Senate voted by a lopsided 60 to 33 to permit payment for abortions under a broad "medically necessary" standard in 1978. Earlier that week the House had voted 238 to 182 to retain the strict Hyde amendment language.

And on the same August 4th day, the Defense Department revealed that it had funded 12,687 abortions at military hospitals between September 1, 1975, and August 31, 1976. The Pentagon policy was to fund abortions for members and dependents for reasons of physical and mental health. The *Washington Post* story reporting military abortion statistics also noted that federal employees were entitled to abortions under the general health plans, but no records were kept of the number of abortions performed for them and their dependents.

In this state of chaos and division, the House and Senate left Washington for their August recess. When the Congress reconvened in September, high on its agenda was the House and Senate Conference on the Labor-HEW appropriations bill.

There are two ways to block federal funding of a particular activity otherwise authorized. One is to pass a statute that prohibits the federal government from acting. Such legislation must be referred to the authorizing committees of the Senate and the House; normally those committees would be required to hold hearings and report the legislation before it was eligible for consideration on the floor. That can be a long and tedious process—with no certainty that the legislation will ever get to the floor of both Houses for a vote. The authorizing committee can block consideration by simply holding the bill.

The other way to block federal funding for a specific purpose is through the appropriations process, either by not providing funds, or by attaching a rider to an appropriations bill, stating that none of the appropriated funds can be spent for the proscribed activity. The appropriations rider has the same practical force as authorizing legislation, and it offers a significant advantage to legislators: Each year the appropriations bills for the executive departments must be reported by the appropriations committees and acted on by the Congress if government is to continue functioning. The disadvantage is that, unlike substantive, authorizing legislation, the appropriations rider comes up for review each year.

Until the mid-1960s, there were few such riders. By and large, House and Senate parliamentarians ruled them out of order because "substantive legislation" was not permitted on appropriations bills. But as the government funded more activities, the lines between substantive legislation and limits on the uses of federal funds became increasingly hard to draw. The more controversial the activities funded by the appropriations bill, the more frequent the attempt to restrict spending by riders.

No bill attracted more politically aggressive, true-believing interest groups than the annual HEW appropriations bill. It had become honey for a host of political bees: riders prohibiting loans or grants to students who crossed state lines to incite to riot (a hangover from the Vietnam War), forbidding the use of funds for busing, limiting the use of funds to obtain civil rights enforcement information from schools. Senator Warren Magnuson, Chairman of the Senate Appropriations Committee, told me during my first month in office, "Joe, you won't recognize the appropriations hearing for HEW. It has attracted the Goddamnedest collection of kooks you ever saw. We've got to stop all these riders. Make them go to the authorizing committees." But Magnuson's outburst was to prove nothing more than exasperated hope. For during the fall of 1977, he would be involved in the bare-knuckled, prolonged fight over the abortion rider on the HEW appropriations bill.

Some facts about abortions also helped inflame the issue. In 1975, the nation's capital had become the first city in America where abortions outnumbered births. As the congressional recess ended in September 1977, the District of Columbia government revealed that in 1976, legal abortions obtained by District residents totaled 12,945—an unprecedented one-third more than the city's 9,635 births. And 57 percent of the abortions—7,400—were paid for by the Medicaid program before the Hyde amendment went into effect on August 4. The high abortion rate in Washington, D.C., reflected the nationwide abortion rate among blacks, which was double that among whites.

With the Congress returning to Washington, the pro-abortionists moved to counter the right to life roses. On September 7, pro-abortion leader Karen Mulhauser announced a campaign to mail coat hangers to Representative Daniel Flood, the Pennsylvania Democrat who chaired the HEW appropriations subcommittee, and other anti-abortion members.

The first meeting of the House and Senate all-male cast of conferees on September 12 broke up almost as soon as it started. Magnuson and Massachusetts Republican Senator Edward Brooke (who, like Packwood, strenuously fought to fund abortions under Medicaid) vowed that they would not return to the conference table until the House voted on the Senate version of the abortion rider. House Committee Chairman Flood initially refused. But, under pressure from his colleagues who feared that funds for important HEW programs and paychecks for federal employees would be interrupted if no appropriations agreement were reached, Flood took the Senate proposal to fund abortions where "medically necessary," to the House floor. On September 27,

the House overwhelmingly rejected the Senate language, 252 to 164.

Then Flood took Magnuson up on his earlier commitment to compromise if the House would first vote on the Senate language. But Magnuson was not prepared to give much and House conferees ridiculed his attempt to cover genetic disease, with statements that his suggestion would permit abortions where the child had a blue and brown eye. At one point Magnuson proposed limiting funding to situations where the life of the mother was at stake, cases of rape or incest, and situations involving "serious permanent health damage." When I heard about his proposal, I suspected the fine hand of Eunice Shriver. But Flood's initial reaction was scathing. "You could get an abortion with an ingrown toe nail with that Senate language," and it went nowhere.

After House Speaker Tip O'Neill complained that only pro-abortionist Magnuson and Brooke attended the conference for the Senate, thus making compromise near-impossible with the dozen House members usually present, more Senate conferees went to the meetings. The conversation became more civil, but the conferees were no closer to agreement as September 30, the end of the fiscal year and the end of HEW's authority to spend money, arrived.

Up to that point I had decided to stay out of the congressional fight over abortion. The administration view was well known. The President did not want to be part of any compromise that was more permissive than his anti-abortion campaign statements. It was one thing to carry out whatever law the Congress passed, quite another to take an active role in easing the restriction. Carter was committed to the former; he wanted no part of the latter.

Popular sentiment, reflected in the polls, was with the strict House view, and many pro-abortionists realized that. On October 6, for example, Norman Dorsen, head of the American Civil Liberties Union, in opposing a constitutional convention, cited his concern that a nationwide convention might be used to outlaw abortion completely. With that kind of popular support, the House was likely to hold to the strict limits on federal funding for abortions that Carter favored.

Moreover, my conversations with members of Congress had led me to the conclusion that I could be of little, if any, help in drafting the substance of an eventual compromise. Abortion was such a profoundly personal issue that neither I nor a President who, during his first nine months of office, had already lost a good deal of respect on the Hill, would have much influence with individual members.

Only once had I come close publicly to entering the debate during this time. I understood the depth of conviction and humane values that motivated most abortion advocates, but I was deeply offended by the cost-control, money-saving argument pushed by the staunchly pro-abortion Alan Guttmacher Institute, the research arm of the Planned Parenthood Federation of America. In late September, the Institute published a report claiming that the Hyde amendment would cost the public at least $200 million, for the first year of their life, to take care of children who could have been aborted under Medicaid. I wanted to denounce this kind of argument in severe terms: it was appallingly materialistic and represented a selfish failure to confront moral issues as such. But in the interests of being firm yet not provocative I waited until I was asked about it at a press conference to express my views, and then did so in muted tones.

Now, however, I had to get into the congressional fight. On October 1, I was compelled to eliminate all hiring and overtime and virtually all out-of-town travel by HEW's 150,000 employees. I also warned that they might receive only half their pay in mid-October unless the House and Senate resolved the appropriations fight over abortion. It was, so far as we could tell, unprecedented at the time for a department to have no authority to operate or spend money after the first of the new fiscal year.

Despite the situation, the conferees again failed to reach agreement on October 3, and postponed any further action until October 12, after the Columbus Day recess. That postponement jeopardized beneficiaries of HEW programs and the pay of Department employees. Across the nation, state rehabilitation agencies for the handicapped were running out of money to process claims for Social Security disability benefits; New York State would be unable to meet its payroll for employees to process disability determinations; Texas intended to furlough 612 employees on October 12; Idaho would have no money for its nutrition and community services program for the aged.

I called Tip O'Neill and Bob Byrd on October 10th, and asked them to try to break the abortion deadlock in order to avoid severe human suffering. The next day I sent them a letter and made it public. It was, the letter charged, "grossly unfair to hold the vulnerable people of our nation and thousands of federal and state employees hostage" in the congressional dispute over the use of federal funds for abortions. If the Congress could not agree on abortion language, I urged them to pass a Continuing Resolution to give me authority to spend in early 1978 at the end-of-1977 level in order to continue HEW programs that people depend on each day. The Senate opposed a Continuing Resolution because it would also keep the Hyde amendment in effect.

I sent telegrams to the state governors alerting them to imminent funding terminations so they would press their congressmen and senators to act. I asked Labor Secretary Ray Marshall to tell the Congress and the public of the dangers of continuing to hold up 1978 funding, since his department's appropriations were tied to the HEW bill. Marshall announced that further delay could force many states to stop processing unemployment insurance claims and halt federally funded job and health safety programs. At my suggestion, President Carter told the congressional leadership on the morning of October 12 that, while we all recognized what an emotional issue abortion was, the paychecks of federal employees should not be held up while Congress tried to resolve it. House Appropriations Committee Chairman George Mahon warned of "chaos in some parts of our government." By October 13, after wrangling with each other and some spirited debate on the House floor, both legislative bodies passed a Continuing Resolution to provide funds for fifteen days until the end of the month.

On Sunday, October 16, I was scheduled to appear on the ABC-TV program *Issues and Answers*. On the Saturday morning preceding the program, I called the President to review the administration's position on abortion. The President said that his position had not changed since the campaign.

"One issue in sharp dispute is how to handle victims of rape or incest," I said, asking whether he objected to funding abortions for rape or incest victims and referring to his July 12, 1977, press conference. There Carter had said that the federal government "should not finance abortions except when the woman's life is threatened or when the pregnancy was the result of rape or incest. I think it ought to be interpreted very strictly."

I asked the President whether his "very strictly" interpretation was related to the dispute between House and Senate conferees over medical procedures short of abortion for rape or incest performed shortly after the act, as distinguished from outright abortion. Carter said he was unaware of the dispute, but wanted to stay out of it. I said that it might not be possible for me to do that. Then leave the administration position ambiguous on this issue, he suggested. "Above all I want people to understand I oppose federal funding for abortion in keeping with my campaign promise."

The words had the texture of the three dimensions that came into play when Carter discussed abortion with me: his deep personal belief, his sense (particularly in the first year) that he would violate some sacred trust if he did not adhere to his campaign

statements, and his insistence on getting the political plusses out of issues that had such significant political minuses as well.

ABC White House correspondent Sam Donaldson asked the first question on the program the next day: What was the administration's position on abortion? I recited the administration position opposing federal funds for abortions "except where the life of the mother is endangered if the fetus were carried to term, or for treatment as a result of rape or incest."

After Bettina Gregory asked about teenage pregnancy, Donaldson pressed for precision on the issue of rape or incest. "The House position . . . would not even allow abortions to be financed in the case of rape or incest, unless someone comes forward and it can be established that there is not yet a pregnancy that has been medically found. Is that reasonable?"

Trying to satisfy the President's desires, I responded: "In the case of rape or incest, you would assume that the individual would come promptly for treatment and that is a matter of several days. Doctors and experts disagree on it. It can be days or a couple of weeks."

Donaldson noted that the House would allow a dilation and curettage only where an abortion was not involved, and asked if I agreed. I hesitated, then in pursuit of the President's overriding objective to be anti-abortion, responded: "Yes, that is the way I feel; that is the way the President feels. He made that clear during the campaign repeatedly, as you are well aware, covering him during the campaign."

I then recalled my own desire to cool the debate, and added: "This is a very difficult issue; it is a very complex issue; it is a very emotional issue. There are strong feelings on all sides. I think in terms of the nation as a whole what is important is that this issue is being debated in every state in the union . . . in city after city. The way to reach a consensus in a democracy is to have people talk about it, where they live; and that is happening now in this country . . . the issue should be debated in more places than in the House and Senate."

When the Continuing Resolution ran out on October 31, House and Senate conferees agreed to language which would permit federal funding for abortion in cases of rape, including statutory rape of minors, or incest, where a prompt report was made to appropriate authorities. They were still split over Senate language which would permit abortions "where grave physical health damage to the mother would result if the pregnancy were carried to term." By the next day, however, the House conferees wanted only forced rape covered. The Senate conferees were furious, and the conference broke up in acrid charges of bad faith. This skirmish marked the first time the House conferees had agreed on abortion, as distinguished from treatment before the fact of pregnancy was established, in any rape situation. Nevertheless, with their conferees unable to agree, the House and Senate voted another Continuing Resolution, giving members a three week respite from the issue until December 1.

But there was no respite from the demonstrations. Without fail, during the week pickets marched outside HEW. The signs got more vivid; the crude printing crueler. There were the color pictures from *Life* magazine and the roses and hangers, which had become calling cards for the protagonists. The rhetoric was increasingly sprinkled with harsh accusations of "murder" by each side— of killing unborn children by Medicaid abortion, or poor mothers by back-alley abortion. Some placards accused me of being a "murderer of poor women."

Wherever I went, pickets greeted me. When I spoke in Oregon at a Democratic political fundraiser, several hundred demonstrators from both sides paraded outside the Hilton Hotel. The Oregon Legislative Emergency Board was scheduled to decide in ten days whether to replace lost federal abortion funds with state money. The pro-abortionists angrily accused me of trying to inject my own views into the

Oregon fight, which I had not heard of until arriving in Portland.

The sincerity of the Oregon demonstrators and others like them took its toll on me: earnest pleas of both sides were moving. None of the lighthearted sidebars that accompanied most demonstrations—even some during the Vietnam War—were present during pro- and anti-abortion rallies. When I avoided demonstrators by going out a side entrance, as I did that evening in Oregon, I felt like a thief in the night, denying these committed marchers even the chance to know they had been at least heard, if not heeded.

The most vehement demonstration took place in New York City's Greenwich Village on Saturday afternoon, November 12. It was my most draining emotional experience over the abortion issue.

New York University President John Sawhill invited me to receive NYU's University Medal. The award ceremony was to consist of a brief talk and an extended question and answer period. As the day approached I was told that pro-abortionists planned a major demonstration. When I arrived at the NYU Law School in Washington Square, there were several thousand demonstrators. They were overwhelmingly pro-abortion; the handful of right-to-lifers there said they had heard of the demonstration only the evening before and had no chance to mobilize their supporters. Bella Abzug reviled the "white-male dominated White House." Speaker after speaker attacked me for "imposing my Roman Catholic beliefs on poor women." "Our bodies, ourselves" protesters chanted to the beat of a big drum. "Not Califano's."

The crowd was so large and noisy, I could hear it clearly when I entered the law school around the block from the demonstrators. As I reached the back entrance, ACLU Chairman Norman Dorsen, a friend of twenty-five years, greeted me with a broad smile on his face. "It took Califano to bring the sixties back to NYU," he cracked. We all chuckled at that welcome, which broke the tension for the next few minutes.

When Dorsen, who was to moderate the question and answer period, Sawhill, and I entered the auditorium, my right arm and hand were in a cast, held by a sling, due to an operation on my thumb the week before. The auditorium was crushingly overcrowded. Every seat was taken; every inch of wall space lined with standees. The antagonism of the audience was so penetrating I could physically feel it as I sat on the elevated stage. Even the cast on my arm will evoke no sympathy here, I thought.

Sawhill spoke first about me. He then turned to give me the medal. As I rose to receive it, the last row of the audience unfurled a huge pro-abortion banner across the back of the auditorium. Fully half the audience stood and held up hangers, many with ends that had been dipped in red nail polish. When the medal was presented, at least a hundred people in the audience turned their backs to me. Many of them remained in that position throughout the entire ninety minutes of my speech and the question and answer session that followed.

The question period was largely devoted to abortion, with many emotional statements and speeches. None, however, struck me more forcefully than that of an intense woman who picked up on a comment I had made earlier that year. On the Sunday, March 20, NBC program *Meet the Press,* Carol Simpson had queried me at length on abortion and the adequacy of the administration program for alternatives to abortion. In the course of one extended response, I observed: "I have never known a woman who wanted an abortion or who was happy about having an abortion. I think it is our role to provide for those women the best we can in terms of family planning services, of day care centers for their children, of health, and prenatal services to make sure children are born healthy, and all the decent things in life that every child in this country deserves, whether it is health care or a clean home or a decent schooling, and we will do our best to do that."

To my left, about halfway down the aisle in the NYU auditorium, a woman rose to the microphone. Her head was tilted sideways, her eyes spilled over with anger, even hatred. "Look at me, Mr. Califano," she shouted with defiant emotion. "I want you to see a woman who wanted an abortion. I want you to see a woman who was happy at having an abortion. I want you to see a woman who had an abortion two weeks ago and who intends to have another abortion."

The room fell into total silence as the tone of her voice became that kind of gripping whisper everyone can hear even when they don't want to: "I want you to go back to Washington knowing that there are women who are happy to have had abortions, knowing that there are women who want abortions. I don't ever want you to make a statement like the one you made saying that you have never known a woman that wanted to have an abortion or never known a woman who was happy about having an abortion. You have now met one."

So draining was the emotional experience at NYU, that afterward, when I got into the car to Kennedy Airport to depart for England, Germany, and Italy to look at national health programs—my first trip abroad as Secretary of HEW—I instantly fell asleep and did not wake up until the driver shook me to say we had arrived at Kennedy.

The abortion issue followed me to Europe. There were questions in England and the Italians were in the midst of their own volatile parliamentary debate on the issue. The latent suspicion of my Catholicism again surfaced in Rome. Immediately after my audience with Pope Paul VI, several reporters called at the Hassler Hotel to see if the Pope talked to me about abortion. He had not mentioned the issue. His focus was on the failure of the food-rich nations such as the United States to feed the world.

I returned to Washington on Thanksgiving eve. I knew the abortion issue would erupt again when the latest Continuing Resolution expired. But I was not prepared for the news the *Washington Post* brought me on the

Sunday after Thanksgiving. Connie Downey, chairperson of an HEW group on alternatives to abortion, had written a memo expressing her views to her boss, Assistant Secretary of Planning and Evaluation Henry Aaron. The *Post* headlined the most sensational portion of an otherwise typical HEW memo: TASK FORCE HEAD LISTS SUICIDE, MOTHERHOOD, AND MADNESS: ABORTION ALTERNATIVES CITES IN HEW MEMO.

The memo, written more than four months earlier on July 18, contained this paragraph: "Abortion is but one alternative solution to many of the problems . . . which may make a pregnancy unwise or unwanted. . . . It is an option, uniquely, which is exercised between conception and live birth. As such, the literal alternatives to it are suicide, motherhood, and, some would add, madness. . . ."

The memo had never reached me, but its leak provided a dramatic reminder of the potential for turmoil within HEW and raised the curtain on the final act between the House and the Senate on the fiscal 1978 HEW appropriations bill.

Returning from Thanksgiving recess, the House leadership was determined to press for a compromise. They did not want the Christmas checks of federal employees to be short. Appropriations Committee Chairman Mahon called me on November 29 to say he had decided to take the leadership completely away from Flood, who ardently opposed federal funds for abortion. "He's just implacable on the subject," Mahon said, distraught. "I'm retiring, but this kind of conduct is a disgrace to the House. We all look asinine."

In secret negotiations with Senator Brooke, Mahon eventually produced the compromise on December 7. The House voted twice within less than four hours. The first time members rejected a Mahon proposal and voted 178 to 171 to stand by their strict position against all funding for abortions except those needed to save the mother's life. Minutes later Mahon, dejected but determined, won speedy approval of new language from the Rules Committee and

rushed back to the House floor. The House reversed direction and adopted the new and relaxed standard, 181 to 167. Within two hours, with only three of its hundred members on the floor, the Senate acceded to the House language and sent the measure to President Carter for his signature.

Under the measure, no HEW funds could be used to perform abortions, "except when the life of the mother would be endangered if the fetus were carried to term, or except for such medical procedures necessary for the victims of rape or incest, when such rape or incest has been reported promptly to a law enforcement agency or public health service; or except in those instances where severe and long-lasting physical health damage to the mother would result if the pregnancy were carried to term when so determined by two physicians."

Senator Brooke described the outcome as "not really acceptable to either side, but it makes some progress." Representative Hyde said that the measure "provides for the extermination of thousands of unborn lives." Senator Javits called the action "a major victory for women's rights." ACLU Chairman Dorsen characterized it as "a brutal treatment of women with medical needs for abortion." Any relief I felt at seeing at least some resolution was lost in the knowledge that the protagonists would rearm to battle over the regulations I had to issue.

As soon as President Carter signed the $60 billion appropriations bill on December 9, it landed on my desk, for the final provision of the compromise language stated: "The Secretary shall promptly issue regulations and establish procedures to ensure that the provisions of this section are rigorously enforced."

The antagonists turned their attention to me. Magnuson and Brooke wrote and called with their permissive interpretation. Robert Michel, ranking Republican on the Appropriations Committee, wrote with his strict view. Dan Flood called and other members—and their even more aggressive staffs—pressed for their interpretation of words such as "medical procedures," "promptly reported," "severe and long-lasting physical health damage," and "two physicians."

There was no way in which I could avoid becoming intimately involved in making key decisions on the regulations. I decided personally to read the entire 237 pages of self-serving and often confused congressional debate and to study the ten different versions of this legislation that were passed by either the House or the Senate.

To assure objectivity, to balance any unconscious bias I might harbor, and to reduce my vulnerability to charges of personal prejudice, I assigned the actual regulation writing to individuals who did not share my strong views about abortion and, more importantly, who stood up for their own views and did not hesitate to tell me when they thought I was wrong. The bulk of the work was done by Richard Beattie, the Deputy General Counsel of HEW, and HEW attorneys June Zeitlin and David Becker, all of whom opposed any restrictions on federal funding of abortions. I also asked the Attorney General to review independently the regulations we drafted at HEW. Once they were in effect, I would establish a detailed auditing system to assure compliance and fulfill the congressional mandate "to ensure that the provisions of this section are rigorously enforced."

Finally, I decided not to consult the President about the regulations. Carter had enough controversial problems on his desk without adding this one. My responsibility under the Constitution and under our system of government was to reflect accurately the law passed by the Congress. Neither Carter's personal views nor mine were of any relevance to my legal duty to ascertain what Congress intended and write regulations that embodied that intent.

In pursuit of my overall goal of cooling the temperature of the debate, I wanted to issue the regulations more "promptly" than anyone might expect. Not relying solely on my own reading of the congressional debates, I asked the lawyers for a thorough analysis of the legislative history. We then spent hours discussing and debating what the Congress intended on several issues, frustrated by the conflicting statements in the congressional record. We determined that for rape and incest victims, the term "medical procedures" as used in this new law now clearly included abortions; that a "public health service" had to be a governmental, politically accountable institution; that short of fraud we should accept physicians' judgments as to what constituted "severe and long-lasting physical health damage"; that the two physicians whose certification was required must be financially independent of each other; and that the rape or incest victim need not personally make the required report to public authorities. We resolved a host of other issues as best we could against the backdrop of the heated and confusing congressional debate. They were wearing days, because I felt the law was too permissive, and its provisions were in conflict with my own position. I revisited many decisions several times, concerned, on overnight reflection, that I had bent too far to compensate for my personal views and approved inappropriately loose regulations, or that I was letting my personal views override congressional intent.

By far my most controversial determination was to define "reported promptly" in the context of rape and incest to cover a sixty-day period from the date of the incident. Even though the Attorney General found the judgment "within the permissible meaning of the words within the Secretary's discretion," there was a storm of controversy over this decision.

There were widely varying interpretations on the floor of the House and the Senate. Most of the legislative history on the Senate floor was made by pro-abortion Senators Magnuson and Brooke. They spoke of "months" and "ninety days" to make the period as long as possible. On the House side, Mahon and other proponents of the compromise spoke of "weeks" and "thirty days" as they cautiously maneuvered this difficult piece of legislation to passage. On the floor of Congress, pro- and anti-abortionists could express their views and protect their constituencies. But I had to select a number of days and be as certain as possible that it would stick.

After extensive internal discussion and spirited argument within the department, I concluded that a sixty-day reporting period was within the middle range of the various time limits mentioned in the debates. The dominant issues during debate were access to abortions and prevention of fraud. The sixty-day period was long enough for a frightened young girl or an embarrassed woman who might not want to report a rape or incest, or one in shock who psychologically could not, to learn whether she might be pregnant and to make the report to public authorities. Sixty days was also prompt enough to permit effective enforcement of the law.

I was ready to issue the regulations during the third week of January 1978. On Monday, January 23, the annual March for Life to protest the 1973 Supreme Court abortion decision was scheduled to file past HEW en route from the White House to the Capitol. I decided to delay issuing the regulations until later in the week. The participants were outraged at the House-Senate compromise. As march leader Nellie Gray saw it, "The life issue is not one for compromise and negotiation. Either you're for killing babies or you're against killing babies."

I issued the regulations on January 26. Attorney General Bell concluded that they were "reasonable and consistent with the language and intent of the law." The *New York Times* editorialized that I had "done [my] duty. . . . He has interpreted the nation's unfair abortion law fairly. . . . On several controversial issues Mr. Califano and his lawyers have performed admirably, hacking their way through a thicket of ambiguities in the law that passed a bitter and divided Congress in December after months of heated debate."

The right to life lobby disagreed. Thea Rossi Barron, legislative counsel for the National Right to Life Committee, called the regulations an example of "a rather blatant carrying out of a loophole to allow abortion on demand." The pro-life groups were particularly disturbed about the sixty-day reporting period for victims of rape or incest. But the most severe critic of that provision was Jimmy Carter.

In testifying before the House Appropriations Committee on the morning of February 21, 1978, less than a month after issuing the regulations, Chairman Flood and Republican Robert Michel pressed me to provide an administration position on tightening the restrictions on abortion.

I called the President during the luncheon break. The President wanted the reporting period for rape or incest shortened. He was "not happy" with the sixty-day time period in the regulations. "I believe such instances are reported promptly," he said coolly.

I told him that the sixty-day period was my best judgment of what Congress intended in the law. Carter "personally" believed sixty days permitted "too much opportunity for fraud and would encourage women to lie."

"But what counts is what the congressional intent is," I argued.

The President then said he thought the regulations did not require enough information. He particularly wanted the doctor to report to Medicaid the names and addresses of rape and incest victims. The President was also inclined to require reporting of any available information on the identity of the individual who committed the rape or incest. Carter said, "Maybe some women wake up in the morning and find their maidenhead lost, but they are damn few. That actually happened in the Bible, you know."

"Perhaps we can tighten the reporting requirement" I responded, somewhat surprised at his Biblical reference. "Do you have any strong feelings on the legislation itself? "

Carter expressed some strong feelings: "I am against permitting abortions where long-lasting and severe physical health damage might result. I think that might permit too much of a chance for abuse and fraud. I want to end the Medicaid mills and stop these doctors who do nothing but perform abortions on demand all day."

When I testified that afternoon, I gave the House Appropriations Subcommittee some indication of the administration's views and agreed to submit a letter with the administration's position the next day.

After preparing a draft, I called the President and reviewed my proposed letter for the committee word by word. The letter set the administration position as stricter than the December compromise of the Congress. The administration opposed funding abortions in situations involving "severe and long-lasting physical health damage to the mother." The President and I compromised on the rape and incest paragraph: "In the case of rape or incest, we believe that present law requires the sixty days specified in the regulation as the period Congress intended for prompt reporting. In order to reduce the potential for fraud and abuse, it may be advisable to reduce that period to a shorter period of time."

Just as he was hanging up the phone, Carter again directed me to tighten the reporting provisions on rape and incest. "I want rules that will prevent abortion mills from simply filling out forms and encouraging women to lie."

I changed the regulations to require that the names and addresses of both the victim and the person reporting the rape or incest, and the dates of both the report and the incident, be included in the documentation for Medicaid funding. This change drew immediate fire from the National Organization for Women's National Rape Task Force, but it was well within my discretion under the law and consistent with the congressional intent.

Yet the President was still not satisfied. He wanted the sixty-day reporting period shortened, regardless of congressional intent. He raised the issue again two months later at the Camp David Cabinet summit of April 17, 1978, sharply criticizing "the regulations HEW issued on abortion" among a series of actions by Cabinet officers with which he disagreed.

The concern of the President and others that the regulations were too loosely drawn in the rape and incest area has not turned out to be justified. During the first sixteen months under the law and regulation until shortly before I left HEW, only 92 Medicaid abortions were funded for victims of rape or incest. The overwhelming majority of Medicaid-funded abortions—84 percent of 3,158 performed—were to save the life of the mother; 522 were to avoid severe and long-lasting health damage to the mother. Eunice Shriver's estimate of 1,000 to 1,500 Medicaid-funded abortions each year was not too far off, particularly when compared with the 250,000 to 300,000 abortions estimated to have been performed annually under Medicaid in the absence of any funding restrictions.

I came away from the abortion controversy with profound concern about the capacity of national government, in the first instance, to resolve issues so personal and so laced with individual, moral, and ethical values. The most secure way to develop a consensus in our federal system is from the bottom up. But once the Supreme Court established a woman's constitutional right to an abortion against the backdrop of federally funded health care programs, the issue was instantly nationalized. As each branch acted—the Congress with the Hyde amendment, the executive with its regulations, and the Supreme Court in its opinions—the mandates from the top down generated as much resentment as agreement. This is true even though, by 1978, many states had more restrictive provisions on abortion funding than the national government.

In 1978, the Congress extended abortion funding restrictions to the Defense Department budget. In 1979, it applied an even stricter standard to both HEW and Defense appropriations, by eliminating funding in cases of long-lasting physical health damage to the mother, thus funding abortions only when the life of the mother is at stake or in cases of rape or incest, as Carter and I proposed for HEW in February 1978. The Supreme Court in the *McRae* case upheld the constitutionality of the Hyde amendment in June of 1980, concluding that the right to an abortion did not require the government to provide the resources to exercise it and that the Congress could restrict the circumstances under which it would pay for abortions. Months later, the Senate and House agreed to place tighter restrictions on Medicaid funding of abortions. Under the 1981 appropriations legislation, such funding is permitted only where the mother's life is at stake, in cases of rape reported within 72 hours and in cases of incest. That legislation permits the states to be even more restrictive; they are "free not to fund abortions to the extent that they in their sole discretion deem appropriate." Similar language was attached to the Defense appropriations bill.

Conforming the Defense and HEW appropriations bills provides the same standards for most of the federal funding arena. So long as the Congress acts through the appropriations for each department, however, rather than by way of across-the-board authorizing legislation, there will be inconsistencies. Even within HEW, the abortion funding policy has been a quilted one. The restrictions do not apply to disabled citizens whose health bills are paid by Medicare, because that program is financed out of Social Security trust funds, not through the HEW appropriations bill. Nor do the funding limits apply to the Indian Health Service; though administered by HEW, funds for the Indian Health Service are provided in the Interior Department appropriations bill. The Congress has begun to move to prohibit the use of federal funds to pay for abortion through federal employee health insurance. The inevitable challenges in court to new restrictions and the recurrent debate in the Congress assure continuing turmoil and controversy over the abortion issue.

In personal terms, I was struck by how infinitely more complex it was to confront the abortion issue in the broader sphere of politics and public policy in our pluralistic society than it had been to face it only as a matter of private conscience. I found no automatic answers in Christian theology and the teachings of my church to the vexing questions of public policy it raised, even though I felt secure in my personal philosophical grounding.

I was offended by the constant references to me as "Secretary Califano, a Roman Catholic" in the secular press when it wrote about the abortion issue. No such reference appeared next to my name in the stories reporting my opposition to tuition tax credits favored by the Catholic Church or my disputes with the Catholic hierarchy on that issue.

I was dismayed by the number of Catholics and diocesan papers that attacked me for the regulations I issued on abortion. Their attack so concerned Notre Dame president, Father Theodore Hesburgh, that he urged me to speak about the conscience and duty of a Catholic as a public official at the commencement in South Bend in 1979. The assumption of many bishops that I could impose my views on the law passed by the Congress reflected a misunderstanding of my constitutional role at that stage of the democratic process. As it turned out, like the President's, their assumption that the sixty-day reporting period for rape or incest constituted a legal loophole was as ill-founded in fact as it was in law.

Throughout the abortion debate, I did—as I believe I should have—espouse a position I deeply held. I tried to recognize that to have and be guided by convictions of conscience is not a license to impose them indiscriminately on others by one-dimensionally translating them into public policy. Public policy, if it is to serve the common good of a fundamentally just and free pluralistic society, must balance competing values, such as freedom, order, equity, and justice. If I failed to weigh those competing values—or to fulfill my public obligations to be firm without being provocative, or to recognize my public duty once the Congress acted—I would have served neither my private conscience nor the public morality. I tried to do credit to both. Whether I succeeded is a judgment others must make.

Abortion in South Dakota
Jillian P. Dickert

In the two years after the United States Supreme Court handed down its 1989 decision on the Missouri abortion case, *Webster v. Reproductive Services,* the national battle over abortion rights raged on at the state level. By permitting greater regulation of abortion by states that could show a "compelling state interest" in the life of a fetus—including standards relating to where, how, and under what circumstances abortions could be performed—*Webster* opened a floodgate of state legislative activity on the abortion issue. Several states—such as Pennsylvania, Utah, Louisiana, and the territory of Guam—strove to tighten their abortion statutes under the new standards. Meanwhile, other states—including Maryland, Connecticut, and Washington—took *Webster* to mean that a state would be free not only to regulate abortion but also to permit it. These states sought to adopt statutes securing abortion rights independent of Supreme Court direction.

A highly restrictive abortion bill introduced in the South Dakota legislature in January 1991 pushed the midwestern state to the front lines of the national abortion conflict. A test case, House Bill 1126, was designed by the antiabortion National

Reprinted by permission of the Case Program, Kennedy School of Government, Harvard University. Copyright © 1993 by the President and Fellows of Harvard.

Right to Life Committee to ultimately be heard by the Supreme Court in an effort to chip away and possibly overturn the landmark *Roe v. Wade* decision, which ruled that states could not interfere with the fundamental right of a woman to obtain an abortion. In South Dakota, the bill—which aimed to outlaw most abortions in the state—ignited a political firestorm that burned throughout the 1991 legislative session. Lobbying activity by citizens and activists reached unprecedented levels, particularly among antiabortion advocates, as state legislators prepared to go on record on an emotionally and politically volatile issue.

Bearing the brunt of the lobbying pressure was Republican senator Scott Heidepriem of Miller, South Dakota. Heidepriem's influential position as chairman of the Senate Judiciary Committee—which would hold hearings and vote on the abortion legislation in February—placed the thirty-four-year-old lawyer under the political microscope. As chairman, Heidepriem was charged with handling as fairly as possible a bill he staunchly opposed—on legal as well as moral grounds—but that enjoyed widespread support within his district and throughout the state.

BACKGROUND: A POLITICAL LIFE

Politics had always played an important part in Scott Heidepriem's life—indeed, one could say politics was in his blood.

Heidepriem grew up in the South Dakota legislature; his father, Herbert A. Heidepriem, served in the Senate for the first twelve years of Scott's life. The young Heidepriem's political career was marked by a rapid succession of campaign victories in his home state. In 1980, shortly after graduating from the University of South Dakota Law School, Heidepriem ran as an Independent and was elected state attorney for Jerauld County. Running as a Republican just two years later, Heidepriem was elected to the South Dakota House of Representatives. Heidepriem was then reelected to the House in 1984, and after an unsuccessful bid for U.S. Congress in 1986, he again sought and won a seat in the South Dakota House of Representatives in 1988.

In 1989, South Dakota Senator Mary McClure resigned her post to accept a position as White House special assistant for President George Bush. Heidepriem was appointed to take her place in the Senate. Upon his appointment, Heidepriem—then the youngest member of the Senate—was made chairman of the small but powerful Senate Judiciary Committee. (Heidepriem had given up the vice chairmanship of the legislature's Executive Board to move to the Senate.[1]) Then, in 1990, Heidepriem won election to the South Dakota Senate, retaining his post as Judiciary Committee chair for the 1991 session. At age thirty-four, Heidepriem was already considered by many a soon-to-be gubernatorial or congressional candidate.

As Judiciary chairman, Senator Heidepriem—a moderate Republican—sought to downplay partisan politics within the seven-member committee. "My view is that most of the things that state legislatures deal with really shouldn't be partisan. I felt like the Republican party tended to reject the Democrats' agenda automatically and *in toto* without thinking. My view was that we could pick and choose a number of their ideas that were actually good, blend them with our own, get Democrat votes, and

actually have some unifying elements in the process instead of the sort of acrimony that I think tends to make the public sick" of politics. As chairman, Heidepriem tried to develop a leadership style that emphasized fairness and gave room to minority (in this case, Democrat) initiatives and concerns: "It was important to me that minority members of the committee did not feel that their bills were getting shot down just because they were in the minority."

HEIDEPRIEM ON ABORTION

Throughout his political career, Heidepriem's position on the abortion issue was no secret, he considered himself "pro-choice." "I believe there are circumstances where to abort or not should be left to a woman, her physician, and her God," he told the *Pierre Capitol Journal* in 1991. "My view is that there is no perfect answer," Heidepriem explains, "but I've read *Roe v. Wade* a number of times and I'm amazed at how close [Justice Harry] Blackmun gets it right." Heidepriem's views on abortion reflected those of his father—another Republican in favor of abortion rights—and his sister, Nikki Heidepriem, a Washington political consultant of liberal-feminist leanings actively involved in the work of the National Abortion Rights Action League (NARAL). "Nikki was a Republican until the party abandoned women in the 1980 platform," adds Heidepriem.

Heidepriem says he felt anchored in the "pro-choice" position, but as a legislator, he—unlike his sister—never stressed the abortion issue. "I've tried to avoid it," Heidepriem admits. "I've probably done everything I could to get out of the way of it. The only time I address it is when the question's put to me squarely, and then I'll answer it. But I would just as soon not talk about it; I don't like to think about it."

Over time, Senator Heidepriem learned that that wasn't always possible. His large, rural district, which spanned the four central counties of South Dakota's James River

Valley—an area Heidepriem describes as "about five times the size of Rhode Island but with less than 20,000 people"—contained the highest concentration of antiabortion organizations in the state: eight in 1991. Heidepriem believed that many, if not most, of his constituents opposed abortion as did a large number of South Dakota residents. A series of statewide polls taken for Democratic candidates in the 1990 election showed that, on average, approximately 50 percent of South Dakotans believed abortion should never be permitted or permitted only in cases of rape, incest, or "danger to the mother's life."

From the start of his legislative career, Heidepriem felt pressure from his colleagues to take a stand against abortion. Heidepriem recalls an incident in 1984 where the lieutenant governor, the majority leader, and another prominent member of the South Dakota House of Representatives called him into the House chamber after a debate on an abortion bill sponsored by the majority leader. According to Heidepriem, the three men—considered the pillars of the South Dakota Republican establishment—warned him: "Look, we think you have a very promising future in politics. But we want you to know that abortion is one issue you can't straddle the fence on, and we hope we can count on you to be in the pro-life category."

Abortion was "very much an issue" in Heidepriem's 1986 campaign for the Republican nomination for U.S. Congress.[2] (Heidepriem was just twenty-nine years old at the time.) That year, the controversy surrounding President Reagan's enthusiastic support for a "Human Life Amendment" to the U.S. Constitution stating that "life begins at conception" trickled down to the South Dakota Republican primary. Heidepriem found himself the only candidate in the primary field opposed to the amendment. "It ended up being sort of a pivotal issue in the campaign," Heidepriem reflects. "I ran a very aggressive, knock-on-doors type of campaign, and I had only two

people express to me their hope that I was pro-choice, and many on the other side." According to Heidepriem, one of his antiabortion opponents, Dale Bell, "spent about forty thousand dollars in the last two weeks [of the primary] telling the state that I was the only one who didn't [support the Human Life Amendment]. Seventeen days out and we were dead even, and his ads just demolished us." Bell won the Republican primary with 46 percent of the vote, versus 29 percent for Heidepriem.

During Heidepriem's four campaigns for the state legislature, however, abortion rarely became a dominant issue. "Aside from questions at forums and occasional letters to the editor urging my retirement," Heidepriem explains, "no great waves of opposition had been generated"—an outcome Heidepriem attributes to "the lack of a legislative vehicle to serve as a focus for the emotion generated by the issue."

ABORTION IN SOUTH DAKOTA

At the time of Heidepriem's tenure in the Senate, South Dakota was one of an increasing number of states where an abortion, although legal, was extremely difficult to obtain. In the years after the Supreme Court handed down its landmark *Roe v. Wade* decision legalizing abortion nationwide in 1973, just two physicians dared to acknowledge that they performed abortions in the state: Dr. Ben Munson provided services in Rapid City, a town on the west side of the state with a population of about 55,000; and Dr. Buck Williams practiced in Sioux Falls, South Dakota's largest city—approximate population 100,000—located in the state's southeastern corner. In 1990, Munson retired, leaving Williams as the sole physician providing abortion services in a state with a total population of almost 700,000.

In the early 1980s, when both Munson and Williams were in practice, the number of abortions performed in South Dakota peaked at an average of 1,150 to 1,250 abortions per year. The number of abortions declined annually in the 1980s—while increasing in the United States as a whole—and dropped off significantly when Munson retired in 1990. From 1980 to 1987, South Dakota experienced a greater decline in the number of abortions performed than any other state in the country: 38.9 percent versus the national average decline of 8.2 percent.[3] By 1991, with only Dr. Williams performing abortions (Williams limited his practice to the first three months, or trimester, of pregnancy), the number dwindled to 900[4]—the lowest per capita number of abortions performed in any state in the United States.

The paucity of abortion services in South Dakota may have been related to the state's long-standing antiabortion stance. Abortion was outlawed in South Dakota in 1890, and the state had only legalized abortion when compelled to by federal statute under *Roe v. Wade*. Furthermore, although the 1973 South Dakota Codified Laws enacted *Roe*'s provisions in Section 34–23A, "Performance of Abortions," the following "trigger" clause was added: "this chapter is repealed on that specific date upon which the states are given exclusive authority to regulate abortion." Only nine other states included this kind of antiabortion language within their laws legalizing abortion after *Roe*.[5]

During his three terms in the South Dakota House of Representatives, Heidepriem witnessed a few attempts—each one unsuccessful—to alter the state's law on abortion. In the mid-to-late 1980s, two House bills were filed: one would have made it possible for a court to create a "guardian" of the fetus, where the guardian—someone other than the pregnant woman—would have the right to exercise judgment about whether to terminate the pregnancy; the other would have required parental consent for a minor seeking an abortion.[6] Heidepriem opposed both bills. Neither bill made it through the legislature.

In 1990, South Dakota Right to Life (RTL), a state chapter of the antiabortion National Right to Life Committee, introduced a bill that would recriminalize abortion in South Dakota in the event that the Supreme Court chose to return to the states the authority to regulate abortion. South Dakota RTL feared that the state's existing "trigger law" contained loopholes and needed stiffening. During the 1990 state legislative session, high-powered South Dakota lobbyist Jeremiah Murphy met with Senator Heidepriem on behalf of RTL to discuss the bill. Heidepriem was able to convince Murphy that the provisions of the RTL bill were already covered by the state's existing trigger law. Ultimately, RTL elected to pull the bill, but it was not the last time Heidepriem would face the powerful antiabortion lobby.

A TEST CASE

In 1990 and 1991, the National Right to Life Committee continued its efforts to enact antiabortion statutes at the state level, hoping to design a bill that would present a desirable vehicle for overturning *Roe v. Wade*, as many anticipated the Supreme Court would soon do. By 1990, the RTL antiabortion bill of choice was a highly restrictive measure that aimed to ban abortion "as a means of birth control." In 1990 and 1991, this bill was introduced in several states, including Minnesota, Utah, Alabama, Mississippi, Idaho, and Louisiana. The bill was able to make it through the Idaho legislature in 1990 but was vetoed by Governor Andrus. In early 1991, both Louisiana and Utah passed the RTL bill.[7] By August of that year, Louisiana's statute had been declared unconstitutional at the district court level, and the state showed no shyness in continuing its appeals through the court system until the statute could be heard by the Supreme Court. Utah's legislative leaders and governor, on the other hand, prevented their antiabortion law from taking effect in 1991 until the Supreme Court ruled on the constitutionality of Louisiana's statute.

Inspired by November 1990 election surveys showing that a majority of the South

Dakota House of Representatives opposed abortion, RTL viewed the state as fertile territory for its antiabortion campaign. By December 1990, RTL was ready to introduce its model statute prohibiting abortion "as a means of birth control" in South Dakota. RTL had clearly been encouraged by the *Webster* decision: Section 5 of the RTL bill stated its intent to "reasonably and constitutionally . . . regulate abortion in accordance with the current abortion Jurisprudence of the majority of justices of the United States Supreme Court," adding that "the state's compelling interest in unborn life throughout pregnancy justifies preventing the use of abortion as another means of birth control." The bill defined abortion as the "use or prescription of any instrument, medicine, drug, or any other substance or device to terminate the pregnancy of a woman known to be pregnant with an intention other than to increase the probability of a live birth, to preserve the life or health of the child after live birth, or to remove a dead, unborn child."[8]

If made law, RTL's bill would outlaw all abortions in South Dakota except where a mother's health was endangered by her pregnancy; when a "medical judgment was made that the child, if allowed to be born, would have profound and irremediable physical or mental disabilities"; or in cases of rape or incest,[9] if the event had been reported within one week of its occurrence. Under the proposed legislation, persons performing or attempting to perform an abortion would be subject to civil fines of $10,000 for a first "offense," $50,000 for a second, $100,000 for a third, and in excess of $100,000 for the fourth or more. No fine would be assessed against the woman seeking the abortion, nor against persons assisting in the abortion, such as nurses and office staff. The state attorney general, county prosecutors, the pregnant woman, parents of a minor, and the father of the unborn child would all be able to bring legal action under the proposal.

With the freshly-drafted antiabortion bill in hand, Washington-based lawyer Burke Balch, state legislative director of National RTL, flew to South Dakota in late 1990 to meet with several legislators to garner support for the measure. On December 27, Balch, accompanied by South Dakota RTL lobbyist Lori Engel, sought out Scott Heidepriem at his law office in Miller, South Dakota. Heidepriem recalls that Balch and Engel were very excited about the possibilities for their new bill and for a few hours put on "quite a road show" to obtain his endorsement. "Regardless of how you felt in the past," the RTL representatives told Heidepriem, "we don't think you support abortion as a means of birth control." Heidepriem read the proposed legislation on the spot, noting to Balch that it was unconstitutional according to current Supreme Court jurisprudence. Balch agreed and added that it would be declared unconstitutional at both the district and circuit levels on its way up to the Supreme Court. However, Balch explained that, when drafting the bill, he felt encouraged by the recent writings of Supreme Court Justice Sandra Day O'Connor, whose opinions after *Webster* seemed to reaffirm her belief that the state's "compelling interest" in the life of a fetus extended from conception to birth. Balch took it as a sign that Justice O'Connor—whom many considered a swing vote on the abortion issue—would vote to sustain the South Dakota antiabortion bill as a proper expression of a state's compelling interest. Heidepriem was unconvinced. In response, Heidepriem informed both RTL representatives that he was "not supporting legal experimentation with taxpayers' dollars." The meeting ended cordially, but without Heidepriem's endorsement of the bill.

Evidently, Balch and Engel had better luck with other lawmakers. When the 1991 legislative session opened on January 16, 1991, Rep. Harvey Krautschun (R-Spearfish) introduced RTL's antiabortion bill in the seventy member South Dakota House of Representatives with twenty-five House co-sponsors, and twelve of the state's thirty-five senators were already on board. Given the large, bipartisan group of sponsors, passage of the bill in the House was virtually assured. As Heidepriem puts it, "the question was not whether it would pass [the House], but by how wide a margin."

CONTROVERSY

House Speaker Jim Hood (R-Spearfish) assigned the bill—now known as HB 1126—to the House Judiciary Committee for its first hearing on January 31, 1991. Supporters of HB 1126 saw it as a compromise bill, a reasonable and moderate alternative to a complete ban on abortions. "This bill is designed to pass constitutional muster," declared Rep. Krautschun. Senator Richard Bellatti (R-Sioux Falls), the prime Senate sponsor of the bill, agreed. "We've got to be realistic," said Bellatti. "It's unreal to assume that we're going to have a 'human life' amendment."[10]

Several opponents of HB 1126, including Senate Majority Leader George Shanard (R-Mitchell), contended that the bill was a costly and unconstitutional violation of a woman's right to privacy. "I question some of the provisions and practicality of enforcing the law," Shanard stated.[11] Supporters of the bill agreed that it would test the Constitution, but argued, "it's worth the price." "The time has come to do what you think is right, and I think it's right," said Senator Bellatti. "I'm ready to take the consequences."[12]

Given the explosive potential of a bill that would outlaw most abortions, legislators braced themselves for a political firestorm. State Rep. Mary Edelin (R-Vermillion) lamented that the bill would split legislators for the rest of the session: "It's just too bad. . . . People will be divided all session over this, and it will carry over to almost every other proposal. . . . You can't keep it from becoming emotional, and you can't keep it from dividing all of us."[13] House Majority Leader Jerry Lammers (R-Madison) concurred. "It's a hot one," Rep. Lammers said. "You have to put on your flak jacket, because people come at

you from both sides. I'm sure it will be very divisive and the debate will be intense." In response, Rep. Marie Ingalls (R-Mud Butte)—a co-sponsor of the bill—sought to portray the issue as a straightforward one. "It's an issue we vote our constituency, we vote the way people back home want us to vote," Ingalls said.[14]

A POSITION OF POWER

As chairman of the Senate Judiciary Committee and the Senate's only lawyer, Heidepriem was poised to play an influential role in the success or failure of HB 1126. One of just ten Senate committees, the Judiciary Committee was charged with handling the second largest number of bills in the legislature, and it was likely to be the next stop for the antiabortion bill if it passed the House as expected. As Judiciary chair, Heidepriem would have complete power over the committee hearings on the bill, including the authority to schedule the hearings, determine their length and content, and decide when to call for a vote on the bill.

Heidepriem's power over the fate of the bill was restrained somewhat by South Dakota's "smokeout" rule, which enabled lawmakers to force a floor vote on a bill in the full Senate (or House) if the committee voted to table it. In the Senate, twelve of the thirty-five senators (one-third of the chamber) would be required to vote for the smokeout in order to get the bill out of committee. Then, eighteen senators—a simple majority—would have to vote to place the bill on the calendar for floor debate. The smokeout procedure was frequently used for bills dealing with highly partisan issues since both parties claimed at least one-third of the seats in both chambers. At the same time, legislative rules in South Dakota mandated that the session end in no more than forty days, and the entire smokeout procedure could take up to six days. Thus, Chairman Heidepriem would always have the option to hold off a committee vote long enough to make it impossible for senators to use the smokeout rule without a suspension of the rules, which would require a tough-to-obtain two-thirds majority vote in the full Senate.

Although state legislative rules required that a bill be posted before its hearing, there was no rule requiring the committee to post the date and time of its vote. As a result, says Heidepriem, "committee chairs tend to hold controversial bills until the hottest-tempered adversaries have left town, and then they dispose of them." However, Heidepriem, adds, "the chairs generally try to gauge the amount of public interest in any question and then attempt to accommodate that interest, regardless of how they feel about the bill." For his part, Chairman Heidepriem says, "I'd usually wait until we had collected a number of [bills]—say, when ten or fifteen had been assigned to us—then, depending on time and the number of hearings I had, I would try to group the bills by subject matter so that people would not have to come twice. We tried hard to accommodate everyone."

TAKING A STAND

Just two days after the HB 1126 was introduced in the House, Heidepriem came out publicly against the bill. "I applaud the Right to Life movement for what they're trying to accomplish," Heidepriem told the *Aberdeen American News,* "but there is no question about the constitutionality of this proposal. The idea as I understand it would be unconstitutional." "If this bill passes," Heidepriem warned, "it will embroil South Dakota in legal turmoil for years to come." Heidepriem speculated that the law would inevitably be challenged by a woman seeking a legal abortion, and the ensuing court battles would in all likelihood continue until the law could be heard by the U.S. Supreme Court. In the process, Heidepriem estimated, the state would amass court fees from $700,000 to $1 million—even more if the state was required to pay for the woman's

legal expenses. "There are plenty of states wealthier than South Dakota able to spread the cost of that legal creativity upon their taxpayers in a way that's less burdensome," argued Heidepriem, noting that South Dakota typically generated less than $500 million dollars in taxes each year, and the state legislature was required by law to balance the budget annually with a mandated reserve.[15]

Heidepriem's position on the bill was bolstered by state attorney general Mark Barnett, who privately agreed that his office probably could not absorb the costs of a Supreme Court challenge in its $7 million budget.[16] But Rep. Lammers contended that it was premature to worry about the legal costs. "I rather suspect there are all kinds of experts who would come to the rescue of South Dakota and offer their service for free. . . . What we do here may be very important in the history of not only the state but the land."[17] Besides, Lammers maintained, a "lawsuit won't cost anything unless the state loses."[18] Meanwhile, supporters of the bill argued that it was not intended to become a test case in the federal courts. "We strongly believe this is a South Dakota issue, and we'll do everything we can to keep it that way," said lobbyist Lori Engel, apparently hoping to blunt the national attention the issue would receive from NARAL, the National Organization for Women, Republicans for Choice, and other national abortion rights organizations.[19]

In an opinion piece published in the *Faulk County Record* on January 30—one day before the scheduled House Judiciary Committee hearing on HB 1126—Heidepriem made it clear to his constituents that he opposed the bill. "I believe this bill is a serious mistake," Heidepriem wrote. "I cannot justify expending nearly one million dollars for a lawsuit that is an exercise in legal creativity." Heidepriem pointed to the antiabortion bill in Utah, which the governor had signed just five days earlier. "Opponents have pledged to challenge it [the Utah law) all the way to the U.S. Supreme Court. South Dakotans, both for and against legal abortion, should wait for the outcome."

WHAT HAPPENED IN THE HOUSE

On Thursday, January 31, the thirteen-member House Judiciary Committee began its deliberations on HB 1126. Almost two hundred spectators packed the committee room to witness and participate in the hearing. Although it was expected that the panel would easily approve the bill, committee discussion was nonetheless charged with emotion. Throughout the hour-long debate, committee members wrangled over the extent to which *Webster* allowed states the right to regulate abortion. Abortion opponents argued that *Webster* had given states "the right to limit abortion and a compelling interest in the life of the unborn," while abortion rights supporters countered that no majority in *Webster* had stated that there was a compelling interest in fetal viability throughout the pregnancy.[20] On February 5, the House Judiciary Committee approved HB 1126 by a vote of 8–5 and sent it to the full House with minor amendments, setting the stage for what promised to be a heated debate on the House floor.

Two days later—February 7—the mass of spectators returned to the House gallery to witness the floor debates on HB 1126. Hundreds of antiabortion activists wearing "I'm for Life" buttons packed the room as a coalition of five abortion rights groups lobbied representatives behind the scenes. Most expected that the Republican-dominated House would vote to advance the measure to the Senate. (Republicans controlled the House forty-five to twenty-five and men outnumbered women fifty-five to fifteen.)

The spirited House debate lasted about ninety minutes. During the hearing, several amendments to HB 1126 were proposed on the House floor, including a requirement that the South Dakota Department of Health give out free contraceptives at a cost of $807,000; a clause that would abolish the state's death penalty; a plan that would have referred the bill to a public referendum; and a move to set aside $1 million to finance the legal costs involved in defending the bill's constitutionality.[21] None of the amendments was successful.

The House hearing on HB 1126 culminated in a larger-than-predicted margin of victory for the antiabortion bill: 52–18 in favor of the legislation. The overwhelming support in the House was a surprise, with seventeen of the fifty-two "yes" votes coming from representatives who had responded in the 1990 preelection survey that the current law on abortion in South Dakota should not be changed.

One day after the House vote (February 8), Lieutenant Governor Walter Dale Miller assigned HB 1126 to the Senate Judiciary Committee, where Chairman Heidepriem would preside over the next hearing on the bill.[22] Senator Bellatti, the prime Senate sponsor of HB 1126, wasted no time in seeking out Heidepriem on the Senate floor. According to Heidepriem, Bellatti said, "Look, I hope the day will come that I can support you for governor. I consider you a good friend. All I ask is that you be fair with us in scheduling the hearing." Heidepriem pledged his fairness, promising not to manipulate the rule to impede the bill's chance to pass.

Meanwhile, Republican Governor George Mickelson issued a public statement declaring that he "favor[ed] the basic philosophy" of the antiabortion bill and signaled his intention to sign the measure into law if it passed the legislature.[23] Coupled with the bill's overwhelming success in the House, the governor's statement sent shock waves through the ranks of abortion rights activists across the state while adding momentum to an already well-organized antiabortion lobby. The phone calls and letters that had been trickling into senators' offices just one week earlier multiplied in numbers with each passing day as constituents came to grasp the enhanced possibility that abortion could become illegal in South Dakota.

In light of the 52–18 victory in the House, Alcester Democrat and Senate Minority Leader Roger McKellips—who had once predicted that a strong antiabortion proposal would be defeated in the Senate—stated: "Now I think it's going to be close. It may pass."[24] In 1991, Republicans held a one vote advantage in the Senate (18–17) and men outnumbered women twenty-four to eleven. Abortion opponents believed they had at least the minimum eighteen votes for Senate passage and possibly as many as twenty-one. Rick Hauffe, the South Dakota Democratic party's legislative director, predicted that the bill would be decided by one vote in the Senate.

PUTTING ON THE BRAKES

Senator Heidepriem was alarmed by the speed with which the bill barreled through the House. "It was just rolling," Heidepriem recalls. "It was just going and it was going to pass, I thought, unless some people just tried to slow it down a little and get people to think about it." When his office began receiving twenty letters and forty phone messages each day—most in favor of the bill—Heidepriem decided "it was time for me to do what I could to slow the train down a little."

Shortly after the bill passed the House, Heidepriem made public remarks—run widely in the South Dakota press—reiterating his opposition to the bill. "I'm against the bill because it is certain to cost huge amounts of money for no useful purpose," Heidepriem stated. "Once Utah passed their law, they took away any possible reasons for passing an unconstitutional law. Utah's law will be heard before ours. What South Dakota is allowed on abortions will not be determined by our legislation but Utah's legislation."

Several Republican senators were noticeably cool to Heidepriem after reading his comments in the *Pierre Capitol Journal*. Heidepriem was approached by Senator Harold Halverson (R-Milbank), vice chairman in the Judiciary Committee and Senate

president pro tempore. "I saw your picture in the paper," Halverson said, with pointed understatement. To Heidepriem, it was a clear indication that his Republican colleagues were less than pleased that he was actively trying to stop the antiabortion bill. But, Heidepriem recalls, "I didn't think that I could help but announce my feelings about the issue and about the bill. . . . It was one of those things where, going in, we had to get every single undecided vote, and we knew that."

The bill came over to the Senate Judiciary Committee on February 8. Now Chairman Heidepriem was in a position to control when and how the bill would be reviewed. First, Heidepriem wanted the hearing delayed to avert what he described as a "steamroller effect." "I routinely did that with emotional issues," Heidepriem explains. "I didn't want the Senate to make a decision in this crazed atmosphere. I think that's not the proper temperament in which to legislate."

In setting the date of the hearing on HB 1126, Heidepriem sought advice from both supporters and opponents of the bill. "Both [sides] indicated that they might have national people coming in [for the hearing], and I felt that it was necessary to set the day early so that people could make their plans," explains Heidepriem. "I wanted to let both sides contact whomever they wanted to bring in plenty enough time so that no one said, 'I didn't have notice. I couldn't get in.'" According to Heidepriem, opponents of HB 1126 wanted the hearing to be held "as late as possible": "Pro-choice people who were organizing against the bill felt that the longer they had, the better, because they thought that it was a senseless move that would sink in, that people would respond." "They would have been happy if I had tried to use the rules to thwart it," Heidepriem adds.

On the supporting side, Heidepriem consulted with Bellatti, Engel, and former legislator Ed Glasgow, chief lobbyist for the antiabortion Family Values Coalition.

Heidepriem requested that the three agree upon a date for the hearing, but according to Heidepriem, they were unable to.[25] Ultimately, Heidepriem chose to schedule the hearing for Friday, February 22—exactly two weeks after the bill arrived on his desk. For Heidepriem, that date was "later than Lori wanted it and before Ed wanted it, but in plenty of time for them to exhaust their supply of maneuvers." Heidepriem adds that, at the time the decision was made, neither side showed "even a slight expression of disappointment at the scheduling of the hearing."

As judiciary chair, Heidepriem also had the option of setting the committee vote late enough in the session to make a smoke-out—which would force a floor vote in the full Senate if the bill were to fail in committee—virtually impossible.[26] However, Heidepriem chose to require that committee members vote immediately after testimony was completed on the day of the committee hearing. "The Right to Lifers were up against it in terms of time," Heidepriem recalls, "so I said to them, 'I will insist that the committee act in such a way that you aren't denied the chance to use those [smokeout) procedures.'" By setting the vote for the day of the committee hearing—February 22, a full seven business days prior to the mandated last day of the legislative session—Heidepriem allowed supporters of HB 1126 ample time to smoke out the bill if it failed in committee. At the time, Heidepriem felt the committee had a "duty"—given the intense interest in the bill—to decide its vote at that time. "I thought it was important to make the decision in front of the people who care about the question," Heidepriem explains.

PRESSURE BUILDS

As the Senate Judiciary Committee hearing on HB 1126 approached, lobbying activity intensified on all sides. By mid-February, abortion rights groups, including Planned Parenthood and NARAL, were spending thousands of dollars on a barrage of newspaper and broadcast advertisements, hoping to gain ground lost in the House to the well-organized RTL lobby. Meanwhile, South Dakota RTL sought to continue its efforts to mobilize citizens on an even larger scale in the state. Republican and Democratic senators alike were deluged with calls, letters, photographs of aborted fetuses, baby rattles, and plastic fetuses wrapped in pink and blue baby blankets. Several lawmakers reported receiving abusive telephone calls and obscenities written in black crayon on their front doors. The home of one Judiciary Committee member, Senate Majority Leader George Shanard, was vandalized with "baby killer" spray painted in large black letters.

Heidepriem's influential position as chairman of the Senate Judiciary Committee ensured that he would bear the brunt of the pressure. "I don't remember any issue where the lobbying has been this intense during my time in politics," says Heidepriem. By mid-February—a week prior to his committee hearing—Heidepriem's Senate office was receiving up to one thousand letters and phone calls per day, many from within his district but most from outside his district and outside the state. Death threats were leveled against Heidepriem and his family. (At the time, Heidepriem had one three-year-old son, and his wife, Susan, was eight months pregnant.) "Particularly memorable," recalls Heidepriem, "was one full-color, bloodbath photo bearing a Rapid City postmark with this inscription: 'Senator, since you like killing so much, take a look at this, and show it to your pregnant wife.'" The pressure led Heidepriem's family to decide, in consultation with law enforcement officials, to send Heidepriem's wife and son to an undisclosed out-of-state location until the matter was concluded. "I felt better knowing that they were somewhere safe," Heidepriem explains. "My wife is a very strong person, but I would have worried a lot more, and it would have added a whole layer of anxiety."

After an initial antiabortion lead, Heidepriem's mail was split evenly between those for and against the bill. While many of the messages for the senator insinuated that his political future could be in doubt if he took the "wrong" stance on the abortion bill, Heidepriem told the *Pierre Capitol Journal* that the pressure would not change his mind: "There isn't a higher office I want badly enough to cause me to act inconsistently with what I believe is right."[27] Nevertheless, Heidepriem conceded that both the pressure and the emotional intensity of the abortion issue were draining. "People have lost the willingness to respect an opposing point of view. That's what's missing here," said Heidepriem. "It's so frustrating because this process is something I care deeply about. It's an issue that accomplishes nothing positive and has the potential of removing myself and other worthy, thoughtful people from the process. And for what, for what?"

Meanwhile, Heidepriem was lobbied to kill the bill in committee by state representatives who had voted earlier for the measure in the House. It may have been politically safer, Heidepriem told the *Sioux Falls Argus Leader,* for some House members who were "pro-choice" but from antiabortion districts to vote "yes" on the bill and then lobby against its passage in the Senate. "Sure there's politics involved," Heidepriem admitted candidly. "There's a temptation to say, 'Why not?' That temptation is greater in the house of origin."[28]

HEIDEPRIEM'S STRATEGY

As both sides of the abortion debate anxiously awaited the Senate Judiciary Committee hearing on HB 1126, Heidepriem did some lobbying of his own within the committee. Heidepriem approached individually each of his six colleagues—three Republicans and three Democrats—on the Judiciary Committee in order to feel out their positions on the bill and explain his objections to it. As the Senate's only

lawyer in 1991, Heidepriem says he "felt a duty to give them [his] best legal read on the question in an objective way."

Heidepriem sought out committee members on the Senate floor and at the hospitality rooms at the Ramkota River Centre, where senators would discuss informally the issues surrounding the 1991 legislative session—namely, the abortion bill. One-on-one, Heidepriem explained to his colleagues that he believed HB 1126 was unconstitutional and would be held so by the federal district court in Pierre, South Dakota's capital. Heidepriem was confident that, on appeal, the district court decision would be sustained by the eighth circuit court in St. Paul. Thus, Heidepriem contended, the state would need to go all the way up to the Supreme Court and ask it to change its mind on *Roe v. Wade.* Heidepriem explained that, even if that route were taken, a decision would come no quicker for South Dakota than for Utah or Louisiana, which had presented similar questions to the Court. "There was absolutely no sense in doing this," Heidepriem told his colleagues, "unless you wanted to potentially pay a million dollars for a symbolic statement and a secondary opinion from the Supreme Court. But you aren't going to change the policy by doing this. It's not possible."

Given the nature of the bill, Heidepriem endeavored to involve in these discussions key women in the lives of his male colleagues. (Two women, Senate Minority Whip Karen Muenster [D-Sioux Falls] and Freshman Senator Roberta Rasmussen [D-Hurley], also sat on the Senate Judiciary Committee.) For example, Heidepriem spoke frequently with Senators George Shanard and Jim Emery (R-Custer), two potential swing votes on the committee. "When Neva and George Shanard were together, I would begin the conversation with Neva," Heidepriem explains. (Heidepriem learned that Neva Shanard did not like the bill.) "When Elaine and Jim Emery were together, I would begin the conversation with

Elaine, and I would engage her on the [abortion] question. I would try to steer the conversation [to the abortion bill] by saying: 'Isn't it interesting that, here we are, never having to face this question, but we're deciding it for people like Elaine, or you Neva, or my wife Susan? "

If Heidepriem was unable to ascertain a male committee member's position on the bill, he sought out the position of his colleague's wife. For example, Senator Emery took Heidepriem up on his offer to discuss the bill with him. During what turned out to be a long, private conversation, Emery never revealed his position on the bill. Later, on the floor of the Senate, Heidepriem approached Emery and asked him if he had any questions about their previous conversation. Emery did not, so Heidepriem asked how his wife, Elaine Emery, felt about the bill. Emery responded that Elaine did not like the bill. Feeling hopeful, Heidepriem left it at that: "I think that Elaine Emery, aside from being a very impressive person, has a very good relationship with her husband. I thought to myself: 'We are in good shape there.' "

By the time of the hearing, only three members of the Senate Judiciary Committee had publicly stated a clear position on HB 1126. Heidepriem and Shanard[29] had openly opposed the bill, while Halverson had pledged his wholehearted support.[30] On February 21, Roberta Rasmussen— a first-term legislator from a predominantly antiabortion district—suggested that she was leaning against the bill for constitutional reasons. Jim Emery and Democrats Karen Muenster and Paul Symens (Amherst) refused to say how they would vote. Muenster had answered the preelection abortion survey by stating that in most cases a woman should have the right to an abortion. Although a poll commissioned by Muenster in 1990 showed that 70 percent of her constituents supported abortion rights, Muenster said she feared reprisals against her family if she talked about her vote.[31] Symens—like the majority of his constituents—was known to oppose abortion,

but he had expressed reservations about the bill in its current form.[32] However, Symens told the *Aberdeen American News,* "I don't know how it will come out in the Senate. It will be close. I haven't counted votes, but my gut feeling is it will pass."[33]

Publicly, Heidepriem said he was uncertain how his committee would vote on the bill: "I think most legislators are undecided about most bills until they hear the testimony," Heidepriem told the *Pierre Capital Journal* on February 11. Privately, Heidepriem guessed that Muenster and Rasmussen would join Shanard and him in voting against the bill, thus defeating the measure 4–3. Heidepriem says he believed that Symens—a Baptist fundamentalist— would vote for the bill because of his strong religious convictions and the pressure he was receiving from his church.

While Heidepriem's vote on HB 1126 was certain to be "no," politically, it would not be an easy vote for him to make. In an interview published in the *Sioux Falls Argus Leader* the day before the Senate Judiciary Committee hearing, Heidepriem described his situation: "Every now and then these things pop up, and you stare into your open political grave. Then you vote." "That's exactly how I felt," Heidepriem recalls. "I had to say, 'Well, if it all ends here, is this still what you want to do?'" In deciding how to vote on the bill, Heidepriem recalls, "I ultimately had just to ask myself what I thought the proper policy was for the state, and then having decided that issue in the negative on the bill, I had to decide whether I had any business taking that view in light of what I perceived to be overwhelming support for the bill in my rural district. It was never even a close question for me."

THE SENATE JUDICIARY COMMITTEE HEARING

At 10 A.M. on Friday, February 22, Heidepriem called the Senate Judiciary Committee to order as three hundred spectators squeezed into Room 412 of the capitol building. Most attendees were abortion opponents with large "South Dakotans For Life" signs strapped to their bodies. A smaller group of abortion rights advocates donned purple ribbons to express their opposition to the bill.

Heidepriem opened the hearings with a warning that he would not tolerate any disruption of the proceedings, noting that he had ordered a full contingent of the South Dakota National Guard and capitol police to clear the room if necessary. Heidepriem then offered both sides of the abortion debate an expanded, but fixed, format for the hearing. Both proponents and opponents of HB 1126 would be granted one hour of testimony and ten minutes of rebuttal time, followed by ten minutes from general commentators, including a law expert chosen by Heidepriem to address constitutionality issues. Heidepriem would then close the discussion and call for a vote in the committee. Throughout the hearing, committee members would be permitted to ask brief questions.

Heidepriem arranged for Professor David Day of the University of South Dakota Law School to appear as a commentator at the hearing to address the constitutionality issues surrounding the bill. Initially, Heidepriem had requested that Attorney General Mark Barnett address the hearing, but Barnett felt it was inappropriate for him to testify, since he would have to defend the bill in court if it passed the legislature. Long-time South Dakota lobbyist Jeremiah Murphy—considered by many the most influential lobbyist in the state—was highly critical of the decision to invite Day, since Heidepriem was aware that the law professor was not favorably disposed to the bill.

Heidepriem also decided to allow the proponents of the bill to show a film that would provide viewers with a picture of a fetus prior to an abortion. Opponents of the bill begged Heidepriem—who had not seen the film—not to let it to be shown during the hearing. However, Lori Engel assured Heidepriem that the presentation would be in good taste (no bloody fetuses).

Although Heidepriem believed that the film was not "directly on point about the bill," he thought it was fair to let the proponents screen it. "A judge clearly wouldn't have allowed it as relevant evidence, but this wasn't a courtroom," Heidepriem explains. "I made a calculation that you should always err on the side of allowing stuff like that because the price you pay for denying them access is oftentimes greater. And I frankly wanted opportunities to show them that I wanted to be fair about it."

Proponents of HB 1126 testified first, opening with the RTL film. Dr. Calvin Anderson of Sioux Falls screened the video, which depicted what he said was an eight-week-old fetus[34] moving and gesturing in response to external stimulation. "Ladies and gentlemen, that fetus is a prime candidate for an abortion," Anderson said. "I rest my case." Two other physicians testified as well, including the bill's Senate sponsor, Dr. Richard Bellatti—a Sioux Falls anesthesiologist. Bellatti argued that the state had the power to prevent the killing of an unborn child: "You may not choose to kill your child. That makes a farce of choice. . . . Please remember that a life is a life, and abortion kills." Bellatti also addressed directly Heidepriem's stated objection to HB 1126: that the antiabortion legislation was unnecessary in South Dakota since similar bills from Utah and Louisiana would make it to the Supreme Court beforehand. "The Supreme Court has more discretion over its docket and may not accept the pending cases," Bellatti contended. "Thus it would be beneficial for a number of states to pass substantive prohibitions on abortions."

Lori Engel also took the stand to present abortion statistics in defense of the bill. Engel argued that from 1989–90, 1,846 abortions were performed and 100 percent of those were performed as a form of birth control.[35] The committee also heard from two lawyers, both of whom agreed—while conceding that bill would be held unconstitutional at the district and circuit court levels—that there was "a reasonable likelihood that HB 1126 would be held constitutional by the United States Supreme Court should it ever be presented to it for a decision." Both lawyers volunteered to argue the case for the state at no cost. The proponents' final witness, Jeremiah Murphy, asked the committee: "Which side of this fight would Jesus Christ be on if he were here today?" Murphy bet that Christ would vote "on the side of life."

Opponents of the bill were up next. Simon Heller, a lawyer for the American Civil Liberties Union in New York, testified that the bill would fail a constitutional test, which he said would prove expensive for the state. "The local district court in South Dakota will surely find it unconstitutional," said Heller. "You will be certain to lose this case not only in circuit court but in district court as well." Dr. Dean Madison, an obstetrician-gynecologist of Sioux Falls, told committee members of his experience treating women who had had illegal abortions before the 1973 *Roe v. Wade* decision. "There were unbelievable low-life scum out there who would abort these ladies," Madison recalled. "I wish you could pass a law that made abortions go away completely, but ladies and gentlemen, they will be done." Choking back tears, Tilly Black Bear—a Lakota woman from the Rose Bud Indian reservation—reminded the committee that "Indian women cannot access services as readily as privileged women, who are white women. We don't oftentimes have the means to make that trip to Minneapolis."

Several others testified about their personal and tragic experiences at the hands of illegal abortionists. NARAL's star witness was Emmy Award-winning actress Polly Bergen, who was made sterile by a pre-1973 illegal abortion that almost killed her. Bergen described how, as a young struggling actress, she had to borrow $300 to pay for an illegal abortion performed—without anesthesia—by a stranger on the kitchen table of a dark California apartment. Three days after her abortion, Bergen was found dying from loss of blood. "Because of that abortion," Bergen testified, "I was unable to do that which I wanted to do so badly, which was to deliver a child. That could happen to other women—that is, if they don't die." Bergen added: "I don't believe that anyone has the right to tell a woman that she must have an abortion, and I don't think it's right to tell a woman that she cannot have one. . . . No one should be able to make a law that would infringe on the freedom of men and women as to when they will have a family and how large that family will be. That is between them and their God."

Throughout the hearing, the committee remained somber and quiet, asking few questions as several witnesses broke into tears. Hours of wrenching testimony and the presence of hundreds of people demanding a specific result rendered the committee clearly uncomfortable.

After both sides had used up their allotted rebuttal time, Heidepriem closed the hearing and, as promised, called for committee action on the bill. First, Senator Halverson made a motion that the committee approve HB 1126. Several hundred disbelieving eyes stared in awe as Halverson's motion met with silence, failing for lack of a second. Not to be denied, Halverson made a second motion, this time requesting that the committee send the bill to the full Senate without recommendation. Once again, his motion failed for lack of a second. Senator Shanard then moved that the bill be laid on the table. That motion carried 6–1. Halverson was the only senator on the committee to vote against tabling the bill.

After nearly four hours of testimony, the committee took just five minutes, without discussion between members, to reject the bill. Few—Heidepriem included—had anticipated such a lop-sided result. "I was really surprised," recall Heidepriem. "I thought Symens would probably second it. I even thought Shanard would second it as a matter of courtesy. . . . I guess the hearing hardened everyone's position."

When asked later about their votes on the bill, all committee members except Symens acknowledge that their individual minds had been made up on the abortion issue well before the bill was introduced in the legislature. Even Emery—whose position on HB 1126 was unknown to the public before the committee vote—conceded that he simply "voted [his] belief" on the issue. "I don't think I sat and listened to the debate and went back and forth or anything like that," Emery reflects. "I think my mind was probably set before the session."

Symens, on the other hand, told Heidepriem after the vote that it was the toughest one he had cast in his time in politics. Symens says he was convinced that the bill had been poorly written and was basically unfair. "I couldn't see passing a law that would punish a doctor for an action that was asked of him by someone else who had made a decision." At the same time, adds Symens, "I did not necessarily like to have to vote that way because I . . . don't believe in abortion.

THE SMOKEOUT

Immediately after Friday's vote, supporters of HB 1126 began working to force the bill out of committee so that it could be debated in the full Senate before the 1991 legislative session ended seven business days later. A smokeout attempt was planned for the following Monday: "We want to wait until the committee testimony has aired on public TV so some more of the senators can see it," explained Engel. One-third of the Senate chamber, or twelve votes, would be required for the smokeout, and a majority of senators—eighteen votes, the same amount needed to pass the bill—would have to agree to put the bill on the Senate calendar. Several senators, including Shanard—who voted against the bill in committee—speculated that even some senators opposing HB 1126 might still vote to place the bill on the calendar, just to give it a fair hearing.

Heidepriem, meanwhile, agonized over whether or not he should acquiesce to the pressure to bring the bill to a floor vote in the full Senate or use his influence as chairman to try to prevent the bill from being placed on the Senate calendar: "As chairman of the committee, I felt like I had to be fair to both sides even though I didn't have much respect for the theory behind the other side." However, Heidepriem adds, "I considered it an affront to the credibility of the Judiciary Committee that this bill would come out to the Senate floor after suffering a 6–1 defeat. I took the work of the committee very seriously, and thought the committee did an exceptional job in wading through it and thinking about it and withstood tremendous pressure to do what each of us thought was the right thing. So why go on with it?" Moreover, Heidepriem was firmly opposed to the bill: "It was just completely the wrong idea—the wrong way to go at a difficult problem. I thought it was demeaning." "I felt so strongly about it being a mistake for the state," Heidepriem adds, "that I think if everyone in my district had written me, urging me to vote for it, I still would have voted against it."

Several of Heidepriem's colleagues in the Senate informed him that they were being accused of using the process to defeat the bill. "They're just kicking the hell out of us at home," one senator told Heidepriem. "They're saying that we're afraid of the merits of this bill." Others told Heidepriem they felt a need in their districts to give the bill a public hearing. "That made some sense to me: the credibility of the legislature in allowing a broader forum and more discussion," says Heidepriem. Yet, Heidepriem recalls, "I was afraid it might pass. I thought it was dead even. It's not uncommon for people to vote one way on the committee and another on the floor." On the other hand, Heidepriem says, "I was afraid if I tried to prevent it [the bill] from coming out and I failed, it had a better chance of passing."

On Monday, February 25, supporters of the bill were able to smoke the bill out of Heidepriem's committee. Eighteen senators—thirteen Republican and five Democrats—stood up to be tallied in favor of the

procedure. The number of senators supporting the smokeout was comfortably higher
than the twelve votes needed for the procedure and identical to the eighteen votes necessary for the bill to pass the thirty-five-member
Senate. Senator Heidepriem—who did not
vote for the smokeout—downplayed the
effect the eighteen Senate votes might have
on the outcome of the bill. "That means nothing positive or negative," Heidepriem said,
pointing to Senator Emery, who voted against
the bill at Friday's committee hearing but
nonetheless stood in support of the smokeout. In order to get the bill on the calendar,
Heidepriem noted, those eighteen senators
would need to vote yet again. Still, Heidepriem realized, "If they decide to cast a vote in
favor of calendaring the bill, there is nothing
I can do about it. And I feared that if—after
having gone to them and asked, 'Please don't
vote to put this thing on the calendar'—if
I were to lose that procedural vote, I'd be
weaker for the final vote on the bill."

At that point, Heidepriem made a political
calculation. "I believed that the perception
that the abortion bill was kept from the
Senate floor by a procedural technicality was
more damaging than to address it head on."
Heidepriem thus decided to stand on the
floor of the Senate and ask his colleagues to
"strike the not," thereby permitting a full
Senate debate on HB 1126. The motion was
carried 34–1 on Tuesday, February 26, and
the bill was placed on the Senate calendar for
further action that day.

Heidepriem says that he made this
decision after Senator Shanard—who
voted against the bill in the Judiciary
Committee—urged him to bring the bill to
the floor:

> I think probably the thing that tipped it for me
> was when the majority leader—who had hung
> in there and sat on the committee; never wins
> by very much; moderate Republican; strong
> supporter of mine; cares about the process—
> came to me and said, "You know, I think you
> ought to do it. Otherwise, we're all going to
> look like we snuffed out democracy. It's not
> going to end unless we do this thing." Sort of

like closure, I thought. We needed to achieve
closure, and we wouldn't if we just let it stay
there in the committee.

Having made that decision, Heidepriem
admits he was not very happy with it.
"It sort of felt like a defeat. I wanted to run
the committee in such a scrupulously fair
way that both sides would rejoice at the end
and say, 'Well, it's just really fair.' It wasn't
to be; they were in this game to win."

ON THE SENATE FLOOR

That afternoon—February 26—hundreds of
spectators returned to the state capitol for
a Senate hearing on HB 1126, jam-packing
the gallery that overlooked the Senate chamber. No one was certain how the bill would
fare in the full Senate, but most agreed the
vote would be close—perhaps even decided
by a one-vote margin. As a result, lobbying
activity picked up tremendously. Even White
House Chief of Staff John Sunnunu lobbied
Senators Emery and Symens—two potential
swing votes—by telephone from Washington, D.C. According to Heidepriem, "the
mood in the Senate that day was that we had
the power to decide once and for all whether
abortion would be legal in South Dakota."

The Senate debate was aired on television
across the state. Senator Bellatti, the prime
Senate sponsor of HB 1126, began the proceedings with an introduction that was later
described by the *Sioux Falls Argus Leader* as
"The speech of his life." "Abortion is a matter
of life and death," Bellatti reminded his
colleagues. "Current abortion laws sanction
legalized murder. When a woman is pregnant,
her rights are further limited by the life of the
baby." In his floor speech, Bellatti also gave
the first hint that some supporters of HB 1126
were annoyed at Heidepriem's scheduling
of the hearings on the bill. "I'd like to apologize for any discomfort you might have had
waiting for the hearing to take place," said
Bellatti. "We introduced the bill on the first
day of the session, and here we are on the
thirty-fifth day."

When Bellatti finished, several other senators took to the floor to argue for and against HB 1126. One senator, Doris Miner [D-Gregory]—an ardent opponent of abortion—directed her floor remarks to Senator Symens, a potential swing vote on the bill. In a move that Heidepriem describes as "the low point in the debate," Miner read a note she claimed to have been handed to her by Symens' daughter, Stephanie, a legislative intern and a member of South Dakota Right to Life. According to Miner, Stephanie Symens was outraged that a penalty existed for the destruction of an eagle's egg but not for the termination of a human embryo. In her memo, Miner said, Symens "begged" Miner and other senators to "vote for those who can't" vote for the bill.[36]

When it was his turn on the floor, Heidepriem reiterated his position that the other antiabortion bills pending in states such as Utah and Louisiana would provide an abortion test in the Supreme Court, reminding the committee that "abortion will continue legally until and unless the U.S. Supreme Court changes its mind." Heidepriem pointed out that the bill "was drafted in Washington, D.C. It is part of the National Right to Life organization's national agenda." Thus, Heidepriem argued, "the whole question is whether this state wants to be a pawn in the national struggle between these forces." On a more personal level, Heidepriem explained that the birth of his first son three years before reaffirmed his belief in reproductive rights for women. "I have a vivid memory of that day and that is of the incredible physical strength of a woman," Heidepriem said. "That made me think that decisions women make about reproduction are decisions some of us cannot understand." In closing Heidepriem, emphasized, "I mean it when I tell you I stand here for life, for life, but not for this bill."

THE SENATE VOTE

Late in the day on February 26, the moment many had awaited since the session began had finally arrived: the Senate roll call on

HB 1126. The roomful of onlookers was silent as, one by one, each of the thirty-five senators stated their votes. It was not until the very last senator voted that the fate of the HB 1126 became known. With seventeen in favor and eighteen opposed, HB 1126 failed on the Senate floor that day.

The vote cut across party lines. Of the seventeen "yes" votes, twelve were Republican and five were Democrat. Of the eighteen "no" votes, twelve were Democrat and six were Republican. Nine of the eleven women in the South Dakota Senate voted against the bill,[37] eight of the nine women voting against the bill were Democrats. Only one Democratic woman, Doris Miner, voted for the bill. Both Senate party leaders, Democrat Roger McKelliops and Republican George Shanard, opposed the bill. In addition, three senators—Democrats Red Allen and Roland Chicoine and Republican William Johnson—had said before the session that the current abortion law in South Dakota should not be changed but voted to change it under HB 1126.

According to Heidepriem, "no member of the Senate suggested that their vote on the bill was determined by anything other than their view of whether abortion should be regulated entirely by the state or the woman." Heidepriem attributes this to the work of Right to Life, which he argues "so successfully dominated the debate that anything short of a declaration of feeling on the issue would have been perceived all around as a dodge. The mail every senator received demanded not just an absence of equivocation, but the willingness to ignore the very significant cost and constitutional issues on the way to vote." In Heidepriem's view, "arguments stating the fact that the state already had in place a statute which repealed legal abortion when the state was given the exclusive rights to regulate abortion met with puzzlement and were passed over quickly."

Senator Bellatti had a different take on the Senate vote. Noting that two weeks earlier, it appeared he would have enough votes to pass the antiabortion measure, Bellatti attributed the eroded support for the bill to stepped-up lobbying of abortion rights advocates late in the session. Bellatti conceded that some lawmakers had become fed up with the overwhelming number of phone calls, letters, baby rattles, and pictures of fetuses sent by antiabortion activists. "I think people plain just got tired."[38] Still, the experience made Bellatti feel hopeful about the future. "It demonstrated that there is a tremendous grass-roots pro-life effort" in South Dakota, Bellatti explained, adding: "I have no doubt that *Roe v. Wade* will be overturned. Eventually, more and more states are going to fall into line."[39]

Shortly after HB 1126 went down, Senator Elmer Bietz (R-Tripp) signaled his intention to force another Senate vote on the bill. Senator Bellatti firmly rejected the idea. Since senators had made up their minds and were unlikely to change their votes, Bellatti said, "I think there's nothing to be gained by working it over again."[40] Supporters of the bill chose to leave it at that. "Dr. Bellatti just wants it done," said Lori Engel. "In fairness to him, we'll honor his request."[41]

REACTION

Immediately after the Senate vote, Katie Michelman, executive director of NARAL, issued a public statement from Washington hailing the decision. "Today's vote not only safeguards the lives and health of South Dakota women, it also prevents another case from entering the crowded judicial pipeline to the U.S. Supreme Court and threatening *Roe v. Wade*." Meanwhile, Nancy Myers, spokeswoman for the National Right to Life Committee, called the vote "a betrayal by one or two people who were voted into office as pro-life legislators."

Some supporters of the bill blamed Senator Heidepriem for the loss, accusing him of delay tactics resulting in what they viewed as a poor timing of the vote. "It was the delay in committee that killed it,"

Engel contended. "I think Senator Heidepriem had his agenda set and that was it. . . . Heidepriem wanted it killed."[42] Engel's remarks clearly stung Heidepriem, who prided himself as a true believer in the sanctity of the political process. "I gave them every break in the world," defended Heidepriem, noting that he did not offer any amendments to try to cripple or kill the bill in committee. "I think I was just scrupulously fair about the testimony, about witnesses. I let both sides run their show within certain limits. We gave it a fair hearing."

Although Heidepriem was relieved that the antiabortion bill ultimately failed, he felt no joy in the outcome. "There's a level of disappointment about it all," Heidepriem told the *Argus Leader*. "I believe that the Senate succeeded in preventing a bad law from taking effect, but none of us runs for office to stop bad things from happening. I think we all run because we're motivated by positive desires to do good things."

EPILOGUE

When the 1991 legislative session ended in early March, Heidepriem—heeding the advice of his sister—raised $5,000 to conduct a telephone survey of every household in his district to assess the level of political damage that may have resulted from his position on HB 1126. The survey found that 40 percent of Heidepriem's constituents believed the bill should have passed and that Heidepriem should have voted for it. Twenty-eight percent believed the bill should not have passed and that Heidepriem should not have voted for it. A full 32 percent were undecided.

Meanwhile, the South Dakota RTL reported that hundreds of people had signed up to help defeat Heidepriem in the upcoming November Senate race. Ninety-five people volunteered to help Heidepriem win that fall. In the end, however, Heidepriem decided against running for reelection. "Eight years in that process was probably enough," explains Heidepriem, who said his primary reason for not running was to be able to spend more time with his family. Still, Heidepriem admits, his experience with HB 1126 also played a role in his decision: "the events around this bill were so completely out of proportion to any other legislative experience I had had . . . that it made no sense to just go back. It was so enormously taxing—personally, emotionally, politically—that to continue on in the legislature somehow seemed almost secondary." Heidepriem adds:

> I really felt this experience marked me and changed me. This process had meant so much to me; I watched this from my father's lap for the first twelve years of my life, and he had made me feel that this was a noble human experience. Some of that came loose for me in '91. . . . A lot of people go into the legislature and they're fired up about being in the process, excited about having won an election, and you take the oath and sit down in a beautiful chamber and hope someday you'll do something good or big for your state. And I certainly wanted that, too. And so the time comes, and it was high profile and a lot of attention, but somehow, it wasn't what I had in mind.

With no concrete plans to reenter public life in 1993 or 1994, Heidepriem returned to his law practice in Sioux Falls. Nevertheless, he remained active as a political commentator for some local television shows and would not rule out a future run for political office. "It would be silly to say that I'm not going to do it again," Heidepriem says. "It's been a central theme since birth. . . . I grew up with it, and I'm really enjoying not being in it now, but I don't know how long I'll feel that way."

All other members of the Senate Judiciary Committee—with the exception of Karen Muenster, who suffered a back injury that took her out of politics—sought reelection in November 1992. Emery, Halverson, and Rasmussen won handily, though Rasmussen was targeted by antiabortion forces.[43] Shanard was defeated by Democrat Mel Olsen, who did not reveal his position on abortion prior to the election. According to Shanard, "the abortion issue was used against [him] rather substantially" during the campaign, and there was "no question that [his vote on HB 1126] hurt" him.[44] Senator Symens meanwhile, was reelected by a very narrow margin: three hundred out of approximately six thousand votes. Symens' vote on the 1991 antiabortion bill dominated the campaign.

The November 1992 elections shifted the balance of power on the abortion issue in the South Dakota Senate. At least eighteen antiabortion candidates were elected to the Senate—just enough for a majority vote. Few were surprised, then, that the abortion issue resurfaced in the 1993 legislative session. Although, this time, no bill sought to outlaw abortion in South Dakota,[45] a package of House bills seeking abortion restrictions was able to pass the legislature and was signed into law by Governor Mickelson in March 1993. The new abortion restrictions included: (1) a mandatory twenty-four-hour waiting period before any abortion could be performed; (2) one-parent notification (the bill did not include a judicial bypass provision); and (3) a ban on the use of fetal tissue for research and medical treatment in South Dakota. Two of the restrictions—parental notification and the twenty-four-hour wait—were to be challenged in court by Planned Parenthood in 1993.

NOTES

1. According to Heidepriem, Senator Mike Dietrich, then vice chairman of the Judiciary committee, "was understandably put out" that Heidepriem was given the Judiciary chairmanship. But in the end, Heidepriem says, Dietrich "understood what [Heidepriem] was giving up in the House to come over to the Senate."

2. Heidepriem ran for the U.S. House seat left vacant by Democrat Tom Daschle, an abortion rights supporter. Daschle ran successfully for the U.S. Senate that year.

3. Alan Guttmacher Institute, 1987.

4. 700 of the 900 abortions were performed for South Dakota residents.

5. The other states were Idaho, Illinois, Kentucky, Louisiana, Missouri, Montana, Nebraska, North Dakota, and Pennsylvania.

6. South Dakota adopted a parental consent statute in the late 1970s, but its enforcement was immediately restricted by the federal district court. The law remained unenforced in 1991 despite recent Supreme Court rulings that had permitted this type of requirement in other states.

7. Both the Louisiana and Utah laws would prohibit abortion except in cases of rape, incest, protecting the mother's health, or removing a severely damaged unborn child. The doctor performing the abortion would face a felony charge punishable by up to five years in prison, but there would be no penalties for the woman seeking the abortion. The Utah legislature also passed a resolution creating an abortion law task force, promising that the state would help other states fight to overturn *Roe* if Utah's bill failed.

8. Critics of the bill noted that this definition would probably outlaw the intrauterine device (IUD), the "morning after" pill, and certainly the French abortion pill, RU-486. Proponents of the bill suggested that the IUD would not be outlawed, as the woman would not be "known" to be pregnant at the time.

9. In the case of incest, the victim would have to be a minor in order to have an abortion.

10. *Sioux Falls Argus Leader,* Feb. 17, 1991.

11. *Aberdeen American News,* Jan. 19, 1991.

12. Ibid.

13. *Sioux Falls Argus Leader,* Jan. 16, 1991.

14. *Aberdeen American News,* Jan. 19, 1991.

15. Ibid.

16. Ibid., Jan. 17, 1991.

17. Ibid.

18. *Sioux Falls Argus Leader,* Feb. 1, 1991.

19. Ibid., Jan. 16, 1991.

20. Ibid., Feb. 1, 1991.

21. HB 1126 would have been more difficult to pass if any of the proposed appropriations were included. In South Dakota, any measure that included spending authority would require a two-thirds majority, rather than a simple majority, to pass.

22. Miller was asked by Senate Majority Leader George Shanard to direct the bill to the Senate Judiciary Committee. Heidepriem believed that Miller "tried very hard to get the bill sent somewhere other than the Judiciary Committee because he sensed that it would get a more favorable hearing somewhere else."

23. In January, Mickelson had said he held reservations about the constitutionality of the bill.

24. *Sioux Falls Argus Leader,* Feb. 11, 1991.

25. Engel wanted it to be held on Monday, February 18, while Glasgow wanted it to coincide with a Family Values Coalition rally that he was planning for Monday, February 25.

26. For example, Heidepriem could schedule the committee vote for the morning of the last—fortieth—day of the legislative session. (State legislative rules required that the session end in no more than forty days.) Since the required steps of a smokeout could take six days to complete, supporters of the bill would have to suspend the rules—which required a two-thirds majority in the Senate—in order to complete all of the smokeout procedures in just one day.

27. Feb. 11, 1991.

28. *Sioux Falls Argus Leader,* Feb. 21, 1991.

29. Shanard believed that 60 percent of the voters in his district opposed abortion.

30. When Heidepriem ran for Congress in 1986, Halverson supported his opponent because of the abortion issue.

31. Muenster's husband Ted planned to run for governor in 1994.

32. *Sioux Falls Argus Leader,* Feb. 21, 1991.

33. Feb. 17, 1991.

34. After the hearing, Heidepriem was approached by several doctors who believed that the fetus looked more like it was twelve weeks old.

35. South Dakota mandated that a reason be given for every abortion performed in the state. In most cases, the physician performing the abortion would check off the "other" box on the mandatory multiple choice questionnaire for the state. Engel interpreted each questionnaire stating "other" reasons for the abortion as evidence that the abortion was performed for birth control purposes.

36. According to Heidepriem, Stephanie Symens later told her father that she had not written a note to Miner.

37. At the time, the South Dakota Democratic caucus was the only caucus in the United States with a female majority; in 1991, nine out of seventeen Democratic senators in South Dakota were women.

38. *Associated Press,* Feb. 26, 1991.

39. *Sioux Falls Argus Leader,* March 3, 1991.

40. *Associated Press,* Feb. 26, 1991.

41. *Sioux Falls Argus Leader,* March 3, 1991.

42. Ibid., Feb. 27, 1991.

43. Emery's challenger did not actively oppose abortion, and the abortion issue did not figure prominently in his campaign. Rasmussen's campaign benefited from legislative redistricting, which in 1992 put her in a district with fewer antiabortion constituents than in 1991. "If my district had stayed the way it was, I'm afraid I wouldn't have gotten reelected," Rasmussen speculates.

44. However, some of Shanard's Senate colleagues believed that unrelated allegations of impropriety dealt the decisive blow to Shanard's campaign.
45. On March 8, 1993, the United States Supreme Court let stand an appeals court ruling that struck down Louisiana's 1991 antiabortion law, which, like the bill that failed in South Dakota in 1991, sought to ban abortions in most situations and stipulated prison terms for physicians performing abortions.

Regulating Abortion Late in the Term*

"Partial-birth abortion," or dilation and extraction (D&X), is a medical procedure performed during the second trimester of a pregnancy, in which a fetus is vaginally taken out of the womb and discarded.

Some states, like Nebraska, prohibited the procedure decades ago. However, it began to attract public attention in 1995, when Ohio enacted a law banning "dilation and extraction" abortion. Michigan later moved to prohibit what its law called "partial-birth" abortion, and Utah followed suit with a law against postviability "partial-birth" abortion. Collectively, these actions prepared the ground for the prohibition that would become a federal law eight years later. The link between this procedure and abortion, and thus between the bill to ban this procedure and *Roe v. Wade,* created the charged political atmosphere in which the debates took place.

The House of Representatives and the Senate debated the issue extensively, and passed two bills to ban the procedure, both of which were vetoed by President Clinton. In 2000, the Supreme Court struck down in *Stenberg v. Carhart* the 1977 Nebraska law prohibiting partial-birth abortions, along with other types of abortion, upholding *Roe v. Wade.* Writing for the majority, Justice Breyer found that the Nebraska ban violated the Supreme Court precedents in *Roe v. Wade* and *Planned Parenthood v. Casey* because it failed to include an exception to preserve the health of the woman and imposed an undue burden on a woman's ability to choose an abortion (the opinion follows).

The continuing political controversy in Congress focused mostly on a proposed amendment allowing a physician to defend the use of a D&X procedure if "the partial-birth abortion was necessary to save the life of the woman upon whom it was performed, and no other form of abortion would suffice for that purpose."

During the lengthy legislative process, conflicting and mutually exclusive testimony was given. Some professionals claimed that fetuses cannot feel pain; others offered research showing that fetuses do respond to painful stimuli as early as the first trimester of gestation. Professionals declared that in some cases the procedure was necessary to preserve the pregnant woman's life; other physicians claimed that those same cases were unsuitable for this procedure.

Controversy arose over nearly all aspects of the data presented, the justifications given and even the terminology used. Starting at an early stage of the debate, and continuing all through the rocky road to its legislation, supporters and opponents of the bill disputed the types of abortions that tally with the notion of "late-term," and correspondingly how often the procedure

---

*Sigal Ben-Porath wrote the introduction and selected the excerpts presented in this section.

was performed in the United States, with figures varying from a few hundred to tens of thousands a year. (The Supreme Court said in *Carhart* that "There are no reliable data on the number of D&X abortions performed annually. Estimates have ranged between 640 and 5,000 per year.") They disagreed about the reasons for its use—how often was it performed because of a major health problem of the pregnant woman? How often because the fetus was severely deformed? What constitutes a severe deformity for this purpose? They disputed the details of the procedure itself: Does the fetus suffer during the procedure? Does it put the woman's health at risk? Are there reasonable alternatives? Even the term used to describe the procedure was politicized, with supporters of the ban describing it as *late-term abortion* or *partial-birth abortion,* and opponents of the ban preferring the medical terms *dilation and extraction (D&X)* or *dilation and evacuation (D&E).*

Even more controversial was the use of the term *health*: What would be defined as a severe enough risk to the woman's health in order for the procedure to be legal? Should a woman's mental health count as a legitimate reason to perform the procedure? The definition of *health* would prove the most problematic aspect of the legislation to ban the procedure, and served as the main rationale for the president's vetoes.

Some legislators opposed the very idea of a law that would supercede medical decisions made by a physician. Others claimed that it is the responsibility of the legislatures to mark the limits of appropriate medical conduct. Politically speaking, the clash of rights—liberty versus life—that *Roe v. Wade* had suggested continued to frame the debate.

Democrats opposing the ban were concerned about the limitations put on a woman's right to decide whether to continue her pregnancy. Republicans and other supporters of the ban claimed that

they were merely precluding a gruesome, unnecessary medical procedure that killed a human being.

EXCERPTS FROM THE OPINION OF THE SUPREME COURT IN STENBERG V. CARHART (530 U.S. 914)

BREYER, J., DELIVERED THE OPINION OF THE COURT, IN WHICH STEVENS, O'CONNOR, SOUTER, AND GINSBURG, JJ., JOINED.

... Justice Thomas says that the cases just cited limit this principle to situations where the pregnancy itself creates a threat to health. . . . He is wrong. The cited cases, reaffirmed in *Casey,* recognize that a State cannot subject women's health to significant risks both in that context, and also where state regulations force women to use riskier methods of abortion. Our cases have repeatedly invalidated statutes that in the process of regulating the methods of abortion, imposed significant health risks. They make clear that a risk to a woman's health is the same whether it happens to arise from regulating a particular method of abortion, or from barring abortion entirely. Our holding does not go beyond those cases, as ratified in *Casey.*

Nebraska responds that the law does not require a health exception unless there is a need for such an exception. And here there is no such need, it says. It argues that "safe alternatives remain available" and "a ban on partial-birth abortion/D&X would create no risk to the health of women." . . . The problem for Nebraska is that the parties strongly contested this factual question in the trial court below; and the findings and evidence support Dr. Carhart. The State fails to demonstrate that banning D&X without a health exception may not create significant health risks for women, because the record shows that significant medical authority supports the proposition that in some circumstances, D&X would be the safest procedure.

We shall reiterate in summary form the relevant findings and evidence. On the basis of medical testimony the District Court concluded that "Carhart's D&X procedure is . . . safer than the D&E and other abortion procedures used during the relevant gestational period in the 10 to 20 cases a year that present to Dr. Carhart." It found that the D&X procedure permits the fetus to pass through the cervix with a minimum of instrumentation. It thereby "reduces operating time, blood loss and risk of infection; reduces complications from bony fragments; reduces instrument-inflicted damage to the uterus and cervix; prevents the most common causes of maternal mortality (DIC and amniotic fluid embolus); and eliminates the possibility of 'horrible complications' arising from retained fetal parts."

. . .

10. The materials presented at trial referred to the potential benefits of the D&X procedure in circumstances involving nonviable fetuses, such as fetuses with abnormal fluid accumulation in the brain (hydrocephaly) . . . ("Intact D&X may be preferred by some physicians, particularly when the fetus has been diagnosed with hydrocephaly or other anomalies incompatible with life outside the womb") . . . (D&X "may be especially useful in the presence of fetal anomalies, such as hydrocephalus," because its reduction of the cranium allows "a smaller diameter to pass through the cervix, thus reducing risk of cervical injury"). Others have emphasized its potential for women with prior uterine scars, or for women for whom induction of labor would be particularly dangerous.

. . .

Nebraska, along with supporting *amici,* replies that these findings are irrelevant, wrong, or applicable only in a tiny number of instances. It says (1) that the D&X procedure is "little-used," (2) by only "a handful of doctors." . . . It argues (3) that D&E and labor induction are at all times "safe alternative procedures." . . . It refers to the testimony of petitioners' medical expert, who testified (4) that the ban would not increase a woman's risk of several rare abortion complications. . . . The Association of American Physicians and Surgeons et al., *amici* supporting Nebraska, argue (5) that elements of the D&X procedure may create special risks, including cervical incompetence caused by overdilation, injury caused by conversion of the fetal presentation, and dangers arising from the "blind" use of instrumentation to pierce the fetal skull while lodged in the birth canal. . . .

Nebraska further emphasizes (6) that there are no medical studies "establishing the safety of the partial-birth abortion/D&X procedure," . . . "no medical studies comparing the safety of partial-birth abortion/D&X to other abortion procedures" . . . (7) [and an] American Medical Association policy statement that "there does not appear to be any identified situation in which intact D&X is the only appropriate procedure to induce abortion," . . . [a]nd it points out (8) that the American College of Obstetricians and Gynecologists qualified its statement that D&X "may be the best or most appropriate procedure," by adding that the panel "could identify no circumstances under which [the D&X] procedure . . . would be the only option to save the life or preserve the health of the woman." . . .

We find these eight arguments insufficient to demonstrate that Nebraska's law needs no health exception. For one thing, certain of the arguments are beside the point. The D&X procedure's relative rarity (argument (1)) is not highly relevant. The D&X is an infrequently used abortion procedure; but the health exception question is whether protecting women's health requires an exception for those infrequent occasions. A rarely used treatment might be necessary to treat a rarely occurring disease that could strike anyone—the State cannot prohibit a person from obtaining treatment simply by pointing out that most people do not need it. Nor can we know whether the fact that only a "handful" of doctors use the procedure (argument (2)) reflects the comparative rarity of late second term abortions, the procedure's recent development, Gynecologic, Obstetric, and Related

Surgery, at 1043, the controversy surrounding it, or, as Nebraska suggests, the procedure's lack of utility. For another thing, the record responds to Nebraska's (and *amici*'s) medically based arguments. In respect to argument (3), for example, the District Court agreed that alternatives, such as D&E and induced labor, are "safe" but found that the D&X method was significantly safer in certain circumstances. . . . In respect to argument (4), the District Court simply relied on different expert testimony—testimony stating that " 'another advantage of the Intact D&E is that it eliminates the risk of embolism of cerebral tissue into the woman's blood stream.' " . . .

In response to *amici*'s argument (5), the American College of Obstetricians and Gynecologists, in its own *amici* brief, denies that D&X generally poses risks greater than the alternatives. It says that the suggested alternative procedures involve similar or greater risks of cervical and uterine injury, for "D&E procedures, involve similar amounts of dilation" and "of course childbirth involves even greater cervical dilation." . . . We do not quarrel with Nebraska's argument (6), for Nebraska is right. There are no general medical studies documenting comparative safety. Neither do we deny the import of the American Medical Association's statement (argument (7))—even though the State does omit the remainder of that statement: "The AMA recommends that the procedure not be used unless alternative procedures pose materially greater risk to the woman."

. . . We cannot, however, read the American College of Obstetricians and Gynecologists panel's qualification (that it could not "identify" a circumstance where D&X was the "only" life- or health-preserving option) as if, according to Nebraska's argument (8), it denied the potential health-related need for D&X. That is because the College writes the following in its *amici* brief:

Depending on the physician's skill and experience, the D&X procedure can be the most appropriate abortion procedure for some women in some circumstances. D&X presents a variety of potential safety advantages over other abortion procedures used during the same gestational period. Compared to D&Es involving dismemberment, D&X involves less risk of uterine perforation or cervical laceration because it requires the physician to make fewer passes into the uterus with sharp instruments and reduces the presence of sharp fetal bone fragments that can injure the uterus and cervix. There is also considerable evidence that D&X reduces the risk of retained fetal tissue, a serious abortion complication that can cause maternal death, and that D&X reduces the incidence of a 'free floating' fetal head that can be difficult for a physician to grasp and remove and can thus cause maternal injury. That D&X procedures usually take less time than other abortion methods used at a comparable stage of pregnancy can also have health advantages. The shorter the procedure, the less blood loss, trauma, and exposure to anesthesia. The intuitive safety advantages of intact D&E are supported by clinical experience. Especially for women with particular health conditions, there is medical evidence that D&X may be safer than available alternatives. (Brief for American College of Obstetricians and Gynecologists et al. as Amici Curiae 21–22 [citation and footnotes omitted]).

The upshot is a District Court finding that D&X significantly obviates health risks in certain circumstances, a highly plausible record-based explanation of why that might be so, a division of opinion among some medical experts over whether D&X is generally safer, and an absence of controlled medical studies that would help answer these medical questions. Given these medically related evidentiary circumstances, we believe the law requires a health exception.

The word "necessary" in Casey's phrase "necessary, in appropriate medical judgment, for the preservation of the life or health of the mother," 505 U.S. at 879 (internal quotation marks omitted), cannot refer to an absolute necessity or to absolute proof. Medical treatments and procedures are often considered appropriate (or inappropriate) in light of estimated comparative health risks (and health benefits) in particular cases. Neither can that phrase require unanimity of medical opinion. Doctors often differ in their estimation of comparative health risks and appropriate treatment. And Casey's words "appropriate medical judgment" must embody the judicial need to tolerate responsible differences of medical opinion—differences of a sort that the American Medical Association and American College of Obstetricians and Gynecologists' statements together indicate are present here.

For another thing, the division of medical opinion about the matter at most means uncertainty, a factor that signals the presence of risk, not its absence. That division here involves highly qualified knowledgeable experts on both sides of the issue. Where a significant body of medical opinion believes a procedure may bring with it greater safety for some patients and explains the medical reasons supporting that view, we cannot say that the presence of a different view by itself proves the contrary. Rather, the uncertainty means a significant likelihood that those who believe that D&X is a safer abortion method in certain circumstances may turn out to be right. If so, then the absence of a health exception will place women at an unnecessary risk of tragic health consequences. If they are wrong, the exception will simply turn out to have been unnecessary.

In sum, Nebraska has not convinced us that a health exception is "never necessary to preserve the health of women." . . . Rather, a statute that altogether forbids D&X creates a significant health risk. The statute consequently must contain a health exception. This is not to say, as Justice Thomas and Justice Kennedy claim, that a State is prohibited from proscribing an abortion procedure whenever a particular physician deems the procedure

preferable. By no means must a State grant physicians "unfettered discretion" in their selection of abortion methods. . . . But where substantial medical authority supports the proposition that banning a particular abortion procedure could endanger women's health, Casey requires the statute to include a health exception when the procedure is "necessary, in appropriate medical judgment, for the preservation of the life or health of the mother." 505 U.S. at 879. Requiring such an exception in this case is no departure from Casey, but simply a straightforward application of its holding.

THE DEBATE IN THE 108TH CONGRESS

In July 2002 the House defeated radical amendments that included a health clause and passed the Partial-Birth Abortion Ban, titled H.R. 760, for a third time. The debate on the corresponding bill in the Senate, titled S.3., began in March 2003. At one point in the Senate debate, Senator Sam Brownback (R-Kans.) showed a photograph of a twenty-one-week-old fetus he said had been spared an abortion by doctors who operated on him in the womb to correct a birth defect. "Is little Samuel's hand the hand of a person," he said, pointing to the photograph, "or is it the hand of a piece of property?"

During this debate, Senator Boxer (D-Calif.), one of the strongest opponents of the bill throughout the process, proposed an amendment that would have allowed D&X "after viability where, in the medical judgment of the attending physician, the abortion is necessary to preserve the life of the woman or avert serious adverse health consequences to the woman." Ex-Surgeon General C. Everett Koop said that this amendment was a "complete sham." It would "not outlaw a single one of the thousands of partial-birth abortions performed each year."

The amendment was defeated 47–51. The Senate then passed S.3, with one addition. Senator Tom Harkin (D-Iowa) had introduced an amendment to the bill expressing support for *Roe v. Wade*:

It is the sense of the Senate that
(1) The decision of the Supreme Court in *Roe v. Wade* (410 U.S. 113 (1973)) was appropriate and secures an important constitutional right; and
(2) Such decision should not be overturned.

Following the passage of S.3 in the Senate, the president released a statement: "Partial-birth abortion is an abhorrent procedure that offends human dignity, and I commend the Senate for passing legislation to ban it. Today's action is an important step toward building a culture of life in America. I look forward to the House passing legislation and working with the Senate to resolve any differences so that I can sign legislation banning partial-birth abortion into law."

The bill then moved back to the House for discussion and action.

EXCERPTS FROM THE DEBATE IN THE HOUSE

Richard Burr (R-N.C.), March 20, 2003

Mr. Speaker, I rise today in support of a ban on the partial-birth abortion procedure. I firmly believe in the sanctity of human life, and am pleased that my colleagues in the other body have taken this necessary step to protect an unborn child's right to life.

I am pleased to be a supporter and cosponsor of the House version of the Partial-Birth Abortion Ban, H.R. 760. I urge my colleagues to consider the lives of thousands of unborn children each year that are terminated by this callous procedure, children who would be spared by the swift passage of this measure. Beyond H.R. 760, I urge my colleagues to support legislation that further protects the rights of unborn children. I am encouraged that there is great momentum in banning partial-birth abortions, and I am hopeful that the House of Representatives will be able to quickly pass this bill. With passage of legislation outlawing this barbaric practice, we will be taking a significant step in protecting innocent children.

Tom Davis (R-Va.), June 4, 2003

Mr. Speaker, I rise in strong support of H.R. 760, the Partial-Birth Abortion Ban Act of 2003.

Partial-birth abortion is an inhumane procedure which is never necessary to preserve the health of the mother. Indeed, this procedure poses serious health risks to the mother, and it is unnecessarily brutal to the baby. I have heard from numerous physicians that there are other safe methods for terminating a pregnancy when the life of the mother is in danger, and the American Medical Association has stated that partial-birth abortion is not an accepted medical practice.

H.R. 760 addresses the constitutional issues raised by the Supreme Court decision in *Stenberg v. Carhart*. It does so by using a more precise definition of the gruesome partial-birth procedure, clearly distinguishing between this and other forms of abortion. Furthermore, H.R. 760 provides extensive congressional findings which show that a partial-birth abortion is never medically necessary to preserve the health of a woman.

The House has passed this legislation in previous Congresses, yet a final vote did not take place in the Senate or in conference. The Senate recently passed the Partial-Birth Abortion Ban Act. We now have a historic opportunity to pass this legislation and send it to the White House for the President's approval. I strongly support enactment of a ban on partial-birth abortion, and I urge my colleagues to vote in support of H.R. 760.

Sheila Jackson-Lee (D-Tex.), June 4, 2003

This partial-birth abortion bill, H.R. 760, is unconstitutional for the same two reasons that the Supreme Court found other statutes attempting to ban partial-birth abortions unconstitutional.

First, H.R. 760 lacks a health exception which the Supreme Court unequivocally said was a fatal flaw in any restriction on abortion.

Second, the nonmedical term partial-birth abortion is overly broad and would include a ban of safe previability abortions. Banning the safest abortion option imposes an undue burden on a woman's ability to choose, and the life of the mother and the health of the mother, and the mother's ability to give birth in the future.

Finally, let me say this: We want to save lives, H.R. 760 does not.

The House refused to accept the "Sense of the Senate" affirmation of *Roe v. Wade*. The disagreement between the two chambers, as represented by the differences in the language of S.3 and H.R 760, had to be resolved in a conference committee.

Senator Boxer's Effort to Preserve the Affirmation of Roe v. Wade, *September 2003*

I am here tonight speaking about an issue that was resolved in 1973, the right of a woman to choose—the fact that this Senate went on record supporting that right quite recently as part of S.3, that very simple language that simply said *Roe v. Wade* has saved lives, stating it is the sense of the Senate that the decision of the Supreme Court in *Roe v. Wade* was appropriate and secures an important right and such decisions should not be overturned.

That was language in S.3 which also for the first time banned a medically recognized procedure. Senator Harkin and I and a majority of the Senate added this language. . . . [O]ne would think the House of Representatives and the Republican leadership would have said: We want to get this bill to the President's desk. We want to ban this procedure. So let's just take this language. The decision of the Supreme Court in *Roe* was appropriate and secures an important right, and such decisions should not be overturned.

Friends, that was not to be the case. Instead of sending this bill off to the President for his signature, which my colleagues have been wanting to do for a very long time, they say we need to strip out this very simple *Roe* language. . . . Now in order to go to conference, we will have a vote to disagree with what the House did. I hope we will disagree with what they did and take another stand for *Roe*. That is why we are here tonight.

The reason the House will not go along with this, and many in our own Senate will not, the real agenda . . . is to overturn *Roe*. . . . It may show up by saying to a woman in the military: You will have to fly back to the United States on an "as available" basis and spend your own money—nothing to do with your own military pay—to get an abortion. We have said to Federal employees: You cannot use the health insurance that you pay a good part of to get a legal abortion, Legal, not illegal, a legal abortion. Abortion is legal.

My friends, some of them here do not like that. So there has been this huge attempt to narrow this right. So every time we get a chance, when we see these bills come forward that would narrow this right, that would potentially harm women, we offer the Harkin-Boxer amendment in favor of *Roe* . . .

Now, what does *Roe* guarantee to women?

In the decision of the Supreme Court, the Court found that a woman's reproductive decisions are a privacy right guaranteed by the Constitution. But I have to say that even though this right was granted to women, it was not an unbalanced decision. It was a very moderate decision. That is why, in my opinion, the majority of Americans support it.

In the early stages of a pregnancy, the Government cannot intervene with a woman's right to choose. That is it, plain and simple. Guess what. We are not going to be big brother or sister, as the case may be. We are going to allow a woman, her doctor, and her God to make that decision.

But in the later stages of pregnancy, *Roe* found that the Government can intervene, that it can regulate, that it can restrict abortion. We all support that. All of us support that. But there is one caveat—always, always, always. Any law that a State may pass to restrict abortion rights has to have an exception to protect the life of the woman or to protect her health.

THE VOTES IN CONGRESS

In the House and Senate conference, the "Sense of the Senate" clause that supported *Roe* was removed and the bill went forward in the form favored by the House. On October 20, 2003, the Senate passed the bill, affirming the original House bill and banning the procedure. President Bush signed it into law, but opponents vowed to keep fighting in the courts. Their main claim was still that absent a clause allowing for the procedure if required to protect the woman's health, the bill is unconstitutional.

Seventeen Democratic senators voted for the bill, allowing it to pass the last legislative barrier, though some expressed uncertainty afterwards. (The public evidently was in a similar state of uncertainty; a *New York Times* article on October 23, 2003, stated that: "The voters say they do not want partial-birth abortion," said Celinda Lake, a Democratic pollster who tracks the issue. "On the other hand, they do not want anything that would interfere with saving the life or the health of the mother. They have a very hard time figuring out what is at stake here, and what is really the issue," p. A1) Senator Blanche Lincoln, Democrat of Arkansas, told the *New York Times* (in the same article) that she voted for the ban despite the fact that she considers herself "about 99 percent pro-choice." Senator Lincoln said she felt that she was reflecting the views of her constituents. However, she had misgivings about making laws to govern medicine. "Trying to legislate what doctors can do," she said, "is a very dangerous thing."

Other Democrats suggested that they felt the medical procedure was morally flawed. The gruesome descriptions of the procedure by groups promoting the ban apparently contributed to the tendency of citizens and representatives to oppose the procedure.

Senator Tom Daschle, Democrat of South Dakota and the minority leader, told the *New York Times* that after eight years of divisive debate, he was ready to get the matter out of Congress and into the courts. He voted in favor of the ban so that pro-choice groups could go to the Supreme Court and settle the matter. The first hint of the next stage of the battle was given in June 2004, when a federal judge announced that he was going to declare the ban unconstitutional.

THE PARTIAL-BIRTH ABORTION BAN ACT OF 2003

The Congress finds and declares the following:

(1) A moral, medical, and ethical consensus exists that the practice of performing a partial-birth abortion—an abortion in which a physician delivers an unborn child's body until only the head remains inside the womb, punctures the back of the child's skull with a sharp instrument, and sucks the child's brains out before completing delivery of the dead infant—is a gruesome and inhumane procedure that is never medically necessary and should be prohibited.

(2) Rather than being an abortion procedure that is embraced by the medical community, particularly among physicians who routinely perform other abortion procedures, partial-birth abortion remains a disfavored procedure that is not only unnecessary to preserve the health of the mother, but in fact poses serious risks to the long-term health of women and, in some circumstances, their lives. As a result, at least 27 States banned the procedure as did the United States Congress which voted to ban the procedure during the 104th, 105th, and 106th Congresses.

(3) In *Stenberg v. Carhart,* 530 U.S. 914, 932 (2000), the United States Supreme Court opined "that significant medical authority supports the proposition that in some circumstances, [partial birth abortion] would be

the safest procedure" for pregnant women who wish to undergo an abortion. Thus, the Court struck down the State of Nebraska's ban on partial-birth abortion procedures, concluding that it placed an "undue burden" on women seeking abortions because it failed to include an exception for partial-birth abortions deemed necessary to preserve the "health" of the mother.

(4) In reaching this conclusion, the Court deferred to the Federal district court's factual findings that the partial-birth abortion procedure was statistically and medically as safe as, and in many circumstances safer than, alternative abortion procedures.

(5) However, the great weight of evidence presented at the *Stenberg* trial and other trials challenging partial-birth abortion bans, as well as at extensive Congressional hearings, demonstrates that a partial-birth abortion is never necessary to preserve the health of a woman, poses significant health risks to a woman upon whom the procedure is performed, and is outside of the standard of medical care.

. . .

(13) There exists substantial record evidence upon which Congress has reached its conclusion that a ban on partial-birth abortion is not required to contain a "health" exception, because the facts indicate that a partial-birth abortion is never necessary to preserve the health of a woman, poses serious risks to a woman's health, and lies outside the standard of medical care. Congress was informed by extensive hearings held during the 104th, 105th, and 107th Congresses and passed a ban on partial-birth abortion in the 104th, 105th, and 106th Congresses. These findings reflect the very informed judgment of the Congress that a partial-birth abortion is never necessary to preserve the health of a woman, poses serious risks to a woman's health, and lies outside the standard of medical care, and should, therefore, be banned.

(14) Pursuant to the testimony received during extensive legislative hearings during the 104th, 105th, and 107th Congresses, Congress finds and declares that:

(A) Partial-birth abortion poses serious risks to the health of a woman undergoing the procedure. Those risks include, among other things: an increase in a woman's risk of suffering from cervical incompetence, a result of cervical dilation making it difficult or impossible for a woman to successfully carry a subsequent pregnancy to term; an increased risk of uterine rupture, abruption, amniotic fluid embolus, and trauma to the uterus as a result of converting the child to a footling breech position, a procedure which, according to a leading obstetrics textbook, "there are very few, if any, indications for . . . other than for delivery of a second twin"; and a risk of lacerations and secondary hemorrhaging due to the doctor blindly forcing a sharp instrument into the base of the unborn child's skull while he or she is lodged in the birth canal, an act which could result in severe bleeding, brings with it the threat of shock, and could ultimately result in maternal death.

(B) There is no credible medical evidence that partial-birth abortions are safe or are safer than other abortion procedures. No controlled studies of partial-birth abortions have been conducted nor have any comparative studies been conducted to demonstrate its safety and efficacy compared to other abortion methods. Furthermore, there have been no articles published in peer-reviewed journals that establish that partial-birth abortions are superior in any way to established abortion procedures. Indeed, unlike other more commonly used abortion procedures, there are currently no medical schools that provide instruction on abortions that include the instruction in partial-birth abortions in their curriculum.

(C) A prominent medical association has concluded that partial-birth abortion is not an accepted medical practice, that it has "never been subject to even a minimal amount of the normal medical practice development," that "the relative advantages and disadvantages of the procedure in specific circumstances remain unknown," and that "there is no consensus among obstetricians about its use." The association has further noted that partial-birth abortion is broadly disfavored by both medical experts and the public, is "ethically wrong," and "is never the only appropriate procedure."

(D) Neither the plaintiff in *Stenberg v. Carhart,* nor the experts who testified on his behalf, have identified a single circumstance during which a partial-birth abortion was necessary to preserve the health of a woman.

(E) The physician credited with developing the partial-birth abortion procedure has testified that he has never encountered a situation where a partial-birth abortion was medically necessary to achieve the desired outcome and, thus, is never medically necessary to preserve the health of a woman.

(F) A ban on the partial-birth abortion procedure will therefore advance the health interests of pregnant women seeking to terminate a pregnancy.

(G) In light of this overwhelming evidence, Congress and the States have a compelling interest in prohibiting partial-birth abortions. In addition to promoting maternal health, such a prohibition will draw a bright line that clearly distinguishes abortion and infanticide, that preserves the integrity of the medical profession, and promotes respect for human life.

(H) Based upon *Roe v. Wade,* 410 U.S. 113 (1973) and *Planned Parenthood v. Casey,* 505 U.S. 833 (1992), a governmental interest in protecting the life of a child during the delivery process arises by virtue of the fact that during a partial-birth abortion, labor is induced and the birth process has begun. This distinction was recognized in *Roe* when the Court noted, without comment, that the Texas parturition statute, which prohibited one from killing a child "in a state of being born and before actual birth," was not under attack. This interest becomes compelling as the child emerges from the maternal body. A child that is completely born is a full, legal person entitled to constitutional protections afforded a "person" under the United States Constitution. Partial-birth abortions involve the killing of a child that is in the process, in fact mere inches away from, becoming a "person." Thus, the government has a heightened interest in protecting the life of the partially-born child.

(I) This, too, has not gone unnoticed in the medical community, where a prominent medical association has recognized that partial-birth abortions are "ethically different from other destructive abortion techniques because the fetus, normally twenty weeks or longer in gestation, is killed outside of the womb." According to this medical association, the "partial birth" gives the fetus an autonomy which separates it from the right of the woman to choose treatments for her own body.

(J) Partial-birth abortion also confuses the medical, legal, and ethical duties of physicians to preserve and promote life, as the physician acts directly against the physical life of a child, whom he or she had just delivered, all but the head, out of the womb, in order to end that life. Partial-birth abortion thus appropriates the terminology and techniques used by obstetricians in the delivery of living children—obstetricians who preserve and protect the life of the mother and the child—and instead uses those techniques to end the life of the partially-born child.

(K) Thus, by aborting a child in the manner that purposefully seeks to kill the child after he or she has begun the process of birth, partial-birth abortion undermines the public's perception of the appropriate role of a physician during the delivery process, and perverts a process during which life is brought into the world, in order to destroy a partially-born child.

(L) The gruesome and inhumane nature of the partial-birth abortion procedure and its disturbing similarity to the killing of a newborn infant promotes a complete disregard for infant human life that can only be countered by a prohibition of the procedure.

(M) The vast majority of babies killed during partial-birth abortions are alive until the end of the procedure. It is a medical fact, however, that unborn infants at this stage can feel pain when subjected to painful stimuli and that their perception of this pain is even more intense than that of newborn infants and older children when subjected to the same stimuli. Thus, during a partial-birth abortion procedure, the child will fully experience the pain associated with piercing his or her skull and sucking out his or her brain.

(N) Implicitly approving such a brutal and inhumane procedure by choosing not to prohibit it will further coarsen society to the humanity of not only newborns, but all vulnerable and innocent human life, making it increasingly difficult to protect such life. Thus, Congress has a compelling interest in acting—indeed it must act—to prohibit this inhumane procedure.

(O) For these reasons, Congress finds that partial-birth abortion is never medically indicated to preserve the health of the mother; is in fact unrecognized as a valid abortion procedure by the mainstream medical community; poses additional health risks to the mother; blurs the line between abortion and infanticide in the killing of a partially-born child just inches from birth; and confuses the role of the physician in childbirth and should, therefore, be banned.

Comment

Although the events in the Califano case took place early in the debate about policy on abortion, the dilemmas that the decision makers faced then—in many respects more clearly posed than now—continue to create ethical challenges. In the Califano case, Father McCormick helpfully identifies three levels of moral questions about abortion: (1) the personal morality of having an abortion; (2) the political morality of legalizing and funding abortion; and (3) the obligations of public officials in shaping and carrying out the law. We cannot ignore the first level of personal morality in considering our positions on public policy and the obligations of public officials, but these cases focus on the second and third levels.

Begin with the issue of public policy—whether the government should fund abortions for poor women. Note Califano's responses to a representative from the National Women's Political Caucus: "I believe abortion is morally wrong," and "I oppose federal funding for abortion." Must the second position necessarily follow from the first? Senator Packwood and Judy Woodruff suggest that it would be unfair for the government not to fund abortions for the poor as long as they are legal. They thereby attempt to separate the question of whether abortion should be legal from the question of whether the government should subsidize abortion for poor women once it is legal. Assess the responses of Califano and Carter to the defense of federal funding on grounds of fairness. Is there any principle other than fairness that would favor funding? On what moral grounds (if any) can one distinguish between the funding of all legal abortions for poor pregnant women and the funding of only those abortions that terminate pregnancies resulting from rape and incest?

One philosopher has suggested that legalizing abortion but not subsidizing it is a fair compromise between the pro-life and pro-choice positions, although it completely satisfies the moral claims of neither. If a compromise is the best solution to the public policy question, are these the right terms? Should the terms of a fair compromise be more or less generous to poor women? Is a compromise the best way to resolve the public policy question?

Consider the question of whether Califano was correct in thinking that he could act responsibly in public office while personally opposing abortion. Did he use the correct standard—willingness to enforce whatever law Congress passes—in deciding to accept the position? Having accepted the position, did Califano act properly in office? Consider the ways in which his opposition to abortion might have affected his conduct in office, including his public statements. Was he justified in interpreting the intent of Congress as he did in writing HEW regulations on funding abortion? Should he have compromised with the president on the paragraph concerning rape and incest?

The moral conflicts Califano faced might have been even more difficult had Congress instructed HEW to fund abortions through Medicaid. Would Califano then have been justified in doing anything to oppose such a policy? Had Califano been committed to the position that poor women have a right to subsidized abortion, what should he have done in the face of congressional action to the contrary? If both the president and Congress are determined to preserve the Hyde amendment unrevised, are there any circumstances under which someone committed to subsidizing abortions for poor women should accept the office of secretary of Health and Human Services?

As chairman of South Dakota's Senate Judiciary Committee, Heidepriem had the responsibility of overseeing a fair process for considering an antiabortion bill that he opposed on moral as well as legal grounds. Are there any political circumstances under which Heidepriem would have been justified in subordinating procedural fairness to abortion rights, or vice versa? Suppose that Heidepriem had reason to believe that the antiabortion bill had a better chance of passing if it reached the floor for discussion. Would he have been justified in doing his best—within the law and rules of the Senate—to prevent the bill from reaching the floor? Or suppose that everyone in his district had written the senator urging him to vote for the bill. Are there any reasons that his constituents might have offered for their opposition to abortion that would have obligated Heidepriem to vote for the bill?

In light of his support for *Roe v. Wade,* which took the issue of legalizing abortion out of legislatures and into the judicial arena, Heidepriem's critics might question the consistency of his commitment to "make the decision [concerning the antiabortion bill] in front of the people who care about the question." How might Heidepriem defend this commitment and the practical implications for open legislative discussion that he associated with it? Is such a commitment consistent with giving the judiciary authority over the issue of legalizing abortion? Suppose that an open legislative debate led to the passage of the antiabortion bill and its support by the overwhelming majority of Heidepriem's constituents. Would Heidepriem then be obligated to defend the law?

Consider whether Heidepriem's reliance on legal arguments to oppose the bill strengthened his case. What weight, if any, should his colleagues and constituents have placed on Heidepriem's prediction that South Dakota would be embroiled in expensive legal struggles for years to come if the legislature passed the antiabortion bill? If you agree with Heidepriem's pro-choice position, consider what moral weight you would place on the risk of expensive litigation to defend a South Dakota law legalizing abortion in the face of a Supreme Court that had overturned *Roe v. Wade*. Did Heidepriem and his colleagues on either side of the issue overlook any legal or moral arguments that should have been central to public consideration of the bill?

By 2003, when Congress passed the ban on what its supporters called "partial-birth abortion" (and its opponents called by its medical names, such as "dilation and extraction"), the Supreme Court had repeatedly affirmed a woman's basic right to an abortion and also invalidated state laws that regulated abortion without making an exception for women's health or life. Yet this thirty-year history had not dampened the conviction of many abortion opponents that it is immoral and should be illegal. The congressional debate over partial birth abortion brings back into the national political spotlight the moral question of when, if ever, a fetus's right may override a woman's right. It highlights the deep disagreements of both fact and value that divide proponents and opponents of a ban.

To begin to analyze these disagreements, first specify precisely what moral rights are at stake on each side of the debate, and how those rights are valued by each side. Second, determine what factual assumptions divide the disputants, and whether there is an obvious way of resolving even the factual disputes. Third, clearly articulate the grounds on which you would defend your conclusion on the substantive debate about the ban. Next, consider the political ethics of Congress's passing a law that is apparently inconsistent with recent decisions of the Supreme Court on the subject. What are the strongest arguments that proponents of the ban can offer in favor of passing a law that appears to contradict *Stenberg v. Carhart*? What are the strongest arguments that opponents of the ban can offer against doing so? Finally, see if you can find any common ground in this ongoing debate.

It is sometimes suggested that one's position on the procedural question in such cases—whether Congress or the Court should have the final word—is entirely dictated by one's position on the substantive question—which right should prevail. But any adequate political ethics should provide a principled basis for distinguishing these positions. It should keep open the possibility of justifying the view of those who oppose the ban but defer to Congress, and those who favor the ban but defer to the Court. If you agree that the distinction should be maintained, what is the best rationale for it? If you disagree, what limits if any would you place on using any procedural means to achieve the substantive ends you favor?

Federal Funding for Stem Cell Research*

In his first major public policy address, George W. Bush announced that he would make federal funding available for limited research involving stem cells derived from human embryos. He also revealed his intention to create a council to study both the medical and the moral aspects of stem cell research and offer policy recommendations. These announcements initiated a diverse, nationwide discussion of the ethics of stem cell research.

Stem cells are a group of "undifferentiated and unspecialized" cells that have the remarkable capacity to transform themselves into many different cell types in the body (liver cells, for instance, or brain cells, or kidney cells). Stem cells first arise in the human embryo, and as they age and differentiate during the embryo's natural development, they lose some of their capacity to diversify. The most useful stem cells for research are therefore those taken directly from the human embryo in its early developmental stages, or from aborted fetuses. (Embryos are fertilized eggs that have not yet implanted in the womb.) Once harvested from either of these sources, stem cells can be preserved in vitro for an apparently unlimited amount of time—they renew themselves.

Medical researchers have become interested in stem cells for several reasons. In the words of the President's Council on Bioethics: "stem cells and their derivatives may prove a valuable source of transplantable cells and tissues for repair and regeneration. If these healing powers could be harnessed, the medical benefits for humankind would be immense, perhaps ushering in an era of truly regenerative medicine." (The full report of the council

is available as *Monitoring Stem Cell Research: A Report of the President's Council on Bioethics,* January 2004, www.bioethics.gov). The benefits of such a medicine could eventually involve the development of cures for debilitating and congenital diseases like diabetes, Parkinson's disease, and Alzheimer's. None of this is yet possible, however, and scientists disagree somewhat about stem cells' potential medical benefits.

The embryos from which stem cells are extracted are taken from in vitro fertilization (IVF) clinics, which routinely discard and destroy embryos no longer needed by their clients. Scientists use these discarded embryos for their medical research. In doing so, they destroy these embryos—there is no known way of extracting stem cells from an embryo without destroying it. Stem cell research has therefore become an extremely controversial public issue, and the debate over the ethics of stem cell research usually turns on the moral status of the human embryo. Critics of the practice believe that any deliberate destruction of the human embryo is a deeply immoral form of killing. (As mentioned before, stem cells can also be obtained from the bodies of aborted fetuses—and this too raises obvious moral problems for those who oppose abortion.)

A range of answers have been given to the question of the embryo's moral status. Some believe that the embryo possesses the full moral status of an adult human being—it is a genetically complete being which will blossom into a mature human if left alone in the woman's body, and it is therefore morally indistinguishable from an adult person. Others argue that it has no moral status at all—it is a bundle of cells without the capacity for feeling, very much like unfertilized eggs and sperm, and does not yet possess any moral standing. Still others

---

*Alex Zakaras wrote the introduction and selected the excerpts presented in this section.

take an intermediate position, arguing that the embryo has moral salience, but that it is not the moral equal of an adult human being. These critics argue that embryos can be destroyed only for overriding moral reasons (such as the alleviation of human suffering through medical research). These different positions typically give rise to different styles of moral argument.

The problem can be framed in two competing ways, each of which highlights one of the two important moral imperatives at issue in the debate. First, it might be asked whether it is morally permissible to destroy human embryos (or use aborted fetuses) for the purpose of medical research. Second, it could be asked whether it is morally permissible to ban research that could prove powerfully beneficial to sick and dying human beings around the world. These questions achieved a new urgency in 1998, following the publication of two papers (written by American scientists) detailing the methods by which stem cells could be "harvested" from embryos and aborted fetuses.

What follows is testimony before the Senate Appropriations Committee (given just before Bush's 2001 speech), as well as excerpts from a later debate at a session of the President's Council on Bioethics.

HEARINGS BEFORE THE SENATE APPROPRIATIONS COMMITTEE JULY 18, AUGUST 1, AND OCTOBER 31, 2001

SENATOR TOM HARKIN

I have co-sponsored with Senator Specter a bill that would allow federally-funded scientists to derive human stem cells from embryos under three conditions: the embryos must be obtained from an IVF clinic; the donor must have provided informed consent; and the embryo must no longer be needed for infertility treatments. The American Society of Cell Biology has estimated that 100,000 human embryos are

currently frozen in IVF clinics, in excess of their clinical need.

Let me be clear about why we are here, why we have introduced our bill, and why we have fought so hard to make sure that the Federal government supports this research. We introduced this legislation because we want to save lives and to find cures for some of the most debilitating diseases that affect mankind. We have seen the . . . human face of these diseases. We have been moved by the testimony of doctors, patients, family members and advocates that have been touched by Juvenile Diabetes, Parkinson's, ALS and Alzheimer's. . . . That is why we are here. This is not an abstract issue. It is about saving the lives of millions of Americans.

It is imperative that the Federal government support this research. The government has an important role to play in supporting basic science. Basic science will always be under-funded by the private sector because this type of research does not immediately get products onto the market. There is no immediate profit—but there are tremendous long-term benefits.

Equally important are the strict, ethical guidelines that will come with Federal funding. It is important to note that stem cell research in the private sector is not subject to Federal monitoring.. . . .

At many points in our history, religion and science have intersected. And at every point, we have paused to measure our morality and the ancient lessons of religion against our science and the new frontiers we explore. As well we should.

Science must be infused with our morality and humanity. When it is not, it can be more about amusing ourselves with our own ingenuity than pursuing real scientific breakthroughs that improve our lives.

In the case of stem cell research, I strongly believe that we have measured the question carefully, and that it is time to move forward. Where there cannot be new life, there can be new hope—new hope for the thousands of Americans suffering from horrible and debilitating disease that withers the mind and body and robs us of our loved ones. In the case of stem cell research, we can be true to our loved ones and true to our values. In fact, it would be an affront to our values if we did not proceed, with caution, and investigate how stem cell research can better our lives and the lives of all Americans.

SENATOR ORRIN G. HATCH

Today's hearing centers on a major opportunity presented to the biomedical research community: stem cell research. As Nobel laureate and former NIH Director, Harold Varmus, has characterized the situation by saying that, it is not unrealistic to say that [stem cell research] has the potential to revolutionize the practice of medicine.

I would like to take this opportunity to share with you how I came to my decision to support federal funding for embryonic stem cell research.

Over many months, I devoted hours of study to this important issue, reflecting on my spiritual teachings, the law, the science, and the ethical issues presented by embryonic stem cell research.

And let me be absolutely clear: I hold strong pro-life, pro-family values and strongly oppose abortion. I conclude that support of embryonic stem cell research is consistent with and advances pro-life and pro-family values. . . . Let me emphasize four points for you this morning.

First, I think that support of this vital research is a pro-life, pro-family position. This research holds out promise for more than 100 million Americans suffering from a variety of diseases including heart disease, multiple sclerosis, Parkinson's, Alzheimer's, ALS, cancer, and diabetes.

Second, in the in vitro fertilization process, it is inevitable that extra embryos are created, embryos that simply will not be implanted in a mother's womb. As these embryos sit frozen in a test tube, outside the womb, under today's technology, there is no chance for them to develop into a person.

While I have no objection to considering ways to foster adoption of embryos, there are a host of issues associated with this which must be worked out. And while those issues are being considered, the reality today is that each year thousands and I am told the number may be tens of thousands— of embryos are routinely destroyed. Why shouldn't these embryos slated for destruction be used for the good of mankind?

Third, while I understand that many in the pro-life community will disagree with me, I believe that a human's life begins in the womb, not in a petri dish or refrigerator. It is inevitable that in the IVF process, extra embryos are created that will simply not be implanted in a mother's womb. To me, the morality of the situation dictates that these embryos, which are routinely discarded, be used to improve and extend life. The tragedy would be in not using these embryos to save lives when the alternative is that they will be destroyed.

Fourth, there is no guarantee that any stem cell research will reap the benefits we hope, but it is clear that embryonic stem cell research holds tremendous promise. Some hold out adult stem cell research as a good alternative. By all means, we should continue adult stem cell research. But, I do not believe it would be wise to cut off support for embryonic stem cell research, since many eminent scientists believe it is the more promising avenue of research.

While I am not a scientist, my preliminary reading of the report strongly suggests that embryonic stem cell research may have some substantial advantages over adult stem cells at least at this stage of the research.

Consider the following excerpts from the summary of the new NIH Stem Cell Report:

Stem cells in adult tissues do not appear to have the same capacity to differentiate as do embryonic stem cells or embryonic germ cells.

Human embryonic stem cells can be generated in abundant quantities in the laboratory and can be grown (allowed to proliferate) in their undifferentiated (or unspecified) state for many generations.

[R]esearchers have had difficulty finding laboratory conditions under which some adult stem cells can proliferate without becoming specialized.

Current evidence indicates that the capability of adult stem cells to give rise to many different specialized cell types is more limited than that of embryonic stem cells.

However, it is also important to note what the NIH report does not say. It does not say that the promise of embryonic stem cell research obviates the need to pursue adult stem cell research. The report indicates that both embryonic and adult stem cell research hold great promise. I believe that both avenues should be zealously pursued.

In the end, it is my hope that we are able to conduct research that will improve and prolong human life. I truly believe that cures for diseases like diabetes, Parkinson's, Alzheimer's, ALS, diabetes, multiple sclerosis, heart disease, and cancer can be found if we continue with this research. That's why we must take advantage of all ethical and promising types of research. . . .

Mr. Chairman, today we stand on the threshold of a great opportunity. Embryonic stem cell research may be the single, most important scientific discovery in our lifetimes. The most renowned scientists in the country have told us that this research holds forth the promise of treatments and perhaps cures for some of the most debilitating diseases affecting our nation, and the world. I think it would be a mistake to cut off federal support for this research. . . .

MR. RICHARD DOERFLINGER, ASSOCIATE DIRECTOR FOR POLICY DEVELOPMENT, UNITED STATES CONFERENCE OF CATHOLIC BISHOPS

In our view, forcing U.S. taxpayers to subsidize research that relies on deliberate destruction of human embryos for their stem cells is illegal, immoral, and unnecessary.

It is illegal because it violates an appropriations rider (the Dickey amendment) passed every year since 1995 by Congress. That provision forbids funding "research in which" human embryos (whether initially created for research purposes or not) are harmed or destroyed outside the womb. National Institutes of Health guidelines approved by the Clinton Administration nonetheless give researchers detailed instructions on how to obtain human embryos for destructive cell harvesting, if they wish to qualify for federal grants in "human pluripotent stem cell research." Clearly, obtaining and destroying embryos is an integral part of this project, even if the specific act of destroying embryos does not directly receive federal funds. By implementing these guidelines, the federal government would encourage researchers to conduct destructive embryo experiments that are punishable as felonies in some states.

This proposal is immoral because it violates a central tenet of all civilized codes on human experimentation beginning with the Nuremberg Code: It approves doing deadly harm to a member of the human species solely for the sake of potential benefit to others. The embryos to be destroyed by researchers in this campaign are at the same stage of development as embryos in the womb who have been protected as human subjects in federally funded research since 1975. President Clinton's National Bioethics Advisory Commission (NBAC) and its 1994 predecessor, the NIH Human Embryo Research Panel, conceded that the early human embryo is a form of developing human life that deserves our respect. Treating human life as mere research material is no way to show respect.

Finally, this proposal is unnecessary because adult stem cells and other alternatives are already achieving some of the goals for which embryonic stem cells have been proposed, and new clinical uses are constantly being discovered.

In our view, human life deserves full respect and protection at every stage and in every condition. The intrinsic wrong of destroying innocent human life cannot be "outweighed" by any material advantage—in other words, the end does not justify an immoral means. Acceptance of a purely utilitarian argument for mistreating human life would endanger anyone and everyone who may be very young, very old, very disabled, or otherwise very marginalized in our society. However, even the Clinton Administration's bioethics advisors, who denied human embryos the moral status of "person," concluded that they could only be destroyed for research as a last resort, if no alternative course existed.

It cannot be denied that these alternatives are available. To be sure, further study will be needed to determine their full potential. But to fund destructive embryo research now, alongside these morally acceptable alternatives, would be to deny any moral status at all to human embryonic life. For that is what we would do if there were no moral issue at stake. Funding embryonic stem cell research here and now will force all taxpayers to act as though they agree with the international chairman of the Juvenile Diabetes Foundation that human embryos have no more value or dignity than a goldfish.

This view of the human embryo as a goldfish has apparently garnered support from some members of Congress who have generally opposed abortion. Their claim is that human life does not begin until placed in a mother's womb. Biologically, however, this is an absurd claim. An embryo's development is directed completely from within—the womb simply provides a nurturing environment. Scientists tell us it would be technically possible to nurture a human embryo in a man's body by abdominal pregnancy, or in a mammal of another species, or even (someday) in an artificial womb. Upon being born could such a person morally be killed for his or her stem cells, because he or she never lived inside a woman's womb?

A subtly different argument has also emerged to try to justify using embryos from fertility clinics for destructive experiments. While human embryos ordinarily deserve respect, goes this argument, these particular embryos do not, because they "would be discarded anyway" by their parents. But this is, to say the least, fallacious reasoning.

If parents were neglecting or abusing their child at a later stage, this would provide no justification whatever for the government to move in and help destroy the child for research material. We do not kill terminally ill patients for their organs, although they will die soon anyway, or even harvest vital organs from death row prisoners, although they will be put to death soon anyway. Federal law prohibits federally funded researchers from doing any harm to an unborn child slated for abortion, though that child will soon be discarded anyway (see 42 USC Sec. 289g). If people's value depends entirely on the extent to which other people "want" them, they have no inherent value at all. So on reflection, this argument ultimately reduces to the argument of "embryo as goldfish."

The argument also rests on a false premise. The embryos slated for destructive research under the NIH guidelines are those deemed to be "in excess of clinical need" by fertility clinics. This simply means that they are not needed or wanted by their parents for reproduction at present. Parents in this situation are routinely offered several options, including: saving the embryos for possible later use (by far the most frequently chosen), discarding them, or donating them to another couple so they can have a child. The NIH guidelines require that these parents be asked to consider donating their embryos for destructive cell harvesting at the same time that they are offered these other options. Some couples who would otherwise have allowed their embryonic children to live—in their own family or another—will instead have them killed for government research. That is why the adoptive couples of some of these former "frozen embryos" have filed suit against the guidelines. . . .

NIGEL M. DE S. CAMERON, PH.D.,
EXECUTIVE CHAIR, THE CENTER
FOR BIOETHICS AND PUBLIC POLICY,
LONDON, ENGLAND

Two great questions confront the human race at the start of the biotech century. The second, presently only on the horizons of our thinking and yet of incalculable import, will focus our growing capacity to design, determine, transform ourselves and our nature; the incremental progression toward the so-called "post-human" future. The first question is the one that confronts us today: whether we should use members of our own kind, Homo sapiens, in whatever stage of biological existence, for a purpose that is other than the good of the individual concerned; whether we should sanction the use of ourselves, in however early a form, as experimental subjects whose final end is destruction.

Let me offer four observations on our dilemma.

First, it seemed until recently to be widely agreed that human embryos should never be manufactured simply in order to be destroyed through experiment, however worthy the experiment. This principle is, for example, enshrined in the European Convention on Biomedicine and Human Rights, the one international bioethics treaty; and was memorably captured some years ago in a *Washington Post* editorial in the ringing phrase: "The creation of human embryos specifically for research that will destroy them is unconscionable." Yet the Jones' Institute has brazenly announced that they have done just that. And as Charles Krauthammer's recent pro-stem-cell research piece notes, the cloning debate has focused the same issue. The chorus of support for Greenwood-Deutsch has been fed precisely by a scientific-industrial community eager to clone and destroy embryos for scientific-industrial purposes.

The problem, of course, is one of drawing lines; the challenge of consistency. May a line truly be drawn that will permit experimentation on clinically "spare" embryos, a line that will stand forever and in the face, we may expect, of mounting commercial and clinical opportunity that argues for their creation to order? That is of course the compromise that has been floated in various quarters, most notably and seriously by Senator Frist. The level of support for embryo cloning-to-order in Greenwood-Deutsch, and now the timely "ocular proof" of the Jones Institute, suggests the naiveté of such policy hopes, since in the minds of most of those who lead the call for "spare" embryo research only there is only a modest distinction between this politic option and the Jones way. It is a distinction that falls far, far short of what the *Post* designated "unconscionable." It is not, as we might put it, that we believe that further dominoes will fall; they are falling all around us. For the logic of the experimental abuse of "spare" human embryos depends ultimately on so meager a valuation of the embryo itself that their creation-to-order is inevitable. If the embryo is at base object and not in any sense subject, what is to prevent it? It is reported that one celebrity recently announced here on the Hill and in defense of embryonic stem-cell research that the embryo is of similar moral standing to a goldfish.

Second, I do not propose to get drawn into the extensive debate surrounding the relative merits of embryonic and other, typically adult, stem-cells. Plainly, some and perhaps all of the good things that are prophesied to be the fruit of embryonic stem-cells may be attained using adult cells or other means. It is ironic, and to be regretted, that this debate has sometimes seemed to hinge on whether adult stem-cell work is likely to be as fruitful as the embryonic kind, as if the moral question, while of some weight, could be discounted by a certain evaluation of likely relative clinical outcomes. This is a profound moral debate about what we will and will not do to our own kind, for whatever alleged benefit.

Third, I believe that we are losing sight of the middle ground. By that I mean that it is by no means necessary to take the view that the early embryo is a full human person in order to be convinced that deleterious experimentation is improper. There are many possible grounds for such a view— that we do not know if the embryo possesses full human dignity and should therefore be prudent; that the embryo possesses the potential to be a full human person and that such inbuilt potentiality entails profound respect, a view widely held and deeply threatened in this debate; or that membership in our species is enough to distinguish the human embryo from all other laboratory artifacts. Indeed, the widely held view that embryos should not be specially created for experimental purposes itself reveals a strong if undefined disposition to protect the embryo from abuse.

Fourth, let me share my sense of dismay at the degree to which this debate has sometimes degenerated into an iteration and reiteration of the potential benefits of this kind of experimentation, as if those who oppose public funding for what they consider unethical research are either ignorant of or heedless toward disease and its sufferers. The celebrity argument is a sham, an attempt to short-circuit the moral assessment of means by the crass assertion of ends. It is an embarrassment to the cause of ethics in public policy.

For the question we face is distinctly ethical in character. At the heart of our conception of civilization lies the principle of restraint: that there are things we shall not do, shall never do, even though they may bring us benefit; some things we shall never do, though the heavens fall.

As we stand on the threshold of the biotech century, we could hardly confront a decision that is more onerous, since the promised benefits from this technology may be great. Yet that is of course simply to focus the moral question. If there are things that we should not do, it is easy for us to refuse to do them when they offer no benefit. When the benefit they offer is modest, the choice is still not hard. The challenge to morals and to public policy lies precisely here, where the benefits seem great. Yet it is here also that our intuitive respect for the early embryo requires us to pay a price. In a culture fixated with the satisfaction of its needs and the healing of its woes, it has become hard even to say that we shall never, for whatever benefit, experiment on our own kind? Shall we do evil, that good may come?

ARTHUR CAPLAN, PH.D., DIRECTOR, CENTER FOR BIOETHICS, UNIVERSITY OF PENNSYLVANIA

I think in some ways I, too, am going to follow Dr. Cameron's lead. I am not going to spend any time today in my brief remarks going over the benefits, be they from celebrities, or be they from scientists, or be they simply from patients who are suffering with disability or disease. I think we can concede that stem cell research is promising. I think there may be a long road to travel to deliver on that promise, but nonetheless, it seems to me the promise is there, and that can be conceded regardless of discussions about possible alternative strategies.

What I would like to do is focus instead on a couple of ethical points about how I would frame this debate. I have been following it closely, in fact, since I first came before this committee about 9 months ago, I think, to talk about this issue, and, like Dr. Cameron, I, too, have been a little bit put off by some of the tone of the debate. I think people who are arguing for respect for human life are commanding a moral position that is deserving of careful listening. I appreciate the committee soliciting all opinion, but at the end of the day, I think the framework being articulated is not correct.

It would be wrong for sure, morally, to say that we can benefit people who are in need, or future generations, by killing some people today. There is no doubt that a principle we should not break is that we should not murder to benefit. As the Senator knows, this has been a major issue in a related area that he and I have had a chance to talk about, organ donation. We know that we can benefit by making kidneys and livers and hearts available from deceased persons, but we also know that we must not hasten death, cause death, or in any way be involved with death, bringing it about, in order to do the benefit.

On the other hand, people die from many tragic reasons, and we do try, then, to approach individuals and see whether they wish to make something good happen out of these tragic circumstances. There may be suicides, there may be murders, there may be child abuse. There are all kinds of conditions that sadly produce the availability of cadaver organs.

I believe that in this debate there is a moral equation that does not hold, and that is that embryos are either persons, or to be treated as human beings from the moment of conception. I think factually this is not the case. I think that what we are talking about and what most Americans believe is that we have something that is a potential or possible person in the right circumstances. In a dish, in a freezer, that potentiality will go nowhere.

If we look at the circumstance of embryos, and if we look at what our biologists are telling us about understanding the genetics involved in development, we know that many embryos are not ever going to become persons, no matter what we did to them. It is why infertility treatment is so difficult.

The fact that embryos may have genetic errors, if you will, blueprint problems, and many do, and that increasingly, as women age, those are more manifest, making fertility impossible after one reaches their fifties, is an indication that not all embryos have potentiality, so one premise I would put before you

and the subcommittee to ponder is that not all embryos do have the potential to become human beings. We know this.

Second, when we store, freeze, and put them aside, it is often because in the opinion of physicians, these particular embryos are not likely to become persons, and the longer they are kept frozen and stored somewhat diminishes that potential even further.

That means that what we are talking about to begin with is not, if we propose to destroy embryos, necessarily killing. We are talking instead about, if you will, the destruction of potential, possible persons. We are also talking, if you will, about the destruction of many things that have no possibility of becoming persons.

If I am to make a trade-off, then, the other principle I have to follow is, do we make things with the intent of destroying them, or have we a situation where for good motives, people trying to have children, for good reasons, people wanting to have babies, these entities are created and exist, but are no longer wanted. As the Senator is well aware, there is something like 100,000 of these, at a minimum, around the United States. Their fate is never to become children.

I see that as somewhat analogous to the situation with transplant. No one set out to make this situation occur. It is a byproduct of our ignorance and inability to successfully help people who want to have children. We overproduce embryos. They are left behind, and they are ultimately going to be destroyed. If we grant, then, that not all embryos have the potential to become persons, then not all embryos are persons, and that we have, if you will, an enormous number of embryos that never will become persons, and trying to make some good happen from the reality of the existence of those stored embryos, which abound, leads me to one last observation.

We are talking here about research that will involve embryonic stem cells, but we are talking also about research that is relatively new, that relatively few people can do. I have to report to the Senator that in trying to figure out—and you will see this in my written testimony—what number of embryos are we talking about for the next few years to demonstrate the feasibility of this research, I would estimate, if 15 researchers worked with five embryo cell lines, we might be talking about something less than 200 embryos out of 100,000 frozen that their fate is destruction, or permanent storage. It seems to me the moral equation comes out in favor of those who are real, here and now, with real needs and real disabilities and real problems. That promise should be delivered on.

So I would argue, using those facts, and the moral principle that making something good happen out of the reality of something unfortunate exists, the surplus, absolute huge number of embryos that already exist, if we are in a situation, what we are talking about then is possibility of potentiality that will never be actualized, I think it is a trade that this committee should pursue aggressively in order to bring benefits to the American people.

EXCERPTS FROM PRESIDENT GEORGE W. BUSH'S ADDRESS, AUGUST 9, 2001

As I thought through this issue I kept returning to two fundamental questions. First, are these frozen embryos human life and therefore something precious to be protected? And second, if they're going to be destroyed anyway, shouldn't they be used for a greater good, for research that has the potential to save and improve other lives? . . .

On the first issue, are these embryos human life? Well, one researcher told me he believes this five-day-old cluster of cells is not an embryo, not yet an individual but a pre-embryo. He argued that it has the potential for life, but it is not a life because it cannot develop on its own.

An ethicist dismissed that as a callous attempt at rationalization. "Make no mistake," he told me, "that cluster of cells is the same way you and I, and all the rest of us, started our lives. One goes with a heavy heart if we

use these," he said, "because we are dealing with the seeds of the next generation."

And to the other crucial question—If these are going to be destroyed anyway, why not use them for good purpose?—I also found different answers.

Many of these embryos are byproducts of a process that helps create life and we should allow couples to donate them to science so they can be used for good purpose instead of wasting their potential.

Others will argue there is no such thing as excess life and the fact that a living being is going to die does not justify experimenting on it or exploiting it as a natural resource.

At its core, this issue forces us to confront fundamental questions about the beginnings of life and the ends of science. It lives at a difficult moral intersection, juxtaposing the need to protect life in all its phases with the prospect of saving and improving life in all its stages. . . .

In recent weeks, we learned that scientists have created human embryos in test tubes solely to experiment on them. This is deeply troubling and a warning sign that should prompt all of us to think through these issues very carefully.

Embryonic stem cell research is at the leading edge of a series of moral hazards. . . . Researchers are telling us the next step could be to clone human beings to create individual designer stem cells, essentially to grow another you, to be available in case you need another heart or lung or liver.

I strongly oppose human cloning, as do most Americans. We recoil at the idea of growing human beings for spare body parts or creating life for our convenience.

And while we must devote enormous energy to conquering disease, it is equally important that we pay attention to the moral concerns raised by the new frontier of human embryo stem cell research. Even the most noble ends do not justify any means.

My position on these issues is shaped by deeply held beliefs. I'm a strong supporter of science and technology, and believe they have the potential for incredible good—to improve lives, to save life, to conquer disease. Research offers hope that millions of our loved ones may be cured of a disease and rid of their suffering. . . .

I also believe human life is a sacred gift from our creator. I worry about a culture that devalues life, and believe as your president I have an important obligation to foster and encourage respect for life in America and throughout the world.

And while we're all hopeful about the potential of this research, no one can be certain that the science will live up to the hope it has generated.

Eight years ago, scientists believed fetal tissue research offered great hope for cures and treatments, yet the progress to date has not lived up to its initial expectations. Embryonic stem cell research offers both great promise and great peril, so I have decided we must proceed with great care.

As a result of private research, more than 60 genetically diverse stem cell lines already exist. They were created from embryos that have already been destroyed, and they have the ability to regenerate themselves indefinitely, creating ongoing opportunities for research.

I have concluded that we should allow federal funds to be used for research on these existing stem cell lines, where the life-and-death decision has already been made. Leading scientists tell me research on these 60 lines has great promise that could lead to breakthrough therapies and cures. This allows us to explore the promise and potential of stem cell research without crossing a fundamental moral line by providing taxpayer funding that would sanction or encourage further destruction of human embryos that have at least the potential for life.

I also believe that great scientific progress can be made through aggressive federal funding of research on umbilical cord, placenta, adult and animal stem cells, which do not involve the same moral dilemma. This year your government will have spent $250 million on this important research.

I will also name a president's council to monitor stem cell research, to recommend appropriate guidelines and regulations and to consider all of the medical and ethical ramifications of bio-medical innovation. . . .

EXCERPTS FROM THE PRESIDENT'S COUNCIL ON BIOETHICS PUBLIC HEARINGS

SESSION 3: ETHICS OF HUMAN STEM CELL RESEARCH, APRIL 25, 2002

PROF. GENE OUTKA [DWIGHT PROFESSOR OF PHILOSOPHY AND CHRISTIAN ETHICS, YALE UNIVERSITY]

[L]et me just then lay out some of [my] claims . . . and that will get us started at least. . . . I argue that once conceived each entity is a form of primordial human life that should exert a claim upon us to be regarded as an end and not a mere means only.

And I say that it is one thing to allow that we need not yet ascribe full moral standing or equal protectibility to embryos. That is to say, I deny that abortion and embryonic stem cell research are morally indistinguishable from murder.

But I claim on the other hand that it is another thing to instrumentalize embryos through and through when what we intend in the actions we perform exhaustively concerns benefits to third-parties.

And I take that to be one indication of sheer instrumentalization, where the actions that we perform we can only justify, and justify exhaustively by virtue of benefits to third-parties.

That is to say that I deny that abortion and embryonic stem cell research are morally indifferent actions in themselves to be evaluated wholly by the benefits that they bring to others.

I then go on to conclude that to conduct research on embryos that creates them in order to destroy them clashes directly with the judgment that entities conceived have irreducible value.

So that is on the one hand. I want to say that the case for sheer instrumentalization is to be resisted, but on the other hand, I also think that we don't confront a single either/or as some conservatives and some liberals suppose, to the effect that we should forbid all embryonic stem cell research, or we should permit it all.

I consider instead a more nuanced possibility, or at least I think it is more nuanced, where we may distinguish creating for research and only employing for research.

And . . . employing for research allows us to consider in vitro fertilization as a practice in our culture, and employing for research connects with the datum of discarded embryos . . . the original creation of [these] embryos has a non-instrumentalist rationale, namely the promotion of fertility.

So that what we intend does not exhaustively concern benefits to third parties. But yet the aftermath allows us to pursue benefits to third parties when we may do so without from the start creating in order to disaggregate.

And the way that I try to speculate about the pros and cons of this conclusion is to invoke the "nothing is lost" principle, which I think illuminates a morally significant distinction between creation for research and employment for research.

The nothing is lost principle says that . . . although it takes the prohibition against murder seriously, it allows two exempting conditions. The first is . . . that some innocent will die in any case, and the second exempting condition is that other innocent life will be saved.

And applying that to the matter at hand, I say that we cannot choose whom we save in the case of discarded embryos. They will die if we do nothing.

And we cannot save them by killing others or letting others die. Yet, we may save others by virtue of the research. And yet on the other hand, and why this remains incurably in the middle, while the nothing is lost principle permits attention to the possible benefits to third parties from research on discarded embryos, it does not permit the

concern about the status of embryos to recede to a platitude.

And where such concern never has efficacy and can always be trumped, and that is one of my tests about saying that a commitment to in this case embryonic life is serious only if it trumps something whenever there is a conflict.

It does not have to trump on all occasions, but it has to trump on some occasions. And where I want to say it trumps is where it disallows the creation of embryos only and exclusively for the sake of, and in order to, disaggregate them. . . . [Disaggregation refers to a procedure by which the stem cells are extracted for research purposes, and the embryo is destroyed.]

PROF. MICHAEL SANDEL [Professor of Government at Harvard University]: There is something very appealing about [Dr. Outka's] compromise and intuitively persuasive. But since I don't find it persuasive, I want to see if I can press a little bit and offer a concrete case to illustrate why I don't think the principle works, or is persuasive.

The first thing to notice—and this struck me I think only maybe in my second reading of the paper—is that the distinction, the crucial distinction is not as we might think from our common discourse about these subjects, . . . between the IVF fertilized eggs, or embryos, on the one hand, and cloned ones on the other.

. . . The crucial distinction is why the embryo was created. So if we imagine an embryo, a cloned embryo, created for reproductive purposes, [but then not needed by the donor couple], it would be all right to do research on those cloned ones, provided that they were created for the sake of reproduction.

But it wouldn't be all right to use cloned embryos created for the sake of research. Likewise, it would be all right to use embryos created with sperm fertilizing an egg in an IVF clinic, provided that it was created for the sake of reproduction.

But it wouldn't be all right to use an embryo created when a sperm is brought together with an egg in sexual reproduction in a clinic if the purpose of the clinic bringing the egg and sperm together was to create an embryo for research.

So the key here, and what is carrying the moral weight, is not how the embryo was created—but why? . . . the question arises why . . . the motive for creating the embryo determines whether it is permissible to use them for research into diseases.

Now that is the heart of the question; why the motive matters, and why the motive for the creation makes a moral difference. And the way to explore this question would be to put aside cloning altogether.

Let's imagine two cases; of traditional sexual creation of an embryo, or in a clinic, or in a lab. In case one, a woman comes to an infertility center and donates some eggs because she wants to help infertile couples have a genetically related child.

And the clinic brings together her eggs with donor sperm and creates some embryos, some of which are implanted, and some of which wind up being spares. In case two, a woman goes to a clinic or to a lab, and donates eggs for a different reason. She donates them because she wants to support stem cell research to cure Alzheimer's and Parkinson's.

Her eggs are brought together with donor sperm and made available to scientists who are engaged in this research.

In both cases, the motive of the woman who contributes or who donates the eggs is to advance a worthy end; helping an infertile couple have a genetically related child in the first case, and advancing scientific research in the other.

And in both cases, she contributes knowing that at least some of the embryos created from her eggs will be sacrificed, will be discarded or destroyed.

Now, according to the "nothing is lost" principle, what do we say about the availability of these two embryos, or sets, or batches of embryos for research?

Well, the "nothing is lost" principle in the paper tells us that it is okay for scientists to extract stem cells from the first batch, but not from the second. And the question that I have is: why?

The answer that the paper seems to give is, well, in the first case, they are spares. They are excess embryos. But then it is not so clear to me what counts as spare. Well, strictly speaking, a spare is an embryo not needed for reproduction that is going to die anyhow. So we may as well use it for some good. But by that definition of a spare, both batches of embryos are spares.

Once they exist, they both meet the "nothing is lost" principle. It is true that both batches of embryos that we have here are going to die otherwise, and we might as well get some good use out of it.

So that can't be—well, maybe that is too limited of an account of what you mean here by spare embryos, because by that definition they would both be spares, both batches.

So maybe there is a further condition of an embryo being a spare embryo; namely, that it had been created in the first place for the sake of reproduction. That would limit us to batch one.

But then the question is whether that condition adds any moral relevance or interest. The idea must be that the intention of the donor confers some morally relevant difference.

Moreover, a morally relevant difference that somehow filters all the way down to govern what a scientist may morally do. Well, what could that difference be?

How could the motive, the different motives in these that led to the creation of these two batches of fertilized eggs, or of embryos, how might that work? Why would the motive make a moral difference?

Well, there are at least two possibilities that I see from the paper. Maybe the motive makes a difference in the moral status of the embryos that result. Maybe it makes a difference therefore in the respect that the embryos are due. But why would that be? How does the different motive in the two cases confer different moral status on the embryos in batch one than in batch two, such that the ones in batch one are properly open to use, to be sacrificed for a worthy scientific end, but not the ones in batch two? There doesn't seem anything different in the moral status of the embryos in batch one and batch two. Well, maybe the difference then isn't in the moral status of the embryos that result from these different motives.

Maybe the difference is in the way that the scientist who would do the research is complicit in the destruction of the embryos that is a necessary feature of the research. But how does the motive that the donor had in creating the two batches change the degree of complicity of the scientist? . . .

Just because there are some embryos that somebody else has decided to destroy or to discard, why does that remove the complicity of the scientist who does the killing? If the Nazis decided to gather people in the concentration camps and had determined that they be killed, it wouldn't—that fact that they were going to die anyhow, wouldn't justify a doctor coming and yanking out their organs to save some innocent people.

He would not be less complicit or she, that doctor, in doing or in yanking out their organs to do a good thing simply because somebody else had decided that those people would already be killed, regardless of how you regard the moral status of the embryo.

It seems to me the degree of complicity isn't affected by the motive of the person who created the embryo in the first place. Well, the only other possible answer that I can think to the question why does the motive of the donor confer some morally relevant difference on these two batches, is—well, maybe to recur to the underlying intuition of the paper, which is that embryos should be treated as ends, and not only as means. And therefore to sacrifice excess or spare embryos in connection with IVF is morally permissible, because the donor didn't know which of the embryos created would be sacrificed, i.e., treated as a means, even though the donor knew that some would be. But even if that marks out a morally relevant difference for the donor, and the donor's willingness to sacrifice embryos for the sake of various ends, it is not clear how

this makes the embryo that results more open to use by the scientist.

So my question is going back to these two scenarios, these two batches, created for different motives, to test my motive matters, is what moral difference does the motive make?

DR. OUTKA: What I wanted to do was two things. I wanted to take seriously the notion of the injunction that comes to us in religious traditions, but also in some philosophical ones, above all, Kantian ones, that treating people as ends and not merely as means.

And I wanted to say that that generates a certain case for inviolability, and so I connected that injunction to the ethics of killing. So the first thing that we are talking about I think is more the morality of actions, rather than the morality simply of motives.

And I want to say that certain actions may be licit if one can say that the rationale for—let's say in the case of IVF clinics, being in the mess that we are in with respect to them doesn't have to do with actions that we ourselves perform.

We are actually dealing with the after effects of an entire industry, and so that would already distinguish the status of what we are contemplating there from the status of contemplating a direct action ourselves when we do X in order to do Y.

And I want to say that a prime case for treating an entity as instrumental through and through is when we do X in order to destroy them for the sake of the benefits that destruction will bring to third parties.

I want to say that that is an instrumentalist action through and through. So I would prefer to use the language of ends and means, and the morality of actions, and specifically the prohibition against killing, rather than I think the language of motives. . . .

Now, in regard to your very interesting example, of case one and case two, it would be the case that if a woman donates eggs for reproduction, she there is donating her eggs for an end that isn't menial.

I mean, there she is donating her eggs for the sake of a couple who want a child, and so nothing that the couple contemplates, or nothing that she does contributes to a case for creating in order to destroy.

Whereas, if she gives her eggs to support stem cell research—and that is her only reason, so that she is giving her eggs in order to do that—there it seems to me that she runs the risk of violating the thing that I am objecting to, which is creation in order to destroy.

So the relevant fact is not simply that they are both spares. The relevant fact has to do with the morality of the two different kinds of actions.

And where the ends have to then be also distinguished, and you say that both ends are worthy. One is to help a couple, and one is to promote research. But I am precisely objecting to the second kind of so-called worthy end if it means that you may directly create a life in order to destroy it.

Comment

Despite their disagreement about whether the federal government should fund stem cell research, proponents and opponents of federal funding seem to share at least some common ground: each appeals to the importance of preserving human life. Proponents of stem cell research cite the moral worth of the lives of those suffering from debilitating disease who may be aided by the research. Opponents cite the moral worth or sanctity of preserving the unborn lives of embryos that will be destroyed by the very same research. Each side clearly believes that its own appeal to human life carries more weight in deciding the issue than does their opponents' appeal.

Does the moral injunction to preserve human life, or the idea of the sanctity of all human life, provide any guidance in enabling you to determine which side should prevail? Consider whether the debate would be more or less easy to resolve (either in principle or in practice) if the value, worth, or sanctity of human life were not at stake on one side or the other. Even if the idea of the value of human life provides guidance, the question still remains as to whether it is specific enough to resolve the debate. If you think it is, is this because you reject one or the other side's claims about the value of human life that is at stake? Or do you think that other considerations—such as how to compare the two competing values of life—also must be taken into account?

Consider the specific arguments offered by supporters of stem cell research. Many defenders of the research rely heavily on the fact that the embryos used are taken from a pool of those marked for destruction by in vitro fertilization clinics. How does the threat of imminent destruction affect the value of the embryo? The fact that an adult patient is terminally ill, Richard Dorflinger points out, does not license physicians to conduct destructive experiments on his or her body. Is this a good analogy, and why or why not? Next consider whether a moral defense of stem cell research must depend on the claim that the embryos would have been destroyed anyway. Construct the strongest argument you can that stem cell research should go forward even if it depends on destroying embryos that otherwise would become viable. How does the assumption that the cells would be destroyed anyway strengthen the proponent's case?

Consider the argument of the opponents of stem cell research that it is wrong, in Gene Outka's words, "to instrumentalize embryos through and through when what we intend in the actions we perform exhaustively concerns benefits to third-parties." What, if anything, is wrong with using embryos as instrumental "means only"? Should anyone think that this is wrong if he greatly values the fruits of stem cell research but does not attribute to the embryo the value of personhood (or a fully human life)?

Outka joins with proponents of stem cell research in denying that "abortion and embryonic stem cell research are morally indistinguishable from murder." On what grounds, if any, can one deny this and still defend prohibiting the use of embryos as instrumental means only in stem cell research? Consider whether and to what extent opposition to using embryos in a purely instrumental way for medical research depends on: (1) how much or what kind of value is attributed to the embryo as a human life, (2) how much or what kind of value is attributed to stem cell research, and (3) how opponents weigh or compare the two values. Do opponents actually engage in a "weighing" of the two competing values, or does the first clearly trump when compared with the second so that no weighing is either needed or permitted?

Defenders of stem cell research cite the fact that many human embryos under natural conditions fail to implant in the woman's womb. Many are lost through natural processes. The defenders then argue that those who believe that the embryo is a human person should be appalled by this fact, and should be taking steps to preserve each of these naturally "discarded" embryos. They also should be outraged by the treatment of embryos in fertilization clinics, where many are routinely frozen and then eventually discarded. Evaluate the strongest response that opponents of stem cell research can offer to these critics, who implicitly accuse them of hypocrisy at worst or inconsistency at best.

Many proponents and opponents of stem cell research agree that the embryo is not a full human person but that it has some moral standing (value or weight) nonetheless. In virtue of what features can the embryo be accorded some moral standing? Some have argued that the embryo, and subsequently the fetus, gains moral weight (so to speak) as it matures, and begins to acquire the capacity to suffer and the capacity for complex neural activity. Are there degrees of human worth? Or must there be a sharp dividing line, somewhere in the organism's growth, that separates moral worthlessness from full human personhood?

The President's Council on Bioethics conducted numerous hearings and engaged in extensive public deliberations on the subject of stem cell research. Their work received considerable press coverage and resulted in several volumes of published findings. Assess whether and to what extent the public value of such deliberations depends on: (1) the correctness of the council's recommendations; (2) the quality of its deliberations; (3) the representation of diverse perspectives in its deliberations; (4) the ability of participants to reach consensus or otherwise find common ground; (5) the power to make a difference in the political outcome; (6) the ability to achieve ongoing cooperation, even mutual respect, among people who continue to disagree on the subject; and (7) the institution of an ongoing process by which conclusions are reassessed over time.

Ethics without Borders? Clinical Trials of AZT*

Esther Scott

In 1994, researchers in the US and France announced stunning news of a rare victory in the battle against the AIDS pandemic. Studies conducted in both countries had shown conclusively that a regimen of the drug AZT, administered prenatally to HIV-positive pregnant women and then to their babies after birth, reduced the rate of mother-to-infant transmission of HIV by fully two-thirds. The results of the clinical trials constituted "one of the most dramatic discoveries of the AIDS epidemic," the *New York Times* declared,[1] and one of the most heartening as well. The new regimen—known by its study name, AIDS Clinical Trials Group (ACTG) 076 or, often, simply "076"—offered the epidemic's most vulnerable targets, newborns, their best hope thus far of a healthy childhood and a normal life span. The number of infants who might benefit from this research was significant: according to World Health Organization (WHO) figures, as many as five to ten million children born between 1990–2000 would be infected with HIV. In the mid-1990s, it was estimated that HIV-infected infants were being born at the rate of 1,000 a day worldwide.

So impressive were the findings of ACTG 076—and so substantial the difference in the transmission rate between sub-jects given AZT and those given a placebo (8 percent versus 25 percent)—that the clinical trials, which were still ongoing, were stopped early, and all participants in the studies were treated with AZT. In June 1994, after reviewing the study results, the US Public Health Service recommended that the 076 regimen be administered to HIV-infected pregnant women in the US as standard treatment to prevent transmission of the virus.

But while 076 was hailed as a major breakthrough, the celebration was somewhat muted. For a variety of reasons, the new treatment regimen would not likely reach those who most desperately needed it: pregnant women in the developing nations of the world and, most particularly, sub-Saharan Africa, where AIDS was wreaking devastation on a scale unimagined in the West.

BACKGROUND: THE SCOURGE OF AIDS IN DEVELOPING COUNTRIES

As the AIDS pandemic stretched into its second decade, no corner of the globe seemed immune from its deadly touch. Each year added millions from all over the world to the rolls of HIV-infected people, who would number 33.4 million by the end of 1998. But the numbers were not evenly distributed. As the 1990s progressed, the toll of illness and death fell most harshly on developing countries. In 1998, for example, of 5.8 million new cases of HIV infection reported by United Nations AIDS officials, 1.2 million would come from South and Southeast Asia, and a staggering 4 million from sub-Saharan Africa.[2]

For the millions of newly HIV-infected people in Africa, there was little hope of treatment. The expensive drug combinations available in developed countries at a cost of

*This case, condensed and modified for this volume, is based on a hypermedia presentation that includes video and links available on the web at the following address: <http://www.ksg.harvard.edu/case/azt>. It was written by Esther Scott under the supervision of Richard Cash, M.D. and Michael Bennish, M.D., for the program on Ethical Issues in International Health Research, School of Public Health, and the Case Program at the Kennedy School of Government at Harvard University. Funding for the case was provided by the National Institutes of Health. (0999) Copyright © 1999 by the President and Fellows of Harvard College.

roughly $15,000 per person annually were far beyond the reach of most sub-Saharan nations, where per capita expenditures on health care were commonly as low as $5.00 to $10.00 a year.[3] Many clinics in the region were unable to maintain adequate stocks of basic medicines and supplies, let alone the sophisticated drugs used to keep HIV at bay; few had the capacity even to provide screening for the virus, or counseling for those who tested positive.

The lack of facilities and funds made the plight of pregnant women infected with HIV especially poignant. Their numbers were growing steadily: in countries like Uganda, South Africa and Malawi, as many as 40 percent of pregnant women were estimated to be HIV-positive. Untreated, roughly one in four or five could be expected to give birth to an HIV-positive baby; those infants who escaped infection at birth faced roughly a 14 percent chance of becoming infected through breastfeeding.[4] Thus far, hospitals and clinics in the region had been powerless to do anything to protect the babies of HIV-positive women from infection. And, it was widely agreed, the exciting discovery of the 076 regimen did nothing to alter that harsh reality.

THE 076 DILEMMA

Cost was the most obvious barrier separating pregnant women in sub-Saharan Africa from the benefits of the 076 treatment protocol. While not as expensive as the elaborate drug regimen used to treat HIV-infected people in many developed countries, 076 carried a prohibitively high price tag—$800 to $1,000 for the AZT alone—for developing nations. But there were other costs attached to the protocol as well. Screening for HIV, the necessary precursor to treatment, cost roughly $10—the equivalent of annual per capita health care expenditures in many sub-Saharan nations. Moreover, the 076 regimen was a complicated one, involving five daily oral doses of AZT over an average of twelve weeks of pregnancy,

intravenous administration of AZT during labor and delivery, and six weeks of postpartum AZT for the infant. None of the AIDS-stricken nations of Africa could afford the clinical infrastructure or staff to administer and monitor such a complex treatment program. In addition, the great majority of women in the region did not seek prenatal care—if they sought it at all—until well into their third trimester, too late to administer the full 076 regimen.

For all these reasons, there was a general consensus in the international health community that 076 was impracticable in sub-Saharan Africa in particular, and in much of the developing world in general. The question, then, was what, if anything, could be done to bring the benefits of the new treatment to the HIV-infected women of these nations, who, without some sort of intervention, faced the bleak prospect of giving birth to babies whose lives would be blighted by the virus they carried. It was in part to answer this question that the World Health Organization convened an international panel of experts in June 1994 to ponder the implications of 076.

THE WHO RECOMMENDATIONS

The WHO gathering was attended by over fifty research scientists and representatives of funding agencies, drug companies, and drug regulatory agencies from all over the world.[5] After three days of review and discussion, the group issued their findings in a series of recommendations. These began by stating that "the concept" of reducing mother-to-infant transmission by the use of antiretroviral drugs such as AZT (or zidovudine) had been "shown to be valid" by the ACTG 076 studies. However, the WHO panel noted, the results of 076 were "only applicable to a specific population." Regional differences in such variables as viral load (the amount of HIV in the body), transmission rate, and breastfeeding habits could limit the degree to which the results were generalizable; in addition, the panel took note of the cost and difficulties of administration as barriers to wider applicability of the trials. "Therefore," the panel wrote, "no global recommendations regarding the use of [AZT] to prevent MTI [mother-to-infant] transmission of HIV can be made." These reservations notwithstanding, however, the group concluded that "where availability, cost and logistic factors are not limiting factors, [AZT] should be offered to HIV-infected women" to reduce the chances of perinatal transmission.

But, recognizing that availability, cost and logistic factors would make 076 unfeasible in precisely "those parts of the world where most MTI transmission of HIV occurs," the WHO panel urgently called for new research in developing countries that would explore "simpler and less costly drug regimens," which would be "affordable, feasible and sustainable in the same setting." The panel further recommended that the research take the form of placebo-controlled trials— i.e., randomized controlled trials in which the control group, or arm, received "dummy" medication—as the "best option for obtaining rapid and scientifically valid results."

Having set out these and other recommendations to guide new clinical trials, the WHO panel called for "world wide coordination" of the research effort, to ensure that "all pivotal research questions are addressed" and to avoid duplication. The WHO recommendations thus constituted a call to arms of sorts to establish "a global research agenda," as one report put it, with the goal of devising "efficacious regimens that can be safely and widely implemented in the developing world."[6]

FIRST FRUITS

Less than four years later, the first results of the research initiative were made public. The results of the Thai study and, later, the African study (known as the PETRA trials) were hailed by international health officials as potentially offering pregnant women in poorer countries their first realistic hope of an intervention that would help protect their babies from HIV infection. Not only were the short-course regimens cheaper, they were simpler to administer, requiring fewer oral doses and no intravenous injections. "The data, though preliminary," said Dr. Joseph Saba, the UNAIDS official who managed the PETRA trials, "mean we can save a lot of children using several strategies, whichever makes sense for the women, their doctors or the community in which they live."[7]

But although there was general agreement that the study results were promising, there was sharp, often bitter, disagreement as to the cost, in human terms, of the clinical trials. While the studies were still in progress, a heated debate arose over the manner in which they were conducted. However valid their purpose, critics said, the trials were unethical: clinicians were knowingly putting lives at unnecessary risk in pursuit of their research goals.

THE PLACEBO DEBATE

The opening salvo in the battle over the clinical trials was an April 22, 1997, letter to US Health and Human Services (HHS) Secretary Donna Shalala, authored by Drs. Peter Lurie and Sidney Wolfe of the Health Research Group—an arm of Public Citizen, the watchdog organization founded by Ralph Nader. The letter's argument was couched in strong terms. "Unless you act now," it began, "as many as 1,002 newborn infants in Africa, Asia and the Caribbean will die from unnecessary HIV infections they will contract from their HIV-infected mothers in nine unethical research experiments funded by your Department through either [NIH or CDC]." From there, the authors went on to assert that the use of placebos in the nine US-sponsored trials violated international ethical guidelines and HHS's own regulations for the protection of human subjects in international research. Because the 076 protocol had been proven effective in reducing

HIV transmission, they wrote, subjects in the control group of any subsequent clinical trials should be given "effective prophylaxis" to help prevent infection. This standard, they noted, was observed in the US: in two trials of treatments to reduce HIV transmission then being conducted in the US, all the women in the study, including those in the control group, were provided with AZT or other anti-viral drugs. Urging the HHS secretary to order researchers to provide treatment to all subjects in the trials (and to pressure foreign governments to do the same), the letter concluded, "We are confident that you would not wish the reputation of your department to be stained with the blood of foreign infants."

Several months later, on September 18, 1997, Lurie and Wolfe repeated their charges in a highly visible venue: *The New England Journal of Medicine,* one of the most respected medical publications in the US. In the same issue in which their "Sounding Board" article appeared, the journal's executive editor, Dr. Marcia Angell, wrote a strongly worded editorial condemning the use of placebos when "effective treatment exists." Like Lurie and Wolfe, Angell likened the use of placebos in the clinical trials on HIV transmission to the infamous Tuskegee syphilis study, in which poor African-American men in the rural south were denied effective treatment for syphilis so that researchers for the US Public Health Service could study the natural progress of the disease.

Both the letter to Shalala and, in particular, the pieces in *The New England Journal of Medicine* sparked a vigorous defense from researchers and health officials in the US and abroad, who strenuously objected to the harsh characterizations and the public manner of the charges of unethical conduct. Many were angered by the press releases and, in one instance, the press conference Lurie and Wolfe used to accompany their criticism, and by the comparison to the Tuskegee study, which, they argued, was inappropriate and

offensive. More important, they took issue with the substance of the criticism of the clinical trials, countering that the use of placebos accorded with the soundest research principles and established ethical practices.

For the next two years, both sides pursued the debate in professional journals and gatherings, in congressional testimony, and in the media. Almost no one disputed the need to find shorter and cheaper ways to reduce mother-to-infant transmission of HIV in poorer nations, although some lamented the unwillingness of rich ones to subsidize treatment with the 076 regimen in Africa and elsewhere.[8] Rather, the disagreement focused largely on the use of placebos as the comparison arm in the clinical trials. Broadly speaking, arguments for and against placebos could be said to fall into two general categories: the scientific and the ethical.

THE SCIENTIFIC DEBATE

While ethical considerations lay at the heart of the controversy over placebos, their use was criticized, and justified, on scientific grounds as well. Essentially, the position of critics of the clinical trials was summed up by Marcia Angell who, in an October 28, 1997, op-ed piece in the *Wall Street Journal,* entitled "Tuskegee Revisited," wrote "there is no scientific necessity to compare [shorter regimens of AZT] with placebos." The position of supporters of the trials, on the other hand, was articulated by Drs. Harold Varmus and David Satcher—directors, respectively, of NIH and CDC—who wrote, in the October 2, 1997, issue of *The New England Journal of Medicine,* that placebo-controlled studies provided "definitive answers to questions about the safety and value of an intervention in the setting in which the study is performed, and these answers are the point of the research." Within this overall debate over the appropriateness of the study design, a number of issues became the focus of discussion.

THE RESEARCH QUESTION

In their article in *The New England Journal of Medicine,* Lurie and Wolfe argued that researchers were asking the wrong question in their conduct of the clinical trials—"Is the shorter regimen [of AZTI] better than nothing?"—a question which only a placebo arm could answer. Taking the "more optimistic view" that researchers would be capable of designing an effective short course of treatment, Lurie and Wolfe maintained that the better research question was, roughly, "Can the duration of treatment with AZT be reduced without compromising the demonstrated efficacy of the 076 regimen?" This research question, they wrote, could be answered by equivalency studies, in which the proven therapy was the comparison arm against which less expensive or toxic treatments would be measured. Such studies, they added, would "provide even more useful results than placebo-controlled trials, without the deaths of hundreds of newborns that are inevitable if placebo groups are used."

Lurie and Wolfe based their optimism about the likely success of trials of shorter courses of AZT on clinical data about the timing of HIV transmission and on findings from the ACTG 076 study itself, in particular, a "subgroup analysis" from that study, which suggested that the 076 regimen was effective for shorter durations than twelve weeks. The existence of these data, they further contended, disturbed the "equipoise," or uncertainty about the outcome of a trial, that was necessary to justify the use of a placebo arm.

Proponents of placebo-controlled trials, on the other hand, argued that the question these studies asked was more nuanced than depicted by Lurie and Wolfe. The trials in Thailand and sub-Saharan Africa sought to determine not simply whether a shorter regimen of AZT was better than nothing, but

rather, in the words of one analysis, whether it was safe in these populations, and, if so, whether the demonstrated efficacy is large enough, as compared to the placebo group, to make it affordable to the governments in question."[9] To such questions, they maintained, the answers were by no means assured and researchers, therefore, remained in a state of equipoise.

Researchers, many argued, could not confidently apply the results of 076, gathered from trials in two highly industrialized nations, to sub-Saharan Africa, where starkly different conditions—economic, environmental, cultural, and biological—prevailed. "These are two different populations," said Dr. H. M. Coovadia, head of the Department of Pediatrics at the University of Natal in Durban, South Africa, during an appearance on National Public Radio's *Talk of the Nation.* For example, he and others pointed out, women in Africa breastfed their infants, which the subjects in the 076 trials did not. Although breastfeeding increased the risk of HIV transmission, health officials in Africa generally continued to recommend the practice on a number of grounds: the cost of formula; the lack of clean water; the nutritional benefits of breast milk; and, in a culture where breastfeeding was the norm, the risk of being stigmatized by others as an HIV-infected mother. In addition, women in African countries frequently suffered from anemia—a common side effect of AZT therapy—as well as from malaria, genital infections, and vitamin deficiencies, all of which could potentially produce different effects from those observed in the 076 trials in the US and France. Consequently, Coovadia said, he and others were not convinced that 076 was "a sort of universal standard by which you could measure effectiveness to reduce mother-to-infant transmission in all parts of the world."

Similarly, those who favored placebo-controlled trials disputed the contention by Lurie and Wolfe that the 076 subgroup analysis was a useful predictor of the likely effectiveness of shorter courses of AZT. The data from the sub-analysis, they maintained, did not "determine the efficacy of short course treatment" or obviate the need for additional trials.[10] At most, they indicated the direction further research might take.

THE UTILITY OF EXISTING DATA

Both sides of the debate disagreed as well over the use of observational and historical data to provide the base of information that a placebo arm would normally afford. Advocates of placebo-controlled trials argued that past observational studies would not be reliable sources for data on HIV transmission rates and other key factors. The WHO panel had addressed the issue in its June 1994 recommendations, in which it discouraged use of "historical controls" in the clinical trials, citing changes over time in the study population, viral strains, diagnostic tools, and treatment practices. Moreover, many researchers noted, the HIV transmission rate was highly variable from country to country. Without a control group to establish the transmission rate of the site of a clinical trial, says Dr. Neal Halsey of the Johns Hopkins School of Hygiene and Public Health, the results of the study would be "uninterpretable."

Critics, on the other hand, took a different view of the available data. First, some maintained, too much was being made of the potential differences between the subjects in the 076 clinical trials, and those in the sub-Saharan trials; it was unlikely, in their view, that what differences did exist would significantly alter the effectiveness of 076. In addition, they argued, historical and observational records provided ample data. "We do know, in fact, from many, many observation studies," Marcia Angell maintains, "very closely about what the transmission rate is in all parts of the world. We know that in Africa the transmission rate is 20 to 30 percent. What we want to know is whether the short regimen is equivalent to the full 076 regimen."

NEAL HALSEY: You need to have a comparison group whenever you're trying to determine if the intervention is having any effect. Observational studies in multiple countries have revealed rates of transmission as low as 11 percent to as high as 40 percent or even higher. If you don't have a control group and you find that there is a 20 percent rate of transmission, you don't know if you've done any good or not, because you don't know whether or not it would have been 40 percent and you had a 50 percent reduction, or whether it would have been 18 percent without the intervention and now you've got a 20 percent. If you don't have a control group, then you don't know that you've done any good. One of the basic principles of conducting research and putting people through the blood drawings and the inconvenience and everything else, is that the study should provide scientific data that will help in making decisions about what should be done. The absence of a control group would not have permitted any firm conclusions from the studies. That was shown by another study done in Thailand by the local Thai group. They did a study that showed 15 percent transmission in both an intervention and a placebo arm. I've forgotten the exact numbers, but that's approximately what it was. And so their very short-course regimen that they were proposing didn't work. But if they had no controls and they used the magic 25 percent that we had in the United States or that I had observed in Haiti, then they would have said, we had a 10 percent reduction in transmission. But fortunately they had a placebo arm and they were able to say, this doesn't work. . . .

PETER LURIE: Well, arguments of differences between populations have to be made on a case-by-case basis. You can't simply say, Africans are different than Americans. Sometimes they are, sometimes they aren't . . . the burden is upon the researcher, in my view, to prove that the people who are, in effect, the second group of people to have the drug tested upon them are likely to be different. And I don't think that they ever proved that. I mean, they were all polite arguments which amounted to, Africans are different. But you really had to go through each one of those specific arguments and say, was it likely that the groups were so different, that it would reduce the remarkable effectiveness of the 076 regimen down to nothing. And remember, that's what they had to believe, that there was a 50/50 chance, approximately, that it would be reduced to nothing. That's what equipoise means in the case of doing a placebo-controlled trial. . . . If you think that the oral regimen is likely, for some reason, to be different than the intravenous regimen, you don't have to do a placebo-controlled trial to figure it out. All you need to do is to take a limited number of people, certainly no more than 20, and randomize them to either getting the oral or the intravenous, and figure out how much AZT gets into their blood. And if they get about the same amount of AZT into the blood in about the same amount of time, the chances are it's going to be about as effective. . . . That was all that was necessary.

THE ETHICAL DEBATE

As important as the scientific arguments were, it was the ethics of using placebos that dominated the debate over the clinical trials to reduce perinatal transmission of HIV. As both sides sought to elucidate the ethical principles underpinning their position, they had recourse to a number of international guidelines to make their case. The guidelines were essentially voluntary codes, with no mechanism for policing or enforcement; nonetheless, they played a key role—though not necessarily a clarifying one—in the controversy.

THE GUIDELINES

The bedrock of ethical guidelines was the Nuremberg Code published in 1947 in the aftermath of shocking revelations of Nazi medical experiments on human subjects. The code, says Dr. Michael Grodin of the Health Law Department of Boston University School of Public Health, was a very, very important document, a grounding document, which talked about respect for individuals. "Perhaps the most important of the ten

principles articulated in the Nuremberg Code was the notion of informed consent," which required that human subjects be apprised of the nature and risks of the research, and that their participation be strictly voluntary. All subsequent guidelines included the principle of informed consent, although they also incorporated language permitting researchers to seek the proxy consent of authorized representatives in cases where subjects were deemed incapable of giving informed consent on their own. Other key tenets of the Nuremberg Code sought to protect subjects from undue harm and risk.

About two decades later, the World Medical Association (not to be confused with the World Health Organization) issued a series of "recommendations," known as the Declaration of Helsinki, to guide research on human subjects. First adopted in 1962 and revised at regular intervals in subsequent decades, these guidelines included two principles in particular that became focal points in the debate over the placebo-controlled trials in developing countries. One stated that "[c]oncern for the interests of the subject must always prevail over the interests of science and society." The other declared that "[i]n any medical study, every patient—including those of a control group, if any—should be assured of the best proven diagnostic and therapeutic method."

Still later, the Council for International Organizations of Medical Sciences (CIOMS), in collaboration with WHO, issued the International Ethical Guidelines for Biomedical Research Involving Human Subjects. Published in 1993, these guidelines were written to address ethical issues that arose in research involving developed and developing countries, in particular when the host country did not have guidelines of its own. In the course of the controversy over the clinical trials in sub-Saharan Africa, two of the fifteen CIOMS guidelines were frequently invoked. Guideline 8 set out a series of principles for research involving subjects in "underdeveloped countries." Under these rules, researchers were required to ensure, among other things, that "persons in underdeveloped communities will not ordinarily be involved in research that could be carried out reasonably well in developed communities," and that the research was "responsive to the health needs and the priorities of the community in which it is to be carried out." Guideline 15 set out the obligations of both sponsoring and host countries. In the former, the guideline stated, the proposed study should be submitted for ethical and scientific review, and the ethical standards applied "should be no less exacting than they would be" for research in the sponsoring country itself. Following that review, the study would be subject to the scrutiny of the "appropriate authorities of the host country, including a national or local ethical review committee or its equivalent.

In addition to these international codes, researchers in the US were governed by federal regulations on the protection of human subjects, promulgated by the Department of Health and Human Services. Apart from provisions concerning informed consent, these were largely devoted to detailing the make-up and duties of "institutional review boards" (IRBs)—essentially, local review committees established by a university, hospital, or research organization—which were authorized to scrutinize research proposals to ensure they afforded adequate protections for human subjects. IRBs, which were required to include at least one member unaffiliated with the host institution and one with a non-scientific background, were provided with specific criteria to guide their reviews of research proposals. But they were expected to be informed as well by the principles and guidelines contained in the Belmont Report, issued in 1979 by the National Commission for the Protection of Human Subjects of Biomedical and Behavioral Research, which was established in the wake of the Tuskegee scandal. The Belmont Report was notable for delineating three "basic ethical principles," frequently cited in the debate over the clinical trials: "respect for persons," which recognized the

autonomy of individuals, primarily through the mechanism of informed consent; "beneficence," which sought to minimize the risks and maximize the benefits of research; and "justice," in the sense of equitable distribution of the burdens and benefits of research, which included the stricture that research should not "unduly involve persons from groups unlikely to be among the beneficiaries of subsequent applications of the research."

In the case of research conducted in a foreign country, federal policy did make allowances for differences in procedures to safeguard human subjects in the host nation. It was permissible, according to HHS regulations, to observe the standards of the host country, if it was determined that they "afford protections that are at least equivalent to those provided in this policy."

THE ARGUMENTS

To critics, the placebo-controlled trials in sub-Saharan Africa and Thailand violated some tenets of all the major international ethical guidelines, as well as US regulations. Lurie and Wolfe, for example, charged that the trials violated principles 2, 4, 5, and 7 of the Nuremberg Code, which largely dealt with the obligation to shield research subjects from unnecessary harm, as well as CIOMS guideline 15, which set ethical standards for international research. In her editorial, Marcia Angell cited portions of the Declaration of Helsinki in support of her contention that the trials were unethical. To advocates, on the other hand, the placebo-controlled trials met the test of ethical standards that guided US-sponsored research on human subjects. Writing in *The New England Journal of Medicine,* David Satcher of CDC and Harold Varmus of NIH cited the principles of the Belmont Report, in particular those of beneficence and justice, in defense of their agencies' research practices in developing nations. They and others also pointed to guideline 8 of the CIOMS code, which called for responsiveness to local needs in research conducted in developing nations. Within the overarching argument about which ethical principles should inform the conduct of the trials, certain themes consistently emerged.

STANDARD OF CARE

Much of the debate revolved around the question of what standard of care human research subjects were entitled to receive. Both sides agreed that placebo-controlled trials to reduce perinatal transmission would not be permitted in the US, where the 076 regimen was the standard of care for HIV-positive pregnant women; but they disagreed over whether, in consequence, it was unethical to use placebos in countries where the standard of care for HIV transmission was, typically, no treatment. In essence, the argument boiled down to whether the notion of "standard of care" should be defined in universal or local terms.

Critics of the placebo-controlled trials believed that the standards laid out in various international guidelines should be uniformly applicable to all subjects, regardless of local circumstances. Thus, Angell argued in her editorial, the language in the Declaration of Helsinki calling for the "best proven diagnostic and therapeutic method" for all subjects, including those in the control arm, meant "the 'best' current treatment, not the local one." Accepting a "shift in wording" from best to local, she continued, led to an "ethical relativism that could result in widespread exploitation of vulnerable Third World populations for research programs that could not be carried out in the sponsoring country." In addition, she and others noted, the Declaration of Helsinki stressed the primacy of research subjects' well-being over those of science and society. Prevailing local standards did not excuse researchers from their responsibility, under the Helsinki guidelines, to provide the best care to participants in a study.

To critics, the very term "standard of care" was problematic in the context of the debate over the clinical trials; it had been redefined, they charged, from its proper meaning of "normative care" to one that was merely descriptive of local conditions, thus permitting a double standard in research. This dualism violated not only international ethical guidelines—notably CIOMS guideline 15—but federal regulations as well, which required researchers in foreign countries to offer subjects equivalent protections to those they would have in the US.

Proponents of placebo-controlled trials in developing nations believed that the local standard of care was the appropriate, and ethical, measure against which new therapies should be tested. Essentially, their position rested on the principle of beneficence, as articulated in the Belmont Report, and on guideline 8 of the CIOMS code. In testimony before a subcommittee of the House Government Reform and Oversight Committee in May 1997, for example, Satcher argued that "the critical issue . . . has to do with the host country, and the extent to which the research is meeting the needs and interests of the host country and is going to result in benefits for the host country." This meant taking into account the realities of local standards of care in designing clinical studies, with the goal of finding treatment that was affordable and feasible under conditions vastly different from those in the US. Testing new therapies that would undoubtedly fail to match the existing "gold standard" of treatment, advocates of placebo trials argued, would lead to useless results and wasted money. Writing in *The New England Journal of Medicine,* Varmus and Satcher asserted that to enroll subjects "in a study that exposes them to unknown risks and is designed in a way that is unlikely to provide results that are useful" would be to fail "the test of beneficence." In addition, some argued, demanding that the most effective and, often, most expensive regimens be used as a comparison arm could discourage efforts to find treatments that poorer nations could afford.

Some researchers also argued that objections to the notion of local standards of care were largely contextual—that it was discomfort with the economic gap between developed and developing nations that fueled much of the criticism. In contrast, they noted, when the US sponsored clinical trials in developed countries, whose local standard of care permitted the use of a placebo arm, no public outcry was raised.

MARCIA ANGELL: The ethical guidelines and the federal regulations couldn't be more clear. The Declaration of Helsinki couldn't be more clear. But they're honored in the breach because there is an industry at work here, and there is an orthodoxy at work here . . . would I want [my daughter] enrolled in this trial, a placebo-controlled trial, versus a trial in which the control was a full 076 regimen? And that's a no-brainer.

The fact of the matter is that when you enroll people in a trial, you take responsibility for those people—not for the whole world; nobody could take responsibility for the whole world. But you do take responsibility for those people. This is a place where the analogy with Tuskegee is very good. In Tuskegee, men who had syphilis were observed over a period of about 40 years, to see what the natural course of the disease was. It's now understood that that was unethical. At the time, a lot of the same arguments were made that we hear today. The argument was made that these very poor men in the rural south of the United States would probably not get treated anyway. And incidentally, the treatment was not very good, during much of the Tuskegee study, so it wasn't like AZT; it was not nearly as effective. But anyway, the argument was made that these men in the rural South, very poor, would probably not get treated anyway. And so they were no worse off. We hear that argument now. But when President Clinton appropriately apologized to the few survivors from the Tuskegee study, the aging survivors, he didn't apologize to all men in the rural South; he apologized to that group of men for which the Public Health Service had taken responsibility. And the same thing is true of the HIV studies in the Third World. Researchers are not responsible for everybody in the cosmos, but they are responsible for the people that they enroll in their trials. The practical effect of saying, well, if in fact this country is so poor that people don't usually get adequately treated anyway, and so we can give placebos to people in our studies, is that people in the poorest countries of the world would be exploited as guinea pigs for the rest of us. And that is absolutely wrong.

NEAL HALSEY: First of all the welfare of the subjects is at the heart of what everybody's about. I mean the people who were planning these trials; the studies were done to benefit those populations and so that's a very important principle. There are differences in the standards of care in terms of what is generally provided to people in different countries around the world, as evidenced by the amount of money we spend on health care—$2,700 per person per year in the United States in 1990 versus $8 to $710 per person in many developing countries. So there are huge differences in what care people get, but there aren't real differences in the ethics of doing studies. The ethics are the same; the standards of care are different. The basic ethical principle that I follow, and that I think everybody else who has been involved in these studies and in similar work to try to improve the health of people in developing countries, you would never deny somebody care that they otherwise would be getting or should be getting in accordance with their national standards.

PETER LURIE: Standard of care is a phrase that ought to be abolished from our discussion of these kinds of issues. Standard of care is something that speaks to adequate medical care—what is good and known to be effective. . . . But it has been misused by people in these clinical trials to imply that it actually means the care that is given. The care that is given in Africa is not a standard of care, it is sub-standard care. It is bad medical care those people are getting.

NEAL HALSEY: In this country, we have had a recommendation for 40 years that all children should receive pertussis vaccines. In Sweden and Italy, they had lost confidence in the vaccine that they had. So, the officials there no longer recommended the vaccine for all children. That made it possible for the Swedes to do a placebo-controlled trial. Because this is not a recommended vaccine, the United States government, through the National Institutes of Health, funded a randomized placebo-controlled trial of new acellular pertussis vaccines compared to a whole cell vaccine that was made in the United States. In Sweden, a country that is economically better off than we were, the study was completed. It demonstrated that the acellular vaccines worked very well—in fact, better than the whole cell vaccine. This study provided benefits to the United States, but the study was done in Sweden. We paid a foreign country to do a study with collaboration from US investigators, with a placebo, which would never be ethical in the United States. That study did not generate controversy. Public Citizen, Marcia Angell, and others didn't raise any concern. Why? It didn't have HIV, it wasn't in a developing country, it was two developed countries working together. But the principles are the same.

"ETHICAL IMPERIALISM"

In the course of the debate, critics of the placebo-controlled trials were sometimes accused of "ethical imperialism"—that is, of seeking to impose their ethical standards on countries that had made their own judgments on the merits of the trials, based on their particular needs. Many of those who made this charge were health officials and clinicians from developing countries. The host countries in sub-Saharan Africa had played an active role in designing the trials, they said, and were not merely the pawns of sponsoring nations. In a letter to Satcher and Varmus, which they quoted in their *New England Journal of Medicine* article, Edward Mbidde, chairman of the AIDS Research Committee of the Uganda Cancer Institute, wrote: "These are Ugandan studies conducted by Ugandan investigators on Ugandans. Due to lack of resources we have been sponsored by organizations like yours. . . . It is not NIH conducting the studies in Uganda but Ugandans conducting their study on their people for the good of their people." Furthermore, these critics maintained, the clinical trials had been carefully examined by ethical review committees in the sponsoring and host countries; they conformed

to international standards, yet were tailored to suit the realities of medical care in their communities.

Many of the researchers and health officials from sub-Saharan Africa who responded to the criticism of Lurie *et al.* questioned the depth of their understanding of conditions in their countries, sometimes in harsh terms. Writing in the *New York Times* on September 28, 1997, Danstan Bagenda and Philippa Musake-Mudido, a biostatistician and a pediatrician, respectively, from Uganda, asserted: "Those who can speak with credibility for AIDS patients in Africa are those who live among and know the people here or have some basic cross-cultural sensitivity. We are suspicious of those who claim to speak for our people, yet have never worked with them. Callous accusations may help sell newspapers and journals, but they demean the people here and the horrible tragedy that we live daily."

Critics of the trials in sub-Saharan Africa dismissed both the charges of ethical imperialism and the defense of the ethical review process that preceded the studies. Regarding the latter, they questioned the disinterestedness of the review, both at home and abroad, particularly in view of the substantial research money at stake. Moreover, some argued, the researchers and health officials who levied charges of ethical imperialism were not necessarily advocates for the poor citizens of their nations. The term, "ethical imperialism," Angell points out, was not a new one, but rather "an old argument in new clothes." Ten years earlier, she had written an editorial on the issue in *The New England Journal of Medicine,* when questions arose about the appropriateness of seeking informed consent from women in some developing nations, where their husbands or village chiefs normally spoke for them. Then, as now, she and others argued that the charge of ethical imperialism obscured a more insidious danger to developing countries: ethical relativism, which opened the door to exploitation of the vulnerable peoples of the Third World.

H. M. COOVADIA: Our own review process, at least for South Africa, and I speak for both Durban and Johannesburg, is a well-established review process. . . . The ethical committees are constituted by a range of different individuals who reflect different aspects of those societies. So you will have experts on science . . . people who represent the culture of our society . . . people who represent the safety of animals . . . individuals who understand drugs and pharmaceutical constraints . . . university representatives. For example, we have a policy, which I think you would call affirmative action and equal opportunity. We would have such individuals. . . . And I must say that the committee that I have sat on in our university is very well constituted, it's sufficiently experienced, and I think it reflects the broad view of both science and society in their deliberations and in the determinations of what is ethically acceptable and what is necessary for our country.

PETER LURIE: Certainly you have to have IRB approval and if you don't, your study is unethical. Period. But simply because you have it doesn't mean that your study is ethical. Much of the defense has rested upon paragraph upon paragraph of descriptions of all this lengthy ethical discussion that has ensued. But the problem is that very often the ethical discussion has been twisted. The Hopkins people, for example, really they're vetting their own, which is part of the nature of IRBs and creates conflict of interest, and so there's always an incentive, even in this country, to pass on studies rather than have your colleagues have their studies turned down by you. . . . The problem is, particularly in developing countries in which people are starved for cash, where researchers want to do work, and they find it very difficult to get funding to do so, and suddenly along comes the NIH with a placebo-controlled trial, and several million dollars for you to do it, it is very hard to turn that down.

MARCIA ANGELL: These people are very privileged people in societies that nobody would claim are egalitarian. They don't speak for their people, as they put it, any more than the

Public Health Service spoke for their people in the Tuskegee case; after all, these were Americans, too. Do Americans get to do whatever they want to Americans? I don't think so. Do Ugandans get to do whatever they want to Ugandans? I don't think so. I think ethics are universal.

H. M. COOVADIA: . . . do we have, in the face of this HIV epidemic, which is maximum in southern Africa, do we have the resources to deal with it and have we done so? And the short answer is no. And it's not the fault of researchers, indeed it's not even the fault of politicians. There simply is not enough amount of money to do all the things we should be doing. . . . The informed consent we have, do we have the sort of time and resources to give each poor woman who's HIV-infected the consideration that she deserves, the privacy that she deserves, and all that, to make her decision? We don't.

MARCIA ANGELL: The term *ethical imperialism* is interesting because what imperialism means is wealthy nations exploiting poor nations. If you do clinical research in poor nations that you could not do in wealthy nations, that seems to me extraordinarily imperialistic, and that's what is going on. We are going to other countries to find out what we want to know. Now if we do find, as I think we have found, that the short course is as good as the long course, is that going to be used in the countries where this research was being done? I don't think so. Because it's still expensive, which has to do with a lot of factors. It has to do with the drug companies' pricing of these drugs, among other things. I think it's very likely that whatever comes out of these trials will be used in the First World, not in the Third World.

MICHAEL GRODIN: So my main concern in all of this is that, one, people should never be worse off by participating in a research study than they will be if they never participated in the study at all. That's one guideline. And two is that you should only do research that could potentially benefit the population after you're done. Otherwise, you're using them.

[W]hat plan do they have, realistic plan, to make sure that, assuming that the drugs work in a shorter time frame, and cost less, that they will actually become available to the people there?

NEAL HALSEY: [I]t will happen at different rates in different countries throughout the world. Brazil is committed to providing regimens like the short-course regimen to pregnant women. And, as I mentioned, so is Thailand. So the countries that are better-off economically may be able to do this on their own now that we have a low-cost, short-course regimen. The poorest countries won't be able to afford these regimens for a long period of time and it's going to take lower-cost drugs and more resources from international agencies and donor agencies. . . .

I do not agree with the admonition that you shouldn't do a study unless there was a very specific plan to be able to guarantee that it would be made available to everybody in the world or everybody in that country forever after. If we had followed that principle, we would never have measles vaccine available for all children in developing countries, because the first studies of measles vaccines were done in the early 1960s, shortly after we had it here, in West Africa by some very dedicated individuals who documented that the vaccine was effective in those children. But when those studies were first done there wasn't money available to make the vaccine available. The same thing is true of diphtheria, tetanus, pertussis toxoid, DTP. The same thing is true of every other vaccine that has been added to the schedule. If we held to that principle, we would be denying people the potential for those interventions.

REFLECTIONS

When the findings of the CDC study in Thailand were released in February 1998 and the PETRA trials in Africa one year later, both sides in the debate saw vindication. While researchers exulted over the definitive results of the four-week AZT regimen, Sidney Wolfe attacked the study for simply confirming what researchers should have known all along. "This is inexcusable, sloppy research," he asserted. "They have wasted a large number of lives and a huge amount of money."[11] When, the following

year, the PETRA results indicated the effectiveness of an even shorter regimen, Joseph Saba of UNAIDS told reporters that the findings of the study justified the use of placebos. "Without a placebo group," he maintained, "we would have been totally misled. Now we can say with a peaceful mind that we made the right choice."[12] But in a February 10, 1999, letter to the *Wall Street Journal,* Lurie and Wolfe contended that "this study would have reached the same conclusion even if no placebo group had been used. The HIV transmission rates in the more effective treatment arms in the present study (8.600 to 10.8%) are so much lower than the transmission rates in the untreated groups in previous studies in developing countries (generally 18% to 4000), that it would have been easy to correctly conclude that these regimens are effective, even without a placebo."

In any event, the Thai results of February 1998 effectively marked the end, at least for the time being, of placebo-controlled trials to reduce perinatal HIV transmission in developing countries. The CDC suspended the placebo arm of the Thai study, and other trials also halted further recruitment to placebo control groups. Some viewed this as a long overdue step, taken only after unnecessary risk to hundreds of young lives, while others saw it as a possibly premature action, based on too little evidence and too much pressure from critics. Both sides agreed that, although the placebo-controlled trials had ended, the controversy—and its effects—lingered on.

One likely arena in which the debate would continue to be played out was a proposed revision of the Declaration of Helsinki, which began circulating in early 1999. Among the changes being considered in the draft document was one passage which, depending on the viewpoint, represented either an effort to clarify previously vague and unworkable language, or a retreat from universal principles of care. In place of the requirement to assure every patient, including those in the control group, of receiving "the best proven diagnostic and therapeutic method," the proposed revision would assure patients that they would "not be denied access to the best proven diagnostic, prophylactic or therapeutic method that would otherwise be available to him or her." The draft revisions also included, unlike previous versions, guidelines on the "ethical and scientific justification" for conducting placebo-controlled clinical trials.

NOTES

1. Sheryl Gay Stolberg, "US AIDS Research Abroad Sets Off Outcry Over Ethics," *New York Times*, Sept. 18, 1997, p. 1A.

2. *Science*, Dec. 4, 1998, p. 1790. By contrast, 44,000 of the new cases were from North America, and 160,000 from Latin America.

3. According to World Bank statistics, sub-Saharan annual per capita health expenditures ranged as low as $5 in Tanzania to $257 in South Africa, the wealthiest nation on the continent.

4. World Health Organization, "Update on Breastfeeding." [Online] Available at http://www.who.int/chd/publications, June 2, 1999.

5. World Health Organization, "Recommendations from the Meeting on Mother-to-Infant Transmission of HIV by Use of Antiretrovirals," Geneva, June 23–25, 1994.

6. The National Institutes of Health and the Centers for Disease Control, "The Conduct of Clinical Trials of Maternal Infant Transmission of HIV Supported by the US Department of Health and Human Services in Developing Countries," July 1997.

7. Michael Waldholz, "HIV Transmission at Birth Cut in Study," *Wall Street Journal*, Feb. 2, 1999, p. B3.

8. See, for example, George Annas and Michael Grodin, "An Apology Is Not Enough," *Boston Globe*, May 18, 1997, p. C1. In it, the authors decried the "moral failure of wealthy countries" to provide "proven therapies" to prevent HIV transmission in Africa.

9. Robert A. Crouch and John D. Arras, "AZT Trials and Tribulations," *Hastings Center Report*, Nov.–Dec. 1998, p. 27.

10. Neal A. Halsey, Alfred Sommer, Robert E. Black, "Author's reply," *British Medical Journal*, Feb. 14, 1998.

11. Sheryl Gay Stolberg, "Placebo Use Is Suspended in Overseas AIDS Trials," *New York Times*, Feb. 19, 1998, p. A16.

12. Richard Knox, "Treatment Found to Cut Risk of Passing HIV to Newborns," *Boston Globe*, Feb. 2, 1999, p. A3.

Comment

The worldwide AIDS pandemic raises difficult questions of bioethics and public policy that cannot be answered on strictly scientific grounds yet also call for a better understanding of the means and ends of scientific research. Medical research and health care practice have made extraordinary progress over the past decade in treating HIV-positive individuals in affluent countries, increasing the quality of life for HIV-positive patients and the life prospects of infants born of HIV-positive mothers. This progress stands in striking contrast, however, with the excruciating problems that still attend the lives of millions of HIV-positive mothers and their children in far poorer parts of the world. The uneven incidence of the AIDS pandemic across rich and poor societies—and its differential effects on people's lives—highlights the growing health disparities between First World and Third World countries. The controversy that broke out in the medical community over the justice of using placebo-controlled clinical trials for HIV-positive mothers in sub-Saharan Africa put those disparities into sharp ethical relief.

Everyone who has taken sides in the dispute over the AZT trials in Africa acknowledges that if it were not for the economic disparities between Africa and more affluent parts of the world, the dispute would probably not arise. Why, then, is it not sufficient simply to agree that rectifying the economic disparities would resolve the dispute? Consider to what extent it is nonetheless important—both morally and practically—that the parties to this controversy recognize its economic sources.

In the absence of sufficient means to reduce the economic disparities between First World and Third World countries, we need to understand the various ethical considerations at the heart of the dispute over whether a clinical trial of a shorter regime of AZT in Africa should include a placebo-controlled group. The proponents and opponents of the placebo-controlled AZT trials make many different claims, some of which are in conflict, and some of which are not. Try to identify the core disagreement by examining the following claims and assessing their comparative merit:

1. "[W]ould I want [my daughter] enrolled in this trial, a placebo-controlled trial, versus a trial in which the control was a full 076 regimen? . . . that's a no-brainer."
2. Informed consent is sufficient to justify the use of a placebo-controlled trial in sub-Saharan Africa.
3. Medical researchers should be responsive to local needs in developing nations because "you would never deny somebody care that they otherwise would be getting or should be getting in accordance with their national standards."
4. Every subject in a medical experiment should be assured of the best proven diagnostic and therapeutic method available anywhere, not just in his or her own society.
5. Demanding the most effective care available anywhere "could discourage efforts to find treatments that poorer nations could afford."
6. "The care that is given in Africa is not a standard of care; it is a sub-standard care. It is bad medical care those people are getting."
7. "Do Americans get to do whatever they want to Americans? I don't think so. Do Ugandans get to do whatever they want to Ugandans? I don't think so. I think ethics are universal."

The three basic ethical principles stated in the 1979 Belmont Report—respect for persons, beneficence, and justice—are assumed to provide some guidance for assessing clinical trials. How should those principles be interpreted so as to apply to the controversy over placebo-based AZT trials? What does your interpretation of these principles lead you to say about whether the notion of "standard of care" should be defined in universal or local terms? About the merits of the attack on critics of the placebo-based trials for engaging in "ethical imperialism"? What, if anything, do the principles imply about the necessity of informed consent? The sufficiency of informed consent as a standard? What do these principles say about the necessity and sufficiency of the standard of protecting individuals from undue risk?

Consider the strongest response to critics of the trials who argue that the failure to provide the same standard of life-saving medical care to all individuals, regardless of their nationality, violates all three of the Belmont principles. It is disrespectful of persons, not a beneficent response to their needs, unfair to individuals who through no fault of their own are poor, and therefore unjust. The critics conclude that as long as placebo-controlled trials are prohibited in affluent societies for the sake of protecting the welfare of individuals, they must be prohibited in all societies for the same reason. How ethically defensible is the strongest response to this argument?

It is now accepted that researchers or the agencies that sponsor them have an obligation to the subjects *after* trials are completed. "As a general rule, the sponsoring agency should ensure that, at the completion of successful testing, any product developed will be made reasonably available to inhabitants of the underdeveloped community in which the research was carried out; exceptions to this general requirement should be justified, and agreed to by all concerned parties before the research is begun." What is the basis for this obligation? What could be the justification for the exceptions?

All things considered, do you believe that placebo-controlled AZT trials should have been conducted in sub-Saharan Africa? Why or why not? To what extent does your answer depend on your assessment of the feasible alternatives? On what conception of distributive justice does your answer depend? See if you can find common ground on which both critics and defenders of the AZT trials could agree to move forward in providing adequate health care for all citizens in poorer countries.

Recommended Reading

Most of the philosophical literature on abortion focuses on the personal morality of abortion. A good place to start is a widely discussed article by Judith Jarvis Thomson, "A Defense of Abortion," in Marshall Cohen et al. (eds.), *The Rights and Wrongs of Abortion* (Princeton, N.J.: Princeton University Press, 1974), pp. 3–22. John Finnis, "The Rights and Wrongs of Abortion," in *The Rights and Wrongs of Abortion, pp.* 85–113, takes issue with Thomson's qualified defense of abortion. The most comprehensive treatment of the personal morality of abortion is Frances Kamm, *Morality, Mortality* (New York: Oxford University Press, 1993). Margaret Little offers a discussion of abortion as an intimate matter in "The Morality of Abortion," in Christopher Wellman and Rey Frey (eds.), *A Companion to Applied Ethics,* (Cambridge England: Cambridge University Press, 2004). David Boonin attempts to persuade opponents of abortion by appealing to their own premises in *Abortion: A Defense* (Cambridge England: Cambridge University Press, 2002).

A collection that presents a variety of perspectives on most aspects of the abortion question is Louis Pojman and Francis J. Beckwith (eds.), *The Abortion*

Controversy: 25 Years after Roe vs. Wade, A Reader (Belmont, CA: Wadsworth, 1998). For a discussion that combines the personal and political aspects of the abortion question, see Ronald Dworkin, *Life's Dominion: An Argument about Abortion, Euthanasia, and Individual Freedom* (New York: Knopf, 1993). See also Elizabeth Mensch and Alan Freeman, *The Politics of Virtue: Is Abortion Debatable?* (Durham, N.C.: Duke University Press, 1993); and Jeff McMahan, *The Ethics of Killing: Problems at the Margins of Life* (Oxford: Oxford University Press, 2002), ch. 4.

Specifically on the question of what a government's position on abortion should be, see Roger Wertheimer, "Understanding the Abortion Argument," in *The Rights and Wrongs of Abortion*, pp. 23–51; and George Sher, "Subsidized Abortion," *Philosophy & Public Affairs*, 10 (Fall 1981), pp. 361–72. Considerations favoring political compromise are highlighted in Mary Ann Glendon, *Abortion and Divorce in Western Law: American Failures, European Challenges* (Cambridge, Mass.: Harvard University Press, 1987). Amy Gutmann and Dennis Thompson discuss the political ethics of abortion in *Democracy and Disagreement* (Cambridge, Mass.: Harvard University Press, 1996), ch. 2.

On the ethics of democratic representation (which are centrally implicated in the Heidepriem case and indirectly in the Califano case), John Stuart Mill provides the seminal statement. See his *Considerations on Representative Government* (Indianapolis: Bobbs Merrill, 1958), ch. 5–8, 12, and 15. A useful commentary is Hanna Fenichel Pitkin, *The Concept of Representation* (Berkeley: University of California Press, 1972), ch. 7–10. Contemporary discussions of the ethics of representations include Melissa Williams, *Voice, Trust, and Memory* (Princeton, N.J.: Princeton University Press, 2000); Iris Young, *Inclusion and Democracy* (Oxford and New York: Oxford University Press, 2002); Andrew Sabl, *Ruling Passions: Political Offices Democratic Ethics* (Princeton, N.J.: Princeton University Press, 2002); and Arthur Applbaum, *Ethics for Adversaries: The Morality of Roles in Public and Professional Life* (Princeton, N.J.: Princeton University Press, 1999).

On the ethics of conducting medical research in developing countries, including a discussion of the universal guidelines and suggested ways of applying them to varying contexts, see G. B. Tangwa, "Between Universalism and Relativism: A Conceptual Exploration of Problems in Formulating and Applying International Biomedical Ethical Guidelines" in *Journal of Medical Ethics* 2004, 30:1, pp. 63–67. A useful volume is the National Bioethics Advisory Commission's *Ethical and Policy Issues in International Research: Clinical Trials in Developing Countries* (Washington, D.C.: National Bioethics Advisory Commission, January 2001).

Many theoretical perspectives were presented to the President's Council on Bioethics to inform the debate on stem cell research. These materials, including the papers by Paul Lauritzen and Gene Outka, can be found in www.bioethics.gov. The council presented its own report, *Monitoring Stem Cell Research*, which provides a detailed investigation of the background philosophical and scientific issues. The report can be found at http://www.bioethics.gov/reports/stemcell/index.html.